"Go To the Land I Will Show You"

Dwight W. Young

“Go to the Land I Will Show You”

Studies in Honor of Dwight W. Young

Edited by
Joseph E. Coleson
and
Victor H. Matthews

EISENBRAUNS
Winona Lake, Indiana
1996

Library of Congress Cataloging in Publication Data

Go to the land I will show you : studies in honor of Dwight W. Young / edited by Joseph Coleson and Victor Matthews.
p. cm.
Includes bibliographical references and index.
ISBN 0-931464-91-9 (cloth : alk. paper)
1. Bible. O.T.—Criticism, interpretation, etc. 2. Middle Eastern philology. I. Coleson, Joseph, 1947– . II. Matthews, Victor Harold. III. Young, Dwight W.
BS1192.G58 1996
221.6—dc20 96-11018
CIP

The paper used in this publication meets the minimum requirements of the American National Standard for Information Sciences—Permanence of Paper for Printed Library Materials, ANSI Z39.48-1984.⊗™

Contents

SECTION II
ANCIENT NEAR EASTERN HISTORY AND LINGUISTICS

INDEXES

Appreciation

The experience of doctoral studies is unique, and the relationship with a mentor is unique among all relationships. A good mentor pours him/herself into each student—molds, probes, challenges, encourages—and with much wisdom and hard work turns a novice into a scholar. Dwight W. Young was my professor and mentor, and he was among the very best. (I say "was" only because he has retired.) Prof. Young knows biblical and ancient Near Eastern studies, and he cares about his students genuinely and graciously.

His own mentor, Cyrus Gordon, once said that he was the best language student he had ever taught. After bringing him to Brandeis, Gordon said that Young was also the best language teacher he had ever observed. Young's teaching method for languages was purely inductive. He assigned texts for us to prepare. If while we were reading them in class we made mistakes, we were shown what the errors were and how to understand what we were reading. Most of the time this was done with marvelous gentleness and courtesy. Occasionally, when we were lazy or stupid, he showed displeasure and disappointment. I felt this displeasure once and took care not to disappoint him again, not out of fear, but out of chagrin for disappointing him. This is the kind of teacher and human being that Dr. Young is.

I remember vividly Dwight and Barbara Young's gracious hospitality on Thanksgiving Day in their home in Newton during our first year at Brandeis. Most of the Near Eastern and Judaic Studies students were present. As a first-year student, I was honored to be invited to a social occasion in my professor's home, especially for a major holiday.

The next summer the Youngs moved to Gloucester to a pleasant house on a hilltop with a sweeping view to seaward, a view of beauty and grandeur. Several of us helped with the move. For the next three years I drove to Gloucester at least one or two times a week to help with landscaping and other projects. Our workdays followed an interesting and pleasant pattern that, in the years since, I have come to value along with the formal part of my Brandeis education. When I arrived, Dr. and Mrs. Young usually were eating breakfast and would invite me to join them. As we ate and talked, we often watched Hughes Rudd and Charles Osgood on the CBS Morning News. Later I would dig, plant, clean out catbrier, or trim branches to clear a path down by the swampy area (now we would call it a "wetland") at the back of the property, and one spring we built a garden, complete with asparagus and strawberry beds. While I worked, Young would often stand nearby, directing the work and conversing. Our conversations ranged over dozens of subjects of mutual interest, some academic. I learned as much, perhaps, while working in Gloucester as I did in the classroom. I always came away richer in treasure that cannot be spent, lost, or squandered. I have since met many more of Young's students, all of whom continue to have the highest regard for him as a teacher and a gentleman. Learning and common sense, erudition and genuine insight into the human condition are not always found together in one individual. Dwight W. Young epitomizes the balanced scholar.

Dwight Young is not solely a first-rate teacher. He is also a world-class scholar and an expert's expert. There are no more than a handful of ancient Near Eastern and biblical scholars, living or dead, who have approached his erudition. He handles all the Semitic languages, naturally, down to the most obscure detail. In his course on comparative Semitics, he could illustrate a point from any of the regional spoken Arabic dialects as easily as he could from Mandaean, Amharic, or Berber. At one point in his scholarly career, he knew more about Coptic than any other person in the world. He is a rarity among scholars of the ancient Near East, a Semitist who knows Greek, both classical and *koine*. He once learned Sanscrit in preparation for a sabbatical trip to India.

His loyalty to his friends and colleagues is also legendary. I have seen him defend a colleague with an intensity I found almost frightening as a young graduate student, later realizing that this too is the measure of a man. Dwight Young is furthermore a devoted husband and father. The pleasure he and Barbara take in each other's company—their genuine *liking* for each other—imparts a blessing to their guests.

I should reveal that Prof. Young has one weakness, known, of course, to many of his students. His soft drink passion is Dr. Pepper. Though I cannot vouch for its veracity, one (apocryphal?) story has it that when he first came to Brandeis, Dr. Pepper was unavailable in the Boston area, so he shipped in a truckload and stored it in his garage.

In a department of stars, Dwight W. Young was never the flashy one; he *was* the dependable one, the solid one, the accurate one. A witticism I heard concerning two scholars in another field applies as well to Prof. Young: another scholar may be more likely to have published it, but Dwight Young is more likely to have it *right*.

Dwight Young fits the description of the excellent teacher first applied, I believe, to Mark Hopkins. The perfect classroom would be Dwight Young on one end of a log and a student on the other end. Each of his students counts it the greatest of privileges to have sat on the other end of the log with Prof. Young. He made us scholars; he made us better human beings. This volume is a small token of our thanks and esteem for the man.

Dwight W. Young—scholar, thinker, teacher, friend—we salute you.

Joseph E. Coleson
Nazarene Theological Seminary

Publications of Dwight W. Young

"An Unplaced Fragment from Shenute's *Fourth Canon.*" *Journal of Coptic Studies,* forthcoming.

Coptic Manuscripts from the White Monastery: Works of Shenute. Mitteilungen aus der Papyrussammlung der Osterreichischen Nationalbibliothek n.s. 23. Vienna, 1993.

"The Incredible Regnal Spans of Kish I in the Sumerian King List." *Journal of Near Eastern Studies* 50 (1991) 23–35.

"The Influence of Babylonian Algebra on Longevity among the Antediluvians." *Zeitschrift fur die Alttestamentliche Wissenschaft* 102 (1990) 321–35.

"On the Application of Numbers from Babylonian Mathematics to Biblical Life Spans and Epochs." *Zeitschrift für die Alttestamentliche Wissenschaft* 100 (1988) 331–62.

"A Mathematical Approach to Certain Dynastic Spans in the Sumerian King List." *Journal of Near Eastern Studies* 47 (1988) 123–29.

"Observations on White Monastery Codices Attested in the University of Michigan Library." Pp. 763–66 in *Atti del XVII Congresso Internazionale di Papirologia.* Naples, 1984.

"Unpublished Shenoutiana in the University of Michigan Library." *Scripta Hierosolymitana* 28 (1982) 251–67.

"A Ghost Word in the Testament of Jacob (Gen 49:5)?" *Journal of Biblical Literature* 100 (1981) 335–42.

(Editor) *Studies Presented to Hans Jakob Polotsky.* Gloucester, 1981.

"A Monastic Invective against Egyptian Hieroglyphs." Pp. 348–60 in *Studies Presented to Hans Jakob Polotsky.* Gloucester, Mass., 1981.

"The Ugaritic Myth of the God Horan and the Mare." *Ugarit-Forschungen* 11 (1979) 839–48.

"With Snakes and Dates: A Sacred Marriage Drama at Ugarit." *Ugarit-Forschungen* 9 (1977) 291–314.

"The Distribution of *shime* and *hime* in Literary Sahidic." *Journal of the American Oriental Society* 91 (1971) 507–9.

"The Milieu of Nag Hammadi: Some Historical Considerations." *Vigiliae Christianae* 24 (1970) 127–37.

"'Precept': A Study in Coptic Terminology." *Orientalia* 38 (1969) 505–19.
"Unfulfilled Conditions in Shenoute's Dialect." *Journal of the American Oriental Society* 89 (1969) 399–407.
"*ESOPE* and the Conditional Conjugation." *Journal of Near Eastern Studies* 21 (1962) 175–85.
"On Shenoute's Use of Present I." *Journal of Near Eastern Studies* 20 (1961) 115–19.
"Notes on the Root *ntn* in Biblical Hebrew." *Vetus Testamentum* 10 (1960) 457–59.

Abbreviations

General

EA	El Amarna tablet(s)
LB	Late Bronze Age
LXX	Septuagint
MB	Middle Bronze Age
MT	Masoretic Text
NAB	New American Bible
NEB	New English Bible
NIV	New International Version
RS	Ras Shamra texts
RSV	Revised Standard Version

Reference Works

AAT	Ägypten und Altes Testament
AB	Anchor Bible
ABAW	Abhandlungen der Bayerischen Akademie der Wissenschaften
AbB	Altbabylonische Briefe
AcOr	*Acta Orientalia*
AfO	*Archiv für Orientforschung*
AHw	W. von Soden, *Akkadisches Handwörterbuch*
AJA	*American Journal of Archaeology*
AJP	*American Journal of Philology*
AKA	E. A. W. Budge and L. W. King, *The Annals of the Kings of Assyria* (London: British Museum, 1902)
AnBib	Analecta Biblica
ANET	J. B. Pritchard (ed.), *Ancient Near Eastern Texts Relating to the Old Testament* (3d ed.)
AnOr	Analecta Orientalia
ANRW	*Aufstieg und Niedergang der Römischen Welt*
AnSt	*Anatolian Studies*
AOAT	Alter Orient und Altes Testament
AOS	American Oriental Series
ARET	Archivi reali di Ebla—Testi
ARM	Archives royales de Mari

ARMT	Archives royales de Mari Textes
ASORDS	ASOR Dissertation Series
BA	*Biblical Archaeologist*
BAR	British Archaeological Reports
BARev	*Biblical Archaeology Review*
BASOR	*Bulletin of the American Schools of Oriental Research*
BBB	Bonner biblische Beiträge
BBR	*Bulletin for Biblical Research*
BDB	F. Brown, S. R. Driver, and C. A. Briggs, *Hebrew and English Lexicon of the Old Testament*
BETL	Bibliotheca ephemeridum theologicarum lovaniensium
BHS	*Biblia Hebraica Stuttgartensia*
Bib	*Biblica*
BIFAO	*Bulletin de l'institut français d'archéologie orientale*
BiOr	*Bibliotheca Orientalis*
BIOSCS	*Bulletin of the International Organization for Septuagint and Cognate Studies*
BKAT	Biblischer Kommentar: Altes Testament
BR	*Biblical Research*
BSO(A)S	*Bulletin of the School of Oriental (and African) Studies*
BT	*The Bible Translator*
BWANT	Beiträge zur Wissenschaft vom Alten und Neuen Testament
BZ	*Biblische Zeitschrift*
BZAW	Beihefte zur *ZAW*
CAD	*The Assyrian Dictionary of the Oriental Institute of the University of Chicago*
CAH	*Cambridge Ancient History*
CBQ	*Catholic Biblical Quarterly*
CBQMS	Catholic Biblical Quarterly Monograph Series
CHD	*The Hittite Dictionary of the Oriental Institute of the University of Chicago*
CRAI	*Comptes rendus de l'Académie des inscriptions et belles-lettres*
CRRAI	Compte rendu de la Rencontre assyriologique internationale
CTA	A. Herdner, *Corpus des tablettes en cunéiformes alphabétiques*
DISO	C.-F. Jean and J. Hoftijzer, *Dictionnaire des inscriptions sémitiques de l'ouest* (Leiden, 1965)
EncJud	*Encyclopaedia Judaica* (16 vols.; ed. Cecil Roth; Jerusalem: Keter, 1972)
ErIsr	*Eretz-Israel*
ETL	*Ephemerides theologicae lovanienses*
ExpTim	*Expository Times*

FB	Forschung zur Bibel
FOTL	Forms of the Old Testament Literature
Friedrich HW	Friedrich, *Hethitisches Wörterbuch*
GRBS	*Greek, Roman, and Byzantine Studies*
HALAT	L. Koehler and W. Baumgartner et al., *Hebräisches und aramäisches Lexikon zum Alten Testament*
HAT	Handbuch zum Alten Testament
HAW	Handbuch der Altertumswissenschaft
HSM	Harvard Semitic Monographs
HSS	Harvard Semitic Studies
HTR	*Harvard Theological Review*
HUCA	*Hebrew Union College Annual*
IB	*Interpreter's Bible*
IBC	Interpretation: A Bible Commentary for Teaching and Preaching
ICC	International Critical Commentary
IDB	G. A. Buttrick (ed.), *Interpreter's Dictionary of the Bible*
IDBSup	Supplementary volume to *IDB*
IEJ	*Israel Exploration Journal*
Int	*Interpretation*
IOS	*Israel Oriental Studies*
JAAR	*Journal of the American Academy of Religion*
JANES(CU)	*Journal of the Ancient Near Eastern Society (of Columbia University)*
JAOS	*Journal of the American Oriental Society*
JARCE	*Journal of the American Research Center in Egypt*
JBL	*Journal of Biblical Literature*
JCS	*Journal of Cuneiform Studies*
JEA	*Journal of Egyptian Archaeology*
JEOL	*Jaarbericht van het Voorasiatisch-Egyptisch Genootschap: Ex Oriente Lux*
JESHO	*Journal of Economic and Social History of the Orient*
JETS	*Journal of the Evangelical Theological Society*
JHS	*Journal of Hellenic Studies*
JJS	*Journal of Jewish Studies*
JNES	*Journal of Near Eastern Studies*
JNSL	*Journal of Northwest Semitic Languages*
JR	*Journal of Religion*
JRAS	*Journal of the Royal Asiatic Society*
JSNT	*Journal for the Study of the New Testament*
JSOR	*Journal of the Society of Oriental Research*

JSOT	*Journal for the Study of the Old Testament*
JSOTSup	Journal for the Study of the Old Testament Supplement Series
JSS	*Journal of Semitic Studies*
KAI	H. Donner and W. Röllig, *Kanaanäische und aramäische Inschriften*
KAT	Kommentar zum Alten Testament
KBo	Keilschrifttexte aus Boghazköi
KTU	M. Dietrich, O. Loretz, and J. Sanmartín, *Die keilalphabetischen Texte aus Ugarit* (AOAT 24; Neukirchen-Vluyn, 1976)
KUB	Keilschrifturkunden aus Boghazköi
LAPO	Littératures anciennes du Proche-Orient
LCL	Loeb Classical Library
MARI	*Mari: Annales de recherches interdisciplinaires*
MDOG	*Mitteilungen der deutschen Orient-Gesellschaft*
MEE	Materiali epigrafici di Ebla
MIO	Mitteilungen des Instituts für Orientforschung
MRS	Mission de Ras Shamra
MVAG	Mitteilungen der vorderasiatisch-ägyptischen Gesellschaft
NCB	New Century Bible Commentary
NICOT	New International Commentary on the Old Testament
OBO	Orbis biblicus et orientalis
OBT	Overtures to Biblical Theology
OIP	Oriental Institute Publications
OLZ	*Orientalische Literaturzeitung*
Or	*Orientalia*
OrAnt	*Oriens antiquus*
OTL	Old Testament Library
OTS	*Oudtestamentische Studiën*
PAPS	*Proceedings of the American Philosophical Society*
PEQ	*Palestine Exploration Quarterly*
PRU	Le Palais royal d'Ugarit
PTMS	Pittsburgh Theological Monograph Series
PTR	*Princeton Theological Review*
RA	*Revue d'assyriologie et d'archéologie orientale*
RÄR	H. Bonnet, *Reallexicon der ägyptischen Religionsgeschichte*
RB	*Revue biblique*
RechBib	Recherches bibliques
RGTC	Répertoire Géographique des Textes Cunéiformes
RHA	*Revue hittite et asianique*
RIH	J. de Rougé, *Inscriptions hiéroglyphiques copiées en Égypte*

RLA	*Reallexikon der Assyriologie*
RSR	*Recherches de science religieuse*
SBH	G. A. Reisner, *Sumerisch-babylonische Hymnen nach Thontafeln griechischer Zeit*
SBLDS	SBL Dissertation Series
SBLSCS	SBL Septuagint and Cognate Studies
SBLSP	SBL Seminar Papers
SBLSS	SBL Semeia Studies
SBLTT	SBL Texts and Translations
SBT	Studies in Biblical Theology
SBTS	Sources for Biblical and Theological Study
SC	Sources chrétiennes
SEb	*Studi Eblaiti*
Sem	*Semitica*
SJT	*Scottish Journal of Theology*
StBoT	Studien zu den Boğazköy-Texten
TDOT	G. J. Botterweck and H. Ringgren (eds.), *Theological Dictionary of the Old Testament*
THAT	E. Jenni and C. Westermann (eds.), *Theologische Handwörterbuch zum Alten Testament*
TynBul	*Tyndale Bulletin*
TynOT	Tyndale Old Testament Commentaries
UF	*Ugarit-Forschungen*
UT	C. H. Gordon, *Ugaritic Textbook*
VT	*Vetus Testamentum*
VTSup	Vetus Testamentum Supplements
WBC	Word Biblical Commentary
YNER	Yale Near Eastern Researches
ZA	*Zeitschrift für Assyriologie*
ZÄS	*Zeitschrift für ägyptische Sprache und Altertumskunde*
ZAW	*Zeitschrift für die Alttestamentliche Wissenschaft*
ZDMG	*Zeitschrift der deutschen morgenländischen Gesellschaft*
ZDPV	*Zeitschrift des deutschen Palästina-Vereins*
ZTK	*Zeitschrift für Theologie und Kirche*

SECTION 1

Biblical Studies

Ruth 4:17: A Semantic Wordplay

Frederic William Bush

> And the neighbor-women gave him a name, saying, "A son has been born to Naomi!" And they called his name Obed—he is the father of Jesse, the father of David.

The complex name-giving in Ruth 4:17 is so unusual in both form and content, in a number of respects, that it has often been concluded that the text cannot be correct as it stands and, therefore, various conjectural emendations have been suggested.[1] The problems usually alleged as justification for such surgery are: (1) The neighbor-women not only make the statement that ostensibly explains the name (17a–b), but they also name the child (17c). There are no other examples in the OT of anyone other than the mother, or occasionally the father, naming the child.[2] (2) The speech of the neighbor-women in 17b does not contain a phonetic allusion to or other suggestion related to the name Obed, given to the child by them in 17c, as is usually the case in OT accounts of naming (see the study below). (3) Since 17a contains the expression *qārâ lô šēm* and is followed by what appears to be an explanation of a name introduced by *lēʾmōr* 'saying', it appears to be a defective

---

Author's note: The part of the study entitled "The Literary Character and Meaning of Ruth 4:13–17" is adapted from my commentary *Ruth, Esther* (WBC; Dallas: Word, 1996).

1. Thus, for example, Eissfeldt (1965a: 479–80) deletes 17c ("so they named him Obed—he is the father of Jesse, the father of David") and replaces the noun *šēm* 'name' in 17a with the name *Ben-Noʿam* or the like; Rudolph (1962: 69–70) deletes *šēm* 'name' in v. 17a and emends 'they called' in 17b to either 'he (i.e., Boaz)' or 'she (i.e., Naomi) called'; cf. also Gerleman (1965: 38); Joüon (1953: 95); Witzenrath (1975: 23–26); Würthwein (1969: 2–3, 24).

2. 2 Sam 12:25 is not a parallel at all, for there a prophet gives what is probably a symbolic name, not the child's personal name (cf. Witzenrath 1975: 23). Luke 1:59 also provides no help, for there it is a matter of a suggestion by the neighbors, which the parents decline (so Rudolph 1962: 70). Cf. the remarks of Sasson (1979: 273–74).

etiological name-giving and hence the verse contains two such namings.[3] However, it is the contention of this article that the text can be given a coherent interpretation as it stands if one takes into account (1) the literary character and meaning of vv. 13–17, the pericope of which it is a part, and (2) a correct understanding of the syntax of the various formulas for name-giving in the OT. These two areas will be explored first and then the results will be applied to a coherent interpretation of the passage.

The Literary Character and Meaning of Ruth 4:13–17

For all its brevity, compared with the preceding scene in which Boaz negotiates with the nearer-redeemer before the legal assembly in the city gate, this pericope forms the high point and culmination of the book, for it sets forth the resolution of the central problem of the whole narrative, namely, the death, deprivation, and emptiness of the life of Naomi, the "woman . . . left alone without her two boys and without her husband" (1:5), which the first chapter so powerfully portrayed. This can be clearly and unequivocally brought out by an examination of the structure of the scene, set forth in the diagram on the following page.

The boundaries of the scene are marked by the inclusio formed by "and she bore a son" in 13e and "a son has been born" in 17b. The scene itself divides into two episodes. Each episode comprises a narrative statement (A, v. 13; A′, v. 16) followed by a resultant action on the part of the women of the city (B, vv. 14–15, B′, v. 17a–c). It is clear that each of the actions of the women, the first a speech (vv. 14–15), the second a name-giving (v. 17a–c), constitutes a response to the important events related in the preceding narrative statements. Both structure and content unite to confirm this. Even though the events of v. 13 are glad and joyous and constitute the fulfillment of preceding plans and promises, they are nonetheless related in a series of five rapid-fire, staccato-like clauses, the longest of which comprises but four words! This very brevity signals that this is not the point of the scene. Rather, in keeping with the pattern set by all of the preceding scenes, the high point is provided by the speech of the participants—in this case, the speech of the women of Bethlehem. Their threefold speech provides the commentary on and the meaning of the events just related in brief compass. Likewise, in v. 16 it is the touching and tender scene of an old woman's joy in and care for the

3. See Ap-Thomas 1967–68: 370–71; Campbell 1975: 166; Eissfeldt 1965a: 479; Joüon 1953: 95; Witzenrath 1975: 24–25.

The Structure of Ruth 4:13–17

Hebrew	Verse	English	Section
ויקח בעז את־רות	13a.	So Boaz took Ruth	**A** Narrative Statement
ותהי־לו לאשה	b.	and she became his wife.	
ויבא אליה ויתן יהוה לה הריון	c–d.	And he entered to her and Yahweh gave her conception	
ותלד בן	e.	and she bore a son.	
ותאמרנה הנשים אל־נעמי	14a.	And the women said to Naomi,	**B** Speech of the Women
ברוך יהוה אשר לא השבית לך גאל היום	b.	"Blessed be Yahweh, who has not left you today without a redeemer.	
ויקרא שמו בישראל	c.	May his name be renowned in Israel!	
והיה לך למשיב נפש ולכלכל את־שיבתך	15a.	He shall become the one who restores your life and provides for your old age,	
כי כלתך אשר־אהבתך ילדתו אשר־היא טובה לך משבעה בנים	b.	for your daughter-in-law who loves you has borne him—she who is more to you than seven sons!"	
ותקח נעמי את־הילד	16a.	And Naomi took the boy	**A′** Narrative Statement
ותשתהו בחיקה	b.	and held him to her breast	
ותהי־לו לאמנת	c.	and became the one who took care of him	
ותקראנה לו השכנות שם לאמר	17a.	And the neighbor-women gave him a name, saying,	**B′** Action of the Women
ילד־בן לנעמי	b.	"A son has been born to Naomi!"	
ותקראנה שמו עובד	c.	And they called his name Obed.	
הוא אבי־ישי אבי דוד	d.	—he is the father of Jesse, the father of David	

child—a woman so long bereaved and bereft of husband and sons—that triggers the glad cry of the neighboring women that at last a son has been born to Naomi. This cry in turn forms the circumstances that suggest his name, "Obed," literally 'servant', but in context 'guardian, provider', he who will care for and sustain her in her old age (see the discussion below).

These two episodes exhibit strictly synonymous parallelism. Thus, the narrative statements A (13a–e) and A′ (16a–c) are parallel in both form and content: in form—each consists of a series of short, staccato-like, temporally sequential clauses; and in content—each begins with a clause of identical syntactic structure using "to take" (13a and 16a) and each contains a clause of identical syntactic structure using the idiom "And she became to him . . ."

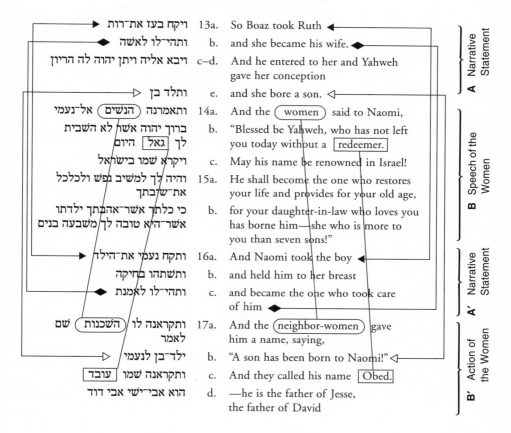

(13b and 16c). The resultant actions B (14a–15b) and B′ (17a–c) are also parallel in form and content: each involves a statement made by the women of the city (14a, 17a); both center their entire attention on the relationship between the newborn child ("a redeemer," 14b; "a son," "Obed," 17b–c) and Naomi (14a, 17b); and each contains the idiom "call his name" (14c, 17a). Indeed, the appended and important appositive in 17d, "he is the father of Jesse, the father of David," provides the fulfillment of the prayer of the women for the newborn infant in 14c, "May his name be renowned in Israel."

The expanded length and fullness of the first statement of the women, B (14a–15b), signals that here is the most important part of the scene. And even though it has the form of words of praise to Yahweh, which is important in its own right, the reason for the women's praise centers on Naomi. The narrative introduction (14a) notes that it is addressed to her, and the second person feminine singular pronominal suffix, referring to Naomi, reverberates six times throughout the women's speech.

As this structure reveals, the central point of the scene describes Naomi's restoration to life and fullness. The speech of the women, who comprise a sort of "female chorus,"[4] devotes itself almost exclusively to describing the significance of the birth of this child for Naomi. Who this child is to be for her they describe first of all by designating him as her "redeemer." Here they use the term in the same sense with which it is used throughout the rest of the book (except for the technical force it carries during the legal negotiations at the gate in 4:1–12), namely, the one responsible to deliver a relative from evil of any kind. We are not left to wonder about the evil from which Naomi needs deliverance, for the women go on (v. 15) to describe him in terms that lack nothing in clarity. He is to be both the "one who provides for her old age" and "the one who restores her life" (15a). The resolution is perfect. Our story has come full circle. Death and emptiness (1:3–5, 21) have given way to life and fullness. The vehicle our author uses to describe this transformation is appropriate in every way: it is the women of Bethlehem, whose delighted cry of recognition in 1:19 triggered Naomi's bitter lament, "Full was I when I went away but empty has Yahweh *brought me back*," and they are the ones who now in jubilant chorus describe the complete reversal of her tragic state and encapsulate her restoration in their happy description of the child as the "one who *brings back* life."

This is in quite striking contrast to the male personnel and concerns that occupied center stage in the previous scene, for this scene is completely dominated not only by women, but by the concerns that are theirs. Yahweh is not celebrated by the female chorus because he has provided a descendant

4. See Porten 1978: 30, 47.

for the line of Elimelech, but because he has not left Naomi without a redeemer to care for her in her need. The female chorus does not see the meaning of this child in the fact that he is the heir of Elimelech and will inherit his property, but in the fact that he restores Naomi to life and will support her in her old age. Nor do they celebrate his identity by crying, "A son has been born to Elimelech," but rather, "A son has been born to Naomi." At every level, then, the point and purpose of this scene is to describe the transformation of Naomi's life from death and emptiness to life and fullness. With the final clause appended to the name Obed, our author leaves the women, the female chorus, and their joyous celebration of Naomi to set forth the status of this child in his own male world, but this only serves to underline all the more dramatically the significance of the reversal of Naomi's fate, for this reversal also redounds to the life and fullness of all Israel: the child who is the means to her restoration was to be the grandfather of the great king David.

The Syntactic Structures of Name-Giving in the Old Testament

If one investigates the examples of name-giving in the OT,[5] the types of syntactic structure that occur are as follows:[6]

§1. The Generic Statement:
*qārā*ᵓ + *šēm* + [*lĕ* + ps/N]
E.g., וַיִּקְרָא הָאָדָם שֵׁמוֹת לְכָל־הַבְּהֵמָה Gen 2:20
'And the man gave (lit. called) names to all the animals . . .'
(Cf. also Gen 26:18, Isa 65:15, Ps 147:4.)

In this use the noun שֵׁם 'name' (plural or singular) is indefinite and stands in the absolute state (that is, it is not modified by a pronominal suffix, nor does it stand in construct with a following noun). The idiom simply makes the general statement that someone "called a name (or names) to a person or object (or persons, objects)."

5. With the exception of Witzenrath 1975: 21–23, the studies of name-giving extant are either brief and incomplete (cf. Eissfeldt 1965a: 479; Hubbard 1988a: 260 n. 40; 1988b: 295; Labuschagne, *THAT* 2.671; Sasson 1979: 164–65, 179) or have another end in view than the syntactic structure (cf. Key 1964: 55–59). Witzenrath's study is deficient in failing to recognize the existence of both the generic name-giving statement (see §1) and one variant of the non-etiological name-giving formula (see §2b below).

6. In the syntactic analysis the following abbreviations are used: ps = pronominal suffix; N = noun; gen. = noun governed by *šēm* 'name' in the construct state (i.e., a *nomen rectum*); PN = personal name. Since it occurs only rarely and only with place-names, the analysis ignores the structure *qārā*ᵓ + direct object + name (cf. Gen 26:33).

§2. The non-etiological name-giving. In this form no explanation of the name is stated. Two syntactic structures occur:[7]

§2a. *qārāʾ* + [*šēm* + ps/gen] + PN
E.g., וַיִּקְרָא אֶת־שְׁמוֹ אֱנוֹשׁ Gen 4:26
'And he called his name Enosh'.
(Cf. also Gen 5:2, 3; 16:15; 17:19; 30:21; 38:3, 4, 5; Judg 13:24; 2 Sam 12:24; 1 Chr 7:16; Job 42:14.)

§2b. *qārāʾ* + [*lĕ* + ps/N] + PN
E.g., וְאָבִיו קָרָא לוֹ בִנְיָמִין Gen 35:18
'But his father called him Benjamin'.
(Cf. also Num 13:16; elsewhere to name places and things, e.g., Gen 1:5, 8, 10; 33:20, etc.)

Form (a) is used most commonly for persons. Form (b) is used twice to rename someone (Gen 35:18, Num 13:16; cf. also the name-giving form in §3b(2) below). Elsewhere it is used to name places and other inanimate objects.

§3. The etiological name-giving. In this form an explanation of the name is given. Two different syntactic structures occur, depending on whether the explanation of the name (a) precedes or (b) follows the name-giving itself, yielding the following types:

§3a. Explanation preceding. When the explanation precedes, the name-giving is syntactically joined by either (1) a *wâw*-consecutive form of *qārāʾ* or (2) the conjunction *ʿal kēn* 'therefore' plus the perfect tense of *qārāʾ*:

Explanation + { (1) *qārāʾ* (*wâw*-consec.) + [*šēm* + ps/gen] / (2) *ʿal kēn* + *qārāʾ* (pf.) + [*šēm* + ps/gen] } + PN

The explanation of the name may be a narrative statement describing an attendant circumstance (e.g., Gen 25:25–26). But predominantly it is a direct speech of one of the principals, most often the mother.

E.g., וַתֹּאמֶר כִּי שָׁמַע יהוה כִּי שְׂנוּאָה אָנֹכִי . . . וַתִּקְרָא שְׁמוֹ שִׁמְעוֹן Gen 29:33
'And she said, "Because Yahweh has heard (Heb. *šāmaʿ*) that I am unloved," . . . and so she called his name Simeon (Heb. *šimʿôn*)'.

7. Cf. Labuschagne, *THAT* 2.671.

In one case, of interest for the Ruth passage, the speech is that of the midwife (Gen 38:27–29):

> . . . there were twins in her womb. And when she was giving birth, one of them put out a hand and the midwife took it and tied a scarlet thread on it, saying, "This one came out first." But when he withdrew his hand and his brother came out first, וַתֹּאמֶר מַה־פָּרַצְתָּ עָלֶיךָ פָּרֶץ וַיִּקְרָא שְׁמוֹ פָּרֶץ [Gen 38:29], she said, "What a breach you have opened for yourself (Heb. *pāraṣtā*)!" And so his name was called Perez (Heb. *pereṣ*).

See also, for syntactic structure (1), Gen 25:25, 26; 29:33; 30:8, 11, 13, 18, 20, 23–24; 38:29, 30; and for syntactic structure (2), Gen 25:30; 29:34, 35; 30:6.

§3b. Explanation following. When the explanation follows, the name-giving formula regularly exhibits the structure noted in §2a above, and the explanation is introduced by the particle *kî* 'for, because':

(1) *qārā*ʾ + [*šēm* + ps/gen] + PN + *kî* + explanation

Again the explanation may be either a narrative statement describing an attendant circumstance (e.g., Gen 3:20) or a direct speech of one of the principals.

> E.g., וַתִּקְרָא שְׁמוֹ רְאוּבֵן כִּי אָמְרָה כִּי־רָאָה יהוה בְּעָנְיִי Gen 29:32
> 'And she called his name Reuben, for she said, "It is because the Lord has seen my misery"'.

See also Gen 3:20; 4:25; 16:11; 41:51, 52; Exod 2:22; Isa 8:3–4; Hos 1:4, 6, 9; etc. There is a variant of this structure in three instances: the explanation is introduced by *lēʾmōr* 'saying', instead of the particle *kî* (Gen 5:29, 30:24; 1 Chr 4:9); in two instances, in addition to introducing the explanation with *lēʾmōr*, the name-giving formula exhibits the variant noted in §2b above, e.g.,

> (2) וַיִּקְרָא לוֹ . . . יְרֻבַּעַל לֵאמֹר יָרֶב בּוֹ הַבַּעַל Judg 6:32
> 'And he called him . . . Jerubbaal, saying "Let Baal take action against him"'.
> (Cf. also 1 Sam 4:21.)[8]

In the vast majority of occurrences of the etiological forms of name-giving, whether type 3a or 3b, the explanation depends on parasonancy,[9] that is, it contains a *phonetic* allusion to or suggestion of the name. Usually the phonetic allusion is very close and obvious, as in the examples cited in §2a above

8. In one instance the explanation is introduced by *wâw*-consecutive plus *ʾāmar*, Exod 2:10; cf. also in the naming of a place, Gen 26:22, 1 Sam 7:12.

9. See Sasson, *IDBSup*, 969.

(Gen 29:33, 38:29). In other cases the allusion is remote and obscure, as in Gen 25:25 where *śĕʿār* 'hair, fur' suggests the name *ʿēśāw* 'Esau', or 1 Sam 1:20 where the wordplay on the name *šĕmûʾēl* 'Samuel' is so obscure as virtually to defy explanation.[10] Most important, however, for the interpretation of Ruth 4:17 is the fact that occasionally a variant of this type of wordplay occurs. In this case the explanation of the name does not depend on parasonancy, that is, on *phonetic* allusion, but on a play on meaning.[11] For example, in Gen 35:18b the name that Rebecca gives to Benjamin, Ben-Oni, 'Son of my sorrow', is explained by the circumstance, related in v. 18a, that her difficult labor resulted in her death. Similarly, in Gen 38:30 the name *zeraḥ* 'Zerah' (as if from *zeraḥ* 'sunrise', cf. 2 Kgs 3:22) is explained by a semantic play on *šānî* 'scarlet thread'.[12]

The Interpretation of Ruth 4:17

Having noted, then, the literary character and meaning of vv. 13–17 and having analyzed the syntactic structures of name-giving in the OT, we turn to a coherent interpretation of 4:17.

To begin, if one compares these attested types of name-giving with Ruth 4:17, it seems clear, as far as the structure is concerned at least, that the text as it stands is an example of the etiological name-giving of type 3a(1):

> Explanation: v. 17a–b
> וַתִּקְרֶאנָה לוֹ הַשְּׁכֵנוֹת שֵׁם לֵאמֹר יֻלַּד־בֵּן לְנָעֳמִי
> 'And the neighbor women gave him a name, saying, "A son has been born to Naomi"'.
>
> Name-giving: v. 17c
> וַתִּקְרֶאנָה שְׁמוֹ עוֹבֵד
> 'And they called his name Obed'.

10. The etymology of the name is clearly related to *šēm* 'name' and *ʾēl* 'God', but the exact meaning is quite unclear. The sense is usually taken to be 'His name is God', which has been interpreted to mean "He over whom the name of God has been said" or "His name (i.e., the name on which the bearer calls in worship) is *ʾEl*" (McCarter 1984). The play is usually taken to be on some form of the verb *šāʾal* 'to ask' that occurs in the explanation (cf. also vv. 27–28).

11. Cf. Witzenrath 1975: 24.

12. Compare also 2 Sam 12:24–25, where Yahweh's name for Solomon *yĕdîdyāh* 'Jedidiah' (i.e., 'beloved of Yahweh') is explained by the preceding statement *wayhwh ʾăhēbô* 'Yahweh loved him'. Note the semantic wordplay in the naming of places and objects in Gen 22:14, 26:21; 1 Sam 23:24–28.

The explanation precedes, consisting of a speech of one of the principals. It is admittedly unusual that this explanation contains the idiom *qārāʾ* + [*lĕ* + ps] + *šēm* and is followed by what could be taken as an explanation of a name introduced by *lēʾmōr* (cf. type 3b(1) above). Hence, a number of scholars have alleged that it is a defective name-giving, in which the noun *šēm* 'name' appears instead of the personal name, and so have resorted to conjectural emendation.[13] Others, seeking to avoid emendation, have rendered the phrase *qārāʾ* + [*lĕ* + ps] + *šēm* by such expressions as "to proclaim his significance,"[14] "to rejoice over him,"[15] or "to establish his reputation."[16] But all such attempts at emendation or reinterpretation fail to recognize that there is actually nothing defective about the form at all.[17] It is simply an example of the well-attested generic name-giving statement described in type 1 above.[18]

13. See nn. 1 and 3 above.

14. Hubbard 1988b: 299–301; cf. 1988a: 13, 14–15. Since there is no "comparable OT usage" (1988a: 14), he posits this meaning partially on the similar sense of the related idiom *qārāʾ šēm* 'to be/become famous' in 4:11, 14 (1988a: 15), but primarily on "consideration of the immediate context itself" (1988b: 300). So also Gray 1986: 402.

15. Campbell (1975: 165–66) argues *ad hoc* that the phrase bears the same meaning as the idiom *qārāʾ šēm* in 4:14, which he renders 'to celebrate', and so "by far the simplest meaning for the beginning of verse 17 is that the celebrating has begun" (p. 166).

16. Sasson 1979: 168. Although Sasson nowhere discusses the meaning of the phrase in v. 17a, it seems clear that he assumes that it bears the same meaning as the idiom *qārāʾ šēm* in 4:11, which he renders 'maintain a reputation' (1979: 156; cf. 164–66). None of these attempts at reinterpretation by Hubbard, Campbell and Sasson, which allude to the usage in vv. 11 and 14, takes into account the very important syntactic difference between the two idioms, namely, the inclusion of the element *lĕ* + pronominal suffix, which clearly and unequivocally makes this an example of the generic name-giving statement (type 1 above). Furthermore, this realization makes quite impossible Sasson's speculative comparison (1979: 233–35) of this idiom with passages in the literature of the ancient Near East in which female deities are assigned "the task of establishing the fate, hence the future, of a newborn male," which newborn "if human is invariably a future king" (p. 233). Since the idiom here does not mean 'establish his reputation' but rather 'give him a name', there simply is no "vestigial motif" (p. 237) present here to be compared with the activities of female birth deities cited by Sasson.

17. In addition, attempts to reinterpret the meaning of the phrase really do not solve the problem that they are in part adopted to solve, namely, the lack of any phonetic allusion between the contents of vv. 17a–b and the name Obed in 17c. Whatever the particular meaning of the phrase adopted in each solution, the unavoidable implication in the resulting sequence is that the first two clauses (17a–b) are intended to provide the explanation for the name (i.e., it is of the type 3a(1) above), and the change in meaning of 17a facilitates nothing in this regard.

18. Hubbard's statement that "the typical naming formula is *qārāʾ šēm* (with attached suffix) + proper name" (1988b: 295) has missed not only the equally valid (but much less frequent) form *qārāʾ* + [*lĕ* + ps/N] + PN (yet see 1988a: 260 n. 40!) but also the existence

The name-giving itself in 17c follows the exceedingly common pattern of type 3a(1).[19] When this and the literary character and meaning of vv. 13–17 are taken into account, the alleged problems of interpretation of the passage as it stands disappear and the text can be given a coherent interpretation that fits the context. The fact that it is the women-neighbors who name the child is, as Hubbard puts it,[20] "literarily appropriate." As our investigation of the literary character and meaning of vv. 13–17 has shown, the author has used the "female chorus" in vv. 14–15 as the fitting vehicle to express the sense of wonder and joy that the birth of this child means in restoring Naomi to life and fullness. Hence, here in v. 17 he has them continue that same theme in their joyful exclamation, "A son has been born to Naomi!" Here our narrator uses his "poetic license"; he does not expect us to take him literally and to believe that it was the neighbor-women who actually formally named the child. What he means by his blatant statement "they (fem. pl.) named him," so utterly in conflict with the fact known to all that the parents (usually the mother) named the child, is that these women "named" him by providing the explanation for his name with their glad cry, "A son is born to Naomi." An analogous situation is provided by the naming of Perez in Gen 38:27–29. Here, as the infant is born, the midwife exclaims, "What a breach you have made!" (v. 27c), and the narrator then relates that the child was named Perez 'breach' (v. 27a).[21] If it had been literarily appropriate in this setting, the narrator could just as well have said, "The midwife gave him a name, saying, 'What a breach you have made,'" for it is this exclamation that provides the explanation for the name. Further illumination that buttresses this understanding has been provided by Hubbard.[22] He notes the parallels between the statement of the women, "A son has been born to Naomi," and the language of Jer 20:15 and Isa 9:5, which he interprets as a "common birth-announcement formula," regularly made to the father who waits nearby during the birth to hear the joyous news. Although the evidence is limited,[23]

of this generic naming statement. Hence his judgment on v. 17a that "recent research has shown it not to be a formula of naming" (1988b: 299) is incorrect.

19. Cf. also type 2a.

20. Hubbard 1988b: 294.

21. *Wayyiqrāʾ šĕmô pāreṣ* could be rendered 'And he (the father?) named him Perez', but is best taken as an example of a Qal passive. In the light of the discussion here, the variant reading of a few Heb. MSS, the Samaritan Pentateuch, the Syriac, and *Targum Pseudo-Jonathan*, *wattiqrāʾ* 'And she named . . .' is of interest. If original, as sometimes alleged, it would produce the same kind of misunderstanding as the text of Ruth 4:17.

22. Hubbard 1988b: 295–99; cf. 1988a: 13–14.

23. The data is at most suggestive and the Isaiah example is fraught with interpretive

it is highly suggestive. Such a setting would be most appropriate to the scene in Ruth.[24] Exercising his literary license, our author underscores the significance of this child for Naomi—she who was childless now has a son—by applying to her the very language of the joyous birth announcement that commonly comes to the waiting father.

Finally, this same setting also provides a reasonably coherent explanation for the objection often raised, namely, that in the explanation in 17a–b there is no phonetic allusion to the name Obed given in 17c. Here we must recognize that the passage does not contain a phonetic wordplay but a play on meaning. This has been cogently argued by Eissfeldt in two articles[25] in which he reverses the view set forth in *The Old Testament*[26] regarding the lack of historical connection between the story of Ruth and the family line of David. Here Eissfeldt argues that tradition gave the names of Boaz, Ruth, and Obed to the author of Ruth as historical celebrities, namely, as ancestors of David, and this fact explains the unevennesses that led him and others to emend v. 17. Obed was known to the narrator as the name of the son of Ruth. Hence, in the statement of the women, "A son is born to Naomi," he could make no wordplay of any kind between the name "Obed" and "Naomi."[27] But, far more to the point, the emphasis in the women's statement is not on "Naomi" but on "son."[28] What the narrator intends is a play based on meaning: the son born to Naomi receives the name Obed 'servant', understood here in the sense of 'provider' (cf. Mal 3:17), since he will show the kindness incumbent on a son for his grandmother. The context for this play on meaning is set by the relationship between Naomi and this "son" already stated with unmistakable clarity in vv. 14–15. Here the women congratulate Naomi because Yahweh has given her a "redeemer," one who "will restore her life and provide for her in her old age."[29] Since the context has already made this clear, the play on meaning between "A son has been born to Naomi" and the name "Obed," otherwise somewhat restrained and remote, is feasible enough.[30]

difficulties; see Hubbard's remarks (1988b: 296–98). However, see the study of Parker (1988: 138–39), who notes in addition a parallel in the KRT epic from Ugarit.

24. So Hubbard 1988b: 298–99.

25. Eissfeldt 1965b; 1966.

26. Eissfeldt 1965a: 479–80.

27. Eissfeldt 1965b: 26–28.

28. Eissfeldt 1966: 47.

29. Ibid.

30. Contra Witzenrath 1975: 282 n. 143 (cf. Rudolph 1962: 70), the fact that Obed is in all probability a hypocoristic or diminutive for a theophoric name (cf. עֹבַדְיָה/עֹבַדְיָהוּ, a name borne by twelve different men in the OT) does not speak against this view, for a semantic play of this kind totally ignores scientific etymology.

Bibliography

Ap-Thomas, D. R.
1967–68 "The Book of Ruth." *ExpTim* 79: 369–73.

Campbell, Edward F.
1975 *Ruth: A New Translation with Introduction, Notes and Commentary.* AB 7. Garden City, N.Y.: Doubleday.

Eissfeldt, Otto
1965a *The Old Testament: An Introduction.* Trans. by P. R. Ackroyd. New York: Harper and Row.
1965b "Wahreit und Dichtung in der Ruth-Erzählung." *Sitzungsberichte der Sächsischen Akademie der Wissenschaften zu Leipzig, Phil.-hist. Klasse* 110: 23–28.
1966 "Sohnespflichten im Alten Orient." *Syria* 43: 23–28.

Gerleman, Gillis
1965 *Ruth, Das Hohelied.* BKAT 18. Neukirchen-Vluyn: Neukirchener Verlag.

Gray, John
1986 *Joshua, Judges, Ruth.* NCBC. Grand Rapids: Eerdmans.

Hubbard, Robert L., Jr.
1988a *The Book of Ruth.* NICOT. Grand Rapids: Eerdmans.
1988b "Ruth IV 17: A New Solution." *VT* 38: 293–301.

Joüon, Paul
1953 *Ruth: Commentaire philologique et éxégetique.* Rome: Pontifical Biblical Institute.

Key, Andrew F.
1964 "The Giving of Proper Names in the Old Testament." *JBL* 83: 55–59.

McCarter, P. K.
1984 *I Samuel: A New Translation with Introduction, Notes and Commentary.* AB 8. Garden City, N.Y.: Doubleday.

Parker, S. B.
1988 "The Birth Announcement." Pp. 133–49 in L. Eslinger and G. Taylor (eds.), *Ascribe to the Lord: Biblical and Other Studies in Memory of Peter C. Craigie.* JSOTSup 67. Sheffield: Sheffield Academic Press.

Porten, Bezalel
1978 "The Scroll of Ruth: A Rhetorical Study." *Gratz College Annual of Jewish Studies* 7: 23–29.

Rudolph, Wilhelm
1962 *Das Buch Ruth.* KAT 18. Gütersloh: Mohn.

Sasson, Jack M.
1979 *Ruth: A New Translation with a Philological Commentary and a Formalist-Folklorist Interpretation.* Baltimore: Johns Hopkins University Press.

Witzenrath, Hagia H.
1975 *Das Buch Rut: Eine literaturwissenschaftliche Untersuchung.* Munich: Kösel.

Würthwein, Ernst
1969 *Ruth, Das Hohelied, Esther.* In *Die Fünf Megilloth.* HAT 18. 2d ed. Tübingen: Mohr.

Joseph, Moses, and the Institution of the Israelite Judicature

Calum M. Carmichael

David Daube, in a historic lecture at St. Paul's Cathedral in London,[1] stated at the beginning,

> All history-writing transfers features of one event or one great personage to another, and, indeed, much history-acting is in imitation of previous occurrences. Whoever nowadays writes about Napoleon is likely to lend him some traits of Caesar, and Napoleon himself—not to mention de Gaulle—would on occasion look to that example. This general phenomenon, that history, whether reflected upon or in the making, harks back to history, is enormously accentuated in New Testament times because, in the then prevalent view, Old Testament events and personages were largely a prefigurement of things to come.

Author's note: It is a privilege to contribute to a festschrift for Dwight Young. He is unfailingly generous in putting his unique scholarly abilities at the disposal of those of us less gifted than he. In recent years he has been engaged in a study of that most puzzling of problems in the book of Genesis, the scheme of numbers used in recording the life spans and epochs of the patriarchs. His initial published results herald a major breakthrough (see "On the Application of Numbers from Babylonian Mathematics to Biblical Life Spans and Epochs," *ZAW* 100 [1988] 331–61; "A Mathematical Approach to Certain Dynastic Spans in the Sumerian King List," *JNES* 47 [1988] 123–29; "The Influence of Babylonian Algebra on Longevity among the Antediluvians," *ZAW* 102 [1990] 321–35). The observations of this essay on another aspect of biblical historiography might be of some interest to him.

1. D. Daube, *He That Cometh* (London: Council of Christians and Jews, 1966) 1. The lecture was historic because, in re-arguing a view put forward some forty years earlier by Robert Eisler, he established decisively the link between the *aphikoman* of the Passover *Seder* and the origin of the Eucharist. For a recent critique, see D. B. Carmichael, "David Daube on the Eucharist and the Passover Service," *JSNT* 42 (1991) 45–67. I introduced Dwight to David Daube in Boston many years ago. Shortly thereafter he invited Daube to give a lecture at Brandeis University on "Dissent in Bible and Talmud," published in *Collected Works of David Daube*, vol. 1: *Talmudic Law* (ed. C. M. Carmichael; Berkeley: Robbins Collection, 1992) 33–44.

The phenomenon in fact is no less pronounced, although less attention has been given to it, when we observe the way in which events in the Hebrew Bible are recounted.

There is a sense in which even the world is re-created after the flood. Lot's drunkenness is like Noah's in that members of the immediate family abuse the *paterfamilias.* Abraham has a problem about who, Isaac and not Ishmael, is to have the right of the firstborn; this problem recurs for Isaac when Jacob wins out over Esau; and Jacob denies the right to Reuben and confers it upon Joseph, whose firstborn son Manasseh is in turn displaced by Ephraim. Or again, Jacob's role as a slave (or quasi-slave) with Laban and with Esau (on meeting up with him Jacob addresses Esau as a servant addressing a master—Gen 32:18, 20; 33:5, 8) has its parallel in Joseph's role as a slave in Egypt, and his experience in turn is repeated in the later lives of all the Israelites in Egypt. Or again, problems of deception in male-female relations recur: Abraham has a problem because his wife is beautiful to behold, and he gives out disinformation that she is his sister and not his spouse; his son Isaac has the same problem with his wife Rebecca; Jacob, in turn, wants the lovely Rachel as his wife but is duped into marrying her not-so-beautiful sister Leah; his son, Joseph, is faced with the problem of the scheming wife of Potiphar. Or again, generation after generation a king's religious stance is compared to a predecessor's.

The story of the Exodus provides a further illustration of how someone writing about one historical episode harks back to preceding events and personages. The writer links, in a way that has not been observed before, the event of the Exodus and its aftermath in which Moses is the foremost player to the immediately preceding event of the nation's experience of famine in which Joseph is the central figure.

First and foremost, we can observe the link between the two episodes by noting that the destiny of both Joseph and Moses was the rescue of their fellow Hebrews from hardship—famine in Joseph's case, enslavement in Moses'. We might add the following less momentous links.

Moses was saved from the river by someone, the pharaoh's daughter, who belonged to a foreign nation. His name supposedly reflects this rescue: "Because I [Pharaoh's daughter] drew [*māšâ*] him out of the water" (Exod 2:10). He ended up as a member of an Egyptian family, not with his own Hebrew family, although his mother, unbeknown to his adoptive mother, was his nurse.

Joseph was taken from the pit, his life saved by a foreign Midianite group, but he too ended up as a member of an Egyptian household. Both Joseph and Moses escaped a direct death: murder in the case of Joseph at the hands of his brothers; drowning in the case of Moses because of the pharaoh's decree. A close relative, Joseph's brother Reuben, Moses' sister Miriam, played a part in delivering each from death.

His fellow Hebrews treated Moses in a hostile way because they saw him as setting himself up as a ruler and judge over them (Exod 2:13, 14). Joseph was met with the hostility of his brothers because of his dreams: "Shalt thou indeed reign over us? or shalt thou indeed have dominion over us?" (Gen 37:8). As a sequel to the respective attacks on their standing among their fellow Hebrews, Moses and Joseph ended up in a neighboring country, Joseph in Egypt, Moses in Midian. In that foreign setting each married the daughter of a priest: Joseph married Asenath, daughter of Potiphera, priest of On (Gen 41:45); Moses married Zipporah, daughter of Jethro, priest of Midian (Exod 2:16–22). Each produced two sons by these unions.

During the time of residence in Egypt, each outdid his Egyptian counterpart and so revealed his superior status to the native-born. Joseph interpreted the pharaoh's dreams when the Egyptian magicians and wise men could not (Genesis 41). Moses (in conjunction with Aaron) outdid the Egyptian "wise men and the sorcerers; . . . the magicians of Egypt" in secret arts (Exod 7:11).[2]

I presume that the role of imitation common to all history-writing provides the general explanation for these links between Joseph and Moses: an author selects incidents and developments for presentation because they are reminiscent of—or made reminiscent of[3]—what has occurred before. We might consider other, specific factors at work in biblical historiography. Writing about the origins of German nationalism, J. J. Sheehan refers to how "The apostles of nationalism were able to create a historical memory of 'liberation' which projected their own enthusiasms on to the nation." He further states, "As is always the case with patriotic myths, the historical memory of liberation took many forms and had many different heroes."[4] The account of ancient Israel's liberation from enslavement in Egypt is, *mutatis mutandis*, less a product of historical fact than of the historical imagination of writers expressing their own beliefs and enthusiasms. What I wish to suggest is that

2. The phenomenon of an outsider standing out in this way is commonplace at all times and places, as for example, in the cases of Napoleon and Hitler. See David Daube's assessment of the phenomenon in *Sons and Strangers* (Boston: Institute of Jewish Law, Boston University School of Law, 1984) 1.

3. For a masterly presentation of the role of imitation in the ancient world at all levels of literary activity, see Thomas L. Brodie, *The Quest for the Origin of John's Gospel* (Oxford: Oxford University Press, 1993) 38–47.

4. J. J. Sheehan, *German History 1770–1866* (Oxford: Clarendon, 1989) 386–87.

the writer (or writers) who elevated Moses to such a supreme position in the legend about the origin of his nation did so by linking him, not just through the universal process of viewing one period of history as a reflection of a preceding one and therefore linking him to Joseph as one hero to another, but in another quite specific, sophisticated way.

Critics have claimed that the legend about Joseph has exerted no further influence on biblical literature. D. B. Redford speaks about the "virtually complete silence of the rest of scripture on the subject of the Joseph story. The romanticized hero of the Genesis story almost never appears elsewhere in the Old Testament outside Genesis and the first chapter of Exodus."[5] M. Niehoff puzzles over the (alleged) fact that in late antiquity the biblical Joseph enjoyed great popularity among Jewish interpreters in contrast to "the rather insignificant role which Joseph plays in the shaping of Israelite religion."[6] We can jettison this common view about the supposed lack of influence of the Joseph story on other biblical material. J. L. Kugel's comments, in turn, are curiously uncritical. At one point he refers to how Joseph "eschews revenge and hatred," how his virtue is supreme. Yet he refers to his "intrigue with their [the brothers'] grain sacks," and, "If he [Joseph] does arrange things so as to give his brothers a scare or two along the way—well, a reader most likely feels that this is only justified in view of their earlier misconduct."[7] We can also jettison claims such as Joseph's unquestioned virtue. The fact is that the writer of the Exodus narrative, taking stock of Joseph's actions, adopts in at least two instances a religious ethical stance that results in a negative judgment on Joseph.[8] One consequence is the further elevation of the legend of the Exodus as a model of divine initiative with Moses idealized more than Joseph.

When Joseph's brothers came to Egypt to obtain food to relieve their hunger, Joseph's power to confer life or death loomed over them time and again. This was true, for example, on their first visit to Egypt, when they stood accused of spying.[9] Unbeknown to them, he was intent on pursuing justice

5. D. B. Redford, *A Study of the Biblical Story of Joseph* (VTSup 20; Leiden: Brill, 1970) 249–50.

6. M. Niehoff, "The Figure of Joseph in the Targums," *JJS* 39 (1988) 234–50.

7. J. L. Kugel, *In Potiphar's House* (San Francisco: Harper, 1990) 13, 14, 22.

8. On just how extensive is the criticism of Joseph's ways, see my discussion of the rules in Exod 23:6–9 in *The Origins of Biblical Law* (Ithaca: Cornell University Press, 1922) 193–203. These rules are formulated precisely in response to Joseph's questionable conduct with his brothers.

9. On the theme of life and death in the Joseph narrative, see W. Brueggemann, "Life and Death in Tenth Century Israel," *JAAR* 40 (1972) 96–109.

because of their original offense against him. To this end he engaged in a transaction with them that involved deception on his part. When providing them grain in return for money, he had the money replaced in their sacks of grain when they were not looking (Gen 42:25, 44:1).[10] Ordinarily, deception in a transaction of this kind takes the form of cheating the recipient out of the full value of the commodity for which he has paid money. Joseph, however, had his own reasons for tormenting his brothers in such a contrary manner.

After the Exodus from Egypt, the Israelites accused Moses of bringing them into the wilderness to kill them with hunger (Exod 16:3). In other words, they saw Moses as exercising the power of life or death over them. Their situation was also like the brothers' in that, while there was no food elsewhere, there was food in Egypt: "When we sat by the flesh pots, and when we did eat bread to the full" (v. 3). The deity caused food to be rained down upon the ground to relieve their hunger. Its distribution proved to be remarkably exact and fair. When measured by the technical quantity, the omer, each family received according to its needs, nothing more, nothing less (Exod 16:18). The narrator places much emphasis on this aspect of the deity's action. He, probably the Priestly redactor, even gives the technical information that an omer is the tenth part of an ephah (Exod 16:36). Unlike Joseph's underhanded dealings in providing his family with grain, the deity's dealings with the Israelite families are open and honest.

Joseph no doubt viewed his resort to deception as a means to a just end in his dispute with his brothers. God's provision of the manna presents a contrasting situation because deceptive practice designed to bring about the resolution of a dispute is totally lacking. Nonetheless, there is a substantial overlap in aim because the deity's eminently fair action is intended to lead to a furtherance of Israel's commitment to law-abiding ways. God's action is comparable to Joseph's in its purpose. The intent of the provision of the food to the Israelites is not just to relieve their hunger, but to inculcate the habit of sabbath observance. This is why two omers of manna, not one as on the previous five days, were provided on the sixth day (Exod 16:5, 22–30). Even then, despite instructions to the contrary, some Israelites tried to gather food on the seventh day. The focus on proper conduct is manifest.

The thrust of the narrative about the manna is not, at least not explicitly, to have the Israelites imitate the example of the deity in their future dealings among themselves by being fair in providing full and just measures of grain. Rather, the curious episode of the deity's procedure is like Joseph's curious

10. At the time of the second occurrence, they had been drinking (Gen 43:34).

but deceitful one. It is an intervention in the lives of hungry Israelites who are to be taught a lesson.

From another angle, we can characterize Joseph's deception involving the replacement of money in the brothers' sacks as a gift with a twist.[11] When the brothers later spoke to Joseph's steward about the matter, the steward told them, "Your God, and the God of your father, hath given you treasure in your sacks; I had your money" (Gen 43:23). The statement is patently false. He did not have their money and they did derive gain from the transaction, but the gain was of a decidedly dubious kind.

Joseph's purpose, as already noted, was to convict his brothers of their original wrongdoing against him. Indeed, the presence of the money in their sacks was to remind them of the profit (*beṣaᶜ*, Gen 37:26) they sought when they decided to sell Joseph to Egypt. On that occasion they were frustrated in their attempt in that they did not actually sell him and acquire money because the Midianite traders had come along and sold Joseph themselves. In a manner consistent with so many subtleties of the story,[12] the money they originally sought for him came to them when they received the grain from Joseph. We might recall how the brothers' bad conscience about their treatment of Joseph was triggered when Joseph, in disguise, insisted that one of them remain behind in Egypt. The requirement immediately reminded them of their original offense against Joseph (Gen 42:21). We might also recall that the reason the brothers sought money for him was because they could not tolerate the idea that, as Joseph's dream portrayed, they were to bow to him as sheaves of grain ("stookies" in the personified, negative sense of Old Scots) bowing down to a sheaf set apart. Immediately after they received the sacks of grain a second time, the brothers paid homage to Joseph, as the dream about the sheaves had predicted.[13]

Joseph's status at the time he was tormenting his brothers was that of vizier of Egypt, a position of leadership recognized by both the native Egyptians and the visiting brothers. In his role as leader, Moses, like Joseph, was

11. On the later rabbinic and early Christian focus on the issue of conduct that is outwardly meritorious but internally flawed, see D. Daube, "Neglected Nuances of Exposition in Luke–Acts," *Principat* 25 (1985) 2329–45.

12. On the tightly knit nature of the Joseph story, see C. M. Carmichael, *Law and Narrative in the Bible* (Ithaca: Cornell University Press, 1985) 282–88; and G. Rendsberg, "Redactional Structuring in the Joseph Story: Genesis 37–50," *Bucknell Review* (1990) 215–32.

13. Like the dream with which the Joseph story begins and which takes in the climactic development of the story is the dream with which Daphne Du Maurier begins her novel *Rebecca*.

intent on justice. To this end, under God's direction (Exod 18:23), he appointed rulers or magistrates to administer it. One of the requirements in the exercise of their judicial function was that they hate (ill-gotten) gain (*beṣaʿ*, Exod 18:21). We might have expected the term *soḥad* 'bribe', although *beṣaʿ* is not inappropriate. The specific God-given requirement that ill-gotten gain be eschewed stands in sharp contrast to the deception that Joseph's steward associated with God when the brothers found money in their sacks. The money was indeed comparable to a bribe in that it was intended to influence Joseph's case against his brothers. The return of the money led to their being accused of its theft (Gen 44:8), which led in turn to Judah telling the disguised Joseph about their original offense against him (Gen 44:14–34). The term *beṣaʿ* 'ill-gotten gain or profit' only occurs in the Pentateuch in Exod 18:21 and Gen 37:26, when Judah had his brothers—with the important exception of Reuben, whose intention was to restore Joseph to his father—agree with his judgment that they should sell Joseph rather than slay him.[14]

There is in fact a larger, substantive link between the etiological account of how a formal judicial system had its origin in ancient Israel (Exodus 18) and the Joseph narrative. The story of Joseph is itself an account of the first dispute ever in the history of the sons of (Jacob) Israel, the very first generation of Israelites. In that this dispute constituted such an important first-time development, its account would have demanded scrutiny of the issues in question. The dispute had begun with a notice about how Joseph brought an ill report of his brothers to Jacob (Gen 37:2). There is no indication of the rightness or wrongness of his report. The dispute escalated, went through all sorts of twists and turns, and did not come to an end until the brothers resolved their difficulties with the vizier of Egypt, who turned out to be Joseph himself.

In that the *paterfamilias* Jacob was biased in favor of Joseph, there could be no resort to some higher human authority, to the *iudicium domesticum*, for example, to resolve the dispute between Joseph and the other sons. For those who exercised their "historical" imagination about the beginnings of Israelite nationhood, the question would be: how did the resolution of disputes among future sons of Israel come to be provided for? The answer would be Moses' institution of 'able men' (*ʾanšê ḥayil*), such as fear God (*yirʾê ʾelōhîm*), men of truth (*ʾemet*), hating unjust gain (*beṣaʿ*)' to be rulers of thousands, of hundreds, of fifties, of tens, and to be judges (Exod 18:21).

14. While the tendency in later rabbinic sources is to exonerate Judah, some (*Genesis Rabba* 85, *Exodus Rabba* 42) view his action negatively, as the biblical narrator certainly did.

It is noteworthy that so much of the language used to define the criteria for these rulers/judges (*śārîm*) is found in the Joseph story. When the brothers eventually settled in Egypt, the pharaoh inquired of Joseph whether there were among them 'able men' (*ʾanšê ḥayil*) who "could be rulers (*śārîm*) over my cattle" (Gen 47:6)—that is, hold a domestic position in the court of Pharaoh. Presumably, in contrast to the low status of the shepherding brothers and the usual restriction on the status of foreigners (Joseph himself being an exception), when the Israelites attained independence there would be need precisely for the abler among them to become rulers over men, not just over herds of animals. The contrast between the situation in Egypt and the situation reflecting Israelite political autonomy may account for the overlap in language we are observing. It is perhaps also worth noting that in both instances two foreigners—Pharaoh and Jethro—are the ones who initiate the organizational arrangements for the Israelites.

In addition to the above examples of shared language between the Joseph and Moses stories, there are two further examples. These two, moreover, concern the resolution of disputes. They are: Moses' institution for the resolution of disputes and Joseph's sham resolution of the dispute between the brothers and himself about spying. Joseph asked whether they were given to the truth (*ʾemet,* Gen 42:16). When he suggested to them a procedure by which they might resolve this particular dispute, he avowed his fear of God (*ʾet-hāʾĕlōhîm ʾanî yārēʾ,* Gen 42:18).

My proposal is that one aspect of the explicit concern with justice in the narratives about the manna in the wilderness and Moses' task of appointing judges is the biblical writer's perceived need to respond to the unsatisfactory way in which justice had been dispensed among the first sons of Israel. Just as the kind of history-writing we are observing suggests a good deal of reflection on the part of the writer(s), so the religious dimension (namely, the role of the deity) that is a pronounced feature of these two narratives is a more obvious indication of reflective activity. Especially with regard to the story of the manna in Exodus 16 we have to ask what possibly could have prompted a writer to have the deity distribute food so precisely that there was conformity to a universal law of giving full and exact weights and measures (Deut 25:13–16; Prov 11:1, 16:11, 20:23). The answer appears to be that the preceding history had told of events and developments in which this kind of problem arose. Consequently, it was deemed important to indicate how the nation should have before it a perfect example—the deity—in the matter of correct weights and measures.

A good deal else in both the stories about Joseph and Moses points to the need to introduce a proper judicial institution. There is Joseph's unjust imprisonment for an action of which he was not guilty, attempted rape. Joseph in turn jailed his brothers for an offense that they never committed (Gen 42:17), just as he forced one of them, Simeon (Gen 42:24), to remain in Egypt as he had been forced to remain there. Moses, like Joseph, set himself up as judge over his fellow Hebrews when two of them were engaged in a brawl, and his judgment sharply raised the point that there was no effective legal machinery to deal with disputes (Exod 2:13, 14).

T. E. Fretheim has also observed the same interrelationship between narratives that I have indicated for certain traditions in the account of the Exodus.[15] He notes that the plagues in Egypt have their reverse analogues in the aftermath of the Exodus.[16] For example, as a result of the first plague in Egypt, the water could not be drunk (Exod 7:24). In Exod 15:23 the Israelites were in a similar situation, but the bitter water was made sweet and the wilderness itself was filled with springs of water.[17] In Exod 9:18, 23 God rained (*mṭr*) hail upon Egypt and it destroyed the sources of food. In Exod 16:4 God rains (*mṭr*) bread from heaven. From one perspective, these sophisticated repetitions of theme are in fact a characteristic of the presentation of many other matters in the Pentateuch. Two examples are how the firstborn loses out in succeeding generations and the occurrence of famine, first in Joseph's Egypt, then in the Egypt of the pharaoh at the time of the Exodus, and last, in the wilderness after the departure from Egypt.

The process in question—a topic in biblical history being taken up in another part of the history—is paralleled in the presentation of biblical law itself. As I have argued elsewhere,[18] the Deuteronomic lawgiver taking stock of Joseph's deceptive transaction and the deity's counter-example in the wilderness has similarly inspired the setting down of the law about false weights and measures (Deut 25:13–16). The combination of the two incidents is what underlies the rule's particular formulation. The lawgiver's reflection on

15. T. E. Fretheim, "The Plagues as Ecological Signs of Historical Disaster," *JBL* 110 (1991) 385–96.

16. The pattern of narration that Fretheim draws attention to is comparable to what S. Bertman uncovered in his analysis of the story of Ruth: "Elements of content, either analogous or contrasting, stand over against each other in the structure of the story and appear thereby to counterbalance one another" ("Symmetrical Design in the Book of Ruth," *JBL* 84 [1965] 165).

17. For the importance in the history of medicine of the curative process exhibited in this story, see David Daube, "Example and Precept: From Sirach to R. Ishmael," *Tradition and Interpretation in the New Testament: Essays in Honor of E. Earle Ellis* (ed. G. F. Hawthorne; Grand Rapids: Eerdmans, 1987) 16–20.

18. Carmichael, *Law and Narrative*, 299–305.

the ethical significance of Joseph's ploy prompted the initial negative statement, "Thou shalt not have in thy bag divers weights, a great and a small. Thou shalt not have in thine house divers measures, a great and a small." The proverbial concern about shortchanging someone in weights and measure was set down as the likeliest parallel in ordinary life to Joseph's extraordinary action. The deity's example in the wilderness prompted the subsequent positive formulation, "Thou shalt have a perfect and just weight, a perfect and just measure shalt thou have: that thy days may be lengthened in the land which Yahweh thy God giveth thee." We might note that Moses promulgated the law to the Israelites in the wilderness (Deut 1:1, 27:2). The lawgiver characterizes the resort to underhanded practices as an "abomination to Yahweh," a phrase he probably employed because Yahweh's activity in the wilderness was viewed as a reaction against the previous practice of Joseph.

There is one especially persuasive indication that we should link the Deuteronomic law on false weights and measures to the narrative in Exodus 16 about the exact provision of manna. I refer to the manifest link that exists between the law in Deut 25:17–19 about the extermination of the Amalekites—the law follows, most haphazardly it might appear, immediately after the law on weights and measures—and the narrative about the Amalekites' dastardly attack on the thirsty Israelites in Exodus 17. That account follows the story about the distribution of the manna in Exodus 16.

There is in fact nothing surprising about the process of certain rules undergoing a change in light of biblical history. The plainest example is the incorporation of the events of the Exodus into the institution of the Passover. It is agreed by all that what was originally an agricultural festival has been transformed into one of historical commemoration. Just so, an ageless rule about weights and measures has been grounded in experiences associated with the beginnings of the Israelite nation. Re-creations of a nation's legal traditions are in fact not uncommon.[19]

Conclusion

It might be worthwhile to put in broader historical perspective the literary process that I have been commenting on. The presentation of both the legal and narrative portions of the Pentateuch reveals a sophisticated, highly developed form of scribal art at some period in Israelite antiquity. This scribal

19. For ancient Athens and seventeenth century England, see D. Cohen, "Greek Law: Problems and Methods," *Zeitschrift der Savigny-Stiftung für Rechtsgeschichte* 106 (1989) 101.

activity is probably the Israelite equivalent of what Meir Malul describes for the ancient Near Eastern legal corpora as a "literary tradition," rather than a "practical legal tradition."[20] The biblical scribes may well have been acquainted with the Near Eastern legal tradition, one that was known well into the first millennium B.C.E.,[21] in a manner comparable to their knowledge of Babylonian mathematics, as Dwight Young has so convincingly demonstrated. In order to set out a distinctive body of Israelite rules, the biblical scribes scrutinized the problems and disputes that they found in their own national traditions about the patriarchs, Moses, the judges, and the kings.

Equally sophisticated is the attention given to the laws and narratives in the Bible around the beginning of the Christian era. Josephus, Philo, and the author of the Letter of Aristeas, while approaching the Pentateuch, or rather Torah, from a milieu in which the Hellenistic rhetorical schools had considerable influence,[22] were in fact accurately focusing on one of its most salient features, namely, the quite definite links between the narrative portions and the precepts. When we turn to the Tannaitic period of rabbinic activity (from about 50 B.C.E. to about C.E. 200), we should analyze *Midrash Halakhah* and *Midrash Haggadah* in light of certain historical developments that have little or no continuity with any biblical precedent. Nonetheless, we should recognize a *typological* parallel between the Tannaites' work on the relationship between law and narrative in their interpretation of the Torah and the activity of the original compilers of the Pentateuch.

20. M. Malul, *The Comparative Method in Ancient Near Eastern and Biblical Legal Studies* (AOAT 227; Neukirchen-Vluyn: Neukirchener Verlag, 1990) 129.

21. See ibid., 105–7 n. 13.

22. See David Daube, *The New Testament and Rabbinic Judaism* (London: Athlone, 1956) 86–89; "Rabbinic Methods of Interpretation and Hellenistic Rhetoric," and "Alexandrian Methods of Interpretation and the Rabbis," *Talmudic Law*, 333–76.

The Peasant Woman and the Fugitive Prophet: A Study in Biblical Narrative Settings

Joseph E. Coleson

Introduction

Plot, character(s), and setting are the trinity of first concerns in literary criticism of narrative writing. While never oblivious to them, biblical and Near Eastern studies have shown a renewed and more mature interest in them as points of diminishing return have been reached with some of the older approaches.

Plot, characterization, structure, poetic, and other literary devices have received much attention in this renewed interest in the literary study of biblical and ancient Near Eastern material. Setting, however, remains relatively neglected.

Setting Described

Writers often attract our attention to and admiration of the settings of their works by skillful description. R. D. Blackmore's description of the Exmoor countryside helped to make *Lorna Doone* one of the best-loved novels of the English language. Thomas Hardy was a master of setting. In *Tess of the d'Urbervilles,* he set

> each stage of Tess's life . . . in its appropriate landscape: her innocence in the tame, mild Vale of Blackmoor; her seduction in the Chase, "the oldest wood in

---

Author's note: It is both a pleasure and a privilege for me to present this study of the use of setting in the books of Ruth and Jonah to Professor Dwight W. Young, my mentor at Brandeis University. Professor Young first aroused my interest in the settings of ancient literatures and gave me the scholarly tools to pursue it.

> England," where, incidentally, she returns at one of her blackest moments only to find her misery superseded by that of the dying pheasants; then her idyllic love affair with Angel in the sensual Paradise garden of Talbothays in the Vale of the Big Dairies; her period of desolation at Flintcomb-Ash, where the unforgiving landscape is as stripped of comfort and vegetation as she is of love and hope; finally, her sacrificial consummation on the altar-stone of Stonehenge.[1]

Hardy went further in his use of setting. He often described settings in such a manner that they virtually became characters in his novels. Hardy said, in one of his introductions to his work, that he used setting in this way purposefully. He intentionally circumscribed the settings of his novels in order that what appeared to be particular might be seen the more effectively to be, in fact, universal.[2] In *Tess of the d'Urbervilles*, the South Wessex countryside and Tess became one. What happened to Tess happened to the country. Both felt it; both reacted. Both were swept away in the changes Hardy saw and described in his corner of England; both Tess's and Hardy's Wessex were destroyed in the end.

Jack London and Stephen Crane are two American authors who come to mind when setting is considered. They, too, used setting so that it acted and reacted in many of the ways human or animal characters did as the plot unfolded. London's North Country was the majestic, proud, implacable foe, a context in which humans and beasts may have survived, but which they never subdued. Crane's battle scenes are the God of War himself, come down to take the measure of the ordinary men who dared to venture into his kingdom.

A few biblical passages utilize setting in similarly powerful ways. Genesis 2 portrays the lost Eden in a few evocative phrases, a setting so sublime that human hearts have ached with the loss through all generations. Eden, with its lost innocence and its lost opportunity, has remained a compelling theme in literature, in painting, and in film.

But more than human hearts have ached. Reflecting upon the Genesis traditions, Paul portrays the entire creation as character, groaning and suffering that loss and awaiting its redemption as a slave groans for freedom or a woman suffers the pangs of childbirth (Rom 8:19–22). Setting becomes character.

Isaiah 35 describes setting to much the same effect. That which human hubris lost will be restored, Isaiah affirmed. It will be a majestic scene, a fruitful scene, inviting but not to be toyed with, a safe place for the simple, a glo-

1. A. Alvarez, "Introduction," in Thomas Hardy, *Tess of the D'Urbervilles* (New York: Viking Penguin, 1978) 11–12.

2. Thomas Hardy, "General Preface to the Wessex Edition," in *Tess of the D'Urbervilles* (New York: Viking Penguin, 1978) 492.

rious adventure for the gifted and the able—for all, a place to delight the whole being, where, in Lewis's happy phrase, the serious business is joy.[3]

Setting Evoked

Setting also may be evoked, rather than described. A writer merely may name the setting, then narrate the action with little or no description at all, trusting the reader's knowledge of that setting to fill in all that is needed of place and atmosphere. This is not carelessness or laziness on the part of the writer; evocation of setting can be a very effective means of drawing the reader into the story.

The biblical writers sometimes use this approach to setting. Two prime examples are the books of Ruth and Jonah. Descriptive words and phrases are employed sparingly for the settings of these two books, though the settings of every one of the four short chapters of each book are vastly different. Yet in both books characters are given very effective descriptions, by the narrators' words as well as by their own speech and action. The lack of description for settings is not due to lack of literary skill. Rather, it is that ancient employment of the skill that allows readers to enter the narrative, as it were, by contributing their own knowledge of setting as they read.

Setting Opened and Enclosed

Another dimension of the skillful and powerful handling of setting is evident in some of the biblical narratives, including Ruth and Jonah. This is the deliberate and powerfully effective alternating of open and enclosed, of public and private settings, to advance both plot and characterization, as well as the reader's involvement in the story and identification with the theological point of view of the story. We will consider these uses of setting in Ruth and in Jonah.

Ruth

Ruth 1:1–5[4] is the prologue and 4:18–22 the epilogue of the book. Leaving them aside, four major episodes comprise the book of Ruth, each in a

3. C. S. Lewis, *The Joyful Christian* (New York: Macmillan, 1977) 228.

4. An earlier version of this part of the present study appeared in *Kardia: A Journal of Wesleyan Thought* 2 (1986) 25–33. I have adapted it with the kind permission of Western Evangelical Seminary, Portland, Oregon.

definite setting that is named and that can be described. These major episodes are 1:6–18; 2:1–17; 3:1–15; and 4:1–12. Each major episode is followed by a minor episode. The minor episodes function both as indicators of the successful resolution of the major episodes that precede them and as transitions to the major episodes that succeed them.

All four major episodes of Ruth are set outdoors. The first minor episode (1:19–22) begins outdoors, in the streets of Bethlehem, but it ends indoors, with Naomi and Ruth entering and settling in Naomi's house. The second (2:18–23) and third (3:16–18) minor episodes are set indoors, in Naomi's house. The fourth minor episode (4:13–17) is set indoors also, but in Boaz's house, not Naomi's.

Of course, this arrangement of four major outdoor episodes, each followed by an essentially indoor minor episode, is a natural development from the agrarian society in which the story is set. But it serves an important dramatic function as well. It makes setting complement and contribute to the development of plot by emphasizing the transitional nature and function of the minor episodes. Thus, the longer narratives of outdoor episodes are filled with physical activity and conversations that evidence tangible results. The shorter narratives of indoor episodes contain much less physical activity (with the exception of the birth of Obed!), and the conversations either report what has already happened or plan and anticipate what will happen. The contrast of the outdoor settings—expansive, open, and unprotected, two of them crowded and busy—with the indoor settings—circumscribed, private, and deliberate—emphasizes that the minor episodes are recesses between the significant events of the major episodes.

The setting of each major episode is named in the Hebrew text of Ruth by a single word that must be translated into English by a prepositional phrase. The Hebrew preposition is attached to the noun in naming three of the four settings. The first setting is designated (1:7) as בַּדֶּ֫רֶךְ 'on the road', the second setting (2:3) as בַּשָּׂדֶה 'in the field'. Only in designating the third setting is the Hebrew preposition not used. However, the setting is named (3:2) as גֹּ֫רֶן, and in English translation both the definite article and the preposition must be supplied, '[at the] threshing floor'. The fourth major setting is named (4:11) בַּשַּׁעַר 'in the gate'.

On the Road (בַּדֶּ֫רֶךְ)

The setting of the first major episode is the road between Moab and Judah. Since we do not know in what part of Moabite territory Elimelech and his family sojourned, we cannot be certain which road this was. However, it was probably the road leading down to the Plains of Moab at the northern end of the Dead Sea and across one of the two fords of the Jordan opposite Jericho.[5] From the Jordan to Bethlehem, three routes are possible, but we may be sure the three women had not yet begun their descent into the Moabite side of the Jordan Rift Valley when Naomi stopped and urged her daughters-in-law to return to their own families.

When Naomi decided to return to Bethlehem, her daughters-in-law accompanied her a short distance out of town as a gesture of politeness, respect, and their affection for her as the mother-in-law whom they had come to love. This action is not surprising, and Naomi showed no surprise. When she felt that they should not tax themselves further, Naomi paused to bid Orpah and Ruth good-by and to pronounce the blessing of Yahweh upon them. The ensuing conversation, the return of Orpah to the town, and Ruth's refusal to turn back all took place in the open countryside of Moab as they paused on the road.

What does setting this episode upon the road accomplish? Ruth and Orpah might just as well have waved good-by from the door of the house or accompanied Naomi only as far as the gate of the town. Orpah could have turned back and Ruth pressed on from either point. One important consideration is that by the time Naomi was well out on the road, her enterprise had been fully launched. For her there was no turning back. This puts into sharper focus the fact that the younger women really were making decisions of lifelong consequence, not just exchanging pleasantries. It has the effect of contrasting even more sharply, if that is possible, the utterly opposite natures of the two decisions.

The dangers of the open road, both realized and potential, likewise amplify the importance of Naomi's and Ruth's decisions. The dangers of the road also increase the thoughtful reader's respect for the courage and the faithfulness of these two women.

Physical dangers from the arid environment faced the two women as they traversed this road. The first problems would have been the provision of an adequate water supply and protection from the sun during the heat of the day. It is true that these considerations would not have caused the women undue anxiety; they knew the country and what was needed to travel safely through it. The point is, however, that provision against these dangers was necessary. Though the dangers were evident, with proper precautions, they could be avoided.

5. George Adam Smith, *The Historical Geography of the Holy Land* (New York: A. C. Armstrong and Son, 1902) 266.

There were other physical dangers to be avoided as well. Venomous snakes, scorpions, predators at night—all these demanded vigilance. An accident—a fall, or even the turning of an ankle—would have been potentially serious to two women traveling alone, as we may assume (though not with absolute certainty) they were.

In time of peace between the people of Moab and the people of Israel, the potential danger from other human beings would have been less. Though banditry always has been a favorite occupation of certain of the inhabitants (particularly the nomads) of the Near East, the extremely stringent code of honor regarding the treatment of women would have been a protection to Naomi and Ruth.

We know from their safe arrival in Bethlehem that no dangers of the road overwhelmed the two women. But at this juncture (the beginning of the journey), all of these dangers and a hundred more were in front of them as potential hazards. Symbolizing and magnifying them all was the fact of the Rift Valley itself, that stupendous, stark, and arid chasm through which the road threaded its narrow, tenuous way. The psychological impact of the Jordan Rift Valley is difficult to impress upon one who has not experienced it personally. George Adam Smith's description probably is the best we have:

> You cannot live in Judaea without being daily aware of the awful deep which bounds it on the east—the lower Jordan Valley and Dead Sea. . . . The depth, the haggard desert through which the land sinks into it, the singularity of the gulf and its prisoned sea, and the high barrier beyond, conspire to produce on the inhabitants of Judaea a moral effect such as, I suppose, is created by no other frontier in the world.[6]

The very geography of the land through which the two women traveled contributed mightily to the momentous nature of Ruth's decision to cast her lot with Naomi, with Naomi's people, and with Naomi's God. Knowing what lay ahead, both of potential dangers and of geography, Ruth did not take her decision lightly. The implacable nature of the journey and the terrain it covered mirrored Ruth's iron resolve never to abandon her beloved mother-in-law. The apparent barrenness of the desert through which the two women passed is also a metaphor for the apparent barrenness of their prospects upon their arrival in Bethlehem.

In terms of story, no story existed until Naomi set out on the road. Ruth's declaration of fidelity would have been virtually meaningless had it been ut-

6. Ibid., 261–62.

tered with Naomi sitting in the house. Spoken in the gate, its force would have been dissipated in the hubbub of competing sound and motion. But voiced on the high road, face to face with Naomi, with Orpah's form receding in the distance and no one else around, it comes down the centuries with breathtaking power. It becomes an event, the climax of this episode.

By setting the conversation and Ruth's decision on the road, the significance of that decision is expanded immeasurably. The road, stretching to the horizon and beyond, through the terrible Valley of the Salt Sea and on to Bethlehem, becomes a metaphor for the procession of consequences resulting from Ruth's decision throughout the years of her own life, down through time, and on into eternity.

In the Field (בַּשָּׂדֶה)

The road is a setting essentially of self-reliance and loneliness, of a certain sense of adventure, and of potential danger. By contrast, the barley field at harvesttime is, for the gleaner, a setting of hard and monotonous but essential work. Loneliness and danger, present or potential, are possible; but they result from the pressure of close, yet hostile and/or competitive, human company, not from its absence.

The fields of Bethlehem probably lay on the slopes and in the valley to the east of the town, though, because Bethlehem was a small town, perhaps not extending to the so-called "Shepherds' Fields" pointed out to pilgrims and tourists today. As often noted, the fields of Bethlehem, through all the biblical period, would not have been separated by strips of uncultivated earth, by ditches, or by fencerows. Rather, each person's field would have abutted his neighbor's so that, except for the boundary stones, they would have appeared to be, all together, one large field.

The season of the barley and wheat harvests, early April through early June, is for all practical purposes the beginning of summer in Judah. Fields of stubble usually are warmer than the surrounding tracts; the fact that the cooling sea breeze usually does not arrive at the ridge (crest or watershed) of the Hill Country until midafternoon or later makes the heat of the day all the more oppressive. Gleaning, with the heat, dirt, and continuous stooping, was not an easy task.

The field at harvesttime also was a very public place. Nearly every able-bodied person would have been involved in one way or another in bringing in the harvest. A letter of the provincial governor Kibri-Dagan to Zimri-Lim, king of Mari on the middle Euphrates in the eighteenth century B.C.E., pictures the situation vividly: "I assembled all the city, [even] down to the children, and sent [them] forth to harvest the barley of the valley."[7]

Everything in this setting worked against Ruth's attaining anything more than her minimal objective of procuring sufficient grain to fend off starvation for herself and her mother-in-law through the coming year. That Boaz should have noticed and intervened on behalf of a foreign widow is remarkable in itself. That he should first have noticed and begun to help her in this setting, inimical as it was to his noticing or taking time to help, strengthens the reader's regard for Boaz's character and God's providential intervention.

At the Threshing Floor (גֹּרֶן)

The Near Eastern threshing floor is a small patch of level ground, its surface hardened originally by packing and tamping and kept hardened by the continual tramping of human and animal feet and the weight of the threshing sledge. (I also have seen a threshing floor whose surface is bedrock.) Threshing floors may be at or near the top of the hill that the town occupies, but they do not have to be. They may be situated partway down the slope, more convenient to the fields. The important factor is not elevation, but that the location is not wind-sheltered, so the afternoon sea breeze can blow unobstructed across it.

In some places in the Near East today, the threshing process continues as it has for millennia. Sheaves of grain are brought to the threshing floor on wagons; they are untied and spread several inches deep on the floor. An ox pulls a sledge around and around the floor. The sledges have sharp stones and/or pieces of metal imbedded in the underside. The weight of the ox and the sledge, combined with the cutting action of hooves and stone or metal, chop the stalks and separate the heads from them.

The straw is forked off later in the winnowing, in the late afternoon and early evening, as long as the sea breeze is strong enough to blow the chopped straw and chaff away from the grain when it is tossed into the air with a wooden fork. With the grain cleansed of most of its impurities, it is shoveled and raked into a heap at the edge of the threshing floor to await a final cleaning with a sieve. This final task is done by the women.

7. Jean-Robert Kupper, *Archives royales de Mari, III: Lettres* (Paris: Musée du Louvre, 1948) 30:12–15. English translation and discussion in Joseph Coleson, *Yaqqim-Addu of Sagaratum: The Correspondence of a District Governor in the Kingdom of Mari* (Ph.D. diss.; Waltham, Mass.: Brandeis University, 1982) 25–26.

Following an afternoon and evening of winnowing and a hearty harvest-time meal with wine, Boaz lay down near the heap of his grain. Other men were there also, but other owners would have been near their own heaps of grain, and servants, if any, would have drawn apart from Boaz in deference to his authority.

The threshing floor thus provided the only setting where privacy for Ruth and Boaz was possible, where she could approach him undetected, and where they could hold an entirely private conversation. Yet privacy even in this setting was not guaranteed. Ruth's coming to the threshing floor did carry with it the risk of detection, which would have meant disapproval, though perhaps not disgrace.

In this episode, the setting plays a crucial role in the advancement of the story. First, it reintroduces the sense of potential danger that had been inherent in the setting of the open road, though no real danger threatened either Boaz or Ruth at the threshing floor. Ruth feared no danger, apparently; she was confident enough that she went beyond Naomi's instruction to her and requested Boaz to marry her and to fulfill the role of kinsman-redeemer for her mother-in-law.

Boaz, by contrast, was frightened, even terrified (that is the meaning of וַיֶּחֱרַד in 3:8) upon awakening and finding a woman at his feet. To some extent, even the modern reader can understand his reaction. It was, after all, the middle of the night and outdoors. Yet the pronoun Boaz used in his startled question was feminine; he recognized that his night visitor was female. His first thought may have been that he was being attacked by the *lilith*, the female night demon.[8] If this was his first impression, Boaz was quickly reassured by Ruth's reply. Yet here again the writer's touch reveals his mastery of setting as an aid to the advancement of story. By recording this detail of Boaz's reaction to being jolted awake, dependent upon setting for its effect, the writer continues to rivet the reader's attention and interest.

The setting of the threshing floor also adds an element of mystery and intrigue that has not been present in the story. Because it follows directly the decidedly unmysterious episode of the harvest field, a sense of intrigue, and hence interest, are here focused even more sharply.

Finally, this setting reintroduces, but more strongly, the sense of adventure and romance inherent in the setting of the open road in the first episode. No longer was there merely the abstract romance of the journey. Now there was the immediacy of a woman and a man who had come to like and respect

8. See the excellent discussion of this point in Jack M. Sasson, *Ruth* (Baltimore: Johns Hopkins University Press, 1979) 74–80.

each other, talking of marriage. The private, nocturnal setting of the threshing floor provided an opportunity for the kindling (or deepening) of romantic interest between Boaz and Ruth. Ruth's night visit to the threshing floor demonstrated her courage, fidelity, and trust in Boaz and his integrity and generosity of spirit toward her, as well. These qualities will be attractive to discerning, mature persons, and in this setting both cerebral and physical attraction undoubtedly were aroused or deepened.

In the Gate (בַּשַּׁעַר)

The gate is the one setting in the story of Ruth whose significance consistently is expounded by commentators. It was the place of highest traffic in and around the town. The stream of passersby would have been heaviest early in the morning and again in the evening. Because it was the place of highest visibility and traffic, the gate became the locus of legal transactions. Early in the morning, Boaz could be sure of finding the town notables—the elders—who acted as judges and other citizens who would serve as witnesses.

This setting, then, provided a suitable audience for Boaz's clever negotiation with the nearer kinsman, by which he persuaded him to relinquish his right to redeem Naomi's land. It also heightens the irony of the kinsman's role in the story. The nearer kinsman, known by name to all in the gate, sought to assure the memory of his name by prudent care of the estate he would bequeath to his own heirs. He ensured instead, by that very act of prudence, that his name would not be preserved, that rather it would be pointedly omitted, from the one record that would have assured him a name of perpetual memory. From the center of attention in the city gate, the center of his universe, he plunged himself into perpetual oblivion.

The setting of the gate also provided for the public witness and affirmation of the private conversation and commitments of Ruth and Boaz, made during the night at the threshing floor. Commitments of this type, though made in private, will be acknowledged and affirmed publicly if they are genuine.

Jonah

Jonah is another book of only four short chapters. As in Ruth, each chapter's events unfold in a distinctively different setting; each setting contributes greatly to the development of the story.

The setting of the first major episode of Jonah is a ship of Tarshish that Jonah boarded at Joppa (1:3–16). The setting of the second episode is the belly of the great fish that God sent to pick up Jonah when the sailors threw him overboard, at his instruction (2:1–11 [Eng. 1:17–2:10]). The third episode is set inside the city of Nineveh (3:3–10); the fourth, in a booth outside Nineveh (4:5–11).

A few general observations may be in order. The setting of the first episode was of Jonah's choosing, as was the setting of the fourth. God chose the settings of the second and third episodes. Thus, there is a kind of chiasm in the settings of Jonah.

In the first episode, Jonah ran away and hid in the "womb," the hold, of the ship as he tried to escape from God and God's directive. Cast out of that womb, he "escaped" to a deeper, more dangerous, more primeval "womb," the belly of the great fish. In the third episode, Jonah progressed a day's journey into the "womb" of the city; the ancient Near Eastern city was crowded, tight, narrow, intimate, womblike. In episode four, Jonah, cast out of the womb of the city by his own anger and self-pity, built himself a booth, a little isolated womb, but God still confronted him in an effort to make Jonah finally "be born," to grow up.

All of these were enclosed, tightly circumscribed settings. All four God used as "space capsules" to thrust Jonah into a wider orbit of vision for his world (though the reader is not told that Jonah achieved that wider vision). God also used these tightly enclosed settings as "re-entry vehicles" for safe return—of the sailors and Jonah from death at sea, of Nineveh from annihilation in God's judgment, of Jonah himself from the poisonous vapors of soteriological exclusivism—the return of all into the world and atmosphere of God and God's love for all people.

Three of these enclosed settings Jonah attempted to use as shelters or refuges in his efforts to avoid and then to thwart God. In the first episode, Jonah sought the shelter of the ship and its hold as an escape from God. In the second, Jonah received the shelter of the fish's belly as salvation from God. In the third, Jonah reluctantly entered the shelter of the city of Nineveh on a mission for God, a mission that he fulfilled as anonymously, as curtly, and as tersely as he thought God would permit. In the fourth episode, Jonah built the shelter of the booth as a retreat from God and as a place to wait and see, still hoping for vindication by God and even for vindication over God.

In Jonah, not only are the four major settings important to the action and the development of Jonah's character, as we are allowed to see it, but also each of these four more narrowly circumscribed, intimate settings is surrounded by a desolate, isolated and isolating, even menacing, larger setting. In chap. 1 this larger setting is the sea, which became not merely menacing but life-threatening as God cast the storm upon it. In chap. 2, the larger setting remains the sea, but now it is the depths of the sea, that mysterious region unknown to human beings in the period when the story of Jonah is set.

The larger setting of chap. 3 is the semi-desert steppe of the Assyrian heartland. In the ancient Near East, the cities usually exercised continuous, effective control for only a limited distance outside their gates. The desert/steppeland, the wild beasts, the pastoral nomads, the weather, the lack of water, the demons who were thought to lurk in the wastelands—all were intimidating potential or immediate foes facing anyone venturing outside the safety and security of the city walls, outside the ordered political structure of the palace and the ordered spiritual structure of the temple.

The larger setting of chap. 4 was still the semi-desert steppeland. But now Jonah was there alone, outside the safety of civilization within the walls of Nineveh. Its menace was a constant companion, and some of it was brought on Jonah by God with a disconcerting immediacy in driving home the lesson of the book.

With these considerations in mind, we now can move to a closer examination of the four settings of Jonah, individually.

In the Hold of the Ship

The book of Jonah opens with God's command to Jonah to go to Nineveh to proclaim the city's destruction. Instead, Jonah went the opposite direction, going down to Joppa and booking passage on a ship going to Tarshish. Jonah's reasons for not obeying God's directive have been variously interpreted; they are not the focus of this study.

The ship on which Jonah sailed was undoubtedly a normal seagoing vessel of the general Phoenician type. These were about thirty feet long; this one had a deck. Probably the deck had a small cabin, a firepit, and reed, rush, or stick railings. These vessels had sails for use when the wind was favorable. When the wind was unfavorable or when coming in or out of harbor, the sailors rowed. These vessels were very small by modern standards and carried a small crew and limited cargo. Some of the cargo was stowed below the deck in the hold, and some was carried on the deck. The sailors never sailed out of sight of land, unless on the short crossing to Cyprus or other such inter-island crossings. At night they pulled into harbor or simply beached the vessel.

After the ship was under way, Jonah went below deck into the hold, crawled in among the cargo, and went to sleep. In his running from God, Jonah always went down and he always went inside. Jonah went down to Joppa, down into this ship, and down into its hold. All this was in his own attempt to escape from God and the commission God had given him. His physical progression down symbolizes the Hebrew conviction that one cannot go up when trying to get away from God. The only possible direction is down.

The same point is made by the continual inwardness of Jonah's physical movement. His entrance into the ship that would take him away from the land God called his own and then into the hold of the ship symbolizes Jonah's attempt to enter a safe and hidden place, a sanctuary away from God's presence. But just as one cannot go up when attempting to flee from God, one can find no refuge from God, no place where God is not.

God forced the issue by hurling a storm upon the sea. The storm's suddenness prevented the sailors from running the ship into the shore to wait it out. In their desperate attempts to deal with the storm and save their lives, they discovered Jonah in the hold. He was brought out of his "safe" place in the womb of the ship. After further attempts had failed, the men cast him overboard, out of the "womb," into the midst of the sea. From a secret, safe, enclosed, and constricted space, Jonah found himself sinking into the depths of the vast, raging, cold, and unbounded sea. Sometimes in literature, a setting almost becomes a character. Here, the setting almost becomes the plot.

In the Belly of the Fish

The setting of the second episode is also inside: Jonah had been ingested by the fish. Here the safety and security of a womb are suggested even more strongly; the Hebrew word מְעֵי, denoting here the 'belly' of the fish, in some other contexts means 'womb'. Further, as is recognized in every serious study of Jonah, Jonah's prayer in the belly of the fish was not a prayer of supplication for deliverance, but a prayer of thanksgiving for deliverance already experienced. When Jonah found himself enclosed within the belly, the 'womb', of the fish, he knew that he had been rescued from death by drowning.

We are not interested here in the arguments pro and con over the fish. The literary setting, inside the belly of the fish, emphasizes and heightens the power of Jonah's prayer of thanksgiving. Jonah was embraced securely, "enwombed" when he had thought he was entombed. Jonah's only altruistic action in the entire book was to offer himself to be thrown overboard, since he knew God was angry with him, not with the sailors. Even this may not have been enough to render Jonah's motive genuinely altruistic, since had the ship foundered, he would have gone down with it. But at least his action saved the lives of the ship's crew.

In offering himself to be thrown overboard, Jonah had every expectation of being drowned. If he shared the general beliefs of his age, he would have thought his spirit doomed to agelong restlessness, since he would not have been afforded the privilege of a grave. The boundless raging sea would have been his lot forever.

Instead, Jonah found himself rescued, securely kept from the cold, raging waves, the slimy seaweed, and all the other perils of the sea. The belly of the fish was as cozy and secure a refuge as he could have wished. What he had sought in booking passage on the ship of Tarshish, God provided for him in the belly of the fish. Jonah's seeking for inside refuge had paid off.

All this is true except for one thing: Jonah knew God had provided the refuge; he recognized that God had rescued him from certain death. He had seen that death pass before his eyes, felt it enter his lungs. His prayer recited that death vividly, with the immediacy of one who has looked death in the eye and discovered to his astonishment that, this time, death blinked. But God had brought this about; Jonah would have to deal with God again.

Within the Walls of Nineveh

In the third episode, Jonah was back on dry land. But he still was in an enclosed setting, the city of Nineveh. It is hard for people in the modern world to visualize how much this was true. We come closest to it, perhaps, in the wide open spaces of the North American West. Miles and miles of emptiness stretch from horizon to horizon. Dotted here and there are settlements that attract attention not for their size, but precisely because they are dwarfed by the vastness of their setting. This is true even when a number of settlements are within sight of the observer.

The impression on the observer, and especially the feeling of the traveler entering a Near Eastern city, was of coming into a tightly enclosed beehive of activity after being adrift for days or weeks upon the empty vastness of the steppeland. The ancient Near Eastern city (as even the modern, until very recently) was an enclosure.

Nineveh was just such a city, even though it was the second largest city of antiquity. Its total area was approximately 800 acres. Though a number of towns and villages clustered around it, Nineveh was an enclosed, intimate space, especially after Jonah's weeks on the road. As Jonah had been enclosed—"enwombed"—within the hold, the belly, of the ship until forced out by the panic of the ship's crew, as he had been enclosed in the belly of the fish until the fish at God's command vomited him onto the dry land, now Jonah enclosed himself (or tried to) in anonymity in the womb of narrow streets and alleys of the city.

Jonah's message would not allow him to be completely anonymous, but he tried to be as anonymous as possible. He went a day's journey into the city. This need have nothing to do with the celebrated controversy over the size of Nineveh; it could mean simply that Jonah spent a day in the city, wandering here and there through its streets and squares, proclaiming his message.

Even the form of the message as given in the book suggests Jonah's desire to make as little fuss as possible, to be enclosed in the busy city, swallowed by its bustle and anonymity. Jonah's message is five short words in Hebrew. It is probably the shortest, and by all odds the most successful, prophetic oracle, sermon, oration, or speech of any kind ever given.

The message fit the setting and the main character of the story. Jonah did his best to melt into the background wherever he was. He did not want to carry out God's commission. When God forced him to, he did it as inconspicuously as he thought God would allow. All the settings of the book, even the busy setting inside the city of Nineveh, help the reader to feel the impact of this. Though they are (unless the reader pays attention) as anonymous and inconspicuous as Jonah wished to be, the settings contribute enormously to the movement of the plot and to the development of Jonah's character.

In the Shelter of the Booth

Jonah moved outside the city to see what God would do. But he did not surrender himself to the vastness of the extra-urban spaces of which we have spoken already. Jonah built himself a booth or tabernacle, an enclosure (סֻכָּה) within which he could secure himself while he waited out these days. Jonah had chosen the enclosure of the ship. His entry into the enclosures of the fish's belly and the city of Nineveh had been God's doing. Now again he made his own choice to build and inhabit this final enclosure. The settings of Jonah, in this regard, form their own chiastic structure within the book.

The last of Jonah's enclosures was built as a personal shelter against the steppe and against the heat of the season. God even added an important element to this shelter, the *qîqāyôn.* (What kind of plant this was and whether its rapid growth was another supernatural event in the story is immaterial to our discussion.) After the worm destroyed the *qîqāyôn,* Jonah's shelter, which had seemed adequate when he built it, no longer comforted and sheltered him as before.

Jonah then requested (a second time) that God provide him with the ultimate shelter, death. When rescued from death by the shelter of the fish's belly, he had been thankful and happy beyond measure. Now he asked for death in a paroxysm of anger that parodied his joy at his earlier deliverance from death.

In requesting that God take his life, Jonah also became a parody of Elijah and his request (1 Kgs 19:4), because his attitude toward his mission was a parody of Elijah's attitude toward his. Elijah had grieved at Ahab's refusal to curb his wife, Jezebel, knowing that the great manifestation of God's glory on Mt. Carmel would as a result bear little fruit in Israel. Jonah was grieved and angry at the great manifestation of God's mercy that bore abundant fruit in Nineveh. Jonah thought to preserve God's honor through judgment, while God sought to promote his own glory through mercy.

Throughout the story, then, we see Jonah always trying to escape inside but always being brought outside to face God, his own deeds, and his own small attitudes. He was forced out of the womb of the ship's hold by God's pursuit of him in the storm; he was vomited out of the womb of the fish's belly by God's grace in calling him a second time; he was cast out of the womb of the enclosing walls of Nineveh by his own anger and jealousy; he was forced out of the womb of his booth shelter by God's confrontation with him over God's sovereign right to mercy.

Comparisons and Contrasts

Jonah's enclosed scenes compare and contrast with Ruth's open scenes in several interesting ways. On the open road (episode one) Ruth and Naomi faced danger; in the enclosed boat (episode one) Jonah faced danger. In the open field (episode two) Ruth worked and Boaz (ultimately Naomi's redeemer and Ruth's husband) gave her secret assistance to keep the two women from death by starvation. In the enclosed belly of the fish (episode two) God rescued Jonah from death by drowning.

In the open, but secret, threshing floor (episode three) Ruth and Boaz made commitments to each other as prospective bride and groom. In the enclosed, but public, city of Nineveh (episode three) the people of Nineveh committed themselves to God in repentance, a commitment the Bible often portrays metaphorically as a marriage of God with his people.

In the open and public gate of Bethlehem (episode four) Boaz bargained with the unnamed nearer kinsman for the privilege of redeeming Naomi. In the enclosed and isolated booth shelter outside the gates of Nineveh (episode four), Jonah complained bitterly against God (in effect, attempting to bargain with God) because in giving them a chance to repent, God had redeemed the unnamed pagan citizens of Nineveh.

In Ruth the larger outdoor settings *are* the settings. They are not menacing (except perhaps the road). Ruth has in-between, indoor, smaller-scale settings as relief from the larger major settings. In the book of Jonah, while the settings are also outdoors, Jonah is always enclosed: in a ship, in the belly of the fish, in the city, in his booth. And each has an air of danger, some immediate—the ship and the sea—some potential, though still hardly remote—the nearby desert and steppe, the scorching east wind, and so on.

In episodes one, two, and four, God took Jonah out of the enclosed settings to further his purposes. Jonah took himself out of the enclosed setting of episode three (Jonah's exit is recorded in 4:1) to further his own purposes. The reader knows that God's purposes were carried out in the actions following Jonah's exits from the ship and the fish. The structure of the book of Jonah requires the reader both to guess (for Jonah's life) and to decide (for his/her own life) whether God's or Jonah's purposes were/are carried out for Jonah's (and the reader's vicarious) exits from the city and from the booth that God destroyed.

Conclusion

The settings of Ruth and Jonah are very different and serve different roles in the two narratives. But in both Ruth and Jonah, the physical settings make essential contributions to the development of the stories. Each setting makes an important contribution by itself. Together, within each story, in the way that the settings simultaneously build upon and contrast with each other, their impact is as great as the characterization, the development of plot, and the many literary devices so masterfully employed. Indeed, all these would be much the poorer but for the settings.

In Ruth, the settings are largely responsible for moving the story along from the mundane in chaps. 1 and 2 to the slightly mysterious expectation of chaps. 3 and 4, from the adventure of chap 1 to the labor of chap. 2, from the privacy of chap. 3 to the publicness of chap. 4, even from the labor of chap. 2 to the much different labor in the final minor episode of chap. 4. In so doing, the settings help both to sustain and to justify the reader's attention and interest. The settings help to make Ruth a thoroughly satisfying story.

In Jonah, setting moves the story from an overwhelming encounter with the forces of God's creation, to an even more overwhelming encounter with God himself, and with God's intention to show mercy upon his creation. The settings of Jonah reveal the human tendency always to enclose and shield oneself from God and God's grand adventure of grace, as well as God's gracious countering of that tendency in pulling his people out of their shelters, or even destroying the shelters from around them, if necessary, in order to bring them along in the grand adventure.

The settings of the two stories also help to ingrain them thoroughly within the reader's memory. Thus, in Ruth, the understated themes of God's sovereignty and care for his people in the ordinary affairs of life, which may turn out not to be ordinary after all, are not forgotten by the reader. In Jonah, the clearly stated theme of God's sovereignty over and care for all people, even those who do not know him as God, is vividly imprinted upon the reader's memory. Such is the privilege of authors writing, after all, for a religious, didactic purpose. Such is the power of these well-told stories, even in their uses of setting.

Ezekiel 47:13–48:29 as Royal Grant

David H. Engelhard

During the last half century, considerable attention has been devoted to discussion of the biblical-theological issue of "the land." Important contributions to this subject have come from a variety of quarters.[1] Walter Brueggemann boldly asserts that "land is a central, if not the *central theme* of biblical faith."[2] Later, and somewhat more tentatively, he suggests "that land might be a way of organizing biblical theology."[3] This suggestion, coupled with the many significant studies noted, highlights the importance of the land theme for biblical studies.

1. W. Brueggemann, *The Land: Place as Gift, Promise, and Challenge in Biblical Faith* (OBT; Philadelphia: Fortress, 1977); Martin Buber, *Israel and Palestine: The History of an Idea* (London: East and West Library, 1952); W. D. Davies, *The Gospel and the Land: Early Christianity and the Jewish Territorial Doctrine* (Berkeley: University of California Press, 1974); P. Diepold, *Israels Land* (BWANT 95; Neukirchen-Vluyn: Neukirchener Verlag, 1972); D. Gowan, "Losing the Promised Land: The Old Testament Considers the Inconceivable," *From Faith to Faith* (PTMS 31; ed. D. Hadidian; Pittsburgh: Pickwick, 1979) 247–68; A. J. Heschel, *Israel: An Echo of Eternity* (New York: Farrar, Straus and Giroux, 1967); E. Jacob, "Les trois racines d'une théologie de la 'Terre' dans l'ancien Testament," *RHPR* 55 (1975) 469–80; P. D. Miller, "The Gift of God: The Deuteronomic Theology of the Land," *Int* 23 (1969) 451–65; Uriel Tal, "Jewish Self-Understanding and the Land and the State of Israel" [with responses], *Union Seminary Quarterly Review* 26 (1971) 351–81; G. von Rad, "The Promised Land and Yahweh's Land in the Hexateuch (1943)," *The Problem of the Hexateuch and Other Essays* (New York: McGraw-Hill, 1966) 79–93; H. E. von Waldow, "Israel and Her Land: Some Theological Considerations, *"A Light unto My Path": Old Testament Studies in Honor of Jacob Myers* (ed. H. N. Bream, R. D. Heim, and C. A. Moore; Philadelphia: Temple University Press, 1974) 493–508; Hans-Ruedi Weber, "The Promise of the Land," *Study Encounter* 7 (1971) SE/16: 1–16.

2. Brueggemann, *The Land,* 3.

3. Ibid.

The focus of this study is Ezek 47:13–48:29, a prophetic statement about the new allocation of land to an exiled and landless people.[4] Exclusive of the commentaries on Ezekiel, this pericope has attracted very little scholarly attention.[5] Undoubtedly this lack of attention is directly related to the prosaic character of the Ezekiel material. Nevertheless, this pericope invites further investigation, and this occasion to honor Dwight Young is a wonderful opportunity to discuss a biblical topic that is illumined by other ancient Near Eastern documents. We shall demonstrate that it is plausible to identify the form of this pericope as the prophet's[6] adaptation of a royal land grant document.[7]

Previous form-critical work on this passage has yielded conclusions different from and in some respects contradictory to that which will be argued here. Referring to Ezek 47:13–48:29, W. Zimmerli concluded that "in this section, which is in the form of a personal address (second-person plural), there has been incorporated in 47:15–20 a boundary description in an impersonal form," and later asserts that "the text itself does not claim to be a divine speech."[8] R. Hals is more tentative but wrestles with the same problematics mentioned by Zimmerli when he says: "the framework indicates

4. Regarding the limits of the pericope, see Ronald Hals, *Ezekiel* (FOTL 19; Grand Rapids: Eerdmans, 1989) 343; see also W. Zimmerli, *Ezekiel 2* (Hermeneia; Philadelphia: Fortress, 1983) 526.

5. See especially three articles by C. M. Mackay, "The City and the Sanctuary, Ezekiel XLVIII," *PTR* 20 (1922) 399–417; "The City of Ezekiel's Oblation," *PTR* 21 (1923) 372–88; "Ezekiel's Division of Palestine among the Tribes," *PTR* 22 (1924) 27–45. For a more recent study, see M. Greenberg, "The Design and Themes of Ezekiel's Program of Restoration," *Int* 38 (1984) 181–208; J. Levenson, *Theology of the Program of Restoration of Ezekiel 40–48* (HSM 10; Missoula: Scholars Press, 1976).

6. Regarding the authorship of this section, I concur with M. Greenberg's statement "that it is the product of a single mind (and hand) and that, as carrying forward ideas and values found in the preceding prophecies, it may reasonably be attributed to their author, the priest-prophet Ezekiel" ("Ezekiel's Program of Restoration," 181).

7. The seminal work on this subject was written by M. Weinfeld, "The Covenant of Grant in the Old Testament and in the Ancient Near East," *JAOS* 90 (1970) 184–203. Subsequently, additional works have appeared that explore this subject in the Hebrew Bible and in the ancient Near Eastern world: Z. Ben Barak, "Meribaal and the System of Land Grants in Ancient Israel," *Bib* 62 (1981) 73–91; A. Hill, "The Ebal Ceremony as Hebrew Land Grant," *JETS* 31 (1988) 399–406; C. Libolt, *Royal Land Grants from Ugarit* (Ph.D. diss.; University of Michigan, 1985); J. N. Postgate, *Neo-Assyrian Royal Grants and Decrees* (Studia Pohl Series Maior 1; Rome: Pontifical Biblical Institute, 1969); H. Z. Szubin and Bezalel Porten, "Royal Grants in Egypt: A New Interpretation of Driver 2," *JNES* 46 (1987) 39–48.

8. Zimmerli, *Ezekiel 2*, 526.

that this unit is to be seen as a divine speech . . . but . . . it is quite clear that the material enclosed within the unit's framework is impersonal description and not divine speech."[9] If this pericope is indeed a royal land grant document, as I argue here, then both the divine speech framework and the detailed descriptions of boundaries and allotments are integral to this genre.

Most casual readers of Ezek 47:13ff., and surely all commentators, would conclude that it has "all the formality of a legal document."[10] A question soon imposes itself: What type of legal document is reflected here? Following the lead of M. Weinfeld,[11] I argue in this essay that it is appropriate to designate this divine oracle as a prophetic adaptation of an official judicial document type known as the royal grant. While it may yet be proved that this pericope is a complex form or even a combination of forms, the thesis presented here moves the discussion in the right direction.

M. Weinfeld has presented compelling evidence for the existence of the "royal grant" form in the Old Testament. He introduced his discussion with the following statement:

> Two types of official judicial documents had been diffused in the Mesopotamian cultural sphere from the middle of the second millennium onwards: the political treaty which is well known to us from the Hittite empire and the royal grant, the classical form of which is found in the Babylonian *kudurru* documents (boundary stones) but which occurs as such also among the Hittites in the Syro-Palestine area, and in the Neo-Assyrian Period.[12]

Weinfeld described the similarities and dissimilarities of the two types of documents as follows:

9. Hals, *Ezekiel*, 343. The arguments for the claim that this is not divine speech seem to be twofold: (a) the enumeration of details does not require divine speech, and (b) Yahweh is referred to in the third person in 48:9, 10, 14. Variations on this line of argumentation are found in Hals, *Ezekiel*, 343: W. Eichrodt, *Ezekiel* (OTL; Philadelphia: Westminster, 1970) 591; J. Wevers, *Ezekiel* (NCB; London: Thomas Nelson, 1969) 336; Zimmerli, *Ezekiel 2*, 526. The first argument is gratuitous, for such enumeration and details are indeed integral to a royal land grant. As for the second argument, Greenberg ("Ezekiel's Program of Restoration," 186–88) has once again called attention to the fact that the alternation from first to third person within a document is consistent with extra-biblical ancient Near East treaties and instructions and thus is not sufficient evidence for determining redactional activity.

10. Mackay, "Ezekiel's Division of Palestine," 27.

11. Weinfeld, "Covenant of Grant."

12. Ibid., 184–85.

> The structure of both types of these documents in similar. Both preserve the same elements: historical introduction, border delineations, stipulations, witnesses, blessings, and curses. Functionally, however, there is a vast difference between these two types of documents. While the "treaty" constitutes an obligation of the vassal to his master, the suzerain, the "grant" constitutes an obligation of the to his servant. . . . In other words, the "grant" serves mainly to protect the rights of the *servant*, while the treaty comes to protect the rights of the *master*. What is more, while the grant is a reward for loyalty and good deeds already performed, the treaty is an inducement for future loyalty.[13]

Evidence in the Hebrew Bible for the royal grant type is found in the gifts to Abraham (land grant—especially Genesis 15) and to David (dynasty grant —especially 2 Samuel 7).[14] While most of the ancient Near Eastern land grant documents may contain the elements of historical introduction, border delineations, stipulations, witnesses, blessings and curses, none of the examples of this type of royal grant in the Hebrew Bible contains *all* of these elements.[15] Thus the designation of a document in the Bible as "royal grant" is more applicable to the function of the grant than to the literary form and components of the grant. Of the proposed biblical examples, Gen 15:7ff. is probably most like the grant document and attendant ceremony.

This observation is important when considering Ezek 47:13ff. Here, too, the literary components of the grant document are not all readily evident. Nonetheless, the subject matter—the granting of land, which is one of the "most prominent gifts of the suzerain in the Hittite and Syro-Palestinian political reality"[16]—suggests the possibility that this passage may belong to the royal grant genre.

In addition to the general subject matter, other specific considerations bolster this thesis. The following section considers seriatim the essential components of a "land grant" and evaluates their presence or absence in the Ezekiel passage.

1. Land grants typically begin with a preamble or a historical introduction in which the king is referred to as the grantor. In Ezek 47:13ff., the divine

13. Ibid., 185.

14. Ibid., passim. In addition to grants to Abraham and David, Weinfeld indicates that the grants to Caleb (Hebron, Josh 14:13–14) and to Phinehas (perpetual priesthood, Num 25:12–13) may be of this same type.

15. This is not unexpected, for all form critics know that "no two examples of a genre are exactly alike" (G. Tucker, *Form Criticism of the Old Testament* [Guides to Biblical Scholarship; Philadelphia: Fortress, 1971] 13).

16. Weinfeld, "Covenant of Grant," 189.

sovereign, Yahweh, is clearly designated as the donor. His history with the people is alluded to in 47:14, where his previous promissory oath is mentioned. One might observe that this oracle is not mediated by the prophet but is presented as a direct oracle to the people from the sovereign. The "divine speech" framework[17] enhances the suzerain's immediate involvement in this grant and guarantees the fulfillment of his word.[18]

2. The historical "introduction" is imbedded in the passage (47:14) but presented more by allusion than by a direct and explicit statement. The statement "because I swore with uplifted hand to give it to your forefathers, this land will become your inheritance" (47:14b, NIV) serves both as motivation or basis for the suzerain's action and as an affirmation of his long and gracious history with this people. Furthermore, this historical allusion binds the new grant to the patriarchical grant and the Exodus.

That the Exodus is alluded to in 47:14b seems likely when one examines it in the light of Ezek 20:5–6. These verses are a small part of what is essentially a pessimistic presentation of the history of Yahweh and Israel.[19] Ezekiel is instructed to inform Israel that even though they rebelled and disobeyed repeatedly, their God began with them in a very gracious way:

> This is what the Sovereign Lord says: On the day I chose Israel, I swore with uplifted hand to the descendants of the house of Jacob and revealed myself to them in Egypt. *With uplifted hand* I said to them, "I am the Lord your God." On that day I swore to them that I would bring them out of Egypt into a land I had searched out for them, a land flowing with milk and honey, the most beautiful of all lands (Ezek 20:5–6, NIV).

17. Cf. Hals, *Ezekiel*, 343.

18. At this juncture, one might ask why it is necessary to have a "new" land grant, when it had already been given to Abraham. Without wishing to argue the case for or against the conditional or unconditional character of the grant to Abraham, Deuteronomy and the Deuteronomistic history make it clear that possession and/or retention of the land was conditional upon the peoples' obedience and faithfulness and that the grant was revocable in the case of disobedience. The exiles to whom Ezekiel prophesied were frequently reminded that their landless condition was the result of their unfaithfulness and that Yahweh had revoked their usufructuary possession. "Renewal" of a land grant to a succeeding generation is not without parallel in the ancient world; see Szubin and Porten, "Royal Grants in Egypt," 43.

19. For a more complete study of Ezekiel 20, see Y. Hattori, "Divine Dilemma in Ezekiel's View of the Exodus: An Exegetical Study of Ezekiel 20:5–29," *The Law and the Prophets: Old Testament Essays in Honor of J. Oswald Allis* (ed. J. Skilton; Philadelphia: Presbyterian and Reformed, 1974) 413–24.

The literary shorthand of Ezek 47:14, "I swore with uplifted hand to give it to your forefathers," is surely intended to remind the hearer of Yahweh's promissory word and the great power ("outstretched arm") he demonstrated in the Exodus and brought to completion in the Conquest. The historical prologue is very terse but no less evocative.

Yahweh's relationship with his people did not begin with the Exodus, but with his oath-bound ("uplifted hand") grant to their ancestors.[20] Whether Exod 6:8 refers to a specific event or functions as a general summary of Yahweh's land promises to the patriarchs, it does nonetheless serve to link the oath alluded to in Ezek 47:14b with the patriarchal period and suggests that this too is part of Yahweh's history with his people.

The historical introduction found in many royal grant documents binds the donor and recipient in a mutual history. Our investigation demonstrates that this element is also present in our passage. It is present in a terse and somewhat implicit manner but stated clearly enough that the recipient of the new grant is fully aware that it comes from one who has been involved in the recipient's history and destiny from the time of the patriarchs.

3. Border delineations, which are prominent in land grant documents, are well attested in our pericope. Ezek 47:15–19 specifies the northern, eastern, southern, and western boundaries of the land grant. While the border towns are not all easily identifiable, there can be no question that the boundaries are given with all the formality of a legal document.

The boundaries of the suzerain's grant in Ezekiel are not as expansive as the territorial limits of the tradition remembered in the grant of Gen 15:18 and other passages,[21] where the land stretches "from the river of Egypt to the great river, the Euphrates." When our passage, however, is compared with Num 34:1–12, it agrees in general on border towns and delineations. There is an inversion of the order in which the boundaries are listed (Numbers 34 beginning with the south and Ezekiel 47 beginning with the north), but this is readily explained by the difference in the route taken into the land. Those coming from Egypt at the time of the Exodus would enter from a southerly direction, whereas those returning from the Exile in Babylon would approach the inheritance from the north. Even though the eastern boundary is the Jordan in both passages, Num 34:13–15 makes allowance for the Transjordan

20. Cf. Exod 6:8: "I will bring them to the land I swore with uplifted hand to give to Abraham, to Isaac and to Jacob. I will give it to you as a possession." Keil and Delitzsch think that this points back to Gen 22:16ff. and 23:6; see C. F. Keil and F. Delitzsch, *The Pentateuch* (Biblical Commentary on the Old Testament; Grand Rapids: Eerdmans, 1949) 1.468.

21. Cf. Exod 23:31; Deut 1:7, 11:24; Josh 1:4.

allotment to the two and one-half tribes, an allotment that is not present in Ezekiel.[22]

While further discussion of the precise boundaries may be interesting and informative, it is not germane for establishing my thesis, namely that this passage follows the form of the royal land grant. The one aspect of the form that is a *sine qua non*, namely boundary delineation, is clearly part of the text in question.

4. Regulations or stipulations respecting the land granted are occasionally attached to the granting document.[23] In keeping with the function of the land grants, the stipulations are usually protective of the recipient and guarantee his use of the property. The regulations found on one boundary stone in which a king grants land to his son are summarized by L. W. King:

> The king, in conferring the ownership of the land upon his son, freed it from all taxes and tithes, and forbade the displacement of its ditches, limits, and boundaries. He freed it also from the *corveé*, and enacted that none of the people of the estate were to be requisitioned among the gangs levied in its district for public works, for the prevention of flood, or for the repair of the royal canal. . . . they were not liable to forced labour on the canal-sluices, nor for building dams, nor for digging out the canal-bed. No cultivator on the property, whether hired or belonging to the estate, was to be requisitioned by the local governor even under royal authority. No levy was to be made on wood, grass, straw, corn, or any sort of crop, on the carts and yokes, on asses or manservants. No one was to use his son's irrigation-ditch, and no levy was to be made on his water-supply even during times of drought. No one was to mow his grass-land without his permission, and no beasts belonging to the king or governor, which might be assigned to the district, were to be driven over or pastured on the estate. And, finally, he was freed from all liability to build a road or a bridge for the public convenience, even though the king or the governor should give the order.[24]

Even a cursory reading of Ezek 47:13–48:29 indicates that similar protective rights and regulations are wanting. To be sure, protective regulatory prescriptions for the land are voiced elsewhere in the Hebrew Bible (laws, prophets, and even wisdom), but not in this pericope.

22. For a more complete and detailed discussion of the boundaries, see G. A. Cooke, *The Book of Ezekiel* (ICC; Edinburgh: T. and T. Clark, 1936) 524–29; Y. Aharoni, *The Land of the Bible* (Philadelphia: Westminster, 1967) 58–72 passim; Mackay, "Ezekiel's Division of Palestine," 27–45; Levenson, *Program of Restoration*, 109ff.

23. Cf. Weinfeld, "Covenant of Grant," 185.

24. L. W. King, *A History of Babylon* (New York: Frederick A. Stokes, n.d.) 248–49.

Stipulations of another sort, however, do appear in this pericope. In the literary subunit of Ezek 47:13–23, one observes two stipulations regulating the grant and its distribution or allotment.[25] The first stipulation is that each tribe shall receive an equal share ("You are to divide it equally among them," 47:14a). Previously each tribe received an allotment, but there was no attempt to make them equal. The size of the tribe and its relative importance in Israel's history do not affect the dimensions of the new apportionment.[26] Many commentators view this as an indication that this passage presents a symbolic or idealized view of the future. Whether or not this conclusion is correct, the royal donor specifies that the tribal recipients of the grant are to receive equal shares. The grantor's territory is not to be marred by inequality and injustice in the allotments made.

Aliens also are to receive an allotment along with native-born Israelites. This second stipulation reads:

> You are to allot it as an inheritance for yourselves and for the aliens who have settled among you and who have children. You are to consider them as native-born Israelites: along with you they are to be allotted an inheritance among the tribes of Israel. In whatever tribe the alien settles, there you are to give him his inheritance, declares the Sovereign Lord (Ezek 47:22–23, NIV).

Whether an interpreter understands this statement as "an interesting example of broad-mindedness"[27] or as the continuation and extension of an already characteristic attitude toward the alien,[28] all are likely to concede eventually that this stipulation is radical, expansive, inclusive, and stunning.[29] Eichrodt's summary of the aliens' previous position is instructive:

> Aliens had, of course, been well treated hitherto and protected against oppression (Ex. 22:21f.; Lev. 19:33; Deut. 24:17); they might own houses (Gen. 19:9) and become rich (Lev. 25:47). This meant that they were to a large extent regarded as members of the congregation and increasingly expected to ob-

25. One might add a third stipulation, namely, the provision for a special oblation in 48:8ff.

26. Cf. Levenson, *Program of Restoration*, 122.

27. J. B. Taylor, *Ezekiel* (Tyndale Old Testament Commentaries; Downers Grove, Ill.: InterVarsity, 1969) 282.

28. Cf. G. C. Aalders, *Ezechiel* (Commentaar op het Oude Testament; Kampen: Kok, 1957) 2.364.

29. Cf. Brueggemann, *The Land*, 143.

> serve the ritual commandments (Exod. 12:19; Lev. 18:26; Num. 19:10) and, if circumcised, were admitted to take their part in festivals (Ex. 12:48) and sacrifices (Num. 15:14, 26). Thus their status gradually kept approaching that of proselytes. Nevertheless, they did not enjoy full rights of citizenship, nor could they hold any property in land (Isa. 22:15ff.).[30]

Undoubtedly this new regulation was of "great social importance" and a "principle with wide implications."[31] Furthermore, the postexilic history of Israel was "ambiguous and marked by conflict precisely because the aliens are given the inheritance."[32] Nonetheless, Yahweh as suzerain includes the foreigners as fellow citizens with his people. The royal grant integrates and engrafts the Gentile with the Israelite. The theological significance of this stipulation is no less evident than the social significance. John Bright has remarked that "the strong feeling persisted, and was voiced by prophets of the Restoration, that he (i.e., Yahweh) means to include foreigners also in his Kingdom (Zec. 2:11; 8:23; Mal. 1:11)."[33] Yahweh's territorial grant of Ezek 47:13ff. substantiates this position found in other prophets.

The presence of these two stipulations may support the hypothesis that this passage is of the royal grant type. However, it must be acknowledged that these two stipulations prescribe the apportionment rather than protect the vassal from outside encroachment. Only secondarily do they protect the vassal (i.e., smaller or less important tribes are protected from unequal treatment and aliens are provided an inheritance to protect them from possible mistreatment and enslavement).

If our discussion of these stipulations is essentially correct, then, although Eichrodt's observation that Ezek 47:22–23 is an interruption "which has no direct connection with the determination of the frontier" is correct, his conclusion that this "must therefore be regarded as a later addition"[34] is not necessary. Stipulations were attached to land grants as a part of the document, and their presence here in Ezekiel need not be surprising or secondary.

5. Two additional elements found in some royal grants and/or boundary-stones (*kudurru*) are the blessings and curses and the list of witnesses. The blessings and curses were inscribed on the *kudurru* and addressed to those who harbored thoughts of removing the stones and encroaching on another's

30. Eichrodt, *Ezekiel*, 592.
31. Ibid.
32. Brueggemann, *The Land*, 143.
33. John Bright, *The Kingdom of God* (New York: Abingdon, 1953) 160.
34. Eichrodt, *Ezekiel*, 592.

territory,[35] that is, they are directed towards "the one who will violate the rights of the king's vassal."[36]

No amount of searching through the Ezekiel pericope, however, will surface any clue of blessings and curses included in this royal grant document. It may be that their absence indicates a time of peace in which there will be no enemies who attack the borders and no encroachers who would remove the boundary stones or in any way diminish the territory.[37] The oracles against the nations (Ezekiel 25–32, 35, 38–39) may function as the literary equivalent of the curses that are frequently contained in the grant to deter territorial tampering. The absence of a list of witnesses is not unusual for biblical covenants and grants. In a monotheistic context in which God swears by himself,[38] one would not expect the "invocation of a third party as divine witness."[39]

Before concluding, there are two further issues that I must address, one briefly and the second more extensively. The beneficiary of the land grant in Ezekiel 47 is the whole nation of Israel, not just an individual. This constitutes a difficulty in the designation of this passage as a "royal grant," since all other evidence indicates that grants were usually made to individuals, not to cities or nations.[40] In a conceptual world, however, in which the collective whole can be referred to as Yahweh's "son" (see Exod 4:22–23; Hos 11:1) and "servant" (Isa 42:19, 44:1, and others), it is not too surprising that here the nation is thought of as an individual. Furthermore, for Yahweh to have granted the land to anyone other than the whole nation at this stage of history would have been unthinkable. Nonetheless, granting the land to the nation as a whole must certainly be viewed as a prophetic adaptation of the genre.

A second issue that requires resolution arises out of Weinfeld's contention that royal grants were given as a "reward for loyalty and good deeds already performed."[41] Although this seems to be the perspective of most of the narratives about the grants to Abraham and David, Weinfeld himself acknowledges that in the Priestly source loyalty is anticipated[42] and is not a matter of

35. Cf. King, *History of Babylon*, 246; A. Leo Oppenheim, *Ancient Mesopotamia: Portrait of a Dead Civilization* (Chicago: University of Chicago Press, 1964) 287.

36. Weinfeld, "Covenant of Grant," 185.

37. This sense of peace is consistent with the ethos of Ezekiel 40–48.

38. Cf. Gen 22:16; Jer 22:5, 44:26, 49:13; Amos 6:8.

39. Meredith G. Kline, *Treaty of the Great King* (Grand Rapids: Eerdmans, 1963) 15.

40. Weinfeld, "Covenant of Grant," 185.

41. Ibid.

42. Ibid., 186 n. 16.

the past. Another author contends that in some instances "the granting of lands became an incentive to loyalty and initiative on the part of the recipients."[43] Past loyalty and anticipated loyalty are not mutually exclusive. In Ezek 47:13ff., however, the land grant is given with the expectation of future loyalty. Any thought that Ezekiel's grant is made on the basis of past loyalty is quickly refuted by the catalog of abominations in chap. 22 and the reminder that those whom the prophet addresses are presently in exile as a consequence of their waywardness.

There are two lines of argument that make it plausible to infer that the divine land grant is given to a new and loyal Israel. The first argument relates to the well-known expression in Ezekiel, "you shall know that I am the Lord."[44] More than sixty times this expression is used in Ezekiel to express the result of some significant act of Yahweh in judgment or grace.[45] It is curious, however, that this expression is absent from Ezekiel 40–48. Could it be that the absence of this expression is meant to suggest that the Israel of 40–48 is the Israel who has come to know the Lord once again and is now a loyal subject? Silence itself is not an adequate foundation for this presumption. However, when this evidence is combined with the description of Israel as a faithful worshiping community and the depiction of Yahweh's returned presence in both temple (43:1–4) and city (48:35), then the inference that Israel is viewed as a holy, loyal nation who knows the Lord is plausible.

A second piece of evidence that points in a similar direction is Yahweh's promise of restoration and renewal initiated by his gracious act announced in Ezekiel 36. There we read:

> For I will take you out of the nations; I will gather you from all the countries and bring you back into you own land. I will sprinkle clear water on you, and you will be clean; I will cleanse you from all your impurities and from all your idols. I will give you a new heart and put a new spirit in you; I will remove from you your heart of stone and give you a heart of flesh. And I will put my Spirit in you and move you to follow my decrees and be careful to keep my laws. You will live in the land I gave your forefathers; you will be my people, and I will be your God (Ezek 36:24–28).

43. Ben Barak, "Meribaal and the System of Land Grants," 74.

44. Cf. W. Zimmerli, *I am Yahweh* (Atlanta: John Knox, 1982).

45. Israel is not the only one who is to know the Lord, for Ammon, Moab, Philistia (chap. 25), Tyre (chap. 26), Sidon (chap. 28), Egypt (chaps. 29–32), Mount Seir (chap. 35), "the nations" (chap. 36), and Gog and Magog (chaps. 38–39) are also said to recognize and acknowledge Yahweh in his mighty acts.

Restored Israel is not the disloyal, rebellious, and faithless Israel who was scattered and carried into captivity. The people will return sprinkled with clean water so that they *are* clean (v. 25). Their external cleansing will be combined with internal renewal—a new heart and a new spirit. A once hardened people ("heart of stone") will become responsive ("heart of flesh") and responsible ("moved to follow my decrees and careful to keep my laws").[46] Yahweh, despised and blasphemed by his people, will again take up residence in their midst ("I will put my Spirit in you") so that the cherished covenant relationship is experienced again ("You will be my people, and I will be your God"). It thus seems plausible to conclude that inasmuch as Israel has been so transformed by the divine initiative, she has become a loyal vassal[47] and the proper recipient of the land grant.

Some aspects of the foregoing presentation strongly support the hypothesis that Ezek 47:13–48:29 is a "royal grant." The subject matter (land) is common in such grants. Furthermore, various elements of the form such as royal donor (Yahweh), historical introduction, border delineations, and stipulations are preserved in this pericope as in other grant documents. Moreover, the issue concerning the loyalty of the grantee, or at least his anticipated loyalty, has been satisfactorily addressed. Even though the absence of an *individual* as recipient and the absence of the blessings and curses leave some questions about the form, the conclusion, that Ezek 47:13–48:29 is patterned after the royal grant documents of the ancient Near East, seems warranted. While there are some departures from the form, they are within the parameters of adaptations allowable without distorting the genre.

46. The Hebrew verbs *hālak* and *šāmar* used here (Ezek 36:27) are terms that Weinfeld ("Covenant of Land Grant," 186) has noted have "come to describe loyal service as a reward for which the gift was bestowed."

47. Levenson (*Program of Restoration*, 39) remarks that in the new exodus there is a striking difference from the first exodus, namely, that "Israel's service is acceptable to God."

The Background of Some Distinctive Values in the Hebrew Bible

Cyrus H. Gordon

The Hebrew Bible embraces such a vast treasury of principles to live by that it would be confusing, if not actually impossible, to cover the subject comprehensively. Nor would an educated public be interested in reviewing all the well-known details, however meritorious their message. For example, "thou shalt not steal" or "thou shalt not bear false witness" or "thou shalt not commit adultery" are well-nigh universal prohibitions whose infractions disrupt and harm society. One can find them in codes that preceded as well as followed the Bible. In no case are they original contributions of Scripture.

In order to establish the originality of anything in the Bible, it is necessary to check whether it occurs in the sources that antedated the Hebrews. We cannot speak of the Hebrew people as a historic entity before the middle of the second millennium B.C.E. Hence if Hammurapi's Code (ca. 1700 B.C.E.) outlaws theft, the biblical commandment prohibiting stealing is not a concept original to the Bible.

We now have such a rich background from discoveries in the "Bible World," including written sources antedating the Hebrews and the Greeks by more than a millennium, that we know that the Hebrew Bible, far from being a primitive beginning, is rather the culmination of a sophisticated international civilization. This does not mean that nothing in the Bible is original. On the contrary, it is precisely because we have a plethora of extrabiblical sources that we can at last single out the great original insights enshrined in the Bible. Moreover, thanks to the extrabiblical sources, we understand the historical setting that provided the soil on which the seeds of Hebrew originality could grow.

Author's note: The material in this essay is substantially the same as that delivered as the Abe and Ida Miller Lecture at Purdue University and published in *Shofar* 12/4 (West Lafayette, Ind.: Jewish Studies Program, Purdue University) chapter 3.

So far, it appears that only the Hebrews, of all the ancient Near Eastern peoples who have left formulations of law, enacted the principle that it was one's duty to help a runaway slave escape, to refrain from turning him over to his master, and to give him every opportunity to support himself as a free man. Throughout the ancient Near East, and indeed throughout much of the world in general, slaves were the private property of their master and, accordingly, an honest citizen was duty-bound to do all he could to return a runaway slave to his owner, as he should with any other kind of lost property (e.g., Hammurapi's Code §§15–20). The Hebrews forbid (instead of requiring) the surrender of a runaway slave to his master. On the contrary, one is to harbor, welcome, and treat him decently (Deut 23:16–17). We can now provide a historical explanation.

There was a widespread people called the ᶜAbiru in the Near East during the second millennium B.C.E. Our documentation concerning them is particularly rich during the Amarna and Ramesside ages (15th–12th centuries B.C.E.). In the Amarna tablets they appear as marauding outsiders who were wresting Canaanite areas from Egypt's sphere of influence. This has suggested some sort of relationship with the Hebrews who conquered the Land after the Exodus. In Egyptian their name is spelled *ᶜpr* and in Babylonian *Ḫa-bi-ru.*

In the Nuzi tablets (in the same Amarna period), the ᶜAbiru appear as outsiders entering into voluntary slavery in the households of established native families. This recalls the slave status of the Jews in Egypt, as well as the institution of the *ᶜebed ᶜibrî* 'Hebrew slave' who can be held only until the sabbatical year whereupon he must be set free unless he elects, of his own free will, to become an *ᶜebed ᶜôlām* 'a permanent slave' in the home of his master (Deut 15:16–17).

In the Ugaritic tablets, there is evidence of ᶜAbiru in the vicinity of Ugarit on the eve of its fall about 1185 B.C.E. We know this because the excavators found an oven full of tablets (UT texts 2059–2113) baked for King Ammurapi (the last ruler of Ugarit). The city fell before the oven was opened to remove the tablets. It was the French archaeologists who excavated the unopened oven and removed the documents, which record an ᶜAbiru presence (UT 2062:A:7). This calls to mind the "Hebrew Conquest" that took place about this time. Ugarit lies far to the north of Joshua's Conquest, but the Bible four times refers to the Promised Land as extending from the border of Egypt to the Euphrates River (Gen 15:18; Deut 1:7, 11:24; Josh 1:4). This might be interpreted to mean that there was a limited Conquest (Joshua's) that became canonical, whereas the "Greater Conquest" embracing northern Canaan as far as the Euphrates was more ephemeral, though it did form part of Israel during the United Monarchy of David and Solomon. (See UT §19.1899, pp. 459–60.)

At Ugarit, tablets emanating from the court of Hattusili III (ca. 1282–1250 B.C.E.) assure the King of Ugarit that ᶜAbiru communities in the Hittite realm would not be permitted to harbor political refugees from Ugarit.[1] Thus we know that the ᶜAbiru protected people who were in trouble at home. The biblical Hebrews were not coextensive with the ᶜAbiru, but rather a segment of them. The historical Hebrews viewed themselves as a confederation of twelve tribes, descended respectively from the twelve sons of Jacob, and regarded the limited area of Palestine as their Land. The ᶜAbiru, on the other hand, appear much earlier in the Old Assyrian and Old Babylonian tablets and are attested all over the Near East, including Anatolia and Egypt during the second millennium. The names *ᶜibrî* 'Hebrew' and ᶜAbiru may be related, but because one or both of them are borrowed they do not follow all of the minutiae of phonetic law operative for native Semitic words occurring in Hebrew or Akkadian.

The Hebrews themselves explained the kindness to runaway slaves and other underdogs differently: it behooved them to be kind because they had been slaves in Egypt. The Hebrews' view of history was the official one in Scripture, according to which all of the Children of Israel had gone down into Egypt, where they were eventually enslaved. Instead of hiding the shame of servitude, they used it as a reason for becoming more compassionate than other people (Deut 5:14–15).

Hattusili's documents unearthed at Ugarit provide us with a new approach to Israel's kindness to the runaway slave and other fugitives from oppression: it appears to be a characteristic of the ᶜAbiru (of which the Hebrews were a part).

When the Ten Commandments tell us not to steal, it echoes many an earlier code. But when it enjoins us not covet, it is making a unique statement among the laws of the ancient (and for that matter, modern) nations. It is a profound insight to realize that coveting precedes the act of theft. The morally superior man does not covet the other fellow's property and therefore is never tempted to steal it. The prohibition not to covet is beyond legality; you cannot punish a person for a bad thought unless it has already led to a bad act. Theft is punishable; coveting is not. The Tenth Commandment ("thou shalt not covet . . .") is unique; "thou shalt not steal" is not. Ugarit has clarified why coveting is forbidden in Hebrew law but not in the other Near Eastern codes.

1. RS 17.238:3–10 in *Palais royal d'Ugarit* 4 (Paris: Imprimerie nationale, 1956) 107–8.

Though trade brings various peoples in contact with each other and promotes the ideal of one world, it has its dangers. A commercial milieu like that in Canaan has the pitfall of materialism that, when unrestrained, robs the individual and society of refined, cultivated, and spiritual values. Ugaritic literature shows that it was a sign of greatness and power for kings and gods to desire things that belonged to others and, if the rightful owners would not yield possession of those coveted articles, the coveting party would stop at nothing, not even murder, to filch them. The most popular goddess in the pantheon, Anath (the sister and beloved of Baal), wanted the wondrous bow possessed by Aqhat. She offered him any price and every inducement—silver, gold, and even immortality—to part with it. He refused rather insultingly, whereupon she had him murdered by a divine assassin and won possession of the bow.[2] Baal is actually celebrated in the Ugaritic myths as coveting land (UT 2001:rev. 1–7) and animals (UT 75:I), which we are specifically forbidden to covet in the Tenth Commandment. The verb used in Ugaritic (*ḥmd*) is the same one used in the Tenth Commandment (Exod 20:17; Deut 5:21). Accordingly, the Hebrew reaction to Canaanite pagan values and religion account for the Tenth Commandment, which is unique in the laws of the ancient Near East.

The polarity of Phoenician and Hebrew values is acted out in 1 Kgs 21:1–27, where the Hebrew king Ahab of Israel, married to the Tyrian princess Jezebel, wanted to buy a vineyard owned by his subject Naboth, because it adjoined the palace grounds. Naboth, like Aqhat, refused to part with his property even though the price offered was generous. But Ahab was a Hebrew reared in Hebrew values. As a Hebrew King (unlike Ugaritic and Phoenician monarchs), he could not seize what rightfully belonged to his subjects. So Ahab could do nothing but sulk. His wife Jezebel saw things differently. If her husband was a king (as she understood the rights of kingship from her upbringing in Phoenician Tyre), no subject had the right to thwart his sovereign's material desires. So she trumped up false charges against Naboth and had him convicted of sacrilege and *lèse majesté*. Naboth was accordingly executed and his estate was confiscated by the Crown and presented to Ahab. In doing this she was emulating her goddess Anath, who had Aqhat murdered so that she could seize his property.

The tragedy was not that a good man (Ahab) was trapped in marriage by a bad woman (Jezebel), but rather that a man and woman of opposing values were united in a hopelessly contradictory union. Jezebel was reared in the Phoenician system of values in which kings and queens (like their gods and goddesses) coveted and obtained what they wanted, regardless of the means.

2. See *Berytus* 25 (1977) 8–9 and 15–20.

Ahab, whatever his weaknesses, was a Hebrew who would not spontaneously seize his subjects' property no matter how much he wanted it. If Ahab was a noble Hebrew king inclined to follow the categorical imperative of his people, Jezebel was a noble Phoenician princess following the example of her goddess Anath. Ugaritic literature portrays Jezebel in the act of *imitatio deae.* The incident reflects the clash of opposing systems.

The uniqueness of the Tenth Commandment among the laws of the ancient Near East did not require the discovery of the Ugaritic tablets. But the explanation of how that unique biblical prohibition arose did in fact require it.

The Sabbath is unique not so much as a day of abstaining from work but as a social institution providing rest to the entire community, including servants and even domestic animals. The sanctity and beauty of the Day of Rest are qualities that the Hebrews gave to it, though the Sabbath had an origin that is not reckoned with in the Scriptural account.

Hesiod's *Works and Days* deals with the notion of lucky and unlucky days. The idea is that some days are auspicious for work and others are not. On the unlucky days of the month, one should avoid embarking on enterprises and on engaging in work, to avoid failure and misfortune. This notion did not start with Hesiod; it appears in Sumero-Akkadian tablets and constitutes the background of the biblical Sabbath.

Two entirely different explanations for the Sabbath are given in the two versions of the Ten Commandments. In Exod 20:11, the rationale given is to rest on the Seventh Day, even as God rested on the Seventh Day after the six days of Creation (= *imitatio dei*). In Deut 5:14–15, the Sabbath is said to commemorate the Exodus from Egypt. Israel must never forget that God saved them from slavery and, therefore, the Israelites must always provide a day of rest for the entire community, slaves included.

It is a sound general principle that in the development of religions, the rituals are primary and the historical or mythological explanations come later. It is not unusual in Scripture to offer alternative explanations. Traditional societies do not require consistency. If there are two or more traditions, all of them are respected. Thus the name Ya^{c}aqob is explained either as Jacob's grasping Esau's heel (^{c}*qb*), or as Jacob's cheating (^{c}*qb*) Esau out of his birthright. Unlike us, the ancient Hebrew did not ask: "which one is right to the exclusion of the other?" This fact is still insufficiently understood today. There are four Gospels, all containing the account of Christ's deeds on earth. There are factual discrepancies among the four Gospels that have perplexed Christians from the start. A modern "historical" approach might eliminate the discrepancies and thus create one consistent "historical" account of Jesus.

Instead, in accordance with Near Eastern traditionalism, all four variants are preserved in the New Testament and are equally revered. Worrying about the discrepancies results when we impose modern attitudes on ancient material.

The significance of the Sabbath does not depend on the pre-Hebraic system of lucky and unlucky days. It depends rather on what the Hebrews did with their pre-Hebraic heritage.

There are a number of developments in the Hebrew Bible that consist of extending to the entire community principles that in the ancient Near Eastern societies were incumbent only on the uppercrust, such as the rulers or the wealthy. Thus Hammurapi's Code (V:15–24, rev. XXIV:59–62) states that the king was destined to promulgate the Law to protect the weak from the strong. In Ugaritic literature it is the duty of the king to defend the widow, the fatherless, and the downtrodden.[3]

What the Hebrews did was to extend this obligation to every member of the community. The principle of social justice is demanded by the Israelite prophets as the one overriding requirement that God demands of every member of the community. Actually, this principle is not really courtroom justice because it means that, in any conflict of interest, the weaker is always right and the stronger is always wrong. Legally, a landlord may be justified in evicting a widow and her orphaned children if she has defaulted on her rent or mortgage payments. But in the Prophetic (and Wisdom) books of the Hebrew Bible, the widow and orphan and downtrodden are always right and the landlord or creditor always wrong. No society or economy could function under a system of Hebrew prophetic social justice, but it is a beautiful ideal needed to temper the harshness of legal justice.[4]

Job was the perfect man who always defended the widow, the orphan, and the downtrodden. We could say of this model human being that he was never neutral; he always defended the weaker against the stronger in any conflict of interest that came to his notice. The prophets would, so to speak, have all of us practice such "social justice" (e.g., Mic 6:8).

3. UT text 127:40–50 (translated in *Berytus* 25 [1977] 58); and UT 1 Aqhat: 19–25 (*Berytus* 25 [1977] 21), 2 Aqhat: 5:4–8 (*Berytus* 25 [1977] 13).

4. The Judeo-Christian tradition has in the course of its long history learned that it is impractical to base an economy on a canonized ideal (that is, the Bible). The Communist world learned this lesson and began to implement it openly only in 1989–90. While Marxist doctrine may have some lofty values and deep insights, it cannot provide a viable economic system. While a meaningful life requires some eternal values, survival in a hazardous and changing world requires some flexibility in *modus operandi.*

The concept of peace is universal. The Hebrew word for 'peace' (*šālôm*) means more than its English translation conveys. It means not only tranquility and lack of strife, but also physical and psychological well-being. But it also includes the concept of international peace among all the nations and tribes of the earth. The ideal, and the formula for achieving it, are enunciated by two different prophets (Isa 2:4 and Mic 4:3) in virtually the same words: "Nation shall not lift sword against nation, nor study the art of war anymore." The formula is absolute disarmament: "They shall beat their swords into ploughshares and their spears into pruning hooks," that is, we must convert all military hardware into useful machinery for helping mankind. So far, this ideal, let alone the only formula for achieving it, has not appeared in prebiblical sources. It is still on the top of our international agenda and we still fail to attain it because we fail to realize that as long as any lethal weapons are around, they can and will be used to kill. So we talk of arms reduction as though by reducing an arsenal of 2000 nuclear bombs to 1000 we have lessened the probability of war or established world peace. How can we explain the Hebraic innovation of requiring international peace so that the world may become a fit place for human life?

Hebrew prophetic ideals began to appear in the literary prophets of the eighth century B.C.E. Before that was the United Monarchy of David and Solomon in the tenth century B.C.E., when Israel became a commercial empire trading by land and sea. Solomon's conquests included the caravan city of Palmyra/Tadmor in the Syrian desert (1 Kgs 9:18 || 2 Chr 8:4). Palmyra is an oasis that served as a stop on the route from Syria to Iraq (that is, from the Mediterranean Levant to Central Asia) until the age of air travel in the twentieth century. Solomon occupied and fortified it to control a vital trade route.

The account of Solomon and the Queen of Sheba (1 Kgs 10:1–13) reflects trade between Yemen and the Mediterranean. She had gold, incense, and precious stones (v. 10) to market in the Mediterranean basin; Israel and Egypt controlled all the land and sea routes through which she might ship her goods. David anticipated Solomon in his treaty with Hiram of Tyre, whereby Israel and the Phoenicians became partners in commerce. Phoenicians needed the use of Israel's overland routes to the Gulf of Aqaba for lucrative trade via the Red Sea and Indian Ocean to South Arabia, East Africa, and India. Indeed Herodotus (I:1) states that the original home of the Phoenicians was along the Red Sea. During the United Monarchy of David and Solomon, Hiram needed Israel to regain access to those sea lanes.

One of the great lessons taught by international trade is that peace is more profitable than war. If caravans and ships are attacked and lost due to international strife and piracy, the merchants and their royal sponsors faced larger losses and fewer profits. Trade teaches an important lesson: for business, peace is better than war. Israel learned this lesson during the good decades of the United Monarchy. That is why the ideal of international peace appears in the prophets *after* the age of Davidic and Solomonic trade.

The Hebrews, being very much in the middle of things, expressed an awareness of being a part of a large cultural network spread over the entire Near East, from Iran to Libya, from the Aegean to South Arabia—embracing the Mesopotamian and Egyptian subcradles of civilization. Palestine was the hub of this ecumene. The Table of Nations in Genesis 10 portrays the interrelationships of the component parts of the ecumene in terms of genealogical kinship. The biblical scheme is quite straightforward: the human race is a single family descended from one man (Noah) and his wife. They had three sons (Shem, Ham, and Japhet) who, with their wives, were saved from the Flood, which wiped out all men and beasts who were not on the ark. This means that all members of the human race are descendants of the same father and mother (Noah and his wife) and are therefore kinsmen. To be sure, children are different from their parents and from their siblings and progeny. None of us is a clone. But we are all related and belong to each other. There is no racism in Genesis. Ham, Shem, and Japheth, as sons of the same two parents, cannot possibly be different races. Genesis 10 (vv. 5, 20, 31) states that the differences among the different peoples descended from Noah are geographical and linguistic, but not racial. Arabs and Hebrews, being Semites (descended from Shem), are more closely related to each other than either is to the Ionian Greeks (whose ancestor is Javan, *Yāwān*, descended from Japhet) and other groups, but ultimately we are all members of the same family and should regard each other as siblings and cousins. Evaluating this concept within the "history of ideas," it becomes evident that the Table of Nations inculcates an indispensable prerequisite for World Peace. Until mankind regards all fellow human beings as brothers, there can be no real One World or universal peace. We are not talking about history or about science, but about attitudes.

There is another factor in the Table of Nations that is too easily missed. The spread of the ecumene was not limited spatially to the Near East; it had marine offshoots. Thus the Greeks had offshoots in the islands (Gen 10:4–5) of the Mediterranean, and the South Arabians had distant offshoots via sealanes on the Indian Ocean (Gen 10:20). This implies navigation, trade, and overseas colonization beyond the Near East.

The quest for knowledge is so widespread that we can call it a trait of mankind in general. Superhuman knowledge is often attributed to different gods. Among various cultures, special classes or castes devote themselves to the quest for knowledge. The Brahmans of India are expected to be learned. The scribes of Mesopotamia were a respected class expected to cultivate the arts and sciences. The Samurai of Japan were dedicated to the cultivation of various arts and virtues, including scholarship. But Israel went further and made it a divine commandment for the entire public to study Scripture daily as a lifelong pursuit (Josh 1:8–9) and to teach the text diligently to the next generation (Deut 6:6–7). This is another example of a virtue (here, the quest for knowledge) that can be found among many peoples—before as well as after the Hebrews of antiquity—but extended in the Hebrew Bible from special segments of society to the entire community.

It is of interest to recall that among the many attributes of God is *ʾēl dēʿôt* (1 Sam 2:3) 'God of Knowledge/Ideas'.

Israel had a wholesome dislike for dictatorship and as a result imposed laws and constitutions on their kings. When Rehoboam succeeded Solomon on the throne of Israel, the people insisted on knowing his policy. They summoned him to Shechem for enunciating that policy and, when he declared that they could expect an iron fist to enforce his will, the Ten Tribes of Northern Israel seceded, leaving to Rehoboam only the South, dominated by Rehoboam's own tribe of Judah (1 Kgs 12:1–24).

The Bible has inherent in it a structure of balance of power. This classical ideal anticipated what Americans call "separation of church and state." The priesthood was restricted to the tribe of Levi. The canonical and sole legitimate king had to be of the tribe of Judah, specifically descended from David, son of Jesse. Any attempt to combine church and state into a single authority was considered usurpation and dictatorship. An extreme example of a case of dictatorship is provided by the Maccabean interlude. A heroic priestly family headed by Mattathias rescued the Jewish community from Seleucid tyranny and paganization and reestablished the Jewish Commonwealth under seemingly strict biblical principles. To do this the sons of Mattathias had to lead their victorious armies and exercise the powers of government, but it ended with the Maccabean dynasty controlling both state and church. It is no accident that normative Judaism (followed by Protestantism) excluded the books of Maccabees from the canon. However noble, necessary, and heroic the Maccabean interlude was, the dynasty violated the principle of balance of power in society.

Another remarkable development within biblical society was the institution of prophecy. I am referring neither to the bands of ecstatic prophets nor to the various guilds of prophets but rather to the individuals who established a reputation for Yahwistic inspiration and, ultimately, verifiable truth.

These prophets were respected by all Israel, from the king down. No matter how unwelcome their words happened to be, they enjoyed "prophetic immunity," by which is meant that they were not to be silenced, let alone put to death, for their teachings.

The "true" prophets were characterized not by their praise of the king, but rather by their criticism and even condemnation of him and his government. This is acted out in numerous passages. For example, in Ahab's court there was a band of court prophets on whom the king could count to give rosy predictions and lavish praise. When Jehoshaphat requested the evaluation of a situation by a true prophet of Yahweh, Ahab stated that there was one, Micaiah by name, who habitually criticized the king and his policies. Micaiah turned out to be the one true prophet with the correct message (1 Kgs 22:1–37).

Jeremiah was not encouraging to the king and the establishment before the fall of Jerusalem at the hands of Nebuchadrezzar in 586 B.C.E. But Jeremiah was right. The king, Zedekiah, did not like Jeremiah's message but respected him and saved him from death.

The clearest case of the true prophet is Amos, who categorically stated that he was not a professional and not a member of a prophetic guild ("I am neither a prophet nor the son of a prophet"). He delivered his message of condemnation and doom to the entire establishment (to both King Jeroboam II and the priest Amaziah). The leaders of the establishment resented Amos's all-too-blunt words but dared not kill him.

"Prophetic immunity" is what made historic writing possible in Israel. No composer of royal annals in Mesopotamia or Egypt dared write anything critical of the crown. It is no accident that Israel developed a tradition of historiography that was impossible among the Mesopotamians and the Egyptians, where anything other than praise for the crown would be unthinkable.

The Bible is not monolithic in viewpoint. Priests, prophets, sages, and others had different points of view. The book of Leviticus embraces a manual for the cultic approach to life's problems. If one has lapsed from the right path, he can be set aright by making the proper sacrifice in accordance with priestly regulations. In a sense, this constitutes a guide book for achieving "peace of mind." Everyone makes mistakes, and Leviticus tells us how to atone and start living again with a clean slate.

For the Psalmist, a more direct and personal appeal to God is necessary. For a prophet like Amos, sacrifices were not what God asks of us, but rather "social justice." For Ezekiel, who was a priest as well as a prophet, both cult and a virtuous personal record were essential.

For the sages in general, wisdom implied prudent living in order to win success and respect. What Torah was to the priest, Wisdom was for the sages. The Torah commands us in God's name not to steal, lie, commit adultery, and so forth. Proverbs tells us that such vices rob us of success, respect, and even life.

Ecclesiastes is a rugged individualist. He admonishes us to study, cherish, and practice the commandments, but to keep an open mind and think for ourselves. He believes in the Golden Mean, in a world where there is a proper time for everything (Qoh 3:1–8). He goes so far as to state that it is a mistake to practice either virtue or vice to excess (Qoh 7:16–17), for either would lead to our undoing. He knows human limitations and reminds us that we are on earth, whereas God is in heaven, and therefore it makes no sense for us to talk as though we know everything (Qoh 5:1). I doubt that Ecclesiastes would be at home in any school of theology that had dogmas or fixed beliefs—let alone philosophical discourses on the nature of God, the soul, or the afterlife. He was an intellectual interested in making the most of life without committing the common mistake of breaking with religion and tradition (Qoh 12:13). Once we discard them, we fall apart.

Obviously, there was a strong ethnic factor in ancient Israel, but not blind chauvinism. Balaam was a prophet of God, though not an Israelite. Cyrus was more than that; God had chosen him, though a Persian, as the Messiah (Isa 45:1–5) to rule the world and implement God's plan. 2 Chronicles (35:2) goes so far as to state that the Egyptian Pharaoh Necho, at Megiddo, was the true mouthpiece of God, while the virtuous Josiah (638–608 B.C.E.), the anointed (= Messiah) of the House of David, was, on that occasion, spiritually too obtuse to recognize God's words spoken through the mouth of Necho.

The Hebrew Bible stresses God's most precious gift, life. Although there is no denial of the existence of the individual after death, the Hebrews (at least prior to the last part of the Hebrew Bible) stressed life on earth. We are commanded to honor our parents, not for any reward in the next world, but that our days may be prolonged here on the land that God has given us.

The reward for goodness is long life and progeny. We go on through our descendants. Joseph was blessed with a long life, during which he lived to see his great-grandchildren (Gen 50:23). The Psalmist (115:7) asks God to help us here on earth because the dead cannot praise God. Ecclesiastes (Qoh 9:4–5) states that the living are better off than the dead, because the living at least know they are going to die, whereas the dead do not even know that much. Death brings release from the woes of this world, but it offers no more than quietude (Job 3:12–19). The ghost of Samuel is not brought down from heaven but raised from the Underworld by a spiritualist (the Witch of Endor), and Samuel resents being disturbed (1 Sam 28:7–25). It is life on earth that the Hebrew Bible stresses, and we are urged to live it well and make the most of it in accordance with the way of life spelled out in Scripture.

With the exception of Egypt, all of Israel's neighbors took a dim view of life and mankind's prospects. Egypt was so tied to its land that it could not effectively spread beyond the Nile Valley because its way of life, values, and traditions were indissolubly tied to its geography and climate. Judaism (as distinct from early Hebrews), Christianity, and Islam owe the concept of a happy afterlife, for those deserving it, to Egypt.

The Hebrews formulated the doctrine that God rules the whole universe and that he has a masterplan of world history. The world began with Paradise, which man lost. Deprived of Paradise, man embarked on the course of history, with all its vicissitudes, wars, disease, and untold sufferings that end only in death. Our historic world is the meeting ground of the forces of good and evil. But it will not last forever. The historic process with all its misery and dislocations will come to an end in the Messianic Age, the kingdom of God on earth, when evil will be banished and a good world will be established for ever and ever.

Before that day comes there will be much havoc, but meanwhile we are not to despair or slacken our efforts. Utter misery and chaos (= Armageddon) precedes that golden age, and the worse things are on earth, the closer we are to the Messianic Age. Accordingly, for the Hebrews (and Jews and Christians after them) life is worth living, because God's plan requires the end of the historic process and the inauguration of the golden age without end.

It is this undying hope and optimism that have kept the biblical religion alive, whereas Mesopotamian, Greek, and Roman paganism have perished.

Primogeniture in Ancient Israel

Frederick E. Greenspahn

Although the Bible has been studied for millennia, it is only in the past century that a continuing stream of discoveries from the ancient world has enhanced our understanding of the broader cultural context from which it emerged. The importance of these resources has been a hallmark of Dwight Young's work, which has also incorporated the insights of contemporary anthropology. It is a pleasure to dedicate this study, which relies heavily on comparisons of these kinds to illumine a particular biblical issue, in his honor.

The Bible is filled with reports of younger sons whose importance outshone that of their older brothers. Indeed, the list of younger siblings who achieved positions of prominence reads like a "Who's Who" of biblical literature, including Seth, Isaac, Jacob and his beloved Rachel, Joseph, Ephraim, Moses, Samuel, David, and Solomon. What makes this collection of younger offspring particularly striking is the widespread consensus that primogeniture was characteristic of Israelite society, a position that conforms well with the common view that firstborns are particularly well-suited for leadership positions.[1]

Joseph Jacobs inferred from this paradox that it was not until after Israel's settlement in Canaan that primogeniture became normative in Israelite culture. Earlier, he maintained, it was younger children who were favored.[2] Biblical stories about an older son's being displaced by his younger brother are, therefore, to be understood as efforts to justify the earlier practice in light of later custom.

1. The first empirically supported statement of this sort was in Francis Galton's *English Men of Science, Their Nature and Their Nurture* (London: Macmillan, 1874) 34–35; the classic survey of the scientific evidence for these kinds of assertions is that of William D. Altus, "Birth Order and Its Sequelae," *Science* 151 (1966) 44–49.

2. Joseph Jacobs, *Studies in Biblical Archaeology* (London: David Nutt, 1894) 46–62.

Jacobs' interest in ultimogeniture was well based. The custom is widely practiced,[3] providing a useful mechanism for societies in which family property is given to children as they mature and establish their own homes to ensure the economic viability of the offspring, who are most likely still to be dependent at the time of their father's demise. However, lack of evidence makes it difficult to ascribe this practice to biblical Israel. Indeed, the Bible offers surprisingly little evidence for any sort of automatic system of inheritance. Succession seems most often to have been determined during a father's lifetime. Jacob's supremacy was ensured by Isaac's blessing, even if fraudulently obtained; similarly, Solomon became king because he had been designated by David. More important is the fact that what biblical evidence we do have is devoted to the transmission of status—a blessing or the crown—whereas ultimogeniture is most often used for the transmission of property.

One reason for the widespread confidence in primogeniture's prevalence in ancient Israel may be an intuitive sense as to the typological development of various inheritance practices. Such certainty is probably misplaced. As a prominent medievalist has observed, it is only "centuries of feudal law and dynastic law [which] have accustomed us to accord [primogeniture] a certain prior right."[4] In fact, it is almost impossible to isolate a theoretical schema as to the historical development of inheritance systems. In the words of one anthropologist, "Patterns of inheritance are . . . historically variable, and not laid down once and for all in some original germ plasm. They constitute adaptive responses to a variety of conditions."[5]

Primogeniture is hardly universal. One survey of thirty-nine unrelated cultures from around the world found only thirteen that grant the oldest child more control of family wealth than other members of the family.[6] The most widely attested pattern does not involve individual succession at all, but collective inheritance through sharing or division of an estate. Even where individual succession is practiced, the decision as to which heir should have primacy is often left in human hands. Nor is paternal descent (which can lead to ultimogeniture as readily as primogeniture) the only automatic principle available for determining a successor. The preferred line may as well be collateral or matrilineal, resulting in inheritance by brothers or brothers-in-law.

3. Cf. Robert Lowie, *Social Organization* (New York: Rinehart, 1948) 151.

4. Marc Bloch, *Feudal Society* (Chicago: University of Chicago Press, 1961) 203.

5. Eric R. Wolf, "The Inheritance of Land among Bavarian and Tyrolese Peasants," *Anthropologica* 12 (1970) 104.

6. Paul C. Rosenblatt and Elizabeth L. Skoogberg, "Birth Order in Cross-Cultural Perspective," *Developmental Psychology* 10 (1974) 53–54.

Even European civilization has not always been characterized by primogeniture. According to Isaeus, fourth-century B.C.E. Athenian "law ordains that all the legitimate sons have an equal right to share in their father's property."[7] Rome's Twelve Tables accord complete equality to all of a decedent's offspring, including daughters.[8] Teutonic peoples also practiced equal division until feudal times.[9] Not until the eleventh century was primogeniture instituted in Britain in an attempt to maintain individually controlled plots of maximal size.[10] Even then, other systems were practiced there as well. Ultimogeniture is widely known as "borough English" because holdings in one section of fourteenth-century Nottingham were transmitted to the youngest offspring even as those in another went to the oldest. Equal division (known as "gavelkind") was characteristic of Kent, while sons themselves determined the prime heir in medieval Saxony.[11]

Although the fact that offices are inherently impartible might lead one to infer that they are not amenable to division and sharing, this is not always the case. Shakespeare's play *King Lear* is based on one of the many examples of a ruler's dividing his realm so that each child could inherit a kingdom.[12] Nor is succession necessarily restricted to a specific family. Sometimes rulership is rotated among various clans or tribes, making it impossible for leaders to be succeeded by their own kin. Even where kinship is a determining factor, a variety of systems is possible. A chief may be followed by either his own or his wife's older brother. The African Gonja stipulate that the deceased may be succeeded by anyone but his own son.[13] Not even dynastic succession always entails primogeniture. A particular family's right to rule may not include a preference for any one individual within that family.

7. Isaeus, "On the Estate of Philoctemon" 25 (LCL, pp. 218–19).

8. Cited by Justinian *Institutes* 2.13.5 in *Remains of Old Latin*, ed. E. H. Warmington (LCL; Cambridge: Harvard University Press, 1979) 3.448–49.

9. Henry S. Maine, *Lectures on the Early History of Institutions* (London: John Murray, 1875) 199.

10. Henry S. Maine, *Ancient Law* (10th ed.; Boston: Beacon, 1963) 222–25.

11. Cf. M. Bloch, *Feudal Society*, 190–210; Paul Vinogradoff, *Outline of Historical Jurisprudence* (London: Oxford University Press, 1920) 276; and Frederick Pollock and Frederic W. Maitland, *The History of English Law before the Time of Edward I* (Boston: Little Brown & Co., 1902) 279.

12. Other examples are noted by Jack Goody, *Succession to High Office* (Cambridge: Cambridge University Press, 1966) 3–8.

13. The various systems are surveyed in Jack Goody's "Introduction" to *Succession to High Office*, 1–56, on which much of what follows is based.

Succession is rarely automatic. The decision may be made through divination, or a preliminary recommendation may require ratification by the incumbent, the ruling family, or the community as a whole. The widespread practice of election from within a pool of eligible candidates, however defined, has the advantage of minimizing the likelihood of incompetence while providing the chosen leader with some level of support from those under him. Some societies allow eligible candidates to fight among themselves in order to determine who will hold office. For 300 years the Ottoman Empire was governed by a "Law of Fratricide," imposed in 1289 by Mehmed II in order to avoid fragmenting his domain.[14] Primogeniture can hardly, therefore, be considered "natural" or even dominant. Anthropologist Robert Lowie speaks of it as relatively rare in "primitive" societies.[15]

Mesopotamian law codes make it clear that primogeniture was hardly universal in the ancient Near East. Numerous legal texts speak generically of "heirs," and some explicitly mandate equal division.[16] Hammurabi refers to brothers' dividing an estate after their father's death (*warka abum ana šimtim ittalku inūma aḫū izuzzū*) and once even specifies that the division be equal (*mitḫāriš*).[17] Although Strabo reports that pre-Islamic Arabs accorded eldest sons a certain priority, they too seem to have allowed all males to inherit, a practice that was only broadened by subsequent Islamic law.[18]

The *šimtu* documents, which stipulate how an estate was to be divided, clearly demonstrate that inheritance was not always automatic.[19] Such agreements presuppose both freedom of disposition as well as the possibility of arrangements other than those primogeniture would require. After identifying

14. A. D. Alderson, *The Structure of the Ottoman Dynasty* (Oxford: Clarendon, 1956; reprinted, Westport, Conn.: Greenwood, 1982) 5–8.

15. R. Lowie, *Primitive Societies* (New York: Horace Liveright, 1920) 248.

16. So already the Lagash texts published by A. Falkenstein, *Die neusumerischen Gerichtsurkunden* (Munich: Bayerischen Akademie der Wissenschaften, 1956–57) nos. 27, 32, 56, 82, and 99 (2.45, 53, 93, 135, 161–62). See also text no. 5 in C. J. Gadd, "Tablets from Kirkuk," *RA* 23 (1926) 126.

17. Code of Hammurabi §165 (lines 39–43; G. R. Driver and J. Miles, *The Babylonian Laws* [Oxford: Clarendon, 1955] 62; see also §§166 and 170). The only exception to this pattern is one passage that allows a father to choose his preferred son (*aplīšu ša inšu maḫru*, lit. 'the heir who [first] meets his eyes'; §165; cf. *CAD* M/1 64).

18. Strabo, *The Geography*, 16.4.25 (LCL 7.364); cf. Asaf A. A. Fyzee, *Outlines of Muhammadan Law* (4th ed.; Delhi: Oxford University Press, 1974) 389–90; and Qurʾan 4:10–12.

19. Cf. Josef Klíma, "Donationes mortis causa nach den akkadischen Rechtsurkunden aus Susa," in *Festschrift Johannes Friedrich* (ed. R. von Kienle et al.; Heidelberg: Carl Winter Universitätsverlag, 1959) 230–40.

one son as *rabû* and another as *ṣeḫrû*, a tablet from Ras Shamra concludes that the inheritance 'will be given to the one who has honored his mother, Bidawa' (*mannumme ina libbīšunu ša ukabbi*[*t*] [f]*Bidawa* [*um*]*mašu ana šuwāti tanandin*).[20]

Several texts explicitly deny using any preferential principle. The best-known formulation is from an Old Babylonian letter that states, *aplūtum ṣeḫertum u rabītum ina Sippar ul ibašši* 'there is no younger or older heir in Sippar'.[21] Similar statements can be found in texts from Nuzi (*kīma mitḫāriš izuzzū rabû u ṣeḫru ina libbīšunu yānu* 'they shall divide equally, with no older nor younger among them') and Ugarit (*yānu rabû yānu ṣeḫrû ina birīšunu* 'there is neither older nor younger among them').[22] The way these assertions are phrased paradoxically betrays an awareness of the very practice they deny, but it raises difficult questions as well. Did they really not have older and younger children in Sippar or Ugarit or Nuzi? Legal documents can alter social facts, but they cannot deny biology.

The terms involved, Akkadian *rabû* and Sumerian gal, are not unusual or obscure words, and most commonly they refer to rank rather than sequence. When applied to animals, *rabû* clearly refers to size; used for functionaries, it is obviously status that is reflected, as in the collective designation of the high gods as *ilāni rabûte*.[23] The term means 'great' and need have no implication for relative sequence at all. It is, therefore, neither surprising nor paradoxical that, after granting priority to an adoptee, one Nuzi tablet states, "Should Akab-shenni's [the adopter] wife bear ten sons, they shall [all] be *rabû*![24]

This explains what has long been regarded as a characteristic idiosyncrasy of ancient Near Eastern law, namely, that fathers may designate their "first-born" on a basis other than biological priority.[25] While texts describing this

20. RS 8.145 lines 25–26, in F. Thureau-Dangin, "Trois contrats de Ras-Shamra," *Syria* 18 (1937) 249–50.

21. F. R. Kraus, *Briefe aus dem British Museum* (AbB 1; Leiden: Brill, 1964) 70 #92.

22. HSS 9:44 lines 13–14, cited by Jonathan S. Paradise, *Nuzi Inheritance Practices* (Ph.D. diss.; University of Pennsylvania, 1972) 129; cf. HSS 19:23 lines 5–6 and 19:17 lines 12–13 (cited by ibid., 68 and 158); and RS 21.23 line 5; no. 81 in *Ugaritica* 5 (MRS 16; Paris: Geuthner, 1968) 173.

23. Cf. Knut L. Tallqvist, *Akkadische Götterepitheta* (Helsinki: Societas Orientalis Fennica, 1938) 14; cf. AHw, 936–38; *DISO*, 271; *UT*, 482; and 2 Kgs 18:17, Jer 39:3, Jonah 1:6, Esth 1:8, Dan 1:30.

24. HSS 5:7, cited by E. A. Speiser, "I Know Not the Day of My Death," *JBL* 74 (1955) 255–56.

25. Cf. Isaac Mendelsohn, "On the Preferential Status of the Eldest Son," *BASOR* 156 (1959) 38–40.

procedure have hardly been ignored, little consideration has been accorded the bizarre nature of the legal fiction they are said to presuppose. It may be reasonable for a father to choose his principal heir, but it would be truly remarkable for him to select which of his children was born first! Lacking other evidence for the primogeniture such texts are said to circumvent, and in light of the broader meaning suggested here for *rabû* and gal, these documents should be understood just as numerous Mesopotamian texts: they identify the holder of that status as a preferred heir; they do not make an arbitrary claim with regard to birth order.

Although succession to office need not follow the same lines as family inheritance,[26] the evidence concerning the transmission of royalty in the ancient Near East does not contradict what has already been described. To begin with, non-lineal systems are well attested. Early in this century, Paul Koschaker found evidence for what he called "fratriarchy," or collateral succession, which persisted in Persia until the Middle Elamite period.[27] Herodotus alludes to a more flexible system in his observation that, "According to Persian Law, the king may not march with his army until he has named his successor."[28] Hittite rulers apparently needed their subjects' consent, at least until dynastic succession was instituted by Telepinus's decree that the successor must be one of the leading princes (*ḫantezzi̯i̯as*);[29] how the ruler would be selected from within that larger group was left vague. Kilamuwa and Panammuwa note their selection from among their father's sons,[30] and Ugaritic mythology reflects a similar practice in El's request that Asherah indicate which of her sons should be elevated to the throne.[31]

26. A. R. Radcliffe-Brown observes that individual cultures typically use similar systems for both (*Structure and Function in Primitive Societies* [London: Cohen & West, 1952] 42).

27. Paul Koschaker, "Fratriarchat, Hausgemeinschaft und Mutterrecht in Keilschriftrechten," *ZA* 41 (1933) 1–89; cf. Dietz O. Edzard, "Sumerer und Semiten in den frühen Geschichte Mesopotamiens," in *Aspects du contact Suméro-Akkadien* (IXe Rencontre assyriologique internationale; ed. Edmond Sollberger) = *Genava* n.s. 8 (1960) 255.

28. Herodotus 7.2 (LCL 3.300–303).

29. Telepinus 2.36, in Inge Hoffmann, *Der Erlass-Telepinus* (Heidelberg: Carl Winter Universitätsverlag, 1984) 32.

30. *KAI* no. 24 lines 131–34 and no. 214 line 15.

31. *CTA* 6 I.43–46. 2 Kgs 3:27 states that the king of Moab was to be succeeded by his *bĕkōr*, but without indicating whether this was typical, much less how that status was achieved.

Near Eastern rulers often claim divine selection.[32] Quite apart from the objectivity of such statements or the underlying procedures, they too imply that selection was not always, or even often, automatic.

Given the ambiguity of this evidence, Israelite primogeniture cannot be taken for granted, nor can it be based on widespread or even ancient Near Eastern practice. Instead, it must be proven out of the biblical text itself, which, as we shall see, offers surprisingly little support for the common presumption that primogeniture was normative and ample indication of a situation that was far more complex. Ironically, this had been sensed as early as the sixteenth century, when opponents of British primogeniture cited the Bible in support of equal division.[33] These advocates of reform certainly did not regard preferential treatment as normative in ancient Israel.

The Bible contains no evidence of exclusive inheritance. Not only is there no law providing any individual with complete control of inheritance to the exclusion of his siblings, but several passages allude to fraternal sharing in a common household.[34] Both Proverbs (13:22) and Ezekiel (46:18) use the plural when speaking of one who "bequeaths (*hinḥîl*) to his children." The freedom implied by such statements underlies biblical depictions of patriarchal blessings as well. Job's estate was to be divided among his sons and daughters. While this distribution seems to rely largely on testamentary discretion, the text's statement that 'their father gave [his daughters] a portion amid their brothers' (*wayyittēn lāhem ʾăbîhem naḥălâ bĕtôk ʾăḥêhem*; 42:15) implies that, even if Job had chosen to exclude his daughters, the estate would still have been divided. Sarah's desire that Hagar be expelled so that "her son not inherit with my son" (Gen 21:10) also presupposes a system of shared inheritance, as does the expulsion of Jephthah from his household (Judg 11:2). Although explicitly exceptional, the story of Zelophehad's daughters confirms this impression with its provision that, in the absence of sons, not one but all daughters serve as substitute heirs.[35] Finally, the divi-

32. Cf. Henri Frankfort, *Kingship and the Gods: A Study of Ancient Near Eastern Religion as the Integration of Society and Nature* (Chicago: University of Chicago Press, 1948) 238–40.

33. Joan Thirsk, "The European Debate on Customs of Inheritance, 1500–1700," in *Family and Inheritance: Rural Society in Western Europe 1200–1800* (ed. Jack Goody, Joan Thirsk, and E. P. Thompson; Cambridge: Cambridge University Press, 1976) 181, 187.

34. Deut 25:5, Ps 133:1; cf. Gen 13:6 and 36:7.

35. Num 27:9–10 and 36:2. Other relatives who can receive an estate in the absence of offspring are likewise stated in the plural. The singular in Num 27:8 is apparently due to the prior use of the singular *ben*, either as a minimal condition or generically.

sion of the land among all the tribes, presented by the Bible as a matter of inheritance by the descendants of Jacob's sons, is based on a similar presumption, with each tribe receiving an allocation.[36]

Deut 21:17–18 is the *locus classicus* for Israelite inheritance. Although the lack of other evidence has forced scholars to use this passage for a broad range of issues, it is concerned with a very specific situation, prohibiting a father from elevating the son of a preferred wife over that of an unloved wife when the latter is already *bĕkōr*. This law is one of many found in Deuteronomy that are intended to protect the weak and the vulnerable.[37] Rather than repairing an abuse whereby fathers fictitiously designated certain children as firstborn in order to circumvent primogeniture, it protects unloved women by limiting their husband's power to deny their sons the status of *bĕkōr* at the time they allocate their belongings (*bĕyôm hanḥîlô ᵓet bānāyw ᵓet ᵓăšer-yihĕyeh lô*), thus demonstrating again that exclusive inheritance was not the issue. Whether a son could be disinherited for some reason other than having a less-loved mother is not stated,[38] nor whether there were acceptable reasons—or times—for making some other son *bĕkōr*.

Although the Bible provides no explicit rules for succession to office, it does offer a wealth of insight into ancient Israelite practice. Aaron may have been the oldest in his family,[39] but there is no evidence that priestly positions were restricted to firstborns. Levi's first three listed offspring—Gershon, Kohath, and Merari—all fathered important priestly lines, as did Kohath's first, second, and fourth sons—Amram, Izhar, and Uzziel.[40] Nor is there any evidence that tribal leadership during the desert period was hereditary, much less that these positions were based on principles of seniority.[41] Other leadership positions in early Israel, as reflected in the books of Judges and Samuel, were also not based on primogeniture. Samuel appointed *both* his sons to be judges (1 Sam 8:1), and Abimelech let the people of Shechem decide,

36. The division was made by lot (Num 34:13–29, Josh 14:2) with no portion presented as inherently preferable to any other and no tribe given automatic first choice in determining which portion would be theirs.

37. See J. van der Ploeg, "Studies in Hebrew Law III," *CBQ* 13 (1951) 35.

38. Cf. Obadiah Sforno at Deut 21:16.

39. The phrasing of Exod 2:1–2 has suggested to some that Moses was once regarded as firstborn. Miriam's relative age is less clear (cf. Martin Noth, *Exodus: A Commentary* [OTL; Philadelphia: Westminster, 1962] 122–23).

40. Exod 6:6–15, Num 3:19. The possibility of fraternal succession in the Herodian period is discussed by E. Bammel, "Die Bruderfolge im Hochpriestertum der herodianisch-römischen Zeit," *ZDPV* 70 (1954) 147–48.

41. Numbers 1–2, 7, 10:14–28, 13, 26, 34; 1 Chronicles 27.

"Which is better for you, to be ruled by seventy men—by all Jerubbaal's sons—or to be ruled by one man" (Judg 9:2), implying that unless its citizens chose otherwise, *all* of Gideon's sons could have ruled over Shechem.

It is widely assumed that Israelite kings were normally succeeded by their oldest sons. Unfortunately, the limited amount of information in the Bible makes it impossible to achieve certainty about this issue. Of the thirty kings who succeeded to the throne in Israel and Judah, the siblings of only seven are named, usually without reference to birth order.

Considering only those for whom information is available, we can note that Saul's sons are listed as Jonathan, Ishvi, and Malchishua in 1 Samuel (14:49); 2 Samuel (2:8) adds Ishbosheth.[42] In 1 Chronicles (8:33, 9:39), however, the sequence is Jonathan, Malchishua, Abinadab, and Ishbosheth (Eshbaal), illustrating the difficulty of using such material to determine seniority.[43] Even if such lists were arranged chronologically, they would provide little support for primogeniture, or any form of automatic succession for that matter. Ishbosheth was made king by Abner (2 Sam 2:8–9), albeit without resistance from his older brothers, assuming Ishvi, Malchishua, and Abinadab to have been older.

The succession following David is not more supportive. One can glean some indication of relative age from the way David's sons are grouped by place of birth, whether they were born in Hebron or Jerusalem. However, the two lists of sons born at Hebron and the three lists of those born in Jerusalem are not identical.[44] Both Absalom and Adonijah claimed leadership, despite being the sons of David's third and fourth Hebronite wives. Those arguing in favor of primogeniture must therefore assume that Chileab had already died when these events took place.[45] In any event, the several Hebronite sons were clearly born before Solomon, who was not even Bathsheba's oldest living son if the list in 1 Chr 3:5 is sequential! The Chronicler surely had no reason to move him to the end of such a list, although one can easily imagine why 2 Samuel might ignore the birth of intervening sons so that

42. Two daughters, described as *habbĕkîrâ* and *haqqĕtannâ*, respectively, are also mentioned in 1 Sam 14:49.

43. The Peshiṭta lists Ishvi instead of Abinadab. Problems with sequence in biblical genealogies are discussed by Marshall D. Johnson, *The Purpose of the Biblical Genealogies, with Special Reference to the Setting of the Genealogy of Jesus* (Cambridge: Cambridge University Press, 1969) 5–16, and Robert R. Wilson, *Genealogy and History in the Biblical World* (New Haven: Yale University Press, 1977) 145–89.

44. 2 Sam 3:2–5, 5:13–16; 1 Chr 3:1–9, 14:3–7.

45. The Peshiṭta gives his name as Caleb (at 2 Sam 3:3). In 1 Chr 3:1 he is called Daniel.

Solomon would appear to have been born immediately after the stillborn fruit of David and Bathsheba's affair.[46]

Biblical descriptions of other Judean kings are equally problematic. The succession of Abijah, son of Rehoboam's second wife as reported in 2 Chr 11:20, may demonstrate the elevation of a favorite wife's offspring,[47] but he is unlikely to have been the king's firstborn. Ahaziah, who is described as his father's youngest son, gained the throne only after his brothers had been taken captive (2 Chr 21:16–22:1). 2 Chronicles also reports that Jehoshaphat "gave dominion (*mamlākâ*) to Jehoram because he was the *bĕkōr*" (21:3), but this does not prove primogeniture to have been binding. Rather than being bound by an automatic principle, his father could have preferred to be succeeded by the *bĕkōr*.

1 Chronicles lists King Josiah's sons in the sequence Johanan, Jehoiakim, Zedekiah, and Shallum (3:15), the latter commonly identified with the son elsewhere called Jehoahaz (2 Kgs 23:30–31; cf. Jer 22:11). Twenty-three when he acceded to the throne, he was followed by his brother Jehoiakim, who was then twenty-five (2 Kgs 23:36).[48] In other words, they did not reign in birth order, nor does Chronicles list them that way. Zedekiah, who is usually considered to have been their brother, must have been younger than either one, since he was only twenty-one at the time of his accession eleven years later; however, he would have been older than his predecessor Jehoiachin, whom the Hebrew text of 2 Chronicles regards as having been his brother (36:10) and whose three-month reign began at the age of eighteen.[49]

Although kingship in both Israel and Judah does seem normally to have passed from father to son, there is no evidence that succession to the throne—or any other office for that matter—was based on primogeniture. Indeed, careful examination of the biblical evidence makes it questionable whether any prince could claim automatic succession. The four-century

46. Some have thought Solomon to have been the son who was adulterously conceived, with the tradition of that child's death having been subsequently constructed to protect his legitimacy; cf. Ernst Würthwein, *Die Erzählung von der Thronfolge Davids: Theologische oder Politische Geschichtesschreibung?* (Zurich: Theologischer Verlag, 1974) 31–32.

47. A similar dynamic is apparent in the preference accorded Isaac, Joseph, and Solomon, and underlies Deut 21:15–18.

48. Whether this was because Jehoahaz, who reigned only three months, had no sons or was a result of foreign intervention is not clear.

49. 2 Kgs 24:8; 2 Chr 36:9 reports him as having been eight. Zedekiah's age is reported in 2 Kgs 24:18, Jer 52:1, and 2 Chr 36:11. Descriptions of him as Jehoiachin's uncle are found in 2 Kgs 24:17, 1 Chr 3:15, and LXX 2 Chr 36:10.

chain of Davidic rulers demonstrates only Judah's acceptance of that dynasty, not how the heir was to be chosen from within it. David chose his own successor. Others were designated by the military or foreign supporters.[50] Numerous kings are said to have been anointed by various functionaries or even the people themselves. Many kings, or would-be kings, such as Absalom, Adonijah, Uzziah, Josiah, and Jehoahaz in the South and Sheba, Rehoboam, Jeroboam, Tibni, and Omri in the North, seem to have needed popular support before they could reign.[51] Admittedly, these procedures may reflect political reality or ritual conservatism, and much of the evidence comes from Chronicles, where the possibility of anachronism cannot be ignored. Still, there is simply no positive evidence that primogeniture was definitive.

The biblical evidence is thus quite different from what is often supposed. Property seems typically to have been divided among the descendent's heirs, most often his sons. Although one son may have been treated preferentially, it is not clear how that son was chosen. Deuteronomy prohibits only one criterion, and this prohibition may be as late as the seventh century. Nor is there evidence for any rigid or automatic system of royal succession. The dynastic principle presumes only that *a* son succeed to the throne, leaving open the choice of which son that would be, as shown by the various struggles for the throne and the involvement of third parties. Because the biblical stories of a younger son's displacement of his older brother cannot, therefore, be interpreted as attempts to justify deviations from some hypothetical norm, they must, instead, be reexamined on their own merits.

50. 2 Sam 2:8–9, 1 Kgs 1:7, 2 Kgs 10:3–5, 23:34, 24:17; cf. Isa 7:6.

51. Cf. C. Umhau Wolf, "Traces of Primitive Democracy in Ancient Israel," *JNES* 6 (1947) 98–108 and Hayim Tadmor, "'The People' and Kingship in Ancient Israel: The Role of Political Institutions in the Biblical Period," *Journal of World History* 11 (1968) 62–66.

An Investigation into the Location of the Laws on Offerings to Molek in the Book of Leviticus

John E. Hartley and Timothy Dwyer

There are eight occurrences of the term מֹלֶךְ 'Molek'[1] in the Hebrew Bible, and five of them come in two passages in Leviticus. The first occurs in Lev 18:21:

ומזרעך לא תתן להעביר למלך
ולא תחלל את־שם אלהיך אני יהוה

And you shall not give any of your seed (children) to transfer to Molek,
for you must not profane the name of your God. I am Yahweh.

Author's note: I wish to express my deep appreciation to Dr. Dwight W. Young for serving as my counselor and guide during the first year of my doctoral program at Brandeis University. He gave me excellent guidance on the approach I should take in my studies. In addition, he introduced me to the wonders of Egyptology, all the way from the Old Kingdom to the era of the Coptic Fathers. I extend to him my hearty thanks for his significant contribution to my education.—John E. Hartley

1. The meaning and form of מֹלֶךְ has been disputed. One position is that this form arose from a transformation in the pointing of the common Hebrew word מֶלֶךְ 'king' to that of the word בֹּשֶׁת 'shame' in order to convey the disgust of a genuine Yahwist toward a pagan deity (e.g., B. Baentsch, *Exodus, Leviticus, Numeri* [HAT; Göttingen: Vandenhoeck & Ruprecht, 1903] 394, and N. H. Snaith, *Leviticus and Numbers* [NCB; Greenwood, S.C.: Attic Press, 1977] 87–88). Another position is that the phrase *lmlk* means a *mlk*-sacrifice (M. Noth, *Leviticus* [OTL; Philadelphia: Westminster, 1974] 148; he is relating the position of O. Eissfeldt [*Molk als Opferbegriff im Punischen und Hebräischen und das Ende des Gottes Moloch* (Beiträge zur Religionsgeschichte des Altertums 3; Halle: Max Niemeyer, 1935)]), but the fact that the people went whoring after מֹלֶךְ (20:5) speaks against this being a word for sacrifice (so Noth). Some scholars, such as G. C. Heider, have come to the position that it is the name of a god that was pronounced according to the pointing in the MT (*The Cult of Molek: A Reassessment* [JSOTSup 43; Sheffield: JSOT Press, 1985] 223–28).

This law stands in the middle of a group of five laws regulating sexual practices: no intercourse with a menstruous woman (v. 19), no adultery (v. 20), no homosexual intercourse (v. 22), and no beastiality, either by a male or a female (v. 23). This group of laws is a supplement to the series of laws regarding incest (vv. 6–17a [18]). The obvious question, then, is why is a law on offering children to Molek included with four laws against illicit sexual intercourse? One reason that this law occurs here is the key term זֶרַע 'seed, children'. This term occurs at the end of v. 20a and provides a fitting tie to v. 21, which opens with ומזרעך 'and from your seed'.[2] In addition, the unlawful acts treated in vv. 19–23 seem to be placed in ascending order of impurity: טמאה 'uncleanness' (v. 20; cf. v. 19), חלל 'profane the name of your God' (v. 21),[3] תועבה 'detestable act' (v. 22),[4] and תבל 'confusion' (v. 23);[5] the ascending order is clear for vv. 20–22, but the lack of knowledge about the full force of תבל does not allow any decision on its relative place among the other three terms for defilement. The law in v. 21 thus stands in the middle of the identifiable progression. This essay will attempt to offer other reasons for the inclusion of this law at this location.

The other references to Molek in Leviticus come in 20:2–6. This passage also stands in relationship to a series of laws regulating incest and other illicit sexual unions (vv. 7–21). The lead law of this series says:

> איש איש בני ישׂראל ומן־הגר הגר בישׂראל אשר יתן מזרעו למלך מות יומת
> עם הארץ ירגמהו באבן (v. 2aβ+b)
>
> Any Israelite or any alien living in Israel who gives any of his children to Molek must be put to death;
> the people of the land shall stone him.

In the next three verses Yahweh states his resolve to punish anyone who 'gives any of his seed to Molek' מזרעו נתן למלך or 'all who play the harlot after him to whore after Molek' כל־הזנים אחריו לזנות אחרי המלך. The reason given

2. Cf. Baentsch, *Exodus, Leviticus, Numeri*, 394; he also takes נתן 'give' as a key word; and Noth, *Leviticus*, 136.

3. Cf. W. Dommershausen, "חלל *ḥll* I," *TDOT* 4.411–12.

4. תועבה describes abhorrent activities that are repugnant to Yahweh, such as idolatry (Ezek 6:9, 11), sacrificing animals with defects (Deut 17:1), human sacrifice (Deut 12:31), and witchcraft (Deut 18:9–14). These activities are viewed as vile because of their total incompatibility with the worship of Yahweh. Cf. P. Humbert, "Le substantif *toᶜēbā* et le verbe *tᶜb* dans l'Ancien Testament," *ZAW* 72 (1960) 217–37, and E. Gerstenberger, "תעב *tᶜb* pi verabscheuen," *THAT* 2.1051–55.

5. The word תבל only occurs here and in Lev 20:12. BDB (p. 117) places it with the Hebrew root בלל 'mix, confuse'. It thus means 'a confusion, a perversion', that is, a twisting of the natural order.

that one may not give a child to Molek is that it 'defiles טמא my (Yahweh's) sanctuary מקדשי' and 'profanes חלל my (Yahweh's) holy name שם קדשי' (v3bβγ). This pericope concludes with a law against necromancy under the terms אבת 'ghosts, mediums' [6] and ידענים 'departed spirits, necromancers'.[7] This last law is not haphazardly attached here, as the usage of certain phrases that occur in the laws about Molek shows, namely, לזנות אחריהם 'to whore after them' (so v. 5)[8] and the penalties ונתתי פני ב 'I will set my face against . . .' (so v. 3a and v. 5a [with ושמתי 'I will put/set'] and והכרתי אתו מקרב עמו 'I will cut him off from the midst of his people' (so v. 3a and v. 5b [without 'from the midst of his people']).

There are three other references to Molek מלך in the MT, but the occurrence in 1 Kgs 11:7 is probably a textual error for מלכם 'Milcom' (BHS). The remaining two are 2 Kgs 23:10, וטמא את־התפת אשר בגי בני־הנם לבלתי להעביר איש את־בנו ואת־בתו באש למלך 'he (Josiah) defiled the Tophet which was in the Valley of Ben-Hinnom, in order that no person might transfer his son or his daughter in fire to Molek', and Jer 32:35aαβ, ויבנו את־במות הבעל אשר בגיא בן־הנם להעביר את־בניהם ואת־בנותיהם למלך 'they built the high places of Baal, which are in the Valley of Ben-Hinnom, in order to transfer their sons and their daughters to Molek'.

The location of these laws against making offerings to Molek in Leviticus in the context of sexual laws primarily against incest raises many questions. The two most prominent are (1) who was Molek and (2) what kind of sacrifices were involved? There has been much scholarly discussion about these offerings to Molek. To answer these questions we shall draw on these studies and in so doing make some contribution to the discussion by recounting the history of

6. H. Hoffner, "Second Millennium Antecedents to the Hebrew *ʾôḇ*," *JBL* 86 (1967) 385–401, and idem, "אוֹב *ʾôbh*," *TDOT* 1.130–34. Hoffner concludes that אוב in the OT has three uses: (1) a special pit that had access to the nether world and through which the deceased could be called up; (2) a deceased spirit; (3) a person skilled in calling up a deceased spirit.

7. ידעוני comes from the root ידע 'know' and means 'a necromancer', one who had a close acquaintance with a departed spirit and was thus able to communicate with that spirit; by extension ידעוני may also mean the 'departed spirit'. It is debated whether or not the two terms stand for two types of practitioners. E. F. de Ward ("Superstition and Judgment: Archaic Methods of Finding a Verdict," *ZAW* 89 [1977] 11) understands that Hoffner's work leads to taking ידעוני for the practitioner and אוב for 'the pit' the practitioner used to call up the ghost.

8. The worship of Yahweh is exclusive. Therefore, when followers of Yahweh serve another god, the Old Testament often refers to this false worship as זנה אחרי 'to play the harlot or whore after. . . .' This metaphor communicates that in doing an act of worship to another god, the people's devotion to Yahweh has waned; such an act is an expression of faithlessness against Yahweh (cf. S. Erlandsson, "זָנָה *zānāh*," *TDOT* 5.101–4).

interpretation. Then we shall make some suggestions as to the reason these Molek laws occur in the context of laws on incest.

Rabbinic tradition held that Molek worship involved the dedication of a child by pagan priests to Molek. In the second century C.E., for example, R. Judah ben Elai commented on Deut 18:10 that the prohibition involved commanding one not to cause his son or daughter to go over to a pagan god. There is some rabbinic tradition that the prohibition in Lev 18:21 involved sexual intercourse with a cult prostitute. As a whole, rabbinic tradition denied that actual sacrifice of the children took place. In 1617 Johannis Selden wrote an essay, *De Dîs Syris*, which defended the position that Molek worship involved the dedication of children, rather than some sort of burning of children. Also in the 1600s, J. G. Schwab (1667), Christiani Ziegra (1684), and Daniel Dietsch (n.d.) wrote studies on Molek (see vol. 23 of *Thesaurus antiquitatum sacrarum*, ed. by Blasio Ugolino). John Spencer, in 1686, was a trend-setter in his postulation that the Molek cult involved actual burning.[9] In the 1800s, Friedrich Münter and F. C. Movers[10] investigated the use of Molek in personal and divine names and introduced the cult of child sacrifice in Carthage as relevant to the question of the cult of Molek in the Bible. Perhaps more influential in the 1800s were the works of G. F. Daumer and F. W. Ghillany,[11] who contended that patriarchal and Mosaic religion involved human sacrifices to Molek, and only later was YHWH distinguished from Molek. Specifically, they saw the commands 'to consecrate' קדשׁ or 'to give' נתן the firstborn to YHWH in Exod 13:2 and 22:8 as originally involving child-sacrifice and then being modified at a later time.

Among studies appearing in the 1800s, the work of A. Geiger was important;[12] he argued for some 25 instances in the OT referring to Molek, an old king-god. W. W. Baudissin made the case for looking to Phoenicia for the origins of the Molek cult in Israel, a view that continues to be championed by some at the present time.[13]

9. J. Spencer, *De legibus Hebraeorum ritualibus et earum rationibus* (2d ed.; Hagae-Comitum: Arnold Leers, 1686).

10. F. Münter, *Religion der Kathager* (2d ed.; Copenhagen: Johann Heinrich Schubothe, 1821); F. C. Movers, *Die Phönizier* (Bonn: Eduard Weber, 1841).

11. G. F. Daumer, *Der Feuer- und Molechdienst der alten Hebräer als urväterlicher, legaler orthodoxer Kultus der Nation* (Braunschweig: Otto, 1842); F. W. Ghillany, *Die Menschenopfer der alten Hebräer* (Nuremberg: Johann Leonhard Schrag, 1842).

12. A. Geiger, *Urschrift und Übersetzungen der Bibel* (2d ed.; Frankfurt am Main: Madda, 1928; orig., 1857).

13. W. W. Baudissin, *Jahve et Moloch: Sive de ratione inter deum Israelitarum et Molochum intercedente* (Leipzig: Fr. Guil. Grunow, 1874).

In this century O. Eissfeldt's work on Molek stands as a landmark.[14] He argued that the term למלך 'for molek' was a technical term for sacrifice; that is, מלך stood for a type of sacrifice, not for a deity at all. Only later in Israel's history, as a result of Josiah's reform, was Molek worshiped as a deity. Many sought to refute his thesis in succeeding years; nevertheless, his work remains a milestone. R. de Vaux[15] followed Eissfeldt in proposing a *molk* type of sacrifice, but de Vaux suggested that the Israelite practice was a misunderstanding of a Phoenician sacrifice. He proposed that the sacrifice was for a king-god, Melek. In 1969, M. Weinfeld revived the hypothesis of ancient Jewish interpreters and others that the Molek cult involved no regular practice of child sacrifice at all.[16] He also denied any connection of this cult with practices in Phoenicia or Carthage. In his opinion, Judah's cult of Molek was actually the dedication of children to Adadmilki, Ishtar, and the King and the Queen of heaven, practiced in the Tophet.

Reacting to an article by Weinfeld in *Ugarit-Forschungen*,[17] M. Smith reasons that a figurative interpretation of Carthaginian texts about the burning of children, as well as of the biblical data, is indefensible.[18] Paul Mosca's Harvard dissertation also challenges Weinfeld and returns to Eissfeldt's position that the references are to a *molk* type of sacrifice.[19] Mosca portrays a cult of child sacrifice, with sources in Phoenicia and Canaan, existing and sanctioned by the official Yahwistic cult up until 722 B.C.E. in the North and until Josiah's reform in the South. A. Green entered the discussion and claimed, however, that the evidence is not conclusive enough either to understand the precise nature of the ritual involving Molek or to understand the connection between Phoenicia and Israel.[20] He limits the role of the cult to times of national emergencies in Israel. A very recent proposal has been put forth by G. C. Heider.[21] His thesis is that the worship of Molek in Israel developed

14. O. Eissfeldt, *Molk als Opferbegriff.*

15. R. de Vaux, *Studies in Old Testament Sacrifice* (Cardiff: University of Wales, 1964).

16. M. Weinfeld, "Moloch, Cult of," *EncJud* (ed. C. Roth; New York: MacMillan, 1971) 12.230–32.

17. M. Weinfeld, "The Worship of Molech and of the Queen of Heaven and Its Background," *UF* 4 (1974) 122–54.

18. M. Smith, "A Note on Burning Babies," *JAOS* 95 (1975) 477–79. Cf. M. Weinfeld, "Burning Babies in Ancient Israel: A Rejoinder to Morton Smith's Article in *JAOS* 95 (1975), pp. 477–79," *UF* 10 (1978) 411–13.

19. P. G. Mosca, *Child Sacrifice in Canaanite and Israelite Religion: A Study in* Mulk *and* mlk (Ph.D. diss., Harvard University, 1975).

20. A. R. W. Green, *The Role of Human Sacrifice in the Ancient Near East* (ASOR Dissertation Series 1; Missoula, Mont.: Scholars Press, 1975).

21. Heider, *The Cult of Molek.*

from a Syro-Palestinian deity Malik, later Milku/i or Molek, which was worshiped as a chthonic deity in Mesopotamia, Mari, Ugarit, and Israel. The cult
was related to deified, often royal, ancestors. It was practiced until the fall of
Judah in 587/6 B.C.E. (with the exception of the times of Josiah and most
likely Hezekiah) and in secret after the return from the exile. In his judgment
the sacrifices were irregular and voluntary, having to do with fertility, and the
cult involved care for the ancestors of the previous inhabitants of the land
(called Rephaim) and the ancestors of the worshipers. The exact nature of the
cult remains mysterious.

This brief discussion of the direction of studies regarding Molek clarifies
the major issues in the discussion. First, does Molek refer to a deity or to a
type of sacrifice? Second, was actual child sacrifice involved? Third, is there a
connection between Phoenician and Carthaginian practices and practices in
Israel? Fourth, was there ever a syncretism between the worship of YHWH
and of Molek in Israel? Fifth, what is the significance of Heider's thesis that
the Molek cult had chthonic characteristics?

The next step to address these questions is to examine other passages that
might shed light on the kind of sacrifice involved. The laws in Exod 13:2 and
13:12–13 require that all the firstborn be holy, that is, they belong exclusively to God. The reason that these verses relate to the discussion of Molek
worship is that the key term of those laws, העביר 'to transfer to', is used in
these laws, specifically, all the firstborn are 'transferred from' the profane to
the sacred sphere. The laws in Exodus treat three categories of firstborn:
sacrificial animals, non-sacrificial animals, and humans. In the opinion of
some scholars, in these laws there are either vestiges of a pre-Israelite firstborn sacrifice of children, or the Canaanites had already adopted a substitute
for the sacrifice of a firstborn child. However, the possibility that a society
would sacrifice all its firstborn children seems to be quite implausible, for
such a practice would deprive that society of a great portion of its strength
for the next generation. In any case, Israel is clearly instructed to 'redeem'
פדה her firstborn children.

Two more laws on giving the first to YHWH are found in Exod 22:28–29
[Eng. 29–30]:

(28) מלאתך ודמעך לא תאחר בכור בניך תתן־לי׃

(29) כן־תעשׂה לשׁרך לצאנך שׁבעת ימים יהיה עם־אמו ביום השׁמיני תתנו־לי׃

You shall not delay (in giving me from) the fullness of your granary and from
the overflow of your vat; you shall give to me the firstborn of your sons. You
shall do the same for your cattle and for your flocks; seven days it will be with
its mother; on the eighth day you shall give it to me.

Some scholars see in this passage the remnants of human sacrifice, for they take the antecedent of the verb יהיה 'shall do' (singular) in v. 29 to be the בכור 'firstborn' of v. 28; otherwise, if the antecedent were 'your oxen and your sheep', this verb would be plural. Furthermore, the verb נתן 'give' does not help decide the issue because it is a very general term; while it could have the meaning of sacrifice, that meaning is not demanded by the term itself. Nevertheless, it can be argued that because the reference in v. 28a is to the first of the granary and the vat, נתן here means 'dedicate', not 'sacrifice'. Thus these laws do not necessarily require 'the sacrifice' of firstborn children. The use of נתן may instead indicate assigning a firstborn child to have a special role for God, like Samuel at Shiloh (1 Sam 1:21–29). Similarly, some have taken Num 18:15a to retain vestiges of a law of child sacrifice. This text reads:

כל־פטר רחם לכל־בשׂר אשר־יקריבו ליהוה באדם ובבהמה יהיה־לך אך פדה
תפדה את בכור האדם ואת בכור־הבהמה הטמאה פדה

Everything of all flesh that opens the womb, both humans and animals, which is to be presented to YHWH, will be yours; however, you must redeem the firstborn of humans, and you will redeem the firstborn of unclean animals.

It is true that the key term הקריב 'draw near, present' frequently is used of the presentation of sacrifice, but it does not always have that meaning (e.g., Num 7:12, where it describes the presenting of vessels and animals as property for the sanctuary). Its sense in this text may then be 'turning over' something to the sanctuary.

Because the verbs נתן 'give' and הקריב 'draw near, present' do not have to mean 'sacrifice', as in the preceding laws, the usage of these terms in the Molek texts does not unequivocally mean that sacrifice was involved in the practice of presenting children to God. Deut 12:31, however, witnesses to some practice of burning children by Israel's neighbors. This text says:

לא־תעשׂה כן ליהוה אלהיך כי כל־תועבת יהוה אשר שׂנא עשׂו לאלהיהם כי
גם את־בניהם ואת־בנתיהם ישׂרפו באשׁ לאלהיהם

You shall not do thus to YHWH your God, because they do for their gods every abomination according to YHWH, which he hates—because they even burn their sons and their daughters in fire to their gods.

The use of שׂרף 'burn' clearly indicates that the sacrifice was consumed by fire. Deut 18:10 expands on this practice. It says:

לא־ימצא בך מעביר בנו־ובתו באשׁ קסם קסמים מעונן ומנחשׁ ומכשׁף

There shall not be found among you one who makes his son or his daughter

> pass through the fire, one who practices divination, one who does soothsaying, or one who interprets omens, or one who practices sorcery.[22]

One interpretation of this verse is that the children were sacrificed at critical times to determine the course of events.[23] Molek is not specifically mentioned in this text; nevertheless, the practice described is pictured as being very similar to the offering of children to Molek (cf. 2 Kgs 3:26–27). What must be noted in this verse is the association of מעביר . . . באשׁ 'cause to be transferred . . . by fire' with various types of divinatory practices and soothsaying. The language here sheds light on the references to Molek in Leviticus. The verb העביר 'cause to be transferred' is the critical term used in Lev 18:21. In addition, the verb 'give' נתן is also used in Lev 18:21, and it is the term for offering in Lev 20:2, 3. As has been stated, in rabbinic tradition the worship of Molek was understood as the transfer of Jewish children either by delivering them to pagan priests or by sexual intercourse ('passing your seed') with a pagan woman. However, is this the limit of the meaning of העביר? The use of באשׁ 'in fire' plus the occurrence of the verb שׂרף 'burn' in other texts favors the position that the sacrifice was actually burned (cf. Num 31:22–23; 1 Kgs 16:3, 17:17). In addition, 2 Kgs 16:3, 17:17, and 21:6 all record that a certain person or the people 'caused [their sons or daughters] to be transferred by fire' העביר . . . באשׁ. It needs to be noted that the latter two references go on to describe various divinatory practices, suggesting that this was one reason for making this kind of sacrifice. 2 Kgs 23:10 supports this interpretation; it records that in his reform Josiah defiled the "Tophet" in the valley of Ben-Hinnom in order to put an end to offering up children to Molek. In this text the sacrificial term is העביר . . . באשׁ 'transfer . . . by fire' and the sacrifice is to Molek למלך. But was the death of children the actual activity of this cult?

Some insight into this last question may come from passages in Jeremiah. This prophet spoke out strongly against the Tophet (e.g., chap. 19). In Jer 7:31 he uses לשׂרף באשׁ את בניהם ואת בנתיהם 'to burn their sons and their daughters with fire' in regard to practices that took place at the Tophet in the valley of Ben-Hinnom; however, he does not use the name Molek. This verse supports the position that the actual burning of children did take place at the Tophet. In 19:5 Jeremiah speaks of the burning of sons by fire, but as whole offerings עלות to Baal. In 32:35 he identifies the high places of Baal with the

22. Cf. the translation by P. Craigie, *The Book of Deuteronomy* (NICOT; Grand Rapids: Eerdmans, 1976) 259.

23. Ibid., 260.

worship of Molek; there sons and daughters 'were transferred to Molek' להעביר . . . למלך. The evidence from Jeremiah then clearly indicates that the actual burning of children took place in the worship of Molek.

Texts in Ezekiel support this position. Ezek 16:21 speaks of slaughtering שחט children and giving them in offerings by transferring them נתן בהעביר. The clinching word is שחט 'sacrifice' with 'my children' בני as the object (see Ezek 20:25–26, 31). This text suggests that the children were ritually killed before they were burned. Ezek 23:37b, which reads את־בניהן אשר ילדו־לי העבירו להם לאכלה 'they have transferred to (their idols) for food their children whom they had borne to me', contributes another word אכלה 'food' to the field of העביר 'transfer'. The conclusion must be clear by now that the term העביר in the context of Molek worship means something beyond dedication; it is a technical term for offering up children as a sacrifice to a god. Moreover, while Ezekiel does not specifically mention Molek, the terms describing the practice of offering children are so similar to the above references that it seems safe to include Molek among the idols mentioned in Ezek 20:31 and 23:37.

As for the question of whether Molek stands for a type of sacrifice or for the name of a deity, the evidence presented favors taking this term as the name of a deity. This conclusion finds support in the phraseology of Lev 20:5: 'to play the harlot after . . .' זנות אחרי, for this language applies more easily to a deity than to a type of sacrifice. Furthermore, Tophet is understood as the place for the worship of specific deities like Molek rather than solely as the place to present a particular type of sacrifice (2 Kgs 23:10). In addition, Weinfeld has convincingly argued that terms such as מלך אמר or מלכאדם, which Eissfeldt, de Vaux, and others claim point only to a *molk* type of sacrifice, are better understood as compound names of an actual deity like Adadmilki, 'Adad the king', to whom children were also burned.[24]

Heider's study takes this position and goes on to show that the inclusion of Lev 20:6, a prohibition regarding the practice of necromancy, with the laws against Molek sacrifice is in accord with references to divination in other passages that deal with Molek and the sacrificing of children (Deut 18:10; 2 Kgs 17:17 and 21:6). From these texts he reconstructs a cult of the dead built on the belief that the dead had a continuing claim on the living, either due to the deplorable existence of the dead or the belief in the ability of the dead to influence events among the living.[25] There is evidence of the existence of such a cult in Canaan and Mesopotamia. A few biblical references also witness to

24. Weinfeld, "Moloch, Cult of," 12.231–32.
25. Heider, *Cult of Molek*, 383–400.

such a cult. Ps 106:28b, for example, speaks of the Israelites' eating sacrifices offered to the dead; this text is an interpretation of the event found in Numbers 25, when the Israelites joined in a Moabite festival. Heider interprets this celebration as a funeral feast, מרזח (cf. Amos 6:7, Jer 16:5).[26] Another passage, Isa 63:3–5a, attests to cultic activities for the dead done in secret places at night, accompanied by eating pork and broth made from unclean things. Heider finds in Ezek 43:7b and 9 reference to cults of the dead like those found at Mari and Ugarit.[27] Molek then, in this interpretation, was closely related to ancestral worship and feasts for the dead. While Heider's position is hard to prove or disprove, his suggestion that worship of Molek involved necromancy, the cult of the dead, and/or divinatory practices makes intelligible the connection of Lev 20:6 about occultic practices in regard to the dead and the statutes against Molek in Lev 20:2–5.

In summary, Molek worship is the offering of infants to a god named Molek by burning on a pyre. While it is likely that some children were burned while living, the variety of texts witnesses to the sacrificing of the infant children before they were burned.[28] As for the location of these laws against Molek worship in the context of sexual offenses, especially crimes of incest, four explanations are proposed: (1) both kinds of offenses are kinship violations; (2) both offenses disregard the personal integrity of the victim and the authority structure of the clan; (3) both offenses involve the greatest pollution and the stiffest penalties; (4) a connection between these acts existed deep in the tribal social consciousness.[29]

26. Ibid., 388–89.
27. Ibid., 392–94.
28. De Vaux, *Studies in Old Testament Sacrifice,* 81.
29. The seemingly unlikely location of the Molek laws has occasioned a number of proposals from critical scholars to account for the composition history of these texts. A selection of these is provided as an example of the variety of explanations set forth. Baentsch (*Exodus, Leviticus, Numeri,* 394) takes the position that a redactor included the laws on Molek sacrifice in Leviticus 20 on the basis that this law carried the same penalty as the other laws listed in that chapter; this redactor inserted the law in Lev 18:21, because of the two key words נתן 'give' and זרע 'seed'. R. Kilian, on the other hand, finds in Lev 20:2 an old and original law, but in his judgment the rest of 20:3–6 is a composite from different sources; in fact the composer of v. 3 did not accept the penalty of death by stoning in the original law (*Literarkritische und Formgeschichtliche Untersuchung des Heiligkeitsgesetzes* [BBB 19; Bonn: Peter Hanstein, 1963] 66–67). Kilian accounts for the Molek law in Lev 18:21 along with the following laws in vv. 22–23a as being taken from the old מות יומת series found in chap. 20 (18:21 from 20:2–3; 18:22 from 20:13; 18:23a from 20:15; ibid., 30). The reason that the Molek law was put in this place in Leviticus 18 is uncertain

First, a consequence of an act of incest is that it disrupts relationships in a clan, bringing long-lasting discord. It needs to be remembered that in a primitive society each person relied on membership in a clan for survival. There was no place for the independent individual; such a person could not keep themselves alive. Sociologist have observed that certain sexual relationships which one society rules as incestuous are permitted by another society with no social disharmony.[30] Nevertheless, once a society defines certain relationships as incestuous and thus taboo, any violation of the standard could bring such conflict among members of the clan that the very existence of that clan would be threatened. This possibility may account for the severity of the penalties for incest found in Leviticus 20, namely the "cut off" penalty, that is, exclusion from the clan (vv. 17, 18)[31] and the death penalty (vv. 10, 11, 12, 13, 14, 15, 16). By removing any member of a clan who had violated an incest law, both the cause of the discord and the threat to the clan's solidarity were removed. Punishing an act of incest was thus a matter of the survival of the clan. This claim, that an act of incest against the accepted standard was socially disruptive, finds support in the account of Tamar, sister of Absalom, a son of David, and Amnon, a son of David by another wife. This account reports that Amnon forced himself on his stepsister (2 Samuel 13). His indiscretion eventually led to his murder at the hands of Absalom. These two acts put a great distance between David and his beloved son Absalom. In time Absalom revolted against David and sought to usurp the kingdom. In the revolt he was killed,

---

except for the connection between the preceding זרע 'seed' in v. 20 and מזרעך 'from your seed' in this law. In contrast to Kilian, A. Cholewiński (*Heiligkeitsgesetz und Deuteronomium*: *Eine vergleichende Studie* [AnBib 66; Rome: Pontifical Biblical Institute, 1976]) finds Lev 20:2ab–5 to be basically a skillfully composed unit from a single hand; on the other hand, he agrees with Kilian that the laws in Lev 18:21–23 were taken over from chap. 20. K. Elliger (*Leviticus* [HAT; Tübingen: Mohr, 1966] 235) finds it very difficult to account for the Molek law in chap. 18. As for the Molek laws in chap. 20, he posits that the author of that pericope freely formulated these laws as an expansion on 18:21, drawing on the distinctive language of vv. 9–21 in order to tie this material closely to its context (ibid., 271–72).

30. Malinoski, for example, found that among the Trobrianders, boys and girls freely experiment with sex without social constraint save that a brother-sister union is strictly guarded against (R. Fox, *The Red Lamp of Incest* [New York: E. P. Dutton, 1980] 36–38).

31. This position follows R. Hutton, *Declarator Formula: Form of Authoritative Pronouncement in Ancient Israel* (Ph.D. diss., Claremont University, 1983) 138–42. Cf. D. J. Wold, "The *Kareth* Penalty in P: Rationale and Cases," *SBL 1979 Seminar Papers* (SBLSP 16; 2 vols; ed. P. J. Achtemeier; Missoula, Mont.: Scholars Press, 1979) 1.1–45; he takes the "cut off" penalty as "a divine curse of extinction visited upon the sinner and his seed" (ibid., 24).

to David's deep sorrow (2 Samuel 15–19). Similarly the offering of a child to Molek would have put a heavy strain on a clan, and one can only imagine the sorrow experienced by the parents, especially the mother, who offered a child to Molek. Such sadness could settle over all the living children and other members of the clan. While the religious zeal of the parents who made the offering would dull their pain and perhaps that of some clan members, it is doubtful that it soothed all members. Thus it is postulated that sacrifices to Molek produced significant dissidence in a clan, similar to that caused by incest.

Second, just as an incestuous relationship both disregarded the honor of a female member of the family and the authority of the male who was responsible for her protection, so sacrifice to Molek also disregarded the right of the child and the proper respect due a deceased relative. Only the latter phrase needs any clarification. As argued above, there was a close tie between sacrifice to Molek and necromancy. Necromancy for the masses was closely associated with the family, that is, a family member diligently sought to communicate with a deceased relative. But from the perspective of genuine worship of Yahweh, it was unseemly to arouse or disturb a departed ghost (cf. 1 Sam 28:15). A deceased relative was to be remembered with honor, but never to be revered. The mores and laws of ancient Israel were designed to prevent any form of ancestral worship. Since sacrifices to Molek crossed this barrier against ancestral worship, they violated the way the deceased were to be regarded.

Third, both of these practices were viewed by Leviticus 18 and 20 as abhorrent. All wrongdoing is defiling; however, the more gruesome a wrongdoing the greater was the degree of pollution. Ancient Israel viewed illicit sexual offenses and incestuous relationships among the most defiling transgressions (compare on Lev 18:18–23, above). Lev 20:9–21 relates the defiling nature of illicit sexual unions; the act of lying with a daughter-in-law is תבל 'confusion, perversion' (v. 12);[32] homosexual intercourse is תועבה 'a detestable thing' (v. 13);[33] the taking (marrying) of a woman and her daughter is זמה 'a lewd act' (v. 14);[34] intercourse with a sister or a half-sister is חסד 'a disgrace' (v. 17).[35] Like these sexual offenses, the offering of a child to Molek had double polluting force. It both טמא 'defiled' the sanctuary, rendering

32. Cf. n. 5.

33. Cf. n. 4.

34. Cf. S. Steingrimsson, "זמם *zmm*," *TDOT* 4.89–90.

35. Normally Hebrew חסד means 'loyal love', but twice חסד occurs with the meaning 'disgrace, something shameful' (here and Prov 14:34). This use of חסד probably comes from a different root (*HALAT* 323).

ineffective the place where sinful humans sought reconciliation with God, and it חלל 'profaned' Yahweh's name, for it usurped from him, the author of life, his primary prerogative over life and death. This language reveals that sacrifices to Molek were among the most miasmic. Thus these two categories of sins are regulated in the same context, for both were violations of family members and fraught with pollution.

The fourth reason is rooted deep in the social consciousness of the Israelite tribes. R. Fox reports that the Chiricahua, an American Indian tribe of the Southwest, equated incest and witchcraft as the gravest violations of the social and of the spiritual realms, respectively.[36] It is amazing that the inclusion of Molek worship with incest in two passages in Leviticus is in accord with the perspective of another people so distant in time and place. This external witness from another culture suggests that the union of these two transgressions, which seem so disjunctive to the Western mind, was not at all disjunctive to kinship-oriented cultures. This suggestion offers fertile ground for further investigation. It is set forth here in the hope that other students of ancient cultures may have observed this pattern or some variation of it in their studies, and thereby they may enter the discussion to throw more light on these biblical texts.

This essay reaches four conclusions. First, the laws regarding Molek worship are appropriately set in the context of laws regulating incest and other illicit sexual acts. Second, sacrifice to Molek was the burning of children who had been sacrificed to a god named Molek. Third, these sacrifices to Molek were sometimes made for the purpose of divination. Fourth, these sacrifices threatened a clan's solidarity.

36. Fox, *The Red Lamp of Incest*, 32–34.

Balaam Son of Beor in Light of Deir ʿAllā and Scripture: Saint or Soothsayer?

Walter C. Kaiser, Jr.

Few personalities in the biblical tradition exhibit a more challenging problem for determining the source of their authority than Balaam, son of Beor. At least two distinct evaluations of his skills and roles exist in the biblical text and in the recently discovered inscription from Deir ʿAllā.[1] On the one hand, Balaam is described as a prophet who has access to Yahweh himself and

1. H. J. Franken, "Texts from the Persian Period from Tell Deir ʿAllah," *VT* 17 (1967) 480–81; J. Naveh, "The Date of the Deir ʿAllā Inscription in Aramaic Script," *IEJ* 17 (1967) 256–58; J. Hoftijzer and G. van der Kooij, *Aramaic Texts from Deir ʿAllā* (Leiden: Brill, 1976); Jacob Hoftijzer, "The Prophet Balaam in a 6th Century Aramaic Inscription," *BA* 39 (1976) 11–17; A. Caquot and A. Lemaire, "Les textes araméennes de Deir ʿAllā," *Syria* 54 (1977) 189–208; Helmer Ringgren, "Bileam och inskriften fran Deir ʿAllā," *Religion och Bibel* 36 (1977) 85–89; Joseph Fitzmyer, "Review of *Aramaic Texts from Deir ʿAllah*," *CBQ* 40 (1978) 93–95; J. Naveh, "Review of *Aramaic Texts from Deir ʿAllā*," *IEJ* 29 (1979) 133–36; G. Garbini, "L'iscrizione di Balaam Bar-Beor," *Henoch* 1 (1979) 166–88; M. Delcor, "Le texte de Deir ʿAllā et les oracles bibliques de Balaʿam," *VTSup* 32 (1981) 52–73; J. C. Greenfield, "Review of *Aramaic Texts from Deir ʿAllā*," *JSS* 25 (1980) 248–52; Stephen A. Kaufman, "Review Article: *The Aramaic Texts from Deir ʿAllā*," *BASOR* 239 (1980) 71–74; P. Kyle McCarter Jr., "The Balaam Texts from Deir ʿAllā: The First Combination," *BASOR* 239 (1980) 49–60; Helga and Manfred Weippert, "Die 'Bileam'-Inschrift von Tell Dēr ʿAllā," *ZDPV* 98 (1982) 77–103; Jean Koenig, "La declaration des dieux dans l'inscription de Deir ʿAllā (I,2)," *Sem* 33 (1983) 77–88; Andre Lemaire, "Fragments from the Book of Balaam Found at Deir ʿAllā," *BARev* 11/5 (1985) 26–39; idem, "L'inscription de Balaam trouvée à Deir ʿAllā: Epigraphie," in *Biblical Archaeology Today: Proceedings of the International Congress of Biblical Archaeology* (Jerusalem: Israel Exploration Society, 1985) 313–25; V. Sasson, "Two Unrecognized Terms in the Plaster Texts from Deir ʿAllā," *PEQ* 117 (1985) 102–3; JoAnn Hackett, *The Balaam Text from Deir ʿAllā* (HSM 31; Chico, Calif.: Scholars Press, 1984); idem, "Some Observations on the Balaam Tradition at Deir ʿAllā," *BA* 49 (1986) 212–22.

to Yahweh's plan to make Israel the instrument of divine blessing for all the nations. This presentation occupies the main narrative in Numbers 22–24. In many parts of this narrative, Balaam certainly appears to be one of Yahweh's obedient servants, even though he surprisingly originates not from Israel but from a non-Jewish heritage.

Juxtaposed alongside this description is another estimate of the same man. In this depiction he is seen as a seer who is blind to the opposing presence of Yahweh's angel (Num 22:22–30). Worse still, he is specifically remembered in the biblical tradition as "Balaam, son of Beor, who practiced divination" [*haqqôsēm*] (Josh 13:22).

Attempts to unravel this puzzle have had a long and rich scholarly heritage, but in an attempt to make a contribution to the continuing discussion, I offer one more solution. It is also a distinct delight to honor my teacher and friend, Professor Dwight W. Young, for his many hours of dedicated research and instruction while I attended Brandeis University.

Balaam's Homeland

That Balaam was a real person and not a legendary figure seems to have been clarified by the discovery of the inscriptions at Deir ᶜAllā in modern Jordan. On Friday, March 17, 1967 a Dutch expedition led by Henk J. Franken from the University of Leiden uncovered traces of letters on small pieces of plaster. The excavation site, Deir ᶜAllā, lay about halfway between the Dead Sea and the Sea of Galilee, approximately one mile north of a tributary of the Jordan River called the Jabbok in biblical times but known as the Zerqa today.

The plaster fragments eventually were arranged in two "combinations" or groups and dated around 850 B.C.E. It was thought that Deir ᶜAllā may have been a center of religious instruction. If this hypothesis is correct, it may supply one of the reasons why these combinations refer to "Balaam son of Beor" at least four times. In what many regard as an Aramaic text, Balaam is called "a seer of the gods" to whom "the gods came . . . at night and [spoke to] him." In spite of the fragmentary state of the text and a whole spate of unresolved issues surrounding these plaster inscriptions, they have added a new dimension of reality to the person and deeds of Balaam.

Balaam's home, according to Num 22:5, was in "Pethor, which is near the river [Heb. *hannāhār*], in the land of his people" [Heb. *ᵓereṣ bĕnê ᶜammô*]. Traditionally, Pethor has been located on the west bank of the Euphrates River about twelve miles south of Carchemish. Pethor is identified with the

Pedru listed in the topographical lists of Thutmose III (fifteenth century B.C.E.). It is also equated with a site spelled *Pitru*, a city captured by Shalmaneser III in 857 B.C.E.[2]

Not all interpreters are happy with the identification of the Euphrates as the river cited by the biblical text. Some translators have emended the Hebrew text from *ʿammô* to read *ʿammôn* in Num 22:5, a reading that is supported by the Samaritan Pentateuch, the Vulgate, the Syriac text, and several manuscripts of the Masoretic Text.[3]

Now that we have discovered these inscriptions in the old territory of the Ammonites, not far from the river Jabbok, there is a strong presumption in favor of the thesis that "Ammon" is the preferred reading for the present translation, 'his people'; it would follow that the Jabbok is "the river" intended, not the Euphrates. It is true, of course, that *ʾereṣ bĕnê ʿammô* 'the land of the sons of his people' as an expression for 'his homeland' is less usual than the more standard phrase *ʾereṣ môladtô* (Gen 11:28, 24:7, 31:13; Jer 22:10, 46:16; Ezek 23:15; Ruth 2:11). However, no such site as Pethor is known in the area of Ammon. Should an identification be made for this region of modern Jordan, everything in this proposal would fit very nicely.

Other translators have emended 'his people' (*ʿammô*) to read 'Amaw' (*ʿammāyw*), the name of a city listed in a fifteenth-century inscription from Alalakh. While this reading does not appear to be any better validated than the reading 'Ammon', it does suggest another memory of the fact that Amaw was in the general area of Carchemish. The historical witness to Balaam and the general region from which he came is again strengthened.

Accordingly, for the moment we will continue to locate this Pethor near the Euphrates River. However, should a Pethor turn up near the Jabbok in the old territory of the Ammonites, it will be clear that what are regarded at present as inferior textual readings do indeed represent the correct *Vorlage* of the Hebrew text of Num 22:5. It would also be clear, in that case, why Balak, king of Moab, went out to meet Balaam at Moab's northern border (Num 22:36).[4]

2. See A. L. Oppenheim, *ANET,* 278. See also A. S. Yahuda, "The Name of Balaam's Homeland," *JBL* 64 (1945) 547–51; W. F. Albright, "The Home of Balaam," *JAOS* 35 (1915) 386–90; and idem, "Some Important Recent Discoveries: Alphabetic Origins and the Idrimi Statue," *BASOR* 118 (1950) 16 n. 13.

3. B. Kennicott, *Vetus Testamentum Hebraica* I (Oxford, 1776). He lists codices 84, 325A, 612, primo 80, 136, 211, 325, 355, 507, 569, forte 196, 546, 618, abrasum "*nun*" 428, 488, primo *ʿmn* 516. But as J. Lust ("Balaam, an Ammonite," *ETL* 54 [1978] 60) points out, "None of these manuscripts, however, are to be dated early."

4. Ibid., 61.

Balaam's Profession

Prior to the discovery of the Deir ᶜAllā texts, many depended on Philo's description of Balaam in his *Vita Mosis* (1.264) as the most insightful analysis of his profession:

> Now there was at that time living in Mesopotamia a man famous for divination who had been initiated into divination in all its forms, but among them [these forms of divination] he inspired awe by means of his great proficiency in augury.[5]

Philo's depiction of Balaam son of Beor as a specialist in divination now finds support, it is alleged, from the Deir ᶜAllā Texts (hereafter DAT). Particularly in DAT I: 3–9 there is a reference to what some judge to be ornithomancy. The context, however, is filled with lacunae and is reconstructed in several spots. In JoAnn Hackett's translation it reads:

> (3) And Balaam arose the next day. . . . And his people came up to him [*and said to*] him, "Balaam, son of Beor, why are you fasting and crying?" And he sa(5)id to them: "Sit down! I will tell you what the Šadda[yyin *have done.*] Now, come, see the works of the gods! The g[o]ds gathered together; (6) the Šaddayyin took their places as the assembly. And they said to Š[ ]: . . . For the swift re(8)proaches the griffin-vulture and the voice of the vultures sings out. The st[*ork*] the young of the NḤṢ-bird(?) and the claws up young herons. The swallow tears at (9) the dove and the sparrow [. .] the rod, and instead of the ewes, it is the staff that is led.[6]

The DAT I is so fragmentary, however, that it is difficult to be certain that augury or any alleged proficiency in divination by means of birds is what is intended here.

The points at which the DAT materials and the biblical traditions coincide are these: (1) Balaam is called a 'seer' (*ḥāzē(h)*; DAT I:1); (2) he received his divine communications at night (*ba-laylah*; DAT I:1); (3) it appears that his prophecy was contrary to what the hearers had expected ('but he was not ab[le to] and he wept grievously' (*wa-lā-yaku*[*l*] *wa-bakā(h) yabke(h)* (DAT I:3–4); and (4) it seems that the people received a curse instead of the blessing they had expected ("Let him cross over the House of Eternity, the

5. Michael S. Moore. *The Balaam Traditions: Their Character and Development* (SBLDS 113; Atlanta: Scholars Press, 1990) 66. See Moore's discussion of this text.

6. Hackett, *Balaam Text*, 29.

house where the traveler does not rise and the bridegroom does not rise, the house . . . and the worm from the tomb"; DAT II: 6–8).

Though these similarities are impressive, they hardly amount to a convincing case at the present time. Too many of the readings are still conjectural to be sure of even the present list of comparisons. And even when the list of coincidences has been established, there is the matter of primary and secondary location of materials. Could it be that Balaam was remembered five to seven centuries after the Mosaic period and turned into a local hero in the Ammonite territory? This may explain why a local school for cultic studies would be the context for copying the text on its walls.

There is more to the argument, however. The fact still remains that Balaam is described in the MT of Josh 13:22 as a 'soothsayer' (*haqqôsēm*). If his homeland is to be placed in Mesopotamia, as I argued in the previous section, this prophet came from the same locale where we have discovered a small group of letters (in the large Mari cache) dedicated to prophetic utterances.[7]

Here is where the problem of the alleged overlap of roles intensifies. Does Balaam carry out the role of a seer/prophet or does he also play the role of exorcist? The strain of containing such diametrically opposite roles in one person can be seen in the Yahwistic abhorrence of both divination and exorcism (Deut 18:9–14). In fact, so strong is this conflict of roles that injunctions against both *qsm* and *nḥš* are placed in Balaam's own mouth in Num 23:23.

Ever since Julius Wellhausen's day, many have raised suspicions about this verse.[8] But it is doubtful if anyone can demonstrate that this was a gloss introduced into the text to harmonize what otherwise would appear to be an irreconcilable contradiction. The precise significance of the terms *qsm* and *nḥš* are not fully known, but it is clear that they are from the realm of magic and relate to "divination" and "obtaining omens." In Num 23:23 Balaam emphasizes that God had brought Israel out of Egypt precisely because "there is no omen against Jacob, nor is there any divination against Israel." I have translated the preposition *be* as 'against', but some may wish to render it as 'in'. From the perspective of history, the latter is impossible; hence 'against' seems

7. See Herbert B. Huffmon, "Prophecy in the Mari Letters," *BA* 31 (1968) 101–24; E. J. Young, "Extra-biblical 'Prophecy' in the Ancient World," in *My Servants the Prophets* (Grand Rapids: Eerdmans, 1952) 193–205; S. Daiches, "Balaam—a Babylonian *bārû*: The Episode of Num 22.2–24.24 and Some Babylonian Parallels," *Assyriologische und archäologische Studien Hermann von Hilprecht gewidmet* (Leipzig: Hinrichs, 1909) 60–70; René Largement, "Les oracles de Bileam et la mantique suméro-akkadienne," *Memorial du cinquantenaire 1914–1964* (Paris: Travaux de l'Institut de Paris, 1964) 37–50.

8. Julius Wellhausen, *Die Composition des Hexateuchs und der historischen Bücher des Alten Testaments* (3d ed.; Berlin: Goschen, 1899) 111.

preferable. If this rendering is correct, it claims either that "there is no enchantment or soothsaying that has any power against Israel, for Israel receives her information by means of revelation" or that "there is no need of these things" because Yahweh gives Jacob and Israel revelation at the appropriate times.[9]

But this explanation conveniently forgets the fact that the delegation of Moabite and Midianite chiefs summoned Balaam's services with 'fees for divination in their hand' (*qĕsāmîm bĕyādām*, Num 22:7). Is it any wonder, then, that Josh 13:22 referred to Balaam as 'the soothsayer' (*haqqôsēm*)?

It must be noted, however, that the text of Scripture only *reports* that this is how the delegation referred to Balaam's honorarium. In no passage does it *teach* that the biblical narrator or Balaam agreed with these terms or that he ever received 'fees for *divination*' for his services. In fact, the phraseology of the report may be related to the fact that Balaam later regretted his inability to perform at the level of King Balak's expectations, and thus the tragic events of Numbers 25 ensued as a sort of redeeming of Balaam's reputation and his fees from another perspective.

This scenario accords with traditions of what happened that are much closer to the events than we are in the twentieth century. Deut 23:4–5 claims:

> Because they did not meet you with food and water on the way when you came out of Egypt, and because they hired against you Balaam the son of Beor from Pethor of Mesopotamia to curse you, [no Ammonite or Moabite shall enter the assembly of the Lord, even to the tenth generation]. Nevertheless, the Lord your God was not willing to listen to Balaam, but the Lord your God turned the curse into a blessing for you because the Lord your God loves you.

The way that the biblical text resolves the role conflict of Balaam is to set Balaam, the prophet who cannot and will not go beyond anything that the Lord commands him (Num 22:8, 18, 35, 38; 23:12, 26; 24:2, 13, 15–16), in contrast with Balaam, the one who advises Israel's disobedience in the cult of Baal Peor (Num 31:16: "Behold, these [women] caused the sons of Israel, through the counsel of Balaam, to trespass against the Lord in the matter of Peor, so the plague was among the congregation of the Lord."

Michael Moore feels that this resolution is a bit too "neat and tidy."[10] In his view, it is unrealistic to resolve the role-strain geographically (one role in Moab and another in Midian).

9. Young, *My Servants the Prophets*, 22–23.
10. Moore, *The Balaam Traditions*, 119.

But this does appear to be the way the text before us outlines the sequence of events: Balaam moved from Moab to Midian. This solution does distinguish between a "simultaneous" and a "successive" role enactment. People do not, as a matter of fact, always stay in character and finish their lives exactly as they began them or as they were perceived and functioned through most of their formative and adult years. The contention here is that a sequential explanation is the best and least complicated accounting for all the factors listed in the text.

The only possible objection that could arise would have to be based on a discrediting of the pieces of data that we have relied on to suggest successive roles for Balaam: the data could be viewed as later glosses and thus be disallowed, considered as deliberate attempts to remove an embarrassing situation from the orthodoxy of the text. Yet, even this explanation must not enjoy a more privileged position than the one we have given. To doubt and to suspect harmonization is part of our heritage as sons and daughters of the Enlightenment, but it proves very little other than cultural predilections and one's own hermeneutical circle.

It would be better to let the text, as we have received it, stand on its own terms until convincing evidence exists that secondary readings were introduced into the narrative. This is nothing less than the application of the American system of jurisprudence (the text is innocent until proven guilty) over other forms wherein one is guilty until proven innocent.

Balaam's Character and Demise

"Few traditions in the Hebrew Bible," opined Michael Moore, "manifest so great a degree of internal conflict as do the Balaam traditions. The simple task of designating who Balaam was and what he did in Israelite history appears to have been one of the most delicate and complex issues Israelite students ever had to face."[11]

There can be little doubt about the pluralistic portrayal of Balaam's character and roles both in the biblical materials and in the DAT tradition. Each of the following roles must be examined: "seer," "oneiromantic," "oracle-reciter," "priest," and potential "sorcerer" or "exorcist." Admittedly, Balaam is not a simple, but a very complex figure.

Seer. In two separate incidents, Balaam is represented as seeking the will of God regarding King Balak's request (Num 22:8, 19) in nocturnal dialogues.

11. Ibid., 116.

During the third and fourth oracles, Balaam intones this affirmation: "The oracle of one . . . who sees a vision from the Almighty" (*maḥăzēh šadday yeḥĕzeh*; Num 24:4, 16). In his second oracle, he claimed the function of a seer, for he promised to tell King Balak 'the word that [God] causes me to see' (*dĕbar mah yarʾēnî*; Num 23:3).

This is not to claim that Balaam's eyes were always open to all things; indeed, he had to have his eyes divinely opened after missing the divine opposition that even his donkey detected! Num 22:31 notes, "Then the LORD opened Balaam's eyes, and he saw the angel of the LORD standing in the road with his sword drawn." This, however, is perfectly in keeping with the distinction frequently made in the biblical materials: it is not the seer or the prophet that is inspired; it is only the message that he speaks and the word given to him that can claim that quality. Therefore, the fact that Balaam functioned once and again as a seer or a prophet of Yahweh in no way prejudices the case regarding other pronouncements of his; one cannot assert on this basis that anything or everything that he may say or do subsequent to functioning as a seer of Yahweh also participates in the same quality or level of authentication.

For example, Nathan functioned as a prophet of God. But in 2 Sam 7:5–11 he had to retract his earlier off-handed endorsement of King David's desire to build a house for God. In v. 2, Nathan spoke his own opinion, but in vv. 5–11 he acted as God's agent, using the prophetic formula: "This is what the LORD says." Accordingly, not everything a prophet says is inspired, but only what he sees or speaks when acting on behalf of God.

Both DAT and the Bible depict Balaam as performing the role of a seer, but performance of a role on several occasions must not be confused with magical control of a function that can be demonstrated on demand. In Numbers 22–24, all of Balaam's abilities as a seer he credits to Yahweh. In fact, "Even if Balak gave [him] his palace filled with silver and gold, [he] could not do anything great or small to go beyond the command of the LORD [his] God" (Num 22:18).

Oneiromantic. In the Ancient Near East, the practice of going to the temple of the god to "incubate," that is, to provoke a divination by means of a dream is well known.

In Balaam's case, all that is said in the biblical text is that he "saw" the word he received from God. He does not appear to have done anything special to induce the message other than to request it. Furthermore, it is never referred to as a dream.

Given the parameters within which Israelite "prophecy" was juxtaposed to "divination," it is most doubtful that Balaam functioned as diviner of dreams in his meetings with King Balak. Whether the tradition of Balaam at Deir ʿAllā depicts Balaam as an ornithomantic (diviner by means of bird extispicy) or a rhabdomantic (divining by means of a rod or wand) must await a clearer reading of the broken texts from Deir ʿAllā.[12]

It is difficult to demonstrate Balaam's involvement in these practices from the biblical texts. This is not to assume that Balaam remains in character throughout the whole narrative. But, on the other hand, we cannot assume that the Deir ʿAllā tradition remained pure in all its recensions and is therefore to be preferred over what we now have in the biblical text. Each of these assumptions is filled with logical pitfalls and should be avoided.

Some feel that indirect evidence for Balaam's oneiromantic role enactment may be found in Num 22:5. Instead of translating v. 5 'Balaam son of Beor, who was at Pethor', the Syriac renders *pĕtôrâ* as *pšwrʾ* (= *happōtēr*) 'the interpreter'. Likewise, *Targum Neofiti* has *ptwrh* 'the interpreter'.

On the contrary, this textual evidence is not persuasive. Furthermore, the vocable *ptr* has been identified as a proper name for a village on the Sagur tributary of the Euphrates River, as attested in the Annals of Shalmaneser III.[13] The mention of "Balaam son of Beor from Pethor in Aram Naharaim" in Deut 23:4 gives further confirmation to reading this word as a place-name 'Pethor' and not as a function 'the interpreter'.

Evidence for the fact that there was some ambiguity over the reading of *pĕtôrâ* can be seen in *Targum Pseudo-Jonathan*, which attempts to give a harmonization of the two readings: "[Balaam's] residence was in Padan, which is Petor (*ptwr*), a name signifying an interpreter of dreams (*pytr ḥlmyʾ*)." But no case is made for Balaam being an interpreter of dreams or a diviner as such.

Oracle-reciter. Balaam did indeed give four major oracles and two directives, based upon his request to accompany the Moabite and Midianite delegations that came to him. But none of these situations is described in a way that implies that the "answers" were given by any kind of magico-specialist techniques.

Balaam's mediatorial role evidences none of the associations that some of the Syro-Palestinian seers customarily demonstrated. Yahweh remained sovereign over his word and the conditions under which it was sent. That word could not be forced, induced, or magically wormed out of a reluctant, or otherwise occupied, Lord of the word.

12. Ibid., 69–86.
13. J. B. Pritchard (ed.), *ANET,* 278.

The source of Balaam's oracles is identified when it is reported that "the Spirit of God came upon him" (Num 24:2). It was "The LORD [who] put a message in Balaam's mouth" (Num 23:5, 16). This appears to be no different than the claims that are made by many of Israel's prophets. The message, then, was what was "exhaled" or "inspired." The men did not function mechanically, as if it were dictated to them, but they were "taught" it, thereby bringing into play all the individual characteristics, personalities, and vocabularies of these unique servants of God.

Priests. There is nothing unusual about a prophet also functioning as a priest. Jeremiah and Ezekiel both came from priestly families, though they served as prophets. Samuel is regularly described as one who offered sacrifices at the high places when he traveled his regular circuit of ministry.

Whether Balaam also functioned as a priest at the sites where the altars were set up for him by King Balak cannot be determined for certain. It appears that Balaam ordered seven altars as well as seven bulls and rams to be sacrificed at the site where the seer would give his oracle; but the offering is regularly described as being Balak's offering, not Balaam's (Num 22:40; 23:1–2, 15, 29).

Exorcist/Sorcerer. The most troublesome text for the sequential view of Balaam's behavior and character is Num 24:1: "Now when Balaam saw that it pleased the LORD to bless Israel, he did not resort to sorcery as at other times, but he turned his face towards the desert." It is the expression *liqraʾt nĕḥāšîm* 'to meet omens' or 'to call [the gods] by means of omens' that is the surprising feature of this text. This appears to contradict chap. 23, in which Balaam did not seek omens but claims to have said only "the word that [Yahweh] caused [him] to see" (Num 23:3). Hence, this would be a change in his source of information and in his strategy.

When did Balaam resort to seeking omens or looking for auguries? The Hebrew expression is *kĕpaʿam bĕpaʿam* 'as time after time', as in 'year after year' (1 Sam 7:7–16) or 'new moon to new moon'. Hence, 'time by time' can only mean that he behaved as he did in former times, or as usual. The Greek text renders it 'according to his custom'.

Two possibilities present themselves: (1) augury and sorcery had been his usual style of operating in the past, prior to taking this assignment to curse Israel, or (2) his purpose in retiring on the previous two occasions, though not expressly stated, was to practice in private the magical arts common to sorcerers in hopes of obtaining the desired result for the pleasure of King Balak. Since we have no evidence indicating that this was his reason for retiring, this text can only refer to what had been Balaam's usual manner of operation prior to this assignment.

The original word for 'enchantments', 'omens', or 'auguries' seems to be closely related to the Hebrew term for 'serpent' (*nāḥāš*). The connection between divination, augury, omens, and the serpent are often made in the biblical and ancient Near Eastern world. Therefore, the phrase 'to meet enchantment or omens' implies a meeting with the deity for the purpose of making him or her more propitious by means of certain mysterious ceremonies.

The amazing fact is that all of this is described within six verses of the clear declaration of Num 23:23—"There is no sorcery (*nāḥāš*) against Jacob, no divination against Israel"—and that was in the body of Balaam's second oracle!

'According to that time' (*kāʾēt*, Num 23:23), that is, at the right time, God revealed his mind to his people. No one could unfold the future from signs in the texture of nature or from inexplicable events in human or animal life. Omens, sorceries, and divinations were useless against Israel.

Conclusion

Will the real Balaam please stand up? Was he a saint or a soothsayer?[14] The answer remains as complex as ever. The scarlet trail of Balaam's sins have left an indelible mark over the pages of Scripture (Num 31:8–16; Deut 23:5–6; Josh 13:22, 24:9–10; Judg 11:25; Mic 6:5; Neh 13:2; 2 Pet 2:15; Jude 11; Rev 2:14). In spite of all of this, it is also a fact that Balaam functioned in a most positive way in Numbers 22–24. He is directed solely by Yahweh in the main story (Num 22:18, 20, 35, 38; 23:3, 5, 12, 16; 24:13–14). When God says he must bless Israel, Balaam can, and does, do nothing else besides.

It is in chap. 25 where the true, if not the real, Balaam begins to stand up. The later Balaam reverts to previous form by counseling a disappointed Moab and Midian in accomplishing what they wanted to achieve by cursing, but failed. Yahweh himself will judge his own people if they can be enticed into sinning.

The scenario that seems to make the best sense out of all the data was proposed by William Foxwell Albright many years ago. He concluded that Balaam must have become "a convert to Yahwism, and that he later abandoned Israel and joined the Midianites in fighting against the Yahwists."[15]

14. George W. Coats, "Balaam: Sinner or Saint?" *BR* 18 (1973) 21–29.

15. William F. Albright, "The Oracles of Balaam," *JBL* 63 (1944) 233. Coats ("Balaam: Sinner or Saint?" 24) and James A. Wharton ("The Command to Bless: An Exposition of

This explanation seems to fit all the complex pieces the best. It is clear from Num 31:8 that Balaam son of Beor was killed in a subsequent battle between Israel and the Midianites. It is also clear that Balaam was found in the company of five other victims of Israel's battle—the five kings of Midian!

But what is even more convincing is Num 31:15–16: "Have you allowed all the women to live?" Moses asked them. "They were the ones who followed Balaam's advice and were the means of turning the Israelites away from the LORD in what happened at Peor, so that a plague struck the LORD's people." The text, then, provides the main key to unlocking the answer to the question, "What became of Balaam after he four times blessed Israel in King Balak's presence?"

Unable to curse Israel, Balaam advised the Moabites and Midianites to entice Israel to sin. Baal Peor seems to be tied into religious prostitution and worship of one's dead ancestors (Ps 106:28–29; Hos 9:10). Apparently, Baal Peor was the god who was worshiped in the city of Beth Peor (Deut 3:29, 4:46). Peor appears to be the Hebrew and Phoenician spelling of the word *paḫura*, which occurs in hieroglyphic Luwian. It is the Hurrian word for 'fire', and some form of the root seems to underlie the Greek *pyr* 'fire'; hence the phrase Baal Peor could be rendered 'Lord of fire'.

What was Balaam: a saint or a soothsayer? All the evidence makes a strong case for the fact that he gained his reputation by divination and soothsaying. Somewhere along the line he also appears to have come into contact with Yahwism, for his prayers and protestations have a genuine orthodox ring about them. Consequently, at the peak of his Yahwistic period, he proved to be a most useful and noteworthy instrument in the hands of Yahweh himself. Tragically, his days did not end well, but in an attempt to please all parties he helped those who had originally engaged his services; not by cursing their enemy Israel, but by joining them and giving them malicious advice on how to seduce Israel into attracting the wrath of God.

Balaam ended his days in a very awkward position. Of course, we are not able to determine anything about the real nature of Balaam's spiritual state or his ultimate allegiances from this, for God alone knows the heart. But it surely does not look good, and it is no wonder that Scripture constantly uses his name as a household word for falling away from the faith (2 Pet 2:15; Jude 11; Rev 2:14).

Numbers 22:41–23:25," *Int* 13 [1959] 41 n. 10) did not agree with Albright's suggestion. They warned against harmonizing all the diverse stages in the history of the Balaam tradition into a single layer. Of course, the reverse warning must also be issued: be careful of layering into multiple traditions what may indeed have been a single biography.

Offerings Rejected by God: Numbers 16:15 in Comparative Perspective

Baruch A. Levine

Introduction

In the course of preparing the Anchor Bible Commentary to the book of Numbers, I encountered two suggestive themes capsulized in a single verse. Each of the themes led me to extensive evidence, and together they clarified the nexus of source criticism and the comparative method. Far from being incompatible or unrelated, these methodologies often nourish one another. The verse in question is Num 16:15:

(15a) *ʾal tēpen ʾel minḥātām*
(15b) *lōʾ ḥămôr ʾeḥād mēhem nāśāʾtî wĕlōʾ hărēʾōtî et ʾaḥad mēhem*

(15a) Do not turn toward their offering(s);
(15b) I have never misappropriated the mule of even one of them, nor have I ever harmed a single one of them.

This verse occurs within a discernible textual unit of the book of Numbers, chaps. 16–17, which are comprised of several literary strands. Their composite character allows us to explore the interaction of source criticism

---

Author's note: The discussion following is offered in tribute to my learned teacher, Dwight W. Young, who impressed upon all of his students the importance of linguistic competence for the proper interpretation of ancient Near Eastern literature. The student of the Hebrew Bible never ceases to be amazed at the close affinity of biblical literature to the themes and diction of ancient Near Eastern creativity preserved in any number of languages.

This article is based on a paper delivered at the annual meeting of the American Oriental Society in Atlanta, Georgia, in March, 1990.

and the comparative method. Comparative insights shed light on the cultural provenance of their components, the building blocks of historiographic narrative, whereas source analysis enables the scholar to trace phases in the formation of the biblical text.

The latter part of v. 15 (labeled 15b) has received more attention than the former part (labeled 15a). Verse 15b has been correctly compared to the *apologia* of the cult-prophet Samuel preserved in 1 Samuel 12, especially the statement of 1 Sam 12:3. In almost the same words as those in Num 16:15b, Samuel asserts his integrity before the assembled Israelites. Analogues to the negative confession have been identified in ancient Near Eastern literature. A classic example from the Egyptian mortuary texts is entitled by its translator, John A. Wilson, "The Protestation of Guiltlessness" and is taken from the *Book of the Dead.*[1] In the Amarna correspondence we find the following statement of a vassal to his suzerain, which rhetorically recalls the protestations of both Moses and Samuel: "Furthermore: Let the king, my lord, inquire if I have misappropriated a single human, or if a single ox, or if a single mule from him!"[2] To these examples, we may add the biblical rite of entry into sacred precincts, formulated most clearly in Psalm 15. The diction of the negative confession was appropriate in diverse situations.

It is Num 16:15a which will concern us here, however. We shall investigate two of its aspects: theme and diction. Viewed as a theme, v. 15a pronounces a curse of sorts. Moses calls upon God to reject the offerings of those who were his enemies, thereby punishing them for having opposed him. In terms of diction, that is, the choice of *how* to express the intended thought, v. 15a reflects the idiom of liturgy and resembles a petition to a deity. The subtle interaction of theme and diction will lead us to differing, though related, genres of ancient Near Eastern literature.

Source Criticism

The immediate context of Numbers 16–17 pertains to an insurrection against Moses and Aaron, the divinely endorsed leaders of the Israelite people. The words of v. 15 are addressed to God by Moses in fear and anger after two leaders of the rebellion, Dathan and Abiram, had defied Moses' authority.

1. See the introduction and translation by John A. Wilson, "The Protestation of Guiltlessness," *ANET,* 34–36.

2. See J. A. Knudtzon, *Die El-Amarna Tafeln* (reprinted, Aalen: Zeller, 1964) 1.849, no. 280, lines 24–29.

Now, anyone who reads chaps. 16–17 holistically, as a unified literary composition, would tend to understand 16:15a in relation to what follows in vv. 16–24 of the same chapter. In vv. 16–24 we read that the leaders of the rebellion were commanded to present themselves for a cultic ordeal, in the course of which they would offer incense at the entrance to the Tent of Meeting. The ordeal would settle the issue of Israelite leadership. By rejecting the offerings of the insurgents, God would announce his will in the matter, and once again he would endorse Moses and Aaron as his chosen ones. Interpreted in this way, Moses' angry plea that God reject the *minḥâ* of the enemies referred to the imminent *minḥâ* of the cultic ordeal, the very one projected in vv. 16–24 of the same chapter. Usage of the term *minḥâ* seals the link.

This reading of chap. 16 is valid, to be sure, and represents one of the views expressed in medieval Jewish exegesis, which poses the logical question of which *minḥâ* is intended in v. 15a.[3] The structuralist, ever intent upon bringing out the inner coherence of the final literary product, might be content to inquire no further. For the source critic, however, the textual makeup of chap. 16 (and of chaps. 16–17, taken together) is both problematic and promising. Source analysis shows that Numbers 16–17 exhibit the blending, or "braiding" of a least two literary strands, the JE and the P narratives, respectively. Most source-critics would assume a diachronic relationship between the JE and P sources, according to which JE represents an earlier strand, available to the narrators of P, who modulate its content and expand upon its themes.

"JE" is the siglum given to a composite Pentateuchal source comprised primarily of J (= *Jahvist*, in German), presumed to be of Judean origin, and E (= Elohist), presumed to be of northern Israelite origin. Most scholars date the completion of JE to the seventh century B.C.E., with its primary sources, J and E, traceable to earlier centuries. P (= *Priesterschrift*, in German) is the siglum given to the writings of the priestly school of biblical Israel, undoubtedly produced in more than one stage. Although there is disagreement on the dating of P, we may regard it as subsequent to JE for purposes of this discussion.[4]

3. See J. Milgrom, *Numbers* (JPS Torah Commentary; Philadelphia: Jewish Publication Society, 1989) 134 sub Num 16:15; and 313, in the notes for chap. 16, numbered nn. 35–39. Milgrom refers to traditional Jewish commentators who discuss the frame of reference intended in this verse.

4. For a discussion of the priestly source and its relation to the other components of Torah literature, see my commentary, *Leviticus* (JPS Torah Commentary; Philadelphia: Jewish Publication Society, 1989) xxv–xxx.

It is possible to identify the respective input of JE and P in chaps. 16–17. In effect we have two principal happenings. (1)There is a rebellion instigated by Dathan and Abiram and a third, largely unknown Reubenite, against Moses. The JE material is concentrated in 16:12–15, 25–34. (2) There also is an internecine conflict within the Levitical clans led by Korah, a leader of the clan of Kohath. The issue in this priestly version was the sole right granted to the Aaronides, of the Amramite clan of Levites, to the Israelite priesthood. This determination relegated the other Levitical clans to a considerably lower status. The P material is concentrated in 16:3–11, 16–24, 35, and all of chap. 17.[5]

In order to blend these two narratives, the priestly writers reworked 16:1–2 so as to recast the rebellion in conformity with their agenda, thereby obscuring its original basis. Priestly writers likewise inserted the name of Korah into several JE passages, to maintain a modicum of consistency. In effect, P superimposed its agenda, namely, the endorsement of the uniquely legitimate Aaronide priesthood, upon one of a series of challenges to Moses' leadership, one that initially had nothing to do with Aaron or the status of the Levites.

Bearing in mind that v. 15 is part of the JE narratives (vv. 12–25), the source critic realizes that at one stage in the formation of the biblical text, v. 15 was not followed by vv. 16–24, but most likely by vv. 25–34. When JE resumes in v. 25, it tells of an act of divine punishment wherein the insurgents and their households were swallowed up alive. Pursuant to a horrendous suggestion by Moses, God created a fissure in the earth. Not to be outdone, P has the insurgents meet their death in a conflagration (16:35).

The upshot of the above source analysis is that Moses' curse stated in 16:15a did not originally refer to a cultic ordeal involving an offering, but was intended to suggest something else to the reader.

The Theme of Cultic Rejection

Moses' petition in 16:15a recalls statements in the curse sections of ancient Near Eastern treaties and royal inscriptions. After all, insurrection was an offense often stipulated in treaties and royal inscriptions as incurring the punishment of the gods. Before citing comparative evidence on the theme of cultic rejection, we should note several innerbiblical reflexes of this theme.

5. Chapter 17 exhibits internal literary problems that need not concern us here. Most likely, the ordeal of the tribal "staffs" (17:16–24) represents a separate, priestly tale.

In terms of diction, the only other biblical source that employs the precise idiom *pānâ ʾel . . . minḥâ* 'to turn toward . . . an offering' is Mal 2:13, although the theme itself is expressed through other images quite frequently in biblical literature.

Malachi, the anonymous postexilic prophet, decried the corruption of the Levitical priesthood serving in the restored temple of Jerusalem:

> And this you must do, in addition: You must cover the altar of the LORD with weeping and moaning, because there will be no further turning toward the offerings (*mēʾên ʿôd pĕnôt ʾel hamminḥâ*), nor their favorable acceptance from your hand (*wĕlāqaḥat rāṣôn miyyedkem*).

In addition to restating the theme of cultic rejection, which was the punishment Moses wished upon his enemies, Mal 2:13 significantly extends the diction of acceptance and rejection to include the idiom: *lāqaḥ min yād* 'to receive from one's hand'. This will prove to be a link to the comparative evidence soon to be discussed.

The theme of cultic rejection recalls the disposition of the diverse sacrifices offered by Cain and Abel according to Gen 4:4b–5a:

> *wayiššaʿ YHWH ʾel Hebel wĕʾel minḥātô, wĕʾel Qayin wĕʾel minḥātô lōʾ šāʿâ*
> The LORD turned toward Abel and toward his sacrifice, but toward Cain and toward his sacrifice He did not turn.

In this statement, the verb *šāʿâ*, rather than *pānâ*, expresses this 'turning' of the neck or the face toward a person or away from him, or by extension, toward or away from one's prayer or sacrifice.

'Receiving from one's hand' expresses acceptance of gifts in several biblical contexts: in Gen 33:10–11 the reference is to Jacob's gift to Esau and in 1 Sam 25:35–36 to Abigail's gift to David. Most instructive are the words of Manoah's wife, Samson's mother-to-be. She understood the phenomenology of sacrifice better than her husband. Reacting to a theophany that terrified her husband, she said:

> Had the LORD indeed sought to cause our death, he would hardly have received from our hand (*lōʾ lāqaḥ miyyādēnû*) burnt offerings and offerings of grain, nor would he have announced all of these things to us at this time.

Following leads of theme and diction brought me to the recently discovered inscriptions from Tell Fekherye, in which similar statements of cultic rejection occur. These royal inscriptions, found in the area of Gozan across the

Ḫabur River from Tell Ḫalaf, preserve parallel Aramaic and Assyrian versions. They have been dated to the ninth century B.C.E., albeit with a degree of uncertainty.

Adad-itʾi, governor of Gozan and its constituent towns, admonished in the following words any person who would efface his name from the appurtenances of the Adad temple:

> *mrʾy hdd lḥmh wmwh ʾl ylqḥ mn ydh*
> May my lord, Hadad, his food and his water not receive from his hand.

In the Assyrian text we read as follows:

> [d]IŠKUR *be-li* NINDA-*šú* A-*šú la i-ma-ḫar-šú*
> Adad, my lord, his food and his water, may he not accept it.

This curse is repeated with reference to the goddess Šala, Adad's consort.[6]

A similar curse is expressed in the inscription of Panammuwa I, found at Zinjirli and dated to the first half of the eighth century B.C.E. It is written in the so-called Yaudian dialect and preserves both the ideal, positive formulation of acceptance and the negative, maledictory formulation of rejection.

First, we present a positive statement, in which the king speaks of his own special relationship with the gods:

> *wbymy ḥlbṫ*[*y*]-*d̈ṫ-ʾhb*
> *lʾlhy wmt yqḥw mn ydy*
> *wmh ʾsʾl mn ʾlhy*
> *mt yt*[*n*]*w ly*
>
> And during the days of my succession (?) x[= gifts, offerings] I proffered
> to the gods (or: "to my gods"), and they always received them from my hand(s).
> And whatever I asked of the gods (or: "of my gods"),
> they always granted me.[7]

Contrast the above with what Panammuwa has to say concerning any of his successors who fail to honor him in the future:

6. See H. Abou-Assaf, P. Bordreuil, and A. R. Millard, *La Statue de Tell Fekherye, Études Assyriologiques* (Cahier 7; Paris: Recherche sur les Civilisations, 1982) 23, in the Aramaic version, lines 17–18′, and 14, and in the Assyrian version, lines 28–29. Also see the alignment of the two versions on p. 65.

7. See J. C. L. Gibson, *Textbook of Syrian Semitic Inscriptions* (3 vols.; Oxford: Clarendon, 1975) 2.66, no. 13, lines 12–13. My translation differs from Gibson's in some respects, and the same is true of the following citations in n. 8.

*wyz[bḥ. hdd. zn. wl*ᵓ*. yzk]*
r ᵓ*šm. pnmw. . . . . . . -zbḥh.*
*w*ᵓ*l. yrqy. bh. wmz. yš*ᵓ*l.* ᵓ*l.*
ytn. lh. etc.

and he offers sacrifice to this same Hadad, but does not pronounce the name of Panammuwa—[may Hadad not receive] his sacrifice, nor view it with favor; and whatever he asks, may he (=Hadad) not grant to him.[8]

Notwithstanding the fragmentary condition of the text, we are able to observe in the above citations expressions of the theme under discussion. When we combine the preserved contents of both citations, the positive and negative reflexes, we emerge with a binary projection of considerable impact.

The Panammuwa inscription brings us face to face with the interaction of theme and diction of which we spoke earlier. The positive formulation is liturgical in its diction, expressing the language of prayer and incantations, which speak of the acceptance of prayer and sacrifice from worshipers favored by the gods. The negative formulation, on the other hand, calls one's attention to the curse sections of treaties and royal inscriptions. Based on an admittedly partial search, we have the impression that the theme of cultic rejection is relatively rare among the punishments that the gods are called upon to impose. For the most part, treaties and royal inscriptions threaten disease and devastation, the denial of progeny or their extinction. I have not found the theme of cultic rejection in the Aramaic Sefire treaties or in the Neo-Assyrian treaties, either.

Denial of Cultic Access

Related to the theme of the rejection of sacrifice and prayer is the denial of cultic access, most often expressed as exclusion from entry into the presence of the gods, in a temple. This theme is evident in some of the Neo-Assyrian treaties. The so-called "Esarhaddon's Succession Treaty" enables us to define the implications of the denial of cultic access in treaty curses. There is a series of curses pronounced against any who violate the terms of the treaty:

8. Again in Gibson, ibid., 2.67–68, parts of lines 21–23. The restorations in the text are virtually certain, because the full formulas are evident elsewhere. The bracketed insertion in the translation is, however, merely an educated guess as to what the missing text said.

> [d]30 *na-an-nar* AN-*e u* KI.TIM *ina* SAḪAR.ŠUB-*pu li-ḫal-lip-ku-nu ina* IGI DINGIR.MEŠ *u* LUGAL *e-rab-ku-nu a-a iq-bi ki-i sír-ri-me* MAŠ.DA *(ina)* EDIN *ru-up-da*
> May Sin, the brightness of heaven and earth, clothe you with *skin disease*, and forbid your entry into the presence of the gods or king. Roam the desert like the wild ass and the gazelle![9]

It is clear that being denied entry into the presence of the gods and the king was part of a more extensive set of punishments. What links this type of curse logically to the theme of cultic rejection is precisely the reference to the presence of the gods: being barred from the temple would make it impossible to participate in sacrificial worship, to petition the gods, initially.

Liturgical Diction

What renders liturgical diction so appropriate for treaties and royal inscriptions is the direct involvement of the gods. Functionally, ancient Near Eastern curses are petitions to gods urging them to do certain things. This dynamic encourages the appropriation of liturgical diction by the ancient scribes in formulating their curses.

A good illustration of this process occurs as part of a lengthy oration attributed to Esarhaddon in what is known as a *Gottesbrief*, a letter addressed to the god Aššur, Esarhaddon's patron. The letter reports on the activities of Esarhaddon with respect to the king of Shupria, with whom he had problems. The latter was begging Esarhaddon to forgive him for offenses he had committed. Esarhaddon is informing Aššur that he had flatly rejected these entreaties. Historically, the reference is to the situation following the Assyrian subjugation of Shupria in 673 B.C.E. Shupria was a region lying in the northwest reaches of the Tigris, west of Lake Van and almost due north of Tell Ḫalaf.

In his letter to the god Aššur, Esarhaddon berates the king of Shupria for his treaty violations. Esarhaddon refuses to forgive the king of Shupria, a policy he is certain will please Aššur:

> *[ṣu]-ul-le-šú ul áš-me*
> *un-ni-ni-šú ul al-qí*

9. See S. Parpola and K. Watanabe, *Neo-Assyrian Treaties and Loyalty Oaths* (SAA 2; Helsinki University Press, 1988) 45, no. 6, lines 419–21. Also see the restored text on p. 22, no. 4, lines 16–17, which relates to the same theme.

ul am-ḫu-ra šu-up-pi-šú
[š]ab-šu ki-šá-di ul ú-tir-raš-šum-[m]a
[u]l ip-šaḫ-šú ez-ze-tú ka-ba-ti
[a]g-gu lìb-bi ul i-nu-uḫ-ma
re-e-mu ul ar-ši-šú-ma
ul aq-bi-šú a-ḫu-la[p]

His request, I did not hear;
His supplication I did not receive;
I did not accept his prayer;
My averted neck I did not turn back toward him;
I did not assuage for him my angry feelings;
My raging heart did not rest;
Friendship I did not show him;
I did not say to him: "Forgiven."[10]

Arrogating to himself the right to speak as a god would speak, Esarhaddon (more accurately, the author of the *Gottesbrief*) appropriates liturgical diction. A literary commentary on Esarhaddon's speech would cite the literature of prayer and incantations. Exclamatory *aḫulap* 'Forgive! Help! Redress!' as well as idioms referring to assuaging the angry heart and to turning the neck toward and away from another are typically liturgical and are frequent in the genre of prayers known as ŠU.IL.LÁ 'the lifting of the hands'. What is rashly denied by Esarhaddon to his enemy is precisely what a prayerful worshiper seeks.[11]

Conclusions

The suggestiveness of Num 16:15a might have been missed had we been content to interpret Numbers 16–17 in purely holistic terms. Responding to

10. See R. Borger, *Die Inschriften Asarhaddons Königs von Assyrien* (AfO Beiheft 9; Osnabruck: Biblio-Verlag, 1976) 104, lines 33–35.

11. See E. Reiner and H. G. Güterbock, "The Great Prayer to Ishtar and Its Two Versions from Boğasköy, *Journal of Cuneiform Studies* 21 (1967) 255–66, esp. 256 n. 6 for bibliography. On p. 260, lines 27–30 of the Neo-Babylonian version of the prayer to Ishtar have a litany wherein four successive entreaties begin with the invocation *a-ḫu-lap-ki be-let* AN-*e u* KI.TIM 'Have mercy, Lady of heaven and earth!' For examples of petitions in ŠU.IL.LÀ prayers, see S. Langdon, *Babylonian Penitential Psalms* (Paris: Geuthner, 1927) 16–17, "The Psalm to Enlil" (reverse, K.5098 and K.4898), lines 23–24; p. 29, "Penitential Prayer to Aya" (K.4623), lines 17–26; pp. 80–81, "Penitential Psalm to a Goddess" (K.101, reverse), lines 3–9.

questions raised by source analysis, we have been able to pursue comparative leads of considerable interest.

Having disassembled the text, broken it down into its component sources, it now behooves us to inquire what the priestly elaboration of the JE narrative contributes to our understanding of that earlier source itself. Apart from superimposing the priestly agenda, may we view the priestly source as a commentary on the JE narrative, as a particular interpretation of it?

For one thing, the priestly writers inform us how they understood cultic rejection phenomenologically: though Moses called upon God to reject the sacrifices of his enemies in the JE narrative, in the priestly narrative it is God who acts out that rejection by rendering his verdict in the cultic ordeal. He convicts those who had opposed his chosen leaders of the people, imposing a death sentence on those whose offering he rejects.

A curious interaction becomes evident: JE's reference to cultic rejection is suggestive, if somewhat metaphorical. Cultic rejection is one way of expressing divine wrath that results in destruction. The priestly writers took this threat literally! All biblical traditions enunciate the ideal state, the sought-after response from God: *rāṣôn* 'favorable acceptance'.[12]

12. I am grateful to D. O. Edzard, T. Frymer-Kensky, and W. W. Hallo for their helpful comments in response to my paper after it was delivered at the American Oriental Society meeting.

The Hannah Narrative in Feminist Perspective

Carol Meyers

The road from Samuel's birth to his emergence as one of the great national leaders of ancient Israel is marked by several complex narratives. All of these serve to prepare the reader or audience for the role Samuel will ultimately play in the critical and momentous transition of Israel from its tribal existence to its monarchic political structure. As is often the case for such pivotal figures, the prefiguring of Samuel's national prominence involves a birth and childhood narrative. Thus, willy-nilly, a woman—the mother of the man destined for greatness—enters the biblical story.

Hannah is introduced in the second verse of 1 Samuel 1 and appears throughout the narrative of that chapter. Her role in the Samuel story culminates in the poem, attributed to her in its superscription, of 1 Sam 2:1–10.[1] Finally, a postscript to her role in the story of her son's birth and dedication to Yahweh comes in 2:21, which records the birth of Samuel's five siblings—three more boys and also two girls.

According to the biblical tale, Hannah was one of two wives of a prominent Ephraimite named Elkanah. Unlike her co-wife Peninah, Hannah had no children. Although her inability to conceive apparently did not dampen her husband's love for her, she suffered from the taunting of Peninah. Her distress was particularly acute during the family's annual trek to Shiloh, where Elkanah's differential allotment of the sacrificial portions—only one portion to Hannah, for she was only one individual—caused her to weep and left her unable to partake in the sacrificial feast (1 Sam 1:8).

1. This poem is usually called the Song of Hannah for reasons summarized by P. K. McCarter, *I Samuel* (AB 8; Garden City, N.Y.: Doubleday, 1980) 74. Most exegetes suggest that the song has been inserted into the narrative. A tenth-century date has been proposed by D. N. Freedman, "The Song of Hannah and Psalm 113," *ErIsr* 14 (*H. L. Ginsberg Volume*; 1978) 56–69.

In the context of one of these trips to Shiloh, Hannah was overcome with distress, offered an ardent prayer to Yahweh, and then made a vow. If God would answer the prayers and provide a son to her, that child would be dedicated to Yahweh. Eli, the priest at Shiloh, encouraged her and sent her home with her family, whereupon she conceived and gave birth to Samuel. Hannah's next trip to Shiloh involved handing over her child to the care of Eli and giving voice to her eloquent prayer of thanksgiving and praise.

Embedded in this narrative is a verse (1 Sam 1:24) describing the sacrifice brought to the sanctuary at Shiloh at the time that Samuel was entrusted to the priests at the "house of Yahweh at Shiloh." This verse provides two pieces of information about the ritual act it records: it lists the commodities brought to the sanctuary;[2] and it gives Hannah an integral role in the presentation of these materials, along with her son, to the sanctuary.

Neither Hannah's actions in this verse nor her position in the narrative has ever figured very prominently in the traditional historical-critical, form-critical, or even the more recent literary-critical treatments of the books of Samuel or of the Samuel story. The commentaries do not subject Hannah's role to special exposition. Indeed, by the very titles they assign to 1 Samuel 1 (or 1 Samuel 1–3),[3] they obscure the prominent position of Hannah in the opening section of the books of Samuel. Yet, this narrative in general and 1 Sam 1:24 in particular contain valuable information when considered from the perspectives of feminist biblical analysis.

Traditional modes of biblical scholarship do not entirely ignore the fact that Hannah was a woman. However, feminist inquiry involves posing ques-

2. These are examined in C. Meyers, "An Ethnoarchaeological Analysis of Hannah's Sacrifice," *Pomegranates and Golden Bells: Studies in Biblical, Jewish, and Near Eastern Ritual, Law, and Literature in Honor of Jacob Milgrom* (ed. D. P. Wright, D. N. Freedman, and A. Hurvitz; Winona Lake, Indiana: Eisenbrauns, 1995) 77–91.

3. Some examples of the way commentaries label this narrative are: "The Legitimacy of Samuel" (1 Samuel 1–3), in W. Brueggemann, *First and Second Samuel* (IBC; Louisville: John Knox, 1990) 10–28; "Birth and Dedication of Samuel" (1 Samuel 1), in G. B. Caird, *The First and Second Books of Samuel*, in *IB* (Nashville: Abingdon, 1953) 2.876–82; "Samuel et Éli" (1 Samuel 1–3), in L. P. Dhôrme, *Les Livres de Samuel* (Paris: Gabalda, 1910) 16–45; "Samuel's Birth Narrative" (1 Samuel 1), in R. P. Gordon, *1 & 2 Samuel* (Old Testament Guides; Sheffield: JSOT Press, 1984) 23–24; and "The Child Asked of God" (1 Sam 1:1–20) and "Samuel Comes to Eli" (1 Sam 1:21–2:11), in H. W. Hertzberg, *I & II Samuel* (OTL; trans. J. S. Bowden; London: SCM, 1964) 10–28. But cf. "Hannah's Trial and Trust" (1 Sam 1:1–18) and "Hannah's Faith Rewarded" (1 Sam 1:19–28), in W. G. Blaikie, *The First Book of Samuel* (Expositor's Bible; New York: Armstrong, n.d.) 1–24.

tions that diverge from those that have long prevailed in biblical studies as the result of the long-dominant sociology of the discipline. That is, biblical studies have been traditionally pursued more in seminaries than in universities and more by men than by women.[4] Androcentric orientation and bias have thus tended to preclude attention to the Bible as the product of a living community of women as well as men. And theological agendas, albeit perhaps subconscious, have interfered with recognition of women's initiative and deed in the ritual sphere. Hannah's role has been marginalized or trivialized or ignored. Furthermore, all too often her actions in bringing a sacrificial offering to a major national shrine have been viewed as atypical, or, worse, the text has been reviewed as corrupt.

Consideration of the place of Hannah as a woman in the poignant narrative of 1 Samuel 1 will thus be a central focus rather than a side issue of this inquiry. Her position as one of the small company of prominent biblical females serves as an introduction. Then, rather than examine the quest for maternity that serves as the theme for the narrative and that has been treated as an annunciation type-scene in recent literary and feminist analyses,[5] we will take a close look at "Hannah's Sacrifice," a designation used here to describe Hannah's trip to Shiloh with ritual offerings, as well as with her young son. This episode within the well-known biblical tale provides a rare opportunity to recognize and evaluate a woman's ritual act. Since the primary actor in the sacrificial passage of 1 Sam 1:24 is a woman,[6] in contrast to the overwhelming predominance of males in cultic contexts in the Hebrew Bible, a feminist perspective is *de rigeur* in considering Hannah's sacrifice.

1 Samuel 1—A Woman's Story

That the first chapter in the books of Samuel is a woman's story can be established first by examining the personnel involved. The cast of characters in 1 Samuel 1 includes five individuals: the Ephraimite Elkanah; his two wives,

4. See C. Meyers, *Discovering Eve: Ancient Israelite Women in Context* (Oxford: Oxford University Press, 1989) 6–23 for a discussion of contemporary biblical scholarship with respect to the social sciences and to gender. See also D. C. Bass, "Women's Studies and Biblical Studies: An Historic Perspective," *JSOT* 22 (1982) 6–12.

5. See R. Alter, *The Art of Biblical Narrative* (New York: Basic Books, 1981) 82–87, and A. Brenner, *The Israelite Woman: Social Role and Literary Type in Biblical Narrative* (Biblical Seminar 2; Sheffield: JSOT Press, 1985) 92–98.

6. Textual variants make the identity of the person offering the sacrifice somewhat ambiguous, but the case for that person's being Hannah is a strong one. See discussion below.

Hannah and Peninah; the priest Eli; and the infant Samuel. Eli and Samuel become prominent in the succeeding chapters. Elkanah is introduced in v. 1, ostensibly as the focus of the ensuing narrative. Of the two women, Peninah plays only a minor role. But Hannah plays a major part in the tale, so much so that the narrative of Samuel's birth could as well be called the Hannah Narrative.

Hannah's prominence is evident in several ways. For one thing, her name is mentioned fourteen times between 1 Sam 1:1 and 2:21. Samuel, whose acclaimed birth is apparently the motivation for the narrative, is named only three times. Peninah also appears three times, and her husband is named eight times. Interestingly enough, given the association formed here between Samuel and his eventual priestly role, Eli is mentioned ten times. Still, Hannah's name appears more frequently than does Eli's and as often as those of all members of her family combined.

Hannah's name is also prominent in comparison to the appearance of the names of other major female figures in the Hebrew Bible. Not surprisingly, given the focus on prenational family "history" in the Genesis narratives, the matriarchs are the women whose names are most frequently mentioned in the Hebrew Bible. The name Sarah/Sarai, for example, appears some 55 times, Rebecca 30 times, Rachel 46 times, and Leah 34 times. Women appearing in all other contexts, no matter how important they may have been, are named far less frequently, if they are named at all.[7] For example, Miriam's name appears only 15 times, Deborah's 9 times, Yael's 6 times, Bathsheba's 10 times, Michal's 16 times, and Huldah's twice. With 14 mentions, Hannah features prominently among the major female figures of the Hebrew Bible.

The first group of women—the matriarchs—figure extensively because of their maternal roles. For the second group, the focus is on some other aspect of their lives; this is true even for Bathsheba, though of course her role as Solomon's mother cannot be ignored. Hannah fits into the latter group (all prominent biblical women other than the matriarchs of Genesis) with respect to frequency of mention. That is, she is hardly mentioned as often as are the female ancestors of the Genesis narrative. Furthermore, although her maternal function is certainly the focus of the narrative, she also belongs to the second group thematically speaking: a dimension of female behavior other than maternity is a significant part of the Hannah story.

7. Esther, as the central figure of a biblical book ten chapters in length, is not included in this statement. But note that Ruth, also the main figure in a biblical book, is mentioned only 12 times (though Naomi, perhaps the true heroine of that book, is named 22 times).

Hannah's prominence as a named individual is also noteworthy in light of the overall pattern of female names—or lack thereof—in the Hebrew Bible. The names of Israelite women represent only 8%, a small percentage, of attested Israelite personal names.[8] Many females who figure in narratives are not named at all. In the epic traditions of Joshua through Samuel, the story of Samson's birth bears some similarity to that of Samuel: in both, a barren woman conceives a child, who is then dedicated to Yahweh, and sacrifices and prayers are part of the sequence of events in both tales. Yet the mother of Samson is denied the visibility of a named individual; she remains the wife of Manoah throughout the narrative. Similarly, the tragic story of Jephthah's daughter (Judges 11) involves remembering the event but not the name of the virgin who was offered as a burnt offering in fulfillment of her father's vow. With biblical texts so restrained in giving women personal names, Hannah's named visibility allows her a modicum of individuality, despite her role as wife to Elkanah and mother of Samuel.

Another dimension of naming likewise offers exceptional status to Hannah: she is one of a series of biblical women who name their offspring. The accounts of women naming their children are found in narratives dealing with the premonarchic period of Israelite history.[9] The role of women in giving names is apparently indicative of an authoritative social role, at least within the family setting, since the child receiving the name thereby comes under the influence of the namegiver.[10] Certainly the details of the Hannah-Samuel story depict a mother making decisions about the future of her child; Hannah participates in the social authority implicit in the giving of a name.

8. I. Ljung, *Silence or Suppression: Attitudes toward Women in the Old Testament* (Acta Universitatis Upsaliensis; Uppsala Women's Studies, Women in Religion, no. 2; Stockholm: Almqvist and Wiksell, 1989) 27. Ljung bases her calculations on the material in M. Noth, *Die Israelitischen Personennamen im Rahmen der gemeinsemitischen Namengebung* (BWANT 3/10; Stuttgart: Kohlhammer, 1928), which lists 1426 personal names, of which 1315 are those of men, resulting in a percentage of 9% for female names. However, Noth includes extrabiblical materials, such as the Elephantine letters, which have proportionately more female names. Ljung apparently excludes extrabiblical names in considering the figures for the Hebrew Bible.

9. Ljung, *Silence or Suppression*, 17, 18–27. Ljung also notes the general absence of women as name-givers in P narratives and as part of the generational chains in P's genealogies.

10. See J. Pedersen, *Israel: Its Life and Culture* (2 vols; London: Oxford University Press, 1926) 245–49. Ljung (*Silence or Suppression*, 103 n. 14) refers to H. Ringgren's observation (in *Israelite Religion*) that knowing someone's name affords some sort of control; she also suggests that the patriarchal impulse to name wells, springs, and places represents not only etiological expression but also the establishment of rights of control.

This discussion of names and naming practices with respect to women in the Hebrew Bible reveals a distinctive role for Hannah. Likewise, several literary features of the 1 Samuel 1 narrative present her as an active person rather than as a passive, dependent female. In looking at all the verbs associated with the noun 'woman' in the primary history (Genesis through 2 Kings), Ljung found that 'woman' was the subject of verbs exactly the same number of times (51) as it was the object of verbal forms.[11] In the 1 Samuel narrative, Hannah is the subject of the verb more than three times more often than she is the object. The narration of her story makes Hannah a social actor and imbues her with a dynamic quality not typical of most texts dealing with women.

The frequent use of dialogue and direct speech in the construction of the Hannah story also affords her the measure of visibility and individuality that is a concomitant of reported speech more so than of descriptive narration. In his perceptive discussion of dialogue in the Hebrew Bible, R. Alter emphasizes that direct speech functions to reveal nuances of character and relationships and that spoken language, in transferring the nonverbal thought into words, is an effective mechanism for revealing the essence of the speaker.[12] In light of this, it is worth noting that there are ten instances of recorded speech in the 28 verses of 1 Samuel 1. Hannah is the only character in the chapter to be part of each of these dialogic episodes: six times she is the speaker (to God, Eli, Samuel, and Elkanah), and four times she is addressed by another (twice by Elkanah and twice by Eli). In contrast, Elkanah speaks only twice and is spoken to but once; Eli also speaks only twice and is addressed twice; and Samuel is spoken about just once (to God? to the household?) when he is named in 1:19. Hannah's character is thus revealed far more fully than that of any of the other participants in her story.

In addition, Hannah's dialogic centrality culminates in the ten verses of poetry attributed to her. None of the other persons featured in 1 Samuel is credited with poetic utterance except for Samuel, for whom only one poetic passage, two verses in length (1 Sam 15:22–23), is recorded. The latter, along with Hannah's song, are the only poetic passages in all of 1 Samuel. Hannah is thereby distinguished, as are relatively few other biblical personages, by association with poetic speech.

Hannah's Sacrifice

This discussion of Hannah's prominence in 1 Samuel 1 serves as a background to a consideration of her role in bringing sacrificial materials to the

11. Ibid., 113.
12. Alter, *The Art of Biblical Narrative*, 66–70.

shrine at Shiloh. The MT of 1 Sam 1:24 portrays her as weaning her son and then taking him, along with the bull, flour, and wine, to the house of Yahweh. However, the LXX and probably also 4QSam[a] have a much fuller text, which presumes that Elkanah also went up to Shiloh, that *he* brought the sacrifices, and that the two of them together offered the sacrifice.[13]

The reasons that some prefer the LXX/4QSam[a] over the MT can be related to certain ambiguities in identifying the agent of the vow and its fulfillment. In 1 Sam 1:11, Hannah makes a vow; 1 Sam 1:21 has Elkanah fulfilling a vow, one that is not previously mentioned; and in 1 Sam 1:27 Hannah refers to the terms of her vow. The role of Elkanah in this votive language is difficult. Is he participating in Hannah's vow or fulfilling one of his own, which is otherwise not mentioned? These questions are not easily resolved. But removing the agency of the sacrificial act from Hannah (with the LXX and 4QSam[a]) does not resolve the issue either, and in the process, it deprives Hannah of a cultic role that legitimately belongs to her. It is easier to consider the circumscribed cultic activities for women at the time of the LXX and 4QSam[a] as a basis for their textual expansion than to forego the MT, which reflects Hannah's premier role in the sacrifice of 1:24.

Hannah's sacrificial agency, as expressed by the MT, is congruent with the prominence she holds in the narrative of 1 Samuel 1 as described above. It is also consistent with what can be inferred about female participation in cultic events, as suggested in recent feminist biblical scholarship.

Hannah's activity in making a vow and bringing sacrificial goods to Shiloh is probably best understood in the context of family religion. Indeed, the spectrum of cultic behavior revealed in 1 Samuel 1 reveals the private, personal piety of Elkanah and his family and should not be considered an early version of the pilgrimage festivals prescribed in pentateuchal legal texts. Indeed, such visits for prayer and for making and keeping vows, precisely because they represent family ritual rather than public or institutional cultic activity, are not mentioned at all in the Pentateuch.[14]

Hannah's sacrifice thus stands as an example of women's religion as it existed at some point early in the history of Israel. The dominant and official roles in the Israelite cultus were reserved for males, but public cultic office

13. So McCarter, *I Samuel*, 56–57, following a suggestion (personal communication) by F. M. Cross. Cf. Cross's hypothesis, in "A New Qumran Biblical Fragment Related to the Original Hebrew Underlying the Septuagint," *BASOR* 132 (1953) 15–26, about 4QSam[a] as *Vorlage* of the LXX. McCarter accepts the LXX as original in his translation.

14. So M. Haran, *Temples and Temple-Service in Ancient Israel* (Oxford: Clarendon, 1978; reprinted, Winona Lake, Indiana: Eisenbrauns, 1985) 304–7. Haran's view is similar to that of Pedersen, *Israel*, 376–82, 385.

and official ritual events were not the sum total of religious practice in ancient Israel or in any society for that matter. That the preeminent male role in Israelite ceremonial life was not so comprehensive as to deny other family members direct activity in the cultic sphere has long been noted.[15] Indeed, there has been a tendency to view male and female roles as being virtually the same except for the matter of priestly eligibility, despite gender differentials in certain texts prescribing specific cultic activities.[16]

The older studies granting some importance to women's religious behavior have now been enhanced and given a firm theoretical base by an approach that examines such behavior in light of anthropological data dealing with gender and religion.[17] Perhaps the most important methodological lesson to emerge from the quest to reconstruct the role of Israelite women in cultic activity is that biblical materials are insufficient, since they are mostly centered on the male-dominated public life of Israel, and the biblical record may even present a distorted picture of a social reality quite at variance with the formal canonical stance. It is becoming increasingly clear that women everywhere have critical roles to play in religious life, even if those roles are ignored or minimized in the public record.[18]

The validity and autonomy of Hannah's actions, as an example of family religion, should not be questioned. Her sacrifice comes as the result of the vow that she made during a family pilgrimage to Shiloh. Although a legal text in Numbers (30:6–8) appears to make a woman's vow subject to the veto of her husband, there is no indication that Elkanah acted in this way in 1 Samuel. That law may be later than the activities recorded,[19] and the very

15. As, for instance, by C. J. Vos, *Women in Old Testament Worship* (Delft: Judels and Brinkman, 1968) 49.

16. One of the first examples of this perspective is I. Peritz, "Women in the Ancient Hebrew Cult," *JBL* 17 (1898) 111–48.

17. Two articles by P. Bird are programmatic in bringing the analytical perspective of anthropological gender studies to bear upon the consideration of the religious roles and activities of both men and women in ancient Israel: "The Place of Women in the Israelite Cultus," *Ancient Israelite Religion* (F. M. Cross Festschrift; ed. P. D. Miller, P. D. Hanson, and S. D. McBride; Philadelphia: Fortress, 1987) 397–420; and "Women's Religion in Ancient Israel," *Women's Earliest Records from Ancient Egypt and Western Asia* (BJS 166; ed. B. S. Lesko; Atlanta: Scholars Press, 1989) 283–98.

18. For a striking example from the contemporary world, see S. S. Sered, "Conflict, Complement, and Control: Family and Religion among Middle-Eastern Jewish Women in Jerusalem," *Gender and Society* 5 (1991) 10–29.

19. So J. T. Willis, "Cultic Elements in the Story of Samuel's Birth and Dedication," *ST* 26 (1972) 59. Willis also points out that even if the MT of 1 Sam 1:21 is correct in

existence of such a law is probably a good indication that women in early Israel were indeed accustomed to making and carrying out their own vows. Furthermore, Hannah's autonomy in making a vow at Shiloh is authenticated by the fact that pilgrimages and concomitant votive acts are two of the most characteristic religious acts of women observed in ethnographic research.[20]

By vowing that her son will be dedicated to Yahweh and by bringing a sacrifice along with her son in fulfillment of that vow, Hannah's religious actions bridge the realms of private and public religious life. Her motivation is individual, personal, and wrenchingly private. Acts prompted by similar profound feelings must surely have been carried out by countless Israelite women; yet those of Hannah are uniquely visible. Biblical tradition has preserved her tale, because it enters the public realm—partly because she interacts with the leading priestly figure of the day at the major shrine of the premonarchic era and partly because her behavior adumbrates the national prominence of Samuel. Although some feminist biblical critics would emphasize the barren-woman type-scene of the Hannah story as an indication of female behavior in the service of patrilineal if not patriarchal interests,[21] it seems that the national purview of this tale transposes it beyond the sexual politics of domestic life and into the realm of national service. The private *is* the public in this instance; were it not so, Hannah would be as invisible as her sisters.[22]

Furthermore, Hannah's visibility comes at a time of political dysfunction in Israelite history. It is precisely in biblical texts dealing with the premonarchic period that most of the examples of women in significant public roles are clustered. In such decentralized eras, marked by social upheavals, and with no dominant national power structure, women frequently emerge as significant social actors. At the very least, their status is usually higher than

---

attributing a vow to Elkanah (although many text critics would delete "his vow"), his vow could not have been the same as his wife's.

20. See the sources cited in Bird, "Women's Religion," 297 n. 37.

21. E. Fuchs, "The Literary Characterization of Mothers and Sexual Politics in the Hebrew Bible," *Feminist Perspectives on Biblical Scholarship* (SBL Centennial Publications 10; ed. A. Y. Collins; Chico, Calif.: Scholars Press, 1985) 118–19, asserts that these type-scenes all promulgate a patriarchal ideology, with male and female in a power-structured relationship that subordinates women.

22. For another instance of female religious activity in the public domain in biblical Israel, see C. Meyers, "Of Drums and Damsels: Women's Performance in Ancient Israel," *BA* 54 (1991) 16–27.

in more stable periods, for it is just at such unsettled times that all persons with marginal access to power find themselves able to transcend the normal criteria that might otherwise limit their actions.[23]

A woman's visibility and centrality in the Hannah narrative of 1 Samuel 1 and her agency in a ritual act thus reveal an otherwise hidden aspect of women's cultic life. In addition, Hannah's sacrifice signifies an instance of female activity, albeit related to maternal functions, with national implications. By the very individuality of her characterization and behavior, she is represented as contributing to the corporate welfare of ancient Israel. Although the Hebrew Bible as the story of Israel may be primarily the story of men, occasionally women such as Hannah can be discerned. Such women may be the exceptions in terms of the canonical record; but they should hardly be considered unique within the dynamics of daily life, at least in the rural context of ancient Israel.[24]

23. See the discussion of these dynamics, and works cited, in J. A. Hackett, "Women's Studies and the Hebrew Bible," *The Future of Biblical Studies: The Hebrew Scriptures* (SBLSS; ed. R. E. Friedman and H. G. M. Williamson; Atlanta: Scholars Press, 1987) 141–64. Cf. the discussion of the private-public dichotomy in C. Meyers, *Discovering Eve,* 173–76.

24. See C. Meyers, "The Family in Early Israel," *The Family in Ancient Israel and Early Judaism* (Religion, Culture, and Family Series; ed Leo G. Perdue; Louisville: Westminster/ John Knox, forthcoming).

Messianism in First and Second Zechariah and the "End" of Biblical Prophecy

Eric M. Meyers

One of the most striking aspects of the study of the canonical book of Zechariah is the relative quietistic tone of its messianic passages, notwithstanding the strong eschatological thrust of chaps. 9–14. This tone stands in marked contrast to the exaggerated tenor of the book of Haggai, which in its final oracle, 2:20–23, uniquely and explicitly focuses on a historical figure, Zerubbabel, to express its support of the Davidic dynasty in a memorable eschatological prophecy:[1]

> 'On that day'—Oracle of Yahweh of Hosts—'I will take you, O Zerubbabel ben-Shaltiel, as my servant'—Oracle of Yahweh—'and I will set you as my signet. For you have I chosen'—Oracle of Yahweh of Hosts (2:23).

Though the setting of Haggai's oracle is 520 B.C.E.—after the temple's refoundation—the strong words of the prophet no doubt reflect the period of malaise just prior to the accession of Darius I, when it was still uncertain who would accede to the Persian throne and who would rule over the province of Yehud.[2] Haggai expresses the ardent hope that Zerubbabel, scion of King David and King Jehoiachin, will one day assume a role that extends far beyond the governorship of the newly constituted subprovince of Yehud. Despite the fact that Zerubbabel is addressed as *peḥâ* 'governor', in recognition

1. All translations in Haggai and Zechariah 1–8 are taken from the author's commentary with C. L. Meyers, *Haggai, Zechariah 1–8: A New Translation with Introduction and Commentary* (AB 25B; Garden City: Doubleday, 1987). The use of the term "my servant" in reference to Zerubbabel here and in reference to Moses in Mal 3:22 can hardly be coincidental. Not only does it seem that there is an attempt to harmonize the last books of the scroll of the twelve minor prophets but that we have a kind of *inclusio* or envelope construction between Haggai and Malachi.

2. Ibid., xxxiff., 66–70, and 82–84.

of his civil leadership in tandem with the high priest, Joshua, Zerubbabel is labeled "servant," a term used to describe the ideal role of an Israelite ruler in close relationship to Yahweh, normally reserved for David. Similarly, the designation "signet" marks the incumbent governor as one destined to carry out the divine will.

The eschatology is heightened in the oracle, especially in vv. 21 and 22: ". . . I am about to shake the heavens and the earth, [22]and I am going to overthrow the throne of foreign kingdoms. . . ." The depiction of a changed future presupposes a major disruption of the present order to be succeeded by Davidic rule. However, for Haggai, there was no expectation that Zerubbabel in the present would do anything but serve in the dyarchic scheme of theocratic rule in which the Davidic governor would stand in at the temple refoundation ceremony—a role normally reserved for the king—but in his capacity as appointed governor and not future royal leader.[3] For the followers of Haggai the disparity between reality and anticipated, hoped-for future was great, and so the prophet alone of the prophets names an historical personage, Zerubbabel, to fulfill God's eschatological design.

Subsequent references to Zerubbabel in First Zechariah, some by name (4:6–10) and some by epithet such as "shoot" (3:8 and 6:12) indicate that Zechariah more than Haggai has adopted a language and rhetorical style that is more directed at advocating—rather than just accepting—the dyarchic program of leadership recognized already in Haggai 1:1. In such a plan the only instance in which Zerubbabel is singled out by name (4:6–10) he is exhorted to hold back in the exercise of power: " [6]This is the word of Yahweh to Zerubbabel: 'Not by might and not by power, but with my spirit,' said Yahweh of Hosts." The tone and intent of this passage contrast strongly with

3. Ibid., 9–16. Though the scholarly literature is replete with suggestions that Zerubbabel was really a king waiting for the appropriate moment to lead a rebellion seeking independence from the Persian Empire, there is no exegetical or extrabiblical support for this hypothesis. Though Haggai's messianic expectations are more heightened than Zechariah's, it would be a misreading of events and of the text to understand Zerubbabel's role in such a way. If we take into account some of the demographic studies and population estimates that have been made regarding Yehud in the Persian period, we could see in an instant that planned rebellion was sheer folly. In his doctoral dissertation, Charles Carter estimates that there were only 6,200 people in the early Persian period (pre-450 B.C.E.) and around 10,000 after. Though there were Jews scattered among the Gentile population around Yehud, the majority remained in a tiny area throughout Achaemenid times and could scarcely have even provided a threat to the empire by itself. See Carter's unpublished 1990 Ph.D. dissertation, *The Temple Economy in Ancient Israel: Socio-Economic Analysis of the Biblical Tithing* (Duke University).

Hag 2:20–23, and one can only speculate what has brought about the change.

If First Zechariah (chaps. 1–8) and Haggai were initially promulgated or presented as a composite work intended for presentation at the rededication of the Second Temple, as the author has contended elsewhere,[4] then it is especially significant for such a variance in eschatological emphasis to be preserved in Haggai–Zechariah 1–8. Since so little time elapses between the call of Haggai and the onset of the partially overlapping career of Zechariah,[5] it is reasonable to conclude that Haggai's success in evoking such a positive response among the citizenry was partially responsible for their acceptance of the new religio-political pattern that Zechariah espoused so eloquently. In any event, all manner of direct reference to Davidic rule disappears in First Zechariah after chap. 4, and the final oracle of chap. 6 makes only the most indirect statement about the future ruler,[6] who in any case, will have the priest alongside him:

> Behold there is a man—Shoot is his name—and from his place he will shoot up and build the Temple of Yahweh. He will build the Temple of Yahweh; and he will bear royal majesty and sit upon his throne and rule. A priest will be on his throne, and there will be peaceful counsel between the two of them. (vv. 12–13)

This reading of the text requires very little change, if any, in the Masoretic Text. At 6:11 we leave the plural "crowns" intact and at 6:14 we read the singular 'crown' or *hāᶜăṭeret*, which requires no consonantal changes in the text at all and is supported by the Septuagint and Peshiṭta.[7] The crowning scene is the last utterance of the prophet on the monarchic issue, and in this final oracle of Part Two of First Zechariah the unmentioned Zerubbabel is relegated to be a symbol of the future, as the prophet suggests that a Davidic governor only anticipates a future Davidic king. The oracle in chap. 6 also

4. Ibid., lii–lxiii.

5. Haggai's career begins August 29, 520 B.C.E. (Hag 1:1) and ends December 18, 520 B.C.E. (Hag 2:10, 20). Zechariah's career begins in October 520 (Zech 1:1) and the latest date in the book is December 7, 518 (Zech 7:1). The overlap in careers is surprising, but the short length of Haggai's ministry is even more surprising.

6. The dropping of Zerubbabel's name and the substitution of Davidic epithets for him is taken as proof that the Persians quashed the rebellion and did away with the governor who really wanted to be king.

7. For a detailed discussion of this see Meyers and Meyers, *Haggai, Zechariah 1–8*, 349–56.

seems to suggest a growing role for the priestly ruler, as is surely anticipated in chap. 3. Indeed, the language of Zech 3:8 is much stronger and more specific with respect to the role of the Davidic governor: "I am indeed bringing my servant the Shoot." Chapter 6 seems deliberately vague and intended to deflate the final burning embers of monarchist feelings that might have existed at the time and that might have been stimulated by the fact that Zerubbabel had participated in the ceremony of refoundation.[8] As has already been pointed out, however, such hopes were not grounded in any sense of realism, because the population in Yehud at this time was insignificant and would have made even the staunchest monarchist hesitate to advocate independence, let alone rebellion.

The obvious meaning of these subtle textual and rhetorical shifts is that reluctantly but nonetheless realistically and pragmatically both prophets, but especially Zechariah, saw it in the best interests of the restoration community to support the Achaemenid-sponsored theocracy of Yehud as the only viable way of reestablishing the Jewish community of returnees to the Holy Land again. But clearly the Persians could not allow a monarchist entity to exist in Yehud when all other areas were being brought into the satrapal organization installed by Darius I.[9] The clear interest of Persian strategy was to install rulers loyal to them and yet who were supported and appreciated within their own cultures. In this respect the Persian solution to Judean hopes for reestablishing the old order was both farsighted and appropriate, for the dyarchic pattern of rule harks back to Israel's premonarchic period when Moses and Joshua led the people into Canaan and Aaron and his successors organized the religious affairs of the people.

Though we can never be absolutely certain why the figure of Zerubbabel drops out of the book of Zechariah, it is highly unlikely that some sort of

8. The ceremony of refoundation is not to be confused with the ceremony of rededication of the Second Temple in 516/15 B.C.E. Rather, it is equivalent to the laying of the cornerstone and ceremonial laying of a foundation deposit. This refoundation leaves numerous textual echoes in both Haggai and First Zechariah, perhaps the clearest of which is Hag 2:18, 20, dated to December 18, 520 B.C.E.

9. There is a large secondary literature on the role of Darius I and the reorganization of the satrapies. J. M. Cook, *The Persian Empire* (London: Dent/New York: Schocken, 1983) passim, provides an excellent analysis of Achaemenid politics. My former graduate student, Kenneth G. Hoglund, in his 1989 Duke University Ph.D. dissertation entitled *Achaemenid Imperial Administration in Syria-Palestine and the Missions of Ezra and Nehemiah*, goes well beyond Cook in examining the ramifications of Persian policies on the internal affairs of Yehud. His dissertation has now been published (SBLDS 125; Atlanta: Scholars Press, 1992).

political rebellion took place under his leadership. The new colony of Yehud was tiny and not yet on its feet economically and would have stood no chance of challenging the might of Persia. Whatever caused Zerubbabel's governorship to end around the end of the sixth century B.C.E., it now seems as if he were not the last of the Davidides to assume an important political or administrative post in the Persian territory of Yehud. As a result of the discovery and publication of a hoard of bullae and two seals of the early restoration era, we are able to fill in the list of governors until Nehemiah (445–433 B.C.E.).[10] It was a certain Elnathan, *pḥwᵓ*, who succeeded Zerubbabel as governor.[11] However, Elnathan apparently served jointly with Shelomith, his *ᵓāmâ*, and she was Zerubbabel's daughter (1 Chr 3:19).[12]

Avigad's preferred interpretation of the meaning of *ᵓāmâ* is that it connoted the status of wife (e.g., Gen 21:10, 12–13) but with the added meaning of 'officer' or 'administrator', an honorific title used by spouses of important individuals. Inasmuch as there were two Davidic sons available to succeed Zerubbabel, that is, Meshullam and Hananiah, it is most significant that Shelomith is called to public office, in all probability to keep the Davidic name in the public eye but at the same time making it quite clear that in the Persian Empire there was no turning back to the old monarchist pattern and that royalty played a more symbolic role than anything else. Still, a woman was chosen over two viable male candidates, and such a decision indicates first that monarchist feelings were running high although realistically focused on the future, and second, that appointing or arranging through marriage a Davidic co-regent for the governor would somehow be a constructive way of dealing with the royal family.

Precisely how long Shelomith and Elnathan ruled together is not clear, since we are dependent upon Avigad's paleographical analysis. Nonetheless, we now know that there were two additional governors prior to Nehemiah, Yohoᶜezer and Ahzai. A reasonable conjecture is that Elnathan and Shelomith held office for at least a decade into the fifth century, and possibly longer. The circumstances surrounding the transfer of power from governor to governor are not at all clear, but we would assume that all of them remained loyal to Persia. The succession in the high priesthood was also very complex, and judging from the attacks on the temple cult in the book of

10. See N. Avigad, *Bullae and Seals from a Post-exilic Judean Archive* (Qedem 4; Jerusalem: Hebrew University Institute of Archaeology, 1976).

11. See chart in Meyers and Meyers, *Haggai, Zechariah 1–8*, 14.

12. See my essay, "The Shelomith Seal and Aspects of the Judean Restoration: Some Additional Reconsiderations," *ErIsr* 17 (*Brawer Volume*; 1985) 33–38.

Malachi and Isaiah 56–66, corruption of the priestly high office came fairly soon after the end of Joshua's term of office. The material in Second Zechariah (chaps. 9–14) indicates that there was chaos at the political level as well, and that even the prophets had become corrupt. Whatever the reasons for such a dramatic reversal in the fortunes of the Jews of Yehud, a measure of irredentism was sure to take root on the one hand, along with a strong assimilationist tendency on the other.

A decline in the political fortunes of Yehud is clearly reflected in the decline of prophecy as it had been known in Israel before, but especially in the cessation of the composition of prophetic books and in the rise of anonymous authorship in the deutero-prophetic corpus. Cross has been most explicit about the decline of prophecy by linking it to the demise of the monarchy. Haggai and Zechariah are really the last gasps or swansong of prophecy: a "last flicker of the old prophetic spirit at the time of a royal pretender."[13] But as I have written before, prophecy was being transformed not so much by inner community struggle into "prophetic eschatology" and apocalypticism but by the closer association of prophecy and priesthood (e.g., Hag 2:10–14 and Zech 7:3ff.).[14] The idealization of the priest in Malachi (2:7) and the linkage between the "Torah of Moses" and Elijah's future role (3:22–24) in the ending to the book also suggest that the reforms of Ezra were consonant with these developments: "He [Ezra] saw the Torah as a means of acquiring the holiness without which Yahweh's eschatological glory could not break in (cf. Malachi). . . . His attempt to set up a twelve-tribe amphictyony in Israel . . . followed the organization recorded in the Priestly writing (Num. 1–10); but it was also in accordance with prophetic voices (Isa. 49.6; Ezek. 37.15ff)."[15]

Whatever the reasons for the decline of prophecy no one can doubt the tremendous difficulties that faced the generation prior to Ezra and Nehemiah.[16] The challenge of rebuilding the temple had been met in an earlier

13. F. M. Cross, Jr., *Canaanite Myth and Hebrew Epic* (Cambridge: Harvard University Press, 1973) 223.

14. E. Meyers, "The Use of Tora in Haggai 2:11 and the Role of the Prophet in the Restoration Community," *The Word of the Lord Shall Go Forth: Essays in Honor of David Noel Freedman in Celebration of His Sixtieth Birthday* (ed. C. L. Meyers and M. O'Connor; Winona Lake, Ind.: Eisenbrauns, 1983) 70. Cf. also my remarks, "The Persian Period and the Judean Restoration: From Zerubbabel to Nehemiah," *Ancient Israelite Religion: Essays in Honor of Frank Moore Cross* (ed. P. D. Miller, P. D. Hanson, and S. Dean McBride; Philadelphia: Fortress, 1987) 509–21.

15. K. Koch, *The Prophets, Vol. 2: The Babylonian and Persian Periods* (Philadelphia: Fortress, 1986) 187.

16. See the excellent summary article on this topic by T. W. Overholt, "The End of Prophecy: No Players without a Program," *JSOT* 42 (1988) 103–15; reprinted in *"The Place*

generation, but the blessings promised by the prophet Haggai still did not flow (2:15–19; cf. Zech 3:8–10). A real leadership vacuum existed at every level, though perhaps the Persians did not allow another Davidic leader to be appointed for good reason. After all, the first half of the fifth century was a critical period in Achaemenid history. The Greeks began to flex their muscles and had already succeeded in establishing trading emporia up and down the eastern Mediterranean. By 460, however, the threat of the loss of Persian holdings in the Levant was made greater by the Egyptian satrapal revolt and its aftermath:

> As such, the decade of 460–450 B.C.E. represented an extraordinary crisis in imperial control of the eastern Mediterranean sphere, a crisis that called forth extraordinary efforts to suppress the Egyptian revolt and to keep Athenian naval power from gaining a military advantage over the empire. Nor was the perception of a threat completely removed by the Peace of Callias, since in 440 B.C.E. there were still concerns over a possible clash between these two antagonists.[17]

The ultimate success of the Greek navy in stemming Persian threats to control the western Mediterranean was one of the major turning points in Western history. It has been memorialized in the magnificent words of Aeschylus' play *The Persians*:

> Nations wail their native sons,
> Who by Xerxes stuffed up hell;
> Many heroes, Persia's bloom,
> Archers, thick array of men,
> Myriads have perished.
> Woe, O King of noble strength.
> Cruel! Cruel! Asia kneels.[18]

How this epochal struggle had impact on Yehud and the canonical process has not yet been sufficiently investigated. Hoglund has attempted to evaluate its impact on the books of Ezra and Nehemiah and has demonstrated how the missions of Ezra and Nehemiah contributed toward greater control and security in the region. In doing so, he has collected the archaeological evidence of forts and fortresses from this era in Palestine and the greater Levant

---

Is Too Small for Us": The Israelite Prophets in Recent Scholarship (SBTS 5; ed R. P. Gordon; Winona Lake, Ind.: Eisenbrauns, 1995) 527–38.

17. Hoglund, *Achaemenid Imperial Administration*, 303–4.

18. From *The Complete Greek Tragedies* (trans. D. Grene and R. Lattimore; Chicago: University of Chicago Press, 1959) 252.

to indicate the tightening grip of Persian imperial rule at the time. Nehemiah's refortification also fits in well with such a scheme.

It is my contention that such formidable events as the ones that had impact on the Levantine world in the mid–fifth century for a generation or more would have had to directly influence the course of events within the leadership of Yehud and within the circles of prophets who ultimately assumed control of their own words and utterances and of the words of their forbears. Second Zechariah, or perhaps more aptly, Deutero-Zechariah, no doubt reflects some of these dramatic changes. Its references to the Davidic line therefore are especially helpful in assessing the pulse of postexilic Hebrew messianism on the eve of the missions of Ezra and Nehemiah. Its remarkable depiction of the righteous king in Zech 9:9–10 is especially informative of the mindset of fifth-century Yehud.

The question of the date and original setting of chap. 9 has occupied biblical scholars for many years, and suggestions for a date have ranged from the eighth century B.C.E. to the second century B.C.E. (Maccabean times). Moreover, vv. 9–10 have been appropriated by the New Testament to depict Jesus' triumphal return to Jerusalem (Matt 21:5–9). The reader of Second Zechariah, however, must surely be struck by the quiescent, though triumphal, tone of the messianic oracle that has been appropriated by Matthew. The two verses stand in sharp contrast to the warlike language that surrounds it, which has led Hanson, among others, to identify the larger piece (9:1–17) as a "divine warrior hymn."[19]

By any standard of measure, chap. 9 is pure poetry, and in this formal respect also stands in marked contrast to the rest of the book of Zechariah and the books of Haggai and Malachi as well.[20] Its distinctive poetic character and elevated oracular style suggest that it played a unique role in the shaping of the canonical book of Zechariah and, in particular, the messianic passage (9:9–10) seems to provide an important link with earlier messianic passages in First Zechariah in which a future righteous king figures so centrally (e.g.,

19. P. D. Hanson, *The Dawn of Apocalyptic* (Philadelphia: Fortress, 1976) 292. Since this article was prepared, my second Anchor Bible volume (with C. L. Meyers) has appeared: *Zechariah 9–14* (AB 25C; New York: Doubleday, 1993); the reader is referred to that volume for greater exegetical detail. See also now D. L. Petersen, *Zechariah 9–14 and Malachi* (OTL; Louisville: Westminster/John Knox, 1995).

20. In terms of prose particles, the percentage in Zechariah 9 is 1.35%, in comparison to 18.7% for Haggai and 15.8% for First Zechariah; so Meyers and Meyers, *Haggai, Zechariah 1–8*, lv–lvi. See also F. I. Andersen and D. A. Forbes, "Prose Particle Counts of the Hebrew Bible" *The Word of the Lord Shall Go Forth: Essays in Honor of David Noel Freedman in Celebration of His Sixtieth Birthday* (ed. C. L. Meyers and M. O'Connor; Winona Lake, Ind.: Eisenbrauns, 1983) 165–83.

4:7, 6:12–13, etc.). It is even possible that the editor or redactor of chap. 9 or even the compiler of the book of Zechariah has inserted these verses into the divine warrior hymn in an attempt to make it more compatible with the earlier materials of Zechariah. In fact, the ending of v. 8, "for now I am watching with my own eyes," is very reminiscent of First Zechariah's familiar expression "to lift up my eyes and see," which occurs some eighteen times, and thus the end of v. 8 may provide an editorial link for the possible insertion of vv. 9–10.

The pacifistic, quietistic tone of this passage is so different from the rest of the material in Second Zechariah, and even from the end of the book of Malachi (3:22–24), where Moses becomes the "servant" of God and Elijah the sign of the eschatological "Day of Yahweh," while at the same time so obviously "Davidic," that it seems fairly certain that the divine warrior hymn has been purposely adjusted to suit larger theological aims and purposes. The first purpose seems to have been to align the beginning of Second Zechariah with the material in First Zechariah. The second purpose was to express clearly an optimistic view of the future in familiar Davidic language but with new theological meaning. It is also quite possible that the recent events in Yehud had led to such a revision and that the servant songs of Isaiah may have actually influenced the author of these verses, as Mason has suggested (cf. Isa 55:3–5).[21] The well-known ideal-king passage of Isaiah of Jerusalem (Isaiah 11) has been replaced in Second Isaiah's more generalized view of a "spiritual centre from which the rule of Yahweh would go forth to the ends of the earth."[22] Second Zechariah's obvious dependency on Psalm 72 should also be noted, especially v. 10b, where the refrain "from sea to sea" depicts the extent of the domain of God's elected one (cf. also the similar thematic elements in Zeph 3:14 and Zech 2:14 ff.).

If vv. 9–10 of chap. 9 of Zechariah seem to have been inserted to correspond better with the muted messianism of First Zechariah, or perhaps the

21. R. Mason's most detailed statements regarding Zechariah 9–14 are unfortunately contained in his excellent unpublished doctoral dissertation at the University of London in 1973: *The Use of Earlier Biblical Material in Zechariah ix–xiv: A Study in Inner Biblical Exegesis.* I would like to express my sincere appreciation to Professor Mason of Regents Park College, Oxford, for his work, to which I am much indebted. The reader is referred to his published essays on this general subject and to his commentary, *The Books of Haggai, Zechariah and Malachi* (Cambridge Commentary on the New English Bible; Cambridge: Cambridge University Press, 1977). The present reference is to his dissertation, p. 61.

22. J. Mauchline, "Implicit Signs of a Persistent Belief in the Davidic Empire," *VT* 20 (1970) 303. The changed character of the Davidic emphasis should not detract from its persistent royal theme, which is represented best by the procession of a king upon a mule, one of the most persistent motifs in ancient Near Eastern literature.

poem or hymn that constitutes the entire chapter or portion thereof was chosen or inserted at the beginning of Second Zechariah because of the verbal congruences or thematic similarities to First Zechariah, then it is not surprising to find other aspects of the deutero-Zecharianic corpus that exhibit similar features.[23] Together with C. L. Meyers, I have indeed argued for such affinities between Zechariah 7–8 and the book of Haggai, a correspondence that suggested a common editor and publication.[24] In the case of Second Zechariah such linkages between chap. 9 and 2:10–17, for example, or with 4:6–7, merely suggest that the compiler of the canonical book of Zechariah was mindful of where he or others, possibly disciples of Zechariah himself, had decided to place the hymn and were prepared, it would seem, to make modest editorial adjustments and some inserts.

The remaining passages in Zechariah that make repeated reference to the Davidic dynasty (12:7, 8, 10, 12; and 13:1) are very complex and seem to allude to the hard times of the Davidic line after Shelomith—surely long after Zerubbabel's governorship. Indeed, chap. 12 seems to indicate its complete disapproval of existing leadership in Yehud, reflecting an entirely new condition that was lacking in First Zechariah. On the contrary, First Zechariah focuses almost entirely on the matter of evincing support for the dyarchic leadership of the early postexilic period and its specific incumbents. As in the book of Malachi, so in Second Zechariah the question of failed leadership is very much at the center of the prophetic mind. It is surprising, therefore, that the messianism of chap. 12 is also muted. Though the figure of the house of David plays a very special role in the messianic scheme, it is not an exclusive one:

> Then I will pour out, on the house of David and on the rulers of Jerusalem, a spirit of favor and supplication, so that they will look to me concerning the one they have stabbed. They will mourn for him as one mourns for an only child and grieve for him as one grieves for a first-born (Zech 12:10).

The most informative aspect of this verse is that the Davidic house or scion will not alone be free to extend his imperial rule. Rather, the "house of David" will join with the rest of the community in the repentance that will help effect the changes. In addition, the "house of David" will work jointly with the "rulers of Jerusalem"[25] in bringing about change in the future. This

23. This is Mason's overall thesis for his treatment of Second Zechariah; see his essay, "The Relationship of Zech 9–14 to Proto-Zechariah," *ZAW* 88 (1976) 227–39.

24. See Meyers and Meyers, *Haggai, Zechariah 1–8*, lii–lxiii.

25. The translation of *yôšēb* as 'ruler' follows the usage in Zech 8:20 and is most often misunderstood as 'inhabitant'. For an explanation of this usage see Meyers and Meyers,

is hardly the traditional concept of a Davidic messiah who in Isaianic terms could certainly establish his kingdom to the ends of the earth (Isaiah 11; Ps 12:7–8). In light of this openness to the "rulers of Jerusalem," it is possible to speculate that even in chap. 9 there may be an allusion to the rule of a Davidide with priests, as the ending of the hymn refers to the end of time when "gemstones of a crown will shine on his (God's) land" (Zech 9:16), an image that is highly reminiscent of First Zechariah's stones of the temple (e.g., Zech 2:15; 3:9; 4:7, 10)[26] and symbols of priesthood. The use of the word "stone" at the beginning of this oracle thus can hardly be coincidental: ". . . I will make Jerusalem a burdensome stone for all the peoples" (Zech 12:3), the expression "burdensome stone" functioning as another link with First Zechariah and evoking echoes of the many stones used in his symbolic vocabulary.

The use of the term "house of Judah" or "chiefs of Judah" in vv. 4 and 5 must be understood as referring to the interdependence of the leadership of Judah (i.e., Yehud) with the Davidic leader, who together would reestablish their community with God's support and encouragement. Verse 6 clearly expresses the prophet's disappointment with the religious and political leadership, cleansing the temple with a "fire-pot" and the environs with a "fire-torch," the former an allusion to the laver of the temple[27] and the latter to Samson's exploits.[28] The fact that v. 7 places Judah first before the "house of David" and the "rulers of Jerusalem" in the eschatological drama need not be understood in any other way but to emphasize Yahweh's role in such a plan of deliverance.

> On that day Yahweh will protect the rulers of Jerusalem so that the weak one among them on that day will be like David, and the house of David will be like God, like the Angel of Yahweh before them (v. 8).

As one might expect, the comparison between the "house of David" and God created some difficulties for the ancient translators, who desired no such exaggerated claims for David's house.[29] Mason correctly turns to the book of Exodus for help in understanding this curious and unique expression.[30]

Haggai, Zechariah 1–8, 437; and N. Gottwald, *The Tribes of Yahweh* (Maryknoll, N.Y.: Orbis, 1979) 512–34. See also now C. L. Meyers and E. M. Meyers, "The Future Fortunes of the House of David: The Evidence of Second Zechariah," in *Fortunate the Eyes That See: Essays in Honor of David Noel Freedman in Celebration of His Seventieth Birthday* (ed. A. B. Beck et al.; Grand Rapids: Eerdmans, 1995) 207–22.

26. Cf. Isa 28:16.

27. Exod 30:18, 28, 31; 39:39; 40:7, 11, 30, etc.

28. Judg 15:1–5.

29. For example, the Targum translates here: 'The house of David shall be like princes and shall flourish like kings'.

30. On this difficult point, see Mason, *Earlier Biblical Material in Zechariah*, 227ff.

When Moses complains that he is unable to speak properly God's words, God reassures him that Aaron will be his stand-in:

> He shall speak for you to the people; and he shall be a mouth for you, and you shall be to him *as* God (Exod 4:16).

Though the preposition in Exodus is *l* and in Zechariah it is *k*, the purpose of the text is similar enough: to show that just as the roles of Moses and Aaron are complementary under God's aegis, so too does the house of David stand in a complementary way to the rest of the Judean leadership in the period when a purified and proper leadership will be returned to their appropriate roles. The addition of the phrase "like the Angel of Yahweh before them" echoes Haggai (1:13) and First Zechariah (1:11,12; 3:1, 5, 6) and anticipates Malachi (2:7; 3:1[2]) later. It is the only occurrence of the expression "Angel of Yahweh" in Second Zechariah, a fact that can hardly be accidental and may be another imprint of the final compiler of the book of Zechariah, who followed the lead of the redactor of First Zechariah, both of whom influenced the author or redactor of the book of Malachi.

Chapter 12 therefore cannot merely be viewed as an "apocalypse molded by the inner-community struggle"[31] but as a creative response to a power struggle or vacuum that had impact on all Yehud sometime towards the end of the first half of the fifth century B.C.E. when the priesthood was corrupted, as depicted in the book of Malachi, and when the governorship in non-Davidic hands lapsed into an unacceptable pattern of leadership. Though we know no details of this period, except for Avigad's governor list, the extent to which conditions had changed from Zerubbabel to Nehemiah suggests a situation of great malaise in Yehud prior to the beginning of the second half of the fifth century. The Dirge for the Fallen (vv. 12–13) indicates a desire to go back to the once-successful postexilic pattern of dyarchic leadership, taking v. 12 as signifying Davidic leadership (Nathan as David's son: 2 Sam 5:14) at the governor level and v. 13 as signifying priestly leadership (Shimei as descendent of Levi: Exod 6:17 and 1 Chr 25:7). The refrain about "women by themselves" seems to indicate the unique role played by women in the ancient Near East and even today in the mourning process and may in fact refer to an actual group of professional keeners.

31. Hanson, *Dawn of Apocalyptic*, 354; here Hanson sees the inner struggle as one between visionaries and hierocrats, that is, supporters of the old prophetic view versus the newer supporters of a theocratic and establishment point of view. Whatever has contributed to the collapse of Yehud's leadership, it is not reflected in the demographics of the time; see n. 3 above.

The renewal of God's favor ("a spirit of favor and supplication," v. 10) is followed by an act of contrition and mourning for "the one they have stabbed." The text is very difficult at this point and there is little consensus among the commentators about its meaning. The change from the third person to the first person is very abrupt and the Hebrew is awkward, with the object preposition occurring before the relative. Many commentators merely remove the object marker *ʾet*. Similarly, emending the preposition *ʾel* ('to' or 'concerning') to the third person from the first person alleviates much tension, as is the case in John 19:37: "They will look to the one whom they have pierced."[32] Most commentators through the ages have sought to identify the "stabbed one" with various martyrs of biblical and postbiblical days, ranging from Josiah to Zerubbabel, Jeremiah to Judah Maccabee. A wide array of others take the suffering servant of Isaiah (52:15–53:12) to be the favored interpretation, and subsequently as the messianic figure predicted in the New Testament.[33]

Mason has pointed to Ezekiel 36 in helping to explain the overall context of chap. 12.[34] Because Zechariah points to a period of renewal and regeneration following the military adventure that ultimately spared Jerusalem and Judah—possibly a reference to an abortive attempt at establishing independence in Yehud that fortuitously resulted in the sparing of the Holy City and yet in imposing stricter Persian controls—the dirge continues and concludes, in my opinion, with Zech 13:1: "On that day there will be an open fountain for the house of David and the rulers of Jerusalem, for [cleansing] sin and impurity." This verse may also do double duty as the opening of chap. 13. The image of the cleansing of impurity with water is very priestly and in keeping with the recounting of cultic abuses noted in Malachi, which probably is to be dated about the same time as Second Zechariah. Such a period of cleansing, if properly understood here, certainly justifies the retention of the first-person suffix in Zech 12:10 (". . . so that they look to me [Yahweh] concerning . . ."). It matters little to us whether the "stabbed one" was a historical personage or not; the expression still supplies a compelling metaphor for understanding the alienation of certain elements from the leadership of the people.[35]

32. So Hanson, *Dawn of Apocalyptic*, 356–57, and H. G. Mitchell, *Haggai–Zechariah* (ICC; Edinburgh: T. and T. Clark, 1912) 334–35.

33. The older interpretations are collected by Mitchell, ibid., 331–33, and the more recent ones by Mason and others. See, for example, W. Rudolph's commentary, *Haggai-Sacharja 1–8—Sacharja 9–14—Maleachi* (KAT; Gütersloh: Mohn, 1976) 216ff.

34. Mason, *Earlier Biblical Material in Zechariah*, 238.

35. Cf. Ezek 36:25.

The diatribe attacking prophecy in Zech 13:2–5 suggests a complicity of certain prophetic elements in supporting whatever abortive event(s) toward the mid–fifth century precipitated the crisis to which Second Zechariah repeatedly refers. The defilement of the cult and the rampant idolatry that followed are the results of the bad leadership that included priests (Mal 2:8) and prophets (Zech 13:2) and those leaders responsible for the general loss of direction (Zech 12:2–9), viewed from a prophetic standpoint. Obviously, the one(s) responsible for preserving the oracles of Second Zechariah, possibly the same as the one(s) who put together the oracles of Malachi, believed in the correctness of the position adopted in these works. This viewpoint is consistent with the books of Ezra and Nehemiah, in which Ezra is depicted as a second Moses and his reforms and activities are placed on a par with the Exodus itself. Moreover, Ezra himself, while condemning present practices and initiating reforms, maintained his firm belief in the power of prophecy to effect changes within society, even within the framework of a strong and evil empire.[36]

In trying to recreate the social setting that could have led to such a new situation by ca. 450 B.C.E., one is hard pressed to find it solely in Yehud, and perhaps this has been one of the problems of recent scholarship. The Jewish community of Yehud, numbering between 8,000–10,000 individuals at the time, was not exclusively confined to that territory. The biblical data, especially the data contained in Ezra and Nehemiah, depict a rather large province that extended to Kadesh-Barnea in the south to Hazor in the northeast and Ono in the northwest. The eastern border would have been the Jordan River. An examination of actual sites and attested finds from them, however, suggests a much more confined area, with the key sites being Jericho in the northeast, En-Gedi in the southeast, Beth-Zur in the southwest, with the Shephelah excluded on the west.

Once we extend our geographical and demographic purview a little, allowing for interregional differences and tension as well as for a more dominant Gentile influence upon the Jewish population in those areas, it becomes easier to imagine the changed circumstances of the fifth century. The dyarchy could probably effectively deal with problems internal to Yehud, especially earlier in the postexilic period in the restoration era, but it would not

36. K. Koch, "Ezra and the Origins of Judaism," *JSS* 19 (1974) 189; *The Prophets, Vol. 2.* See also now my essay, "The Crisis of the Mid–fifth Century B.C.E. Second Zechariah and the 'End' of Prophecy," in *Pomegranates and Golden Bells: Studies in Biblical, Jewish, and Near Eastern Ritual, Law, and Literature in Honor of Jacob Milgrom* (ed. D. P. Wright, D. N. Freedman, and A. Hurvitz; Winona Lake, Ind.: Eisenbrauns, 1995) 713–23.

be able effectively to cast its administrative controls over areas outside of Yehud. Since so much of the administrative infrastructure related to taxation and was related to the temple itself as the general population grew in the Persian era, it became less and less possible to control a system that was centered in Jerusalem but was so dependent on communications that were far away. It is certainly in the non-Yehud setting that the issue of intermarriage carries a special sense of urgency.

It can hardly be coincidence that Second Zechariah ends its eschatological drama with a call for celebration of the Feast of Booths, that is, Succoth (Zech 14:16–19). There is support for the special importance assigned to this festival in the rabbinic recognition of it as "the feast" of chief importance in Second Temple times.[37] This is a bit surprising in view of the fact that Passover, which falls in Nisan at the Old Babylonian spring New Year, seemingly has a more central place in Jewish tradition, both in First Temple times and post-70 C.E. times.[38] Yet it is at the time of the Feast of Booths that Ezra reads from the Law in the square before Water Gate (Neh 8:1–3) and proclaims the Torah as the binding law of the land. I am not suggesting that chap. 14 of Zechariah has been influenced by the author or compiler of Ezra and Nehemiah or vice versa. For the moment, however, it is at least worthy of consideration that some editorial adjustments to the canonical book of Zechariah, possibly through this curious use of the Feast of Booths, is one such way that the works were brought into closer harmony.

The Book of the Twelve was presumably put together sometime in the second half of the fifth century.[39] It seems appropriate that the concluding verses of the book of Malachi, the last of the twelve, concludes with eschatological words of praise to Moses and Elijah:

> Remember the torah of Moses my servant, which I commanded him at Horeb, over all Israel, statutes and ordinances. I will indeed send you the prophet Elijah before the great and awesome day of the Lord comes (3:22–23).

37. In Mishnaic Hebrew, Succoth is called *heḥag*; see tractate *Succoth*, etc.

38. For the definitive treatment of Passover, see B. M. Bokser, *The Origins of the Seder: The Passover Rite and Early Rabbinic Judaism* (Berkeley: University of California Press, 1984). However, the book of Deuteronomy, by calling in 31:9–13 for the public reading of the Torah every seven years at the Feast of Booths, elevates Succoth to great importance in the pre-exilic period.

39. David Noel Freedman has treated the subject of the entire Hebrew canon, including the Book of the Twelve, in *The Unity of the Hebrew Bible* (Ann Arbor: University of Michigan Press, 1991). The volume is the result of his distinguished professor lectures delivered on campus in 1989. See also the unpublished 1979 Yale University dissertation of Dale A. Schneider, *The Unity of the Book of the Twelve.*

Moses the archetypal prophet and unique mediator of God's words becomes similar to Ezra the lawgiver, a second Moses. Elijah, the only prophet to ascend to heaven, symbolizes the return of the prophetic spirit before the end of time. In later Jewish and Christian tradition Elijah is the forerunner of the messiah, and in the Passover service developed by the rabbis after 70 C.E. Elijah becomes the substitute Moses who has been entirely eliminated from the retelling of the story of Passover.[40] In short, the ending of the Book of the Twelve, like the content of Second Zechariah and Ezra and Nehemiah, underscores the centrality of the law, the continuing role of prophecy, and the relevance of the Exodus paradigm signified in a new emphasis on the Feast of Booths, at which time Jews actually relived the Exodus by sleeping in booths that reminded them of the severe conditions that accompanied them after leaving Egypt.

The practical realities of Persian politics being what they were in fifth-century Palestine meant that fewer and fewer realistic hopes could be attached to a future messiah of the house of David; even Deutero-Isaiah seems to have achieved such a course. The Davidic line became more and more a symbol of future hope that was quite remote from the present. Chapter 9 of Second Zechariah endorses the quietistic vision of First Zechariah, whose realistic sensibilities enabled the Second Temple to be completed and rededicated. Davidic expectations remained only beneath the surface of Yehudite thoughts during the fifth century, and apparently a leadership struggle toward mid–fifth century once again flamed hopes of a renewed Davidic leadership. Or, could it be that such feelings of a Davidic restoration emanated also from those Jews living outside Yehud, but in Palestine, for whom keeping their religion was a continuous challenge in light of the cosmopolitan culture that was engulfing them on all sides? But as in First Zechariah, it had to be a leadership tied closely to priesthood and prophecy and the rebuilding of Jerusalem. Hence, it is no wonder that the last of the fifth-century historiographers, the Chronicler, places so much emphasis on the achievements and accomplishments of the house of David in relation to the development of the worshiping community of Yehud.[41]

40. I.e., in the traditional *Haggadah*. To the best of my knowledge only the *Reconstructionist Haggadah*, organized and edited by Mordecai Kaplan, has reintroduced Moses into the narrative; so Kaplan, *The New Haggadah* (New York: Behrman House, 1942).

41. P. Ackroyd, "History and Theology in the Chronicler," *Concordia Theological Monthly* 38 (1967) 501–15.

The Kerygmatic Structure of the Book of Isaiah

John N. Oswalt

In his book *The Formation of Isaiah 40–55*, Roy Melugin concludes that, while Isaiah 40–55 is composed of originally independent discourses, they have not been arranged in a chance or haphazard manner. Rather, they have been put in this order because of the specific message that the author or editor wished to communicate.[1] Melugin uses the New Testament Greek term *kerygma* 'message' to define this organizing principle.

It is my conviction that this conclusion applies to the book as a whole, not merely to the portion often labeled Deutero-Isaiah. Whatever we may conclude about the date and authorship of the various parts of the book, it is not now in its present form because of chance or because of such mechanical matters as word similarities. Rather, the various components are in their present shape and organization because of the theological points that the author(s) and/or editor(s) were trying to communicate.

Fortunately, the older position that chaps. 40–55 and 56–66 were composed as independent books without any necessary dependence on Isaianic writings preceding them has mostly faded away.[2] I say "fortunately" because such a position stems more from the early enthusiasm for source criticism, which sought to find independent sources behind every document, than it does from an attempt to understand the present book.[3]

An interim attempt to explain the phenomenon of the present book was the school hypothesis. This theory saw the present unit as the result of a

1. Roy F. Melugin, *The Formation of Isaiah 40–55* (BZAW 141; Berlin: de Gruyter, 1976) 175.

2. For an example of the older position, see O. Eissfeldt, *The Old Testament: An Introduction* (trans. P. R. Ackroyd; Oxford: Blackwell, 1965) 304, 332–46.

3. Eissfeldt dismisses the entire question of the origin of the present book in less than a page (ibid., 345–46).

school of prophets who were committed to studying and transmitting the Isaian corpus. Eventually, new books were written by members of the school, which, while still independent of First Isaiah (and later, Second Isaiah), nonetheless show the influence of the great eighth-century prophet's thought and outlook. Ultimately, other members of the school combined their colleagues' work with that of the master.[4] However, as Clements and others have recently noted, the existence of such a school is both unprecedented and unattested.[5] There is no evidence in support of the hypothesis except the present form of the book, which gave rise to the hypothesis in the first place and which can be better explained in other ways.

Recently, a number of studies showing the interdependence of the various sections of the book have appeared.[6] First Isaiah is not ignorant of Second Isaiah or even Third Isaiah. This observation is not new, but whereas it used to be said that these passages were insertions from the second or third Isaianic "sources," it is now argued that First Isaiah *in its present form* reflects a thoroughgoing impact of the ideas of the last twenty-seven chapters.[7] Furthermore, it is asserted that these last chapters were never meant to stand alone but were written in the full knowledge of the earlier work(s) and with the intent of bringing the ideas found there to their full development.[8] The implications of these findings for date and composition have been profound. Many now argue that the present book is the product of a thoroughgoing revision that took place sometime during the fifth century B.C.E. At that time the material was ordered and reordered in such a way as to give a theological unity to the whole.[9] However one may receive this last suggestion, the new

4. W. L. Holladay, *Isaiah, Scroll of a Prophetic Heritage* (New York: Pilgrim, 1987) 18. This book is an excellent example of the atomistic tendencies in critical studies that have reduced the book of Isaiah, and others, to collections of often artificially and accidentally collected phrases and sentences.

5. R. E. Clements, "The Unity of the Book of Isaiah," *Int* 36 (1982) 119.

6. P. R. Ackroyd, "Interpretation of the Babylonian Exile: A Study of 2 Kings 20, Isaiah 38–39," *SJT* 27 (1974) 329–52; Walter Brueggemann, "Unity and Dynamic in the Isaiah Tradition," *JSOT* 29 (1984) 89–107; Brevard S. Childs, *Introduction to the Old Testament as Scripture* (Philadelphia: Fortress, 1979) 216–25; R. E. Clements, "Unity of the Book of Isaiah," 117–29; idem, "Beyond Tradition-History: Deutero-Isaianic Development of First Isaiah's Themes," *JSOT* 31 (1985) 95–113; R. Rendtorff, "Zur Komposition des Buches Jesaja," *VT* 34 (1984) 295–320; Christopher Seitz, "Isaiah 1–66: Making Sense of the Whole," *Reading and Preaching the Book of Isaiah* (ed. C. R. Seitz; Philadelphia: Fortress, 1988) 105–26.

7. Ibid., 113–14.

8. Rendtorff, "Komposition des Buches Jesaja," 320.

9. For example, see John W. Watts, *Isaiah 1–33* (WBC 24; Waco, Texas: Word, 1985).

recognition of the wholeness of the book can only be greeted with enthusiasm. The dissection and fragmentation of one of the great pieces of world literature, not to mention one of the great pieces of theological reflection, has been nothing less than scandalous.

Scholars have identified several indications of the literary unity of the present book. Some of these relate to terms and concepts, such as, for instance, the even distribution of the phrase "the Holy One of Israel" throughout the book (12 occurrences in chaps. 1–39; 13 in chaps. 40–55).[10] Clements has also noted the recurrence of the theme of "deaf and blind," especially in relationship to Israel, in the various segments of the book (6:9–10; 35:5–6, 7; 42:18–20; 43:8; 50:4–5; 55:2–3; see also 63:17).[11] Rendtorff has pointed out the presence of "comfort," a leading idea in chaps. 40–52, at such key junctures as 12:1 and 61:2.[12] The importance of redeemed Zion is another concept that is found throughout (1:27; 4:5; 12:6; 28:16; 29:8; 30:19; 33:20; 34:8; 35:10; 40:9; 46:13; 51:3, 11, 16; 52:1–2, 8; 59:20; 60:14; 61:3; 62:11; 66:8).[13] It has also been observed that the hymnic portions of 40–48 closely resemble the preexilic psalms (as do the similar portions of chaps. 1–39).[14] Two other concepts worth mentioning are "wait" (8:17; 25:9; 26:8; 33:2; 40:31; 42:4; 49:23; 51:5; 59:9, 11; 60:9; 64:4) and rebellion (1:2, 20, 23, 28; 24:20; 30:1, 9; 36:5; 43:27; 44:22; 50:1, 5; 53:5, 8, 12; 57:4; 58:1; 59:12–13, 20; 63:10; 65:2; 66:24).

But beneath and around these hints of the unity of the book is a conceptual unity that gives shape and substance to what must otherwise remain somewhat ephemeral. By this I mean that, lacking a central theological concern and purpose, the presence of these repeated terms and concepts proves little. But if such a concern can be identified, then these elements become confirmatory evidence and take their places as component parts of a larger whole.

Melugin's phrase *kerygmatic structure* is a happy one for Isaiah, I believe. For without question, Isaiah is a kerygmatic book. It might be urged that all of the prophets are kerygmatic in their strong emphasis upon proclamation

10. J. J. M. Roberts, "Isaiah in Old Testament Theology," *Int* 36 (1982) 131–33; "The Holy One" with reference to God occurs a total of 35 times, 18 in 1–39 and 17 in 40–66. As noted above, 25 of these are "the Holy One of Israel," one is "the Holy One of Jacob," 3 times it occurs with a pronoun referring to Israel, and 6 times it stands alone (3 in 6:3).

11. Clements, "Unity of the Book of Isaiah," 125.

12. Rendtorff, "Komposition des Buches Jesaja," 298–99.

13. Ibid., 305–9.

14. Claus Westermann, *Isaiah 40–66* (OTL; Philadelphia: Westminster, 1969) 56, 59.

of both judgment and salvation. But Isaiah is more so. From the opening verse to the last, the book resounds with calls to hear, to attend, to deal with, to take action. The prophet is depicted as proclaiming a message that demands response. Moreover, it is a message of good news, not only, as is especially the case, in chaps. 40–55, but long before that. The message to Ahaz, though not received as such, was intended to be good news: "God is with us; we need not fear Rezin and Pekah" (7:4–10). But even before that, the announcement of salvation is clearly an integral part of the introduction (chaps. 1–5), not only in chap. 1 (vv. 16–19, 26–27), but also in 2:1–5 and 4:2–6. Moreover, that note of hope caps each succeeding segment (chaps. 6–12 end with chaps. 11–12; chaps. 13–24 are followed by chaps. 25–27; chaps. 28–35 close with chaps. 32–35, etc.). All this is brought to a climax in chaps. 60–66, which, without denying the people's inability to save themselves (63:1–65:7), nevertheless insist upon the absolute triumph of the grace of God.[15] Thus, if the message of any book has a claim to the term "kerygmatic," Isaiah's does.

But what precisely is the message of Isaiah? When we look to the first five chapters of the book, which most scholars, regardless of their convictions on authorship, believe were written to introduce the present book, two aspects are likely to catch the reader's eye. The first is the dramatic interchange between light and dark, judgment and hope. The judgment passages are almost unremittingly dark, from the bitter injunction to turn away from useless, dying humanity in 2:22, to the call for the howling winds of battle to destroy a nation so far gone as to call evil good (5:20, 26–30). Against this backdrop, the hope passages are almost unbelievably bright. They speak of a nation clean and pure, sheltering beneath a benevolent God (4:2–6), to whom all the nations will come to hear how the Creator intended them to live (2:1–5).[16] The sense of contrast between these emphases is heightened by the way in which they are alternated with each other. After chap. 1, which is largely judgmental, except for two brief rays of light (vv. 18–19, 26–27), comes hope in 2:1–5. But then we return to judgment in 2:6–4:1. This is followed by hope again (4:2–6), which gives way yet again to the judgment that closes the segment (5:1–30).

The second aspect that will impress the reader in these introductory chapters is the shocking abruptness with which these interchanges occur. There

15. As one more element in all of this, remember that the prophet's name is *yišaᶜ +yah*—'Yahweh saves'.

16. Calling the Mountain of the Lord the highest mountain of the world is a figurative way of calling him the Creator.

are no transitions whatsoever from judgment to hope, or back again—this in a book that is noted for such smooth transitions that scholars cannot agree in given cases whether the transitional statement is to be interpreted with the previous segment or with the following one.[17] Yet here there are no transitions, and we must ask why. Surely it will not do to posit a construction by mechanical means (e.g., similar words in two otherwise unrelated pieces) or by chance. This would be as if to say that one motif follows another in Beethoven's Fifth Symphony because both happen to have been written in the same key, or because the one happened to fall from a student's composition book at the moment the master was in need of another phrase. No, the abrupt juxtaposition of these kinds of ideas, whatever their ultimate source, not once, but twice, in these opening chapters, whether done by author or editor, must be seen as an indication of intent.[18] Furthermore, the inclusion of the prophet's call only after these introductory chapters must be taken into account.

What does the structure and content of these chapters say about the kerygmatic intent of the book, about the way in which the author or editor wishes us to read the book? Without question it speaks about the inescapability of divine retribution. This is clear both by the way chap. 1 concludes and by the way chap. 5 concludes the introduction. Whatever the distant future may hold, it is *through* judgment, not around it. Whatever the ultimate destiny of Israel and Judah, their immediate destiny is one of destruction.

But against this bleak backdrop stands another certainty equally as real, one whose absolute nature is not mitigated in any sense by the certainty of destruction. This certainty is the realization of the Exodus promises: God's people will be holy, as he is, experiencing his continual guidance and protection (4:2–6; cf. Exod 19:3–6; Num 9:15–18). Whatever may come upon the nation in retribution for their rebellion (chap. 1), their pride (2:6–4:1), and their corruption of moral truth (5:1–30), God's promises will not fail.

17. Some of the debated transitional passages are 1:9, 2:5, 6:1–13, 9:1[2], 17:9, 30:18, 32:5, 44:6–8, 45:23, etc.

18. While I insist that this kind of structuring is indicative of intent, I am very skeptical of hypotheses that depend on identifying elaborate structures, such as chiastic parallelism, extending over several chapters or even over the whole book. Not only do all these proposals seem to me to depend on misusing some of the data sooner or later, they also do not seem to take enough account of the way the motifs of the book appear and reappear. Thus, it is possible to create any number of these "structures," each one plausible and each one differing from the rest. An example in point is J. Goldingay's "The Arrangement of Isaiah 41–45," *VT* 29 (1979) 289–99.

But to what purpose are those promises? Was the covenant with Israel merely a fiat of divine love, one manifestation of that eternal Tao that reveals itself to other cultures in other ways? Hardly! The placement of 2:1–5 could not be more telling. The God of Israel is the *only* manifestation of the Tao, and his law was given to the Israelites so that it might be transmitted to the entire world. They cannot perform this function if they are filthy and blood-stained, but cleansing and holiness are not ends in themselves, either. Rather, they are necessary conditions if the ultimate end of the promises—worldwide acknowledgment of the God of Abraham, Isaac, and Jacob—is to be attained.[19] Furthermore, this acknowledgment is expected to result in a rule of peace and equity (see also 9:5–6[6–7], 11:3–9, 25:6–9, 42:1–4).

Thus, the opening chapters of Isaiah tell us how we are intended to read the book. We are intended to see that as sure as destruction is apart from some radical and continuing change of moral direction (1:16–20), restoration is equally sure. But restoration is for a purpose, the purpose of revealing God to the world and drawing the world to him.

Investigation of the placement and distinctive content of chap. 6 confirms this judgment. The central focus of this chapter is the revelation of God in his moral perfection and in his world-filling glory. God must be known, both in his own essential character and in his relationship to the world. But this revelation can only be destructive to sinful humanity. Thus, Isaiah's response to the experience is not that he is limited, or finite, or even mortal, but that he is unclean and so cannot exist in God's presence. This parallels the judgment passages in chaps. 1–5. Alongside the Holy One of Israel (1:4; 5:19, 24; cf. 6:3) the hubris of humanity (1:31; 2:7–8, 11, 17) that fuels our rebellions (1:2–4, 3:9) would be laughable if it were not so hideous.

It is very significant that it is his lips and the lips of his countrymen that the prophet recognizes to be unclean. What else can this signify but the sense that the glory of God demands to be declared, but cannot be, either by him

19. Controversy continues to rage over whether Isaiah is "truly" universalistic. See H. M. Orlinsky, *Studies in the Second Part of the Book of Isaiah* (VTSup 14; Leiden: Brill, 1967) 97–117. But unless conjectural emendation is resorted to and offending parts are excised, it seems to me beyond any qualification that the present book teaches that the God of Jerusalem is the sole God of the world and that the whole world must eventually come to him in submission, either voluntary or coerced. (Along with this passage, see 19:23–25, 25:6–8, 45:5–6, 66:18–19.) Whether this end is envisioned as resulting from Jewish "missionary" activity or simply as a result of God's activity on behalf of his people may be argued. But I do not think that the nature of the expected outcome can be disputed. See my chapter entitled "Israel's Mission to the Nations in the Prophets," *Through No Fault of Their Own* (ed. J. Sigountos; Grand Rapids: Baker, 1991) 85–95.

to his people, or by his people to the world, because of a fundamental uncleanness of their lives? Thus, the experience of cleansing—a gracious act on the part of God, both unbidden and undeserved—is immediately followed by the commission to speak. Cleansing is not for its own sake, but for the purpose of communication. But communication cannot take place until cleansing, a cleansing by fire (cf. 4:4), has taken place.

Thus chap. 6 is in its present place in the book to answer the questions raised by the shocking oscillations of chaps. 1–5. As the reader careens back and forth between grimmest judgment and highest hope, he or she must ask, "But how can this Israel, proud, rebellious, corrupt, become that Israel, clean, holy, displaying the truth for which all hunger?" Chapter 6 provides the answer. When the nation of unclean lips has shared the experience of the man of unclean lips, they can declare to the world the glory he has declared to them. Thus, chap. 6 is not merely the call of the prophet; it is the call of the nation.

This equation (cleansing is for declaration) emerges with special clarity again in chaps. 40–48. It is present in the intervening chapters, as will be seen below, but in more muted ways. In chaps. 40–48 Israel is in the position of Isaiah in 6:5. They are undone. Their fundamental uncleanness has delivered them over to destruction and they, like him, can see no other possible outcome than dissolution and disappearance. But completely unexpectedly, as unexpected as the seraph's words after the coal has seared Isaiah's lips, comes the announcement of forgiveness, cleansing, and commission (40:1–11).[20] The captive Judeans will be restored; far from being cast off, they are called God's chosen servants.[21] What will these servants do? In chaps. 40–48 (with the exception of 42:1–9, on which see below), they do nothing. They are strictly recipients of the unmerited grace of God. But by receiving that grace they become the vehicle whereby God will demonstrate to the world that he alone, the deity of little, defeated Jerusalem, is deity of the whole world.

The point just made needs to be emphasized, and this can be accomplished by comparison with Ezekiel 34–48. There too the message of gracious, undeserved restoration is declared. But there, except for one brief

20. The MT makes it plain that Jerusalem is the messenger of good news, not the recipient, in 40:9. Note the similarities between chap. 6 and 40:1–11. But 40:1–11 is not an independent call narrative. It assumes chap. 6 and builds on it. See Seitz, "Isaiah 1–66," 109.

21. Almost certainly the sense of "servants" in these passages is that of performers of religious service. This is the equivalent of holy priesthood in Exod 19:6. See Pss 100:2, 102:23[22], 134:1–2, 135:1–2.

though important passage (36:16–36), the stress is solely upon the return and its blessed character. Here in Isaiah the emphasis is quite different. Here the point of Ezek 36:16–36 is expanded to the entire section. Virtually all of chaps. 40–48 is given over to a discussion of what the restoration of Israel will demonstrate to the nations about God. Israel, without doing anything but receiving God's cleansing grace (40:2, 41:10, 44:1–5, 46:12–13, 48:9–11), will not only be the evidence to prove that God alone is God (41:25–29, 43:8–13, 44:6–8, 48:14–15), but also the evidence to cause the nations to come to Jerusalem in acknowledgement of him (45:14, 22–25).

The final section, chaps. 60–66, confirms this understanding of the *kerygma* of the book. Although it is not as widely agreed that this section was written as a conclusion to the book as it is that chaps. 1–5 were written as an introduction,[22] nevertheless, there is something of a concluding emphasis. The opening verses (60:1–3) make the point and set the tone. The glory of God has risen on Israel and its brightness will draw all nations to that dawning.[23] Thus, the promises of chaps. 1–5 are realized. It is sometimes urged that the picture here is not of co-religionists or converts but of captives.[24] Surely this element is present (e.g., 60:11–12, 14; 61:5; 63:6; 64:2), but it is by no means the only or even the dominant note. The light to the nations concept not only opens the segment, as just pointed out, but also closes it (66:18–19, 23). Jews will travel the world over to proclaim the glory (cf. 6:3, 40:5–6) of God with the result that the dispersed Jews will be sent home in triumph as an offering to the Lord, and all will join in worshiping him. Nor is this emphasis merely confined to the opening and closing of the section, important as that is. It also appears within the segment at 61:9, 11 and 62:2. The point of these verses is, to be sure, not that the Jews will proselytize the nations. But what they will do is entirely consistent with 2:1–5 and 43:8–13: the nations will be moved to acknowledge God's lordship and saviorhood when they see how he has redeemed and purified his people.[25]

22. The uncertainty largely stems from the failure of these chapters to summarize the themes of the preceding chapters quite as completely as one might expect in a purposefully written conclusion. Also, it seems to introduce a certain amount of new material (especially in 63:1–65:7).

23. For those who believe that this is more than empty rhetoric, the coming of Christ, in whom the glory of God dwelt bodily (John 1:14) and because of whom all the nations have come to Jerusalem, fulfills the meaning of this passage precisely.

24. So Orlinsky, *Second Part*, 36.

25. For further discussion of the issue of captives versus converts see my article, "Israel's Mission to the Nations."

In the light of the foregoing observations, a strong case can be made that the kerygmatic message of the book centers on Israel's servanthood. To be sure, this actual terminology is only prominent in chaps. 40–55. But as I have tried to show, the sense in which servanthood is used there, especially in 40–48, is precisely the same as the sense of chaps. 1–6 and 60–66. It is as the chosen are graciously redeemed from their just judgment that the world will come to acknowledge God. It is as Israel accepts its role as servant of God that this goal, elucidated at the beginning of the book, reemphasized in the middle, and reiterated at the end, could be achieved.

With this realization in mind, we can now look at the rest of the book and see to what extent other sections complement and develop this theme. In chaps. 7–39 the nations, and Israel's relation to them, is the special focus. The great question is: will Israel trust the nations to insure its future, or will it trust God? The historical sections, chaps. 7–12 and 36–39, stand at either end as mirror images of each other.

In chaps. 7–12 Israel refuses to trust God in the face of Rezin's and Pekah's threats. Instead of being a light to the nations, demonstrating to them God's trustworthiness, Israel turns for its hope to the very kingdoms of humanity it was to have led to God. As a result, Isaiah has to tell Ahaz that Assyria (whom Ahaz has trusted in place of God) will turn on him and destroy Israel. But the true test of God's trustworthiness, Isaiah then says, is that in spite of all this rebellion, God will graciously reestablish the house of David, restore his people from captivity, and establish his universal kingdom. It is when the people will have reaped the just results of their foolish choices and yet have received God's totally unmerited deliverance that they will be able to cry, "I will trust and not be afraid" (12:2). Furthermore, it is out of this deliverance that they will declare to the nations the exalted name and glorious deeds of the Holy One of Israel (12:4–6).

Chapters 36–39 move in a diametrically opposite direction. At the outset, the response is one of trust. The predicted outcome of Ahaz's choice is at hand—the Assyrian lion is clawing the door. Should Hezekiah surrender? God's answer through Isaiah is, "No, trust me" (37:6–7, 22–35). Hezekiah does trust God and the army of the mightiest nation in the world is destroyed. In place of the lack of trust in chaps. 7 and 8, here is a clear manifestation of a lesson learned and of the validity of that lesson. But whereas the lack of trust and consequent destruction in 7:1–10:4 became a basis for a proclamation of eventual salvation in 10:5–11:16, here the movement is in the opposite direction. Chapter 39 concludes with a prophecy of destruction at the hands of the Babylonians. What is happening? Two significant points need to be made. First, chaps. 38 and 39, which detail Hezekiah's mortality and fallibility, make it painfully clear that he is not the promised Messiah of 9:5–6 [6–7] and 11:1–5. The miraculous deliverance might make it appear so, but he is not. For the ultimate confirmation of the truth that God is with us (7:14), that he is trustworthy, we must look to another. Our trust is in God, not in any expression of human perfectibility.

The second point that these chapters make relates directly to what we are identifying as a dominant motif of the book. According to 39:1, the reason the Babylonian envoys visited Jerusalem was because they had heard of Hezekiah's recovery from his illness. In other words, this was the time to perform the task of 12:1–6: to declare to the world the wondrous name and the glorious deeds of God, to announce absolute and unreserved trust of him. In fact, Hezekiah failed to do so. Instead of magnifying God, he magnified himself (cf. Num 20:10–12). Trust is a way of life, not a one-time or a two-time declaration, and Hezekiah typifies the short-term trust of the nation that would eventually result in its own destruction. Thus, we may argue that both chaps. 7–12 and 36–39 are governed by the concerns we have already identified: the witness of redeemed servant Israel, both pivoting around the theme of trusting the nations or trusting God. Chapters 7–12 move from negative to positive while chaps. 36–39 move from positive to negative. In so doing each sets the stage for what is to follow.[26]

Chapters 7–12, with their promise that God will deliver from the nations, raise the question of whether he can really do this. Chapters 13–35 insist that he can and use several literary structures to make the point. Chapters 13–23 consist of oracles against the nations which assert that all nations, not only Israel, are accountable to God. When God desires to restore his people, he can be trusted to do so, for no nation can stand in his way. Chapters 24–27 insist that all history, not merely Israel's, is under the dominion of God.[27] Chapters 28–33 use the examples of contemporary history to show the folly of the alliances a craven and corrupt court is advocating and conclude with the promise that the True King who will give right counsel is coming. Finally, the entire section is concluded by chaps. 34–35, which sum up the options in graphic form: turning the world into a desert if we refuse to trust

26. Chaps. 36–39 are also a fitting conclusion to chaps. 7–39 because they confirm what Isaiah had prophesied and show that he was right when he declared that God could be trusted. For further discussion of these points see my *The Book of Isaiah, Chapters 1–39* (NICOT; Grand Rapids: Eerdmans, 1986) 627–98.

27. As noted above, it is in 25:6–8 that the redemption of all people on "this mountain" (cf. 2:2–3, 66:20) is declared. History will culminate in redemption for all who will submit.

God (chap. 34); and having God turn our desert into a garden if we will turn back to him and trust him in the end (chap. 35).

Thus we can say that, within the larger movement of the book, chaps. 7–39 establish the basis for servanthood. The basis is the sovereign grace of God, which means that humans can trust him and nothing else. Furthermore, the division also illustrates the fundamental problem that was first exposed in chaps. 1–5: the idolatrous tendency of human pride to deify human glory and accomplishment, putting our trust in what is temporal, mortal, and fallible, instead of in the transcendent Creator to whom Israel's eventual deliverance would bear witness.

Chapters 36–39, while concluding the earlier division, also point the way to what follows. This is not merely in the more superficial sense of predicting the coming exile, but on a deeper, more ideological level.[28] Again, a question is raised that falls to the next section to answer. That question is, "Who is the Deliverer?" If indeed Hezekiah is representative of his people in the short-term nature of his trust, who will be the ideal king of chaps. 9 and 11? If Hezekiah is not Immanuel, then who is?

Furthermore, these chapters raise another question that calls for an answer in this book. Isaiah has insisted in the most absolute of terms that this God is God of the whole world, able to deliver any who trust in him from any threat. This had certainly seemed true in the case of Assyria. But now the prophet says that God will not deliver Jerusalem from Babylon. Does this not call into question the whole theme of the book? How can the people of God testify to the world about the complete trustworthiness and absolute incomparability of Yahweh of Jerusalem if they are captives in Babylon? As chaps. 1–39 are now structured, it is impossible for chap. 39 to be the conclusion of the book. It would not be a conclusion, but a negation of all that the book claimed.

In fact, chaps. 40–66 are a necessary part of the message that was introduced in chaps. 1–6. They show that the new situation after 586 B.C.E. will not negate what was said in chaps. 7–39. God is so far from being overcome by the new historical situation that he can use the new situation to do something previously unheard of—deliver a captive people from exile. The new situation will provide an even better platform for demonstrating to the nations that the God worshiped on Mt. Zion is indeed their God, the only God. Furthermore, it is in this context that the completely unmerited grace of God can provide motivation for service. The stunning word that the Babylonian

28. See Ackroyd, "Interpretation of the Babylonian Exile," for additional reflection on this topic.

captivity did not mean abandonment by God was exactly what was needed to move the Judeans to put into actual practice the trust that had been so clearly taught in chaps. 7–39.

But what about the deliverer? If not Hezekiah, then who? Is Cyrus the promised Messiah? Beyond this, chaps. 40–48 raise their own question. How can sinful Israel become servant Israel? How can the nation of unclean lips be made the bearer of God's truth? Is it merely the fires of judgment that will take care of the problem? Or is something more at stake? Here we must consider the role of the "suffering servant." Undoubtedly, this is the single most controversial issue in the book. Literally hundreds of books and articles have been written on the topic in the last century alone. Thus, it is impossible even to offer a complete review of the alternatives here, much less solve the problem. We can only ask readers to consider again the evidence that two different servants are discussed between 41:8 and 54:17. The identity of the one servant is quite unmistakable: it is the nation of Israel. And all those instances where the nation is unquestionably referred to have the fearful servant merely being encouraged with promises of the benefits of servanthood.

But there are other references in which the identity of the servant is not obvious, and in these (42:1–9, 49:1–12, 50:4–11, 52:13–53:12) the servant's vocation is to bring justice and salvation to the earth (42:1–4, 49:6), light to the nations (42:6, 49:6, 50:10–11), and deliverance to the people, Jacob (42:6, 49:5–6, 53:4–9). The dominant characteristics of this servant are humility, uncertainty, misunderstanding, and pain (42:2; 49:4, 7; 50:4–6; 53:1–9). All of this is so enigmatic that Duhm proposed that these so-called "Servant Songs" were not a part of the original chaps. 40–55.[29] While this judgment has largely held sway ever since, there has been no unanimity about the origin of the songs or their function, either in their original format or after having been edited into the present structure.[30] The three figures most often identified as this "suffering servant"—the nation, Cyrus, and the prophet himself—all have one or more problems in the above descriptions that must be explained away.

The point that I would like to make here is that an examination of the material in chaps. 49–55, where three of these four passages occur, shows a major emphasis on the means and the fact of deliverance (note the repetition

29. B. Duhm, *Das Buch Jesaia* (Göttingen: Vandenhoeck & Ruprecht, 1892) 311–13.

30. James Muilenburg ("Isaiah, Chapters 40–66," *IB* [Nashville: Abingdon, 1956] 5.406–8) argued that the "Servant Songs" were an integral part of chaps. 40–55. Recently T. N. D. Mettinger (*A Farewell to the Servant Songs: A Critical Examination of an Exegetical Axiom* [Lund: Gleerup, 1983]) has insisted on the same conclusion.

of "the arm of the Lord": 51:5, 9; 52:10; 53:1; cf. also 59:1). Gone are the disputations with the gods in which the possibility of deliverance from Babylon is established. Here the issue revolves around Israel's sin and God's willingness to deliver in spite of that previous condition. Two different atmospheres can be identified. In chaps. 49–52, deliverance is being anticipated and Jerusalem is being encouraged to believe it can happen. In chaps. 54–55, there is a lyrical call to participate in a deliverance proleptically seen as having occurred. It can hardly be accidental that the segment that falls between these two is 52:13–53:12. What all of this indicates is that whoever this servant is, he is equated with the means by which Israel's servanthood is made possible. In chaps. 40–48, the means is Cyrus, except in 42:1–9, where the servant is described in terms like those ascribed to the Messiah in chap. 11. The servant described in chaps. 49–53 does not resemble Cyrus in any degree. This suggests that the deliverance the Israelites require is more than simply from Babylonian captivity. That the problem is Israel's sin is intimated in 50:1 and 51:1–3, 7. This is confirmed by the repeated references to suffering for sin, iniquity, and transgression in 53:5–12.

In sum, I would argue that chaps. 49–55 deal with the deliverance from captivity to the nations and from what prompted that captivity, as was first predicted in 4:2–6 and followed up on in 11:10–16. Israel's witness to the nations depended on the evidence of God's power and his faithfulness. The identity of Cyrus is perfectly clear, but the identity of the other deliverer is almost purposely enigmatic. Nevertheless, the function of the person seems clear. He offers himself in order to deliver from that which Cyrus cannot. It seems a telling comment that chap. 55, just prior to its mention of being a witness to the peoples and calling the nations together because of God's glory given to them (vv. 4–5) refers to the everlasting covenant with David. Is this an identification of the suffering servant with the Davidic Messiah? So it would seem. Thus chaps. 49–55 tell us that the ultimate means of Israel's servanthood is the self-giving of the servant who is the ideal Israel (49:3).

The section of the book remaining to be discussed is chaps. 56–59. Here we are reminded again that deliverance from Babylonian captivity does not automatically constitute one a servant of God. Unless there has also been a deliverance from sin to righteousness, from transgression to faithfulness, one is no better than a foreigner or a eunuch. In fact, foreigners and eunuchs can be very effective servants of God, if they will live in ways that are consistent with God's character (56:3–8). Birthright and physical characteristics no longer define acceptability. Behavior is now the only criterion (57:3–4, 11–13). Thus, there is here an indication that the outreach to the nations that was forecast in 2:1–5 is already at work in the community. The segment closes with the admission by the prophet on behalf of the people that they are unable to do right or to bring justice in and of themselves (59:9–15a). Unless God delivers them by himself and imparts his spirit to them, they will be unable to speak the message of judgment and deliverance (59:15b–21).

I have argued that the single most dominating theme of the present book of Isaiah, the one that gives shape to the message of the book and thus to the book itself, is that of servanthood. But it is a particular approach to servanthood. Israel is called to be the means whereby the understanding of God that it has received—that the God of Jerusalem is the sole Lord of History, the only Judge and only Savior—should become known to the whole world. This is only possible by means of an accurate knowledge of God and a life that is an accurate reflection of his character. Chapters 1–6 lay down these basic ideas. Chapters 7–39 reveal to the servants the essential trustworthiness of God and show that there is nothing and no one else who is worthy of such trust. They also reinforce the ideas of God's absolute sovereignty and his utter righteousness. The glory of humanity, as seen in the great nations of the earth, is as nothing in comparison to the Lord's. If Israel is to fulfill its function of servanthood, learning the lesson of God's trustworthiness is essential.

Chapters 40–48 demonstrate God's election of the Israelites and explain how their deliverance from political oppression will be the evidence of God's uniqueness. These evidences of undeserved love will provide the motivation for servanthood. Chapters 49–55 address the problem of the means of servanthood. There is a deeper obstruction to servanthood than bondage or oppression. What shall be done about the sin that put them into bondage in the first place? Here it is the servant who becomes the Arm of the Lord to set them free.

It might be expected that Isaiah's message is completed with the great hymn of salvation in chap. 55. But it is precisely because of the nature of his message that the book cannot end there. The Jews must not be permitted to believe that their servanthood is carried out merely because they have experienced the hand of salvation from the bondage of the past. Their mission to the nations will fail if there are no clear evidences of God's unique character in the changed lives of his servants. Thus, one of the recurring themes of chaps. 56–66 is the inability of humans to live the life of God, but the divine ability to do in them what they cannot do in themselves. God will make of them a light to the nations. If chaps. 49–55 deal with the work of God *for* his servants, these chapters focus upon his work *in* his servants, all to the end that, because of his glory (6:3; 35:2; 60:1, 9, 19; 66:18–19) shining in them, the whole world might come to recognize God as the only God (60:3, 60:19).

The book of Isaiah, in a way almost unparalleled in any other biblical book, reveals a complete picture of God: sovereignty, creativity, purposefulness, trustworthiness, faithfulness, justice, grace, holiness, glory, and patience. Surely the book's purpose is to declare God's uniqueness and to call people in every age to experience his deliverance and to share in the task of demonstrating his uniqueness to the watching world.

The Cohesive Issue of mišpāṭ in Job

Carl Schultz

A key, if not the key, to understanding the purpose and arrangement of the book of Job is the concept of divine justice.[1] The legal pattern of Job is critical to the understanding of its message. The primary Hebrew word employed by the writer(s) to denote justice is *mišpāṭ*.[2] While it is common to all the participants except Zophar,[3] it is used with a variety of nuances that help to document the development of the book's ideas about God's involvement with Job's sufferings and the shifting of Job's own attitude toward his suffering.

When the various components of this book are analyzed it becomes quite clear that the issue of this book is the suffering of righteous Job. The critical word here is *righteous*. The issue is not simply suffering, but suffering that is non-retributory. While deserved suffering presents a problem, it is entirely different from the suffering under consideration in this book. In fact, this is the very reason why the comforters are at least ineffective and at most offensive in their presentations. They have chosen to eliminate the critical word *righteous* in their treatment of Job, and thus their retributory explanation is inappropriate and is unequivocally rejected.

When the word *non-retributory* is appropriately emphasized, the centrality of divine justice in this book becomes more apparent. There must be some reconciliation between divine justice and this undeserved suffering. While, as noted above, the comforters deny any tension here, Job is acutely aware of it and seeks an answer. It is to this answer that the book moves.

1. Sylvia H. Scholnick, "The Meaning of *Mišpāṭ* in the Book of Job," *JBL* (1982) 521–29.

2. Other roots expressing a nuance of justice that are used in Job are: *ṣdq*, 19 times; *yšr*, 7 times; *tmm*, 16 times.

3. Eliphaz in 22:4; Bildad in 8:3; Job in 9:19, 32; 13:18; 14:3; 19:7; 23:4; 27:2; 31:13; Elihu in 32:9; 34:4, 5, 6, 12, 17, 23; 35:2; 36:6, 17; 37:23; Yahweh in 40:8.

While the Prologue indicates that Job is being tested and thus focuses on his suffering and reaction, the Dialogue shows that in reality it is God who is on trial, and it zeroes in on his nature and his relationship to the world.[4] Ultimately it is not Job's integrity that is being tested, but God's integrity. Can God indeed be said to exercise *mišpāṭ*? God's reputation is more at stake in this book than Job's, but they are so interwoven that they cannot essentially be separated.

Thus, even though some have denied it,[5] there is an effort in this book to arrive at a theodicy,[6] that is, a vindication of the justice of God. This is not to deny the importance of the issue of disinterested religion[7] or to minimize the significance of the personal revelatory encounter that Job experienced at the end of the book.[8] These elements are crucial and critical but not comprehensive in themselves. Since the writer poses and tolerates the question of theodicy, it is only reasonable to expect him to move to an answer. As Tsevat observes: "The Book of Job without an answer to its problem would constitute a literary torso, an anthology of verbalized doubts; it would betray an utter lack of appreciation of the controlling conceptions which are everywhere in evidence in the work. . . ."[9]

Not only does the idea of divine justice enable us to understand the purpose of this book, but it also casts considerable light upon the complex arrangement of this book. Scholars in general question the unity of Job, seeing it as the product of several stages of development. The poetic exchanges between Job and the three comforters (chaps. 4–31) are seen as an addition to the original prose story about Job. The Elihu pericope (chaps. 32–37) is considered not only late, but also inferior and extraneous. The three major poems on wisdom (28:1–28), on Behemoth (40:15–24), and on Leviathan (41:1–

4. David N. Freedman, "Is It Possible to Understand the Book of Job?" *Bible Review* 4/2 (April, 1988) 26–33, 44.

5. H. H. Rowley, *Job* (NCB; Grand Rapids, Mich.: Eerdmans, 1980) 19. Cf. Samuel Terrien, *Job, Poet of Existence* (London: Nelson, 1957) 21.

6. The English word *theodicy* comes from two Greek words: *theos* ('God') and *dikē* ('justice').

7. Terrien argues that the essential and primary question of Job is not theodicy, but true worship; Samuel Terrien, *Job* in *IB* (New York: Abingdon, 1954) 3.913–14.

8. Cf. George Fohrer, *Introduction to the Old Testament* (New York: Abingdon, 1965) 334. Fohrer contends that the issue is not an explanation for undeserved sufferings but rather the question of *how* a sufferer should conduct himself. This interpretation has appeal and may be a secondary theme, but the whole book clearly struggles with the "why" of undeserved suffering.

9. Matitiahu Tsevat, *The Meaning of the Book of Job* (New York: KTAV, 1980) 80.

34) are considered late and only loosely attached. The Yahweh speeches (chaps. 38–41) are seen by some as a late addition that obscures the meaning of the book.[10]

While the development of the book is not crucial to this paper, the arrangement of the book is. Granted that there have been several stages of development, the final arrangement as we now have it is not the product of chance or confusion. This is not to deny the problems associated with structure or to dismiss consideration of them. Rather, it is to argue that in its present form, the book reflects a scheme and builds to a climax. This paper seeks to show that the issue of divine justice is a cohesive factor and that, by noting it throughout the succeeding sections of the book, a plan and pattern will emerge.

The Prologue: Divine Justice Unquestioned

While the Hebrew word *mišpāṭ* is not found in this section, the issue of divine justice is raised. Though the first two chapters present Job as just,[11] they make no such claim for God. In fact, the details of God's dealings with *śāṭān*, his willingness to accede to Job's suffering, and his inclination to protect his own interests while seemingly reducing Job to an expendable pawn, raise serious questions about divine justice. Job, necessarily oblivious of these details, seems to assume that God is just in all that he does.[12] This seems to be the intent of his well-known utterances in these chapters: "The Lord gave and the Lord has taken away" (1:21) and "Shall we receive good at the hand of God and shall we not receive evil?" (2:10).

Even more important in this narrative section are the significant points that the writer establishes about God, the world, and Job. These are foundational and critical to the subsequent consideration of God's justice in the book.

10. For a treatment of the stages in the development of this book, see Rowley, *Job*, 8–18.

11. As will be noted shortly, Job is said to be *yšr* and *tm*. In these chapters, Job appears in a better light than God.

12. Job's assessment of God's activity in the Prologue may not have a judicial thrust as much as it has a sovereign one. The emphasis may not be so much forensic as it is executive. As Scholnick shows, God seems to emphasize this executive dimension in his speeches, but if this is the case, the book essentially begins where it ends and this negates the need for the lengthy poetic section ("Meaning of *mišpāṭ*," 521).

God Is Presented as Sovereign

In the opening chapters God presides over the nameless angels[13] who "present themselves," that is, literally 'stand over', as servants stand before the seated master.[14] Obviously, God is not one of them but is clearly distinct from and over the angels. Though not called a son of God, *śāṭān* is among them. He challenges the disinterest of Job's religion but cannot take any action until authorized by God. It is God who allows Job to suffer. This is clear to the reader, but not to Job, for obvious reasons. Nowhere other than here in the Prologue is *śāṭān* referred to in the book. When Job speaks of his suffering he invariably assigns it to God.

The above observations are critical to the question of divine justice. The absence of other gods (polytheism) and of an evil being equal to God (dualism) immediately eliminates these as possible explanations for Job's sufferings. The exclusivity of Yahweh results here as elsewhere in the Hebrew Bible in his being the effective force in all matters.

Since the singularity of God should have meant coherence and consistency of purpose, issues arose in monotheism that would not have been found in polytheism. As Gottwald observes:

> In the ancient Near East, various aspects of power, justice, and mercy can be exhibited in one or another deity, emphasizing now this or now that attribute or activity and even uniting them momentarily in one deity in formal analogy with Yahweh, without necessarily bringing to the fore the question of how the sum total of divine manifestations are to be understood. In Israel, however, the fact that these manifestations exhibit the attributes and purposes of a single god pushes the question of the coherence of what is revealed farther into the foreground of communal consciousness. On the one hand, this means a heightened sense within the Israelite society of being confronted by a consistently purposing and revealing god; and on the other hand it means that serious problems of theological comprehension and of communal praxis and self-understanding are provoked in Israel when there is a prolonged absence of divine manifestations where they are expected, or when natural and historic-social developments unexpectedly contradict the understood purposes and attributes of deity. This opens the road to that consuming passion for theodicy.[15]

13. Even the word *śāṭān* here is probably more a designation than a name. His role or function is that of an accuser.

14. Rowley, *Job*, 31. Cf. Marvin Pope, *Job* (AB 15; Garden City, N.Y.: Doubleday, 1973) 9. Pope suggests that the idea here is of angels positioning themselves as courtiers before a king.

15. Normal K. Gottwald, *The Tribes of Yahweh* (Maryknoll: Orbis, 1979) 687. It needs to be noted that while the site of this book and the homes of the participants are not located in Israel, the writer(s) are reflecting an Israelite perspective. While the dating of Job

God Is Seen as Active in the World

Not only does God know what is happening on earth (1:8), he is keenly interested, taking pleasure in Job's commitment. In fact, it is this awareness and satisfaction that leads to the wager.

Throughout the poetic dialogue, Job is aware of the divine activity. He states that God has zeroed in on him, creating his suffering. Nowhere is this better observed than in 7:17–18, where Job expresses a parody of Ps 8:4. The psalmist is honored by God's attention; Job is distressed by it. Job argues that God makes too much of man, devoting too much attention to him.

The fact that God permits *śāṭān* to function in the world also reflects his involvement with the world. Clearly, in the mind of the writer(s) God has not absented himself, he has not abdicated. Having created the world and being responsible for its management, he takes the world seriously. While he has a responsibility to the world of nature and animals, his primary concern is man.[16] His relationship is not so much with the land as it is with man.[17]

The emphasis here in Job as in other wisdom literature is upon this world, the world of the here and now, the world of the living. This is where the struggle is and this is where the resolution will be realized. No appeal is made to an afterlife, hence the inclusion of the epilogue where the sufferings of Job are relieved and his fortune and family restored.

The above observations relative to God's involvement with the world are critical to the question of divine justice. There is no tendency in Job toward deism. In contrast to Psalm 14, where the fool does not sense any need to reckon with God and where God for all practical purposes does not matter, the book of Job clearly reflects an active God who is responsible for the events that happen. This involvement intensifies the issue of divine justice.

Job Is Presented as Righteous

While space does not permit a detailed consideration of Job's righteousness, the fact of it is quite apparent. Even a casual reading of the text will

---

is difficult, it probably was written during the time of the monarchy when, as Gottwald observes, the coherence of the divine manifestation was a problem. It was perhaps this climate that gave rise to this book.

16. In the Yahweh speeches it is noted that the Lord is creator of the earth (38:4–7), of the sea (38:8–11), and of time (38:12–15). He is the master of land and sky (38:16–38) and the protector of wild animals (38:39–39:30).

17. Gottwald, *Tribes of Yahweh*, 688. Never is God called the "God of Canaan" or "God of the land of Israel" or "God of the land of Judah" or the "God of Shechem" (or any other city).

show it. His goodness is described in universal terms. He was blameless ('complete') and upright ('straight'). These two words used together indicate thorough rectitude.[18] The third quality ('feared God') suggests that Job was religious, devout. The final quality ('shunned evil') indicates a deliberate rejection of evil and thus means 'moral'.

So critical is Job's righteousness that the writer presents it in the opening verse of the book, then has God attest to it (1:8; 2:3), and also the wife of Job (2:9). Even *śātān* does not challenge it. The significance of this has already been noted. If Job can be shown to deserve his sufferings, as his friends insist, the book loses its meaning and purpose. In the words of Andersen: "The book of Job loses its point if the righteousness of Job is not taken as genuine."[19]

The assessment of Job's character is critical to the question of divine justice. It is Job's apparent innocent suffering that raises the question of divine justice.

The Presentation of the Comforters: Divine Justice Sustained

Eliphaz, Bildad, and Zophar, well steeped in conventional theology,[20] insist that God has given Job exactly what he deserves. When they use *mišpāṭ*, they clearly have in mind moral recompense. They explain Job's sufferings by a cause and effect relationship, beginning with the effect, from which they deduce the cause. To them the issue is not God's integrity, but Job's sins. Suffering does not happen unless sin has been committed. Job's extreme suffering indicates commensurate sin on his part.

Neither Job nor his friends were aware of the events described in the Prologue. While insisting on his righteousness, Job did not know that God considered him righteous. The comforters, on the other hand, deny Job's righteousness, also not knowing that God reckoned Job righteous. The wager between God and *śātān* had to be kept from Job in particular for the proposed test to be valid. Given the assessment of Job's character found in the Prologue, the comforters with their traditional theology, are at best straw

18. Cf. Ps 25:21, 37:37; Prov 29:10.

19. Francis I. Andersen, *Job* (TynOT; Downers Grove, Ill.: InterVarsity, 1976) 66.

20. The deuteronomic idea of history was that the nation always got what it deserved (Deuteronomy 28). In Judges the nation is subjugated or delivered, depending upon its relationship to the Lord. This collective idea is individualized by Job's friends.

men. Their ideas are *de facto* dismissed before they are given, but since they represent the orthodox view on suffering, they are granted opportunity to speak.

The causal relationship enables the comforters to assume Job's guilt from his suffering. In the words of Eliphaz: "Think now, who that was innocent ever perished? Or where were the upright cut off? As I have seen, those who plow iniquity and sow trouble reap the same" (4:7–8). Job's sufferings are clear evidence that he is guilty of sin, even as his children's deaths are proof of their sin (8:4).

While the comforters are initially content to sustain Job's guilt by virtue of his suffering, they are forced finally to catalog his sins. While Job at one time probably shared a common theological position with his friends, his recent experiences caused him to reassess his theology. As a result, the friends' contention of his guilt based upon his suffering is not convincing to Job. This leads to the listing of Job's sins by Eliphaz (22:6–9).

The sins listed are those most likely associated with the rich and powerful and, hence, allegedly practiced by Job during his earlier, successful years. He is accused primarily of social sins: taking away the garments of the needy for their inability to pay their mortgage (22:6), withholding water from the weary and food from the hungry (22:7), and oppressing the widow and orphan (22:9).

Not only are these charges denied by the writer, who labels Job "upright," but they will also be refuted by Job himself (31:16, 17, 19). Job's innocence must be maintained if the purpose of the book is to be realized, but in the process, the issue of divine justice is intensified.

The Protestation of Job: God's Justice Questioned and Challenged

As mentioned above, Job is oblivious of God's positive assessment of his character. While his inherited theology suggests guilt, his empirical information argues otherwise. He never once questions the source of his suffering. He believes that God is punishing him, but without reason. Thus Job charges God with injustice, with reaching a verdict of guilty without allowing him to speak on his own behalf.[21] Thus Job, desirous of defending himself, uses *mišpāṭ* in the sense of 'litigation' and 'case', rather than 'moral recompense', as employed by the comforters.

21. Andersen's claim that Job believes that God's justice is simply delayed, but not denied, is not very convincing (*Job*, 191).

Job's challenge and appeal to God for clarification of the nature of divine justice is not novel. Abraham, too, was concerned with divine justice, asking relative to the destruction of Sodom and Gomorrah: "Wilt thou indeed destroy the righteous with the wicked? . . . Far be it from thee to do such a thing, to slay the righteous with the wicked! Far be it from thee! Shall not the judge of all the earth do right?" (Gen 18:23, 25). Abimelech, following his abortive relationship with Sarah, cried out: "Lord, wilt thou slay an innocent people? . . . in the integrity of my heart and the innocence of my hands have I done this" (Gen 20:4, 5). The judgment ("you are a dead man") seemed unjust to Abimelech, who had been misled by Abraham. Habakkuk struggled with Babylon's success, questioning: "Thou who art of purer eyes than to behold evil and canst not look on wrong, why dost thou look on faithless men, and art silent when the wicked swallows up the man more righteous than he?" (1:13). He concluded, "The law is slacked and justice never goes forth. For the wicked surround the righteous, so justice goes forth perverted" (1:4).

Desiring justice, Job wants to enter into litigation with God, but senses the impossibility of this, because God is "not a man" as he is.[22] Given his background, his functioning in the judicial system of his community (15:7, 29:12, 31:21), it is not surprising that he would consider litigation. While at first this seems impossible, his continued suffering and the repetitious charges of his friends necessitate such a move. He finally identifies God as his opponent (13:3) and states that he has prepared his *mišpāṭ*—his case (13:18).[23]

God's response to Job's challenge is not immediate. No litigation results, even though he has pressed charges against God (19:7). In particular, he has charged God with *ḥāmās*, a technical word for wrongdoing. In Prov 4:17 this word refers to that which has been secured by illegal means. Thus Job may be charging God with unlawful seizure of his property.[24] This legal procedure would cast Job in the role of plaintiff and God in the role of defendant.

So far in our consideration of Job's pursuit for divine justice, our legal metaphor has seen Job as the plaintiff and God as the defendant. This is indeed the interpretation followed by many scholars.[25] But, as Dick cautions, we need to

22. Job 9:32. Here the idiom *bôʾ bĕmišpāṭ* is used. While it literally means 'go to the place of judgment', it is better translated 'enter litigation' here. A similar meaning is found in Ps 143:2, where the possibility of appearing before God is accepted; Scholnick, "Meaning of *mišpāṭ*," 524.

23. Here the word *mišpāṭ* means 'case'. A similar use can be found in 23:4 ("I would lay my case before him"), in Num 27:5 ("Moses brought their [Daughters of Zelophehad] case before the Lord"), and in 2 Sam 15:4 ("Every man with a suit or case might come to me").

24. Scholnick, "Meaning of *mišpāṭ*," 525.

25. Cf. B. Gemser, "The *Rib* or Controversy-Pattern in Hebrew Mentality," *Wisdom in Israel and in the Ancient Near East* (VTSup 3; Leiden: Brill, 1955) 135.

be careful "in sharply delineating the roles of plaintiff and defendant, for ancient documents are often unclear in distinguishing these relationships, and a too rigid imposition of this modern distinction might be anachronistic."[26]

Further complicating the issue is the fact that God is involved and alternately assumes different roles. This can be demonstrated by Job's desire for an umpire (9:33),[27] a witness,[28] and a vindicator (19:25).[29] God seems to be designated by all these terms. Even though Job knows that God is also the accuser, the judge, and the executioner, he nevertheless appeals to God and thus is appealing from God to God.[30]

Granted these difficulties, Dick is nevertheless correct in seeing Job also cast in the role of defendant.[31] Job's speeches indicate that he believes God has developed a case against and found him guilty. He has already been judged in some previous unaccountable and unannounced juridical proceeding. There is simply no other way for him to account for his losses than to recognize them as punishment.

The comforters also understandably see Job in the role of the defendant. They too believe that Job has already been judged and found guilty. While Job struggles with this verdict, the comforters are convinced that justice has been done (8:3). As has already been noted, Eliphaz in his concluding speech reminds Job of this divine litigation (22:3) and defends the verdict by itemizing Job's sins that led to this judgment (22:5–9).

Convinced of his innocence, Job demands a writ of particulars, suggesting that God has indicated proceedings against him. In 13:23 Job requests that the nature and number of charges against him be specified.[32] He is convinced

26. Michael Brennan Dick, "The Legal Metaphor in Job 31," *CBQ* (1979) 37–50.

27. The term *umpire* is seen by some as a 'negotiator' or 'reconciler' who brings quarreling people together, one who would "lay his hand upon . . . both" as a common friend (Andersen, *Job*, 151). However, *môkîaḥ* is better rendered 'arbiter' (KJV has archaic 'daysman'). When used with *bîn*, as in Gen 31:37 (cf. Job 16:21), *môkîaḥ* is a legal term and seems to refer to a judge. The location of the function of the *môkîaḥ* "in the gate" demonstrates that its domain is in *jus civile.*

28. Here God is clearly referred to, because shed blood cries out to him (Gen 4:10).

29. While the term *gôʾēl* designates the 'redeemer' and hence one who does not necessarily function within the court setting, when used of God it can suggest a defender of justice (Prov 23:10–11). Further, in the Job passage under discussion, the *gôʾēl* is said to 'stand' (*qûm*), suggesting a court setting (cf. Ps 1:5) where the witness stands to testify.

30. This appeal from God to God may reflect a struggle between two differing conceptions of God in Job's mind (Rowley, *Job*, 121).

31. Dick, "Legal Metaphor," 38.

32. The desire for precision can be seen in Job's use of three words for sin: *ʾāwôn*, derived from the verb 'to err'; *ḥaṭāʾât*, a noun related to the verb meaning 'to miss the mark'; and *pešaʿ*, from the verb meaning 'to rebel'.

that he is not guilty of any crime (*ḥāmās*, 16:7). But there is no response from the Lord (30:20).

The silence of the Lord drives Job to extreme action—the use of the oath of clearance. In the world of the Old Testament, this oath was taken by the accused, but was only invoked after all rational means of proof had been exhausted.[33] The use of nonrational proof brought the deity into the process, which is precisely what Job wanted.[34]

The very form of the oath of clearance indicates its terribleness: "If I did or shall do this, or if I did not or shall not do this, then may God punish me." Ordinarily ellipsis occurs, that is, the apodosis ("then may God punish me") is omitted. The reason for this is quite apparent: there was always the possibility of an unintentional factual inaccuracy. An inaccuracy could set in motion the mechanism of punishment for perjury that the oath envisages. Caution truncated the oath, but Job was so desperate that he threw caution to the wind and frequently included the apodosis (31:8, 10, 22, 40).

In this same chapter, with these oaths of clearance, Job registers his formal request for a writ of particulars: "Oh, that I had one to hear me! Here is my signature! Let the almighty answer me! Oh that I had the indictment written by my adversary" (31:35)! Dick sees this request as a legal appeal of a defendant for a formal hearing through the assemblage of a tripartite judicial board. The "one to hear" Dick identifies as the judge, the "adversary" as God, thus casting Job as the defendant.[35] The role of the judge here is to force the adversary to produce written charges.[36] Job wants to know what his crime is. He believes that he will be able to prove his innocence (31:36–37).

In his desperation, Job not only used the oath of clearance, but he also employed the institution of the hue and cry (*vox oppressorum*, Ps 30:9–10).

33. There is no evidence in the Old Testament that a witness ever took an oath; Hans Jochen Boecker, *Law and the Administration of Justice in the Old Testament and the Ancient Near East* (Minneapolis: Augsburg, 1980) 35.

34. Given the nonrational character of the oath of clearance, it is not surprising to note that its provenance was the cult rather than the local court (Num 5:12–28). This does not mean that the trial became exclusively a cultic process. Rather, it is likely that the priests functioned in conjunction with the local court.

35. Dick, "Legal Metaphor," 48–49. Blank also argues that the oaths of clearance in this chapter can be seen as a part of Job's formal petition; S. H. Blank, "An Effective Literary Device in Job XXXI," *JJS* (1951) 105–7.

36. In Hebrew trials the witnesses and the judge were not necessarily different people. This was also true of the plaintiff and judge. The accuser could function as judge and pronounce sentence on others (cf. Jeremiah 26). Boecker, *Law and the Administration of Justice*, 34–35.

This was a basic cry for justice and assistance by the dispossessed and oppressed. Anyone hearing such a cry was obligated to respond. Job made such a cry, obviously wanting a divine response: "O earth, cover not my blood, and let my cry find no resting place" (16:18). Job must have had in mind the phrase in Gen 4:10: "The voice of your brother's blood is crying to me from the ground."

All of Job's legal efforts indicate the centrality of divine justice in this book.

The Adjudication of Elihu: Divine Justice Qualified

The role of Elihu in this book is difficult. He appears abruptly, makes his presentation, with no reply from Job, and then just as abruptly disappears. No reference is made to him in the Prologue or Epilogue. His speeches (chaps. 32–37) could be removed from the book without being missed. Following Job's employment of the oath of clearance, as noted above, one would have expected the response of Yahweh to follow immediately. The source and purpose of these chapters are therefore understandably debated.

Perhaps Elihu should not be cast in the role of a protagonist, but rather in the role of adjudicator.[37] He begins with his assessment of the comforters' arguments—"there was none that confuted Job" (32:12)—and subsequently says of Job: "Job speaks without knowledge, his words are without insight" (35:35). If Elihu is seen as the human adjudicator, then Yahweh could be viewed as the divine adjudicator. Note his assessment of the dialogue: "You (comforters) have not spoken of me what is right, as my servant Job has" (42:7).

Elihu shows great awareness of the previous speeches. In contrast to the other participants, who only occasionally refer to previously spoken words, Elihu freely quotes from and alludes to the earlier speeches.[38] His remarks can be seen as a commentary on the earlier presentations.

More significantly for this paper, Elihu seems to play a pivotal role in the understanding of divine justice. He will go beyond the comforters and Job in his treatment of divine justice but will fall short of Yahweh's explanation. His purpose is to serve as a transition between the traditional explanation of divine justice and the authentic one given by Yahweh himself.

37. Andersen, *Job*, 51.

38. D. N. Freedman, "The Elihu Speeches in the Book of Job," *HTR* (1968) 51–59.

As Scholnick observes, Elihu will use the word *mišpāṭ* as a judicial term in three different ways: like Job, as 'litigation' (32:9) and 'case' (34:4–6; 35:2), and like the comforters, as 'moral recompense' (34:12).[39] He will assess Job's case, noting the key arguments that Job has advanced (33:9–11, 34:5–6, 35:2).

He notes Job's forensic language[40] but insists that God cannot be subject to litigation (34:23). Rather, God administers justice through a system of moral retribution. This is done without warning and investigation (34:24). God simply does not hold public sessions of judgment, as Job would have liked (24:1).

Elihu concludes his speeches with a picture of God as sovereign ruler of nature (36:24–37:24). Here he senses that God is not simply judge, but also sovereign: "The Almighty—we cannot find him; he is great in power and justice" (37:23). He associates *mišpāṭ* with the idea of power (*kōaḥ*). This is the first time this happens in the book.[41] God must not be simply viewed as a judge, but must also be seen as sovereign king. *Mišpāṭ* is not simply jurisprudence; it is also sovereignty. Divine justice cannot be treated apart from divine sovereignty.

The Adjudication of Yahweh: Divine Justice Explained

The issue of divine justice is a critical issue in the Yahweh speeches at the end of the book. Failure to recognize this has resulted in charges that these chapters are at best irrelevant to the suffering of Job and to the book itself. To be sure, these chapters do not provide Job with the bill of particulars that he had demanded. Nor do they provide him opportunity to question Yahweh. Earlier Job had requested: "Then call, and I will answer; or let me speak and do thou reply to me" (13:22). Such a choice was not available to him. Yahweh did all the questioning.

The legal nature of this divine encounter is stressed at the beginning of both speeches: "Gird up your loins like a man, I will question you, and you shall declare to me" (38:3, 40:7). Even as Jeremiah had been instructed to gird up his loins (Jer 1:17) in preparation for a legal encounter with Israel, so now Job is told to ready himself for a legal encounter with Yahweh. "To gird

39. Scholnick, "Meaning of *mišpāṭ*," 525.

40. He uses the idiom *hlk bammišpāṭ* (34:23), which is similar to the one employed by Job, *bwʾ bammišpāṭ* (9:32, 14:3).

41. Scholnick, "Meaning of *mišpāṭ*," 526.

up the loins" may be an idiom for the belt-wrestling ordeal, which was used at Nuzi for settlement of a case where there was conflicting testimony.[42]

In these speeches Yahweh refers to *mišpāṭ* only once (40:8), but the concept of divine justice is clearly central to these speeches. This has been the issue of the book and here in its culmination it does not seem likely that it would be ignored. What then does Yahweh say about divine justice? Three positions, not radically different from one another, will be considered.

He Denies Justice[43]

Tsevat claims that the speeches of Yahweh demonstrate that "no retribution is provided for in the blueprint of the world, nor does it exist anywhere in it. None is planned for in the nonhuman world. Divine justice is not an element of reality. It is a figment existing only in the misguided philosophy with which you have been inculcated. The world in which you and the friends are spun is a dream. Wake up, Job!"[44]

Tsevat reasons that once the principle of *quid pro quo* is rejected, once the idea of the possibility of justice is given up, the issue of injustice disappears, because injustice can only exist when justice is possible.[45]

Tsevat summarizes his position by imagining an equilateral triangle at the vertexes of which we have G (God), J (Job), and R (Retribution). The book of Job tells us that we cannot maintain these ideas simultaneously. In fact, the purpose of the book is to show that from necessity one of the three will have to be eliminated.[46]

The friends maintain G and R, while eliminating J. Job is inclined to give up G while keeping J and R.[47] God retained G and J, but he eliminated R. God denies the truth of retribution in nature, in extra-societal situations. Note Tsevat's words:

> But the Book of Job does more than demythologize the world; it also "demoralizes" it, which is to say, makes it amoral. It completes the process whose

42. Cyrus H. Gordon, *Ugaritic Literature* (Rome: Pontifical Biblical Institute, 1949) 134. Cf. *HUCA* 23 (1950) 131–36.

43. Tsevat, *Book of Job*, 100. He notes that roots that express the idea of justice (*ṣdq*, *yšr*, *tmm*) are omitted in Job's journey through the world.

44. Ibid., 100.

45. Ibid., 98.

46. Ibid., 104–5.

47. Tsevat notes that Job was enmeshed in contradictions and, while he despairs of God, he never actually surrenders God.

first phase is known to the reader of the Bible from the opening pages of Genesis: the removal from the conceptual world of an order of superhuman beings independent of the Deity. And it extends it by the denial of the realization of moral values—values deriving from the Deity, to be sure—other than realization effected by man. This new world is as harsh as it is simple, for in it man is deprived of the protection he enjoyed in a world saturated with myth and morality and populated with powers to which he might turn with a view to rendering them favorable to his well-being, foremost by his leading of a meritorious life.[48]

He Redefines Justice

This position, particularly as advanced by Buber, stresses differences between human justice and divine justice:

> Not *the* divine justice, which remains hidden, but *a* divine justice, namely that manifest in creation. The creation of the world is justice, not a recompensing and compensating justice, but a distributing, a giving justice. God the Creator bestows upon each what belongs to him, upon each thing and being, in so far as he allows it to become entirely itself. . . . The just Creator gives to all His creatures His boundary, so that each may become fully itself. Designedly man is lacking in this presentation of heaven and earth, in which man is shown the justice that is greater than his, and is shown that he with his justice, which intends to give to everyone what is due to him, is called only to emulate the divine justice, which gives to everyone what he is.[49]

Von Rad's approach is similar in that he maintains that God can root justice where he pleases:

> It is not as if God were bound to some norm of right, so that there was, as it were, an umpire who, in case of a dispute between God and man, could engage both to observe the rule (Job 11:32f.). JAHWEH is so full and powerful that he himself determines what is right, and is always in the right against man.[50]

A serious problem with this position is the definition of justice as that which is freely and appropriately given. Generosity is not normally understood as the definition of justice, particularly not when it comes to large doses of suffering. Von Rad and Buber have sought to retain divine justice, but by means of a definition not normally accepted.

48. Tsevat, *Book of Job*, 102.
49. Martin Buber, *The Prophetic Faith* (New York: Harper and Brothers, 1949) 194–95.
50. Gerhard von Rad, *Old Testament Theology* (2 vols.; New York: Harper and Brothers, 1962) 1.413.

He Expands Justice

Scholnick's position is not too radically different from the above positions. Her main stress is that divine justice is not limited to jurisprudence, but also includes sovereignty:

> Yahweh's appearance before the hero and his friends signals his acceptance of the challenge for litigation. But in his testimony, rather than pressing charges or presenting a defense, God focuses on the more fundamental question of the nature of divine justice. Excluding any mention of man's system of justice through litigation, he speaks instead of his own authority over the universe, which he labels *mišpāṭ* in 40:8. His concern for Job is expressed through teaching him that justice goes beyond the human legal system to include a system of divine kingship.[51]

Scholnick, while recognizing that the majority of the occurrences of the root *špṭ* in the Hebrew Bible fall into the forensic category, notes that there are many that refer to governance, such as the reference to the king in 1 Sam 8:9.[52] Here the jurisdiction of the king allows him to draft, to enslave, and to appropriate property.

While the writer of Job uses both meanings for *mišpāṭ*, in the speeches of Yahweh the emphasis is clearly upon sovereignty. This accounts for his treatment of nature. Yahweh is the creator and the sustainer of nature. He is indeed the Ruler of the World. Thus he rebukes Job for challenging his *mišpāṭ*, his sovereignty: "Will you even put me in the wrong? Will you condemn me that you may be justified?" (40:8).

Like the monarch described in 1 Sam 8:10–15, Yahweh has the right to appropriate property as he chooses, without consulting the owner. Such appropriations need not be seen as punishment. Yahweh is suggesting to Job that his loss of wealth, family, and health is not divine punishment, but divine appropriation.

Job's Response: Divine Justice Accepted

An assessment of Job's response to Yahweh's speeches is pertinent to our consideration.

Curtis, moving backward from Job's response to the speeches of Yahweh, also sees an emphasis on sovereignty in Yahweh's presentation. In fact, he sees

51. Scholnick, "Meaning of *mišpāṭ*," 521–22.
52. Ibid., 522.

such an emphasis on the divine prerogative here that he reasons that Job has no choice other than to reject Yahweh. Curtis rejects the traditional translation of 42:6, rendering it: "Therefore I feel loathing, contempt, and revulsion toward you, O God; and I am sorry for frail man."[53] Job simply cannot accept Yahweh's unlimited and unanswerable power. The speeches of Yahweh do not solve, but rather compound Job's problem.

While some of Curtis's linguistic arguments in 42:6 are compelling, his conclusion requires him to deny unity to the book. He goes so far as to argue that the prose sections not only give the setting of events and provide a happy ending, but that they have been added to deliberately mislead the reader. The Epilogue, with its accepted ending and divine approbation of Job, intentionally conceals Job's decisive rejection of Yahweh.[54] This tension between the poetic and prose sections should not be resolved by adjusting the poetic conclusions to those of the prose. While this suggestion may be valid, it is not necessary.

Job does not reject God but rather rejects his efforts at litigation. The root *nḥm*, translated 'repent', has a forensic use in prophetic lawsuit literature and can mean 'retract' (cf. Jer 15:6). Cyrus Gordon suggests that *nḥm* in 42:6 may be used "apparently in the sense of a judge retracting and lightening his decision."[55] Job thus now may be rejecting some of his earlier comments and his insistence on litigation.

> The hero no longer wishes to continue his case when he realizes that there is a dimension of justice outside of the court which supersedes the purely forensic. . . . What Job learns is that the divinely ordained justice in the world is God's governance. Job speaks at the end of the drama, not as an innocent hero who rejects the divine Judge for improperly accusing him of wrong doing, but as an enlightened and humbled man who accepts an all-powerful King. His acceptance is based on a full understanding that *mišpāṭ* integrates the ideas of human jurisprudence and divine sovereignty.[56]

Conclusion

Divine justice is indeed a concern of each of the participants in this book. It is the issue that gave rise to the book and it is the unifying and cohesive

53. John B. Curtis, "On Job's Response to Yahweh," *JBL* (1979) 498–511.
54. Ibid., 510.
55. Cyrus H. Gordon, *Legal Background of Hebrew Thought and Literature* (M.A. Thesis, University of Pennsylvania, 1928).
56. Scholnick, "Meaning of *mišpāṭ*," 529.

factor around which the various sections have been organized. While the development and organization of this book is exceedingly complex, there is no need to deny a unified purpose that finds its center in divine justice.

Whether divine justice is defended (comforters), questioned/denied/accepted (Job in his various stages), or redefined (Elihu and Yahweh), it still remains the central issue of the book. These varied responses to divine justice show its centrality and cohesiveness, because all the participants feel a need to address it. Raised in the Prologue, the issue of divine justice dominates the entire book.

Center Structure in the Center Oracles of Amos

R. Bryan Widbin

The Structure of Amos

The problem of literary structure in the book of Amos continues to attract the attention of biblical scholars.[1] Even a casual reader can detect the reason: it is hard to miss the book's recurring speech patterns, which offer tantalizing clues for instant rhetorical and stylistic analysis. Yet equally apparent is the halting movement and interrupted development of many of its passages, defying a quick and easy solution to the organization of the book. Is it any wonder so many return to the oracles of Amos for a closer look?

A number of studies of structure in Amos have attempted to unravel the mystery of the overall design of the book.[2] James Limburg's analysis of "divine speech formulas" represents one of the more productive attempts at

1. A useful survey of the literature is provided in A. G. Auld, *Amos* (Old Testament Guides; Sheffield: JSOT Press, 1986) 50–59.

2. See the sections on structure in the commentaries by James L. Mays, *Amos* (OTL; Philadelphia: Westminster, 1969); E. Hammershaimb, *The Book of Amos* (Oxford: Blackwell, 1970); Hans Walter Wolff, *Joel and Amos* (Hermeneia; Philadelphia: Fortress, 1977); Gary V. Smith, *Amos: A Commentary* (Library of Biblical Interpretation; Grand Rapids: Zondervan, 1989); and Francis I. Andersen and David Noel Freeman, *Amos* (AB 24A; (New York: Doubleday, 1989). Also see Robert Gordis, "The Composition and Structure of Amos," *Poets, Prophets and Sages* (Bloomington: Indiana University Press, 1971) 217–29; Robert B. Coote, *Amos among the Prophets: Composition and Theology* (Philadelphia: Fortress, 1981); Hartmut Gese, "Komposition bei Amos," *Congress Volume, Vienna 1980* (VTSup 32; Leiden: Brill, 1981) 74–95; K. Koch et al., *Amos: Untersucht mit den Methoden einer strukturalen Formgeschichte* (3 vols.; AOAT 30; Neukirchen-Vluyn: Neukirchener, 1976); William A. Smalley, "Recursion Patterns and the Sectioning of Amos," *BT* 30 (1979) 118–27; Adri van der Wal, "The Structure of Amos," *JSOT* 26 (1983) 107–13.

defining major discourse units in Amos.[3] Limburg observes that these formulas, 49 in number, are clustered in heptadic sets that divide the book into 7 units along the natural contours of the oracles. The distribution of these sets identifies the book's literary building blocks, as demonstrated in the following arrangement: (1) 1:1–2 (book introduction: *dibrê ᶜāmôs . . . way-yōᵓmer*); (2) 1:3–2:16 (14 formulas); (3) 3:1–15 (7 formulas); (4) 4:1–13 (7 formulas); (5) 5:1–6:14 (7 formulas); (6) 7:1–8:3 (7 formulas); (7) 8:4–9:15 (7 formulas).

The above structure has important implications for the various parts of Amos as well as for the book as a whole. For instance, the successive "Woe" appeals in 5:18–6:14, usually thought to be independent of surrounding materials, are tied within the structure (unit 5) to the "hear this word" address of 5:1–17. Also, the so-called appendix of consolation in 9:11–15, regardless of its date and origin, is incorporated by this structure (unit 7) into the essential prophetic message.

But beyond this, the structure lays a sound foundation for a broader division of the book. When intersected with other patterns (see chart 1), the seven divine speech units become the components of three major sections of the book.[4] This complex structure results in a more reliable identification of the major sections of Amos. It also encourages us to go on and pursue the matter of the internal cohesion of each of these sections. One might argue that this enterprise should take priority over the confined analyses of smaller units of material, especially since part of the meaning of these smaller units derives from their function as elements in a larger literary framework.

In many ways, the most appealing major section for analysis is section B, 3:1–6:14. One notices immediately in chart 1 that this section is centered or

3. James Limburg, "Sevenfold Structures in the Book of Amos," *JBL* 106 (1987) 217–22. By "divine speech formulas" Limburg refers to "those stereotyped expressions that introduce or conclude sayings identifying them as words of the Lord" (p. 217). The book attests *ᵓāmar* formulas (27), *nĕᵓūm* formulas (21), and a single *dibbēr* formula = 49 total.

4. This "seven-into-three" arrangement of materials is far from uncommon in Amos. One notes that the oracle against Israel in 2:6–16 is constructed in three sections (Israel's crimes, vv. 6–8; divine acts of grace, vv. 9–13; consequences of judgment, vv. 14–16), consisting of seven clauses each. The center section, vv. 9–13, is given a climactic eighth clause for prominence: 2:13, "I will split you apart as a cart splits when full of sheaves," identifying the expected earthquake as a final act of grace. One will note that the arrangement of seven-plus-one first-person clauses in vv. 9–13 is organized into three units by the introductory *wĕ(hinnēh) ᵓānōkî* (vv. 9, 10, and 13). These patterns are wonderfully reminiscent of the three heptadic divine speech sets in 3:1–6:14, the center section of the book.

Chart 1

A. 1:1–2:16, "For three crimes, . . . I'll not relent."[a]
(2 divine speech sets = 14 formulas)

B. 3:1–6:14, "hear this word!"[b]
(3 divine speech sets = 21 formulas)

C. 7:1–9:15, "YHWH showed/Amos saw."[c]
(2 divine speech sets = 14 formulas)

a. This familiar recurring formula is found in 1:3, 6, 9, 11, 13; 2:1, 4, and 2:6, in a seven-plus-one arrangement (see n. 4).
b. This recurring formula is prominent in 3:1, 4:1, and 5:1.
c. One will note that the collection of visions in the final section of Amos is patterned with a sevenfold recurrence of the verb *rāʾâ*: 7:1, 4, 7, 8; 8:1, 2; 9:1.

placed in relief by an additional divine speech set, perhaps indicating its prominence in the book. Furthermore, since scholars often regard the organization of oracles in 3:1–6:14 as the least coherent in Amos,[5] a fresh look at these materials as a whole would seem particularly appropriate. This is the purpose of the present study.

The Center Oracles: Amos 3:1–6:14

Structural analyses of materials in Amos 3:1–6:14 usually begin by isolating a unit of text, whether by the recurring introductory formulas, 'Hear this Word' (*šimʿû ʾet haddābār*, 3:1, 4:1, 5:1) and 'Woe' (*hôy*, 5:18, 6:1), or by some other device.[6] This approach has certain advantages, of course, but

5. E.g., Mays, *Amos*, 14; in reference to this section he comments, "the collectors apparently took oracles which had the same introductory words and used them as headings of small sequences of approximately equal length. Beyond this there is no demonstrable scheme to the arrangement, historical, geographical, or thematic."

6. Cf., e.g., Marjorie O'Rourke Boyle, "The Covenant Lawsuit of the Prophet Amos: III 1–IV 13," *VT* 21 (1971) 338–62; Jan de Waard, "The Chiastic Structure of Amos V 1–17," *VT* 27 (1977) 170–77; J. Lust, "Remarks on the Redaction of Amos V 4–6, 14–15,"

these advantages are limited to the unit under analysis and, therefore, cannot reveal potential relationships with other units in the section.

By contrast, this study focuses on one way in which the widely diverse materials of Amos 3:1–6:14 find unity. One might even regard this feature as the major cohesive device within the section. My intention is to show that the whole of 3:1–6:14 is organized inextricably in an extended chiasm, or palistrophe.

Now, the suggestion that a palistrophe exists in these materials is not exactly new. Jan de Waard observed this structure more than a decade ago in his perceptive analysis of 5:1–17 (see letters G–K below, chart 2).[7] But what has not been appreciated is that the palistrophe actually extends to all of the materials in 3:1–6:14, in effect, giving the center oracles a comprehensive center structure.[8] Whether by coincidence or not, this structure consists of 21 subsections, corresponding exactly to the number of divine speech formulas in the section (see chart 2).

A Palistrophe in the Center Oracles

In this portion of our study we will examine the thematic and linguistic parallels that inform the palistrophe of 3:1–6:14 and so attempt to justify the arrangement shown in chart 2. Our discussion will be limited to A/A′ through F/F′, or those subsections that heretofore have not been treated.[9]

OTS 21 (1981) 129–54; Yehoshua Gitay, "A Study of Amos's Art of Speech: A Rhetorical Analysis of Amos 3:1–15," *CBQ* 42 (1982) 293–309; N. J. Tromp, "Amos V 1–17: Towards a Stylistic and Rhetorical Analysis," *OTS* 23 (1984) 65–85.

7. De Waard, "Chiastic Structure," 170–77; letters G through K in the palistrophe depend heavily on de Waard's analysis.

8. Prior to the appearance of de Waard's analysis, J. Lust submitted an article for publication in which he proposed in a closing footnote, albeit without justification, a chiastic scheme for 4:1–6:7 ("Remarks on the Redaction of Amos," 153–54 n. 103). Though this was a step in the right direction, in my estimation it misses the inclusion of chap. 3 and the rest of chap. 6 in the structure. At the other extreme, William Smalley felt that the entire book of Amos could be organized in a single chiasm, with 5:8c as its center ("Recursion Patterns," 22). Beyond the subsections in chap. 5, which depend heavily upon de Waard's analysis, his proposal is unconvincing. Moreover, Smalley's suggestions for subsections in 3:1–4:13 and 5:18–6:14 are entirely at odds with those proffered in the present study.

9. For a full discussion of 5:1–17 and parallels G/G′–K, see de Waard, "Chiastic Structure," 170–77, and esp. Tromp, "Amos V 1–17," 56–84. Also cf. Lust, "Remarks on the Redaction of Amos," 129–54, and Gary V. Smith, "Amos 5:13: The Deadly Silence of the Prosperous," *JBL* 107 (1988) 289–91.

Chart 2

A Argument: YHWH's Relationship with Israel as a Basis for Judgment (3:1–11)
  B Exhibit: An Image of Death and Worthless Leftovers (3:12)
    C Sworn Testimony: Divine Punishment of Jacob Coming (3:13–15)
      D Named in Indictment: Self-Indulgent Women in Mt. Samaria (4:1–3)
        E Condemnation: Cultic Activities (4:4–5)
          F Past Judgments Reviewed: Significance Missed (4:6–13)
            G Lament: Funeral Songs in the City (5:1–3)
              H Exhortation: "Seek YHWH" (5:4–6)
                I Accusation: Contempt for Innocence/Poverty (5:7)
                  J Hymn: He Who Creates Light and Water on the Earth (5:8a–b)
                    K YHWH IS HIS NAME (5:8c)
                  J′ Hymn: He Who Flashes Destruction on the Fortress (5:9)
                I′ Accusation: Contempt for the Innocent/Poor (5:10–13)
              H′ Exhortation: "Seek Good" (5:14–15)
            G′ Lament: Funeral Sounds in the City (5:16–17)
          F′ Present Judgment Announced: Significance Missed (5:18–20)
        E′ Condemnation: Cultic Activities (5:21–27)
      D′ Named in Indictment: Self-Indulgent Men in Mt. Samaria (6:1–7)
    C′ Sworn Testimony: Divine Punishment of Jacob Coming (6:8)
  B′ Exhibit: An Image of Death and Worthless Leftovers (6:9–10)
A′ Argument: YHWH's Relationship with Israel as a Basis for Judgment (6:11–14)

A/A′ Argument: 3:1–11 // 6:11–14

At first glance, the subsections 3:1–11 and 6:11–14 would seem to have little in common.[10] The former is a rather lengthy address characterized by

10. Not all will agree with my delineation of these subsections. I admit that in some respects a more natural division of chap. 3 would be after v. 8, and again after v. 12, based on the triadic repetition of the introductory verb *šmᶜ*, vv. 1, 9, 13. Also, some may like to see 6:11 (beginning with *kî*) joined as a concluding comment to 6:9–10. There is a rhetorical validity to these observations. However, the comprehensive palistrophe of 3:1–6:14 develops alongside, not necessarily identical with, the three complete "Hear This Word" addresses in these oracles. This demands an alternative display of the data. One may observe as well that 3:1–11 // 6:11–14 could break down palistrophically as follows: A 3:1–2 // A′ 6:14 (Raising of a Nation); B 3:3–8 // B′ 6:12–13 (Rhetorical Questions involving animals); C 3:9–11 // C′ 6:11 (Destruction of Fortresses). In my estimation, however, the proposed arrangement is more appropriate to the single idea that each subsection as a whole conveys: the shared relationship of YHWH and Israel implies judgment as well as blessing.

Chart 3

3:1–2	6:14
Opening:	*Closing*:
Against you, O House of Israel[a] (*ʿălêkem bêt yiśrāʾēl*) which I brought up (Hiphil *ʿly*) from the land of Egypt	Against you, O House of Israel (*ʿălêkem bêt yiśrāʾēl*)[b] I will raise up (Hiphil *qm*) a nation
Comment:	*Comment*:
saying (*lēʾmōr*) only you (*ʾetkem*) I know	says (*nĕʾūm*) YHWH, God of Hosts they will fight you (*ʾetkem*)

a. 3:1; reading LXX, *oikos Israel* (= *bêt yiśrāʾēl*), versus MT, *bĕnê yiśrāʾēl.* Error due to abbreviation.

b. The phrase *ʿălêkem bêt yiśrāʾēl* occurs nowhere else in Amos, though it seems to be reflected in 5:1, *ʾānōkî nōśēʾ ʿălêkem qînâ bêt yiśrāʾēl* 'I am raising against you a dirge, O House of Israel', as part of a coexisting structure. The triadic movement of 3:1, 5:1, and 6:14 would have YHWH raising Israel in deliverance, raising a dirge for her expected demise, and finally, raising another nation to accomplish this demise. The idea of YHWH as the mover of all nations for benefit and judgment also occurs in 1:6, 15, and 9:7.

imperatives and persuasive references to Israel's historic past. The latter, on the other hand, is a succinct, emphatic statement of the coming judgment of YHWH. But in spite of their apparent differences, these subsections deal with precisely the same issue in remarkably similar ways.

First, we observe that 3:1–2 opens the initial "Hear This Word" address in the center oracles with an ironic salutation and comment. It is surely no coincidence that 6:14 mirrors 3:1–2 in the closing of the final "Hear This Word" address. This effectively forms an *inclusio* for the whole of the center oracles (3:1–6:14) (see chart 3).

A second, more obvious correspondence between the two subsections is the use of rhetorical questions for the purpose of refuting Israel's preconceptions about herself and YHWH (3:3–8 // 6:12–13). But the connections do not stop at the mere use of this form. We are impressed that (1) both sets of questions are structured in a sequence with *hă* and *ʾim* as introductory markers (cf. 3:3–5 with 6 // 6:12a with b), (2) both sets of questions conclude with a summary explanation introduced by *kî* (3:7 // 6:12c), (3) both sets of questions argue from analogy with animals in their habitats, whether natural or unnatural (lions in the forest or den, birds on the ground [3:3–5] // horses on a crag, an ox in the sea [6:12][11]), and (4) both sets of questions imply the issue of military conquest in order to assert YHWH's sovereignty over all nations (3:6, and cf. *lkd* in 3:4b, 5b // 6:13).[12]

In the summary explanations, or *kî* clauses, an additional item occurs that increases our conviction that subsections 3:1–11 and 6:11–14 are related. According to 3:7, YHWH does 'nothing' (*lōᵓ . . . dābār*) without revealing his plan to prophets. In context (3:6), this plan involves the divine judgment of Israel in the form of military disaster. In the companion 6:13, the power-hungry Israelites are said to be "rejoicing in *lōᵓ dābār*," an ironic pun on the place-name, Lo-Devar, which was conquered by Israel, and its supposed meaning 'nothing'.[13] The point is that Israel's pride in her own military superiority ignores the fact that YHWH is the one responsible for her victories. The reference to Lo-Devar in 6:13 then furnishes an application of the general assertion of 3:7 that it is indeed YHWH who accomplishes the 'nothing' of conquest and that it is according to the plan revealed through his prophets.

A third set of correspondences between the two subsections occurs in 3:9–11 and 6:11. These materials emphasize two things: (1) the disintegration of buildings, particularly those associated with wealth and power, and (2) the scattered remains of these edifices.

In 3:9–11, the 'fortresses' (*ᵓarmĕnôt*) of Ashdod and the 'fortresses' of Egypt are summoned to bear testimony against 'fortresses' in Israel that store up violence and plunder. According to the oracle, the Israelite 'fortresses' soon will be reduced to what they store, relatively insignificant articles available to a conquering foe. Their doom is imaged in a subsequent illustration

11. Accepting the commonly proposed division of the text, *bĕbāqār yām*. However, in light of the context, Alan Cooper's proposed emendation is most attractive: *ᵓim yaḥărôš babbiq[ᶜâ] rēm* 'Does a wild ox plow in the Valley?' (Alan Cooper, "The Absurdity of Amos 6:12a," *JBL* 107 [1988] 725–27). His point is that *selaᶜ* and *biqᶜâ* refer respectively to the Edomite stronghold conquered by Amaziah of Judah (2 Kgs 14:7; 2 Chr 25:12) and the Lebanese Beqaᶜ, both presently in Israelite control. They represent the southern and northern limits of territory controlled by Jeroboam II, also depicted in 6:14 as the Wadi of the Arabah and Lebo-Hamath (cf. 2 Kgs 14:25). Accordingly, the riddle is: "Real horses do not scamper across crags, and real wild oxen cannot be yoked to the plow. . . . Yet the Israelite 'horses' did indeed overrun Sela, just as their 'wild oxen' plowed up the Beqaᶜ." This proves irrefutably YHWH's involvement in these "unnatural" conquests.

12. See Cooper, "Amos 6:12a," 725–27, for a compelling discussion of this point.

13. See Wolff, *Amos*, 288, for the identification of Lo-Devar.

of bits and pieces of a victim left in a lion's mouth after it attacks (3:12). This illustration is then reapplied in the same verse to the so-called "deliverance" of the Israelites, or those who reside in Samaria. They will be like the broken furniture of a house after the house itself has been destroyed. This final image causes us to recall the opening of the oracle in 3:1, which proclaimed, "Against you, O *house* of Israel."

We also note that three enemies are referred to in vv. 9–11: a conquered Egypt (cf. 3:1), an insignificant Ashdod (a play on *šōd* 'plunder', 3:10), and an unnamed enemy (Assyria) who will reduce Israel to leftovers. This parallels exactly 6:13–14, which names two conquered foes, Lo-Devar and Qarnayim, along with an unspecified 'nation' (*gôy*, Assyria) who ultimately will swallow up Israel's conquests.

In comparison now with 3:9–11, 6:11 asserts that YHWH will command the demolition of 'the big house into splinters' (*habbayit haggādôl rĕsîsîm*) and 'the little house into scraps' (*habbayit haqqāṭōn bĕqīᶜîm*). As in 3:9–11, this comment is attached to an illustration, this time of "leftovers" (relatives!) in a house reduced by the death of its owners (6:9–10). But here, instead of leading into the illustration, the comment applies it (*kî*, 6:11). One should not miss the movement from 3:9–11 to 6:11. The deserved plundering of the political and economic establishment of Samaria will result in the decimation of all life in Israel, whether wealthy or poor.

Before concluding our discussion of A/A′, we must observe the internal organization of the opening/closing subsections of the palistrophe. In reference to one another they develop chiastically, or in an a b c // c′ b′ a′ pattern, perhaps signaling the palistrophe (see chart 4).

Finally, in addition to the ideas, metaphors, and linguistic elements that unite the subsections, 3:1–11 and 6:11–14 also are united by sameness of theme: YHWH's prerogative and activity stand behind what happens in the world, particularly as it concerns affairs between nations. The misguided notion that nations themselves can control their own destinies is rendered patently absurd.

Both 3:1–11 and 6:14 are constructed basically as arguments. The rhetorical questions (a theoretical argument) and references to Israel's history, both former and recent (a practical argument), are designed to gain the general consent of a premise: YHWH's relationship with Israel has produced the benefits of her position in the world. Forced to concede this, Israel cannot escape the conclusion that, just as certainly, YHWH may reduce that position. In the palistrophe, the practical, concrete, and immediate presentation of 6:11–14 draws the specific implications of the more theoretical, metaphorical, and historical presentation of 3:1–11.

Chart 4

	3:1–11		6:11–14
a	Raising up a Nation (Israel) to know her (3:1–2)	c′	Demolition of Houses (6:11)
b	Rhetorical Questions (3:3–8)	b′	Rhetorical Questions (6:12–13)
c	Demolition of "Houses" (3:9–11)	a′	Raising up a Nation (Gentile) to fight her (6:14)

B / B′ Exhibit: 3:12 // 6:9–10

Whereas the connections between 3:1–11 and 6:11–14 were not immediately obvious, the relationship between 3:12 and 6:9–10 presents no such problem. Each subsection concocts a brief illustration of the undeniable death and disaster about to befall Israel. Amos 3:12 continues the lion imagery of 3:4, 8, while 6:9–10 anticipates the demolition of all homes in Israel, both of the wealthy and the poor.

A closer look at these brief passages reveals that they share a number of rather interesting elements in common. First, both are concerned with the idea of death and particularly with the figure of a dissected corpse. Making an issue of worthless, surviving elements serves to emphasize the finality of disaster. In 3:12, the shepherd 'will deliver' (*yaṣṣîl*) only 'two shank bones' (dual, *kĕrāʿayim*) and a body part (*ʾōzen* 'ear') from the lion's mouth. In 6:10, a relative enters a house 'to deliver' (*lĕhôṣîʾ*) 'bones' (*ʿăṣāmîm*) from a body part (dual, *yarkĕtê*, lit. 'thighs' → recesses) of the house.

Second, in 3:12 the figure of pieces of a ravaged animal is used as an analogy for pieces of furniture[14] in an Israelite house and even for the Israelites themselves. But what the analogy lacks is the vivid details of an event. This is

14. Reading the problematic *bdmšq* as *bad mšq* 'part of the leg' (of a bed); see Smith, *Amos*, 123 n. 76.

provided in the companion 6:9–10, through the image of a relative entering a house ravaged by death in order to collect its (human) 'remains'.

Finally, the oracular introduction to the analogy in 3:12 (*kōh ʾāmar* YHWH *kaʾăšer*) finds a counterpart in 6:9–10 in a constant reference to speaking in the empty house of the dead (*wĕʾāmar laʾăšer . . . wĕʾāmar . . . wĕʾāmar*), and in particular 'the mentioning of the name of YHWH' (*lĕhazkîr bĕšēm* YHWH) in these circumstances. In my estimation, these rather ingenious plays make the association of subsections 3:12 and 6:9–10 virtually incontrovertible.

C/C′ Sworn Testimony: 3:13–15 // 6:8

The opening words of 3:13–15 and 6:8 provide an immediate sense of the relatedness of these subsections. Both begin with legal formulas announcing a statement by YHWH. It may be that in C/C′ the prosecutor of A/A′ and the exhibitor of B/B′ is taking the stand in his own behalf. It is worth noting how similar the vocabulary in these introductions are (see chart 5). But one particular item deserves special mention: the reference to Israel as "Jacob" in 3:13. This title is relatively rare in Amos, occurring only twice in the center oracles. It is hardly a coincidence that these two references to "Jacob" in the center oracles are distributed between companion subsections 3:13–15 and 6:8. Supporting the prophet's invitation for the nations to bear witness concerning the crimes of "the house of Jacob" (3:13), YHWH declares in 6:8b that he abhors "the pride of Jacob." A connection like this one, involving an unusual feature in the text, is particularly helpful in establishing the palistrophe.

After the legal introductions we find a second point of contact between subsections 3:13–15 and 6:8. This is provided by the divine statements themselves. Not only are the statements similar in content, dealing with the removal of the cultic and political machinery of the kingdom,[15] they are identical structurally as well. Both begin with anticipatory clauses containing a nonfinite verb form with a first-person pronoun (3:14a // 6:8b),[16] and con-

15. Recall that in the initial set of subsections, 3:9–11 referred frequently to the 'fortresses' (*ʾarmĕnôt*) of nations (4 times), while 6:11 referred to 'the big house' (*habbayit haggādôl*) and 'the little house' (*habbayit haqqāṭōn*). Here it is just the opposite: 3:15 refers to 'the winter house' (*bêt hāḥōrep*), 'the summer house' (*bêt haqqayiṣ*), 'ivory houses' (*bāttê haššēn*), and 'many houses' (*bāttîm rabbîm*) (= 4 times), while 6:8c refers to 'fortresses' (*ʾarmĕnôt*).

16. Amos 3:14a, *kî bĕyôm poqdî pišʿê yiśrāʾēl ʿālāw* 'indeed, when I punish him (= Jacob, cf. 3:13) for the crimes of Israel, . . .' // 6:8b, *mĕtāʾēb ʾānōkî ʾet gĕʾôn yaʿăqōb* 'I, having abhorred the pride of Jacob. . . .'

Chart 5

3:13	6:8a
Hear and bear witness	Adonai YHWH has sworn
concerning (*bĕ*)	by (*bĕ*)
the house of Jacob	himself
Says (*nĕᵓūm*) Adonai YHWH	Says (*nĕᵓūm*) YHWH
God of Hosts	God of Hosts

tinue with two main clauses introduced by consecutive first-person suffix conjugation forms (3:14b–15 // 6:8c–d).[17] The greater length of 3:14b–15 is due to the intrusion of two parenthetical clauses after each of its main clauses for the purpose of specifying the result of the main activity.

The relationship between these subsections is fairly clear. Both present a testimony of YHWH's intent to remove the cultic and political barriers that prevent recognition of his sovereignty. Amos 3:13–15 is proclaimed publicly with an emphasis on the demonstration of his intention; 6:8 focuses on its inner, motivational aspects.[18]

D/D′ Named in Indictment: 4:1–3 // 6:1–7

Apparently J. Lust was the first to recognize a similarity in subject matter between 4:1–3 and 6:1–7.[19] A closer look reveals that, in fact, a number of items draw these oracles together and incorporate them into the palistrophe.

As Lust has noted, their common topic cannot be missed. Both vividly portray in condemning fashion self-indulgent women (4:1–3) and men (6:1–7) lounging in the lap of luxury on the upper crust of society. But as we have seen before, the points of comparison between subsections in this palistrophe do not stop at related subject matter. In fact, the strongest connection here is

17. Amos 3:14b–15: *ûpāqadtî ᶜal mizbḥôt bêt ᵓēl . . . wĕhikkêtî bêt hāḥōrep ᶜal bêt haqqayiṣ* 'I will punish the altars of Bethel . . . and I will dash the winter house and summer house' // 6:8b–c *ᵓarmĕnōtāyw śānēᵓtî wĕhisgartî ᶜîr ûmĕlōᵓāh* 'I hate his fortresses, and I will close down the city along with its contents'.

18. Cf. E/E′ 4:4–5 // 5:21–27, two oracles condemning Israel's worship with the identical movement between the passages as in 3:13–15 // 6:8.

19. Lust, "Remarks on the Redaction of Amos," 153–54 n. 103.

what, on the surface, would seem to be a meaningless detail: the residence of the men and women. Their "ivory tower," as it were, is 'in Mount Samaria' (*běhar šōmrôn*, 4:1 // 6:1). It is significant that, while the plural, *hārê šōmrôn*, is amply attested, the singular, *har šōmrôn*, occurs only in Amos 4:1 and 6:1 in the entire Hebrew Bible.

In the extended portrait of the men and women, textual correspondences abound. (1) Both portraits are organized with a sequence of participles: a series of three for the women[20] and a series of six for the men.[21] (2) The women are called 'cows of Bashan' (*pārôt habbāšān*, 4:1); the men are said to eat 'calves from the pen' (*ᶜăgālîm mittôk marbēq*, 6:4b). (3) The women order their husbands, 'Bring me!' (*hābîᵓa*, 4:1c); but it is to the men that the Israelite people regularly 'come' (*ûbāᵓû*, 6:1b). (4) The desire of the women is 'that we may drink' (*wěništeh*, 4:1c); but the men are 'drinkers' (*haššōtîm*, 6:6) of wine by the barrel.

Correspondences continue in the announcement of punishment. (1) In both portraits the penalty is exile. (2) The women will be sent away 'to the last of you' (*ᵓaḥărîtěken*, 4:2b); the men, as the 'elite' (*rēᵓšît*, 6:1b, 6) will go 'first' (*běrōᵓš*, 6:7). (3) The women will go 'one in front of the other' (*ᵓiššâ negdāh*, 4:3); the men will go 'at the front' (*běrōᵓš*, 6:7). (4) The women will go through 'breaks' (in the wall?) (*pěrāṣîm*, 4:3); the men are 'breakers(?)' (*happōrětîm*, 6:5) like David in their musical skill, but do not grieve over the 'brokenness' (*šēber*, 6:6b) of Joseph. (5) As the women will be carried away in *sîrôt* ('hooks'(?), 4:2b), so the drunken lollygagging of the men *wěsār* ('will end,' 6:7).

Seemingly in every clause we are granted more insight into the depraved consumerism of 4:1–3 through the penetrating analysis of corrupted leadership in 6:1–7. The combined portraits of dominating women who demand the wine of "their masters" and invidious men who eat the "calves" of their "cows" is an image of society turned to feeding on itself.

E / E′ Condemnation: 4:4–5 // 5:21–27

As with the previous set of subsections (D/D′), the correlation between 4:4–5 and 5:21–27 is obvious. These oracles condemn the false cult of Is-

20. Amos 4:1b, *hāᶜōšěqôt* 'the oppressors'; 4:1c, *hārōṣěṣôt* 'the crushers', 4:1d, *hāᵓōměrōt* 'those who have a say'.

21. Amos 6:1b, *habbōṭěḥîm* 'those who have security'; 6:3, *haměnaddîm* 'ones who dismiss'; 6:4a, *haššōkěbîm* 'those who lie down'; 6:4b, *hāoᵓōkělîm* 'eaters'; 6:5, *happōrěṭîm* 'those who devise'; 6:6, *haššōtîm* 'those who drink'.

rael. Though they are somewhat uncomfortable in their immediate literary surroundings, they fit together perfectly within the structure proposed here.

The ironic call to worship in 4:4–5 parodies Israel's enjoyment of religious formalism. She is invited in a series of seven imperatives to "enter" (the shrines), "commit crimes," "commit more crimes," "bring" (lavish, inappropriate offerings), "offer" (unauthorized sacrifices), "identify" and "let (all) hear" (your intention to worship); all because "this is what you love to do, O people of Israel" (4:5b). These imperatives seem to have an antithetical parallel in the seven religious activities that God refuses to acknowledge in 5:21–24.[22] Listed there are festivals, solemn occasions, holocausts, tribute offerings, well-being offerings, the racket of songs and the plucking of harps.

The final, climactic imperative *hašmîʿû* 'let hear' (4:5) stands out for a reason beyond its placement in the series. It has a counterpart, *lōʾ ʾešmaʿ*, which occurs in a similar series as the climactic, fourth negated prefix conjugation form (first person) in 5:21b–23. In this passage, YHWH's response to the frenzied religious activity of Israel is presented: "I don't enjoy" (your occasions), "I don't want" (your holocausts and tribute offerings), "I don't regard" (your fatted well-being offerings), and 'I don't hear' (*lōʾ ʾešmaʿ*, 5:23) (the plucking of your harps). The contrast between Israel's passion for the cult and YHWH's rejection of its empty forms is stressed in the final line of 4:4–5 and in the initial line of 5:21–27: 'you love . . .' (*ʾăhabtem*) // 'I hate' (*śānēʾtî*).

Issues related to cultic observance are the source of frequent interplay between these subsections, especially in the matter of sacrifice. In 4:4b, Israel is encouraged ironically to perform 'your sacrifices' (*zibḥêkem*) every morning and bring the triennial tithe every three days. But in 5:25, YHWH reminds Israel that frequency of ceremonial activity is of little consequence. For who can forget that she was sustained for forty years in the wilderness without these communal 'sacrifices' (*zĕbāḥîm*)?

Another correspondence worthy of mention is the ironic invitation in 4:5 to desecrate the *tôdâ* and *nĕdābôt*, both occasions of the *šelem*, which, according to 5:22b, YHWH does not regard. And finally, it should not be overlooked that the first three imperatives of 4:4–5 call the Israelites to Bethel and to Gilgal (if the latter does not refer to the shrine itself at Bethel[23]), the site of their cultic sins. Amos 5:24 proposes a desired alternative to this useless pilgrimage in a delightful wordplay on *haggilgāl* (4:4): "Let justice 'roll'

22. Cf. Limburg, "Sevenfold Structure," 219–21, for a discussion of the multiple sets of seven and seven-plus-one figures in the oracles of Amos. Limburg includes 4:4–5 and 5:21–24 in his discussion (p. 220).

23. See the discussion in Lust, "Remarks on the Redaction of Amos," 142–43.

(*wĕyiggal*) like water; uprightness like a rushing wadi." Amos 5:27 then completes the pun with the inevitable results if they continue supporting the shrine: "I will send you into exile" (*wĕhiglêtî*). In a most dramatic way, 5:21–27 provides YHWH's response to the cultic priorities of Israel referred to in 4:4–5.

F/F′ Judgments Reviewed/Announced: 4:6–13 // 5:18–20

Our discussion ends with a consideration of the parallels between companion subsections 4:6–13 and 5:18–20. As with A/A′ 3:1–11 // 6:11–14, these subsections of the palistrophe seem to have little in common. Actually, the oracles are strikingly similar, if not in amount of material, at least in their subject matter and organization.

Amos 4:6–13 is presented in five major units, with a final statement of consequence including a hymn fragment.[24] The lyric of the hymn moves through a series of five active participles that praise the name of YHWH and at the same time balance the entire oracle. The five major units of the oracle are easily distinguished by the recurring formula *wĕlōʾ šabtem ʿāday nĕʾūm YHWH* 'but you did not turn to me, oracle of YHWH' (4:6, 8, 9, 10, 11). They are also grouped triadically in a 2+2+1 framework.[25] That is, lack of food (4:6) and lack of water (4:7–8) form a subunit (cf. *wĕgam ʾănî / ʾānōkî* introduction for both); blight/mildew (4:9) and plague (4:10) form a subunit; the cataclysm reminiscent of Sodom and Gomorrah fittingly stands alone as the third subunit (4:11).

The subject matter of 4:6–13 is as transparent as its form. The oracle rehearses five stereotypical judgments that failed to bring Israel to repentance. In every instance, YHWH's efforts, in spite of their severity, proved resistible for Israel. But the oracle does not end there. Verses 12–13, in a valiant appeal for repentance, promise one final effort by the incomparable YHWH to effect inescapable judgment. The five participial names in the hymn assure us that YHWH himself is able to produce what his calamities have not. 'The one who makes (even) the dawn dark' (*ʿōśe šaḥar ʿēpâ*) surely is capable of anything.

On the opposite wing of the palistrophe is 5:18–20, a brief oracle about the Day of YHWH. Though it cannot compare with the elaborate strains of 4:6–13, its materials are woven together just as tightly. The introductory

24. On pentadic groupings in Amos, see Coote, *Composition and Theology*, 66–78.

25. A similar format may be proposed for the five vision reports in 7:1–9:15. For a brief discussion, see Smith, *Amos*, 215–16.

"Woe" pronouncement is followed immediately by a rhetorical question that picks up the "Day of YHWH" theme (5:18b). Both the structure of this question and its vocabulary match the final line of the oracle (5:20), forming an *inclusio* for the analogy within: 5:18, "What do you want with the Day of YHWH? It is darkness, not light!" // 5:20, "Is not the Day of YHWH darkness, not light; blackness with no gleam whatsoever?" It seems that we are meant to recall here the reputation of YHWH, described in 4:13 as the one who blackens the dawn.

What unfolds within the oracle (5:19) are five brief acts dramatizing a man's attempt to escape a series of threatening situations. (1) He flees the mouth of the lion, (2) only to be approached by the bear; (3) so he goes home, (4) puts his hand against the wall, (5) and the snake bites him. These acts are distinguished by four *waw*-conjunctions and are organized triadically. Not only does the series identify three animal threats (each defined in the poem for recognition), but one finds again the 2+2+1 triadic framework that was employed in 4:6–11. The threats of the lion and the bear form the first subunit, the entering of the house and leaning against the wall form the second subunit,[26] and finally, in the climactic subunit, the snake bites the man.

As in 4:6–13, the issue again is the attempt to sidestep judgment, a point illustrated in the five-act play of 5:19. But a more basic point seems to be that Israel, in a misconception about the Day of YHWH, has forfeited her best opportunity for repentance. Consequently, she will experience this day as her doom, another point established in the final act of the illustration.

As in previous subsections, the second passage provides a response to issues raised in the first passage. The confusing (and rather ambiguous) 4:12 is pivotal for understanding how this works in this section of the palistrophe. The verse announces the consequences of Israel's failure to turn to YHWH in spite of repeated opportunities. YHWH says, "Therefore this is what I will do to you, O Israel; because I will do this to you, prepare to meet your God, O Israel!" The demonstratives are left without referents in the passage—a most unusual situation. In my estimation, this can be resolved satisfactorily (and simply)[27] by assuming that they refer to "the Day of YHWH," which will be

26. One may recall here the point of correspondence in B/B′ 3:12 // 6:9–10. In the former subsection, the illustration revolved around pieces of a victim in a lion's mouth. In the latter, a relative searched for surviving elements within a house of death. The first two subunits appear to pick up this "animal-house" interchange for similar reasons.

27. Contra Wolff, *Amos*, 222; Wolff posits in "thus" a nonverbal pointing to the destroyed altar at Bethel. Nor is there any reason to support the notion that Amos has in mind the statement of punishment in 3:2; see Smith, *Amos*, 147.

introduced in the companion subsection of the palistrophe.[28] This also makes sense of the reference to "meeting your God" in v. 12, especially if "the Day of YHWH" was conceived of as a moment in which YHWH would manifest himself within history to do battle with his opponents.[29]

But none of this solves the problem of the hymn fragment in 4:13. We will not attempt a full discussion of that question here, since to do it justice the fragment must be addressed in conjunction with 5:8–9 and 9:5–6, which is beyond the scope of the present study. However, we have noted that the fragment contains a reference to YHWH as the "darkener of dawn"—perhaps the clearest semantic parallel to 5:18–20, wherein "the Day of YHWH" is identified twice as "darkness, not light." Perhaps what we have in 4:13 and 5:18–20 are actually alternative ways in which the sinful people of Israel may "meet" their God. And it may be that these alternatives were introduced earlier in the form *liqraᵓt* 'to meet' (4:12).

Commentators are agreed, with good reason, that the form *liqraᵓt* is not related to *qrᵓ* but to *qry*, though the LXX and the Peshiṭta opt for the former, reading 'to call, proclaim'. But it is conceivable that both were intended in an ingenious wordplay. The content of the hymn introduces a sovereign God who holds creation in his hands, is not bound to Israel as patron, and therefore may be responsible for visiting judgment upon her. But we should not dismiss too quickly the fact that the hymn also offers Israel a vehicle whereby she may "proclaim" the name of her God and so *legitimately* escape judgment.[30] Therein lies the alternative. Israel may prepare herself "to name" her God in recognition of his sovereign power and right to judge. Or she must be prepared to suffer the consequences of "meeting" him on his day when "the snake will bite" and there will be no escape.

If this is at all the sense of 4:12–13 (// 5:18–20), it explains why the palistrophe continues its development to a center point in the refrain of the hymn: *YHWH šĕmô* (5:8c). In 3:1–5:8b, the oracles are theoretical or categorical. Often they present what might be, but need not be, if Israel will turn to YHWH in an authentic recognition of his sovereignty. What better way for cult-loving people to do this than in the form of a hymn. But in 5:9–6:14, the words are real with a finality about them. All implications are drawn, and their immediacy horrifies us. In effect, these words describe now what must be.

28. J. Lust seems to have been the first to recognize this connection between 4:12 and 5:18–20; cf. Lust, "Remarks on the Redaction of Amos," 153 n. 103.

29. For options regarding "the Day of YHWH," see among others, Smith, *Amos*, 178–80.

30. See Deut. 32:3, for *qrᵓ* (with accusative) used of 'proclaiming' the name of God in his power over creation.

Baruch, the Ideal Sage

J. Edward Wright

Why was the Greek *Apocalypse of Baruch* (*3 Baruch*) ascribed to Baruch, the companion of the prophet Jeremiah? The pseudepigraphic attribution of the Jewish apocalypses to notable figures from the Hebrew Bible is an issue that prevents us from identifying and understanding better the actual authors of these works and their audiences.[1] I propose to address this problem by surveying the several Baruch pseudepig rapha to gain a more complete appreciation of the character of the Baruch who was being presented in the literature attributed to him. What will emerge from this study is the development of the character of Baruch toward that of an "Ideal Sage." Michael Stone has described the place and the nature of the ideology of the "Ideal Sage" in Early Judaism.[2] Building on his treatment, I shall trace the development of the portrayal of Baruch in the biblical materials pertaining to him and in the several Baruch pseudepigrapha.

In pseudepigraphic literature the narrative framework is the skeleton that binds together the visions, paranesis, testaments, etc.; it is how the author integrated the constituent components into a literary whole.[3] Moreover, the

1. Standard treatments on the vexing issue of pseudepigraphy are Norbert Brox, ed., *Pseudepigraphie in der heidenischen und jüdisch-christlichen Antike* (Darmstadt: Wissenschaftliche Buchgesellschaft, 1977) and Wolfgang Speyer, *Die literarische Fälschung im heidenischen und christlichen Altertum: Ein Versuch ihrer Deutung* (HAW 1.2; Munich: Beck, 1971).

2. "Ideal Figures and Social Context: Priest and Sage in the Early Second Temple Age," *Ancient Israelite Religion: Essays in Honor of Frank Moore Cross* (ed. Patrick D. Miller Jr., Paul Hanson, and S. Dean McBride; Philadelphia: Fortress, 1987) 575–86. Note also Jacob Neusner, "Sage, Priest, Messiah: Three Types of Judaism in the Age of Jesus," *Judaism in the Beginning of Christianity* (Philadelphia: Fortress, 1984) 35–44.

3. This has been pointed out by Divorah Dimant, "The Testament as a Literary Form in Early Jewish Pseudepigraphic Literature," *Proceedings of the Eighth World Congress of Jewish Studies: Division A, The Period of the Bible* (Jerusalem: World Union of Jewish Studies, 1982) 79–83.

narrative framework relates the new work to an already developing literary corpus allegedly written by the ancient sage. When readers encounter a new pseudepigraphon, they do so with an understanding of the traditions that are developed in the narrative settings of earlier texts. The selection of the particular pseudonym itself is not based solely on the character's biblical reputation, but also for what it had become in the minds of the people since or outside of the biblical material. Each new text adds something to the portrayal of the character and, thus, the character develops. For example, little is made of Enoch in the Bible, but apparently he was the focus of a wealth of traditions that circulated alongside the scanty biblical account.[4] Ezra fares well both in and outside of the Bible.[5] The same obtains with Daniel.[6] The character of Baruch develops as time passes and can be shown in the various works pertaining to Baruch.

Baruch in the Bible: The Book of Jeremiah

In Jer 32:12–16 Baruch witnesses or certifies the land transaction between Jeremiah and his cousin Hanameel in what appears to be a normal scribal function. Baruch next appears in chap. 36, where he is involved in the production and reissuing of Jeremiah's sermons. In this activity he appears as a type of editor of Jeremianic materials.[7] In Jer 43:1–7 Baruch is charged with

4. See P. Grelot, "La legend d'Henoch dans les Apocryphes et dans la Bible: Origin et signification," *RSR* 46 (1958) 5–26, 181–210; cf. Grelot, "La géographie mythique d'Henoch et ses sources orientales," *RB* 65 (1958) 33–69; James VanderKam, *Enoch and the Growth of an Apocalyptic Tradition* (CBQMS 16; Washington: Catholic Biblical Association, 1984); H. L. Jansen, *Die Henochgestalt* (Oslo: Jacob Dybwd, 1939); and Ithamar Gruenwald ("Jewish Apocalyptic Literature," *ANRW* 2.19.11 [ed. Wolfgang Haase; Berlin: de Gruyter, 1979] 89–118).

5. See Robert A. Kraft, " 'Ezra' Materials in Judaism and Christianity," *ANRW* 2.19.1 (ed. Wolfgang Haase; Berlin: de Gruyter, 1979) 119–36.

6. See Carey A. Moore, *Daniel, Esther, and Jeremiah: The Additions* (AB 44; Garden City, N.Y.: Doubleday, 1977).

7. The idea that Baruch was editor of Jeremiah stems in large measure from attributing excessive importance to this story as indicative of what actually happened in the publishing of the Jeremianic corpus. Robert P. Carroll (*Jeremiah* [OTL; London: SCM, 1986] 44–45, 61) notes that one must be cautious not to attribute too much creative activity to Baruch based solely on the few scattered and not entirely clear passages involving him. It appears that the idea that Baruch was the editor and biographer of Jeremiah is an idea not fully warranted by the text and one that has nevertheless led to a great deal of speculation regarding his involvement in the production of the book of Jeremiah.

provoking Jeremiah to proclaim words against the people who proposed the Egyptian sojourn as a way to avoid the exile to Babylon. These people then take Jeremiah and Baruch to Egypt forcibly.[8] Finally, in chap. 45 Jeremiah delivers an oracle directly to Baruch. Baruch apparently sought "great things" for himself. God said he should not do so, but should await the realization of the promise that he would give him his life as "booty" wherever he would go. Overall, Baruch appears as little more than the great prophet's recorder in the Hebrew or Masoretic version of the book of Jeremiah.

In the biblical materials, Baruch appears only in the book of Jeremiah. As is well known, the Greek version of Jeremiah represents a substantially different version of this book from the Masoretic Text: the Greek textual tradition is not simply a revision of the Masoretic Text, but represents a wholly different textual tradition of the book.[9]

In the Masoretic textual tradition, Baruch appears to be an aide to the prophet Jeremiah, performing customary scribal functions, that is, transcribing the prophet's oracles, certifying land transactions, and delivering the prophet's oracles to audiences on the prophet's behalf.[10] Due to the placement of the "Oracles against the Nations" section to an earlier position in the Greek version, the events involving Baruch appear at the end of the book in this version. This arrangement gives a different slant to the relationship between Jeremiah and Baruch from the one presented in the Masoretic Text. Baruch is the last person addressed by God in Greek Jeremiah 51,[11] the penultimate chapter

8. There is considerable variety in the traditions about the exile of Baruch. The biblical account has him going unwillingly to Egypt. According to *2 (Syriac) Apocalypse of Baruch* (see 10:1–3) and the *Paraleipomena Jeremiou*, he remained in Jerusalem while Jeremiah went to Babylon. The opening verse of the book of Baruch notes that Baruch went to Babylon. *Pesiqta Rabbati* has Baruch going to Babylon but eventually returning to Jerusalem; see 26:6 and 33:1–2.

9. See Emanuel Tov, *The Septuagint Translation of Jeremiah and Baruch: A Discussion of an Early Revision of Jeremiah 29–52 and Baruch 1:1–3:8* (HSM 8; Missoula: Scholars Press, 1976), and "L'incidence de la critique textuelle sur la critique littéraire dans le livre de Jérémie," *RB* 79 (1972) 189–99; Jerald G. Jansen, *Studies in the Text of Jeremiah* (HSM 6; Cambridge: Harvard University Press, 1973); and Louis Stulman, *The Other Text of Jeremiah: A Reconstruction of the Hebrew Text Underlying the Greek Version of the Prose Sections of Jeremiah with English Translation* (Lanham, Md.: University Press of America, 1985) 1–5; idem, "Some Theological and Lexical Differences between the Old Greek and the MT of the Jeremiah Prose Discourses," *Hebrew Studies* 25 (1984) 18–23.

10. On Baruch as a scribe with considerable social standing, see J. R. Lundbom, "Baruch, Seraiah, and Expanded Colophons in the Book of Jeremiah," *JSOT* 36 (1986) 107–8 and the literature cited there.

11. This material is found in chap. 45 of the Hebrew text.

of the book. Here God delivers to Jeremiah an oracle intended for Baruch, an oracle in which Baruch is told not to seek "great things" for himself but to rely on God's promise that he will grant him his life as a "booty" wherever he goes. This enigmatic statement,[12] its placement at the end of this version of the book, and the fact that it is a communication directed from God to Baruch via Jeremiah, suggest that the Greek version is giving special attention to Baruch at this point. True, the Masoretic Text has this same material, but the placement of it at the end of the work in Greek Jeremiah suggests that the author wants to indicate the emergence of Baruch as the successor to Jeremiah, the one who would lead the people in the great prophet's absence.[13] This arrangement of the material does not simply indicate the authorship of the work,[14] but testifies to the emergence of Baruch as the successor to Jeremiah.[15] If, according to Tov and others, Greek Jeremiah represents a more pristine form of the book, then what has taken place is that the Masoretic Text has arranged the material in part to denigrate the position of Baruch vis-à-vis

12. *2 Bar* 13:2–6 seems to be a gloss on this passage in Jeremiah: "Stand on your feet, Baruch, and hear the word of the mighty God. Because you have been astonished at that which has befallen Zion, you will surely be preserved until the end of times to be for a testimony. This means that if these happy cities will ever say, 'Why has the mighty God brought upon us this retribution?,' you and those who are like you, those who have seen this evil and retribution coming over you and your nation in their own time, may say to them that the nations will be thoroughly punished."

13. P.-M. Bogaert, "De Baruch à Jérémie: Les deux rédactions conservées du livre de Jérémie," *Le livre de Jérémie: Le prophète et son milieu, les oracles et leur transmission* (ed. P.-M. Bogaert; BETL 54; Louvain: Louvain University Press, 1981) 168–73, notes that the order in the LXX suggests that Baruch is not only the witness to the proclamation of the oracles of Jeremiah, but that he is promised by God that he will also be around to be the witness to their fulfillment. Moreover, the arrangement in the MT is intended to make Jeremiah look like not only the author of the oracles but also of the entire book itself.

14. So Bogaert, "De Baruch à Jérémie," 173; cf. Bogaert, "Le personnage de Baruch et l'histoire du livre de Jérémie: Aux origines du livre de Baruch," *BIOSCS 7* (1974) 19.

15. This is not to deny that the passage has some relationship to ancient scribal practices and conforms to the pattern of a colophon; see Lundbom, "Baruch, Seraiah, and Expanded Colophons," 99–101. In Lundbom's opinion, the two versions of the book of Jeremiah known to us in the LXX and the MT were the results of the editorial activity of Baruch and his brother Seraiah in Egypt and Babylon respectively. While the reliability of the tradition that Baruch went into and remained in Egypt with Jeremiah cannot be fully substantiated, it is nonetheless interesting to see that the two versions of Jeremiah close with their alleged editors being addressed in the fifty-first chapter of each of the two versions, Baruch in the LXX and Seraiah in the MT. The last chapter (chap. 52) is a narrative account of the fall of Jerusalem. Cf. Lundbom, *Jeremiah: A Study in Ancient Hebrew Rhetoric* (SBLDS 18; Missoula: Scholars Press, 1975) 25–27, 111, 118–20.

Jeremiah.[16] Both versions of Jeremiah end with a narrative account of the fall of Jerusalem based on 2 Kgs 24:18–25:30. Because of the order of its chapters, in Greek Jeremiah Baruch is the last person addressed in the text by God before the account of the fall of Jerusalem.

So, already in the biblical material, specifically in the Greek version, there is a clear attempt to portray Baruch as the successor to the prophet Jeremiah, a person who has his own claim to being a leader of the people.[17] In the subsequent Baruch pseudepigrapha, the character of Baruch is developed toward that of an ideal sage, each text beginning from what had preceded it and adding its own elements.

The Book of Baruch

This is an anonymous work consisting of several components that existed and circulated independently and that gradually were juxtaposed to create a new piece of literature. The text as a whole or its component parts became associated with the book of Jeremiah and was not known separately as "the book of Baruch" until the eighth century in the Latin church.[18] The testimony of the Greek church is ambiguous. Some Greek fathers quote passages from the book of Baruch but attribute them to "Jeremiah." Others cite the source of their quotation as "Baruch." Some are completely inconsistent, citing the source once as "Jeremiah" and then as "Baruch" in the very same work.[19] The whole and/or parts of this book would not have been associated

16. Bogaert, "De Baruch à Jérémie," 170–71; although he does not accept the idea of a denigration of Jeremiah in the LXX, he notes that the MT at 36:26 reads "Baruch the scribe and Jeremiah the prophet" while the LXX 43:26 reads "Baruch and Jeremiah." While this may be an example of the expansionistic tendencies of the MT (so Tov, *Septuagint Translation*, and "L'incidence"; and Jansen, *Studies*), might it not also be due to the MT's attempt to delineate clearly between the roles of Baruch and Jeremiah, while the LXX is attempting to make them seem more like equals? Note also Bogaert, "De Baruch à Jérémie," 171–72, where he details other differences between the MT and LXX that may have some bearing on the portrayal of the relationship between Baruch and Jeremiah.

17. In a Coptic Jeremiah apocryphon often entitled "The History of the Captivity in Babylon," Baruch is portrayed as the betrayer of Jeremiah, the one responsible for the prophet's imprisonment. See K. H. Kuhn, "A Coptic Jeremiah Apocryphon," *Le Muséon* 83 (1970) 116–17.

18. See P.-M. Bogaert, "Le nom de Baruch dans la littérature pseudépigraphique: L'apocalypse syriaque et le livre deutérocanonique," *La littérature juive entre Tenach et Mischna: Quelques problèmes* (ed. W. C. van Unnik; RechBib 9; Leiden: Brill, 1974) 56–72, esp. 61–72.

19. Bogaert, "Nom de Baruch," 65–66.

with Baruch until the introduction was added, because it is only in this narrative introduction that we find Baruch's name.[20]

In the narrative introduction we find that the exiles are seeking to do their best in Babylon and that they wish their brethren in Jerusalem to pray that they will enjoy the favor of their overlords Nebuchadnezzar and Belshazzar. Here Baruch speaks to the people as a prophet or other type of leader. This is evident from the fact that the king and "all" the people gather to hear his words and respond to them in a penitential manner. He appears like Ezekiel or Jeremiah in that people gather around him to hear "the word of the Lord" (Jer 25:1–2, 26:7; Ezek 8:1, 33:30–32).

The prayer of Bar 1:15–3:8 portrays Baruch as a penitent who prays like Daniel. The text of this prayer is a patchwork of excerpts from Daniel 9.[21] In this prayer, Baruch appears as one who has accepted the Deuteronomistic explanation of the fall of Jerusalem and the exile of the people.[22] As such he fits in well with the piety promulgated through such characters as Daniel: he accepts God's punishment of the disobedient people as just and, in an attitude of sincere penitence, he asks for divine forgiveness of his and his people's sins. He then requests restoration to the land based on his sincere pleading for forgiveness. The parallels cited by Tov in his text and translation of the book of Baruch show that already in the late second or early first century B.C.E. Baruch was portrayed as a person who had accepted the Deuteronomistic interpretation of history. This is seen in the use of the quotations and allusions to Deuteronomistic materials and to the use of materials from the prophets Daniel and Jeremiah in particular.[23] This prayer, then,

20. Bogaert, "Le personnage de Baruch," 20, notes that even with the introduction the work is better associated with Jeremiah and not Baruch because the οὗτοι οἱ λόγοι of Bar 1:1 refers back to Jeremiah, the book immediately preceding this one in the Bible, or perhaps the book of which this is a part.

21. For the links with Daniel in this prayer, see the notes in *The Book of Baruch* (ed. and trans. Emanuel Tov; SBLTT 8; Missoula: Scholars Press, 1975) 15–27, and L. E. Tony André, *Les Apocryphes de l'Ancien Testament* (Florence: Osvaldo Paggi, 1903). On the question of the possible relationships between the Book of Baruch and the Theodotion translation of Daniel, see Tov, "The Relations between the Greek Versions of Baruch and Daniel," *Armenian and Biblical Studies* (ed. Michael E. Stone; Jerusalem: St. James Press, 1976) 27–34.

22. Note the same deuteronomistic interpretation of history in *2 Baruch* 77.

23. Thus the original composition was made sometime after the composition of Daniel in the Maccabean period. Tov (*Septuagint Translation*, 165–67) dates the translation into Greek of Jeremiah and the book of Baruch to sometime before 116 B.C.E. based on the evidence of Ben Sira. Moreover, he dates the revision of the Old Greek translation of these books to the latter part of the second or early part of the first century B.C.E.

portrays Baruch as a person of Daniel-like piety. He is in the tradition of pious people who were concerned for the exiles and the state of the holy city.[24]

In addition to presenting Baruch as a Daniel-like repentant saint, Bar 3:9–4:4 portrays Baruch as offering a poem in praise of Wisdom. Here he calls people to pursue "Wisdom," which is presented in a fashion that recalls Proverbs 1–8. In addition, this section equates Wisdom and Torah, an equation made also by Ben Sira (24:23). The one who seeks after Wisdom also follows the precepts of Torah.[25] This section of the book of Baruch adds a wisdom element to the developing persona of Baruch.[26] He has become a Second Temple Period sage who is devoted to a "Wisdom" that combines all the learning of the past with the new "Wisdom," which is equivalent to Torah obedience.[27]

The book closes (4:5–5:9) with a paranetic discourse in which Baruch encourages the people to take heart, obey the commandments of God, and prepare themselves for a return to the land, because the God who banished them for disobedience will just as quickly restore them for obedience. He appears as a leader who encourages the people who, though still in exile, are nevertheless faithful to their God and are anxiously awaiting their repatriation.

The book of Baruch alone does not explain how Baruch the scribe became the apocalyptic seer of *2* and *3 Baruch.*[28] If Tov is right, and at least the first section of the book of Baruch was appended to the book of Jeremiah by the late second or early first century B.C.E., then what is happening is that the people writing the *Baruch* pseudepigrapha are attributing their work to a character who was developing from a scribe to a great sage.

Paraleipomena of Jeremiah

There are some discrepancies in the parallel narrative accounts of the events surrounding the fall of Jerusalem in the *Paraleipomena Jeremiou*[29] and

24. Note that a prayer of similar tone is offered by Ezra, another "scribe" and leader of the people in Ezra 9:5–15.

25. See Daniel J. Harrington, "The Wisdom of the Scribe according to Ben Sira," *Ideal Figures in Ancient Judaism* (ed. G. W. E. Nickelsburg and John J. Collins; SBLSCS 12; Chico, Calif.: Scholars Press, 1980) 181–89.

26. J. Schreiner, *Baruch* (Die Neue Echter Bibel; Altes Testament 14; Würzburg: Echtger, 1986), dates this section to ca. 200 B.C.E.

27. See Gerhard von Rad, *Wisdom in Israel* (New York: Abingdon, 1978) 240–62.

28. See P.-M. Bogaert, *Apocalypse de Baruch: Introduction, traduction du syriaque et commentaire* (Sources Chrétiennes 144–45; Paris: Du Cerf, 1969) 259 n. 1 and 453.

29. Quoted from *Paraleipomena Jeremiou* (ed. Robert A. Kraft and Ann-Elizabeth Purintun; SBLTT 1; Missoula, Mont.: Society of Biblical Literature, 1972).

Syriac *Baruch*;[30] these discrepancies involve the relationship of Jeremiah to Baruch. I will here outline the texts as they portray the direct contrasts between these two characters.

Paraleipomena Jeremiou	*2 (Syriac) Baruch*
It came to pass, when the children of Israel were taken captive by the king of the Chaldeans, that God spoke to Jeremiah saying: Jeremiah, my chosen one, arise and depart from this city, you and Baruch, since I am going to destroy it because of the multitude of the sins of those who dwell in it. For your prayers are like a solid pillar in its midst, and like an indestructible wall surrounding it. Now, then, arise and depart before the host of the Chaldeans surrounds it. . . . And the Lord said to Jeremiah: Since you are my chosen one, arise and depart the city, you and Baruch, for I am going to destroy it because of the multitude of the sins of the people who dwell in it. . . . Arise, then, and go to Baruch, and tell him these words. . . . And Jeremiah ran and told these thing to Baruch (1:1–3, 8–11; 2:1).	And it happened . . . that the word of the Lord came to Baruch, the son of Neriah, and said to him: Have you seen all that this people are doing to me, the evil things which the two tribes which remained have done—more than the ten tribes which were carried away into captivity? For the former tribes were forced by their kings to sin, but these two have themselves forced and compelled their kings to sin. Behold, therefore, I shall bring evil upon this city and its inhabitants. . . . This, then, I have said to you that you may say to Jeremiah and all those who are like you that you may retire from this city. For your works are for this city like a firm pillar and your prayers like a strong wall. (1:1–2:1)

These two texts have the following elements in common: (1) a mention of the direct address of God to the person—"God spoke to Jeremiah" (*Paraleipomena Jeremiou*), and "the word of the Lord came to Baruch" (*2 Baruch*); (2) a declaration about the multitude of the sins of the people being the cause of the impending judgment—"since I am going to destroy it (i.e., the city) because of the sins of those who dwell in it" (*Paraleipomena Jeremiou*), and "Have you seen all that this people are doing to me, the evil things which the two tribes which remained have done. . . . Behold, therefore I shall

30. Quoted from A. F. J. Klijn, "2 (Syriac Apocalypse of) Baruch," *The Old Testament Pseudepigrapha* (2 vols.; ed. James H. Charlesworth; Garden City, N.Y.: Doubleday, 1983–85) 1.615–52.

bring evil upon this city and its inhabitants" (*2 Baruch*); and (3) a statement regarding the effectiveness of the prayers or works of Jeremiah, Baruch, and their associates.[31] These two texts differ, however, when it comes to the details of who told whom what to do. In the *Paraleipomena Jeremiou* God addressed Jeremiah directly ("God spoke to Jeremiah") and instructed him to go and tell Baruch what to do. In *2 Baruch*, however, just the reverse is the case: Baruch is the recipient of the divine word ("the word of the Lord came to Baruch"), and God commands him to go and tell Jeremiah what to do. The accounts of how Jeremiah learned that he should go with the exiles to Babylon are likewise contradictory.

Paraleipomena Jeremiou

> And the Lord said to Jeremiah: . . . And you, Jeremiah, go with your people into Babylon and stay with them, preaching to them, until I cause them to return to the city. But leave Baruch here until I speak with him. . . . While Jeremiah was still weeping for the people, they brought him out with the people and dragged them to Babylon. But Baruch put dust on his head and sat and wailed this lamentation, saying: . . . When he had said this, Baruch departed from the city, weeping and saying: Grieving because of you, Jerusalem, I went out from you. And he remained sitting in a tomb, while angels came to him and explained everything that the Lord revealed to him through them.
> (3:14–16, 4:6–12)

2 (Syriac) Baruch

> And it happened after seven days that the word of the Lord came to me and said to me: Tell Jeremiah to go away in order to support the captives unto Babylon. You, however, stay here in the desolation of Zion and I shall show you after these days what will happen at the end of days. And I spoke to Jeremiah as the Lord commanded me. He, then, went away with the people, but I, Baruch, came back and sat in front of the doors of the Temple. . . .
> (10:1–5)

31. Note that the personal pronouns here indicate the piety of the several people involved and not just that of Jeremiah or Baruch; note the plural ὑμῶν in *Par Jer* 1:2, not the singular σοὺ; it is *ʿbdykwn* in *2 Bar* 2:2, not the singular *ʿbdyk*. One would expect to see the singular form of the personal pronouns were the author intending to refer to either Jeremiah or Baruch alone. Note that while *ʿbdʾ* means generally 'deed', 'work', or 'act', there is also the meaning of 'worship', 'adore', or 'service'; see Gustaf H. Dalman, ed., *Aramäisch-Neuhebräisches Wörterbuch zu Targum, Talmud und Midrasch* (Frankfurt: J. Kauffmann, 1901) 290.

It is clear that the two texts have different perspectives on the relationship between Jeremiah and Baruch. According to the *Paraleipomena Jeremiou*, God speaks to Jeremiah and tells him directly that he is to go to Babylon with the others and that he should tell Baruch to remain in Jerusalem. Shortly thereafter we read that God reveals things to Baruch that the angels then interpret for him. The account in *2 Baruch*, on the other hand, has God speaking to Baruch and telling him to instruct Jeremiah to go to Babylon, instructions that Jeremiah dutifully follows. In addition, here God tells Baruch to remain in Jerusalem so that he can teach the seer what will happen "at the end of days." In *2 Baruch*'s account of the fall of Jerusalem, there seems to be a point made of the greatness of Baruch's piety over that of his contemporaries. *2 Baruch* 6–9 has Baruch alone witnessing the invasion of the angels to break down the walls of the city and to hide the sacred vessels. In *Paraleipomena Jeremiou* both Baruch and Jeremiah witness this. This appears to be part of the attempt to limit the role of Jeremiah or to emphasize the emergence of Baruch as a successor to the great prophet in this text.

In another instance, Baruch says that he was the one who took several leaders of the people to the Kidron valley in order to tell them what he had heard from God, a message to which they responded with lamentation.

> And I went away and took with me Jeremiah and Adu and Seraiah and Jabish and Gedaliah and all the nobles of the people. And I brought them to the valley of Kidron and told them all which had been said to me. And they raised their voices and they all lamented. And we sat there and fasted until the evening (*2 Bar* 5:5–7).

Paraleipomena Jeremiou and *2 Baruch* exhibit a discrepancy regarding the nature of the relationship between Jeremiah and Baruch. It is clear from the very close verbal links between these two texts in these passages that they drew on a common source for the traditions about Baruch, Jeremiah, and the fall of the holy city.[32] Given the overall prominence of Jeremiah in Jewish and Christian tradition, we may assume that the work that has Baruch appearing equal to or superior to Jeremiah is trying either to promote Baruch over Jeremiah or, more probably, is trying to show how Baruch succeeded Jeremiah as a qualified recipient of divine oracles.[33] These texts, therefore,

32. G. W. E. Nickelsburg ("Narrative Traditions in the Paraleipomena of Jeremiah and 2 Baruch," *CBQ* [1973] 60–68) shows conclusively that *2 Baruch* and *Paraleipomena Jeremiou* are drawing on a common source.

33. Note *2 Bar* 33:1–3, where a command given to Baruch by Jeremiah is quoted; in it the prophet tells Baruch to remain in Jerusalem and to teach the people while Jeremiah

reflect the transition that was indicated already in Greek Jeremiah: Baruch became Jeremiah's successor, the one who took up the prophetic mantel in Jeremiah's absence.[34]

Second (Syriac) Baruch

This apocalypse dates roughly to the same period as *Paraleipomena Jeremiou*, shortly after the destruction of the temple by the Romans in 70 C.E.[35] Baruch is portrayed here as the successor to Jeremiah. One way in which the author presents Baruch as in continuity with the biblical prophets is by using a phrase to introduce the divine oracles addressed to Baruch that was the classical formula for introducing a message from God: 'the word of the Lord came to Baruch' (*hwʾ ptgmʾ dmryʾ ʿl brwk*) (1:1, 10:1, etc.).[36] As much as the divine word "came" to Jeremiah (היה דבר־יהוה אל ירמיה; compare Jer 1:2, 4, 11, 13; 2:1, etc.), so, this author would have us understand, has Baruch received divine oracles. Thus, Baruch is in the line of the classical prophets.

After his first address to the leaders of the people informing them of what God was revealing to him, Baruch begins to go away from them, and they respond with the following words:[37]

---

is in Babylon. This seems to go against a strict rewriting of the relationships in favor of the priority of Baruch over Jeremiah in this book. The quoted material occurs nowhere in *2 Baruch* or elsewhere in the Baruch literature to my knowledge. So, the contradictory traditions about the relationship between Jeremiah and Baruch occur even within this single text.

34. Perhaps Baruch was not the only one regarded as Jeremiah's successor according to *Paraleipomena Jeremiou*, for whenever Jeremiah addresses Baruch in this book he speaks to both Baruch and Abimelech, apparently viewing the two as each equally his disciples or replacements while he is in Babylon (see 7:16, 32; 8:7; 9:7–8, 26, 29, 32). The passage 9:23–29 is of particular importance, because here Jeremiah delivers to both Baruch and Abimelech "all the mysteries which he had seen" from God.

35. P.-M. Bogaert ("Le nom de Baruch," 60, 71–72) thinks that *2 Baruch* was the first book to bear the name Baruch and that all the others developed from this one.

36. See Gerhard von Rad, *The Message of the Prophets* (New York: Harper and Row, 1965) 66–67.

37. Attention to the words of the people whom a seer addressed will, it seems to me, help us a great deal in determining the social setting of these works. For an attempt to locate the social setting of *1 Enoch* 1–36, "The Book of the Watchers," see Martha Himmelfarb, "From Prophecy to Apocalypse: The Book of Watchers and Tours of Heaven," *Jewish Spirituality: From the Bible through the Middle Ages* (World Spirituality: An Encyclopedic History of the Religious Quest 13; New York: Crossroad, 1986) 154–62.

> And it happened after having said all these words to them that I, Baruch, went my way. And when the people saw that I went away, they raised their voices and lamented and said: Where are you going from us, Baruch, and do you leave us as a father who leaves his children as orphans and goes away from them? . . . And now, if you abandon us too, it would have been better for all of us that we shall die first, and that then you should abandon us. And I answered and said to the people: Heaven forbid that I should abandon you or that I should go away from you. But I shall go to the Holy of Holies to ask from the Mighty One on behalf of you and Zion so that I may receive in some ways more light, and after that I shall return to you (*2 Bar* 32:8–9, 33:3–34:1).

The people thought that Baruch was about to leave them for good and were fearful of being left without a leader.[38] Their response indicates how highly they valued his presence. This response also indicates how the author of this text perceived his role vis-à-vis the people he was addressing or those who would subsequently read this text. He intended that the readers put themselves in the position of the people addressed by Baruch and that they view him as a divinely inspired seer and this text as the product of divine revelation.

In *2 Baruch* 44–45 Baruch addresses the leaders of the people a second time, telling them that he is about to leave this world. Their response to this announcement shows how they regard him as their inspired interpreter:

> And my son and the elders of the people said to me: Did the Mighty One humiliate us to such an extent that he will take you away from us quickly? And shall we truly be in darkness, and will there be no light anymore for that people who are left? For where shall we again investigate the Law, or who will distinguish between death and life for us? And I said to them: I cannot resist the throne of the Mighty One. But Israel will not be in want of a wise man, nor the tribe of Jacob, a son of the Law. But only prepare your heart so that you obey the Law, and be subject to those who are wise and understanding with fear. And prepare your soul that you shall not depart from them. If you do this, those good tidings will come to you of which I spoke to you earlier, and you will not fall into the torrent of which I spoke to you earlier.
> (*2 Bar* 46:1–6)

Here Baruch is the inspired or the divinely authorized interpreter of Torah to whom the people turned for the correct interpretation of the Law. He has

38. According to *Par Jer* 9:1–12, when Jeremiah appeared to have died, the people responded in a manner similar to this; James D. Tabor (" 'Returning to the Divinity': Josephus's Portrayal of the Disappearances of Enoch, Elijah, and Moses," *JBL* 108 [1989] 225–38) points out that in the Greco-Roman world when a holy person "returned to the divinity," those who followed him or her would respond with tears and weeping.

the ability to "distinguish between life and death," that is to tell which things please God and lead to salvation and which displease him and, therefore, lead to death. Such a role is attributed to Moses in Deut 30:11–20 (cf. *2 Bar* 19:1–4). The author of *2 Baruch* viewed himself and wished his readers to view him as one of those later inspired interpreters to whom people should turn for instruction in Torah. Even though Moses would pass away, and after him Baruch, God would provide other teachers to take their place. In this community of inspired teachers like Moses and Baruch the author of this work positions himself.

Baruch is consistently portrayed as a Moses-like figure in *2 Baruch*.[39] He embodies Wisdom and Torah, and his fidelity to the Law is irreproachable (*2 Bar* 38:2–4). God gave revelations to him just as he did to Moses.

> For he showed him (i.e., Moses) many warnings together with the ways of the Law and the end of time,[40] as also to you; and then further, also the likeness of Zion with its measurements which was to be made after the likeness of the present sanctuary (*2 Bar* 59:4).[41]

Just as Moses saw "many warnings," so too did Baruch. In chap. 76 Baruch is told by an angel to ascend a mountain before he leaves the earth in order that God might show to him all manner of mysteries. Such an experience is modeled on the events in the last days of the life of Moses (see Deut. 32:48–52 and 34:1–8).[42] He is told that he will depart this world but not via death, an idea that directly parallels a tradition that Moses did not die but ascended to heaven from Mt. Nebo.[43] In chap. 84 Baruch appears as a mediator of another Moses-like Covenant.[44]

39. This has been pointed out by Frederick James Murphy, *The Structure and Meaning of Second Baruch* (Atlanta: Scholars Press, 1985) 117–34.

40. There was a tradition that God showed also this to Moses: "Do not read עד הים האחרון 'unto the hinder sea', but עד היום האחרון 'unto the last day'. This means that he showed to him all the world from the day it was created until the day when the dead will became alive." See *Sifre Deut.* 357 (ed. L. Finkelstein) 426.

41. Note that a model of the sanctuary was revealed also to Ezekiel in great detail according to Ezekiel 40–48.

42. See Murphy, *Structure and Meaning*, 23.

43. See S. E. Loewenstamm, "The Death of Moses," *Studies on the Testament of Abraham* (ed. G. W. E. Nickelsburg, Jr.; SBLSCS 6; Missoula, Mont.: Scholars Press, 1976) 185–217. Compare *2 Bar* 84:1–11.

44. Murphy, *Structure and Meaning*, 27; he entitles this chapter "Baruch renews the covenant which Moses established," 25.

> Now, I gave you knowledge, while I still live. For I have said that you should particularly learn my mighty commandments[45] which he has instructed you. And I shall set before you some of the commandments of his judgment before I die. Remember that once Moses called heaven and earth to witness against you and said, "If you trespass the law, you shall be dispersed. And if you shall keep it, you shall be planted." And also other things he said to you when you were in the desert as twelve tribes together. And after his death you cast it away from you and, therefore, that which has been said before has come upon you. And now, Moses spoke to you before it befell you and, behold, it has befallen you for you have forsaken the Law. Also I, behold, I say to you after you suffered that if you obey the things which I have said to you, you shall receive from the Mighty One everything which has been prepared and has been preserved for you. Therefore, let this letter be a witness between me and you that you may remember the commandments of the Mighty One, and that it also may serve as my defense in the presence of him who has sent me. And remember Zion and the Law and the holy land and your brothers and the covenant and your fathers, and do not forget the festivals and the sabbaths. And give this letter and the traditions of the Law to your children after you as also your fathers handed down to you (*2 Bar* 84:1–9).

Here Baruch claims a direct continuity between Moses and himself. He is communicating divine commandments to the people just as Moses had done. Moreover, he reiterates the promise to the people that if they are diligent to obey the Law, they will be blessed.

Not only is Baruch the inspired interpreter, but he also insured that his teachings would be passed on accurately to succeeding generations by appointing select successors who would be invested with his authority.

> And I, Baruch, went from there and came to my people and called my firstborn son and the Gedaliahs, my friends, and seven of the elders of the people and said to them: Behold, I go to my fathers in accordance with the way of the whole earth. You, however, do not withdraw from the way of the Law, but guard and admonish the people who are left lest they withdraw from the commandments of the Mighty One (*2 Bar* 44:1–3; cf. 84:9).

Here we see the beginning of the transfer of the role that Baruch has been filling to the other leaders of the people. The passage continues with Baruch exhorting these leaders to follow the ways of the Lord and to be sure to guide the people in them, because the way of the Torah is the way of life. I think the author would have considered himself, or would like his readers to consider

45. Probably read "the commandments of the Mighty One," as in one manuscript.

him, to be one of these successors and thus authorized to speak in the name of Baruch. In addition, it is truly telling to observe the high value that the author is attributing to his words: these teachings are able to make the one who reads and follows them live, that is, they are the means of salvation.[46]

The people respond similarly to another of Baruch's farewell discourses in which he gives a brief deuteronomistic explanation of the captivity and then tells those remaining with him in Jerusalem[47] that they must behave righteously or else be prepared to suffer the same consequences. To this the people respond with the following words:

> And the whole people answered and they said to me: Everything which we can remember of the good things which the Mighty One has done to us we shall remember, and that which we do not remember he knows in his grace. But do this for us, your people: Write also to our brothers in Babylon a letter of doctrine and a roll of hope so that you might strengthen them also before you go away from us. For the shepherds of Israel have perished, and the lamps[48] which gave light are extinguished, and the fountains from which we used to drink have withheld their steams. Now we have been left in the darkness and in the thick forest and in the aridness of the desert. And I answered and said to them: Shepherds and lamps and fountains came from the Law and when we go away, the Law will abide. If you, therefore, look upon the Law and are intent upon wisdom, then the lamp will not be wanting and the shepherd will not give way and the fountain will not dry up (*2 Bar* 77:11–16).

The importance of these inspired leaders in the ideology of this book is illustrated further by *2 Bar* 85:1–4, which is part of the just-mentioned letter to be sent to the nine and one-half tribes in exile:

> Further, know that our fathers in former times and former generations had helpers, righteous prophets and holy men. But we were also in our country, and they helped us when we sinned, and they intervened for us with him who has created us since they trusted in their works. And the Mighty One heard them and purged us from our sins. But now, the righteous have been assembled, and the prophets are sleeping. Also we have left our land, and Zion has been taken away from us, and we have nothing now apart from the Mighty One and his

46. That someone could either claim authority to give peculiar teachings, or that a teacher could authorize another to spread about his teachings, is behind the questions addressed to Jesus in Matt 21:23–27.

47. On the whereabouts of Baruch, see n. 9 above.

48. According to *2 Bar* 59:1–2 the "lamp" is the Law that was promulgated by Moses, Aaron, Miriam, Joshua, and Caleb.

> Law. Therefore, if we direct and dispose our hearts, we shall receive everything which we lost again by many times.

From this one may conclude that the inspired interpreter, though not mentioned in the immediate context, is the one who will now guide the community in the proper observance of Torah.[49]

That the various groups within Judaism developed on the basis of differences in the interpretation of the Torah is clear. An example of this is Jesus, who is often presented as giving new interpretations to the ancient, authoritative Scriptures. In Matt 5:21–48, several times Jesus says "you have heard it said . . . ," then cites a commandment from the Torah, and then says "but I say to you . . . ," and then gives a new interpretation of the meaning of the particular commandment. Here he is an inspired interpreter of Torah who regards himself as giving the real or divinely-intended meaning of that passage. Jesus' interpretations of the Torah and their concomitant practices led to disputes with other Jewish leaders. This is evident in the debate with some Pharisees over the ritual cleansing of hands prior to eating (Matt 15:1–3 and parallels). Each of the two groups represented here had its own approach or interpretation of what was intended by the relevant biblical passages.

Paul's place in the debates between Early Christianity and its Jewish contemporaries, as well as his place in the internal Christian debates, was determined by his interpretation of Scripture. Regarding himself as the inspired interpreter and teacher, he often warns his followers to remain faithful to the teachings that he delivered to them and not to be led astray from them by other, "false" teachers (see 1 Cor 11:2; Col 2:8; 2 Thess 2:15, 3:6; 1 Tim 6:3–4). The Teacher of Righteousness at Qumran appears also to have functioned as the group's inspired interpreter. He was inspired by God to interpret the Bible and to reveal other divine mysteries (cf. 1QpHab II 1–10, VII 3–5, 17–VIII 31; 1QH II 13–15). The Qumran sectarians, like Paul and his followers, set themselves against all those whose biblical interpretations and concomitant religious practices conflicted with theirs.

Baruch is presented in *2 Baruch* as this type of divinely-inspired interpreter of Torah.[50] The people who follow his interpretations and other teachings do so because they believe his are the only teachings that correctly interpret the

49. The inspired interpreter is a constituent element in the persona of the wise sage figure described by Michael Stone in "Ideal Figures and Social Context."

50. Compare Gwendolyn B. Sayler, *Have the Promises Failed? A Literary Analysis of 2 Baruch* (SBLDS 72; Chico, Calif.: Scholars Press, 1984) 110–18.

Torah and that alone lead to salvation. The apocalypse is part of this collection of inspired documents; its teachings are to be regarded as coming directly from God via Baruch.

Conclusions

Baruch is presented in the Masoretic textual tradition of the book of Jeremiah as the scribal aide to the prophet Jeremiah. Although this was a highly respected profession, the portrayal in the MT shows clearly that Jeremiah is the prophet and that Baruch is his helper; Jeremiah in every way holds the lead role, while Baruch remains a secondary character.

The Greek recension of the book of Jeremiah presents a transition in the relationships between Jeremiah and Baruch. Here Baruch emerges as Jeremiah's successor. The Book of Baruch, an addition to Greek Jeremiah, portrays Baruch as a Daniel-like penitent saint and man of Wisdom who addresses the people as one of their leaders, much like Daniel and Ezra.

2 Baruch adds another element to the persona of Baruch: now he has become a visionary and inspired sage. Assuming the priority of 4 Ezra, Baruch is portrayed as an Ezra-like sage who engages in disputes with God over issues of theodicy. In several passages of this work there is evident a social context where Baruch appears as the inspired interpreter of Torah upon whose divinely inspired teachings the people depend for eternal life.

To return to my initial question, I now ask, "why was *3 Baruch* so attributed?" It appears from the preceding study that the character of Baruch evolved from the historical figure to that of an "Ideal Sage" during the Second Temple Period. He was thought to be a very pious man of great learning. Believing that Baruch had already received a "historical apocalypse" (that is, *2 Baruch*), the author of *3 Baruch* thought it appropriate to attribute this text to him. Like Enoch he could be portrayed as having received both a "historical" and an "otherworldly journey" apocalypse.[51] He had become an "Ideal Sage."

The sage had a prominent position in Early Judaism. According to Ben Sira (chaps. 38–39), he was respected for his wisdom, piety, and knowledge of Torah. The shift in ritual practice within Judaism during the Second Temple Period from sacrifice to study of the authoritative documents is

51. For definitions and descriptions of these types of apocalypses, see John J. Collins, "The Jewish Apocalypses," *Semeia* 14 (1979) 34–35, 41–42.

reflected partially in the rise of the synagogue as a place for Jewish gathering and learning.[52] Here one could learn the Torah from one who had mastered it. The canonical literature attests the place of Ezra as a wise and learned scribe (Ezra 7:10). As I hope I have shown, the literature of the Second Temple Period attests the development of Baruch toward that of an "Ideal Sage."

52. See Lee I. Levine, "The Second Temple Synagogue: The Formative Years," *The Temple in Late Antiquity* (ed. Lee I. Levine; Philadelphia: American Schools of Oriental Research, 1987) 7–31.

SECTION 2

Ancient Near Eastern History and Linguistics

Some Unrecognized North Syrian Toponyms in Egyptian Sources

Michael C. Astour

Egyptian topographic lists and historical records of the New Kingdom served as the earliest available—and for a long time the only—source of North Syrian toponymy of the Bronze Age. In the absence of contemporaneous local documentation, the Egyptian toponymic material was often misunderstood and gave rise to a distorted image of the ethnohistory of North Syria.[1] Later epigraphic discoveries at Ugarit, Mari, Alalaḫ, Ḫattušaš, and more recently at Emar and, above all, at Ebla have greatly increased the toponymic data at our disposal and have helped to correct the obsolete views that continue to persist.[2] Even so, the Egyptian material (which also has grown in volume in the last decades) has retained its importance for the toponymist and historical geographer. Some of its data remain unique, and others represent the only Late Bronze mentions of Eblean place-names from Early Bronze III. On the following pages, I shall endeavor to clarify a number of hitherto unrecognized Egyptian entries pertaining to Northern Syria. These will be arranged in the chronological order of the inscriptions in which they appear.[3]

Author's note: abbreviations used in this article include the following:

AT	siglum for Alalakh Text(s)
TM	siglum for tablets from Tell Mardikh–Ebla
SSAU IV	Manfred Dietrich and Oswald Loretz, "Die soziale Struktur von Alalaḫ und Ugarit (IV): Die É = *bītu*-Listen aus Alalaḫ als Quelle für die Erforschung der gesellschaftlichen Schichtung von Alalaḫ im 15tn Jh. v.Chr.," *ZA* 60 (1970) 88–123 [cited by no. of text and line]
VE	siglum for "Il Vocabolario di Ebla," published in MEE 4

1. See Astour (1977) 124–25.

2. See Astour (1988a).

3. The transliteration from Egyptian group writing follows the system applied for the Medinet Habu list of Ramesses III in Astour (1968), explained there on p. 749 and in the chart on p. 751. A comprehensive chart for all topographic lists may be compiled at a later opportunity.

A. Thutmose I's Gate at Karnak[4]

3. *Ḏə-ʾu-ni*:[5] ^{uru}*Za-ú-na* AT 352:4; SSAU IV 21:15′; also ^{uru}*Za-ú-ti*/*Za-i-ti*/*Za-i-te*/*Za-i-it* in other Alalaḫ IV texts. A town of the land of Mukišḫe, not far from its capital Alalaḫ. Recurs in the Annals of Shalmaneser III as ^{uru}*Gil-za-ú*[6] and possibly as *Za-ì-ti*^{ki} at Ebla.[7] It is now Zau (Arabic) or Zev (Turkish, 14 km south-southeast of Antakya, on the road from that city to Ǧisr eš-Šuġr, in the Ǧebel Quṣeyr, which was known as the Boxwood Mountain in the second millennium B.C.E.[8] It was the abundance of precious wood that attracted the troops of Thutmose I there during his victorious expedition to Northern Syria.[9]

B. Thutmose III's Naharina List

The Naharina List, though it includes the names of several non-Syrian places within the sphere of Mitannian domination, remains the richest single Egyptian source on North Syrian toponymy. A new critical edition of the Naharina List is highly desirable. Here will be given only those of its entries that appear in the Ebla texts but are not attested in any other Bronze Age records. When comparing the Eblaic names with their Egyptian counterparts, written down some 900 years later, the following considerations should be taken into account:

(a) Differences of vocalization, a common phenomenon in Semitic onomastica, are already attested in Eblaic toponymy.
(b) Some cases may be due to the imprecision of Egyptian syllabic notation, one aspect of which is vocalic metathesis.

4. Engraved, along with *Q-d-m* and *Tu*$_5$*-na-p* (Tunip), on extant blocks from a dismantled gate at Karnak. Published by Redford (1979). For the attribution to Thutmose II rather than to Amenhotep I, see Bradbury (1985a) 76–77; (1985b).

5. Redford sought a similar name in several ancient sources but overlooked the Alalaḫ texts.

6. See Röllig, *RLA* 3.375. It was located on the route of Shalmaneser III's retreat from Qarqar to a place where he "mounted boats and went into the sea," which must have taken place at the mouth of the Orontes in the loyal kingdom of Patin (Unqi).

7. ARET IV 2 §23, if NI = *ì* (most common value at Ebla).

8. The name of the town, derived from Akkadian *zaʾu* '(fragrant) resin' fits well its location.

9. Cf. Astour (1989) 15–16.

(c) Lack of distinction between voiced, unvoiced, and emphatic consonants, and insufficient differentiation between sibilants in Eblaic orthography, which is similar to Old Akkadian but less consistent.
(d) Simultaneous use of simple and affixed forms of names both at Ebla and in later periods.
(e) Addition, in the middle third of the second millennium, of one or more Hurrian formatives (*-ḫe*, *-ni*, *-na*, *-šše*, *-we*, *-zzi*) to Semitic place-names.

126. *Ru-gə-bə₄* : *Ur-ḫu-bù*^{ki} ARET VIII 524 §39; ARET VII 152:I:6; 153: obv.III:10.[10] Egyptian *g* transcribed the Semitic and Hurrian sound *ġ*.[11] In cuneiform script, *ġ* was rendered by *ḫ*-holding signs. It may be assumed that this was the case with the Eblaic name. There is no root RḪB in Semitic; RḤB is out of the question, because *ḥ* was not noted by *ḫ*-holding signs in Eblaic; thus, there only remains a derivation from RĠB in one of its Ugaritic, Arabic, or Hebrew (> R^{c}B) meanings.

142. *Ru-r-t-ya* : *Lu-la-tù*^{ki} ARET III 467:rev.VI:6; *Lu-la-ti*^{ki} ARET VIII 524 §13.[12] Possibly modern Lulīyeh on the Sağur River.

153. *Śu-bə-qə* : *Šu-bù-gú*^{ki} ARET VIII 523 §32; *Šu-bí-gú*^{ki} 524 §24.

168. *Ḫu-ṯə-rə-ḏú* : *Ḫu-za-rí-um*^{ki} ARET III 457:rev.VI:4. Recurs in the eighth century as ^{uru}*Ḫu-za-ar-ra*, one of the cities of Unqi (Plain of Antioch and neighboring hills), Annals of Tiglath-pileser, Rost (1893) I, 24 line 144, now Ḥazreh. KÁ *Ḫu-za-ri* Em 296:1 (name of a gate or city quarter in thirteenth-century Emar) has no relation to the place-name in question but derives from a personal name (cf. *Ḫu-uz-za-ra* AT 179:27; 192:3).[13]

203. *ᵓA-ya-ta-wá* : *Á-i-tù*^{ki} ARET II 5 §44; "Culto" 1:rev.IX:9: *A-i-tù*^{ki} ARET VII 156:obv.IV:2.

10. ARET VII has reached me during the preparation of this article, but its editor, Alfonso Archi, had kindly sent me a copy of its index of geographical names in October, 1987.

11. See C:20 below.

12. Thus in the index of geographical names, but *lu-la-si*^{ki} in the text. The photograph of the tablet (pl. XXXI) allows the discernment of *ti* in the box obv.IX:4.

13. The initial group of the Egyptian entry could be read *ḫa* or *ḫu*; *ḫu* was chosen by analogy with Eblean and Neo-Assyrian spellings. Groups with *ṯ*, which normally transcribed the Semitic samek, could also stand—against Rainey (1980) 339 but with Albright (1934) passim and most students of Egyptian topographic lists—for Semitic *z* and the Anatolian phoneme expressed by cuneiform *z*-holding signs.

205. *Tu$_5$-ᵓu-bᵓə* : *Tù-u$_9$-bù*^{ki} TM.75.G.1451:rev.II:12;[14] TM.75.G.1669: rev.VI:8;[15] TM.75.G.2377:obv.III:4 ("Little T."), obv.III:7–IV:1 ("Great T."), with duplicate TM.75.G.2379;[16] TM.75.G.1410.[17] *Tu$_5$-ᵓu-bè* was identified with ^{uru}*Tu-ba*$^{(ki)}$ of the Alalaḫ VII tablets;[18] however, the latter, a royal appanage of the kingdom of Yamḫad, appears at Ebla, also as a client kingdom, written *Tù-ub*^{ki}.[19] The clearly marked glottal stop in *Tuᵓubu* (both in the Eblaic and the Egyptian spellings) points to a name of a different derivation.

207. *Ši-na-rə-ka-ya* : *Ša-na-ru$_{12}$-gú*^{ki} TM.75.G.1451:rev.I:2;[20] ARET III 57: III:8; 774:obv.I:1; and variants.[21]

213. *ᵓA-rə-sə* : perhaps *A-la-sú*^{ki} ARET II 14:XI:5; *Al-la-su$_{11}$*^{ki} ARET III 732:V:8. However, the final syllables of the Eblean names may as well be read, respectively, *-zu* and *-zú*, which would not have been transcribed by Egyptian *s*, phonetically identical to *ś* at the time of the New Kingdom.

221. *ᵓA-tu$_5$-rə* : *A-du-úr*^{ki} TM.75.G.1462:obv.III:2;[22] ARET VIII 521 §§12, 19, 22; *A-du-ur*^{ki} ARET VIII 540 §19; *A-du-lu*^{ki} ARET VIII 522 §10; 523 §28; 525 §30; and in some unpublished texts.

223. *ᵓÍ-si-tə* : *Ì-sa-tù*^{ki} TM.75.G.5188:rev.III:5 = MEE I 4139; perhaps *Ì-za/sà-a-tù*^{ki} ARET VII 155 (5 times).

225. *ᵓÉ-nu*: If it transcribed the toponym in its cuneiform (i.e., Akkadian) pronunciation *īnu/ēnu*, meaning 'eye' or 'spring', then there is a possibility that the same place-name was recorded at Ebla as *A-nu*^{ki} (*anu* being the Eblaic pronunciation of Semitic *ᶜayn-*),[23] ARET VIII 522 §19; 526 §10, and ideographically as IGI^{ki} ARET VIII 523 §33; TM.75.G.2420:88 (treaty between Ebla and *A*-BAR.SAL$_4$^{ki}).[24] In the treaty, IGI^{ki} is listed among sixteen

14. Published by Archi (1981) text 2.
15. Published by Archi (1980) 11–14.
16. Published by Archi (1979) 107–8.
17. Quoted by Pettinato (1986) 369 under MEE I 848.
18. Albright and Lambdin (1957) 120.
19. See Matthiae (1979).
20. Published by Archi (1981) text 2.
21. These include *Sa-na-ru$_{12}$-gú*^{ki}, *Ša-na-lu-gú*^{ki}.
22. Unpublished, except for a passage quoted in Archi (1984) 229 n. 2; but a full list of the toponyms in this text was kindly supplied to me by Archi.
23. See VE 712, 715, 723, 728b; cf. Krebernik (1982–83) II, 27 *ad* VE 712; Fronzaroli (1984) 136, 143.
24. Published by Sollberger (1980). The edition of the text by Pettinato (who reads *A-šur$_y$*^{ki} for *A*-BAR.SAL$_4$^{ki}) has not appeared, or reached me, as of this writing, but I am

cities[25] claimed by the king of Ebla as being "in his hand." One of them is Carchemish, which suggests that the remaining fifteen cities, and *A*-BAR.SAL$_4$^{ki} itself, were located in or near the area of the great bend of the Euphrates. The hieroglyphic Hittite stele 1 §10, from Tell Aḥmar (ancient Til-Barsib, capital of Bīt-Adini, 14 miles southeast of Carchemish on the opposite bank of the Euphrates), mentions a country Ana (*Á-na*^{REGIO}, §10) in which the royal author's grandfather had died.[26] This agrees with the probable location of Eblean Anu.

226. *ʾA-ta-bʾə-na* : *A-da-ba*$_4$^{ki} ARET VIII 529 §7; *A-da-bù*^{ki} TM.75.G.1451:obv.V:13;[27] *ʾÀ-da-bà*^{ki} TM.76.G.295.[28] Since Egyptian *t* in the fifteenth century also rendered Semitic *d*, and cuneiform DA at Ebla was read both *da* and *tá*, the phonetic value of the dental does not influence the analogy between the cuneiform and the hieroglyphic writings of the place-name.

227. *ʾA-šə̌-mə$_4$-bə̀* : *A*$^{?}$*-šúm-ba*^{ki} TM.75.G.1964:obv.II:1.[29]

228. *ʾA-tə-ka-rə* : *A-da-gàr*^{ki} TM.75.G.1451:rev.VI:13.[30]

230. *ʾA-ta-rə-nu* : *A-dar-a-nu*^{ki} ARET III 104:rev.II:7.

253. *Pá-pá-ʾa* : *Ba-ba*^{ki} (or *Pá-pá*^{ki}) TM.75.G.1320.[31]

282. *Mə́-šə̌-wá* : *Maš-a*^{ki} ARET III 193:VI:2; ARET IV 15 §49: ARET VIII 538 §24; TM.75.G.1399 §28;[32] TM.75.G.2233;[33] *Ma-ša-ù*^{ki} TM.75.G.1410.[34]

---

obliged to him for allowing me to peruse the manuscript of 1983. *A-nu*^{ki} and IGI^{ki} appear in very similar groupings of cities.

25. Two (according to Pettinato) or four (according to Sollberger) city names have been lost.

26. New edition by Hawkins (1980). His guess that Ana may represent the land of Ḫana on the middle Euphrates cannot be accepted, for the pharyngeal in Ḫana was the strong phoneme *ḫ*, which would not be elided in Hittite hieroglyphic writing. Nor is *A-na-i-tá*^{REGIO} in Tell Aḥmar 2:6 the city of Ḫanat (second millennium) or Anat(u) (first millennium), modern ᶜĀnah: it is much too far from Bīt-Adini for its king to "settle it." It is rather a Semitic feminine ethnic adjective from the same *Á-na*^{REGIO}. Perhaps *ʾA-nu* in the list Simons XIV:34 (Seti I) is the same place as NL 225.

27. Published by Archi (1981) text 2.

28. Quoted in MEE I 6505–11.

29. Published by Archi (1981) text 3.

30. Ibid., text 2.

31. Quoted in MEE I 758a.

32. An excerpt of this text was published by Zaccagnini (1984) 198–201.

33. Quoted in MEE I 1671.

34. Quoted in Pettinato (1986) 365 under MEE I 848.

283. *ʾÍ-in-rə-ka*: *Il-la-ga*^{ki} ARET VIII 524 §7; 525 §44; TM.75.G.10019: rev.II.[35]

291. *Tə-kə-ən-wə* : *Du-gan*^{ki} (or *Tù-kan*^{ki}) TM.75.G.1281:IV:3.[36] The Eblean city should probably not be equated with *Tkn* in the kingdom of Ugarit, PRU II 26:rev.15; PRU V 76:27; *Tkny* RIH 83/2:29; cuneiform ^{uru}*Ta*$^{!}$*-ku-ni* PRU VI 93:15; LÚ.MEŠ *Ta-ku-*[*ni*] PRU III 231:IV:40.[37]

292. *Tə-ru-ḫá* : perhaps *Da-ra-ḫa-tù/ti*^{ki} ARET III 93:IV:2; MEE II 37: rev.IX:8; TM.75.11100:rev.I:3′;[38] *Dar-ḫa-tù/tum/ti*^{ki} ARET I 8 §40; 16 §§3, 4; ARET III 584:IV:4, V:4; *Da-ar-ḫu-ù*^{ki} ARET VIII 527 §9.[39]

293. *ʾÚ-rə-nà* : *U*$_9$*-ra-na-a*^{ki} MEE II 13:obv.VI:1; 35:rev.IV:6; 43:obv.X:9; TM.75.G.1353 §14;[40] *U*$_9$*-ra-na-an*^{ki} TM 75.G.1293:obv.VI:1;[41] *Ù-ra-an*^{ki} TM.75.G.2377:obv.V:35.[42]

294. *Rə-mə́-ən-na-ya* : *Lum-na-an*^{ki}/*Lum-na-nu*^{ki}/*Lu-mu-na-an*^{ki}/*Lu-mu-na-nu*^{ki} One of the principal client kingdoms of Ebla, mentioned too frequently to list the occurrences here.[43]

298. *ʾA-rə-šə́-*[. .]: It is tempting to compare *ʾÀ-la-šu-bí*^{ki} TM.75.G.2420: 76;[44] *A-ra-su-bí*^{ki} ARET VIII 523 §40.

307. *Ku-rə-mi-tə* : *Gur-mi-tù*^{ki} ARET III 82:VIII:1.

308. *ʾA-mi-ku-u*⟨*n*⟩[45] : *A-ʾà-mi-gú*^{ki} ARET II 28:III:2.[46]

315. *ʾÙ-ka-mə́* : *Ù-ga-mu*^{ki} ARET IV 19 §20.

344. *ʾA-d̠a-ən-nu*$_5$: *ʾÀ-za-an*^{ki} An important city of the royal domain of Ebla, the textual occurrences of which must be omitted here for the same rea-

35. Quoted in MEE I 4922.
36. Published by Archi (1984) text 4.
37. Both readings are found in Weselius (1983).
38. Quoted in MEE I 5040.
39. Omitted in the index of geographical names of the volume.
40. Published by Milano (1980) 12–15.
41. Published by Archi (1987a) 67–72.
42. Published by Archi (1979) 107–8.
43. See the indexes of geographical names in ARET I, II, III, IV, VII, VIII; MEE I, II; Pettinato (1986) 380–81.
44. See B:225 and n. 24 above.
45. On the final, incompletely carved group see Albright and Lambdin (1957) 121, entry 36. They identified the place with ^{uru}*A-ma-ak-wa-an* AT 56:3 (Alalaḫ VII); but the latter is probably a different site.
46. The text has *A-ʾà-mu-gú*^{ki}, but the index of geographical names has *A-ʾà-mi-gú*^{ki}. The position of the box in question on the photograph (pl. XXIII) makes it illegible.

son as in no. 294 above, except for the variants *ʾÀ-za-n*[*u*^{ki}] ARET III 952: III:2 and *ʾÀ-za-ni* ARET VIII 538 §17.

398. *Rə-təp* : *La-da-bí-ià*^{ki} TM.75.G.1558:III:5;[47] *Lu-da-ba-ù*^{ki} TM.75.G. 1975:obv.III:3;[48] *La-du-bí*^{ki} TM.75.G.1353 §30;[49] *Li-da-ba*$_4^{ki}$ ARET III 747:II:7; *Li-ti-ba*$_4^{ki}$ ARET III 197:VI:2; 261:III:6; 861:2:9; *Lá-da-ba*$_4^{ki}$ ARET VII 94:obv.I:2. It belonged to the district of Luatum, which agrees with its appearance in the eighth-century hieroglyphic Hittite stele from Jekkeh as *La-tà-pa-ti*^{URBS}.[50]

C. Amenhotep II's List (Simons List VI)

This list originally comprised twenty-four place-names, but ten of them are lost and six are damaged. The remaining names (including the easily restorable Nos. 1 and 2)[51] are well known and were, or may have been, visited by the Pharaoh during his expeditions of years 3, 7, and 9. They are not listed in any particular geographical sequence. Four items of the list merit our attention.

13. *Ḫa-rə-bu* has been generally assumed to represent Ḫalab (Aleppo), as it does, for example, in NL 311. But Amenhotep II, unlike his father, never reached Ḫalab: the interval of fourteen days between his crossing of the Orontes near Qaṭna and his entry into Niya "on the return of His Majesty southward to Egypt," as indicated on his stele,[52] is much too short for it. It is, of course, quite possible that Amenhotep II included Ḫalab simply for reasons

47. Published by Archi (1984) text 10.
48. Published by Archi (1980) text 1.
49. Published by Milano (1980) 12–15.
50. Meriggi (1967) text 28:19.
51. Upper and Lower Reṯenu, traditional designations of Palestine and Syria.
52. Amenhotep II's Karnak stele (erected by himself) and Memphis stele (copied, with additions, under Thutmose IV) have been published in a synoptic and commented edition by Edel (1953). The fourteen days in question are not accounted for in the steles. I discussed one aspect of Amenhotep II's itinerary (his alleged march to Ugarit) in Astour (1981a) 13–14. The distance to be covered, by the most direct and practicable roads, from the Orontes ford at er-Restān to Aleppo and from Aleppo to Qalᶜat Muḍīq (Apamea-Niya) amounts to a minimum of 351 km. This, divided by 14, gives us 25 km for a daily stage—a not impossible figure, provided that the army marched without ever slowing down or stopping for battle, rest, or collection of tribute or booty, which is patently unreal. If one takes off even as little as three days for these purposes, the average daily march goes up to 32 km, which seriously exceeds the normal length of a stage of ancient armed forces on a sustained expedition.

of vainglory. But the sober and realistic character of the surviving part of the list does not favor such an assumption. Amenhotep II's *Ḫa-rə-bu* may rather be equated with the homonymous city mentioned in the Papyrus Anastasi I along with Ṣumur and wrongly believed to be Aleppo,[53] but which can now be identified with *Ḫal-bá*^{ki} in the land of the Amurru, at the foot of Mt. Lebanon, near ^{uru}*Ar-dá-at*^{ki}, named in the "letter of the general" found at Ras Shamra (RS 20.33),[54] the medieval and modern Ḥalba in northern Lebanon.[55] The question, "On which side of it (Ṣumur) is *Ḫa-rə*⌜*b*$_x$⌝?" makes little sense with regard to Aleppo, which is 200 km away from Ṣumur in a straight line and at least half as far again by road; but it makes perfect sense with regard to Ḥalba, which is only 20 km distant from Tell Kazel (ancient Ṣumur). This location of Amenhotep II's *Ḫa-rə-bu* would imply that on the outbound leg of the expedition of year 7 his army was transported by sea to one of the harbors of northern Phoenicia and marched from there to the Orontes via the Eleutherus River gap; and that is exactly how his father, Thutmose III, led his invasions of inner Syria after the conquest of northern Phoenicia.

18. *Ḥə̂-ḏə̂-rə̂*: etymologically identical with biblical *Ḥaṣôr* but corresponding to *Ḫa-ṣú-ra*(*-a*)^{ki} of the Mari texts, a site that was located in northern Syria and whose name has been preserved by the village *Ḥāṣūr* on the return route of Amenhotep II from Niya to Qidšu; see Astour (1991).

20. ⌜*ʾA*⌝-⌜*qə̂*⌝-⌜*tu*$_5$. On the traces of the damaged signs, see Simons *ad loc.* My restoration of the name, made around 1970, has been confirmed by Edel's new publication (in consonantal transliteration only) of Amenhotep III's topographic list from Soleb, in which the entry XI:B:2 appears as *ʾqt.*[56] I consider it an Egyptian rendering of alphabetic *Aġt* UT 111/CTA 69:5; UT

53. Papyrus Anastasi I was published in hieroglyphic transcription by Gardiner (1911); translation, with bibliography, by J. A. Wilson, *ANET*, 475–79. Much of the papyrus deals with geography of central and southern Syria and of Palestine in a roughly north to south sequence. The reading of the damaged last sign of the name under consideration as *b*, doubted by Gardiner, was accepted by Wilson, *ANET*, 477 and Helck (1971) 315; both rendered the name "Aleppo."

54. Published by Nougayrol (1968) text 20. See also Rainey's study (1971). It dates to the final phase of the Hittite-Egyptian war under Ramesses II, when the hostilities took place in the maritime zone of Amurru.

55. Thus identified by Schaeffer (1968) 679–81. For the reading *Ḫal-ba*^{ki} rather than *Ḫal-pa*^{ki}, see Rainey (1971) 137. It is a rather common North Syrian toponym, meaning 'hill' (Ugaritic *ḫlb*).

56. Edel (1980) 67. Giveon (1964) 252 complemented *iq(r)*, where *i* (= Edel's ʾ) corresponds to my *ʾa*. This item has not been included in the Aksha and Amarah West lists.

113/CTA 73:14; PRU II 81:16; PRU V 58:II:38; 147:10′; KTU 4.553:5′; ethnic *aġty* KTU 4.748:10; syllabic [uru]*A-ḫa-tu* PRU IV 95:9; 111:10; 134:16. Egyptian *q* transcribed not only Semitic *q* but also (along with *g*) the Semitic and Hurrian phoneme *ġ*.[57] The town of Aġatu belonged to the Transorontian district of the kingdom of Greater Ugarit.[58] It formed a joint fiscal and military unit with Dumatu and Qamanuzi, and since the position of the latter is known (see F: 101 below), Aġatu must have been located in the same area, near Sarmīn and Idlib, immediately north of the Ǧebel Zāwiyeh massif.

21. *Śəm-*[*r*]*ə*!. The first sign, M_{21} according to Gardiner's sequence (three reeds growing side by side), had the phonetic value *śəm*.[59] We should assume that it was thus used in writing the name in question. Of the second sign, which was narrow and horizontal, only the vertical stroke beneath it has been preserved. This fits only two signs of group writing, *rə* and *ru*. Either of these, but preferably the former, would equate the completed name with alphabetic *šmry*[60] UT 111/CTA 69:4; UT 113/CTA 94:8, 10; PRU II 81:4; 181:13; PRU V 44:8; 58:II:37; KTU 4.762:7; RIH 83/47+51+56;[61] syllabic [uru]*Šá-am-ra-a* PRU VI 77:7; 105:8′; [uru]*Šà*[*m*]*-r*[*a-a*] PRU VI 111:6. Note the perfect correspondence between Ugaritic *š* and Egyptian *ś* in the transcription. The town of Šamrā, now Bešmārūn,[62] is located in the same narrow

57. See Helck (1971) 537. But his rule that *ġ* was rendered by Egyptian *q* at the beginning or end of a word and by Egyptian *g* in the middle of a word imposes an unnecessary stricture. One can adduce several cases that contradict it.

58. On the territorial subdivisions of the kingdom of Ugarit and our basis for their geographical allocation see Astour (1981b), with map.

59. Gardiner (1957) 482.

60. The letter No. 30 in the chart of the Ugaritic alphabet, UT §3.3, is transliterated there and in most other publications on Ugarit and Ugaritic as *ṯ*. This is correct inasmuch as the Ugaritic phoneme thus written is genetically related to Proto-Semitic unvoiced interdental *ṯ*. But it was not pronounced as such in Ugaritic, as evidenced by (a) its position in the Ugaritic ABC tablet in the place of Phoenician-Hebrew *šin*, (b) its definition by cuneiform *ša* in PRU II 189, (c) its use in transcriptions of Akkadian, Egyptian, and Hittite words and/or names, (d) its use in alphabetic Hurrian texts for the Hurrian phoneme *š* (e) its survival as *š* in modern derivations of Ugaritic toponyms that contained this letter. Therefore, wherever I am allowed by the editors, I transliterate it by *š*. This is especially called for in the present paper, in which *ṯ* stands for a quite different Egyptian phoneme.

61. General information on the tablet RIH 83/47+51+56 (list of twenty towns of Ugarit) and three of its toponyms have been adduced by Bordreuil et al. (1984) 427.

62. The prefix *be*/*bi*/*ba* is the Aramaic word for 'house', very common in North Syrian toponymy and often attached to pre-Aramaic place-names. The name has also been noted as Tell Šemārūn on the map compiled by Lieut. Froment (1930).

area as Aġatu, 9 km to the west-northwest by west from Idlib, dominating the northern entrance to the fertile and well-populated valley of er-Rūǧ.[63] Aġatu and Šamrā thus mark the northernmost points of Amenhotep II's incursion into northern Syria, the places where he turned west from his previous northbound march and then south, through the er-Rūǧ and Orontes valleys to Niya (Apamea). Such a route—unlike one having its turning point at Aleppo—is perfectly feasible in fourteen days.[64]

D. Amenhotep III's Kom el-Hetan D_N List

The topographic lists from Amenhotep III's funerary temple at Kom el-Hetan have been published by E. Edel.[65] A new fragment of the socle D_N was discovered subsequently; it carried three ovals with place-names (right 1 and left 1 and 2), which Professor Edel kindly communicated to me in his letter of February 7, 1972. Here I shall deal only with the surviving names carved on socle D_N, one of the five extant inscribed socles of the temple.

Right side 1. *Śə-ən-gə-rə*: this alternative designation of Babylonia is well attested and needs no elaboration.

2–6. Destroyed. Then follow five names prefixed with *pa*, the Egyptian definite article masculine, a not infrequent device in Egyptian recordings of place-names.[66]

7. *Pa-ʾa-rə-mu*. The resemblance to the later ethnonym Aram, Arameans is purely coincidental.[67] This ethnonym is not attested before the late twelfth century. In the context of the Kom el-Hetan lists, the name must stand for a specific site. Depending on the reading of *rə*, it may be compared either to Eblean *A-la-ma*^{ki} ARET III 78:rev.IV:2 = ^{uru}*A-la-ma* AT 42:3, 4; 319:3

63. The lake or lagoon of Balūᶜa in the middle of er-Rūǧ, recently drained by the Syrian government, was of recent origin. See Froment (1930) 291.

64. The distance from er-Restān to Qalᶜat Muḍīq, on a route that bypassed the Ǧebel Zāwiyeh massif from the east and north, amounts to 252 km. If one deducts two days for rest, the average daily march would be 21 km; if three, 23 km—quite normal figures, conforming to those of Amenhotep II's return leg from Niya.

65. Edel (1966), with summaries of previous partial publications, careful hand copies of the inscriptions, and an extensive commentary.

66. Several examples are cited by Edel (1966) 27. One may add *p3-Knᶜn*, a designation of Gaza, Helck (1971) 275, and *p3-Ḫa-ti* 'the Hatti(-land)' in the stele of *Wśr-Śt.t*, Helck (1955); cf. Helck (1962) 280.

67. Their identity, though, was maintained by Edel (1966) 28–29.

(Level 7) = ^{uru}*An-la-ma-*[*a*] in Unqi at the time of Tiglath-pileser III;[68] or to Eblean *Ar-ra-mu*^{ki} ARET III 795:III:11; TM.75.G.1444:VI:11.[69] There were also towns in the kingdom of Ebla named *A-rí-mu*^{ki}, *A-rí-ma-mu*^{ki}, *Ar-*ᵓ*à-mu*^{ki}, and so forth.

8. *Pa-*ᵓ*a-ru-un-ra-wə-ya*;[70] that is, *pa-Arullawiya* or *pa-Alullawiya*, which would in both readings correspond to the Eblean place-name variously written *A-ru*$_{12}$*-lu*^{ki} ARET II 18 §5; ARET IV 2 §§8, 21; TM.75.G.243;[71] TM.75.G.246;[72] *A-lu-lu*^{ki} ARET I 6 §54; TM.75.G.1586;[73] *A-lu-ru*$_{12}$^{ki} ARET II 13 §17; *A-lu-úr*^{ki} TM.75.G.1569.[74] Whatever the spelling, it appears in association with a group of towns that formed a distinct territorial unit, apparently located to the north and northeast of Aleppo. According to its area under cultivation, the town in question must have been, at the time of the Ebla archives, the largest in its district. Another possibility, closer in time to the Egyptian record, is $^{[u]ru}$*A-lu-ul-la* PRU IV 9:11′; ^{uru}*A-lu-ul-li* 10:3′;[75] alphabetic *Ull* UT 113/CTA 71:19; PRU II 81:12; PRU V 76:42; ethnic singular *ully* RIH 78/3:rev.2′; plural *ullym* UT 313/CTA 94:6. It is now Tell Halūl in the er-Rūǧ valley.

9. *Pa-śə-rə-ṯəs*. The final group, not used elsewhere in group writing, is cited in Gardiner's S_{24} as a semi-ideogram meaning 'tie', 'bind', and derivatives. Edel apparently considered it a determinative. However, *śə-rə* has no such meaning in either Egyptian, Semitic, or Hurrian. Perhaps *ṯəs* was intended to be read phonetically and in the resulting **Śarṯise* could be interpreted as a formation with the Hurrian *-šše* of the Eblean place-name *Sa-ar-zu*^{ki} ARET III 106:rev.IV:5; *Sa-ar-zú*^{ki} ARET II 28 §3; TM.75.G.2233.[76]

68. Rost (1893) 1.85 (III R No. 3) 2.34. A new, updated, and augmented edition prepared by H. Tadmor appeared in July, 1995 (though copyrighted 1994: *The Inscriptions of Tiglath-Pileser III* [Jerusalem: Israel Academy of Sciences and Humanities, 1994]).

69. Published by Edzard (1981a).

70. The fourth group is *n* with two of the three short vertical strokes which give it the value *ən* (i.e., *n* preceded by a vowel that reiterates the final vowel of the preceding group); the third stroke was not carved because the head of the recumbent lion of the following group (*ru*) intruded into the space. The fifth group, 'mouth' and 'eagle' (for *ra*?) is unique; perhaps the eagle was intended to stand with *wə*.

71. Quoted by Pettinato (1986) 355 under MEE I 67.

72. Ibid., under MEE I 70.

73. Quoted in MEE I 1024.

74. Quoted in MEE I 1007.

75. These texts (respectively, RS 17.62 and RS 17.366) are copies of the list of localities transferred from Mukiš to Ugarit by Šuppiluliumaš; cf. Astour (1969) 398–405 and (1981a) 21 and n. 101, with certain adjustments.

76. Quoted in MEE I 1671.

10. *Pa-rə-šə-wá-šə̌.* The final *-šə̌* cannot represent Hurrian *-šše*, which is systematically transcribed in Egyptian records by *ś/s*-holding groups. No onomastic parallels suggest themselves, unless one assumes that the oval contains two names,[77] both known at Ebla, namely, *Ra-áš*^{ki} TM.75.G.2420:80;[78] ideographically SAG^{ki} ARET VIII 522 §2; 523 §33; 541 §30; MEE II 44:rev. II:1; ethnic *Ra-sa-yu-um*^{ki} in a Mari tablet;[79] and *Wa-si-am*^{ki} ARET VIII 524 §39; cf. *Wa-ʾà-su*^{ki} ARET IV §58.

11. *Pa-*[.]*a-wə-ka.* Impossible to complete and identify.

12. *A-šú-rə.* Looks superficially like Assur, but cannot be equated with that famous city, the name of which is always spelled in Egyptian records with *ś* (sometimes reduplicated),[80] conforming to Ugaritic *aṯrym* 'Assyrians' PRU II 89:3. It even appears thus written at Kom el-Hetan itself, list A_N, left:13. Perhaps one may instead compare the Eblean *A-su-úr*^{ki} ARET III 159:obv. III:2′–4′; *A-sur*$_x^{ki}$ TM.75.G.2165 and TM.75.G.2233.[81]

13–17. Lost.

Left side 1. The oval contains two place-names:

1a. *Mə-dú-rə* : *Mdrʾ* (*Madōrā), a city of the kingdom of Arpad, stele I:A:34 of the eighth century Sfireh treaty,[82] possibly already mentioned at Ebla as *Ma-du-lu*^{ki} TM.75.G.1444:VIII:3;[83] *Mu-du-lu*^{ki} TM.75.G.1625:rev.I:1.[84]

1b. *Ku-rə-ka-nə* : ^{uru}*Kar-kum-m*[*a*] KUB XIX:rev.8′,13′, a border city of the Hittite appanage of Carchemish.[85] It is associated with ^{uru}*Zi-ri-pa*, which Ar-

77. As in the entry left: 1 below, in the Medinet Habu list Nos. 5, 7, 37, 49, 59, 60 (cf. Astour [1968] s.vv.), and in Soleb VI:b:4 (cf. Edel [1980] 67).

78. See n. 24 above.

79. Quoted, without siglum, by Dossin (1939) 994–95 (reprinted in Dossin [1983] 163–64). The man so designated was a Benjaminite; hence, his home town is supposed to have been located on the upper flow of the middle Euphrates. The spelling with *s* follows the Amorite pronunciation.

80. See, among others, Albright (1934) 56, item D:1; Helck (1971) 258, 279.

81. Place-names quoted in, respectively, MEE I 1603 and 1671. The reading *sur*$_x$ for the composite sign ŠÁR×MAŠ is given in the Ebla sign list MEE III 52 No. 66, also published by Archi (1987b); it is confirmed by the spelling *Sur*$_x$*-gal*^{ki} for the Sargonic *Su-ur-gal*^{ki} in both the Ebla and the Abū Ṣalābīḫ copies of the scholarly geographic list MEE III 56 No. 111. At Ebla, *s*- and *š*-holding signs frequently interchange. *Sur*$_x$ is found only at Ebla; but the Old Akkadian pronunciation of its homophone SUR was *sur.*

82. Dupont-Sommer (1958) 18; cf. p. 49.

83. Published by Edzard (1981a).

84. Published by Archi (1981) text 1.

85. Transliteration and commentary by Forrer (1926) 48–56. Most of Forrer's geo-

chi recognized in Eblean *Zi-rí-ba*^{ki} in the district of Luatum, TM.75.G. 1975:rev.IV:3,[86] and in the partially overlapping list of "seventeen towns in the hand of the king of Ebla," TM.75.G.2136:obv.II:1.[87] The district of Luatum was located in the northern part of the crown domain of Ebla, astride the Turkish–Syrian border, west of the Sāǧūr River.[88] Karkumma should then correspond to the important Bronze Age mound at Körküm or Körkün, where a hieroglyphic Hittite stele of an eighth-century king of Carchemish was found.[89] *Kurkana* is a variant of *Karkumma* with a vocalic metathesis[90] and the frequently attested interchange of endings in *m* and *n*.[91]

2. *Bá-bi-rə*: Babylon, repeated in entry 11.

3–7. Lost.

8. [. .]-*da-tə*: Edel tentatively: [Ar]data$^{?}$. As a simple possibility among many, one may restore [*Da*]$^{?}$-*da-tə*; cf. *Da-du-ti*^{ki} in the district of Luatum, TM.75. G.1975:obv.V:1;[92] *Da-da*^{ki} ARET VIII 529 §26 (in a similar context).

9. [. .]-*mə-mə*$_5$-*ya*. Only a vertical stroke remains of the first group. Edel's tentative restoration [Ku]mmiya$^{?}$ (a temple city of Tešub in northern Transtigris) is compatible with this vestige and with the inclusion of Transtigridian entities (Arrapḫa, Lullu, Pabḫi) in other display lists. *Ru* and *ʾən* are also graphically compatible, and one may think of Eblean EN-*ma-mu*^{ki} TM.76.G. 156,[93] in which the first sign can be read *en* or *ru*$_{12}$.

10. [. .]-⸢*bə́*⸣-*ḫə-rə-kə-nə-ṯə*. Here, too, we are dealing with more than one name. The acephalic first half is beyond restoration; it is dubious whether *ḫə-rə* is a complete toponym, corresponding to *Ḥa-rə* in Thutmose III's Palestine List 77. For the second half, *Kə-nə-ṯə*, two hypothetic parallels may be proposed. (a) We may take it as an unsuffixed variant of *Kə-n-ṯù-tə́* Palestine List

graphical equations in the text are now obsolete, among them the identification of Karkumma with the Neo-Hittite and Neo-Assyrian Gurgum.

86. Archi (1981) text 1; cf. p. 2.

87. Published by Pettinato (1978) 51–52.

88. On my reasons for this location, see Astour (1988b) 143 n. 29; cf. B:398 above.

89. Alkim (1969) 7; Archi et al. (1971) No. 124; Hawkins (1974) 72.

90. In fact, the Egyptian and the Hittite forms of the toponym faithfully reproduce the plant name from which it is derived as it appears in Akkadian (*kurkanû*) and in West Semitic (Heb. *karkôm*, Aram. *karkōmā*, Arab. *kurkum-*).

91. Cf., for example, at Ebla: *Ar-zi-ga-mu*^{ki}/*Ar-zi-ga-nu*^{ki}; *A-ba-ti-mu*^{ki}/*A-ba-ti-nu*^{ki}; *La-la-mu*^{ki}/*La-la-ni-um*^{ki}; *I-da-ì-mu*^{ki}/*I-da-i-nu*^{ki}. It is also known in biblical Hebrew onomastica.

92. See n. 86 above.

93. Quoted by Pettinato (1986) 366 under MEE I 6368.

93 = *Ki-in-ṯú-tà* Kom el-Hetan, list B_N, left:3. Its exact location is not known, but from its position in both lists, it seems to have belonged to southern or south-central Syria. This does not fit very well the pronounced north-Syrian character of list D_N. (b) Or, if preference is to be given to the geographical context, *Kə-nə-ṯə* could be equated with *Ga-ni-šu*^{ki} in the already mentioned (1b above) Eblean list of seventeen northern towns, TM.75.G.2136:obv.IV:1; *Ga-ne-su*^{ki} ARET I 8 §34; TM.75.G.10022:obv.II.[94] It is not the Cappadocian Kaniš[95] but ^{uru}*Ka-an-ni-š*[*e*] KBo XVIII 151:rev.4,[96] a north-Syrian town in the vicinity of the royal city of Ḫaššu(wa) that I identify with the excavated site of Tilmen Hüyük, east of Islâhiye. There arises the question of the Egyptian rendering of the final sibilant by *ṯ* (which normally corresponds to West Semitic *samek*), while the phoneme denoted by *š* in cuneiform Hittite was invariably transcribed by Egyptian *ś* under Ramesses II. The answer lies probably in the frequent interchange *s*/*š* between and within Semitic languages (especially in Akkadian). In particular, the root to which the toponym may be attached, appears as KNS in Hebrew and KNŠ in Aramaic.[97]

11. *Bá-bi-rə*: once again, Babylon.

12. *Ḫa*/*Ḫu-bu-śə* : *Ḫa-bù-sa-an*^{ki} TM.75.G.1975:obv.III:2; *Ḫu-bù-ša-an*^{ki} TM.75.G.2136:obv.II:2, that is, in both related lists cited in entries 1a, Ib, 8, and 10 above. By its name, as well as because it belongs to the district of Luatum, the town can be identified with the large Tell Ḥabeš,[98] 14 km east of Kilis and 4 km north of the Syrian border. U. B. Alkim's survey disclosed Early Bronze, first millennium, and classical wares there,[99] but surface collection of sherds often fails to reflect the full history of occupation of a site.[100]

13–14. Lost.

94. Quoted in MEE I 4925. *Ga*-NE-*su*^{ki} can also be transliterated *Ga-bí-su*^{ki}, as was done (originally) by Pettinato in MEE I and by Archi in ARET I. If I prefer *Ga-ne-su*^{ki}, it is because in ARET I 8 it is immediately preceded by *Za-bur-rúm*^{ki} (§33), which appears in the list of the seventeen towns (obv. III:2) along with *Ga-ni-šu*^{ki} (obv. IV:1).

95. As asserted by Pettinato (1979a) 111, (1986) 306–7, and elsewhere.

96. Transliteration, translation, and discussion by Ünal and Kammenhuber (1974), who ascribe it to the time of Ḫattušiliš I or Muršiliš I. In my opinion, the frequent mentions of plague assign it rather to the ill-fated Syrian expedition of the next Hittite king, Ḫantiliš.

97. Cf. also the triple spelling of a biblical toponym: *Mikmāš*/*Mikmāś*/*Mikmās*.

98. This Arabic form of the name was used in Ottoman census documents. It was Turkicized Tilhabeş, then renamed Yananköy, Yavuzli and, according to the map *Alep* 1:200,000, Taşlica.

99. Alkim (1969) 7. General description: Archi et al. (1971) No. 202.

100. Cf. Parrot (1953) 326; von der Osten (1955) 7; Kohlmeyer (1981).

E. Amarah West, East Wall Insert

It is generally recognized that the list of Asian place-names at Amarah West and its partially extant copy at Aksha, both from the time of Ramesses II, were either pirated from the topographic list of Amenhotep III at Soleb or derived from a common original.[101] However, entries Nos. 29–45 on the east wall of the Amarah temple stand apart; none of them is repeated on the north wall or appears at Soleb. This insert must go back to a different source from well before the reign of Ramesses II. It seems to display a certain geographical unity, and most of its names do not recur in other Egyptian records.

29. *Ka-śə-ya* : ^{uru}*Ka-aš-še* AT 313:4 (Level IV), perhaps same as Kassa, a village near Antioch attested ca. C.E. 600, and/or the Eblean town *Ga-sa*^{ki} ARET III 119:rev.VI:5; 124:I:1; 129:I:2; 401:rev.III:7; 964:rev.IV:1; TM.75.G.543;[102] TM.75.G.1451:obv.I:6.[103] TM.75.G.1767:obv.IV:1, rev.II:5;[104] TM.76.G.340.[105]

30. *Tu*$_5$*-r-rə-śə-tə* : ^{uru}*Dur-ra-sú*^{ki} AT 180:7; ^{uru}*Dur-ra-sú* AT 307:1 (both Level IV); *Du-ra-su*^{ki} TM.75.G.1964:obv.III:2′.[106]

31. *Mu*$_6$*-rə-ə* ⟨*n*⟩$^?$. Of the last group, only the three vertical strokes remain, as though the lapidary omitted the *n* above them. If it is thus amended, the resulting name would resemble *Mú-rə-nù-śə* in Ramesses III's Medinet Habu list, southern tower, No. 38, in which the final group is the Hurrian suffix *-šše*. However, that list is composed mainly of non-Syrian toponyms,[107] and no similar name has so far been provided by cuneiform records. Therefore the location of this entry remains uncertain.[108]

101. The existence of the Amarah West list was announced by Fairman (1939) 141; in his 1940 article he promised that "they will shortly be published in detail" (p. 165). But they were only published, along with the Aksha list, in hieroglyphic hand-copies by Kitchen (1979) 211–17. Of the Soleb list, drawings of very few items have been published so far; they have been reproduced in various places by Schiff Giorgini (1965); see also Simons (1937) list IX. Giveon (1964) provided the complete list in consonantal transliteration. A useful synoptic chart of the Amarah West, Aksha, and Soleb lists was presented by Edel (1980).

102. Quoted in MEE I 211.

103. Published by Archi (1981) text 2.

104. Published by Archi (1980) text 1.

105. Quoted in MEE I 6512.

106. Published by Archi (1981) text 3.

107. Cf. Astour (1968), in which many details need correction.

108. There is a ruin near the town of Qarāṭī, 21 km southeast of Ma^{c}arret en-Nu^{c}mān, variously called on maps and in medieval and modern geographical works Tell

(32. *Qə-hə-qə*: an African name, repeated here out of context from the beginning of the Amarah West list, No. 6).

33. *Ma₅-ṯə̂-wa*ₓ-[*t*]ʾə. Edel's drastic emendation to *Mš*ᵎ*w*[*š*], the Libyan tribe called Maxyes by the Greeks, does violence to the transmitted name both phonetically and graphically.[109] According to Kitchen's drawing, there is no room in the last group of the name, right of the eagle, for the long sign *š*. If we restore in the gap the short sign *t* (Gardiner's X_1), we obtain a perfect transcription of ᵘʳᵘ*Ma-zu-wa-ti* KBo I 1:rev.17′, one of the cities transferred by Šuppiluliumaš to the expanded appanage kingdom of Carchemish. This was a major city with a long history. It is first attested at Ebla both as *Má-zú*ᵏⁱ ARET VIII 526 §11, and under the composite name *Tin-ma-za-ù*ᵏⁱ TM.75.G.1975:rev.II:6; *Ti-na-ma-zu*ᵏⁱ TM.75.G.2136:obv.II:3, in the district of Luatum (see D:12 above, with further cross-references); then at Alalaḫ IV as ᵘʳᵘ*Tin*ᵎ*-na-ma-zu-wa*[110] AT 180:13. It reemerges in the mid–eighth century as *Mzh*, a city of the kingdom of Arpad, in Sfireh stele I:A:34 (cf. D: left:1a); then, immediately after the fall of Arpad to Assyria, the king of Carchemish, Kamanas, in the hieroglyphic Hittite stele from Jekkeh (cf. B:398 above), added "lord of the land of *Ma*ₓ*-zá* ᵁᴿᴮˢ" to his title "ruler of Carchemish."[111] This means that Tiglath-pileser III rewarded the loyal vassal state, Carchemish, with the northern part of the abolished kingdom of Arpad

---

Murān, Tell Murrān, Tell Muarān, Tell Marrān, and Tell ᶜUmrān. But the small size of the tell and the uncertainty of its name advise caution. A different possibility is to think of *Mu-ru*₁₂ᵏⁱ, an important city of the kingdom of Ebla, at times a royal appanage, often associated with cities of the northern district of Luatum, which reemerges at the time of Shalmaneser III as ᵘʳᵘ*Mu-ú-ru*, a provincial capital of the kingdom of Arpad, located near its northern border. It may correspond to the large mound at Tibil, where the road from Aᶜzāz to Gaziantep crosses the Syrian–Turkish border. If so, either the three strokes should be ignored or the amended entry is to be considered a suffixed variant of Muru.

109. Except for his identification of the bird with a damaged head in the third group as an eagle rather than as an owl, as in Kitchen's copy.

110. The reading *tin* for the first sign is mine. Wiseman, in the typewritten transliteration of some unpublished Alalaḫ texts (of which he kindly sent me a photocopy in 1967), read ᵘʳᵘ*Ši-qa-ma-zu-*[*we*]; Dietrich and Loretz (1967) 535 read ᵘʳᵘ*Ar-ma-zu-we*. Hawkins's (1983) attempt to identify the hieroglyphic Hittite Masuwari—a name or epithet of Tell Aḥmar—with imperial Hittite Mazuwati is wrong on several accounts, of which the most obvious is the fact that Tell Aḥmar was not inhabited between ca. 2000 and 1000 B.C.E.

111. The reading *Ma*ₓ*-zá* for the earlier VITULUS-*í* has been ascertained, for the first sign, by its occurrence in *Ma*ₓ*-li-zi* ᵁᴿᴮˢ = Assyrian Malidi/Melidi, Aramaic *Mlz* (Hawkins [1974] 75; Hawkins and Morpurgo-Davies [1975] 122), and for the second, by the revaluation of certain hieroglyphic Hittite signs presented by Hawkins, Morpurgo-Davies, and Neumann (1974).

(which included the area of Jekke) as an entity with its capital at *MzhlMa*$_x$-*zá*. By combining these pieces of evidence, we come to the conclusion that Maza/Mazuwati was the enormous Oylum Hüyük, by far the largest in the region between A^{c}zāz and Gaziantep, at a distance of 6 km east of Kilis, 8 km west of Tell Ḥabeš, and 14 km northwest of Jekkeh.[112]

34. *Nu-b̀ə-rə̀*. A similar place-name, vocalized *Na-bu-rə*, appears in the Medinet Habu list, Nos. 64, *120. Because of the presence there of numerous north Mesopotamian toponyms, I identified it with Middle Assyrian ^{uru}*Na-bu-la*, Neo-Assyrian ^{uru}*Na-bu-lu*, which has since then been uncovered at Girnavaz, 4 km north of Nusaybin.[113] However, *Nu-b̀ə-rə* may have been a homonymous city in northern Syria, in accordance with the rest of the identifiable places in the Amarah insert. There is a town Nūbul, near the eastern slope of Ǧebel Sim^{c}ān and just west of the Aleppo-A^{c}zāz highway, with a large mound where a broken relief in Neo-Hittite style (now in the National Museum of Aleppo) was found.[114] Moreover, it carried its modern name at least as early as the Neo-Assyrian period. The Sfireh stele I:A:34 lists a city of the kingdom of Arpad the name of which was transliterated by Dupont-Sommer as ⸢*M*⸣*blh*.[115] But the hand-copy of the relevant part of the inscription, by J. Starcky,[116] shows the trace of the half-erased letter to be closer to *n* than to *m*. Nūbul, of course, lies within the borders of the old kingdom of Arpad.

35. *Rə-d̲ə*: Eblean *La-za*^{ki} ARET I 8 §38; *La-su*^{ki} ARET III 35:obv.VI:3; *La-za-ù*^{ki} 531:III:1; *La-zú*^{ki} 565:I:2; Alalaḫ Level IV ^{uru}*La-aṣ-ṣi*$^{(ki)}$ AT 179:2, 197:2, 233:16, 329:3, 341:12; ^{uru}*La-ṣi*$^{(ki)}$ 145:1, 223:13,14, 338:2; ^{uru}*La-aṣ* 287:13; DUMU *La-aṣ-ṣi* 147:II:38.

112. Archi et al. (1971) 153. Alkim (1969) 7 noted: "As it may be the centre of a kingdom it has been decided to excavate this mound as soon as work in the region of Islâhiye is finished." But Alkim's next assignment was in the area of Bafra on the Black Sea. Only several years after his death in 1987 did a Turkish archaeological team start excavating Oylum Hüyük; see note in *Nestor* 15:6 (Sept. 1988) on the report by Engin Özgen on the Tenth International Symposium of Excavations, Surveys and Archaeometry, Ankara, May 23–27, 1988.

113. Astour (1968) 742 E:r. Cf. *RGTC* 4, 201; Parpola (1970) 258 s.v. Napulu; Mellink (1985) 554.

114. Matthers et al. (1981) 16 (visited by the British survey team but not sampled for sherds); Saouaf (*1974) 265 and fig. 153.

115. Dupont-Sommer (1958) 18 (*m* in the transliteration marked with a dot to show its damaged state), 20, 49 (in both places without reservation).

116. Ibid., pl. IV.

36. *ʾA-bu-*⸢x⸣. The vestige of the last sign looks in the hand-copy like a small square or quadrangle with a missing bottom line. Restoring it as *p* makes little sense onomastically. Perhaps it is the lower square of *ś* (Gardiner Aa$_{18}$); then *ʾA-bu-*⸢*śə*⸣$^{!?}$ might be compared to Eblean *A-ba-šu*^{ki} TM.75.G.1430:I: 3;[117] *A-ba-su*^{ki} TM.75.G.274:I:3;[118] *ʾÀ-ba-sa*^{ki} TM.75.G.1558:obv.VI:3;[119] *A-ba-zu*^{ki} ARET I 6 §54; ARET IV 5 §47; 20 §32; ARET VII 145:obv.III: 4; TM.75.G.246;[120] *A-ba-šu-nu*^{ki} TM.75.G.1451:rev.III:2;[121] *A-ba-zu-nu*^{ki} ARET III 595:III:2. It belonged to the same district north of Aleppo as entry D:right:8 above. The identification, of course, remains tentative.

37. *ʾA-r*[. . .]*-ya-b*$^{?}$. The last group is uncertain; too much is lost for an identification.

38. *D̲ə*-[. . . .]. Too little remains for an identification.

39. *Wə*$_{x}$*-pa-tə-ə*[*n*]: cf. *Wa-bílpi*$_{5}$*-tù*^{ki} ARET VII 152:obv.III:5; 155:rev.I:5. The survival of the initial *w* in a Semitic name (root WPY) in Late Bronze Syria is unusual.

40. *ʾA-du-ni-tə*. Edel's tentative identification with Adana in Cilicia ignores the existence of a place-name that is closer to the one in question and belongs to an area with which the Egyptians were much more familiar than with Cilicia. It has been known as *A-da-na-at*^{ki} AT 8:37 (Alalaḫ VII) since 1953. Since then it has emerged in the Ebla texts both in the same form *A-da-na-at*^{ki} TM.75.G.1390,[122] and closer to the Egyptian mention, *A-da-ne-tù*^{ki} ARET III 682:obv.I:5; ARET VII 156:obv.V:7, and *ʾÀ-da-ni-tù*^{ki} ARET II 5 §§5, 43, 46; "Culto" 1:obv.V:18–19; 4:obv.II:6–7.[123] It appears more often as *ʾÀ-da-ni*^{ki}. The vocalization *du* instead of *da* may be due either to the imprecision of Egyptian group writing or the sporadic occurrence in Late Bronze northern Syria of the south Canaanite vocalic pattern in the personal names ^{m}*A-du-ni-*^{d}U at Ugarit[124] and *A-du-ni-a-bi-ia* on the inscribed

117. Published by Fronzaroli (1980).
118. Quoted in MEE I 4225.
119. Published by Archi (1984) text 10.
120. Quoted in Pettinato (1986) 352 under MEE I 70; also under MEE I 68, 1508, 6456.
121. Published by Archi (1981) text 2.
122. Quoted in Pettinato (1986) 352 under MEE I 828.
123. Published by Pettinato (1979b). In the quoted passages it appears in the formula ^{d}*Ra-sa-ap ʾÀ-da-ni-tù*^{ki}; elsewhere ibid., texts 1 and 3, and formula is ^{d}*Ra-sa-ap ʾÀ-da-ni*^{ki} (15 times). This confirms the identity of the suffixed and unsuffixed forms of the name.
124. PRU III p. 196 (RS 15.42 + 15.110:II:20).

torso found at Sfireh.[125] From the fact that the locality later belonged to the Transorontian district of Ugarit[126] and from its position on Shalmaneser III's itinerary in 853,[127] it follows that it corresponds to Ad(d)ana of the Roman period, modern ed-Dānā, 6 km north of Maᶜarret en-Nuᶜmān and 15 km southwest of Tell Mardīḫ-Ebla.

41. *Má-ku-śə*: Edel suggested Mukiš, the ancient region of the Plain of Antioch and surrounding hills, with Alalaḫ as its capital; but he recognized the difficulties with the vowel of the second group and especially with the sibilant of the third, which according to the Ugaritic spelling *Mgšḫ*, should have been *š́* in Egyptian transcription. The toponym should rather be understood as **Maku* (or **Magu*) with the Hurrian formative *-šše*. Its pre-Hurrian basic part may be compared to [*M*]*a*$^{?}$*-ga-*⌜*ʾà*⌝$^{?\ ki}$ TM.75.G.1975:rev. III:1, better preserved in the composite name *Gi-ga-*⌜*ma*⌝*-ga-*⌜*ù*⌝^{ki} ibid.:obv.III:6,[128] both in the district of Luatum.[129] It probably recurs as *Ma*$_5$*-ki*^{WRITE}*-ʾì* G:274 below.

42. Lost.

43. *Má-wa*$_x$-[..]. The missing final group must have been low and narrow, possibly *ʾí* or *tə*. Both, if substituted for the missing group, conform to toponymic parallels: for *Má-wa*$_x$-*[*ʾí*], cf. *Má-wá-ʾi* G:281 below; for *Má-wa*$_x$-*[*tə́*], cf. *Ma-wa-ti-um*^{ki} TM.75.G.11007,[130] *Ma-a-ʾà-at*^{ki} ARET III 3:obv. V:6, and *Ma-a-i*^{ki} ARET I 13 §32 (rev.I:17), all of which are probably variants of the same place-name.

125. The inscription was published by Dossin (1930); Arnaud (1987). The torso has been dated to 1550–1350 by Matthiae (1962) 32. The nominal list from Ugarit (n. 124) includes several persons who are attested elsewhere as Ashdodians; hence ^{m}*A-du-ni-*^{d}U (Adonibaal) may have been a southerner. But *A-du-ni-a-bi-ia* was a local prince, certainly a native of North Syria.

126. ^{uru}IGI-*A-da-na-a* PRU VI 80:7.

127. ^{uru}*A-de-en-nu* in the Monolith Inscription, ^{uru}*A-da-a* (to be completed ^{uru}*A-da-*⟨*na*⟩*-a*) in the corresponding passage on the Balawat Gates; see Parpola (1970) 3.

128. Published by Archi (1981) text 1.

129. The Eblaic vocable *ma-ga-um* appears in the Sumerian-Eblaic vocabulary (MEE IV) in the entries VE 1246′a and 1246′b. On the reading of its Sumerian counterparts and its meaning 'oar', see Civil (1987) 143, 150 and n. 25. In Akkadian, *makkû* means 'pole, stake'.

130. Quoted in MEE I 4947. Cf. *in ma-wa-tim*, Pettinato (1979b) text 2:obv.III:27, IV:27; text 4:rev.III:4, VII:21, always without the determinative of place but listed by Pettinato among toponyms. Lack of this determinative occurs with several known place-names in the "Culto" texts.

44. *Qə-ʾa-wə́-d-nu*$_x$. One cannot but agree with Edel's emendation to *Qə-d̲ə-wə́-d-na* 'Kizzuwadna'. Until the publication of the Amarah lists, Egyptian mentions of Kizzuwadna appeared only in the records of Ramesses II dealing with the Hittites. It is thus probable that this name was added to the insert at the time of its engraving. On the other hand, Kizzuwadna was as much a north-Syrian as an Anatolian state in the fifteenth century, so its occurrence in a list dating from that time cannot be excluded.

45. *Sə-ḥa-śə-pa-wə-nu.* Totally unknown and incomprehensible. Edel radically emended to *Tꜣ*$^!$ *Šꜣsw pꜣ-wnw /Pwnw* 'Land of the Shasu-Bedouins of Wanu/Pawanu', on the model of the five Shasu-lands of the main body of the Amarah list, Nos. 92–97, partially preserved on column IV of the Soleb temple.[131] *Wnw* occurs in some so-called stereotypic lists of Seti I but is unidentifiable.[132]

F. Amarah West, Main Body

Most entries in the main body of the Amarah West list and their extant counterparts at Soleb cause few problems of identification. For Amarah West Nos. 92–97, see n. 131; for Soleb XI:B:2, see C:20 above. Three more entries will be discussed here.

East Wall 49. *ʾ[A]-rə-wi-šə* = North Wall 86. *ʾA-rə-wi-šə-na* Cf. *I-lá-wa-sá-na*^{URBS} in the hieroglypic Hittite Mara IV stele, a city conquered by a ninth-century king of Gurgum.[133] The shift *a* > *i* can be explained from Luwian phonetics.[134] The toponym is Hurrian, with cognates at Nuzi,[135] and thus goes back to the second millennium.

88. *ʾU-rə-kə-*[*ʾa*] *m*$^?$. The erased sign to the left of the owl was a narrow one. It may have been Gardiner M_1 (tree), which formed with the owl-sign the group *ʾam* (as in the Palestine List 85). Thus restored, the name reminds one

131. These five items are discussed in Astour (1979).

132. Cf. Helck (1971) 308.

133. Meriggi (1967) No. 34:4,12. The initial vowel sign, transliterated *a* in that work, has been rendered by *i* in accordance with the revised readings of some hieroglyphic Hittite signs by Hawkins, Morpurgo-Davies, and Neumann (1974). The sign *wa* could also stand for *wi.*

134. Hawkins, Morpurgo-Davies, and Neumann (1974) §4.6, with numerous examples, including *Imatu* for the non-Luwian toponym *Amatu* (Hamath).

135. ^{uru}*Al-la-i-wa-aš-wa,* Fisher (1959) No. 39; ^{uru}*Al-la-i-še,* SMN 2580:9. The voiced Hurrian sibilant *ž* (noted in careful cuneiform writing by a single *š*) was transcribed by Egyptian *š.* The constituent elements are *alla*(*i*) 'lady, queen' and *waš* 'to bring'; cf. Laroche, *Glossary,* s.vv.

of Mount Ulik(k)am(m)a in the list of forty mountains in the Hurro-Hittite Ḫišuwa ritual.[136] This mountain is thought to have been personified as the stone giant Ullikummi who, rising from the sea, threatened the gods assembled on Mount Ḫazzi (Ǧebel Aqraᶜ).[137] It was suggested that Mount Ulik(k)am(m)a stood on the Cilician coast opposite Mount Ḫazzi.[138] But the nearest mountain close enough to the coast of Cilicia is ca. 300 km in a straight line away from Ǧebel Aqraᶜ, which does not make for a good juxtaposition. The Ḫišuwa ritual contains several north-Syrian oronyms beside Mount Ḫazzi, and Mount Ulik(k)am(m)a could have been one of the summits of the southern Amanus ridge within the view of Ǧebel Aqraᶜ. On the other hand, if the toponym in question is read with an *r* rather than *l*, it may be compared to *U*$_9$*-ra-gú*^{ki} in TM.75.G.5152:III:4,[139] assuming a variant with the toponymic suffix *-am*(*u*), which is rather frequent in Eblean place-names.[140]

101. *Qə-mə̀-d̠ə̀-nu*$_4$*-ꜣ-n̓ə*. Some signs are evidently misplaced in the engraving. The eagle (*ꜣ*) should stand after, not before, the red crown sign (Gardiner S$_3$), forming the group *ná*. One may also suppose that the group *nu*$_4$ should have stood before *d̠*, which would result in the emended **Qə-mə̀-nu*$_4$*-d̠ə-ná*, that is, *Qamanuzina = Ugaritic alphabetic *Qmnz* UT 109/CTA 66:8; UT 113/CTA 71:15; PRU II 81:11′; 176:5′; 181:9; damaged but recognizable PRU 58:II:35; 147:8′; KTU 4.553:3′; ethnic *qmnzy* UT 312/CTA 89:5,8; PRU II 80:3; syll. ^{uru}*Qa-ma-nu-zi* PRU III 32 (RS 15.81):3; PRU VI 80:8; ^{uru}*Qa-ma-nu-zu* PRU VI 105:7′. It was a town of the Transorontian district, closely connected with *Aǵt*/^{uru}*A-ḫa-tu* (see C:20 above); its name has been retained by the village Qamīnās (or Qumīnāz), but its ancient site was probably at Tell Danit̠, 2 km to the north.

G. *The Onomasticon of Amenemope*

This long collection[141] of appellations of different objects of the world, including numerous Egyptian and foreign place-names, was composed at the

136. On these mountains, see Otten (1969); Dinçol (1974). For the mentions of Mount Ullikama see *RGTC* 6, 453. Spellings: *Ú-li-ig-ga-ma, Ú-li-kám-ma, Ú-li-ka-am-ma.*

137. A full, critical edition of the Song of Ullikummi (Hittite translation of a Hurrian original) was given by Güterbock (1951–52).

138. Otten (1969) 254.

139. Quoted in MEE I 4025–4126.

140. In addition to the Eblean toponyms mentioned in n. 91 above, cf. *A-rí-ma-mu*^{ki}, *Da-ga-na-am*^{ki}, *Gi-bí-ra-mu*^{ki}, *Gur-ru*$_{12}$*-uš-dam*^{ki}, *Ḫa-za-nu-ma*^{ki}, *Na-za-rí-am*^{ki}.

141. Published with an extensive commentary by Gardiner (1947).

very end of the Twentieth Dynasty, but its compiler utilized earlier sources. The list of foreign peoples, countries, and towns covers the entries 243–94. We single out ten hitherto unexplained toponyms.

253. *ꜣAr-ru-ru.* This is a shorter form of either the entry D:right:8 or of ^{uru}*A-ru-ri-ia*^{ki} AT 201:15; 328:2; ^{uru}*A-ru-ri-e* 157:4; 187:9; ^{uru}*A-ru-ri* 152:6′ (all of Alalaḫ IV).

271. *Ḫu-ur-má.* Gardiner, advised by Sidney Smith, thought about Hittite (and Old Assyrian) Ḫurma in southeastern Anatolia. However, a homonymous ^{uru}*Ḫu-ur-mu* is attested in Unqi (which was largely coterminous with the earlier region of Mukiš) at the time of Tiglath-pileser III.[142] It may be detected in the Naharina List 179 as *Ḫù-rə-*[*mə*]$^{?}$[143] and probably in an Eblean list of towns, if one reads *Ḫur-ma-tù*^{ki} in TM.75.G.1669:rev.V:2.[144]

274. *Ma*$_5$*-ki*^{WRITE}*-ꜣì.*[145] See E:41 above.

280. *Tꜣ n Śə-ər-ku* ‘the land of Ś’. S. Smith compared Hittite Šerigga (in Kizzuwadna near Kummanni). Eblean *Šar-ga*^{ki} TM.75.G.10127:rev.III[146] and Alalah IV ^{uru}*Šar-ku-ḫé* AT 180:35; 185:16 are preferable both onomastically and geographically.

281. *Má-wá-ꜣi.* See E:43 above.

282. *ꜣÌ-ir-má-ꜣu*$_4$. This is a characteristically Eblean toponymic formation with the ethnic suffix *aꜣu.* At Ebla, the name appears in the variants *Ì-rìm*^{ki} ARET IV 3 §59; 7 §44; TM.75.G.2367:obv.III:12;[147] TM.75.G.5188;[148] TM.76.G.257:VIII:14;[149] in the epithet ^{d}BE *Ì-rìm*^{ki};[150] ^{d}*Ir-mu*[151] (shorter form of the preceding epithet); *Ìr-mu-ut*^{ki} ARET II 22:III:5. The “War Bulletin” (n. 147) locates the city in the Euphrates valley, apparently upstream

142. III R No. 3:34 = Rost (1893) pl. 27, p. 85.

143. As hinted, without elaboration, by Albright (1940) 2.28 and n. 33. The Onomasticon of Amenemope had not yet been published at that time. Helck (1971) 308 considered “certain” the equation of Amenemope 271 with the Anatolian Ḫurma.

144. Archi (1980) 11–14.

145. Concerning the determinative, Gardiner compared Nos. 212 and 450 of the onomasticon, “both of these entries writing initial *Mk* as though it were the particle ‘behold’.”

146. Quoted by Archi (1985) 78 No. 136.

147. Published by Pettinato (1980); with a different interpretation, by Edzard (1981b). I prefer the transliteration *Ì-rìm*^{ki} rather than *Ì-rúm*^{ki} for reasons of comparative toponymy.

148. Summarized under MEE I 4139.

149. MEE I 6469.

150. Pettinato (1986) 362 cites it under MEE I 1301 (TM.75.G.1863).

151. Quoted in MEE I 1008.

from Emar. It may correspond to ^{uru}*I-ri-ma-aš* PRU IV 117 (RS 17.369B+*x*+17.69):obv.7′,15′,rev.9, a city under the jurisdiction of the Great King of Ḫatti.

283. *ʾA-ru-ku*: Eblean *ʾÀ-ru$_{12}$-gú* ^{ki} ARET I 8 §31; 13 §§31–32; 14 §14; ARET III 51:V:4; 178:rev.IV:8; 458:obv.III:5; 465:obv.VII:6; ARET IV 15 §36; 17 §72; MEE II 32:obv.IX:3; TM.75.G.1329;[152] TM.75.G.1386;[153] TM.75.G.1498;[154] *ʾÀ-ru$_{12}$-ga* ^{ki} ARET III 734:rev.II:12; *Ar-u$_9$-gú* ^{ki} ARET II 28 §6; ARET III 538:III:2; ARET IV 23 §§20–21; TM.75.G.2377:rev.I:1.[155]

288. *Ta-ar-wa-ʾi*: Eblean *Tár-wa* ^{ki} ARET III 464:obv.III:3; ARET VII 38: obv.I:4; also in *Tár-wa-ša-ḫa* ^{ki} ARET I 5 §26; *Tár-wa-ša-ḫu* ^{ki} ARET VIII 31 §28 (in which the second component recurs independently as *Ša-ḫa-a* ^{ki} ARET I 7 §27). The same toponym probably recurs at Alalaḫ IV as ^{uru}*In-tar-we-e* AT 223:38; ^{uru}*In-ta-ra-we-e* AT 138:1; 343:28 (in which *in-* should be understood as 'spring').

293. *ʾÁ-ha-bú* (from West Semitic ʾHB 'to love'): cf. Eblean *A-a-bù-tù* ^{ki} ARET III 527:rev.V:1.

294. *Bə$_x$-gə-ru-qə*. Assuming that final *qə* represents the Hurrian suffix *-ḫe*, pronounced voiced after a vowel and written *-ġ* in Ugaritic, one may compare the basic part of the name to Eblean *Ba-ga-ra* ^{ki} ARET I 8 §38.

Conclusion

The comparative material presented in this contribution leads to two observations: (1) the importance of the unprecedented great number of already published Eblean place-names for the study of the north-Syrian historical toponymy, and (2) the high degree of survival of those place-names through a thousand years of turbulent history.

152. Quoted in MEE I 767.

153. Quoted in MEE I 824.

154. Cited in Pettinato (1986) 355 under MEE I 1498.

155. Published by Archi (1979), along with its duplicate TM.75.G.2379, where this toponym appears in rev.II:8.

Bibliography

Albright, William F.

1934 *The Vocalization of the Egyptian Syllabic Orthography.* AOS 5. New Haven: American Oriental Society.

1940 New Light on the History of Western Asia in the Second Millennium B.C. Part I, *BASOR* 77: 20–32; Part II, *BASOR* 78: 25–31.

Albright, W. F., and T. O. Lambdin

1957 New Material for the Egyptian Syllabic Orthography. *JSS* 2: 113–27.

Alkim, U. Bahadir

1969 Recent Archaeological Research in Turkey: Islâhiye Region. *Anatolian Studies* 19: 6–7.

Archi, Alfonso

1979 Diffusione del culto di ^{d}NI-*da-kul. SEb* 1: 105–18, 2 plates.

1980 Notes on Eblaite Geography. *SEb* 2: 1–16, 4 plates.

1981 Notes on Eblaite Geography II. *SEb* 4: 1–17, 7 plates.

1984 Allevamento e distribuzione del bestiame ad Ebla. *SEb* 7: 45–81, 10 plates. [Reprinted from a preprint from *Annali di Ebla* I (1980); actually appeared in 1988.]

1985 Les rapports politiques et économiques entre Ebla et Mari. *MARI* 4: 63–83.

1987a Reflections on the System of Weights from Ebla. Pp. 47–89 in C. H. Gordon, G. Rendsburg, and N. H. Winter (eds.), *Eblaitica 1.* Winona Lake, Ind.: Eisenbrauns. [Transl. of "Considerazioni sul sistema ponderale di Ebla," which appeared in 1980 as a preprint from *Annali de Ebla* I.]

1987b The "Sign-List" from Ebla. Pp. 91–113 in C. H. Gordon, G. Rendsburg, and N. H. Winter (eds.), *Eblaitica 1.* Winona Lake, Ind.: Eisenbrauns.

Archi, Alfonso, Paolo Emilio Pecorella, and Mirjo Salvini

1971 *Gaziantep e la sua regione: Uno studio storico e topografico degli insediamenti preclassici.* Incunabula Graeca 48. Rome: Ateneo.

Arnaud, Daniel

1987 L'inscription du torse viril M.6525 de Sfiré (Syrie). *Aula Orientalia* 5: 143–44.

Astour, Michael C.

1968 Mesopotamian and Transtigridian Place Names in the Medinet Habu Lists of Ramses III. *JAOS* 88: 733–52.

1969 The Partition of the Confederacy of Mukiš-Nuḫašše-Nii by Šuppiluliuma: A Study in Political Geography of the Amarna Age. *Orientalia* 38: 381–414, folding map.

1977 Continuité et changement dans la toponymie de la Syrie du Nord. Pp. 117–41 (+ folding map) in *La toponymie antique: Actes du Colloque de Strasbourg, 12–14 juin 1975.* Leiden: Brill.

1979 Yahweh in Egyptian Topographic Lists. Pp. 17–34 in *Festschrift Elmar Edel.* AAT 1. Bamberg.

1981a Ugarit and the Great Powers. Pp. 3–29 (+ folding map) in Gordon D. Young (ed.), *Ugarit in Retrospect: Fifty Years of Ugarit and Ugaritic.* Winona Lake, Ind.: Eisenbrauns.

1981b Les frontières et les districts du royaume d'Ugarit (Éléments de topographie régionale). *UF* 13: 1–12.

1988a Toponymy of Ebla and Ethnohistory of Northern Syria: A Preliminary Survey. *JAOS* 108: 545–55.

1988b The Geographical and Political Structure of the Ebla Empire. Pp. 139–58 in Harald Hauptmann and Hartmut Waetzoldt (eds.), *Wirtschaft und Gesellschaft von Ebla: Akten der Internationalen Tagung, Heidelberg 4.–7. November 1986.* Heidelberg: Heidelberger Orientverlag.

1989 *Hittite History and Absolute Chronology of the Bronze Age.* Studies in Mediterranean Archaeology, Pocket-book 73. Partille, Sweden: Åstroms.

1991 The Location of *Ḫaṣurā* of the Mari Texts. *Maarav* 7: 51–65.

Bordreuil, Pierre, et al.

1984 Les découvertes archéologiques et épigraphiques de Ras Ibn Hani (Syrie) en 1983: Un lot d'archives administratives. *CRAI* (1984) 398–438.

Bradbury, Louise

1985a Nefer's Inscription: On the Death Date of Queen Ahmose-Nefertari and the Deed Found Pleasing to the King. *JARCE* 22: 73–95.

1985b The Tombos Inscription: A New Interpretation. *Serapis* 8: 1–20.

Cagni, Luigi, ed.

1987 *Ebla 1975–1985: Dieci anni di studi linguistici e filologici: Atti del Convegno Internazionale (Napoli, 9–11 ottobre 1985).* Naples: Istituto Universitario Orientali.

Civil, Miguel

1987 The Early History of ḪAR-ra: The Ebla Link. Pp. 131–58 in Cagni 1987.

Dietrich, Manfried, and Oswald Loretz

1967 Zur Ugaritischen Lexikographie (II). *OLZ* 62: 533–51.

Dinçol, A. M.

1974 Über die Hydronomie und Oronomie Anatoliens zur Zeit der Hethiter. *Berytus* 23: 29–40.

Dossin, Georges

1930 Une inscription cunéiforme de Haute Syrie. *RA* 27: 85–92.

1939 Benjaminites dans les textes de Mari. Pp. 981–96 in *Mélanges syriens offerts à M. René Dussaud,* volume 2. Paris: Geuthner.

1983 *Recueil Georges Dossin: Mélanges d'Assyriologie (1934–1959).* Akkadica Supplementum 1. Leuven: Peeters.

Dupont-Sommer, André, avec la collaboration de M. l'abbé Jean Starcky.

1958 *Les inscriptions araméennes de Sfiré (Stèles I et II).* Paris: Imprimerie Nationale.

Edel, Elmar

1953 Die Stelen Amenophis' II. aus Karnak und Memphis mit dem Bericht über die asiatischen Feldzüge des Königs. *ZDPV* 69: 97–176, plates. 1–5, 7.

1966 *Die Ortsnamenlisten aus dem Totentempel Amenophis III.* BBB 25. Bonn: Peter Hanstein.

1980 Die Ortsnamenlisten in den Tempeln von Aksha, Amarah und Soleb im Sudan. *Biblische Notizen* 11: 63–79.

Edzard, Dietz Otto

1981a Der Text TM.75.G.1444 aus Ebla. *SEb* 4: 35–60.

1981b Neue Erwägungen zum Brief des Enna-Dagan von Mari (TM.75.G.2367). *SEb* 4: 89–97.

Fairman, H. W.

1939 Preliminary Report on the Excavations at ʿAmarah West, Anglo-Egyptian Sudan, 1938–9. *JEA* 25: 139–44, plates 13–16.

1940 Review of Simons 1937. *JEA* 26: 165–68.

Fisher, Loren R.

1959 *Nuzi Geographical Names.* Unpublished Brandeis University dissertation.

Forrer, Emil

1926–29 *Forschungen.* Vols. 1/1, 1/2, 2/1. Berlin: Selbstverlag.

Froment, Lieutenant

1930 Carte touristique et archéologique du caza de Ḥārem. *Syria* 11: 280–92, plate 48.

Fronzaroli, Pelio

1980 Il verdetto per A'mur-Damu e sua madre (TM.75.G.1430). *SEb* 3: 65–78, 1 plate.

1984 Materiali per il lessico eblaita, 1. *SEb* 7: 145–90 [actually appeared in 1988].

Gardiner, Alan H.

1911 *Egyptian Hieratic Texts. Series I, Part I: The Papyrus Anastasi I and the Papyrus Koller together with the Parallel Texts.* Leipzig [reprint Hildesheim: Olms, 1964].

1947 *Ancient Egyptian Onomastica.* 3 volumes. Oxford: Oxford University Press.

1957 *Egyptian Grammar: Being an Introduction to the Study of Hieroglyphs.* 3d rev. ed. Oxford: Ashmolean Museum.

Giveon, Raphael

1964 Toponymes ouest-asiatiques à Soleb. *VT* 14: 240–55.

Güterbock, Hans Gustav

1951–52 The Song of Ullikummi: Revised Text of the Hittite Version of a Hurrian Myth. *JCS* 5: 135–61; *JCS* 6: 8–42.

Hauptmann, Harald, and Hartmut Waetzoldt, eds.

1988 *Wirtschaft und Gesellschaft von Ebla: Akten der Internationalen Tagung, Heidelberg 4.–7. November 1986.* Heidelberg: Heidelberger Orientverlag.

Hawkins, J. D.
1974 Assyrians and Hittites. *Iraq* 36: 67–83.
1980 The "Autobiography of Ariyahina's Son": An Edition of the Hieroglyphic Luwian Stelae *Tell Ahmar* 1 and *Aleppo* 2. *Anatolian Studies* 30: 139–56.
1983 The Hittite Name of Til Barsip: Evidence from a New Hieroglyphic Fragment from Tell Ahmar. *Anatolian Studies* 33: 131–36.

Hawkins, J. D., and A. Morpurgo-Davies
1975 Hieroglyphic Hittite: Some New Readings and Their Consequences. *JRAS*: 121–33.

Hawkins, J. D., Anna Morpurgo-Davies, and Günter Neumann
1974 *Hittite Hieroglyphs and Luwian: New Evidence for the Connection.* Nachrichten der Akademie des Wissenschaften in Göttingen I, Philol.-hist. Klasse, Jahrgang 1973, Nr. 6. Göttingen: Vandenhoeck & Ruprecht.

Helck, Wolfgang
1955 Eine Stele des Vizekönigs *Wśr.Śt.t. JNES* 14: 22–31, plate 2.
1962 *Die Beziehungen Ägyptens zu Vorderasien im 3. und 2. Jahrtausend v. Chr.* Ägyptologische Abhandlungen 5. Wiesbaden: Harrassowitz.
1971 *Die Beziehungen Ägyptens zu Vorderasien im 3. und 2. Jahrtausend v. Chr.* Ägyptologische Abhandlungen 5. 2d ed. Wiesbaden: Harrassowitz.

Kitchen, Kenneth A.
1979 *Ramesside Inscriptions,* volume 2, fasc. 4. Oxford: Blackwell.

Kohlmeyer, Kay
1981 "Woven man nicht sprechen kann": Grenzen der Interpretation von bei Oberflächenbegehungen gewonnenen archäologischen Informationen. *MDOG* 113: 53–79.

Krebernik, Manfred
1982–83 Zu Syllabar und Orthographie der lexikalischen Texte aus Ebla. Part I: *ZA* 72: 178–236; Part II: *ZA* 73: 1–47.

Laroche, Emmanuel
1978–79 *Glossaire de la langue hourrite.* Part I: *RHA* 34 (1976); Part II: *RHA* 35 (1977).

Matthers, John et al., eds.
1981 *The River Queiq, Northern Syria, and Its Catchment: Studies Arising from the Tell Rifa'at Survey 1977–79,* part I. BAR International Series 98(i). Oxford: British Archaeological Reports.

Matthiae, Paolo
1962 *Ars Syria: Contributi alla storia dell'arte figurativa siriana nelle età del Medio e Tardo Bronzo.* Centro di studi semitici, Serie archeologica 4. Rome: Università di Roma.
1979 *Du-ub*^{ki} di Mardikh IIB1 = *Tu-ba*^{ki} di Alalakh VII. *SEb* 1: 115–18.

Mellink, Machteld J.
1985 Archaeology in Anatolia. *AJA* 89: 547–67, plates 61–66.

Meriggi, Piero
1967 *Manuale di eteo geroglifico: Parte II—Testi—1ª serie: I testi neo-etei più o meno completi.* Rome: Ateneo.
Milano, Lucio
1980 Due rendiconti di metalli da Ebla. *SEb* 3: 1–21, 6 plates.
Nougayrol, Jean
1968 Textes suméro-accadiens des archives et bibliothèques privées d'Ugarit. Pp. 1–446 in *Ugaritica*, volume 5. Paris: Geuthner.
Osten, Hans Henning von der
1955 Bemerkungen zu einer Art anatolischer Ruinenstätten, den "Hüyüks." *Jahrbuch für Kleinasiatische Forschungen* 3: 1–17.
Otten, Heinrich
1969 Die Berg- und Flusslisten im Hišuwa-Ritual. *ZA* 59: 247–60.
Parpola, Simo
1970 *Neo-Assyrian Toponyms.* AOAT 6. Kevelaer: Butzon & Bercker / Neukirchen-Vluyn: Neukirchener Verlag.
Parrot, André
1953 *Archéologie mésopotamienne,* II: *Techniques et problèmes.* Paris: Albin Michel.
Pettinato, Giovanni
1978 L'Atlante Geografico del Vicino Oriente Antico attestato ad Ebla e ad Abū Ṣalābikh (I). *Or* 47: 50–73, plates 7–12.
1979a *Ebla: Un impero inciso nell'argila.* Milan: Arnoldo Mondadori.
1979b Culto ufficiale ad Ebla durante il regno di Ibbi-Sipiš. *OrAnt* 18: 83–215, plates 1–12.
1980 Bolettino militare della campagna di Ebla contra la città di Mari. *OA* 19: 231–45, plates 14–15.
1986 *Ebla: Nuovi orizzonti di storia.* Milan: Rusconi.
Rainey, Anson F.
1971 A Front Line Report from Amurru. *UF* 3: 131–49.
1980 Linguistic Notes on Thutmose III's Topographical List. *Scripta Hierosolymitana* 28: 335–59.
Redford, Donald B.
1979 A Gate Inscription from Karnak and Egyptian Involvement in Western Asia During the Early 18th Dynasty."*JAOS* 99: 270–87.
Rost, Paul
1893 *Die Keilschrifttexte Tiglat-Pilesers III nach den Papierabklatschen und Originalen des Britischen Museums neu herausgegeben von . . .* 2 volumes. Leipzig: E. Pfeiffer.
Saouaf, Soubhi
*1974 *Alep, son histoire, sa citadelle, ses monuments antiques et son musée.* 4th ed. Aleppo: n.p., n.d. (ca. 1974).

Schaeffer, Claude Frédéric Armand
1968 Commentaires sur les lettres et documents trouvés dans les bibliothèques privées d'Ugarit. Pp. 607–768 in *Ugaritica*, volume 5. Paris: Geuthner.
Schiff Giorgini, Michela, en collaboration avec Clément Robichon et Jean Leclant
1965 *Soleb I: 1813–1963*. Florence: Sansoni.
Simons, J.
1937 *Handbook for the Study of Egyptian Topographic Lists Relating to Western Asia*. Leiden: Brill.
Sollberger, Edmond
1980 The So-Called Treaty between Ebla and "Ashur." *SEb* 3: 129–55.
Ünal, Ahmed, and Anneliese Kammenhuber
1974 Das althetitische Losorakel KBo XVIII 151. *Zeitschrift für vergleichende Sprachforschung* 88: 157–80.
Weselius, J. N.
1983 Two Notes on Ugaritic Toponyms. *UF* 15: 315.
Zaccagnini, C.
1984 The Terminology of Weight Measures for Wool at Ebla. *Quaderni di Semitistica* 13: 189–204.

A New Coptic Fragment of the Book of Hebrews

Charles W. Hedrick

A fragment containing part of Heb 1:1–13 was discovered at Edfu in Upper Egypt and received into the Coptic Museum in Cairo on April 1, 1938. It was given the registration number 862 and was, at the time I first saw it, one of two large fragments in a plexiglass container bearing the same registration number. The fragment comes from a Coptic codex having two columns to a leaf. At its widest point the extant parchment measures 20.2 cm high and 8.0 cm wide.[1] But a measurement of the widest part of the reconstructed text demonstrates that the leaf, at its widest point, was originally more than 22 cm wide. By estimating the amount of space that it took the scribe to write 8 lines, which is approximately the amount of text lacking in lacunae at the bottom of column one and at the top of column two on the hair side of the fragment, we may conclude that the leaf was originally more than 29.0 cm high.[2]

1. The measurement was taken by Samiha Abd El-Shaheed, First Curator of Manuscripts at the Coptic Museum.

2. My estimation of the original size is clearly not exact. The estimate is based on a reconstruction of the text from photographs that were not one-to-one with the parchment. From the photograph that I myself made in the Coptic Museum and reproduced in 8″ × 10″ prints, I made a "mock-up" of the leaf by tracing the reconstructed text from the extant text, using the extant lettering as a control. Using this method on the hair side of the fragment, we find that the lines of the reconstructed text are 9–11 letters in length. When compared to Horner's text, the hair side of the fragment is lacking 77 letters in lacunae between column one (ending 1:2[-]) and column two (beginning 1:[-]3). Therefore 7–9 lines are lacking in the lacunae at the bottom of the first column and the top of the second column. On the flesh side, the lines of the reconstructed text are 9–12 letters in length. When compared to Horner's text, the flesh side of the fragment is lacking 100 letters in the lacunae between column one (ending 1:9[-]) and column two (beginning 1:11). Therefore there are 8–11 lines in the lacunae at the bottom of the first column and the top of the second column. I base my estimates on measurements from the hair side of the fragment. My photographs are about 1.5 cm smaller than the original.

Since sheets at the outside of a quire (i.e., at the beginning and ending of a codex) are wider, it appears that this tractate, the book of Hebrews from which the fragment comes, probably fell toward the end of the codex.[3] To some extent this is confirmed by the numeral "two" (ⲃ̄) that is written beside the title of the text, [ⲧⲡⲣⲟⲥ] [ϩⲉⲃⲣⲁⲓⲟ]ⲩⲥ on the hair side of the leaf. Apparently, the scribe numbered the tractates in the sequence in which they fell in the codex. Hence, the book of Hebrews was the second tractate in the codex. The first tractate would have ended in the lacuna at the top of the first column on the hair side, though no traces of the lettering of that tractate are now extant.

The language of the text is standard Sahidic and apparently followed the text as reconstructed by Horner rather closely.[4] There are several places, however, where this text diverges from Horner's reconstruction.[5] On the basis of a comparison of literary hands, the fragment may date as early as the fifth century C.E.

The fragment was identified as part of the book of Hebrews in 1984 by Robert A. Kraft on the basis of photocopies of photographs that I supplied. Working with a computer base of the Sahidic New Testament as reconstructed by Horner, Kraft searched rapidly through Horner's text for a sequence of letters similar to those that appeared on the fragment. He managed to identify the fragment as deriving from the book of Hebrews after only a few minutes of searching.

SIGLA

H = G. Horner, *The Coptic Version of the New Testament in the Southern Dialect*

δ = British Museum papyrus fragment Heb 1:1–2:4, 6–9.

Bo = Bohairic

om = omits

3. See James M. Robinson, *The Facsimile Edition of the Nag Hammadi Codices: Introduction* (Leiden: Brill, 1984) 55. I am assuming on the basis of the measurements of the Nag Hammadi Codices that 22 cm is the wider measurement.

4. G. Horner, *The Coptic Version of the New Testament in the Southern Dialect Otherwise Called Sahidic or Thebaic* (7 vols.; Oxford: Clarendon, 1911–24) 5.3–6.

5. See the critical notes to the reconstructed text below.

Hair Side

Hebrews 1:1–2 [-]

[ⲧⲉⲡⲣⲟⲥ]
[ϩⲉⲃⲣⲁⲓⲟ]ⲩⲥ ⲃ̄

(1:1) |[ϩⲛ̄ ϩⲁϩ ⲙ̄ⲙⲉⲣ]ⲟ̣ⲥ
[ⲁⲩⲱ ϩⲛ̄ ϩⲁϩ] ⲛ̄
[ⲥⲙⲟⲧ] ⲉⲁⲡⲛⲟⲩ
[ⲧⲉ ϣⲁ]ϫ̣ⲉ ⲙ̄ⲛ̄ ⲛ̄
[ⲉⲓⲟⲧ]ⲉ ⲛ̄ϣⲟⲣⲡ̄
[ϩⲛ̄ ⲛⲉⲡⲣⲟ]ⲫⲏ
(1:2) [ⲧⲏⲥ· |ⲛ̄ⲑⲁⲏ]ⲛ̄
[ⲛⲉⲓϩⲟⲟⲩ ⲁϥ]ϣ̣ⲁ
[ϫⲉ ⲛ̄ⲙ̄ⲙⲁⲛ ϩⲙ̄]
[ⲡϣⲏⲣⲉ ⲡⲉⲛⲧ]
[ⲁϥⲕⲁⲁϥ ⲛ̄ⲕ]ⲗⲏ
[ⲣⲟⲛⲟⲙⲟⲥ][ⲙ̄]ⲡⲧⲏ[1]
[ⲣϥ̄· ⲡⲁⲓ ⲟⲛ ⲛ̄]ⲧⲁϥ

Hebrews 1: [-]*3–5*

(1:3) [ϣⲁϫⲉ] ⲛ̣̄[ⲧⲉϥ]
[ϭⲟⲙ] ⲉⲁϥ[ⲉⲓⲣⲉ]
[ⲙ̄]ⲡ̣[ⲧ]ⲃ̣ⲃⲟ ⲛ̣̄[ⲛⲉⲛ]
ⲛⲟⲃⲉ ⲉⲃⲟⲗ̣ [ϩⲓⲧⲟ]
ⲟⲧϥ̄ ⲁϥϩⲙ[ⲟⲟⲥ]
ϩⲓ ⲧⲟⲩⲛⲁ̣[ⲙ ⲛ̄]
ⲧⲙⲛ̄ⲧⲛ[ⲟϭ ϩⲛ̄ ⲛⲉⲧ]
(1:4) ϫⲟⲥⲉ |ⲛ̣̄[ⲑⲉ ⲉⲧϥ]
ⲥⲟⲧⲡ̣̄ [ⲉⲛⲁⲅⲅⲉ]
ⲗⲟ̣[ⲥ ⲧⲁⲓ ⲟⲛ ⲧⲉ]
ⲑⲉ̣ [ⲛ̄ⲧⲁϥ ⲕⲗⲏⲣⲟ]
ⲛ[ⲟⲙⲉⲓ ⲛ̄ⲟⲩⲣⲁⲛ]
ⲉ[ϥϣⲟⲃⲉ ⲉⲣⲟⲟⲩ]
(1:5) |ⲛ̄ⲧⲁ̣[ϥϫⲟⲟⲥ ⲅⲁⲣ]
ⲛ̄ⲛⲓⲙ̣ [ⲛ̄ⲛⲉϥⲁⲅ]
ⲅⲉⲗⲟⲥ ⲉ̣[ⲛⲉϩ]
ϫⲉ ⲛ̄ⲧⲟⲕ [ⲡⲉ ⲡⲁ]
ϣⲏⲣⲉ ⲁⲛⲟⲕ ⲁ̣[ⲓ]
ϫⲡⲟⲕ ⲙ̄ⲡⲟⲟⲩ
ⲁⲩⲱ ⲟ̣ⲛ̣ ϫⲉ ⲁ̣ⲛ̣[ⲟⲕ]
ϯⲛⲁϣ̣[ⲱⲡⲉ ⲛⲁϥ]
ⲉⲩⲉ̣ⲓ̣[ⲱⲧ ⲛ̄ⲧⲟϥ]
[2]ⲇⲉ̣ [ϥⲛⲁϣⲱⲡⲉ]
ⲛ[ⲁⲓ ⲉⲩϣⲏⲣⲉ]

1. ⲙⲡⲧⲏⲣϥ] δ; ⲉⲡⲧⲏⲣϥ, H
2. ⲇⲉ] δ, om H

Flesh Side

Hebrews 1:[-]6–9[-]				*Hebrews 1:11–13*
[ⲟⲩⲟⲩⲱ]ϣ[ⲧ̅ ⲛⲁϥ		1		
[ⲧⲏⲣⲟⲩ] ⲛ̅ϭⲓ ⲛ̣[ⲁⲅⲅ]		2		
[ⲉⲗⲟⲥ] ⸢ⲙ̣̅⸣ⲡⲛ[ⲟⲩ]ⲧⲉ̣		3		
ǀ [ϣⲁϥ]ϫⲟⲟⲥ ⲙⲉⲛ	(1:7)	4	(1:11)	ǀⲛⲧ]
[ⲛ̅ⲛⲁ]ϩⲣⲛ̅ ⲛ̅ⲁⲅⲅⲉ		5		ⲟ̣[ⲟⲩ ⲥⲉⲛⲁϩⲉ ⲉ]
[ⲗⲟⲥ ϫ]ⲉ ⲡⲉⲧⲧⲁ		6		ⲃⲟ̣[ⲗ ⲛ̅ⲧⲟⲕ ⲇⲉ ⲕϣⲟ]
[ⲙⲓⲟ ⲛ̅]ⲛⲉϥⲁⲅⲅⲉ		7		ⲟⲡ̣ [ⲁⲩⲱ ⲛ̅ⲧⲟⲟⲩ]
[ⲗⲟⲥ ⲙ̅ⲡ]ⲛ̅ⲁ̅ ⲛⲉϥ		8		ⲧ[ⲏⲣⲟⲩ ⲛ̅ⲑⲉ ⲛ̅ⲟⲩ]
ⲗⲉⲓⲧⲟⲩⲣⲅ]ⲟⲥ ⲛ̅[1]		9		[ϩⲟⲓⲧⲉ ⲥⲉⲛⲁⲣ̅ⲡⲗ̅]
[ⲟⲩϣⲁϩ ⲛ̅ⲥⲁⲧⲉ] ǀⲛ̅	(1:8)	10	(1:12)	ϭⲉ ǀⲁ̣[ⲩⲱ ⲕⲛⲁⲧⲟⲩⲏ][2]
[ⲛⲁϩⲣⲙ̅ ⲡϣⲏⲣ]ⲉ		11		ⲧⲟ̣ⲩ [ⲛ̅ⲑⲉ ⲛ̅ⲟⲩⲣ̅]
[ⲇⲉ ϫⲉ ⲡⲉⲕⲑⲣ]ⲟ		12		ϣⲱⲛ̣ ⲛ̣̅ⲥ̣[ⲉϣⲓⲃⲉ][3]
[ⲛⲟⲥ ⲡⲛⲟⲩⲧ]ⲉ		13		ⲛ̅ⲧⲟⲕ ⲇ[ⲉ ⲛ̅ⲧⲟⲕ]
[ϣⲟⲟⲡ ϣⲁ]ⲉ̣ⲛⲉϩ		14		ⲟⲛ ⲡⲉ· ⲁ̣[ⲩⲱ ⲛⲉⲕ]
ⲛ̅ⲧⲉ ⲡⲉⲓⲉⲛ]ⲉϩ		15		ⲣⲟ̣ⲙ̣[ⲡⲉ ⲛ̅ⲛⲉⲩⲱϫⲛ̅][4]
[ⲁⲩⲱ ⲡ]ϭ̣ⲉⲣⲱⲃ ⲙ̅		16	(1:13)	ǀⲛ̅ⲧ[ⲁϥϫⲟⲟⲥ ⲇⲉ]
[ⲡⲥⲟ]ⲟⲩⲧⲛ̅ ⲡⲉ		17		[ⲛ̅ⲛⲓⲙ ⲛ̅ⲛⲉϥⲁⲅⲅ]
ⲡϭ̣ⲉ̣ⲣⲱⲃ ⲛ̅ⲧⲉⲕ		18		[ⲉⲗⲟⲥ ⲉⲛⲉϩ ϫⲉ]
ⲙⲛ̅ⲧⲉⲣⲟ vv ǀⲁⲕ	1:9	19		[ϩⲙⲟⲟⲥ ϩⲓ ⲟⲩⲛⲁ]
[ⲙ]ⲉⲣⲉ ⲧ̣[ⲇ]ⲓ̣ⲕⲁⲓⲟ		20		ⲙ [ⲙ̅ⲙⲟⲓ ϣⲁⲛϯⲕⲱ]
[ⲥⲩⲛⲏ ⲁⲕ]ⲙⲉⲥⲧⲉ		21		ⲛ̅ⲛ[ⲉⲕϫⲁϫⲉ ⲛ̅ϩⲩ]
[ⲡϫⲓ ⲛ̅ϭⲟⲛ]ⲥ̅ ⲉⲧ		22		ⲡⲟ̣[ⲡⲟⲇⲓⲟⲛ ⲛ̅ⲛⲉⲕ]
[ⲃⲉ ⲡⲁⲓ ⲁϥⲧ]ⲁ̣ϩⲥⲕ̅		23		[ⲟⲩⲉⲣⲏⲏⲧⲉ

1. ⲛⲟⲩϣⲁϩ] Bo; ⲛϣⲁϩ, H δ
2. ⲧⲟⲩⲏⲧⲟⲩ] ⲥⲟⲟⲩϩⲟⲩ, H
3. ⲣϣⲱⲛ ⲛⲥⲉϣⲓⲃⲉ] ⲣϣⲱⲛ [ ], H
4. ⲛⲉⲕⲣⲟⲙⲡⲉ ⲛⲛⲉⲩⲱϫⲛ] ⲛⲉⲕⲣⲙⲡⲟⲟⲩⲉ ⲥⲉⲛⲁⲱϫⲛ, H

From Head to Toe in Hittite: The Language of the Human Body

Harry A. Hoffner, Jr.

There are approximately seventy known Hittite words for parts of the human body.[1] Most are marked with the Sumerian determinative UZU 'flesh'.[2]

Although no single passage contains anywhere near the entire repertoire of seventy terms, several magic rituals for removing evils from suffering clients contain a representative group.[3] The same curative spell is repeated over each body part. The fact that the enumeration starts with the head and ends with the feet prompted my title "From Head to Toe in Hittite." Since there is nothing intuitive about proceeding from the top down, we must conclude that this was part of a cultural given in ancient Ḫatti.

Author's note: My first teacher of ancient Near Eastern languages was Dwight W. Young, who initiated me as a 22-year-old into the mysteries of Biblical Hebrew and Classical Arabic at Dallas Theological Seminary in 1956–58. During the years 1960–63 he taught me Akkadian, Egyptian, and Coptic at Brandeis University and inspired me with his exacting scholarship. With great pleasure I dedicate this study to him as my teacher, my colleague, and my friend.

The substance of this paper was presented at the 1990 national meeting of the American Oriental Society in Atlanta, Georgia, as part of a panel on The Language of the Body.

1. Most were listed in Hoffner 1967.

2. Thirty examples can be found in Reichert 1963: 140–41. Additional examples can be found in texts published since 1963.

3. Two of these, KUB 9.34 and duplicates (CTH 448.1) and KUB 9.4 (CTH 760), have recently been treated by Hutter 1988: 24–32 and Beckman 1990.

Human, Divine, and Animal Physiognomy

Hittite lists of male and female apparel share very few items,[4] but differences in anatomical terms between two sexes are limited to words for the sex organs: penis, testicle, vulva, and woman's breast. The same word (*parḫa-*) was used for 'nipple' in both sexes.[5]

Since deities were usually conceived in anthropomorphic terms, they obviously had the same inventory of body parts as human beings. In the Illuyanka Myth, the Storm-god loses his heart and eyes.[6] In the Telepinu Myth the bee is instructed to sting the hands and feet of the sleeping god.[7] In the Song of Kumarbi, Kumarbi bites off the genitals of the god Anu.[8] In innumerable scenes in the Song of Ullikummi, a god prepares to travel by taking a staff in his hand and putting shoes on his feet.[9]

The Distribution of the Terms

For some body parts several different terms coexisted. The penis could be called *pišnatar*, *lalu*, *ḫapušaš*, and possibly also *ḫarniu*. Two terms have been claimed as referring to the testicle: *arki-* and *tašku-*, but the latter is less certain than the former and may designate the scrotum. The head was properly *ḫaršar*. But in an Akkadian-Hittite lexical list Akkadian *rēšu* is glossed not by *ḫaršar* but by a unique word *ḫalanta*.[10] And the skull or cranium was called *tarnaš*.[11]

For some body parts there was a single shared term. In many languages there are separate words for the 'leg' and 'foot'.[12] But in Hittite a single term,

4. Hittite terminology for the items of male and female attire was thoroughly investigated and discussed by Goetze 1955.

5. Cf. CHD s.v.

6. *ANET* 126, left column.

7. *ANET* 127, left column; Hoffner 1990, text 2, version 2, §5.

8. *ANET* 120, right column with note 1.

9. *ANET* 121, right column.

10. Friedrich, *HW* 46.

11. Hoffner 1977.

12. The following examples are taken from Afro-Asiatic languages. In Akkadian *šēpu* 'foot' is distinguished from *išdu* and *purīdu* 'leg'. Modern Literary Arabic uses *qadam* for 'foot' and *rijl* or *sâq* for 'leg', but dialectally *rijl* is also used for 'foot'. In Middle Egyptian *wᶜrt* likewise covered both areas. And in both ancient and Modern Hebrew the word *regel* denotes both 'leg' and 'foot'. Among the classical Indo-European languages (Greek and

padaš, which is related to Latin *pes, pedis*, Greek *pous, podos*, and English 'foot', denotes either the foot or the entire leg.[13] Similarly, the word *keššar* 'hand' can also denote the entire arm.[14] A common noun *kalulupaš* 'digit' was used for both the finger and the toe. Speakers who wanted to distinguish the two did so by adding the words 'of the hand' or 'of the foot'. The fingernail and toenail were likewise denoted by a single word, *šankuwai-*.[15] The same noun, *šarḫuwanza*, in the singular denotes the stomach of a dog and in the plural the unborn child of a woman who has miscarried.[16]

For some parts of the body there was an indirect or descriptive term, a euphemism. As one might suspect, it is secondary sex characteristics that are most commonly designated by euphemisms. The vulva is once described in the Ullikummi Myth as *katta=kan kuit ḫarzi* 'what she has below'.[17] The penis is often referred to as *pišnatar* 'manhood'. A rarely attested word for the penis is *ḫapušaš*, which also denotes a plant 'stem' or 'stalk'.

Certain anatomical terms arose as words taught to very young children (German *Lallwörter*). Some have an onomatopoetic quality. The word for 'tongue' *lalaš* is phonetically appropriate, in that the tongue is the primary articulator of the sounds of its own name. Less obvious is the case of 'lip', Hittite *puriš*, whose initial stop is a bilabial and whose initial vowel is rounded and fronted, causing the pursing of the lips. In the English 'tooth' and Latin *dens, dentis* the articulation at the dental ridge is conspicuous, although strangely the Hittite word for 'tooth' *kaka-* contains no dental stop. The word for the windpipe (trachea) *ḫuwaḫḫurti-* with its *ḫ*'s and *w* has a distinctly "windy" sound.

Latin) distinct terms are used (πούς/*pes* versus σκέλος/*crus*). But note C. D. Buck's observation: "Some words [in Indo-European languages] which meant originally only 'foot' have been extended to designate the 'leg' also (like 'hand' > 'arm', 4.31)" (1949: 241).

13. Cf. CHD sub *pada-*.

14. In laws dealing with assault and battery (§§11–12) the texts speak only of breaking the *keššar* and *padaš* (Friedrich 1959 and *ANET* 189). And since fractures of entire limbs are much more common than fractures of hands or feet, it is probable that here and in other passages these terms refer not to 'hand' and 'foot', but 'arm' and 'leg'. But compare Laws of Eshnunna §§44–45, where Goetze (*ANET* 163) translated 'hand' and 'foot'. Neither 'hand/arm' nor 'foot/leg' is mentioned in the corresponding battery clauses of the Code of Hammurapi §§196ff., the same ground being covered by the term 'bone' §§197–99.

15. KUB 4.47 i 13–14 ('nails of the left hands and feet').

16. Friedrich 1959 and *ANET* 190 §§17–18 and *ANET* 193 §90.

17. Güterbock 1952: 12–13 (*JCS* 5: 146–47). The phrase is left untranslated by Goetze in *ANET* 121, right column.

Words taught to children are also occasionally euphemisms. One of the Hittite words for the penis is *lalu*, which—with its playful reduplicated syllables—almost certainly was the particular term taught to children.

Metaphorical Extension of the Terms

In many languages terms for body parts have extended meanings. We speak of the 'head' or 'foot' of the bed or of the two 'arms' and the four 'legs' of a chair or of a table. Hittite too possessed beds with four[18] and kneading troughs with three[19] *padiyalliš*, a term clearly derived from the word *padaš* 'foot, leg'.[20] As we do, the Hittites referred to heads (*ḫaršar*) of grain.[21] We call the small hole in the needle its 'eye'. They spoke of the tiny holes in a sieve as its 'thousand eyes' (IGI.ḪI.A = *šakuwa*).[22] A clove of garlic, which looks like a canine tooth, was called a *kaki-* ('tooth').[23]

In his autobiographical apology, King Ḫattušili III tells how, after he had won an especially important battle, he 'built a hand' ŠU-*an*[24] *wetenun*. This has been understood to refer to a victory monument, perhaps a stela. The use of the Hebrew word 'hand' (*yad*) to refer to such a monument in the Hebrew Bible[25] and the recovery of small upright stone monuments on which raised hands are chiseled in relief[26] support this interpretation of the Hattušili passage.

Pastries were sometimes molded in the shape of human body parts (ears, tooth, tongue, and so on). In one text an elaborate pastry is described as depicting 'the mouth, the tongue and twelve teeth'![27]

Most languages build idioms on anatomical terms. In English we say "Don't stick your nose into my business," or "He is sniffing around in my things." We can also say "I'm all ears," or that someone "has a lot of cheek."

18. KBo 13.260 iii 23.
19. KBo 19.129 obv. 22.
20. Cf. CHD sub *pada-* and *padiyalli-*.
21. Otten, StBoT 8, pp. 36–37, lines 19–20 ('heads of barley . . . heads of wheat').
22. KUB 9.6 i 2–4. Cf. Popko 1974: 181–82 and CHD sub *pattar* and *šakui-*.
23. Hoffner (1974) 109.
24. Although I am well aware of the alternative transliteration ŠU.AN or ŠU.DINGIR proposed by Otten (1981), I am not persuaded by it.
25. 1 Sam 15:12 (NIV): "Saul has gone to Carmel. There he has set up a *monument* in his own honor."
26. See the stela from Hazor pictured, among other places, in Negev 1976: pl. 25.
27. Hoffner 1974: 208 below.

Hittite too had idioms that employed anatomical terms. The phrase *aiš duwarna-*, literally 'to break the mouth', meant 'to divulge a confidence'.[28] Similarly, *aiš anda ḫamenk-* 'to bind up the mouth' meant 'to force someone to remain silent'.[29] These idioms remind us of the expression "my lips are sealed." The phrase *nu=kan kuelka iššaz karpta* 'he lifted from the mouth of someone' 'he contradicted the statement or command of someone'.[30]

The combination *ḫanza ḫar-*, literally 'to hold the forehead', meant 'to support' someone. There is no similar English idiom known to me, but Akkadian *rēšam kullum* (lit. 'to hold the head') has the similar meaning 'to take care of, be at the disposal of'.

In the law code if someone injured another accidentally, or at least without premeditation, it was said *keššaršiš waštai* '(only) his hand is at fault'.[31]

Some anatomical terms are extended to refer to aspects of the psyche. The word 'heart' can designate several things. (1) It is the seat of emotions and desire: *kardiaš=šaš* 'that of his heart' means 'his desire/wish'.[32] In Hittite, wishes arise from the 'heart'. This shades over into affection in the expression *kardiaššaš* DUMU 'the child of his heart', that is, 'his favorite child'. The words for 'anger' and 'angry', *kardimmiyaz* and *kardimiyawanza,* contain the word 'heart' *kard-*.

(2) Another mental state is reflected in the compound word *šallakardatar* —literally meaning 'great-heartedness'—which has been translated by some as 'arrogance'. The German *Hochmut* by coincidence has made a tempting literal equivalent. To be sure, the word's usages show that it is a blameworthy trait. Yet from the words of a civil servant being investigated for embezzlement we can see that the word denotes one of the less serious faults, one that is not premeditated, for he describes the behavior for which he is being

28. Von Schuler 1957: 14, 20 left column; Friedrich, *HW* ² 1.48 bottom right; Puhvel 1984–: 1.16.

29. So probably in *apāš=ma* KA×U.ḪI.A-*uš anda ḫamankta* KUB 14.4 ii 10 (Neu 1976: 304–5, Puhvel HED 1 17, cited without translation or comment in Friedrich, *HW* ² 1.50 right).

30. One of these is KUB 26.9 + Bo 69/1256 iv 9–11 (edited by Otten 1983: 136–37): 'You, the *ḪAZANNU* official, must keep the regulations of Ḫatti just so' *nu=tta=kan uddana*[*z*] *lē kuiški karpzi* 'and let no one contravene your word'. Otten construed *=tta* as an accusative, translating: 'und niemand soll *dich* von dieser Sache abhalten' (emphasis mine).

31. See laws 3, 4, 5, and 7. The standard edition is Friedrich 1959. English translation by A. Goetze in *ANET* 189.

32. Sommer 1938: 93–94; Friedrich, *HW* 103 sub *kard-*.

charged as follows: 'It was carelessness (*šallakardatar*) on my part, but not a deliberate plan (*kupiyatiš*) to defraud'.[33]

(3) The heart was also the seat of courage. A Hittite draft for a letter to a member of the Assyrian court, commenting on the accession of a new Assyrian king, says: 'God has given him heart'.[34] Undoubtedly the sense of 'heart' here is 'courage'.[35] In the second version of the Old Hittite Myth of Illuyanka,[36] the dragon at first defeats the Storm-god and takes from him his heart and eyes. The incapacitated Storm-god has no more courage (heart) and cannot intimidate a foe with his fierce eyes. He can only concoct a plan to be carried out by his mortal son cleverly to regain his heart and eyes as the "bride-price" given to a live-in husband. In the New Hittite myth "The Song of Kumarbi,"[37] the god Kumarbi menaces the god Anu, and it is said 'now Anu could not withstand Kumarbi's eyes, so he fled'. Here the eyes stand for the intimidating gaze of Kumarbi.

(4) The heart was also the seat of self-awareness, which is reflected in the idiom *kardi=šši piran mema-* 'to speak before one's heart', which means 'to think' or 'deliberate', that is, to say to oneself.[38]

The term *genzu* 'lap' is somewhat like Akkadian *rēmu* and Hebrew *raḥămîm* in that 'to take *genzu*' means 'to take pity on (someone)'. This suggests that the anatomical zone of the *genzu* was considered the seat of compassion and pity. A king who showed no mercy was not *genzuwalaš*, that is, he did not make use of his *genzu*.

A particularly intriguing case is the word *karat-*. Both Kammenhuber and Otten originally wished to equate it with *kard-* and translate it 'Leibesinneres'. In recent years, newly published evidence has made that equation unlikely. On the one hand it is known in the plural to denote a physical body part that can be 'eaten up' by disease. It is also attested with the determinative for 'flesh' (UZU).[39] The part also exists in animals and as such could

33. This text is edited by R. Werner (1967).

34. DINGIR-LUM-*ši maḫḫan* ŠÀ-*er piyan ḫarzi* KUB 23.103 rev. 8ff., commented on by Sommer 1938: 68.

35. CAD L 170b cites two Middle Babylonian extispicy texts in which *libbu* has the meaning 'courage'.

36. The most easily available translation is by Goetze in *ANET* 125–26. The latest edition is by Beckman 1982: 11–12. A new English translation appeared in Hoffner 1990.

37. Entitled "Kingship in Heaven" in *ANET* 120–21; titled "The Song of Kumarbi" in Hoffner 1990.

38. Cf. CHD L–N 260 sub *mema-* 9a.

39. [U]ZU*ka-ra-ta* 103/x i 6, cited in Otten 1969: 27.

be eaten by humans. These facts point to an internal organ of some kind. But in the Old Hittite tale of the Queen of Kanesh we see a different use. Her sons whom she has not seen for years return, and the text says that the gods had put in/on them another *karat-*, here in the singular, so that the mother did not recognize them. One expects here some term for overall appearance, or even possibly our word 'character'. Another psychological use of the term, this time in the plural, occurs in the Madduwatta Text, where the king speaks of the 'valiant *karatau*[*š*] of my troops'.[40]

Physical Disabilities

Temporarily or permanently disabled persons occasionally play a major role in literary texts. We have already mentioned the case of the Storm-god as described in the Illuyanka Story. In the Song of Ḫedammu the goddess Šauška successfully weakens her brother's enemy, the sea monster Ḫedammu, by dancing and singing before him naked. But when she tries this same tactic in the later Song of Ullikummi against the Stone Monster, a wave rises from the sea to inform her that the monster is blind and deaf and thus immune to her charms. We are reminded, of course, of Odysseus and the Sirens.

That Hittite law sometimes required the blinding of criminals as a punishment we learn not from the laws themselves, but from outside references, such as the Ma at letters.[41] Other forms of physical mutilation were performed on slaves found guilty of certain crimes.[42] Injuries inflicted on persons not guilty of such crimes were themselves punishable by law. The laws[43] refer to examples of blinding (laws §§7–8), knocking out teeth (laws §§7–8), battering the head (§9), breaking an arm or a leg (§11), biting off the nose (§13), tearing the ear (§15). For all these injuries, monetary compensation was required and, in some cases, the provision of medical care (§10).[44]

The malfunction or dysfunction of some part of the body was expressed in the picturesque words *tapuša pait* 'it went to the side'. This implies that 'to go straight ahead' was the term for proper functioning of the body. The idiom *tapuša pait* applied to a body part first appeared in the account of King

40. KUB 14.1 + KBo 19.38 rev. 41; cf. Otten 1969: 27.

41. Alp 1980: 39–42; cf. Otten 1979: 276.

42. Sturtevant 1935, "Instructions for Priests," col. i 29–30; *ANET* 207, right column below.

43. Edited in Friedrich 1959; translation in *ANET* 166.

44. On the provision of medical care in law 10, see Watkins 1976. On Hittite medicine in general, see Güterbock 1962 and the edition of the medical texts by Burde 1974.

Muršili's hysterical aphasia, where the king says *aiš=a=mu=kan tapuša pait* 'my mouth went to the side'.[45] Understandably, some interpreters considered that the phrase might quite literally describe muscle failure or paralysis on one side of the face such as can be a secondary result of a stroke or of Bell's palsy. But the phrase has now occurred in another context where it describes the failure of the mouth, the eyes, and the nine body parts.[46] The phrase 'the nine body parts', like the more common one 'the twelve body parts, probably refers to the aggregate of all human body parts. Since it follows the specific mention of the mouth and the (two) eyes, it might even be understood as obtained by subtraction of these three from the stereotyped total twelve. Nowhere to my knowledge in published texts does a list of exactly twelve body parts occur. Scholars generally understand the term as an arbitrary number, similar to the phrase 'the Thousand Gods', which denotes the entire Hittite pantheon.

For example, the well-known list from KUB 9.34[47] begins with the words 'I arrange the twelve body parts'. The speaker then proceeds to mention (1) the head, (2) the cranium, (3) the ear(s), (4) the shoulder, (5) the upper arm, (6) the arm/hand, (7) the fingernail, (8) the rib, (9) the genitals, (10) the *ḫupparatiyatiš*, (11) the testicle, (12) the penis, (13) the leg/foot, (14) the sole, (15) the toenail, (16) the musculature, and (17) the blood. 'I have arranged his twelve body parts' the speaker concludes, after he has listed seventeen!

The Language of Significant Symbolic Gestures Frequently Included Body Parts

(1) The eyes: *ḫaššuš šakuwa iyazzi* 'the king makes eyes' occurs often in the descriptions of the liturgy of the great festivals. It indicates a signal that the king makes to functionaries that they should proceed with the next activity.

(2) The hands: *ḫaššuš keššaran dai* 'the king places the hand' is a second common gesture. Sometimes the words 'from a distance' (*tuwaz*) are added, implying that the gesture was usually made with a nearby referent. This is a gesture of authorization, permitting someone else to perform an act on the king's behalf, usually the slaughter of a sacrificial victim. The Hittite gesture has been compared to biblical *sāmak yādāyw.* On several occasions in the texts a king speaks of raising his hand to a deity. The Hittite verbal expres-

45. First edition by Götze and Pedersen 1934.
46. The text is KUB 44.4 rev. 7–8. It is edited and discussed by Beckman 1983: 185.
47. For example see Hutter 1988: 32–33, lines 22ff.

sion is *keššaran šara ep-*. This can be a gesture of taking a vow. But it is also seen on royal reliefs as a simple sign of worship or homage to the deity who sits or stands opposite the king. Kings tell with pride how a deity has 'seized me by the hand'. The gesture is shown on several royal reliefs.[48] The deity who stands behind the king reaches around him to hold him by the upraised wrist. In the formula of blessing and good wishes found in letters it is sometimes said 'may the gods hold their arms around you and protect you'.[49] This same gesture of protection is referred to in the treaties, where the vassal is urged figuratively to hold his arms around the Hittite king. One passage is particularly interesting, since it also contains a comparison: 'As your own soul is dear to you, so that you hold your arms about it, so may the life of the king be dear to you, so that you hold your arms about the king's life'.[50]

(3) The knees: taking to the knees is to us such a self-evident sign of submission and veneration that we hardly think of it as significant. Hittite possessed several verbs for kneeling or prostrating oneself: *genuššariya-* actually contains a word for 'knee' (*genušša/i-*). The word *ḫaliya-* is something done at the feet of the person venerated. An interesting expression used to show supplication is *nu=za genuššuš epzi.* This used to be translated 'he (the supplicant) seizes his (the other man's) knees'. But a proper consideration of the crucial role played by the reflexive particle *=za* has led to the improved translation 'he betakes himself to his (own) knees', that is, he falls to his knees.

(4) The word 'head' could stand for the entire person or life. Hittite vassals were commanded to protect the 'head' of the Hittite king.[51] A person who paid compensation for a serious injury often had to pay a certain number of 'heads', by which subject persons (slaves) are probably meant.[52]

The Body as a Whole

The term for the body as a whole was *tuekka-*, which occurs in either the singular or plural to designate a single body. As we use the word 'body' by extension to designate a group of people, so in a difficult passage from the Hittite laws the term *tuikkant-* describes a group of people to which the culprit belongs.[53]

48. See Bittel 1976: 218–19, pls. 252–53.
49. Hagenbuchner 1989.
50. Friedrich 1926 and 1930.
51. Friedrich 1926 and 1930.
52. Cf. Güterbock 1961.
53. Friedrich 1959 §49 and pp. 98–99; Goetze in *ANET* 191 §49 (translating 'community').

A dead body was designated by other words: either the adjective 'dead' *akkant-* or the rare noun *anšaššiwi-*.[54] The usual Akkadogram for *tuekka-* is *RAMĀNU*. But in the lexical texts *tuekka-* was used to translate rather inaccurately other Akkadian words as well: *zīmu* 'appearance, looks, countenance' is an example. Since the same word *tuekka-* is used in the horse-training texts for the bodies of horses,[55] it is clear that it was not specialized for humans.

Cleanliness and the proper care of the body was obligatory for priests and temple personnel.[56] But from the prayer of Prince Kantuzzili we gather that guarding the body against ritual defilement was a virtue for any pious person.[57]

In order to pacify an angry god, one had to remove magically certain evils from the god's 'body'.[58] In the same way the rituals make it clear that evils attacked a mortal by entering his body.[59]

It was believed that an impotent man could be cured by sleeping in the sanctuary of the goddess Uliliyašši. As the impotent man slept, he would experience in a dream the goddess coming to him in her body, showing him her eyes, and sleeping with him.[60]

Although the previous example shows that the concept of the god's body was not limited to an image, in one text 'the garments that have grown old on the god's bodies' obviously refers to the clothing on the cult images.[61] The terms 'body and soul' sum up the entire person, whether it be a god or a human being. In a prayer to the Sun-god, a suppliant says he is 'your body and soul's servant', meaning 'your personal servant'.[62]

Since one's body is one's most intimate possession, a *tuekkaš uttar* 'matter of the body' comes to mean 'a personal or confidential matter'.[63] The eunuchs who guarded the intimate life of the king were said to 'touch the sacred body of the king'.[64] The ultimate value that an individual places upon

54. This word is a Hittite translation of the Akkadian entry *ŠALAMTU* in the vocabulary KBo 1.51 rev. 13.

55. Kammenhuber 1961.

56. Cf. "Instructions for Temple Officials" in *ANET* 207.

57. *ANET* 400, right column, above.

58. KUB 17.10 iii 9–11 (Telepinu myth, OH/MS), translit. Laroche 1969: 34.

59. Second Mast. iii 6–7, ed. Rost 1953: 356–59.

60. Full edition by Hoffner 1987: 279, §15; translation *ANET* 350, left column.

61. KUB 17.21 i 19–20 (prayer of Arn. and Asm., MH/MS), ed. Lebrun 1980; English translation, *ANET* 399.

62. FHG 1 + KUB 36.79 ii 21–22; also KUB 30.10 obv. 9 (translated 'thy favorite servant' in *ANET* 400, right column, above).

63. Kammenhuber 1964: 171.

64. KUB 26.12 + KUB 21.42 iv 33–34, ed. von Schuler 1957: 28–29.

his own body is used as an appeal to servants: 'Just as you hold you own bodies dear, your own wives, children and families, so in the same way you must hold the king's law (*šaklai-*) dear and administer it well'.[65] The sequence is revealing: the dearest thing is one's own body, and after that wives, children, and other relatives.

65. KUB 13.20 i 30–31.

Bibliography

Alp, S.

1980 Die hethitischen Tontafelentdeckungen auf dem Masat-Höyük: Vorläufiger Bericht. *Belleten* 44/173: 25–59, pls. 1–4.

Beckman, G.

1982 The Anatolian Myth of Illuyanka. *JANES(CU)* 14: 11–15.

1983 *Hittite Birth Rituals.* StBoT 29. Wiesbaden: Harrassowitz.

1990 The Hittite "Ritual of the Ox" (CTH 760.I.2–3). *Or* 59: 34–55.

Bittel, K.

1976 *Die Hethiter.* Munich: Beck.

Buck, C. D.

1949 *A Dictionary of Selected Synonyms in the Principal Indo-European Languages.* Chicago: University of Chicago Press.

Burde, C.

1974 *Hethitische medizinische Texte.* StBoT 19. Wiesbaden: Harrassowitz.

Friedrich, J.

1926 *Staatsverträge des Hatti-Reiches in hethitischer Sprache*, part 1. MVAG 31/1. Leipzig: Hinrichs.

1930 *Staatsverträge des Hatti-Reiches in hethitischer Sprache*, part 2. MVAG 34/1. Leipzig: Hinrichs.

1959 *Die hethitischen Gesetze.* Documenta et Monumenta ad Orientis Antiqui Pertinentia 7. Leiden: Brill.

Goetze, A.

1955 Hittite Dress. Pp. 48ff. in Hans Krahe (ed.), *Corolla linguistica: Festschrift F. Sommer.* Wiesbaden: Harrassowitz.

Götze, A., and H. Pedersen

1934 *Muršilis Sprachlähmung.* Det Danske Videnskabernes Selskab; hist.-filol. Meddelelser 21/1. Copenhagen: Levin & Munksgaard.

Güterbock, H. G.

1952 *The Song of Ullikummi: Revised Text of the Hittite Version of a Hurrian Myth.* New Haven: American Schools of Oriental Research.

1961 Further Notes on the Hittite Laws. *JCS* 15: 17–23.
1962 Hittite Medicine. *Bulletin of the History of Medicine* 36: 109–13.

Hagenbuchner, A.
1989 *Die Korrespondenz der Hethiter.* Texte der Hethiter 15–17. Heidelberg: Carl Winter.

Hoffner, H. A., Jr.
1967 An English-Hittite Glossary. *Revue hittite et asianique* 25: 7–99.
1974 *Alimenta Hethaeorum.* AOS 55. New Haven: American Oriental Society.
1977 Hittite Lexicographic Studies, 1. Pp. 105–11 in M. de Jong Ellis (ed.), *Essays on the Ancient Near East in Memory of Jacob Joel Finkelstein.* Hamden, Conn.: Archon.
1987 Paškuwatti's Ritual against Sexual Impotence (CTH 406). *Aula Orientalis* 5: 271–87.
1990 *Myths of the Hittites.* Writings from the Ancient World 2. Atlanta: Scholars Press.

Hutter, M.
1988 *Entsühnung und Heilung: Das Ritual der Tunnawiya für ein Königspaar aus mittelhethitischer Zeit.* Göttingen: Vandenhoeck & Ruprecht.

Kammenhuber, A.
1961 *Hippologia hethitica.* Wiesbaden: Harrassowitz.
1964 Die hethitischen Vorstellungen von Seele und Leib, Herz und Leibesinnerem, Kopf und Person. *ZA* 56: 150–222.

Laroche, E.
1969 *Textes mythologiques hittites en transcription.* Paris: C. Klincksieck.

Lebrun, R.
1980 *Hymnes et prières hittites.* Homo Religiosus 4. Louvain-la-Neuve: Centre d'histoire des religions.

Negev, A.
1977 *Archaeology in the Land of the Bible.* New York: Schocken.

Neu, E.
1976 Review of J. Friedrich and A. Kammenhuber, *Hethitisches Wörterbuch* (Heidelberg: Carl Winter, 1975). *Indogermanische Forschungen* 81: 298–305.

Otten, H.
1969 *Sprachliche Stellung und Datierung des Madduwatta-Textes.* StBoT 11. Wiesbaden: Harrassowitz.
1981 *Die Apologie Hattusilis III.: Das bild der Überlieferung.* StBoT 24.Wiesbaden: Harrassowitz.
1983 Der Anfang der *ḪAZANNU*-Instruktion. *Or* n.s. 52: 133–42.
1988 *Die Bronzetafel aus Boğazköy: Ein Staatsvertrag Tutḫalijas IV.* StBoT Beiheft 1. Wiesbaden: Harrassowitz.

Popko, M.
1974 Notes on Hittite Vocabulary. *JCS* 26: 181–82.

Puhvel, J.
1984– *Hittite Etymological Dictionary.* Trends in Linguistics: Documentation. Berlin: Mouton.

Reichert, P.
1963 Glossaire inverse de la langue hittite. *RHA* 21: 59–143.

Rost, L.
1953 Ein hethitisches Ritual gegen Familienzwist. *MIO* 1: 345–79.

Schuler, E. von
1957 *Hethitische Dienstanweisungen für höhere Hof- und Staatsbeamte.* AfO Beiheft 10. Graz: Ernst Weidner.

Sommer, F., and Falkenstein, A.
1938 *Die hethitisch-akkadische Bilingue des Ḫattušili I. (Labarna II.).* Abhandlungen der Bayerischen Akademie der Wissenschaften, Philosophisch-historische Abteilung 16. Munich: Bayerischen Akademie der Wissenschaften.

Sturtevant, E. H., and G. Bechtel
1935 *A Hittite Chrestomathy.* Philadelphia: Linguistic Society of America.

Watkins, C.
1976 Sick-Maintenance in Indo-European. *Ériu* 27: 21–25.

Werner, R.
1967 *Hethitische Gerichtsprotokolle.* StBoT 4. Wiesbaden: Harrassowitz.

The Scission and Ascendancy of a Goddess: Dīrītum at Mari

Paul Y. Hoskisson

W. Lambert has rightly stated: "From the earliest times [in the cuneiform world, Mesopotamia] scholars had begun to organize the pantheon into a united whole, and in the process they began to equate similar deities."[1] While the scholars were thus busily making order, the people were obviously creating new entities for the scholars to organize. For instance, J. J. M. Roberts has pointed out that Annunītum as an epithet of Ištar "could also be used independently as a designation for the deity, at least by the time of Šar-kali-šarrī. After the Old Akkadian period this is the only way it does occur, which suggests that the epithet split off and became an independent deity. The new goddess, however, retained her former character as war goddess."[2] I will demonstrate that the Old Babylonian Mari goddess Dīrītum, like Annunītum, went through an analogous transformation. She began as a local *Erscheinungsform* of Ištar, established her own identity distinct from other Ištar *Erscheinungsformen* at Mari, and rose to prominence, perhaps even preeminence, in the pantheon of Mari.

There can be no doubt that Dīrītum was an Old Babylonian *Erscheinungsform* of Ištar at Mari. As W. Leemans has pointed out, "Ištar was often named after a place of her cult," and he cites, as examples from Mari, Dīrītum, Hišamītum, and Kišītum.[3] This certainly would be sufficient reason for identifying Dīrītum with Ištar, but there is proof: in the Old Babylonian text ARM 24 263, she is explicitly equated with Ištar. The first five lines of this tablet read:

Author's note: I have used the standard abbreviations for Mari materials.

1. W. Lambert, "The Gula Hymn of Bulluṭsa-rabi," *Or* 36 (1967) 108.

2. J. J. M. Roberts, *The Earliest Semitic Pantheon: A Study of the Semitic Deities Attested in Mesopotamia before Ur III* (Baltimore: Johns Hopkins University Press, 1972) 147.

3. W. Leemans, *Ištar of Lagabe and Her Dress* (Studia ad tabulas cuneiformes collectas a F. M. Th. de Liagre Böhl pertinentia 1/2; Leiden: Brill, 1952) 36.

1. ^{d}*eš$_4$-tár*
2. ^{d}*eš$_4$-tár di-ri-tum*
3. *an-nu-ni-tum*
4. ^{d}*da-gan*
5. ^{d}*be-el ma-tim*[4]

From the name in line 5, it is clear that a nomens rectus in this list requires inflection in the genitive case. Thus "Ištar-Dīrītum" cannot be read as the construct chain "Ištar of Dīrītum," but, rather, Dīrītum must be read as an appositive to Ištar, "Ištar, the One of Dīr,"[5] confirming her name as an appellative of Ištar. Dīrītum was Ištar, albeit the Ištar originally at home in the city of Dīr.

In the kingdom of Mari, the antiquity of the cult of Ištar, from which Dīrītum and other Ištar *Erscheinungsformen* sprang, is well attested. Of the 25 gods listed in the Old Babylonian text PANTHEON,[6] Ištar is among the 5 deities[7] who appear in texts from all three Mari periods represented by tablets. She is well attested during the Old Babylonian period. In the immediately preceding Early Old Babylonian period, she occurs in the first line of the pantheon list TDM 3.[8] This alone should be sufficient to demonstrate the traditional nature of Ištar.[9] In addition she is attested in several pre-Sargonic

4. This text was first published by P. Talon, "Un nouveau pantheon de Mari," *Akkadica* 20 (1980) 12–17, as T. 186.

5. Dīr is about eleven km south of Mari, and Zurubbān is between Terqa and Mari. See ARM 16/1, pp. 41 and 9, respectively.

6. For the original publication of this Mari text see G. Dossin, "Le pantheon de Mari," in *Studia Mariana* (ed. A. Parrot; Leiden: Brill, 1950) 41–50. For a more recent discussion of the pantheon of Mari, see W. G. Lambert, "The Pantheon of Mari," *M.A.R.I.* 4 (1985) 525–29.

7. Adad, Šamaš, Dagan, Ninhursanga, and Ištar. If Ea = Enki at Mari, then the number is six.

8. First published by M. Lambert, *Syria* 47 (1970) 247, 249ff., #3. Lambert gave no date for this tablet in the original publication. However, the ductus is clearly older than Old Babylonian. The use of *ú* for a conjunction would date this tablet to the Early Old Babylonian period. P. Steinkeller has confirmed this dating in a private communication. For more recent discussions of the Mari "šakkanakku" texts and with some discussion of dating see *M.A.R.I.* 4 (1985) 147–343 (numerous articles); and M. Anbar's review of these *M.A.R.I.* 4 articles in *BiOr* 44 (1987) 174–76.

9. Unfortunately Ištar is not on the other Early Old Babylonian pantheon text, T. 142, though she may have been listed in the first few lines, which are broken in the extant tablet. This text was first published by G. Dossin, *RA* 61 (1967) 97–104, who dated it to the Ur III period. I. J. Gelb ("Thoughts about Ebla," *Syro-Mesopotamian Studies* 1 [1977] 10),

votive inscriptions, albeit in the form ^{d}*iš-tár-ra-at,*[10] or written INANNA plus an expansion, for example, INANNA.UŠ.[11] Even though it is not known what her pre-Sargonic names signify,[12] it is clear that the cult of Ištar at Mari can be traced back to the pre-Sargonic period. Given the antiquity of the cult of Ištar at Mari, it would not be surprising to find various locations, such as Dīr, where her cult had long taken root within the Old Babylonian Mari kingdom and produced local *Erscheinungsformen.*

The goddess Dīrītum appears first and only on tablets dated to the Old Babylonian period.[13] Yet already in this period she and/or her cult had become quite prominent in the kingdom of Mari. Indeed, with the exception of ARM 24 263 (where her connection with Ištar is made certain—"Ištar, the One of Dīr," as noted above), in the Old Babylonian period she always appears simply as Dīrītum, "The One of Dīr." Therefore, in the circles represented by the textual material from Mari, Dīrītum had reached the level of recognition where it was not necessary to ask, "Which One of Dīr?" In addition, perhaps the most telling indications of Dīrītum's prominence are that the king of Mari was present in Dīr from the sixteenth to the nineteenth of the month Kiskissum for the Dīrītum festival, that other kings and officials attended,[14] and that the festival was probably held every year at the same time with the king of Mari in attendance.[15]

however, has stated that "to all appearances" T. 142 belongs to the post-Ur III period. J.-M. Durand ("À propos du 'Panthéon d'Ur III à Mari,'" *RA* 74 [1980] 174–76) has commented on this text without discussing the dating, except to say "à la suite de l'*editio princeps.*" See also n. 8 above.

10. André Parrot, *Mission archéologique de Mari, Vol. III: Les temples d'Ishtarat et de Ninni-zaza* (Paris: Geuthner, 1967) 309–30. For this name, see D. O. Edzard, "Pantheon und Kult in Mari," *La civilisation de Mari* (CRRAI 15; ed. J.-R. Kupper; Paris: Les Belles Lettres, 1967) 53.

11. See also the forms INANNA X ZA.ZA and INANNA-*zàr-bat,* discussed by Edzard, "Pantheon und Kult," 53–54. For a short discussion of ZA, etc., see W. G. Lambert, "Addenda to W. G. Lambert, 'The Pantheon of Mari,' (*M.A.R.I.* 4 [1985] 525–29)," *M.A.R.I.* 6 (1990) 644.

12. Edzard, "Pantheon und Kult," 53.

13. Dīrītum appears already on tablets from the Yaḫdun-Lim period. For instance, see ARM 22 233:16.

14. In ARM 25 276, the author wrote to the king, Zimri-Lim, that he was sick and would not go to "the offering of Dīrītum."

15. The dates of the sacrifices for Dīrītum have been ingeniously assembled by M. Birot, "Simahlânê, Roi de Kurda," *RA* 66 (1972) 131–36. Using the texts discussed here and others, he pieces together the evidence for the king's presence in Dīrītum for the festival from the sixteenth to the nineteenth of Kiskissum. Birot goes on to present evidence

Other texts show that royal attention to Dīrītum was not limited to the king's presence at her festival. The king of Mari, Zimri-Lim, took interest, for whatever reason, in the cult of Dīrītum to the extent that he issued an order to his official Addu-dūri not to be idle but to "let the matter concerning the offering of Dīrītum be accomplished."[16] The king also received reports from court officials concerning Dīrītum. For instance, Baḫdi-Lim reported to Zimri-Lim that he had issued strong orders to the effect that "all of it, the offering of Dīrītum, shall be offered in Mari."[17] The pervasiveness of her cult is indicated by the fact that other events were dated by reference to the dates of her festival. For example, in ARM 7 263 iv:10′–15′, six(?) sheep are mentioned as an offering of the/a king at the time of Dīrītum.[18] And ARM 26 458:8 dates the loss of some cattle to "after the offering of Dīrītum."[19]

Given the antiquity of the cult(s) of Ištar at Mari and the fact that Dīrītum is an *Erscheinungsform* of this goddess, and given the prominence of Dīrītum in Old Babylonian Mari, it is not surprising that the cult of Dīrītum appears to have spread beyond her namesake city, Dīr, to at least two other cities, the city of Mari itself and the city of Zurubbān. M. Birot has gathered ample evidence for her cult in the city of Dīr.[20] The evidence for the other

---

that the festival was held yearly at that same time. He also theorizes that the king personally took part in the yearly festivals of the various gods at their cult centers. See also the summary in I. Nakata, *Deities in the Mari Texts* (Ph.D. diss., Columbia University, 1974) 152–54. For a discussion of the Ištar festival at Mari, see my *Cult in Mari* (Ph.D. diss., Brandeis University, 1986) 139–41 and n. 11, where I suggest that the Ištar festival celebrated during the month of Kiskissum during Yasmaḫ-Addu's reign became the Dīrītum festival during the subsequent Zimri-Lim period.

16. The text reads: *ṭēm nēqêtim ša* [d]*dīrītim lū šutaṣbut* (ARMT 10 142:25–31). I read (with G. Dossin) the stative of a Štn-stem from *ṣabātum* in line 30. AHw 1070b, citing this passage, reads an infinitive, *šutaṣbutam*. The meaning of the sentence is not altered by either reading. For Štn *ṣabātum* meaning 'to bring together and prepare, realize' see AHw 1070b.

17. The text reads: *kalûšu nīqum ša* [d]*dīrītim* [*in*]*a mari*[ki] *inn*[*aqqi*] (ARM 6 74:5′–6′). I have read the signs *i-n*[*a-aq-qí*] as an N-stem. For another N-stem of *naqûm* at Mari see ARM 13 111:14, according to AHw 345a. J.-R. Kupper, ARMT 6 74, translated: 'il [offrira]'. See also ARM 26 475:6–7.

18. That the phrase *inūma dīrītum* indicates 'at the time of the offering of Dīrītum' is proven by M11299 (AAM2):6 (cited in ARM 26, p. 122 n. 12) 1 gu_4-uš $siskur_2$-re lugal *ša i-nu-ma ḫa-a-ia-ar* [d]*di-ri-tim*.

19. ARM 22 204 rev. ii:15–16 connects economic activities for Dīrītum with the king. Other texts detail economic activities concerning Dīrītum but do not connect these activities with the king or other official circles, other than the fact that the transactions are recorded on tablets found at Mari.

20. Birot, "Simahlânê, Roi de Kurda." Add to the reference in this article ARM 26 199:17–18.

two sites is sparse but conclusive. Because she occurs in PANTHEON 10, and because the deities of this text are mentioned as deities of Mari in lines 28–30, there must have been a cult center for her at Mari. It is from this possible cult site at Mari that the *āpilu*-priest of Dīrītum, Qišti-dīrītim, went to the gate of the palace in Mari to prophesy.[21] Zurubbān, the other possible cult location for Dīrītum, in addition to Dīr and Mari, is mentioned in ARM 9 77:3–4, where Dīrītum is the recipient of gold and silver. The other occurrences of Dīrītum without geographic specification can probably be assigned to either Mari or Dīr.

It remains to be demonstrated that Dīrītum plausibly rose to preeminence, possibly eclipsing the goddess of her beginnings, Ištar, during the reign of Zimri-Lim. The initial indications for Dīrītum's preeminence over Ištar come from the PANTHEON text, a list of sheep offerings for the temples of Mari. Of the 25 deities on this list, 10 receive 6 or more sheep and the other 15 receive either 2 or 1 sheep. If there had been a continuum of 1 to 7 sheep consigned, it would be easy to suspect but difficult to prove that the number of sheep a god was assigned corresponded with the deference accorded that god at Mari. The disparity, however, of consigning to the gods either 6 (and in the case of Dīrītum, 7) or 2 (or less) sheep would seem a priori to indicate that the former gods were more favored than the latter. If this initial, credible indication of the standing of the gods on this list can be corroborated by other means, and if Dossin's reading of '7' sheep for Dīrītum in line 10 is correct,[22] then she would be the most honored deity on the list.

There is a nearly perfect correspondence between the number of sheep consigned in PANTHEON and the level of cultic activity of the various deities of Old Babylonian Mari. Of the 10 who receive at least 6 sheep according to this tablet, all 10 are prominent in the cultic life of Old Babylonian Mari; with the exception of Ištar, those that receive 1 or 2 sheep are not prominent in the cultic life of Old Babylonian Mari.[23] In addition Ištar is the only traditional

21. ARM 26 208:5–7.

22. Dossin is undoubtedly right. Given the total of 87 sheep in the summary, and subtracting the known number of sheep in the other lines (87 − 66 = 21), 21 sheep remain for the total of lines 10–13. It seems likely that the numbers to be expected would be similar to the numbers already listed for the other recipients on the list, that is, 1, 2, or 6. The parts of the signs that are preserved in lines 11 and 13 easily allow, indeed almost require, the reading '6'. This leaves 9 sheep to be distributed between lines 10 and 12. Traces of the sign for '2' exist in line 12 in the extant text, according to the cuneiform copy of G. Dossin in the original publication and, therefore, with Dossin, '2' should be read in the gap in that line. This leaves 7 sheep for the goddess Dīrītum in line 10.

23. Hoskisson, *Cult in Mari*, 476–81.

god of Mari[24] on the list who does not receive 6 sheep. As I. Nakata has pointed out, "this is somewhat surprising," given other evidence of her cultic activity at Mari.[25] On the basis of two other Mari "Pantheon" lists, the Early Old Babylonian text TDM 3 and the Old Babylonian ARM 24 263 (both discussed above), in both of which Ištar occurs in the first line of the text, followed by other prominent Mari deities,[26] Ištar was the most honored deity of Mari. In addition to the evidence from PANTHEON, Ištar does not appear in the consignment text ARM 23 264, though three erstwhile Ištar *Erscheinungsformen* do: Dīrītum, Hišamītum, and Annunītum.[27]

Clearly, Dīrītum's absence on any tablets earlier than the Old Babylonian period must indicate, barring some future contrary discovery, that even as an *Erscheinungsform* of Ištar she had not yet come into (noticeable?) existence. In this case, as suggested above, ARM 24 263 represents a stage when Dīrītum had clearly come into her own, but was still very much an *Erscheinungsform* of Ištar. The placing of "Ištar Dīrītum" immediately following "Ištar" on this list seems to indicate that at the time of the composition of this Old Babylonian tablet her position was second only to Ištar's.

In conclusion, before or at the inception of the Old Babylonian period at Mari, Dīrītum separated from her beginnings as a local *Erscheinungsform* of Ištar in Dīr. The transition stage between *Erscheinungsform* and independence is represented by the tablet ARM 24 263:2, where she appears as Ištar Dīrītum. All other tablets from Mari witness to her independence, at least in name. If, as suggested above, the number of sheep consigned to each god in PANTHEON is indicative of standing,[28] then Dīrītum, with seven sheep, was the most honored god on the Mari list and eclipsed Ištar. In a few other texts, Ištar seems to have fallen somewhat out of favor, perhaps toward the end of the Zimri-Lim era. Perhaps Dīrītum rose to prominence, if not preeminence and royal favor, because she issued through her *āpilu*-priest at Mari favorable predictions for the king and throne of Mari (ARM 26 208:5–7).

24. That is, those gods who are attested in the pre-Sargonic, the Early Old Babylonian, and the Old Babylonian periods and who are prominent in the Old Babylonian period.

25. Nakata, *Deities in the Mari Texts*, 292.

26. These texts list the same gods in the first five lines (numbering according to TDM3), except for the insertion of "Ištar Dīrītum" in ARM 24 263, between lines 1 and 2, immediately after Ištar.

27. This list could reflect the local cult centers at Terqa and not the cults of the city of Mari. Dīrītum also occurs in ARM 23 consignment texts 279, 303, and 364.

28. Hoskisson, *Cult in Mari*, 479–81.

Messengers and the Transmission of Information in the Mari Kingdom

Victor H. Matthews

Communication is of the essence for any government. In the ancient world, however, the difficulties of travel made the gathering and transmission of information both hazardous and time-consuming. Eventually, it was the nation or state that developed the best military and messenger/spy service that came to dominate an area. During the Old Babylonian period of the early 18th century B.C.E., the kingdoms of Mari and Babylon competed for political hegemony in the Tigris-Euphrates river valley. Each maintained a network of ambassadors and auxiliary personnel to further its political interests in the region. The purpose of this study will be to examine instances in the royal correspondence of the Mari kings that describe the ways in which the messengers, *mar šipri*, were used by the king and local officials to maintain communications and jockey for power with the other states.

Messengers and Their Missions

Messengers can be classified according to several categories. The most common are those who carried tablets from the provincial governors to the palace. This task could be accomplished by military personnel, travelers, or merchants who were conscripted for the job by the king or by local officials.[1] Servants or apprentice members of the diplomatic corps served on occasion as runners, swiftly carrying news from one part of the kingdom to the other.

1. J. N. Postgate (*Taxation and Conscription in the Assyrian Empire* [Studia Pohl 3; Rome: Pontifical Biblical Institute, 1974] 228) discusses the conscription of messengers in the Assyrian Empire. These men worked for both the royal house and provincial authorities when they were active in a provincial area.

This last group was the lowest ranking of the messenger corps. All that was required of them was reliability and speed. ARM 13 131 mentions two runners in the entourage of an envoy from Carchemish. These men, *suḫarum*, stood ready to be dispatched by the *mar šiprim* to announce the imminent arrival of the higher official or carry a preliminary message should the caravan's speed be too slow vis-à-vis the gravity of the news.[2] In another instance (ARM 2 21:15–22) Ibal-pi-El writes to Zimri-Lim at Mari that the *suḫar* of Meptum had carried a tablet to Hammurabi containing a list of the activities of the king of Eshnunna.

Another example of the use of speedy messengers is found in a text[3] dealing with another form of communication, the fire signal, and its limitations. Alarm had risen over the appearance of fire signals and a general mobilization had taken place to repel an invading army. However, as this letter from Išme-Dagan to his brother Yasmaḫ-Adad notes, the problem was a local one, and therefore not all of the cities in the vicinity of Andariq needed to send troops. Now 'swift messengers' *suḫaru qallūtim*, had been sent out with the explanation:

> A large force of the enemy has raided the countryside. This is the reason for the fire signals. However, you [the districts of Hasidanum and Nurrugum] do not need to come help.

Since kings seldom paid state visits to each other's capitals, messengers, functioning as official envoys, served as royal surrogates. This role required them to function as diplomatic couriers, negotiators, and occasionally as emissaries to the gods. This latter role is found in a prophecy text[4] that mentions messengers being sent with reports from the king to the image of Dagan at Terqa.

Embodying as they did the authority and power of their state, messengers were generally treated well by local officials. Their persons were protected, as well as their personal property. Evidence of the concern for a messenger's personal property is found in ARMT 14 58:5–15. Yaqqim-Addu reports to Zimri-Lim that he has investigated the loss of a slave by the messengers of Qatna. He assures his lord that the matter will be taken care of properly to prevent any sort of incident or further complaint.[5]

2. See also ARM 1 93 for the use of relay runners. A. D. Crown ("Tidings and Instructions: How News Traveled in the Ancient Near East," *JESHO* 17 [1974] 264–65) notes that the normal pace for couriers and military officials was 25–30 km per day.

3. G. Dossin, "Signaux lumineux au pays de Mari," *RA* 35 (1938) 182.

4. G. Dossin, "Une revelation du dieu Dagan à Terqa," *RA* 42 (1948) 129, 131.

5. On a more mundane level, ARMT 14 36:5–12 mentions the care and feeding of several asses belonging to the Yamḫadian messenger.

Another sign of the system of courtesy extended to couriers is found in the lists of food rations, garments, and other necessities given to them to meet their needs on the road and to please their master. ARM 12 747 is only one of many[6] texts containing notation of expenditures and provisions given to messengers and other visitors at the palace. This document contains a list of 18 persons, messengers from a number of different states (Yamḫad, Babylon, Eshnunna, Carchemish, and Emar), as well as a priest, singers, and several craftsmen who were given portions of mutton during their stay in Zimri-Lim's palace.

The protocol attached to the gifting of visitors and official representatives was apparently quite strict. When it was violated, the local ruler would be taken to task by the leader of the visiting group and a letter would be sent back to their lord appraising him of the situation. This was apparently the basis for the complaint in ARM 2 76:5–19, 34–38, where Laᵓum reports that an official of King Hammurabi of Babylon had failed to give clothes to part of their delegation from Yamḫad, the *ša šikkim* messengers:

> I spoke on their behalf to Sin-bel-aplim [administrative aide to Hammurabi], saying: "Why do you separate us as if we were robbers? Whose servants are we and whose servants are the *ša šikkim* messengers? We all serve the same lord."

Gifts of clothing were regularly given to messengers who carried presents to administrators and rulers along with their messages. ARM 23 43 describes the awarding of vestments to six messengers (dispersed from the royal storerooms by the palace major-domo Mukannišum) on their way to Qatna. Two of these messengers are mentioned in other texts from this corpus: Hammi-sagis in ARM 23 41:8 and Yarpa-Addu in ARM 23 37:1–3.[7]

In ARM 23 43, these messengers are being entrusted with gifts to be transported from the palace to the court of the Amnanean King Sura-hammu.[8] For instance, a present of two chairs was to be taken to the well-known official Iddin-Numušda[9] and a Yamḫadian garment of fine quality

6. See also ARM 12 10, 21 40:4, 21 68, and 21 189. The last text lists sour bread as one of the journey provisions given to the messengers of Elahut.

7. Hammi-sagis is also mentioned as a messenger from Qatna in ARM 23 41:8. Yarpa-Addu is described as "the man of Qatna" in ARM 23 37:1–3, but he is mentioned in conjunction with Isḫi-Dagan, who is designated as the messenger of Qatna.

8. See ARM 23, pp. 344–54, for a cataloguing of these expeditions, the gifts/tribute they carried, and the diplomatic value attached to them.

9. Iddin-Numušda is also mentioned in ARM 2 133:20–24, where he detains a group of envoys while he awaits further orders from the king.

was to be given to Warad-ilišu, a singer and high-ranking member of the Mari cult community.[10]

Messengers sometimes also carried a letter of introduction (*wurtum*),[11] which served as a passport through foreign territories. If ARM 2 77 is any indication, these ambassadors sometimes even had the power to negotiate treaties and establish economic ties between states. In this letter, Abum-ekin describes some difficult talks with Hammurabi in which the ambassador takes an active part—not just serving as a messenger, but actually disagreeing with Hammurabi over the terms of the treaty.

I suspect that very few messengers had such latitude in their missions. In most cases they simply functioned as representatives, not active participants in royal negotiations. An indication of this is found in Tell el-Rimaḫ text 101. Here Mutu-ḫadki writes to Iltani, the wife of the ruler of Karana, to send a messenger (line 16) to a royal official named Masiya with a request for the return of two serving women. He suggests that the messenger "steadfastly obey Masiya's instructions." This may have been a delicate matter and Mutu-ḫadki may have thought that to appear too forceful would destroy any chances of either the return of the servants or compensation for their loss. A comparison might also be made with the injunction to messengers given by the Egyptian vizier Ptah-hotep.[12] In this 25th-century B.C.E. piece of wisdom literature, the courier is exhorted to fulfill his mission with dispatch and to repeat the full text of the message without personal editorializing. At the same time, he is to be diplomatic in tone and reserved in attitude.

Rules of Conduct and Espionage

The routes taken by these courier-officials took them from one city to the next on the way to their ultimate destination. Along the way, provincial officials took note of their passage and kept a running account of whose ambassadors were going where and with whom.[13] Regular accounts were then sent to the palace, often in what appears to be a form letter (see ARM 6 14 and 17), along with the mundane activities of the district.

10. Warad-ilišu is described as training female singers in ARM 10 126. In ARM 2 134, he is detained by Isḫi-Addu because of unfavorable omens.

11. Crown, "Tidings," 259 n. 82.

12. *ANET* 413, lines 150–60.

13. J. M. Munn-Rankin, "Diplomacy in Western Asia in the Early Second Millennium B.C.," *Iraq* 18 (1956) 107.

ARM 6 15:6–15 is a good example of this type of reporting on the movement of messengers.[14] Here Kibri-Dagan notes the arrival of five diplomats and their escorts from Qatna who were then bound for three separate destinations. ARM 6 23 describes the arrival at Mari of six different diplomatic groups bound for Yamḫad, Qatna, Hazor, and elsewhere. Lines 28–30 in this text also note the imminent arrival of messengers from Yamḫad and Carchemish who were on missions to cities south and east of Mari. Following this same pattern of official reports, in ARMT 14 125:4–9, 21–23, Yaqqim-Addu, the governor of Sagaratum, questions a subject of the king named Burqan who had just arrived, accompanied by his escort, *alik idišū*, from Ilansura. The result was a dispatch describing the envoy's mission that would arrive before he reached Mari.

The use of escorts by messengers is an interesting aspect of their work. Nearly every letter to the king of Mari mentions the number of escorts that accompanied the messenger and where they were from. Some of these escorts were assigned when the courier was sent on his mission, perhaps as guides. Others joined his entourage on the return trip, either being assigned by the ruler of the city visited or by a provincial official along the way. Thus, in ARM 6 14:22–28, Baḫdi-Lim reports the arrival of Yarpa-Addu, a messenger from Qatna on his way to the court at Mari. However, he had arrived without an escort and thus one was assigned to him before he was sent on to meet the king. ARMT 14 117:5–15 contains a similar case in which Halu-rapi, a messenger of Haya-Sumu, was assigned an escort of guards by Yaqqim-Addu before he left Sagaratum. This may have been a matter of protocol or respect for the ruler who had sent the messenger.

There were times, however, when the lack of an escort was due to a deliberate slight by a ruler. ARM 2 73:4–15 reports the displeasure of Hammurabi with the king of Elam. To demonstrate dissatisfaction with the course of negotiations with that country, he refuses to grant an audience to the Elamite messengers and sends them on their way without a proper escort.

Hammurabi's action not only served as a diplomatic gesture but also left these men open to the very real dangers of traveling alone. It seems clear in some texts that the *alik idi*'s role was to protect the envoy from the dangers of the road. Text 45 from Tell el-Rimaḫ states that men were to be appointed to accompany the servants of Napsuna-Addu on their journey to see King Aqba-hammu of Karana. On the other hand, ARM 6 20:6–13 notes that several royal officials had returned safe from their journey, guided on the

14. See also ARM 6 21; 14 33, 101, and 122.

road by Yamur-Addu, a messenger from Yamḫad. In this case, the messenger travels with and functions as the guide-protector of other officials.

The hazards faced by travelers are graphically portrayed in ARM 2 123, where a large party headed by the king's envoy Ili-iddinam was attacked by bandits. Fourteen of their group, including Ili-iddinam and Tulish of Elahut, were killed, and their 10 laden donkeys and a horse were stolen. In a similar case, ARMT 14 86:5–13, another official party was attacked, although this time because they were in the wrong place at the wrong time:

> Kasan, a messenger of Karkemish, Šamaš-redi and his companion, who are subjects of my lord, were en route from Karkemish to my lord. Four Uprapeans, who were skinning a stag, attacked them (and) killed Šamaš-redi and his companion, (but) the man from Karkemish escaped.

These messengers and their companions were attacked by the Uprapeans to cover up their poaching activity. Potential attacks and other dangers may also explain Yaqqim-Addu's assigning of "three reliable men" to guard the Ekallatean messenger in ARMT 14 127:5–17.

The question naturally arises: were the escorts simply bodyguards and guides or did they have other functions as well? Certainly, there was a good deal of suspicion of foreign envoys. As they traveled through the land they could pick up valuable military and economic information for their masters. An escort could at least insure that they did not take side trips and learn more than necessary. This may explain Šamši-Adad's careful orchestration of each leg of the journey by the messengers of Hazor and those of the kings of the Amurru as they traveled to Qatna. He requested that his son Yasmaḫ-Adad entrust them to the messenger of Isḫi-Adad, king of Qatna, perhaps to demonstrate his concern for their welfare and perhaps also to keep a close eye on them.[15]

There are several other indications of a suspicious attitude held toward foreign messengers. For instance, in ARM 2 41:3′–4′, a question is directed to the ruler of Qatna by Zimri-Lim as to why his messengers so often traveled with those of the Assyrian regent of Šubat-Enlil, Išme-Dagan. The latter was Zimri-Lim's political rival, and association with his officials was tantamount to a political alliance.

15. G. Dossin, "Kengen, pays de Canaan," *RSO* 32 (1957) 37–38; A. Malamat, "Northern Canaan and the Mari Texts," *Near Eastern Archaeology in the Twentieth Century* (Nelson Glueck festschrift; ed. J. A. Sanders et al.; Garden City, N.Y.: Doubleday, 1970) 265.

While the system of courtesy was extended to these representatives, political reality required that their missions be strictly monitored and that their persons sometimes be "unavoidably" detained to insure that some information was not too timely. The sophistication of some of the decisions made regarding *mar šipri* are a reflection of the complexity of foreign as well as domestic policy during the Mari period. For example, in a fragmentary text published by C. F. Jean,[16] Yawi-ila, king of Talhiyim (in the upper Baliḫ region), reported that he had detained messengers of Eshnunna and of Qarni-Lim of Asnakkum. These men had been traveling to meet with Adal-šenni, king of Burundum, perhaps to request aid or an alliance in their war against Zimri-Lim. Yawi-ila's action slowed the diplomatic process enough to allow his ally Zimri-Lim to react to this threat and thus thwart the plans of Qarni-Lim.

Placed in context, the messenger very often could be considered a spy. As messengers traveled throughout the kingdom, they were able to assess the effectiveness of local administration, the needs of the villages and towns, and even the sources of discontent in various areas. Their foreign missions were also designed to collect this type of intelligence in rival states, in addition to conducting open diplomatic service. The act of detaining messengers thus became both an occasional necessity and an art, since some attention also had to be given to the possibility that this action could precipitate an international incident.

It is no wonder that governors were careful to document their actions and to write to the king to clarify orders on whether to detain messengers and for how long a time. Yaqqim-Addu's letter, ARMT 14 97:5–14, is typical of this administrative style. He writes:

> Kirip-Seris and Samusa, men of Kurda, and a Babylonian messenger, serving as their escort, have arrived from Kurda. I detained them in Sagaratum.
>
> They have told me that they are bound for Babylon. Now let my lord write to me about whether or not to allow them to proceed.

The very shrewd royal official Baḫdi-Lim writes to the king in ARM 6 19:17–22:

> I detained this man [Yarpa-Addu, messenger from Qatna]. My reasoning was: Perhaps the allied troops have not (yet) assembled before my lord. Thus (if) I send this man to my lord, he will discover this about the troops. Therefore I have detained him.

16. C. F. Jean, "Arisen dans les lettres de Mari," *Sem* 1 (1948) 23.

A final example of the use of detention to delay or damage the effectiveness of intelligence-gathering by messengers is found in ARM 2 133:20–25. A group of messengers on their way to Qatna had been stalled by Idin-Numušda for five days. He now asks whether they can be allowed to depart and notes that they would have to wait somewhat longer, since the caravan they had planned to accompany had already departed.[17]

Conclusion

It can be demonstrated in the Mari texts that the possibilities for service by messengers included many different missions, both in personal service to the royal family and to the state. While some were assigned directly to queens (as in ARM 10 174:13) and princes to carry messages privately to the king, their principal duty was to facilitate communication on all official levels. Their activities were crucial to the administration of the state. Those in power communicated through these underlings on nearly every type of mundane as well as sensitive matter. The timeliness of these messages and their attempts to uphold the authority of their lord in their missions make the *mar šipri* some of the most important officials in the Mari bureaucracy.

17. S. A. Meier (*The Messenger in the Ancient Semitic World* [HSM 45; Atlanta: Scholars Press, 1988] 80–81) cites several texts, including this one, to demonstrate the regularity with which messengers accompanied caravans. Such a practice contributed to safety as well as the maintenance of a more regular, predictable schedule for their missions.

Structure in ***The Wisdom of Amenemope*** *and Proverbs*

Paul Overland

Introduction

Within the Hebrew Bible, the book of Proverbs offers a significant opportunity for comparative research. This owes to several close parallels discovered in an Egyptian sapiential text, *The Wisdom of Amenemope.* Correlations between Prov 22:17–24:22[1] and excerpts of *Amenemope* were observed soon after E. A. W. Budge's publication of the text in 1922.[2]

In the numerous studies comparing *Amenemope* and Proverbs, one element has not consistently been taken into account, namely, the element of structure within *Amenemope* and its relation to parallels in Proverbs.[3] The purpose of this article is to evaluate *Amenemope*/Proverbs parallels in terms of structural significance.

Three aspects of *Amenemope* make it useful for a discussion of structure. First, content in *Amenemope* is grouped around a series of themes. These include

---

Author's note: I am indebted to Dwight Young for introducing me to the field of Egyptology and Hebrew sapiential literature.

1. Prov 22:17–24:22 is bounded by remarks implying a section title in 22:17 and 24:23. The phrase דִּבְרֵי חֲכָמִים 'words of the wise' appears in a summons injunction in 22:17, while גַּם־אֵלֶּה לַחֲכָמִים 'these, too, pertain to the wise' occurs in 24:23. This study is limited to Prov 22:17–23:11, since no firm parallels are found beyond Prov 23:11. When the terms *text* or *document* are applied to Proverbs, they refer to this section.

2. E. A. W. Budge, "The Precepts of Life by Amen-Em Apt, the Son of Kanekht," in *Recueil d'Études égyptologiques Dédiées à la Mémoire de Jean-François Champollion* (Paris: n.p., 1922) 431–46.

3. *Structure* in this study refers to surface structure rather than deep structure.

themes such as Forethought in Speech (chap. 3), the Hot-Tempered Man and the Tranquil Man (chap. 4), and Regard for Land Boundaries (chap. 6).[4]

Second, *Amenemope* was divided into chapters. Chapter enumeration is explicitly mentioned in the epilogue: "See for thyself these thirty chapters, they please, they educate."[5] Thus the chapter division of *Amenemope* can be regarded as an integral part of its formation, dating perhaps to its initial composition, rather than a convenient segmenting of the text imposed on it by a reader who belonged to a later era and culture.

Third, the Egyptian sage arranged his material so that one can often determine the theme of an entire chapter by reading the initial saying. Sayings in chapter-initial position frequently serve as topic sentences for the remainder of a chapter. This will have particular bearing on the comparison with Israelite material.

Before we compare the two documents, however, it will be helpful briefly to review how past scholarship has regarded the relationship between Proverbs and *Amenemope.*[6] Then we will consider the extent to which past studies have utilized the chapter structure of *Amenemope* when comparing the two collections.

Review of Scholarship

Budge, whose publication of *Amenemope* appeared in 1922, concluded that the Egyptian work showed a potential debt to Asian influence.[7] Subsequent scholars advanced the discussion. Some have argued for the priority of

4. For one scholar's list of the thirty themes, see F. L. Griffith, "The Teaching of Amenophis the Son of Kanakht. Papyrus B.M. 10474," *JEA* 12 (1926) 194. No titles appear in the hieroglyphic text, only the enumeration of chapters.

5. Column xxvii, lines 7–8 (*Amen.* 30:1–2), using Griffith's translation ("The Teaching of Amenophis," 224). This epilogue is present even in the earliest copy. In future citations of *Amenemope, column* / line references will be designated by lowercase Roman numerals followed by Arabic numerals (e.g., xxvii 7–8). *Chapter* / line references will be designated by Arabic numerals separated by a colon (e.g., 30:1–2).

6. For a more thorough review of past scholarship, see Glendon E. Bryce, *A Legacy of Wisdom: The Egyptian Contribution to the Wisdom of Israel* (Lewisberg, Penn.: Bucknell University Press, 1979) 15–38.

7. E. A. W. Budge, *The Teaching of Amen-em-Apet* (London: Martin Hopkinson, 1924) 103, cited by R. J. Williams, "The Alleged Semitic Original for the Wisdom of Amenemope," *JEA* 47 (1961) 100.

the Egyptian work.[8] Another view postulated a common Semitic source from which both *Amenemope* and Proverbs drew material. According to this theory, the Israelite sage followed the source closely, while his Egyptian counterpart expanded it considerably.[9] This would account for the Hebrew composition's being more compact than the Egyptian collection.

Some, on the other hand, attempted to demonstrate dependence on a Hebrew original by listing alleged semitisms in the Egyptian composition.[10] R. J. Williams effectively countered this position by adducing equivalent expressions from other Egyptian works, especially from Late Egyptian.[11] The language of *Amenemope* does not reflect standard Middle Egyptian, nor is it clearly Late Egyptian. It includes elements of each. Thus, it was appropriate for Williams to bring Late Egyptian evidence to bear on the question of alleged semitisms.

When similar themes occur in *Amenemope* and Proverbs, *Amenemope* generally offers a more lengthy discussion of the themes than Proverbs. Consequently, some have been inclined to infer that an Egyptian writer used the Israelite document to supply topics that he then expanded with Egyptian coloration.[12] When a mid–first millennium date was still tenable for *Amenemope*, influence stemming from Proverbs remained conceivable. However, the Cairo ostracon 1840 bearing a portion of *Amenemope* has been dated by Černy to

8. Adolf Erman was one of those who considered the Egyptian source older than the Hebrew source. See "Eine ägyptische Quelle der 'Sprüche Salomos,'" *Sitzungsberichte der preussischen Akademie der Wissenschaften, Philologisch-Historische Klasse* 15 (1924) 92.

9. This view was suggested by W. O. E. Oesterley, "The Teaching of Amen-em-opet and the Old Testament," *ZAW* 45 (1926) 9–24. See also Oesterley, *The Wisdom of Egypt and the Old Testament* (London: S.P.C.K., 1927; reprinted, New York: n.p., 1972) 105.

10. R. O. Kevin, "The Wisdom of Amen-em-Apt and Its Possible Dependence upon the Hebrew book of Proverbs," *JSOR* 14 (1930) 115–57. Similarly, Étienne Drioton, "Sur la Sagesse d'Aménémopé," in *Mélanges bibliques rédigés en l'honneur de André Robert* (ed. H. Cazelles; Paris: Bloud & Gay, 1957) 254–80. See also Drioton, "Le livre des Proverbes et la sagesse d'Aménémopé," in *Sacra Pagina: Miscellanea Biblica Congressus Internationalis Catholici de re Biblica* (ed. J. Coppens, A. Descamps, É. Massaux; BETL 12; Paris: LeCoffre, 1959) 1.229–41.

11. Williams, "Alleged Semitic Original," 100–106.

12. Cf. ibid., 100ff., for references to arguments favoring priority of the Israelite document. The principle of expansion from short epigrams to longer sayings was argued for Hebrew sentence literature (without specific reference to *Amenemope* parallels) by J. Schmidt in *Studien zur Stilistik der alttestamentliche Spruchliteratur* (Alttestamentliche Abhandlungen 13; Münster i. Westf.: Aschendorff, 1936) 1. See also William McKane's remarks in *Proverbs: A New Approach* (OTL; Philadelphia: Westminster, 1970) 1–2.

the late Twenty-First Dynasty (ca. 1000–950 B.C.E.).[13] If we regard the mid-tenth century B.C.E. (the Solomonic monarchy) as a *terminus a quo* for Proverbs, the Cairo ostracon effectively establishes that *Amenemope* is not indebted to Proverbs. Any influence must have proceeded from Egypt to Israel.

The fact that the ostracon is a schoolboy copy also contributes to the issue of cross-cultural contact. As a schoolboy text, the probability increases that there were multiple copies in circulation.[14] One of these copies might have reached a scribal school in Jerusalem.[15] The outcome of the *Amenemope*/Proverbs dialogue suggests that the Israelite author at some point had contact with the Egyptian composition, not vice versa.

Throughout preceding studies, scholars have focused attention on parallel concepts and actual expressions found both in the Egyptian and Israelite texts.[16] Their research has not paid attention to the position within the source document from which material appears to have been borrowed. Lack of attention to position in the source document is a significant omission in the present state of Proverbs/*Amenemope* research.

13. Noted by Williams, "Alleged Semitic Original," 106. In another article he remarks that in addition to the Turin, Moscow, and Louvre copies of *Amenemope* (dating to Dynasties 26, 25/26, and 21/22, respectively),

> we must add an unpublished ostracon in Cairo that Černý dated to the late Twenty-First Dynasty. Since the new papyrus and the ostracon are both schoolboy copies, the original composition can hardly be later than the Twentieth Dynasty. We may then assign it with some confidence to the twelfth or even thirteenth century B.C. Hence there is no reason to suppose that the text was unknown in the days of Solomon ("A People Come out of Egypt," *Congress Volume: Edinburgh 1974* [VTSup 28; ed. J. A. Emerton; Leiden: Brill, 1975] 242).

Although never published by Černý, the ostracon has been made available by B. Peterson in *Studia Aegyptiaca* 1 (Budapest, 1974) 323–27. Its contents correspond to portions from col. iii 9 to iv 10 of the British Museum copy.

14. The circulation of sapiential material is attested from the discovery in Boghazköy of an extract from the wisdom text *Subeʾawilum*, which derives from Ugarit (see Bryce, *Legacy of Wisdom*, 81 and 136).

15. Based on Solomon's marriage to a daughter of the Pharaoh (1 Kgs 3:1), we may conclude that there were persons in Jerusalem who could read Egyptian, at least during the united monarchy. Concerning the question of scribal schools in Israel, see James L. Crenshaw, "Education in Ancient Israel," *JBL* 104 (1985) 601–15, and J. P. J. Olivier, "Schools and Wisdom Literature," *JNSL* 4 (1975) 49–60.

16. Compare the following sayings, which provide a remarkably close content parallel: "Surely it [wealth] will make wings for itself, and like an eagle fly heavenward" (Prov 23:5b) and "They [riches] have made themselves wings like geese; they have flown heavenward" (*Amen.* x 4–5).

Many scholars do not comment on the significance of source position because they use only column/line references, thus omitting the Egyptian author's own chapter groupings.[17] Gressmann follows chapter notation for *Amenemope*, yet does so inconsistently, and fails to point out the significance of positioning.[18] McKane indicates that opening lines of Egyptian chapters sometimes parallel Israelite proverbs, yet he does not point out the significance of position consistently. Position is noted for *Amenemope* 2 (Prov 22:22) and for *Amenemope* 9 (Prov 23:4).[19] Dunsmore twice points out significant positioning, but his treatment falters due to imprecise handling of the Egyptian text.[20] Richter observes that material drawn from chap. 1 of *Amenemope* comes from the opening lines of the chapter, but no comment is made on subsequent parallels that demonstrate unusual positioning.[21] Grumach treats *Amenemope* according to chapter groupings but notes significant positioning only in the case of Prov 22:24–25.[22] In a more recent commentary, Otto Plöger indicates chapter numbers for *Amenemope* but only sporadically demonstrates the importance of position within the chapter.[23]

17. E.g., D. C. Simpson, "The Hebrew Book of Proverbs and the Teaching of Amenophis," *JEA* 12 (1926) 232–39; so also Kevin, "Wisdom of Amen-em-Apt," 119ff., and W. Bühlemann, *Vom Rechten Reden und Schweigen: Studien zu Proverbien 10–31* (OBO 12; Freiburg, Switzerland: Universitätsverlag, 1976) 150, and Bryce, *Legacy of Wisdom*, 16 and 66. Bryce's objective is to show that the differences between particular parallel passages may reflect a certain stage along a continuum of adaptation, assimilation, and integration of Egyptian material in Israelite hands (pp. 57–58). He is interested in specific expressions and how they may have been reshaped by the Israelite sage, rather than attending to their location within *Amenemope*. Erman notes chapters but omits verse numbers, leaving unclear the chapter position of a parallel (pp. 87–91). Similarly, A. Alt, "Zur Literarischen Analyse der Weisheit des Amenemope," *Wisdom in Israel and in the Ancient Near East* (ed. M. Noth and D. Winton Thomas; VTSup 3; Leiden: Brill, 1955) 25 n. 4.

18. Hugo Gressmann, *Israels Spruchweisheit im Zusammenhang der Weltliteratur* (Berlin: Karl Curtius, 1925) 37.

19. McKane, *Proverbs*, 377ff.

20. Marion H. Dunsmore, "An Egyptian Contribution to Proverbs," *JR* 5 (1925) 300–308. The two cases referred to by Dunsmore are discussed below under the fourteenth parallel.

21. Wolfgang Richter, *Recht und Ethos: Versuch einer Ortung des weisheitlichen Mahnspruches* (Munich: Kösel, 1966) 17–40.

22. Irene Grumach, *Untersuchungen zur Lebenslehre des Amenope* (Münchner Ägyptologische Studien 23; Berlin: Deutscher Kunstverlag, 1972) 79. Cf. n. 41 below.

23. Plöger, *Sprüche Salomos (Proverbia)* (BKAT 17; Neukirchen-Vluyn: Neukirchener Verlag, 1984). Chapter position is shown in *Amenemope* 9 (Prov 22:24) but is omitted for the following verse of Proverbs (p. 269). Position is given for *Amenemope* 30 (Prov 22:29,

Amenemope/Proverbs Parallels

The objective of this study is to examine the significance of position for *Amenemope* parallels.[24] Before beginning a comparison of parallel passages, I will discuss the contents of *Amenemope* and endeavor to show how the contents pertain to significant positioning.

Amenemope begins with two and one-half columns of prefatory remarks that describe the purpose, author, and intended reader of the composition. Following the preface, the first numbered chapter brings an introductory charge to the pupil (cols. iii 8–iv 2). The instruction proper extends from chaps. 2–29, with chap. 30 acting as an epilogue. In Proverbs, too, there is a distinction between an introductory charge (22:17–21) and the instruction proper (22:22–24:22).

Seventeen sayings in Prov 22:17–24:22 resemble parallel statements in *Amenemope.* The similarity involves thematic correlation at least and often extends to verbal resemblance. Of these seventeen, ten correspond to lines that are significantly positioned in the chapters of *Amenemope.*

By "significantly positioned" it is meant that the material stands at the beginning or end of a chapter. The significance lies in the topic-sentence role often played by chapter-initial lines and in the conclusion or climax that can occur with the closing lines of chapters in *Amenemope.*[25] At times, two consecutive phrases in Proverbs resemble initial and terminal lines of a single chapter in *Amenemope.*[26] This may be described as "telescoping" the material from *Amenemope.* Telescoping represents some of the strongest evidence that the Israelite writer was aware of the structure of the Egyptian document.

In addition to the position of lines within a chapter, the position of lines within the entire document can be significant. This is particularly true when, for example, prologue material in *Amenemope* is found to resemble material

p. 270), but is overlooked for another parallel drawn from the same chapter of *Amenemope* (Prov 22:20, p. 270). *Amenemope* 6 (Prov 23:10a, p. 272), chap. 7 (Prov 23:4a, p. 271), and chap. 23 (Prov 23:1a, pp. 270–71) comprise additional parallels in which Plöger omits chapter position.

24. The position-significance of parallels that are presented below was independently observed by the writer. Confirmation from previous scholarship has been noted whenever possible.

25. The chapter-initial and chapter-terminal position of material in *Amenemope* resembles the notion of framing devices. The use of framing devices has been demonstrated within Proverbs (for instance, see my *Literary Structure in Proverbs 1–9* [Ph.D. diss., Brandeis University, 1988] 76–82 and 395–98).

26. See the seventh and eighth parallels.

located in the Israelite prologue. I will now discuss each parallel, noting any instance of significant positioning.

First Parallel [27]

Prov 22:17–18a	Incline your ear and hear words of wisdom; apply your heart to my knowledge. For it is pleasant if you guard them within you.
Amen. iii 9–11 (1:1–3)	Lend me your ears; hear what is said. Give your heart to interpret them. To put them in your heart is advantageous.

In the first parallel, Proverbs' exhortation corresponds to the initial lines of the first chapter in *Amenemope*. Both documents call the pupil to pay attention to ensuing instruction. This functions as a summons.[28] The Israelite writer adapted lines positioned significantly in both chapter and book setting.[29] As with the source document, so also in Proverbs these lines form the opening charge to the pupil, yielding a close correlation.

Second Parallel

Prov 22:18b	If they are established together on your lips . . .
Amen. iii 16 (1:8)	It shall be as a mooring-post for your tongue.

The second parallel continues the emphasis of a charge to the pupil, rather than a specific instruction. Both texts deal with control of one's speech. In the Hebrew text, the second parallel follows immediately after the first (22:17–18a followed by v. 18b). In the Egyptian text, the second phrase occurs within the same chapter as the first parallel, though separated from it by five lines.

It is not surprising that the second parallel does not bear chapter-initial significance in *Amenemope*, since it extends a concept already captured by a chapter-initial saying (*Amen.* 1:1–3). *Amen.* 1:1–3 and 8 correspond to Prov 22:18a and 18b, since the halves of the respective pairs[30] lie close together in

27. The translations from Hebrew and Egyptian are mine.

28. Compare Prov 1:8; 4:1, 20; and 5:1 for other examples of the summons device.

29. Plöger notes that the lines appear in the first chapter of *Amenemope*, but he fails to comment on their initial position within the chapter (*Sprüche Salomonos*, 267). Erman observes that these words begin the Egyptian writing (or, more precisely, the introductory segment of the composition), although he omits *Amenemope*'s chapter notation ("Eine ägyptische Quelle," 88).

30. That is, *Amen.* 1:1–3 vis-à-vis 1:8, and Prov 22:18a vis-à-vis 18b.

each document and because those halves appear in the same order in each document.[31]

Third Parallel

Prov 22:20	Have I not written to you thirty[32] [sayings] of counsels and knowledge?
Amen. xxvii 7–8 (30:1–2)	You see for yourself these thirty chapters—they please, they educate.

The third parallel produces another case of chapter-initial positioning in *Amenemope.* Relative positions within the entire documents present a correlation as well. Within the framework of 22:17–24:22, Prov 22:20 appears outside the central group of instructions. Prov 22:20 belongs to the introduction. *Amen.* 30:1–2 also stands outside the central group of instructions. Chapter 30 is the concluding chapter. Its contents reflect on the value of the preceding instructions as a whole. The correlation between Egyptian and Israelite document position would have been closer if both parallels occurred either in their respective introductions or in their epilogues.[33] Yet it is not without significance that the location of the Egyptian and Hebrew passages occurs outside the central body of their respective instructions. To this extent the

31. Mention of a "mooring-post" fits well a nautical Egyptian setting (cf. "The Shipwrecked Sailor," line 4 in A. M. Blackman, *Middle-Egyptian Stories* [Bibliotheca Aegyptiaca II; Brussels: n.p., 1932] 41; for an English translation, see Miriam Lichtheim, *Ancient Egyptian Literature: A Book of Readings* [3 vols.; Berkeley: University of California Press, 1973] 1.212). Perhaps his inland Palestine culture prompted the Israelite writer to reword this saying, omitting the maritime allusion. Elsewhere the Israelite sage compared the effects of inebriation with the unsteady footing experienced at sea (Prov 23:35). This shows that he was capable of using nautical terms. The contrast between "to be a mooring-post" and "to be established together" suggests that while the sage could have duplicated the Egyptian phrase, he chose to adapt it to a culture less closely associated with maritime activities.

32. Based on correlation with *Amenemope,* the reading 'thirty' seems preferable to both 'previous', according to the *Kethiv,* and to 'officers' (or 'chief'?), according to the marginal *Qere.* This involves replacing a ו with a י (as in the *Qere* suggestion) and repointing the vowels: שְׁלֹשִׁים in place of שְׁלְשׁוֹם (*Kethiv*) or שְׁלִישִׁים (*Qere*). Cf. C. H. Toy, *A Critical and Exegetical Commentary on the Book of Proverbs* (ICC; New York: Scribner's, 1899) 423; Simpson, "Hebrew Book of Proverbs," 236; McKane, *Proverbs,* 372; Bryce, *Legacy of Wisdom,* 81–86.

33. Erman speculates that other tradents were responsible for relocating the reference to "thirty chapters" from the conclusion of *Amenemope* to its introduction in the copy obtained by the Israelite sage (Bryce, *Legacy of Wisdom,* 19).

third Hebrew parallel resembles *Amenemope* as to its position within the document at large.[34] Thus Prov 22:20 is significant in relation both to chapter and document position.

Fourth Parallel

Prov 22:21b	. . . to return words of truth to him who sent you.
Amen. i 5–6 (prologue lines 5–6)	. . . to know (how) to return the answer to him who spoke; to carry back a report to him who dispatches him.

Like the third parallel, these words in Proverbs still belong to the introductory remarks of vv. 17–21. The instruction proper does not begin until Prov 22:22. Corresponding material in *Amenemope* likewise precedes the main block of teaching (*Amenemope* 2–29). Although the saying does not begin an Egyptian chapter (or prologue, in this case), it may be considered prominent in position since it appears so early in the entire manuscript, within the first six lines. There is a similarity of document position in the two texts.[35]

Fifth Parallel

Prov 22:22	Rob not the poor, because he is poor, neither crush the oppressed in the gate.
Amen. iv 4–5 (2:1–2)	Guard yourself against robbing the poor, against being valorous against the man with a broken arm.

For Proverbs, this fifth parallel comprises the first teaching following introductory exhortations (Prov 22:17–21).[36] The Egyptian parallel similarly appears in the earliest chapter devoted to actual teaching and is found in the initial position of that chapter. In contrast to chap. 2, the preface and chap. 1

34. Erman states that *Amen.* 30:1–2 stands in terminal position with respect to the entire document ("Eine ägyptische Quelle," 92 n. 1). This remark must be understood as referring only to the document position of the *chapter* containing the statement, not the document position of the *statement* itself. Aside from the colophon, the statement bearing actual document-terminal significance appears eight lines later (*Amen.* 30:9–10). This terminal saying also resembles a statement in Proverbs and is discussed below under the ninth parallel.

35. The lines from *Amenemope* draw our attention to the premium that the Nile culture placed upon a dependable statesman or negotiator who would accurately represent a principal's interests. The Egyptian material may help us better understand the sociological dynamics behind Prov 22:21 (McKane, *Proverbs*, 54 and 377).

36. Plöger notes the chapter number for *Amenemope* but omits the line number. Thus the position significance goes unnoticed (*Sprüche Salomonos*, 268).

of *Amenemope* contain a biographical background and introductory exhortations. Because the lines of the fifth illustration are chapter-initial in *Amenemope*, they present a high degree of correlation with the parallel in Prov 22:22.

One aspect of content in these lines distinguishes Egyptian and Israelite cultures. While both teachings involve respect for the defenseless, the legal setting "in the gate" presents an expression that is appropriate for Israelite culture and that does not appear in *Amenemope*. In the Egyptian document, the sage goes on to safeguard the aged as an additional disadvantaged class.

<u>*Sixth Parallel*</u>

Prov 22:23a	For the LORD shall argue their case.
Amen. iv 19 (2:16)	Thou Moon, bring forward his crime!

Amenemope 2 concentrates on advocating the rights of the helpless. The sixth parallel appears in this chapter. It is instructive to note that the painful consequences promised to the aggressor in *Amenemope* 2 reach a climax with the threat of divine intervention (2:16). The Egyptian sage appeals to Thoth, represented by the moon, since he was the god responsible for accounting man's guilt or innocence.[37]

We noted above that the Israelite document first raises the issue of justice for the helpless in Prov 22:22. Is it mere coincidence that, as he proceeded to instruct concerning the disadvantaged, the Israelite sage chose as his next point the concept found at the climax of *Amenemope* 2? In that next point (Prov 22:23a) he warned of *divine* intervention, corresponding to the Moon in the climax of *Amenemope* 2. It appears that the Israelite writer distilled *Amenemope*'s teaching concerning the helpless. He began with the chapter-initial topic sentence in *Amenemope*[38] and continued the teaching with a threat of divine retribution. The Israelite sage made suitable adjustments to reflect his own theology.[39]

<u>*Seventh Parallel*</u>

Prov 22:24	Do not associate yourself with an angry man, nor go in company with a wrathful man.
Amen. xi 13–14 (9:1–2)	Do not make friends with the hot-headed man, nor approach him for conversation.

37. Notice the similarity of *sʾhʾbtȝ*, a legal term for 'impeachment' or 'accusing of crime', and יָרִיב 'to dispute' or 'to argue a case' (Griffith, "The Teaching of Amenophis," 200 n. 7). For *sʾhʾbtȝ* the hieroglyph is .

38. See the fifth parallel above.

39. That is, replacement of Thoth by the LORD.

The seventh parallel in *Amenemope* forms the opening lines for a chapter concerning the hot-headed man.[40] Chapter-initial position suggests that the material was summarized by adopting a topic sentence from the Egyptian document. As the chapter progresses, it is unrestrained speech that brands the person depicted in *Amenemope*. He is destructive as a wolf (9:26), unpredictable as a cloud (9:29), lethal as a crocodile (9:31). The Israelite writer bypasses these similes and resumes with a warning in the following parallel.

Eighth Parallel

Prov 22:25	Lest you learn his ways and catch a snare for your soul.
Amen. xiii 8–9 (9:35–36)	Do not leap to cleave to that [fellow], lest a terror carry you away.

Prov 22:25 concludes the theme of the hot-headed man. It warns the pupil of personal consequences that he may suffer if he associates with a person given to anger. Warning of personal consequences also marks the *Amenemope* parallel. This statement stands apart from twenty-six preceding lines that describe the passionate man without personally implicating the pupil. Because of the personal tone of caution and because of parallel consequences—being snared or carried off—these excerpts form a parallel.

Like the seventh, the eighth parallel occurs within chap. 9 of *Amenemope*, precisely at its conclusion. The telescoping process evident in parallels five and six and again in parallels seven and eight presents one of the most convincing evidences favoring the view that an Israelite writer abridged the Egyptian work.[41]

Ninth Parallel

Prov 22:29	Do you see a man who is skilled in his work? He will stand before kings. He will not stand before obscure men.

40. While Plöger observes that this is the opening statement of *Amenemope* 9 (*Sprüche Salomonos*, 269), he overlooks the telescoping treatment of *Amenemope* caused by the Israelite sage's choice of the ensuing verse.

41. This abridgment is also noted by Alt ("Weisheit des Amenemope," 25 n. 3). He does not point out the important fact of initial and terminal positioning of these lines within *Amenemope* 9, only that they both appear within a single chapter. Grumach, however, does observe that parallels seven and eight derive from the beginning and end of the source chapter (*Lebenslehre des Amenope*, 79).

Amenemope offers no parallel to the cautions of Prov 22:26–27. These lines may represent a restatement of Prov 6:1–5. The prohibition against moving boundaries (v. 28) is discussed below under Prov 23:10–11.

Amen. xxvii 16–17 (30:9–10) If a scribe is skilled in his office, he will find himself worthy of being a courtier.

These lines stand out in *Amenemope* because they form the last verses of the epilogue (chap. 30).[42] Only the two-line colophon occupies a position later than *Amen.* 30:9–10.[43] Such a highly significant position may have inclined the Israelite writer to give special attention to this aphorism.

It is instructive to note that the author of Proverbs neither reserved these lines for the end of his document nor even employed them as the final parallel corresponding to *Amenemope.* Eight more parallels follow. Such a clear break from the document-terminal positioning of material within *Amenemope* (30:9–10) suggests that the author of Proverbs did not feel obliged to imitate slavishly the sequence of material found in *Amenemope.*[44] Rather, he exercised full autonomy over presentation of the foreign material that he deemed worthy of transmission.

Tenth Parallel

Prov 23:1a	When you sit down to eat with a ruler . . .
Amen. xxiii 13 (23:1)	Do not eat bread in the presence of a ruler.

The principle of significant positioning recurs in the tenth parallel. Both passages are concerned with the pupil's demeanor when he dines with a superior. Taken in the larger context, both warn him against untimely indulgence. Reference to table manners before a ruler appears in chapter-initial position in the source document. Consistent with the frequent theme of restraint advised in speech, the Egyptian wisdom writer here allots an eight-line chapter to encourage restraint when enjoying the hospitality of one's superior. The theme continues in the following parallel.

Eleventh Parallel

Prov 23:1b	. . . consider carefully what is in front of you.
Amen. xxiii 17–18 (23:5–6)	Focus your attention on the beverage before you; let it supply your need.

42. While Plöger observes that these lines serve as the concluding sentence to *Amenemope* 30, he does not indicate that, aside from the colophon, they have the added prominence of document-terminal positioning (*Sprüche Salomonos,* 270).

43. The colophon reads, "That is the end. Written by Senu son of the divine father Pemu" (Griffith, "The Teaching of Amenophis," 225).

44. In contrast to this inattention to sequence, the various elements of the curse in Deut 28:27–33 sequentially resemble the maledictions in the vassal-treaties of Esarhaddon (Moshe Weinfeld, "Traces of Assyrian Treaty Formulae in Deuteronomy," *Bib* 46 [1965] 418–20).

In *Amenemope* the eleventh parallel forms the last injunction before an obscure aphorism[45] closing this brief, eight-line chapter. To argue for chapter-terminal prominence would strain the evidence, but one may safely infer that the Israelite writer crystallized two elements drawn from chap. 23 of the source document. Prov 23:1a and b correspond to *Amen.* 23:1 and 5–6, respectively. To these the Israelite sage added several ideas of his own that intensify the severity of the warning (Prov 23:2–3).

Twelfth Parallel

Prov 23:4a	Do not toil after riches.
Amen. ix 10 (7:1)	Do not cast your heart after wealth.

Again in the twelfth parallel, the Egyptian passage appears in chapter-initial position. Chapter 7 of *Amenemope* advises against trying to gather more wealth than one actually needs, especially if acquired illegally. Scholars such as Gressmann and Simpson prefer to correlate this Hebrew proverb with *Amen.* ix 14 (7:5): "Do not be greedy in search of wealth."[46]

The content of the two Egyptian sayings is very similar. However, given the Israelite writer's apparent preference for topic sentences, it seems more reasonable to link Prov 23:4 with *Amen.* 7:1, an Egyptian saying that is chapter-initial.

Thirteenth Parallel

Prov 23:5a	Your eye lights upon it [riches], but it is not there.
Amen. ix 18–19 (7:9–10)	Day dawns and they [riches gained by robbery] are not in your house. One sees their place but they are not there.

Wealth continues as the topic of the thirteenth parallel. *Amenemope* specifies wealth acquired dishonorably (ix 16). In the Israelite document the notion of dishonorable conduct does arise in connection with nearby warnings (that is, "do not rob the poor" in 22:22, and "do not remove landmarks" in 22:28). But it is the ephemeral quality of wealth that persists in the mind of the Israelite sage, whether or not that wealth was acquired lawfully. He seems to have been bothered by inferior life goals more than by simple infractions of justice. Not because of law violations, but because it is an unworthy master, riches will surely vanish.

45. "Even as a noble is great in his office, he is like as a well aboundeth [in] drawings [of water]" (Griffith's translation, "The Teaching of Amenophis," 220).

46. Author's translation; cf. Gressmann (*Israels Spruchweisheit*, 41) and Simpson ("Hebrew Book of Proverbs," 237).

The notion of the mysterious disappearance of wealth is common to both documents. While found within the same Egyptian chapter as the preceding parallel (chap. 7), it lacks prominent positioning.[47] The next parallel extends the idea of wealth.

Fourteenth Parallel

Prov 23:5b	Surely it will make wings for itself, and like an eagle fly heavenward.
Amen. x 4–5 (7:15–16)	They have made themselves wings like geese; they have flown heavenward.

The fourteenth parallel offers one of the most striking correlations between Proverbs and *Amenemope*. Wealth will take wings and elude the miser's grasp. Marion Dunsmore, in a rare reference to position-significance, surmises that Prov 23:4–5 "seems to be a shortened form of chapter vii of Amenemopet [sic], which begins 'Weary not thyself to seek for more' and ends, 'They (riches) have made themselves wings like geese and have flown heavenward.' "[48] This observation holds true, as long as by "shortened" Dunsmore does not mean "telescoped." For *Amenemope* 7 to have been telescoped into Prov 23:4–5, it would be necessary for *Amen.* 7:15–16 to have been located at the end of chap. 7. In fact, these lines are separated from the end of chap. 7 by ten lines.

Chapter-initial significance obtains for *Amen.* 7:1 (parallels Prov 23:4a), as noted above in the twelfth parallel. *Amen.* 7:15–16 (parallel to Prov 23:5b) does not occupy a significant position aside from the fact that, like each of the expressions dealing with wealth, this saying derives from *Amenemope* chap. 7.

It is instructive to note the adaptation of Egyptian fauna to better suit the saying to an Israelite context. Geese fit well an aquatic context such as the Nile valley. Eagles would be more suitable for Israel.[49] This shift is similar to replacement of "Thoth" by "LORD" in the sixth parallel (Prov 22:23a).

47. Lack of prominent positioning is due in part to the fact that chapter-initial position has already been claimed by the previous parallel (Prov 23:5a, parallel to *Amen.* 7:1).

48. Dunsmore, "Egyptian Contribution to Proverbs," 304–5.

49. The word נֶשֶׁר appears twenty-six times in Biblical Hebrew, three of which occur in Proverbs (30:17 and 19, in addition to the present example). On two occasions נֶשֶׁר was chosen despite nautical references in the same verses that might have inclined the writer to select an aquatic bird rather than the eagle (Job 9:26 and Prov 30:19). Cf. BDB 676–77.

Dunsmore views the ensuing caution against fraternizing with a selfish man (Prov 23:6, 8) as a summary of *Amenemope* 11, with chapter-initial correlation (Prov 23:6 and *Amen.* 11:1).[50] If the content were parallel, one could concur with this view and add it to the list of significantly-positioned parallels. However, the content does not correlate with sufficient precision. The Israelite document warns the *gullible onlooker* against being *taken in* by a greedy host, while it is the *crafty onlooker* whom *Amenemope* orders to refrain from *devouring* possessions of the poor. The respective warnings diverge too greatly to be considered parallel. Similarly, no clear parallel may be found in *Amenemope* to correspond to Proverbs' discussion of the fool (23:9).

Fifteenth Parallel

Prov 23:10a	Do not remove the ancient landmark.
Amen. vii 12 (6:1)	Do not remove the landmark on boundaries of the sown field.

In the fifteenth parallel, the *Amenemope* injunction stands in chapter-initial position. A decisive prohibition against altering boundary lines appears twice in Proverbs (22:28 and 23:10) and twice in *Amenemope* (vii 12 and viii 9, both falling within chap. 6). Other allusions to the idea in the same Egyptian chapter include: do not covet another's land (6:3) or trample his furrow (6:23); instead, regard such a trespasser as "an enemy to the town" (6:13) and determine that you will prosper by your own resources, without decreasing those of another (6:21). The parallel continues in the following phrase of Prov 23:10.

Sixteenth Parallel

Prov 23:10b	. . . nor enter the field of the fatherless.
Amen. vii 15 (6:4)	. . . nor throw down the boundaries of a widow.

In the sixteenth parallel, both documents insist on giving special regard to the less fortunate. The identity of the unfortunate person varies between the fatherless child (in Proverbs) and the widow (in *Amenemope*).

There may be a reason for this distinction, although the case is not clear-cut. "Ancient" landmarks in the Hebrew of the preceding phrase call to mind the practice of a family retaining land rights through successive generations. By safeguarding land of the fatherless (Prov 23:10b), the community ensured

50. Dunsmore, "Egyptian Contribution to Proverbs," 305.

transfer of title from parent to child. This concern may explain in part the Hebrew reference to land passed to surviving children, rather than to the surviving spouse, as in the Egyptian case.

Position of parallel sixteen within *Amenemope* 6 is not significant.[51] The theme of care for the poor concludes in Prov 23:11, the final parallel.

Seventeenth Parallel

Prov 23:11	Their redeemer is mighty, he will plead their case against you.
Amen. vii 19 (6:8)	He [the aggressor] will be lassoed by the power of the Moon.

In the final parallel, both documents threaten divine retribution. The Egyptian god Thoth is represented by the moon, as seen earlier in the sixth parallel. Divine influence forms a prominent theme in chap. 6 of *Amenemope*, as evident from the following three examples. First, God is propitiated when one reinforces land boundaries (*Amen.* 6:19–20). Second, the Egyptian is counseled to be aware of the Universal Lord (6:22). Third, the sage assures his audience that God's provision, though small, is better than surplus acquired unlawfully (6:27–28, 6:33–34). Since references to the divine are fairly numerous in *Amenemope* 6, by borrowing this theme in Prov 23:11 the Israelite writer incorporated an idea that was prominent in the source chapter, although it was not significantly positioned.

Summary

The data concerning *Amenemope* and Prov 22:17–24:22 may be summarized as follows. Of seventeen parallels in Prov 22:12–24:22, nine are significant by being positioned in *Amenemope* either *initially* (parallels 1, 3, 5, 7, 10, 12, and 15) or *terminally* (8 and 9). Two of these bear double significance. As well as being chapter-initial, the fifth parallel also forms the initial saying for the entire teaching segment both in Proverbs (22:22–24:22) and *Amenemope* (chaps. 2–29). The ninth parallel is document-terminal in *Amenemope* (excepting the colophon), in addition to being chapter-terminal. Thus, of the first seventeen sayings having *Amenemope* parallels, over sixty per cent are significantly positioned in the source document.

51. Chapter-initial position has already been claimed by the phrase in Prov 23:10a.

Amenemope is unusual, because from antiquity the sayings that reflected a particular theme were grouped into distinct chapters. Such a system of inherent structure is rare for Egyptian wisdom collections. Enumeration of chapters was not part of the initial Israelite composition either. The chapter location of parallel sayings in *Amenemope* suggests that the Israelite writer excerpted statements that would most effectively summarize the longer Egyptian collection.[52] Often this involved the use of topic sentences within established chapter divisions. At times closing sentences were adopted as well.

This pattern of borrowing (and sometimes adapting) significantly positioned phrases implies that the Israelite sage was aware of the way chapters in *Amenemope* tended to be structured, with key sentences appearing toward the beginning and end. In view of the structure evident in other parts of Proverbs, it is not surprising to find that, when he encountered a foreign document that was already structured, the Israelite sage was sensitive to that structure and made use of it as he sought to distill foreign material for the benefit of an Israelite audience.[53]

52. One might propose that the Israelite author should not be credited with taking a complete copy of *Amenemope* and shortening it. Perhaps he possessed an abridged recension produced by yet a different author. This was suggested by Erman (see Bryce, *Legacy of Wisdom,* 19). While this explanation is conceivable, in the absence of any extant abridged recension, it seems more reasonable to conclude that the Israelite author was responsible for shortening the Egyptian composition.

53. For a study of structural devices in Proverbs 1–9, see Overland, *Literary Structure in Proverbs 1–9,* 141–328.

An Historical Overview of Pastoral Nomadism in the Central Euphrates Valley

Wayne T. Pitard

The metamorphosis of the scholarly understanding of nomadism and its role in ancient Near Eastern civilizations has been one of the more dramatic developments in our field of the past two decades. The recognition that anthropological and sociological data are of great value in dealing with this area of study has had a heavy impact on Mesopotamian historical research, as well as on biblical scholarship, where remarkable changes in the study of the early development of Israel have taken place, particularly during the last decade (cf. Gottwald 1979, Lemche 1985, Coote and Whitelam 1987).

Before this revolution, nomads in the ancient Near East were perceived largely as having been major factors in two critical kinds of event in history: (1) the nomads were the primary cause of the downfall of various states and cultures, and (2) they were the primary origin for the distinct cultures that followed these collapses. They were usually portrayed as wild barbarians flowing out of the desert and descending on the settled populations, often wiping them out and bringing urban civilizations to an abrupt end. But at the same time, these nomads were part of a consistent evolutionary process by which they (as members of a primitive lifestyle) eventually and inevitably settled into villages and developed into sedentary, sometimes urban, cultures, often preserving cultural characteristics of the societies they had previously conquered. For many scholars, this process of conquest (or sometimes peaceful migration) and sedentarization answered the question of the origins of the various peoples of the Near East. Whether by invasion or migration, the nomadic tribes ranging out of the great Syrian desert would see the advantages of sedentary life and would settle into villages and towns, their place on the steppe taken by other nomadic groups, which in turn would eventually follow the same process.[1]

This scholarly reconstruction had developed out of nineteenth- and early twentieth-century anthropological research on ancient nomadic life, heavily influenced by studies of the more recent camel nomads of the Near East. The ancient Near Eastern documents themselves appeared to provide crystal-clear examples of nomadic (read: barbarian) invasions and migrations that led to the collapse (or near collapse) of various states in Mesopotamia. Thus the Amorites of the late third millennium B.C.E. were usually depicted as nomadic hordes descending on Mesopotamia and violently bringing about the end of the Ur III civilization (for example, Kramer 1963: 69–70), but afterward adopting Mesopotamian culture and creating the subsequent "Amorite period." And, to a lesser extent, the description of the attack on the city of Agade by the Gutians in the Sumerian poem, "The Curse of Agade" (lines 151ff.), was taken as a paradigm of this type of invasion.[2] The Aramean incursions into Syria and Mesopotamia of the late second millennium also fit the description well. Archaeological evidence, particularly from the transitions between the major periods, was often interpreted by reference to the same scenario. In Palestine, for example, the collapse of the Early Bronze III civilization was commonly attributed to a similar Amorite onslaught (Kenyon 1966; de Vaux 1971: 236–37). And, of course, the two classic reconstructions of the Israelite settlement in Canaan at the beginning of the Iron Age (represented by Alt and Albright) assumed a nomadic origin for the Israelites, disagreeing, however, on whether they had invaded the land or simply migrated peacefully into it.

That this perception of nomadism was inaccurate and too simplistic became increasingly clear, particularly during the course of the 1960s, when more sophisticated anthropological models came to be applied by Near Eastern historians to specific problems associated with the relations between nomads and settled populations. The works of Mendenhall (1962), Luke (1965), Rowton (1973a, 1973b, 1974, 1976a, 1976b, 1976c, 1980), Gottwald (1979), Matthews (1978), Kamp and Yoffee (1980), Lemche (1985), and others have produced a completely different paradigm for understanding the role of the pastoral nomads in Near Eastern history that has been nothing short of revolutionary in its redefinition of the concept of the tribe as an

1. This view is reflected in numerous works on Near Eastern history, including the important works of Kupper (1957, 1973). See also the discussion on this by Luke (1965: 8–38).

2. See Kramer 1963: 37, where the Gutians are called "ruthless and barbaric nomadic hordes."

ethnic group. The ruthless barbarian invaders so commonly appealed to twenty years ago have largely disappeared from current reconstructions of the rise and fall of cultures in the Near East, their place taken by much more complex processes. While the pastoralists surely played a part in such political and social changes, their role is clearly subordinate and not at all as it had been perceived earlier (Yoffee 1988: 50–51, 62).

Reevaluation of our understanding of the nomads has not just affected our view of their role in political change but also the way we look at their role in tribal and ethnic organizations. Previously, groups such as the Amorites, Haneans, Yaminites, and others were identified as primarily nomadic tribal confederations, perhaps with elements that were evolving into sedentary existence (Luke 1965: 8–38 for a summary of earlier scholarship). It has now become clear that these and similar tribal or ethnic groups[3] were in fact complex organizations that included a substantial percentage of members that were sedentary, and that the sedentary members of these groups cannot be viewed as part of an evolutionary transition of the tribes from strictly nomadic to strictly sedentary. The nomadic and sedentary elements were in fact constant components of the ethnic groups, and the ethnic label, such as "Amorite" or "Hanean" or "Yaminite," did not in any way describe the lifestyle or immediate background of the member. In fact, members of a tribe could and did move back and forth between sedentary and nomadic lifestyles (Rowton 1973a, 1973b, 1974; Kamp and Yoffee 1980: 89–94).

Only recently have scholars begun to explore the wide range of socioeconomic possibilities that were available to members of ethnic groups. M. B. Rowton, in his important and influential series of articles on enclosed nomadism and what he called the "dimorphic structure" of tribal groups, emphasized the close connections between the parts of the tribes that lived in villages and those that were pastoralists. His insights have been further refined and transformed by scholars such as Katherine Kamp and Norman Yoffee (1980) and Niels Lemche (1985: 84–163), who have pointed out that ethnic groups are even more complex than the "dimorphic" model allows and that Rowton's insight into the primary dichotomy of the tensions between the pastoralists and nomads on the one hand and the urban centers on the other must be regarded as too simplistic. Kamp and Yoffee (1980: 91–94) have argued that there is no reason to doubt that there was a certain amount of ethnically-related integration between the urban state and the periphery as well. Thus, members of the same ethnic group may have been

3. For a discussion of the terms *tribe* and *ethnic group*, see Yoffee 1988: 50–51.

pastoralist, peasant, city dweller, even urban elite, not in an evolutionary sequence, but contemporaneously.[4]

One of the results of this new interpretation has been the development of a clearer understanding of the complex interactions between the pastoral nomads and the sedentary groups that surrounded them (both peasant and urban). In this paper I will concentrate on a few specific relationships between the urban centers and the pastoralists, as illustrated in the second-millennium texts from the Central Euphrates Valley, as well as in some Assyrian texts of the twelfth and eleventh centuries.

The Central Euphrates Valley provides a rare, moderately detailed glimpse into the role of the pastoral nomads in the history of ancient Near Eastern society because of the extraordinary collections of tablets that have been recovered from several cities and towns in the region. Of course, the central archive is the one from Mari, but the smaller, basically contemporary collections from Tell el-Rimah, Tell Asmar, Chagar Bazar, Terqa, Tell Shemshara, and now Tell Leilan, either have provided new insights into the situation of the early second millennium B.C.E. or promise to. A reiterated word of caution, however, is appropriate, since the texts are far from being comprehensive in their treatment of the pastoralists' role in the affairs of the state. Problems arise from the vagueness that often pervades the letters, since the writers and the recipients had considerably more knowledge of the various situations referred to in the letters than we can extract from them. Thus we may at times misinterpret aspects of the dealings between the state and the nomads, and publication and discoveries of further letters may thus significantly change the picture we draw today. We must also keep in mind the biases of the writers, who were almost always members of the urban elite, and we must bear in mind that the writers themselves may have had some misconceptions about the situations they describe in the letters and that some writers may also at times have intentionally misrepresented the situation to the king in order to protect themselves.

There are three areas of Mesopotamian study in the third and second millennia that are particularly relevant for illustrating the impact of these new insights about the pastoral nomads on historical reconstruction. The first is the role of the nomads in the rise of the Amorite kingdoms in the late third and early second millennia B.C.E. The second is the origin of the Arameans

4. A particularly good example of the presence of an urban elite element in a tribal context is found in Charpin and Durand 1986: 150–52, where an as-yet-unpublished Mari letter is discussed; the letter shows that even King Zimri-Lim of Mari was identified according to his tribal affiliation, "son of Simʾal."

who appear in written texts for the first time in the late twelfth century as inhabiting large areas of the Middle Euphrates and Ḫabur River valleys. The third is the nature of the relationship between the pastoralist elements of the Haneans and Yaminites and the urban power of Mari.

The Nomads and the Amorites

The traditional interpretation of the role of the nomads in the development of the Amorite kingdoms has already been described: an inpouring of nomadic Amorites from the west during the latter years of the Ur III dynasty brought about the collapse of Neo-Sumerian culture. In spite of desperate attempts to keep them out, the Amorites drove into Mesopotamia, causing the downfall of Ur. Upon entering the cultural milieu of Mesopotamia, however, the tribes began to settle into various towns, where they soon became urbanized and formed the new dominant political group (Gadd 1971: 625–28; Hallo and Simpson 1971: 75–77).

This scenario has, however, significantly changed. Beyond the general recognition that the collapse of Neo-Sumerian culture was much more complicated than can be explained by an invasion of nomads, the role of the Amorites has received considerable reassessment. Even in the 1960s it had become clear that by the late third millennium a large number of Amorites were living in the major Mesopotamian cities and were part of the urban social structure. The appearance of these urban Amorites was at first assumed to illustrate the evolutionary stage in which some tribal members were beginning to sedentarize and assimilate into Mesopotamian society (Buccellati 1966: 339–46, 355–62; Bottéro 1971: 562–65). The majority of the Amorites, however, were still thought to be pastoralists who would eventually make the same transition. More recent interpretations, however, argue that it is a mistake to portray the urban Amorites as part of the evolutionary model of sedentarization. Instead, it is more appropriate to recognize that the ethnic group called the Amorites was a very complex entity made up of pastoralist, peasant, and urban elements that had existed side by side for centuries. The pastoralist element of the Amorites was not in the process of dying out, nor was the urban element a newer approach to life that was the sign of the future for the tribe. The evidence, rather, is better interpreted as suggesting that urbanized Amorites were a long-standing ethnic element in many Mesopotamian cities and were not specifically descendants of the pastoralist part of the tribe. Though there indeed were nomadic Amorites as well, dangerous groups that the kings of Ur felt must be dealt with, they were far from being the only

Amorites, or even necessarily a majority of the ethnic group. And they certainly were not the only politically important Amorites, when it comes to the collapse of the Ur III period. The Amorites who gained political control over several cities early in the second millennium are not to be identified as rude nomads fresh from the desert, but rather as well-established members of Mesopotamian society who belonged to the large ethnic group called "Amorites" (Kamp and Yoffee 1980: 89–94). The pastoralists, therefore, are no longer thought of as invaders who brought down Neo-Sumerian civilization and as the founders of the succeeding culture. The Amorites who seized control of several cities no longer need to be identified as pastoralists, but as urban Amorites, Amorites who have maintained their ethnic connections.[5]

The Origins of the Arameans

The Arameans have usually been understood as invaders of the fertile crescent from the Syrian desert during the last quarter of the second millennium B.C.E. This new population conquered much of the Middle Euphrates and the Ḫabur River area, then spread southwest into Syria as far as Damascus and southeast into Babylonia. By the late twelfth century, the Arameans were threatening the very existence of Assyria. This led to major conflicts between the nomads and the Assyrian army.[6] But this view of the rise of Aramean culture is also based largely on preconceived notions about cultural change in the Near East. A careful reading of the Assyrian sources from the twelfth through tenth centuries that mention the Arameans fails to substantiate the entire scenario of an Aramean invasion of northern Mesopotamia. There is no indication in these texts that the Arameans were viewed as invaders. They are simply portrayed as tribal groups with a large component of pastoralists, but also with numbers of members living in their own towns and villages.[7]

5. The tendency of tribal members in an urban setting to lose their ethnic identity over time (Rowton's "detribalization") appears to be more rare than has been previously supposed. See Kamp and Yoffee 1980: 93; Charpin and Durand 1986: 157–76.

6. This scenario may be found throughout the literature. See, for example, Dupont-Sommer (1949: 15–19), who identifies the Arameans with the Aḫlamū, another largely pastoralist group known from the fourteenth century on; Malamat (1973: 134–36), who disputes the identification of the Arameans with the Aḫlamū; and Hawkins 1982: 372–75.

7. Tiglath-Pileser I (1116–1076 B.C.E.), the first Assyrian to mention the Arameans in his inscriptions, describes a campaign in which he destroyed six Aramean towns in the Jebel Bishri region (*ARI* #34).

Nor is there any indication that the campaigns against the Arameans were in response to Aramean aggression against Assyria or other populations in northern Mesopotamia. Tiglath-Pileser states: "I have crossed the Euphrates twenty-eight times, twice in one year, in pursuit of the *aḫlamū* Aramaeans." But there is no compelling reason to assume that these campaigns were part of an attempt to drive back invaders. When one examines the overall strategy of Tiglath-Pileser's military actions, it becomes clear that his desire was to gain control of the major trade routes across northern Mesopotamia, from Syria to Babylonia. The pastoralists of the Middle Euphrates were always a problem for centralized governments because of the difficulty in controlling their activities, which at times included such practices as raiding caravans (see below on Mari). It seems quite likely that the campaigns against the Arameans were designed to discourage the raiding parties, so as to keep the trade routes clear, rather than to discourage further conquests.

One major piece of evidence used to support the theory of a major invasion of Arameans during Tiglath-Pileser's reign is a fragmentary entry from an Assyrian chronicle that is interpreted as describing the invasion of Assyria itself by Arameans during the terrible drought near the end of Tiglath-Pileser's reign (*ARI* ##200–201).[8] H. Tadmor (1958: 133–34; 1979: 12–13) has argued that the chronicle shows that the Arameans not only invaded Assyria, causing a major flight of the population into the mountains of Kirriuri (lines 5′–7′), but that they attacked Nineveh during the drought, captured it, and forced Tiglath-Pileser and his army to flee to Kadmuḫi (lines 10′–13′). However, this reconstruction is actually quite uncertain. What is actually preserved indicates that there was a famine that affected the Assyrians and the Arameans, but it remains entirely unclear whether the Arameans attacked Assyria. Lines 5′–7′ may suggest an attack on something Assyrian, but line 5′, which reads]KUR *Aš-šur ik-šu-du il-qu-ú* '. . . Assyria they captured, they took', is actually far from clear. The phrase]KUR *Aš-šur* may or may not be the direct object of the verb *ik-šu-du*, but it also might be part of the subject, for example, '[the (army?)[9] of] the land of Assyria captured, took . . .' (Grayson 1975: 189). Nor is it entirely clear whether it was the Arameans or the otherwise unmentioned people of Assyria who fled to the mountains of Kirriuri. Lines 10′–13′, interpreted by Tadmor as indicating the capture of Nineveh by the Arameans and the flight of Tiglath-Pileser, is much too broken to be interpreted with confidence. Line 11′, in fact, seems

8. A transcription of the text may be found in Grayson 1975: 189.

9. For the use of the plural verb with *ummānu* in a similar context, see Grayson 1975: 91–92, lines 3–15.

to suggest that the Arameans were getting the worst of a conflict (". . . they became numerous, they seized the houses of the Arameans"). And Tiglath-Pileser's journey to Kadmuḫi is not characterized at all in the text.[10]

During the reign of Tiglath-Pileser's son and second successor, Ashur-bel-kala (1073–1056), there were further conflicts between the Arameans and the Assyrians. But again, nothing in the texts (particularly the so-called Broken Obelisk, *ARI* ##235–47) compels one to assume that the battles were fought to oppose expansionist policies of the Aramean nomads (Wiseman 1975: 467–69; Brinkman 1968: 124–44). These conflicts are likely to have been part of a series of Assyrian offensives designed to gain control over the area north and northwest of Assyria as far as the Euphrates. The common assumption that the battles with the Arameans were desperate attempts to contain the spread of their invasion is entirely conjectural. Again, there is no evidence from the inscriptions to suggest that these Aramean tribes were newcomers to the region. The conflicts that took place in that area were between the Assyrians and whatever groups opposed Assyrian expansion.

Thus, a reanalysis of the evidence that has been used to support the existence of great Aramean invasions indicates that most of it is either quite ambiguous or nonexistent. With the lack of any substantial evidence for a widespread population shift in the areas that became Aramean lands, it seems plausible to suggest that the Aramean groups in general were the Semitic-speaking tribal groups that had lived in Upper Mesopotamia and Syria throughout the second millennium, some as pastoralists, some in villages, towns, and cities. During the times of political instability in that region in the thirteenth and twelfth centuries, some of these Aramaic groups came to political ascendency and formed the Aramean states that are known from the tenth century onward in Syria and Upper Mesopotamia.

It is perhaps worth noting that, while arguing that the Amorite and Aramean pastoralists cannot be characterized as invading hordes that swept over the cultures of the Fertile Crescent, bringing about major population shifts, I am not suggesting that populations of the Near East were completely static

10. This translation is problematic also, however, since one cannot, in the broken context, be sure whether É.MEŠ [KUR *A*] *r-m*[*a-a-ia-e*] is the object of *iṣ*-[*bu*]-*tu* or the subject of a different verb, lost at the beginning of the next line. Tadmor (1958: 134) originally suggested that the line be read: '[Plagues] became numerous, affected the tents of [the Arameans]'. This still seems a plausible restoration of the beginning of the line, although it is, naturally, speculative. Doubts about Tadmor's interpretation of this fragment have been expressed elsewhere; see Wiseman 1975: 462. Brinkman (1968: 387) makes use of Tadmor's reconstruction, but points out in note 2164 that the text is ambiguous and that the interpretation of it remains hypothetical.

during the second millennium B.C.E. or that large pastoralist bands could not have attacked and looted various cities at various times. There is indeed evidence for population movements in the Near East, and these must be taken into account. For example, the ruling stratum of the Neo-Hittite states of northern Syria in the eleventh through eighth centuries clearly migrated from Anatolia, whence their culture largely derived (Hawkins 1982: 372–75; 435–41). The Sea Peoples who settled along the coast of Canaan in the twelfth century were also clearly foreigners. But in these cases the evidence is clear and the archaeological remains indicate the foreign aspects of the societies. On the other hand, there is no clear historical or archaeological evidence for the supposed massive migrations of the Amorites and Arameans from their homelands, and thus it remains inappropriate to postulate such major movements. It does remain possible that Aramean tribes did migrate from the Middle Euphrates region into southern Mesopotamia during the early first millennium B.C.E. But even this is not supported by specific evidence from the sources (Brinkman 1968: 281–85).[11] The rise of the Aramean states in Syria and Mesopotamia cannot be explained by the invasion hypothesis. It must be understood in terms of more complex social, economic, and ecological factors, many of which are at the present time unrecoverable.

Mari, the Haneans, and the Yaminites

When we turn to the relationship between the kingdom of Mari and the pastoralist elements of the Hanean and Yaminite tribal confederations in the

11. It is clear that, during the eleventh century, Arameans and other pastoral groups caused trouble in Babylonia. An inscription of Simbar-Shipak (1026–1009 B.C.E.) describes in quite hyperbolic language the plundering of Sippar and Nippur during the reign of Adad-apla-iddina (Goetze 1965: 121–22, lines 10–14). But in no cases are there inscriptions that portray the nomads as immigrants from elsewhere who attacked cities in order to take over the land. In fact, the Simbar-Shipak inscription emphasizes the booty taken from the cities of Sumer and Akkad rather than the loss of any land. A third inscription that is thought to deal with widespread migration of Aramean groups into Babylonia is from the New Babylonian Chronicle, lines 4′–7′. Line 5′ is restored by Brinkman (1968: 132) as '105 kings of the lands of the A[ḫlamū came into the land] and enjoyed abundance and [prosperity]'. Brinkman points out that his restoration of the critical center of the sentence is based on the understanding of the period as one in which nomadic invasions were endemic (p. 133). As we have seen, the situation may have been quite different, and these tribes may have long been present in Babylonia. On the issue of the damage that barbarian attacks can do to societies, see Bronson 1988.

second millennium, we find in the texts a complex and varying situation that cannot be fully defined from the preserved records. Certain insights may be gained, however, by examining the data, while keeping in mind Shmuel Eisenstadt's insights into the way political centers deal with groups on the periphery of the state (1963: 13–32; 1971: 121–25, 138–45). It was clearly impossible for the kings of Mari to impose direct rule over the pastoralist element within their domain in the same manner that they ruled over the villages. At the same time, it was important to the rulers to maintain as much control as possible, to minimize negative activities such as raiding and to assure that the tribes would not ally themselves with other, rival kings.[12] The pastoralist population was a significant source of economic and military benefit for Mari. The problem was how to take advantage of these benefits. Eisenstadt has pointed out that the political center, in order to extract goods and services (through taxation, corvée, and so on) must legitimize its demands by providing certain services to the peripheral group that will appear to them as a reasonable tradeoff. When such a tradeoff works, there can be a fairly smooth relationship between the center and the periphery. But this relationship is very fragile, can be easily upset, and can lead to serious political consequences, although, of course, the impact of a breakdown between the center and periphery depends on the political importance of the peripheral group.

The Mari letters reflect a very substantial concern of the rulers of Mari to control the pastoralists who lived within the boundaries of Mari's domain, and several mechanisms were employed to do just that, including the appointment of tribal officials as intermediaries between the tribal elements and the government (for example, the *sugāgūtum*),[13] the regular imposition of a census on the tribal groups for purposes of conscription and corvée (Luke 1965: 248–56), the imposition of taxes, the confiscation and control of tribal cult statues (at least in certain cases), which could be obtained by the tribe only with the king's permission (*ARMT* 14:8:5–13; cf. Matthews 1978: 151), and the control of tribal lands, which allowed the Mari rulers to guarantee tribes access to their lands and pasturages or (at least at times) redistribute the land to others (for example, *ARM* 1:6:22–43; Dossin 1939: 984:b:9–12; *ARMT* 13:144:26–30).

These mechanisms met with varying degrees of success among the pastoralist groups under Mari's control. The major ethnic groups that included large

12. See Dossin 1939: 986:a:10ff.; B:6ff.; and Charpin and Durand 1986: 176–79. The latter is a new version of *ARM* 14:84, with substantial new joins.

13. On the office of *sugāgum* see Matthews 1978: 139–53; Talon 1985; Talon 1986: 4–5; and Nakata 1989.

contingents of pastoralists were the Haneans, the Yaminites, the Simʾalites, and, on a more peripheral basis, the Suteans.[14] The archives indicate a substantial difference in the relationship between Mari and each of these groups, a difference that illustrates some of the complexities that exist between urban centers and different ethnic groups on the periphery.

The Haneans, whose villages and pasturelands were all within the domain of Mari (Luke 1965: 244–45), appear to have had much more cordial relations with the rulers of Mari than did the Yaminites. In fact, the kings of Mari took on the title of "king of the land of the Haneans" from the time of Yaḫdun-Lim, whose inscriptions describe the defeat of seven Hanean chieftains early in his reign.[15] The Haneans seem to have been closely involved in several aspects of Mari's political makeup, most notably in the military.

The Yaminites appear to have been much less cooperative with Mari than the Haneans, and there is much less evidence for members of the Yaminite tribal groups participating in the military aspects of Mari. A key factor in their different relationship with Mari is that, while the southern lands of the Yaminites were located within the political sphere of Mari, their northern grazing area was outside Mari's direct influence, along the Baliḫ and the Upper Tigris Rivers (Anbar 1985: 21–23; Luke 1965: 245–48). Thus, unlike the Haneans, who had reason to cooperate more fully with the dominant political power that controlled their lands, the Yaminites needed to steer as independent a course as possible, not being under the full control of either the king of Mari or the rulers of Zalmaqum in the north. This may be part of the reason why there is evidence of considerable resistance by the Yaminites to the census, since census-taking implies government domination. In one case, Shamshi-Adad canceled a census of the Yaminites, largely to avoid a violent showdown, although he still ordered the Yaminite *sugāgū* to assemble their troops anyway, but without the formality of a census (*ARMT* 1:6:5–21). Letters from the reign of Zimri-Lim indicate that while some Yaminite villages submitted to a census, others did not, and that the Yaminite troops

14. The significance of the Simʾalites, the tribe of Yaḫdun-Lim and Zimri-Lim, is just beginning to become clear, since only a small number of references to them have been published so far. Charpin and Durand (1986: 150) have indicated that there are more than sixty unpublished references to this group in the Mari letters.

15. Talon (1986: 2–4) suggested (without knowledge of the letter identifying Zimri-Lim as a Simʾalite) that this title indicates that Yaḫdun-Lim and his family were Haneans. This may be true, if Charpin and Durand (1986: 152–56) are correct in identifying the Simʾalites (as well as the Yaminites) as a subdivision of the Haneans. It should be noted, however, that the evidence thus far presented by them is inconclusive and susceptible to interpretations that would maintain the distinction between these groups.

conscripted on the basis of censuses sometimes simply failed to appear when summoned (for example, *ARMT* 6:30:3–26).

Although we can say with certainty that the pastoralists played a significant part in the Mari military, details of their participation are very spotty. For example, although there are several references to Hanean troops being mustered, there is no indication of what percentage of those troops were taken from the nomadic element of the tribe and what percentage from the villages. Nor do we know what percentage of the entire army was provided by the Haneans and other groups with pastoralist elements, as opposed to nontribal groups in the towns and cities. The numbers found in the texts suggest that the Haneans provided a significant part of the army (often several thousand Hanean troops are mentioned). But at the same time, texts indicate that a king like Shamshi-Adad could muster an army of up to 60,000 in an extreme emergency (a text from Shemshara; see Sasson 1969: 7–11). How many of these were from tribal groups and how many were from the pastoralist elements of those tribes we simply cannot say. Nor is it clear what percentage the pastoralists would comprise during a more normal combat season. Whatever the situation was, it does seem likely that the pastoralists were an important source for military conscription. However, their use in the military was somewhat of a double-edged sword for the urban centers, since the experience in battle gained by the pastoralists could also be used at other times for raiding expeditions.

There are certain other areas in which the pastoralists may have had an impact on the state. One of these is the area of trade. With regard to local trade, it is clear that the pastoralists were very important in providing the foodstuffs and raw materials that are associated with cattle. The close relationship necessary between the pastoralists and the villagers provided for the mutual benefit of trading pastoral goods for agricultural necessities.[16] What is less well understood is whether pastoralists played any significant role in interregional trade as well. Texts suggest that to some extent the regularity in their migrations allowed the pastoralists to carry goods, often easily transportable items such as precious metals, stones, or slaves, from one part of the Near East to another. At the same time, however, the extent of the pastoralist participation in this kind of trade is unknown and may have been fairly minor (Klengel 1977). Our sources will have to be supplemented considerably

16. Cf. Coote and Whitelam 1987: 109–11. Note that Buccellati (1988: 45) argued very briefly that the pastoralist element in the Central Euphrates Valley provided an immense economic resource for the urban centers. Details of his argument are promised in a forthcoming article.

before a clear picture of this aspect can emerge. There is, however, one other area for which we have some evidence of a pastoralist impact on trade, this time a rather negative one. This, of course, was the practice of raiding caravans, which at times could become a serious interference with trade (Klengel 1977: 164–65; Matthews 1978: 104–7). But even here, it is often difficult to distinguish between professional bandit groups and pastoralists (cf. Coote and Whitelam 1987: 92–94).

Summary

What can we say about the role of the pastoral nomads in the history of the Central Euphrates Valley in the late third and second millennia B.C.E.? It seems that in many ways the new understanding has diminished the role and importance of this group. Nomads have basically lost their status as the primary factor in the collapse of civilizations in the Near East, and they are no longer considered to be the primary source for the people who developed new cultures following those collapses. But now they are seen to have played an integral part in the complex social system of that area, a part that was itself complex, because of the wide variety of types of pastoralists and of tribal organization. It was also a part that was of substantial concern to the central governments that ruled the valley, who were forced to create a range of bureaucratic organizations to deal with them that can only partially be defined from our currently available sources. And thus they played a significant role in the political, military, and economic realms of the states in Mesopotamia.

Many aspects of the role of the pastoralist remain obscure. The anthropological and sociological models that have been developed have been helpful, although, as Kamp, Yoffee, and Lemche have argued, they continue to be too simplistic to describe fully the complexities of nomadic existence in the Near Eastern environment. However, the Central Euphrates Valley will continue to be one of the key places where this type of investigation will flourish, as more and more texts emerge from excavations and eventually reach publication.

Works Cited

Anbar, Moshe

1985 La distribution géographique des Bini-Yamina d'après les archives royales de Mari. Pp. 17–24 in J.-M. Durand and J.-R. Kupper (eds.), *Miscellanea Babylonica* (Festschrift Maurice Birot). Paris: Éditions Recherche sur les Civilisations.

ARI = Albert Kirk Grayson, *Assyrian Royal Inscriptions, Part II: From Tiglath-Pileser I to Ashur-naṣir-apli II.* Wiesbaden: Harrassowitz, 1976.

Bottéro, Jean

1971 Syria during the Third Dynasty of Ur. Pp. 559–66 in I. E. S. Edwards, C. J. Gadd, and N. G. L. Hammond (eds.), *The Cambridge Ancient History*, vol. 1, part 2: *The Early History of the Middle East.* Cambridge: Cambridge University Press.

Brinkman, John A.

1968 *A Political History of Post-Kassite Babylonia, 1158–722 B.C.* AnOr 43. Rome: Pontifical Biblical Institute.

Bronson, Bennet

1988 The Role of Barbarians in the Fall of States. Pp. 196–218 in Norman Yoffee and George L. Cowgill (eds.), *The Collapse of Ancient States and Civilizations.* Tucson: University of Arizona Press.

Buccellati, Giorgio

1966 *The Amorites of the Ur III Period.* Naples: Istituto Orientale di Napoli.

1988 The Kingdom and Period of Khana. *BASOR* 270: 43–61.

Charpin, Dominique, and Jean-Marie Durand

1986 "Fils de Simᵓal": Les origines tribales des rois de Mari. *RA* 80: 141–83.

Coote, Robert B., and Keith W. Whitelam

1987 *The Emergence of Early Israel in Historical Perspective.* Social World of Biblical Antiquity 5. Sheffield: Almond.

Dossin, Georges

1939 Benjaminites dans les textes de Mari. Pp. 981–96 in *Mélanges syriens offerts à M. René Dussaud*, vol. 2. Paris: Geuthner.

Dupont-Sommer, A.

1949 *Les Araméens.* Paris: Maisonneuve.

Eisenstadt, Shmuel

1963 *The Political Systems of Empires.* London: Free Press of Glencoe.

1971 *Political Sociology.* New York: Basic Books.

Gadd, C. J.

1971 Babylonia c. 2120–1800 B.C. Pp. 595–643 in I. E. S. Edwards, C. J. Gadd, and N. G. L. Hammond (eds.), *The Cambridge Ancient History*, vol. 1, part 2: *The Early History of the Middle East.* Cambridge: Cambridge University Press.

Goetze, Albrecht

1965 An Inscription of Simbar-Šīḫu. *Journal of Cuneiform Studies* 19: 121–35.

Gottwald, Norman

1979 *The Tribes of Yahweh: A Sociology of Liberated Israel, 1250–1050 B.C.E.* Maryknoll, N.Y.: Orbis.

Grayson, Albert K.

1975 *Assyrian and Babylonian Chronicles.* Texts from Cuneiform Sources 5. Locust Valley, N.Y.: Augustin.

Hallo, William W., and William K. Simpson
1971 *The Ancient Near East: A History.* New York: Harcourt Brace Jovanovich.
Hawkins, J. D.
1982 The Neo-Hittite States in Syria and Anatolia. Pp. 372–441 in John Boardman et al. (eds.), *The Cambridge Ancient History,* vol. 3, part 1: *The Prehistory of the Balkans; the Middle East and the Aegean World, Tenth to Eighth Centuries BC.* Cambridge: Cambridge University Press.
Kamp, Kathryn A., and Norman Yoffee
1980 Ethnicity in Ancient Western Asia during the Early Second Millennium B.C.: Archaeological Assessments and Ethnoarchaeological Prospectives. *BASOR* 237: 85–104.
Kenyon, Kathleen
1966 *Amorites and Canaanites.* London: Oxford University Press.
Klengel, Horst
1977 Nomaden und Handel. *Iraq* 39: 163–69.
Kramer, Samuel N.
1963 *The Sumerians: Their History, Culture and Character.* Chicago: University of Chicago Press.
Kupper, Jean-Robert
1957 *Les nomades en Mésopotamie au temps des rois de Mari.* Paris: Société d'Édition "Les Belles Lettres."
1973 Northern Mesopotamia and Syria. Pp. 1–41 in I. E. S. Edwards et al. (eds.), *The Cambridge Ancient History,* vol. 2, part 1: *History of the Middle East and the Aegean Region 1800–1380 BC.* Cambridge: Cambridge University Press.
Lemche, Niels P.
1985 *Early Israel.* Leiden: Brill.
Luke, John T.
1965 *Pastoralism and Politics in the Mari Period.* Unpublished dissertation. University of Michigan.
Malamat, Abraham
1973 The Aramaeans. Pp. 134–55 in D. J. Wiseman (ed.), *Peoples of Old Testament Times.* Oxford: Clarendon.
Matthews, Victor
1978 *Pastoral Nomadism in the Mari Kingdom (ca. 1830–1760 B.C.).* ASOR Dissertation Series 3. Cambridge: American Schools of Oriental Research.
Mendenhall, George
1962 The Hebrew Conquest of Palestine. *BA* 25: 66–87.
Nakata, Ichiro
1989 A Further Look at the Institution of *sugāgūtum* in Mari. *JANESCU* 19: 113–18.
Rowton, Michael B.
1973a Autonomy and Nomadism in Western Asia. *Or* 42: 247–58.

1973b Urban Autonomy in a Nomadic Environment. *JNES* 32: 201–15.
1974 Enclosed Nomadism. *JESHO* 17: 1–30.
1976a Dimorphic Structure and the Problem of the *ᶜapirû-ᶜibrîm. JNES* 35: 13–20.
1976b Dimorphic Structure and Topology. *OrAnt* 15: 17–31.
1976c Dimorphic Structure and the Tribal Elite. *Studia Instituti Anthropos* 28: 219–57.
1980 Pastoralism and the Periphery in Evolutionary Perspective. Pp. 291–301 in *L'archéologie de l'Iraq: Perspectives et limites de l'interprétation anthropologique des documents.* Paris: Centre national de la recherche scientifique.

Sasson, Jack M.
1969 *The Military Establishments at Mari.* Studia Pohl Series Minor 3. Rome: Pontifical Biblical Institute.

Tadmor, Hayim
1958 Historical Implications of the Correct Rendering of Akkadian *dâku. JNES* 17: 129–41.
1979 The Decline of Empires in Western Asia ca. 1200 B.C.E. Pp. 1–14 in Frank M. Cross (ed.), *Symposia Celebrating the Seventy-Fifth Anniversary of the Founding of the American Schools of Oriental Research.* Cambridge, Mass.: American Schools of Oriental Research.

Talon, P.
1985 Quelques réflexions sur les clans Hanéens. Pp. 277–84 in J.-M. Durand and J.-R. Kupper (eds.), *Miscellanea Babylonica* (Festschrift Maurice Birot). Paris: Éditions Recherche sur les Civilisations.
1986 Les nomades et le royaume de Mari. *Akkadica* 48: 1–9.

Vaux, Roland de
1971 Palestine in the Early Bronze Age. Pp. 208–38 in I. E. S. Edwards, C. J. Gadd, and N. G. L. Hammond (eds.), *The Cambridge Ancient History,* vol. 1, part 2: *Early History of the Middle East.* Cambridge: Cambridge University Press.

Wiseman, Donald J.
1975 Assyria and Babylonia c. 1200–1000 B.C. Pp. 443–81 in I. E. S. Edwards et al. (eds.), *The Cambridge Ancient History,* vol. 2, part 2: *History of the Middle East and the Aegean Region 1380–1000 BC.* Cambridge: Cambridge University Press.

Yoffee, Norman
1988 The Collapse of Ancient Mesopotamian States and Civilizations. Pp. 44–68 in Norman Yoffee and George L. Cowgill (eds.), *The Collapse of Ancient States and Civilizations.* Tucson: University of Arizona Press.

The Imperative "See" as an Introductory Particle: An Egyptian–West Semitic Calque

A. F. Rainey

The Distribution of amur 'Behold'

The most striking expression for "Behold!" or "Look!" in the peripheral Akkadian used by Canaanite scribes is the imperative singular of the verb *amāru* 'to see'. It does not function as a presentation particle in classical Babylonian, but its distribution in the peripheral dialects is of the utmost interest. One finds it numerous times in the texts from Canaan, and it also appears in the Egyptian correspondence (EA 1:28; 162:30, 67) including texts from the thirteenth century B.C.E. that were sent from Egypt to Hattusas.[1]

Author's Note: The ensuing remarks are meant as a small token of the great debt that I owe to Dwight Young. During my student years at Brandeis, he was my teacher for most of the basic language courses that prepared me for my own career: Akkadian, Ugaritic, and Egyptian. In the Ugaritic class, I was often the only student, so he became virtually my private tutor. At those Ugaritic sessions, he also instructed me in the fundamentals of Biblical Hebrew grammar. I hope that the fruits of my research over the years have been some kind of reward for his personal investment in me. I am also indebted to Dwight Young for sending me to study with Professor H. J. Polotsky here in Israel, where I eventually found a position at Tel Aviv University. In turn, during Dwight's trip to Israel as a visiting lecturer in Professor Polotsky's department, I succeeded in infecting him with a love for Historical Geography, which he then taught avidly after his return to Brandeis. So our careers have been intertwined throughout the years. The present topic was selected because I know that Dwight will be interested in it, both for its intrinsic morphosyntactical value and for its relationship to Ramesside Egyptian and ancient Canaanite, both of them subjects that have been close to his heart over the years. These introductory particles, comprised of the imperatives from verbs meaning 'to look, to behold', derive from an age of close contact between the scribes of Canaan and Egypt, namely, the fourteenth and thirteenth centuries B.C.E.

1. Z. Cochavi Rainey, *The Akkadian Dialect of the Egyptian Scribes in the 14th–13th Centuries B.C.E.: Linguistic Analysis* (Ph.D. dissertation, Tel Aviv University, 1987) 228 [Hebrew with English summary].

The example recorded from Ugarit (RS 17.116:21′)[2] is actually in a letter sent from Amurru.[3] The scribes of Ugarit do not seem to have used it.[4] Some examples are cited for Hattusas, but with the exception of a letter from Hattusilis III to Kadashman-Ellil II (KBo I, 10:50), all the texts using *amur* as a presentation particle were written by Egyptian scribes, including the treaty between Ramses II and Hattusilis III (KBo I, 7:passim). In fact, the latter text, an Akkadian translation from the Egyptian original,[5] has a parallel in the Egyptian version on a wall at Karnak (which was a translation of an Akkadian original written in Hattusas).[6] One Egyptian parallel to Akkadian *amur* is the Egyptian imperative *ptr* 'see'! The original text of the Akkadian passage was approximately as follows (with some additions based on the Egyptian parallel passage):

> *a-mur* ^{I}*Re-a-ma-še-ša ma-a-i* ^{d}*A-ma-na* LUGAL GAL LUGAL KUR *Mi-iṣ-ri-i* 〈*i-na ri-ki-il-ti ša na-da-ni*〉 *a-na e-pé-ši ṭe*$_4$*-ma*
> Behold, Ramses, beloved of Amon, the great king, the king of the land Egypt, 〈*is in a treaty of causing*〉 the relationship to come into being. (KBo I, 7:11)

while the corresponding Egyptian entry is:

> *ptr Ḫ-t-s-l pꜣ wr ꜥꜣ n Ḫ-t* [*m*] *nt-ꜥn dỉ.t mn pꜣ sḫr*
> Behold, Hattusilis, the great ruler of Ḫatti is [in] a treaty of making firm the relationship. (Treaty line 8)[7]

Another particle paralleling *amur* in the Egyptian version of the treaty will be referred to below.

That the texts from Canaan employ the imperative of the verb 'to see' is not surprising in the light of the similar use of *rĕʾēh* in Biblical Hebrew. Its status as an independent introductory particle is especially prominent in the

2. CAD A/2 19; J. Nougayrol, *Le Palais royal d'Ugarit IV* (ed. C. F. A. Schaeffer; MRS 9; Paris: Imprimerie Nationale and Librairie C. Klincksieck, 1956) 132–33.

3. S. Izre'el, *The Akkadian Dialect of the Scribes of Amurru in the 14th–13th Centuries B.C.: Linguistic Analysis* (Ph.D. dissertation, Tel Aviv University, 1985) 247 [Hebrew with English summary].

4. J. Huehnergard, *The Akkadian Dialects of Carchemish and Ugarit* (Ph.D. dissertation, Harvard University, 1979) 354–55.

5. A. Spalinger, "Considerations on the Hittite Treaty between Egypt and Hatti," *Studien zur altägyptischen Kultur* 9 (1981) 355.

6. Ibid.

7. K. A. Kitchen, *Ramesside Inscriptions, Historical and Biographical*, vol. 2, fascicle 5 (Oxford: Blackwell, 1971) 227 lines 4–5.

following passage, where a plural audience is addressed while the imperative remains in the singular:

> *rĕʾēh nātattî lipnêkem ʾet hāʾāreṣ*
> Behold, I have placed before the land . . . (Deut 1:8).[8]

The same construction is found in Deut 11:26:

> *rĕʾēh ʾānōkî nōtēn lipnêkem hayyôm bĕrākâ ûqĕlālâ*
> Behold, I am placing before you today a blessing and a curse.

But normally the audience or auditor is addressed in the singular, which corresponds to the singular imperative used to introduce the clause (Deut 1:21, 4:5, 30:15).

The Imperative Function

The original nature of *amur* as an imperative was not really lost. The earliest documented example, from the fifteenth century B.C.E., carries the first common singular accusative pronominal suffix:

> ⸢*i*⸣-⸢*na*⸣*-an-na a-mur-ni i-nu-ma / i-pu-*⸢*šu*⸣ ⸢DÙG⸣.⸢GA⸣ *it-ti-ka*
> Now, behold me, that I will do good for you. (Taanach Text 2:17–18)[9]

On occasion, one finds that the imperative *amur* governs a nominal direct object:

> *a-mur i-pí-iš* / ⸢URU⸣ *Ṣur-ri*
> Behold the deed of Tyre.
> (EA 89:10–11)[10]

> *a-mur ip-ša an-ni-ú ip-ši* ^{I}*Mil-ki-*DINGIR / *ù ip-ši* DUMU.MEŠ *La-ab-a-ya*
> Behold this deed, the deeds of Milkilu and the deeds of the sons of Labʾayu.
> (EA 287:29–30; also apparently EA 288:7–8 where ⟨*a-mur*⟩ must be supplied)

8. P. Joüon, *Grammaire de l'hébreu biblique* (Rome: Pontifical Biblical Institute, 1923) p. 287 / §105d.

9. A. F. Rainey, "Verbal Usages in the Taanach Texts," *IOS* 7 (1977) 46.

10. R. F. Youngblood, *The Amarna Correspondence of Rib-Haddi, Prince of Byblos (EA 68–96)* (Ph.D. dissertation, Dropsie College, 1961) 329.

ša-ni-⌜*tam*⌝ *a-mur ar-na* ⌜*ša*⌝! / [*yi*]*-pu-iš* ^{I}*A-zi-ru*
Furthermore, behold the crime which(!) Aziru has [co]mmitted.
(EA 140:20–21; also possibly EA 106:4; 140:18–19)

even when the object is in extraposition to the ensuing clause:

a-mur / ÌR-*da ša iš-me a-na* {*a-na*} *be-li-šu* /
šul-mu URU-*šu šul-mu* É-*šu* / *šum-šu a-na da-ri-ti*
Behold, the servant who has obeyed his lord:
his city is at peace, his house is at peace, his name endures forever.
(EA 147:48–51)

In the following passage *amur* should probably be supplied:

⟨*a-mur*⟩ *ḫa-an-pa* / *ša iḫ-nu-pu a-nạ mu-ḫi-ia*
⟨Behold⟩ the audacity that they have exercised against me.
(EA 288:7–8)

Associated Particles and Adverbs

An optional addition to *amur* is the enclitic *-mi*. Whether this is to mark the ensuing clause as direct speech, or whether it is the Canaanite enclitic for emphasis, is open to question. Enclitic *-ma* is never used with *amur*. The optional nature of the enclitic with *amur* may be seen from two passages in the same epistle, one with an enclitic and one without it:

a-mur-mi a-na-ku ÌR *ša* ^{I}*šàr-ri*
Behold, I am a servant of the king.
(EA 264:5)

ša-ni-tam a-mur ni-nu a-na mu-ḫi-ka$_{4}$ / 2 IGI-*ia*
Furthermore, behold (as for) us, my (sic!) eyes are towards you.
(EA 264:14–15; for the extraposition see below)

Numerous other examples could be cited; for example:

a-mur-mi ni-i$_{15}$*-nu i*$_{15}$*-ba-ša-nu* / *a-na* ^{KUR}*Am-qí*
Behold, we belong to the land of ᶜAmqi.
(EA 174:8–9; also EA 175:7–8, 176:7–8, 363:7–8)

The affinity between expressions for 'now' and those for 'behold' can be seen in one instance in which a scribe from Tyre used *amur* in a position usually occupied by *anumma*, that is, *a-mur i-na-an-na* 'Behold, now' (EA 147:24).

Certain particles may stand before *amur* at the head of a clause. Now and then, *amur* appears after *šanītam* (EA 140:18, 20; 264:14; 296:9; 330:13; possibly EA 84:42), or after the simple *u* conjunction (EA 179:14, 28; 209:8, 10). And *amur* at the head of a sentence may be followed by another adverb, for example, *panānu* (EA 122:11; 130:21).

Types of Clauses

The kind of sentences introduced by *amur* vary somewhat. There are a few places where *amur* serves to introduce a verbal clause:

> *ù a-mur-mì* ᴵ*Bir*₅*-ia-wa-za* / *uš-ši-ir gáb-bi* URU.DIDLI.ḪÁ LUGAL / EN-*ia a-na* LÚ.MEŠ SA.GAZ.MEŠ
> And behold, Biryawaza has handed over all the cities of the king, my lord, to the men of the ʿ*apīrū*. (EA 189:rev. 9–11)

> *a-mur-mì a-na-ku na-aṣ-ra-ti* [URU]. / DIDLI.ḪÁ LUGAL EN-*ia*
> Behold, I have protected the [cit]ies of the king, my lord.
> (EA 227:5–6)

> *ù a-mur-mì* / LÚ.MEŠ *ḫa-za-nu-ta*ᴹᴱŠ / *ša it-ti-ia* / *la-a ti-pu-šu-na* / *ki-ma ia-ti-ia*
> Behold, the city-rulers who are with me are not doing as I (do).
> (EA 365:15–18)

> *a-mur šar-ri* EN-*ia ša-ka-an* / *šum-šu a-na mu-ṣi* ᵈUTU-*ši* / *ù er-bi* ᵈUTU-*ši*
> Behold, my king, my lord, has placed his name at the sunrise and at the sunset.
> (EA 288:5–7)

Only once is a really complex sentence led off by the particle *amur*:

> ⸢*a*⸣-⸢*mur*⸣-*mi a-na ú-mi tu-ṣú* / *ù i-né-pu-ša-at gáb-bi* / KUR.MEŠ *a-na* LUGAL *be-li-ia*
> Behold, on the day you come forth, all the lands will return to the king, my lord.
> (EA 362:62–64)

However, by far the largest number of clauses introduced by *amur* are nonverbal; for example:

> *a-*[*mur*] GU₄.ME[Š] *it-ti-šu*
> Be[hold], there are oxen with him.
> (EA 92:42)

> *ù a-mur-mi* URU *Ṭú-*[*bi-ḫi*] URU É-*ti a-bi-ia*
> And behold, the city of Ṭô[biḫi] is the city of my paternal family.
> (EA 179:28)

a-mur ni-i-nu / ÌR.MEŠ *šàr-ri*
Behold, we are the servants of the king.
(EA 239:18–19)

a-mur at-ta LÚ *em-qú*
Behold, you are a wise man.
(EA 71:7)

a-mur at-⟨ta⟩ ŠEŠ-*ia*
Behold, yo⟨u⟩ are my brother.
(EA 34:7, from Alashia)

and especially from Jerusalem:

a-mur a-na-ku la-a LÚ*ḫa-zi-a-nu* / LÚ*ú-e-ú a-na šàr-ri* EN-*ia* / *a-mur a-na-ku* LÚ*ru-ʾì šàr-ri*
Behold, I am not (just) a city-ruler, a soldier of the king, my lord; behold I am a companion of the king. (EA 288:9–11)

a-mur KUR URU*Gin*$_6$*-ti-ki-ir-mi-il* KI / *a-na* I*Ta-gi*
Behold, the land of Gath-carmel belongs to Tagi.
(EA 289:18–19)

Many more could be cited (EA 60:6–7, 84:38, 106:18–20, 107:8–9, 117:34, 211:15–17, 254:10, 257:78, 264:5). These are also reminiscent of the use of the Egyptian calque on *amur*, the imperative of *ptr* 'to see'.

ptr wiʾ⌜*m*⌝ *p3wr* ᶜ*3* [*n*] *Ḫ-t ỉrm* [*R*ᶜ*-mss mry Ỉmn*] *p3 ḥk3* ᶜ*3 n Kmt m ḥtpw nfr m snsn nfr*
Behold I, as the great chief [of] Hatti with [Ramses beloved of Amon], the great ruler of Egypt, am in genuine peace and genuine brotherhood.
(Treaty, lines 11–12)[11]

A particularly striking usage of *amur* is to introduce a sentence component, most often the first common singular independent pronoun, standing in extraposition to its clause. A good case in point was EA 264:14–15, cited above. The Byblos letters frequently make use of this construction:

a-mur a-na-ku / *nu-kúr-tu*$_4$ UGU-*ia* 5 MU.MEŠ
Behold, (as for) myself, there has been hostility against me five years.
(EA 106:16–17)

a-mur a-na-ku ia-nu / *ḫa-za-na i-na ar-ki-ti-ia*
Behold, (as for) myself, there is no city-ruler behind me.
(EA 117:9–10)

11. Kitchen, *Ramesside Inscriptions*, p. 227, lines 11–12.

a-mur a-⌈na⌉-ku pa-nu-ia-ma / a-⌈na⌉ a-ra-ad LUGAL
Behold, (as for) myself, it is *my* face that is set to serve the king.
(EA 118:39–40)

These contexts remind us of a similar usage of the introductory particle *ỉr* in Late Egyptian:

ḏd.f ỉr ỉnk wn.ỉ ḥmsỉ.k (wỉ) m pꜣ-pr n A
He said, "As for me, I was staying in the house of A."
(BM 10052, 3)[12]

ỉr ỉnk gr ỉnk ỉn ỉnk pꜣy.k bꜣk
As for me, even me, am I your servant?[13]

And in fact, *amur* does serve as the translation for *ỉr* in the treaty between Ramses II and Hattusilis III. The Egyptian text reads:

ỉr r-ḥꜣt n-ḏr nḥḥ ỉr pꜣ sḫr n pꜣ ḥkꜣ ꜥꜣ n Kmt ỉrm pꜣ wr ꜥꜣ n Ḫtꜣ
As for from the beginning forever, as for the relationship of the great ruler of Egypt together with the great prince of Ḫatti, . . .
(Treaty, line 7)[14]

while the Akkadian is:

a-mur ṭe$_4$-ma ša LUGAL GAL LUGAL KUR *Mi-iṣ-ri-i* / [*qa-du* LUGAL GAL(!)] LUGAL KUR *Ḫa-at-ti ul-tù ⌈dá⌉-ri-ti*
As for the relationship of the great king, the king of the land of Egypt [with(!) the great king], the king of Ḫatti since the beginning . . .
(KBo I, 7:9–10)[15]

The element in extraposition need not be a pronoun:

a-mur É [URU]*Ṣur-ri* / *ia-nu* É-*ti ḫa-za-ni* / *⌈ki⌉-ma šu-a-ta*
Behold, as for the house (= palace) of Tyre, there is no house (= palace) of a city-ruler like it. (EA 89:48–50)

12. J. Černý and S. I. Groll, *A Late Egyptian Grammar* (Studia Pohl: Series Maior 4; Rome: Pontifical Biblical Institute, 1975) 14 §2.1.3, example 14.

13. A. H. Gardiner, *Late-Egyptian Stories* (Brussels: Fondation Égyptologique Reine Élisabeth, 1932) 68, 7; Černý and Groll, *Late Egyptian Grammar,* 14 §2.1.3, example 15.

14. Kitchen, *Ramesside Inscriptions,* 227, lines 2–3; cf. Spalinger, "The Hittite Treaty between Egypt and Hatti," 307 n. 19.

15. The *ša* LUGAL GAL at the beginning of line 10 in KBo 1, 25 probably parallels the *ša* LUGAL GAL in KBo 1, 7:10; the restoration of *qa-du* is based on the parallel Egyptian *ỉrm* 'with', which usually is matched by *qadu* in the Akkadian version; A. F. Rainey and Z. Cochavi Rainey, "Comparative Grammatical Notes on the Treaty between Ramses II and Hattusili III," *Studies in Egyptology Presented to Miriam Lichtheim* (ed. S. Israelit-Groll; Jerusalem: Magnes, 1990) 797 n. 8.

One must also read:

> *a-mur*!(NA) LÚ.MEŠ *ḫa-za-nu-tu* URU.MES *a-na ša-šu-nu*
> Behold, (as for) the city-rulers, they have their cities.
> (EA 118:45–46)

In one unique passage, the extraposition is only made by the repetition of the independent pronoun in the ensuing clause:

> [*a*]*-mur a-na-ku* GIŠ.GÌR.GUB *ša* GÌR-*pe* / LUGAL BE-*ia a-na-ku ù* ÌR *ki-it-ti-šu*
> [Be]hold, as for myself, the footstool of the king, my lord, am I, and his loyal servant. (EA 106:6–7)

Perhaps the most famous text using this construction derives from a Jerusalem letter:

> *a-mur a-na-ku la-a* [LÚ]*a-bi-ia* : *ša-ak-na-ni* / *ù la-a* [MÍ]*ú-mi-ia* / *i-na aš-ri an-ni-e*
> Behold, as for myself, it was not my father that placed me, and not my mother, in this place. (EA 286:9–11)

Concluding Remarks

Many more parallel passages could have been cited for the function of Egyptian *ptr* in syntagmas like those of *amur* in the Amarna texts from Canaan.[16] However, this would not answer the question of a possible priority. Did the Egyptians develop this calque through West Semitic influence, or was it just the opposite? Or did both languages develop independently the use of an imperative from a verb meaning 'to see' in the function of a presentation particle? In discussing the distribution of *amur* as a presentation particle in peripheral Akkadian, it was noted that by far the largest number of examples come from the Amarna letters written in Canaan. Therefore, one may at least suggest tentatively that the idiom is originally West Semitic, specifically Canaanite. There does not seem to be a comparable idiomatic use in Ugaritic, and thus the Akkadian texts from Ugarit do not use *amur* in this fashion. The full documentation for *amur* in the Amarna texts from Canaan has been given here because of the great interest attached to that particular dialect of Akkadian.

16. Černý and Groll, *Late Egyptian Grammar*, 148–49 §9.6.

The Vasilikos Valley: Its Place in Cypriot and Near Eastern Prehistory

Ian A. Todd

Introduction

The Vasilikos valley, located in the Larnaca District adjacent to the southern coast of the island of Cyprus, has been the scene of archaeological fieldwork since the 1940s. Porphyrios Dikaios undertook several small scale excavations of prehistoric sites, but the results were never published in detail. Since the summer of 1976, a multidisciplinary and regionally oriented project, based on the village of Kalavasos and directed by the writer, has been undertaken with the overall aim of illuminating from archaeological sources the nature of life in the valley in all its phases from the earliest occupation virtually until the present day. Excavations have now been undertaken at four separate sites of different periods, the first and most important stage of the field survey has been completed, and various other studies have also been finished or are now in progress. After 14 seasons of excavation, other fieldwork, and publication, the time is now right to summarize the results, to examine the major implications of the research, and to cast a retrospective eye over the work to date.

The village of Kalavasos and the Vasilikos River valley lie almost equidistant from the modern towns of Limassol and Larnaca (fig. 1). The valley is one of a series that runs down to the southern coast of the island from the eastern end of the Troodos mountain range. The village of Kalavasos (elevation ca. 85 m) is located at a narrow point in the valley, approximately halfway between the Kalavasos Dam and the copper mines to the north and the Mediterranean coast 5 km to the south. The only other inhabited villages

---

Author's note: It gives me great pleasure to offer this study in honor of my former colleague, Professor Dwight Young, whose wide-ranging interests encompass archaeology as well as so many other aspects of the ancient Near East.

within the project area are Mari to the south of Kalavasos and Zyyi on the coast to the SE. The valley narrows from the broad coastal strip as it approaches Kalavasos; to the north of the village it widens out again before the higher foothills of the Troodos range are reached. The climate is typically Mediterranean; until the recent introduction of widespread irrigation, much of the land was occupied by fields with olive and carob trees and seasonal cereal growing. In the upper reaches of the valley many of the slopes are uncultivated, and stands of pine and other trees exist. From the geological point of view, the northern part of the valley consists predominantly of igneous rocks, while limestones and marls predominate from north of Kalavasos down to the coast.

The archaeological importance of the Kalavasos area has been known for a number of years since P. Dikaios undertook brief excavations at the Neolithic sites of Kalavasos-Tenta (which he named Mari-Tenta; Dikaios 1953: passim), Kalavasos-Kokkinoyia (Kalavasos Site A; Dikaios 1962: 106–12) and Mari-Paliambela (Dikaios 1953: 319), and at the Chalcolithic site of Kalavasos-Pamboules (Kalavasos Site B; Dikaios 1962: 133–40). Bronze Age tombs were also excavated within the confines of Kalavasos village (Karageorghis 1940–48), and Catling recorded other Early and Late Bronze Age sites in the region in his survey of Bronze Age settlement patterns (Catling 1962). But prior to 1976, no extensive excavation and field survey work had been undertaken in the valley as a whole.[1]

Since its inception, the Vasilikos Valley Project (hereafter V.V.P.) has been designed to bring a multidisciplinary approach to the archaeological problems of the Vasilikos valley and more generally to those of the earlier prehistory of Cyprus.[2] Excavations were initially planned at the Neolithic site of

1. I am most grateful to Dr. Vassos Karageorghis, then Director of the Department of Antiquities, for his initial suggestion of Kalavasos as a possible venue for archaeological research. Sincere gratitude is also expressed to Mr. A. Papageorghiou, presently Director of the Department of Antiquities, to Mr. M. Loulloupis, Curator of Archaeological Museums and Surveys, and to other officers of the Department of Antiquities who aided the project in so many ways. The research has been funded by the National Science Foundation (1976–1979), the National Endowment for the Humanities (1982–1984), the Center for Field Research (1982–1983), the University Research Expeditions Program of the University of California at Berkeley (1984), and the Institute for Aegean Prehistory (1986–1990). I have also benefited personally from awards made by the Fulbright Commission, the Mazer Fund, and the Sachar International Program of Brandeis University. To all of these funding agencies our great indebtedness is acknowledged.

2. For preliminary reports summarizing all activities of the project, see Todd 1977, 1978, 1979, 1982, and 1986a. Two final reports have so far been published (Todd ed. 1986 and

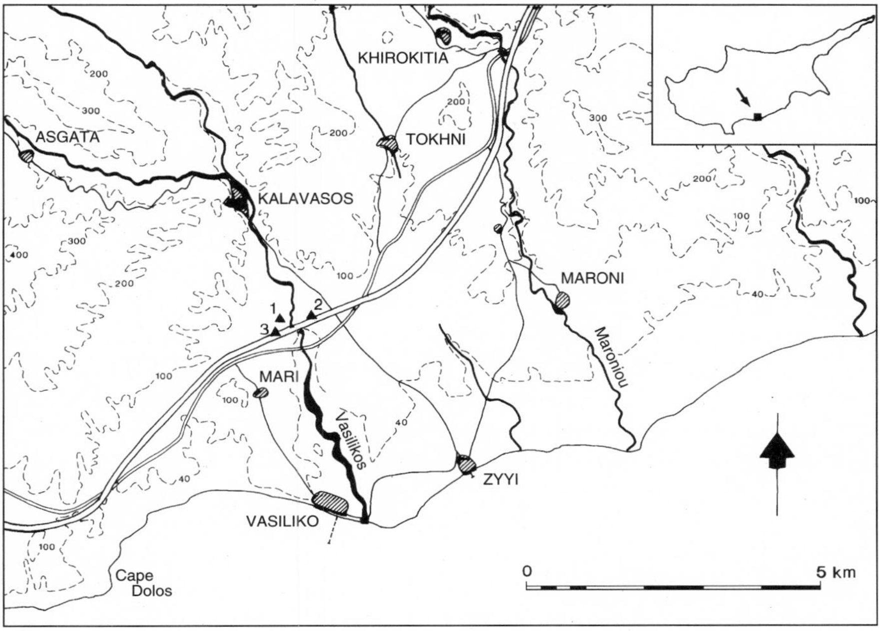

Figure 1. Sketch map of the southern part of the Vasilikos valley and adjacent areas, showing the general location of sites excavated by the V.V.P.
Key to sites: ***1.*** *Tenta;* ***2.*** *Ayious;* ***3.*** *Ayios Dhimitrios;* ***4.*** *Kalavasos village, Bronze Age cemetery.*
Contours are in meters. Drawn by I. A. Todd from an original drawing by A. South.

Kalavasos-Tenta, but excavation of later period prehistoric sites was also envisaged to cast light on changes that occurred following the end of the Aceramic Neolithic phase. During the various excavations in the valley, emphasis has been placed on the retrieval of data pertinent to environmental and economic aspects of the sites; botanical and zoological analyses of the material from all excavated sites have been completed or are currently in progress, and studies of the human geography, geology, hydrology, ethnography, and other aspects of the valley have also been undertaken. Concurrent with the various excavations, the field survey of the Vasilikos valley has been designed, by means of a transect sampling procedure, to recover data from

Todd 1987), and others are in press or almost completed. References to the Ayios Dhimitrios excavations and the field survey are provided below.

which the settlement system of the valley may be reconstructed for all periods from the earliest Neolithic occupation until modern times. The survey, together with the various regional environmental studies, will allow the excavated sites to be seen in the true perspective of the valley as a whole. The regional approach should provide the data for the testing of various hypotheses concerning settlement systems and the interrelationships of sites. It is also hoped that in the future it will be possible to compare entire regional sequences within the island rather than individual sites alone.

While the underlying aims of the project have remained constant since the beginning of fieldwork in 1976, the development of the project has been radically different from that originally envisaged. As outlined in the last preliminary report, excavations at sites other than the Neolithic site of Tenta were always anticipated, but the initial plan was to complete the Tenta excavations and the field survey and to publish both of these activities before proceeding with research at another site. However, in recent years "development" in the valley area has taken place so fast that adherence to such a plan was not feasible. Full advantage had to be taken of opportunities as they arose to clarify the post-Neolithic sequence, especially since the sites in question were about to be at least partially destroyed. During the summer of 1978 the construction of a new building adjacent to the Panayia Church in the center of Kalavasos Village necessitated the rescue excavation of 13 Middle Bronze Age tombs, and late in the same year it became apparent that the Chalcolithic site of Ayious lay in the path of the new Nicosia–Limassol Highway. Test excavation was therefore undertaken at the latter site late in 1978 and a full-scale excavation season was carried out in the summer of 1979, a season that ultimately lasted well into 1980.

During the summer of 1979 it also became apparent that the new highway would pass through Ayios Dhimitrios, a locality to the south of Tenta, in which a scatter of Middle Bronze Age sherds and a large quantity of heavy storage jar (pithos) sherds of unknown date had previously been encountered. A small test pit dug in connection with the new road had revealed the presence of a well-built stone structure, and permission was sought to undertake a small-scale excavation to determine the nature and date of the building to which the structure belonged. It soon became apparent that the building dated to the Late Bronze Age and that the site covered an extremely large area. Since road construction was thought to be imminent, it was decided to mount a major rescue excavation to save as much as possible of the site that lay within the road-line. The excavation lasted from the autumn of 1979 through February 1980, and the results surpassed all expectations. More controlled summer excavation seasons in recent years have concentrated on areas of the site out-

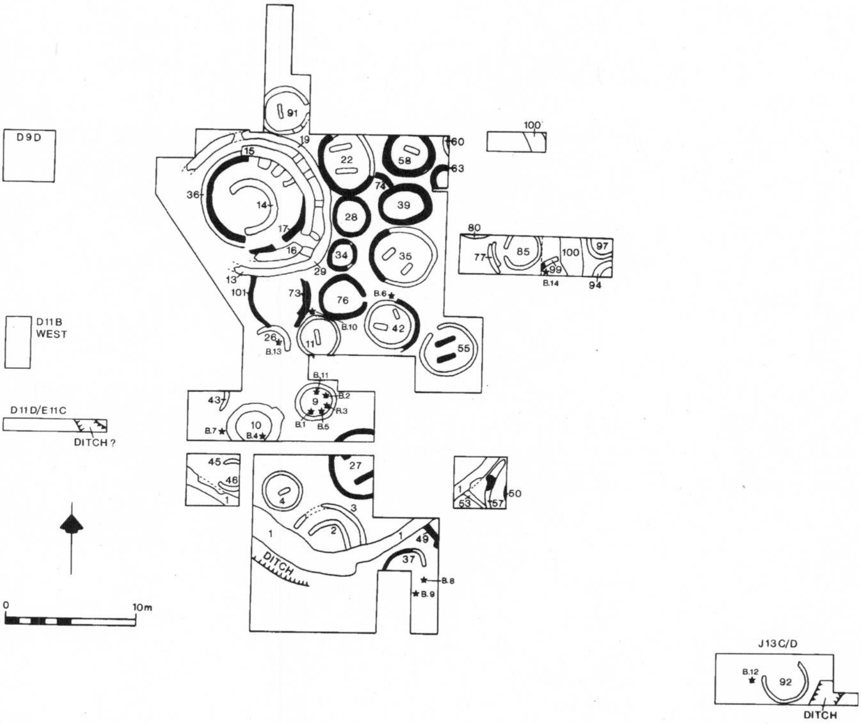

Figure 2. Sketch plan of the Neolithic architecture and other features at Kalavasos-Tenta. The location of human burials is indicated by stars. B = Burial. Numbers without the B prefix refer to structures. Mud-brick walls are shaded, whereas unshaded walls are built of stone. Drawn by I. A. Todd.

side the road-line, especially in the NE Area, where an important public building and a very richly furnished tomb have now been uncovered.

Thus, despite the initial intention of restricting excavation to Tenta until the research there was completed, a great deal more became known about the post-Neolithic archaeology of the valley rather sooner than had originally been anticipated. However, the dilution of effort involved in the excavation of other sites was detrimental to the overall Tenta research program; the final excavation season at Tenta in 1984 did not solve all of the outstanding problems, and further excavation at the site would no doubt provide valuable results. The main phase of the field survey was not completed until the summer of 1989.

Figure 3. Aerial view of Kalavasos-Tenta after the erection of the protective roof, from NW. Photograph by A. Koutas.

Excavations at Kalavasos-Tenta

Five seasons of excavation were undertaken at the Aceramic and Ceramic Neolithic site of Tenta in 1976–1979 and 1984 (figs. 2–4). The architecture and other aspects of the site were summarized in the first volume of the final report (Todd 1987: xvi), from which the following section is derived, with emendations in the light of more recent research.

Figure 4. Architecture of the Aceramic Neolithic period on the upper part of Kalavasos-Tenta with Structure 55 in the foreground, from SE. Photograph by I. A. Todd.

The site consists of occupation deposits on a small natural hill overlooking the Vasilikos valley from its west side. Brief excavation at the site in 1947 revealed the presence of stone architecture of the Aceramic Neolithic period, and numerous curvilinear stone and mud-brick domestic structures were excavated by the V.V.P. on the top and on the southern slopes of the site. The west side of the top of the site was occupied by three successive large buildings, which are differentiated either by their size or the complexity of their plan from other structures on the site. On the east side of the top of the site were at least four rows of dwellings built of mud-brick or stone or a combination of both. In many structures, single or double internal piers probably served to support a partial upper story. At least in an early phase of its existence, the settlement was surrounded by a wide stone wall, with a ditch outside the wall on the southern side of the site. At a later date, but still within the Aceramic phase, the settlement expanded beyond the line of the previous outer settlement wall, but it is unclear whether the enlarged settlement was similarly enclosed.

A total of 14 human burials containing a minimum of 18 individuals was excavated either below the floors of buildings or in open areas outside them.

Figure 5. The sites of Ayious (on top of the plateau on left side of photograph and Pamboules (on top of the plateau on right side of photograph) seen from Tenta, from NW. Photograph by I. A. Todd.

Those buried below house floors were interred in pits, but elsewhere the bodies usually appear to have been deposited in layers of rubbish and were soon covered over. One worked lump of red ochre represents the only artifact deposited with any of the bodies. Examination of the skeletal remains suggests the practice of artificial cranial deformation.

During the Aceramic phase, a wide range of stone containers was in use. Frequently formed of hard stones, the shapes of the vessels are quite sophisticated, with finely formed spouts and handles, and a few are decorated on the exterior. A considerable variety of stone jewelry, often made of picrolite,[3] was also found, together with some bone tools. Imported obsidian, probably from the Çiftlik central Anatolian obsidian sources, occurs as a small percentage of the lithic industry. Only two fragmentary stone figurines were found in contrast to the distinctly larger number found at nearby Khirokitia. Domestic stone equipment, including querns and pounding and grinding stones, occurs frequently, together with a wide variety of axes and other tools. Cereals were grown by the inhabitants of Tenta, and both wild and domestic animals are represented among the animal bones excavated on the

3. Picrolite is a soft blue-green stone available in Cyprus but not locally in the Vasilikos valley. The same material has also been called antigorite and steatite in previous archaeological publications.

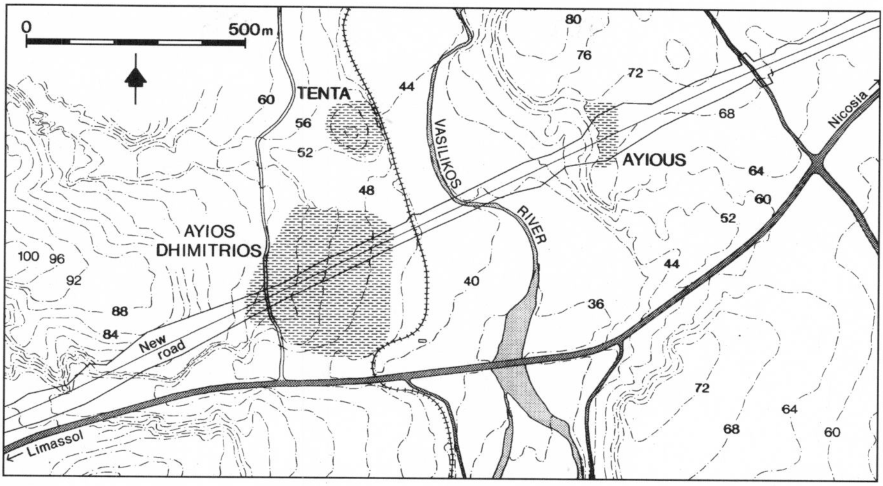

Figure 6. Topographical map showing the location of the sites of Tenta, Ayious, and Ayios Dhimitrios. The site areas are shaded. Contours are in meters. Drawn by A. South.

site. A series of radiocarbon dates suggests that the earliest occupation of the site may date back to the eighth millennium B.C.E., earlier than has previously been proposed for the beginning of the Cypriot Aceramic Neolithic. Some of the later dates (sixth millennium B.C.E.) are more in line with those from other sites such as Khirokitia.

Probably following a lengthy break in occupation, the Ceramic Neolithic/Early Chalcolithic utilization of the site is represented by some pits and deposits containing ceramics on the lower flanks of the site. No remains of standing architecture of this phase were found. Ceramics of well-known Neolithic and Early Chalcolithic types are plentiful, in conjunction with small numbers of artifacts of other materials.

Excavations at Kalavasos-Ayious

The site of Ayious lies in a prominent position on the east side of the Vasilikos valley, ca. 500 m east of Tenta, on the top of a fairly flat-topped plateau (fig. 5; for location see also fig. 6). Dikaios's excavations at Kokkinoyia (Site A) and Pamboules (Site B, also visible in fig. 5), a short distance to the south, in earlier years had indicated a complete lack of standing architecture,

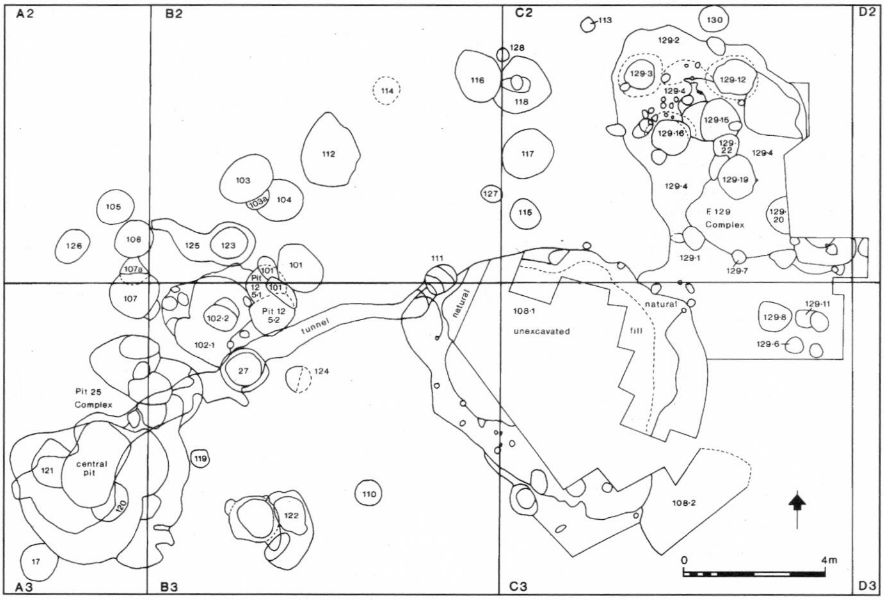

Figure 7. Plan of the Pit 25 complex and adjacent pits in the NW Area at Ayious. Drawn by I. A. Todd from an original plan by P. Croft.

but they revealed a series of sometimes deep pits that were interpreted as pit-dwellings. Those at Kokkinoyia were dated to the Ceramic Neolithic ("Neolithic II") period and those at Pamboules to the Early Chalcolithic ("Chalcolithic I"). Since the Ayious plateau represents a northward continuation of the Kokkinoyia/Pamboules plateau, separated from it only by a sizable gully, it seemed likely that similar features would be found in both areas. I was unimpressed with Dikaios's designation of the pits as "pit-dwellings," and it was thought that excavations at Ayious might clarify the true nature of these features. As soon as it became apparent that a major portion of the Ayious site was endangered by the construction of the new Nicosia–Limassol Highway, test excavations were undertaken in the autumn of 1978 to determine the nature of remains on the site. As anticipated, no standing architecture was encountered, but a large pit was centered by good fortune in one of the soundings laid out on the center line of the new road immediately adjacent to the steep slope down to the valley floor. The omens were, therefore, good for the solution of the problem posed by the pits excavated in earlier years, and a

Figure 8. The C 11 C, 5.1 pit at Ayious with artifacts in situ *on a surface, from east. Photograph by A. Kingsnorth.*

more substantial excavation was started in the summer of 1979, lasting until the early days of 1980.

The final excavation report covering research at Ayious is nearing readiness for publication (Todd and Croft forthcoming), and the results of the excavation are there summarized in the following terms. No clear evidence of standing architecture was found, but pits of varying size were located in several different parts of the site (fig. 7). The larger and deeper pits (fig. 8) range in diameter from 1.5 m to 2.75 m, with a maximum depth of ca. 2.0 m. The fill of these pits frequently contained quantities of lumps of pisé derived either from a collapsed roof or from the destruction of nearby structures, the material from which had then washed into the pits. Compacted earth surfaces occurred in some pits, and on some of these, clusters of artifacts were found, implying at least activity surfaces. Numerous smaller pits were also excavated, some having clearly been used as hearths and others probably for storage.

At the north end of the site a unique complex of pits and underground tunnels was revealed. A large, approximately circular pit (Pit 25) was found

Figure 9. The tunnel between Pit 25 (background) and Pit 27 (foreground) at Ayious, from NE. Photograph by A. South.

to be connected to a small but deep shaft (Pit 27) by a low, narrow tunnel (figs. 7, 9). Another tunnel was located running from the shaft to a small pit (Feature 111) that contained steps and served as the entrance to the tunnel. The fill of this complex contained considerable quantities of domestic refuse including pottery, lithics, and human figurine fragments.

The excavations at Ayious have not provided any conclusive evidence concerning the nature of the site as a whole or the purpose of the larger pits and associated tunnels. Interpretation of the larger pits as pit-dwellings still seems unlikely, although the quantities of domestic debris together with the presence of compacted earth surfaces and possible evidence of roofing might be taken to point in this direction. Some form of specialized activity might be postulated to account for the larger pits, but analyses of the artifacts recovered from them are inconclusive. The designation of the site as a residential village requires the supposition that the houses were built of pisé and other light materials, the only remains of which found by excavation were lumps of pisé washed into some of the pits.

Figure 10. Clay human figurines and fragments thereof found at Ayious. Photograph by A. South.

The very incomplete skeleton of an infant and a few scattered bones constitute the only human remains found on the site, which dates several centuries before the middle of the fourth millennium B.C.E., perhaps slightly earlier than Kissonerga-Mylouthkia in the Paphos region (Peltenburg 1982a). Large quantities of ceramics were recovered from the Ayious excavations, providing good evidence for intra-island regional relationships and variations in the Chalcolithic period, as well as chronological seriation. Chipped stone tools also occurred frequently, together with quantities of ground stone implements and lesser numbers of bone tools, clay figurine fragments (fig. 10), and other artifacts (South 1985). Little evidence was found at Ayious for trade with the mainland, but comparison between the Cypriot sequence and that of Palestine suggests that similar environmental factors in both areas might have led to the adoption of subterranean features, marking a radical change from the solid architecture of distinctly earlier periods in both regions.

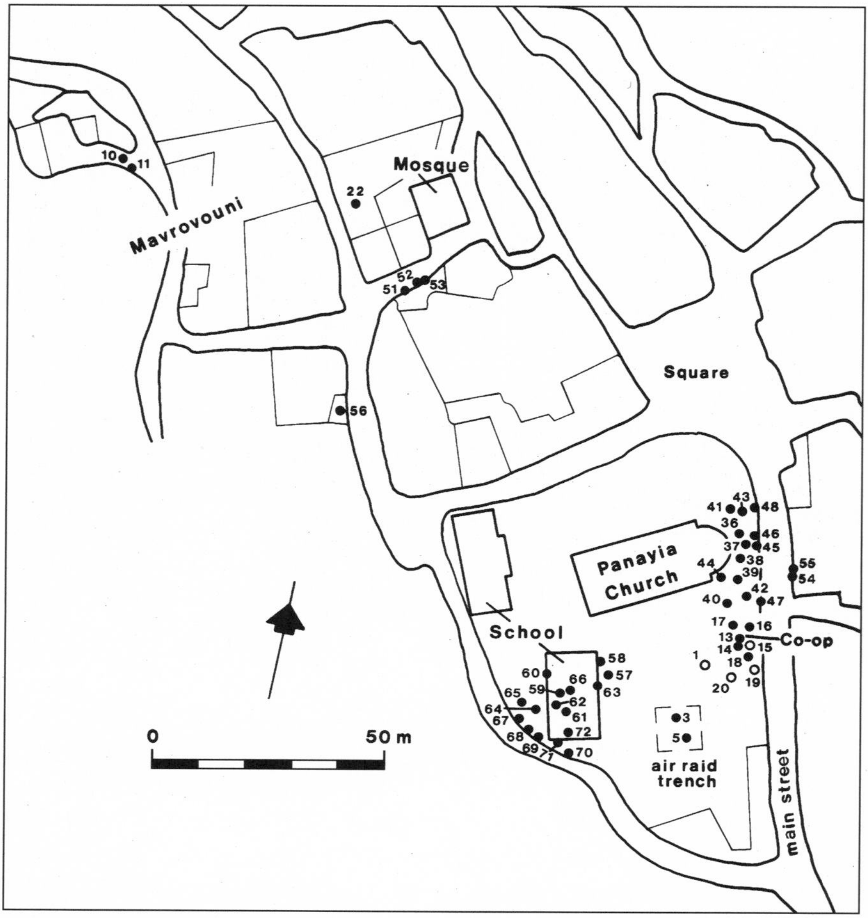

Figure 11. Plan showing the location of tombs in the Panayia Church and Mosque areas of Kalavasos. Solid black circles indicate the exact locations of tombs; open circles indicate approximate locations. Tomb 2 is not shown since its location is too uncertain. Drawn by I. A. Todd with additions from an original plan by D. Pearlman.

Excavations in the Bronze Age Cemetery within Kalavasos Village

The village of Kalavasos has been known in archaeological literature as a Bronze Age cemetery site since Karageorghis' initial publication of a series of

Figure 12. Kalavasos village and the Panayia Church-Mosque area, from the SSW. Photograph by I. A. Todd.

tombs discovered in the 1940s in the Panayia Church area at the center of the village (figs. 11–12) (Karageorghis 1940–48). A further series of tombs was found near the south end of the village in 1961 during the construction of the village cinema (just out of the photograph to the right in fig. 12). Other scattered tombs have also been found adjacent to these areas and near the mosque just to the north of the Panayia Church. The tombs are predominantly of Middle Bronze Age date, although there is an admixture of Late Bronze Age graves, especially in the mosque area. Since the inception of the project the V.V.P. staff have been involved in two separate series of rescue excavations of tombs in the Panayia Church and cinema areas in 1978 and 1987.

During the 1978 summer season, construction of a row of shops and offices immediately east of and below the Panayia Church was commenced. Bulldozing quickly revealed the existence of Bronze Age tombs, and thirteen tombs were ultimately excavated, many of which had been damaged by the machine. The tomb chambers were cut in the natural *kafkalla* (calcrete) and overlying deposits, but little information could be retrieved about their method of entry. The human skeletal remains were mostly disturbed but multiple burials occurred in several chambers. The dead were buried with

Figure 13. Red Polished Mottled large bowl with modeled human and animal figures (K-PC 4) from Kalavasos Village Tomb 36. Photograph by P. Brodie.

comparatively rich grave goods; these are predominantly ceramic (figs. 13–14), but a number of metal tools and weapons were also recovered, in addition to several stone items and several thousand beads, including some of faience. The ceramics were mostly of Middle Bronze Age date, but several Late Bronze Age White Slip sherds were also found, in addition to a series of Iron Age wheel-made vessels found in one tomb. The Middle Bronze Age ceramics indicate that this series of burials spans the entire Middle Cypriot period. Close stylistic parallels with pottery from sites in northern, central, and eastern Cyprus indicate extensive lines of communication across the island. The most elaborate vessel, a Red Polished Mottled large bowl with modeled figures around the rim (fig. 13), belongs to a somewhat rare category of vessels bearing depictions of scenes of daily life, perhaps wine-making and bread-making in this case (Todd ed. 1986: 41–42; cf. Morris 1985: 264–90). Vessels such as the White Painted II juglet illustrated in fig. 14 display connections with the areas of Lapithos and Dhenia in the more northerly region of the island.

Figure 14. White Painted II juglet (K-PC 85) from Kalavasos Village Tomb 36. Photograph by P. Brodie.

Between 1984 and 1987, further tombs were accidentally discovered during construction work in the Panayia Church, mosque, and cinema areas of the village. These were excavated by the V.V.P., in conjunction with the Department of Antiquities.[4] Sixteen tombs (T. 57–72; all Middle Bronze Age) were excavated in the Panayia Church area below and immediately adjacent to the old southern elementary school building, which was demolished (plan, fig. 11). Two further Middle Bronze Age tombs (T. 54–55) were found on the east side of the main village street opposite the church. Four tombs (T. 51–53, 56; three MB and one LB) were found in the mosque area in 1984 and 1986. At the end of 1987, seven more tombs (T. 73–79; all MB) were found immediately north of the cinema (to the south of the area shown in fig. 11).

4. The report on these excavations is currently in preparation and will be published as volume 11 in the Vasilikos Valley Project series.

In all cases the tombs consisted of circular or oval subterranean chambers cut in the soft natural rock or natural soil deposits. The internal measurement of the floors of the chambers varies from a minimum of 1.32 m to a maximum of 2.80 m. The entrances to the chambers were covered with very large, heavy slabs of local stone. Because the tombs were discovered during the course of construction work, the *dromoi* (entrance shafts) were frequently not excavated. The only *dromoi* to be excavated were three examples in the elementary school area near the church where, in each case, three burial chambers opened off the same roughly rectangular *dromos.* Many of the chambers were found completely intact, with their blocking stones still in situ. Clear pick marks were preserved on the walls and ceilings of some of the chambers.

The condition of the human skeletal remains and the grave goods in the tombs varied; at best, the bones and artifacts were found still in their original position, while in other cases there was much evidence of disturbance. The cinema area tombs were predominantly used for single interments, while multiple interments were evidenced in the elementary school tombs near the church. The grave goods consisted mostly of ceramic gifts, with small numbers of metal tools, weapons, and items of personal adornment. Terra-cotta spindle whorls/weights also were found in small numbers, together with an occasional stone tool. Large numbers of tiny faience and stone beads were also found in some tombs.

The ceramics comprise mainly Red Polished Mottled vessels, with smaller number of incised Red Polished III wares. A few Black Topped bowls were found, as well as occasional examples of Black/Brown Polished wares. Red Polished IV was completely absent, and only a very few sherds (and no complete vessels) of White Painted ware occurred. The Red Polished Mottled vessels vary from large amphorae, jugs, and bowls to small bowls. The ceramics generally betray a local origin, but two small incised vessels found in the elementary school area show clear connections with northern and central Cyprus and must be considered imports in a Kalavasos context.

The comparatively good state of preservation of these tombs has provided information, not available from the previously excavated tombs in Kalavasos, about Middle Bronze Age burial customs and the disposition of the dead and their accompanying artifacts. New details of overall tomb morphology and construction methods also came to light. More detailed chronological seriation is now possible within the Kalavasos village cemetery as a result of these recently excavated tombs, and the changing pattern of relationships with other areas of Cyprus has been clarified to a considerable extent.

Excavations at Kalavasos-Ayios Dhimitrios

The existence of a large archaeological site at Ayios Dhimitrios,[5] almost immediately south of Tenta across a small terraced drainage, has been known since the early days of the project, but the chronology of the site and its overall significance only became clear when excavation commenced in 1979. The site lay in the path of the new Nicosia–Limassol Highway, and the central portion, the Central and West Areas, has now been covered over or destroyed by road construction. Excavations in recent years have concentrated on the NE Area on the northern edge of the site outside the road-line, and the excavations have yet to be completed.[6]

The large urban settlement (covering ca. 11.5 hectares) at Ayios Dhimitrios dates to the Late Bronze Age, more specifically to the Late Cypriot IIC phase, ca. 1300–1190 B.C.E. It is located on low-lying, gently sloping terraces ca. 200 m west of the Vasilikos River, 3.5 km north of the coast. The situation is poor, from the defensive point of view, but excellent for trade and communications; it lies at the crossroads of the route linking the eastern to the southern and western regions of the island and the route from the coast northwards to the Kalavasos mines area and the Troodos Mountains.

Excavations have been undertaken in various parts of the site, and substantial stone buildings, all with the same orientation, have been found in all areas. Most of the excavated architecture is clearly dated to LC IIC only, but some buildings in the Western Area might have been occupied at a slightly earlier date. It seems likely that a settlement of the LC IIA–B phases exists somewhere in the near vicinity, the occupants of which used several tombs of this phase found within the LC IIC settlement area. The LC IIC town plan shows a high degree of organization. Several fairly large (ca. 100–350 m^2) multi-roomed buildings, probably private residences of reasonably affluent citizens, front onto at least one long straight street, which leads north towards a large public building (Building X) adjacent to the present NE edge of the site. No definite evidence has yet been found for the existence of a defensive wall. Most buildings were well built, with stone walls (but not ashlar masonry), probably with superstructures of mud-brick, and an upper story.

5. My wife, Alison South, field director of the Ayios Dhimitrios excavations, kindly assisted in writing this section.

6. Preliminary reports on the excavations at Ayios Dhimitrios have been published by South (1980, 1982, 1983, and 1984a). The first of the final excavation reports has been published (South, Russell, and Keswani 1989). For the most recent published notes on the site see South 1988 and 1989.

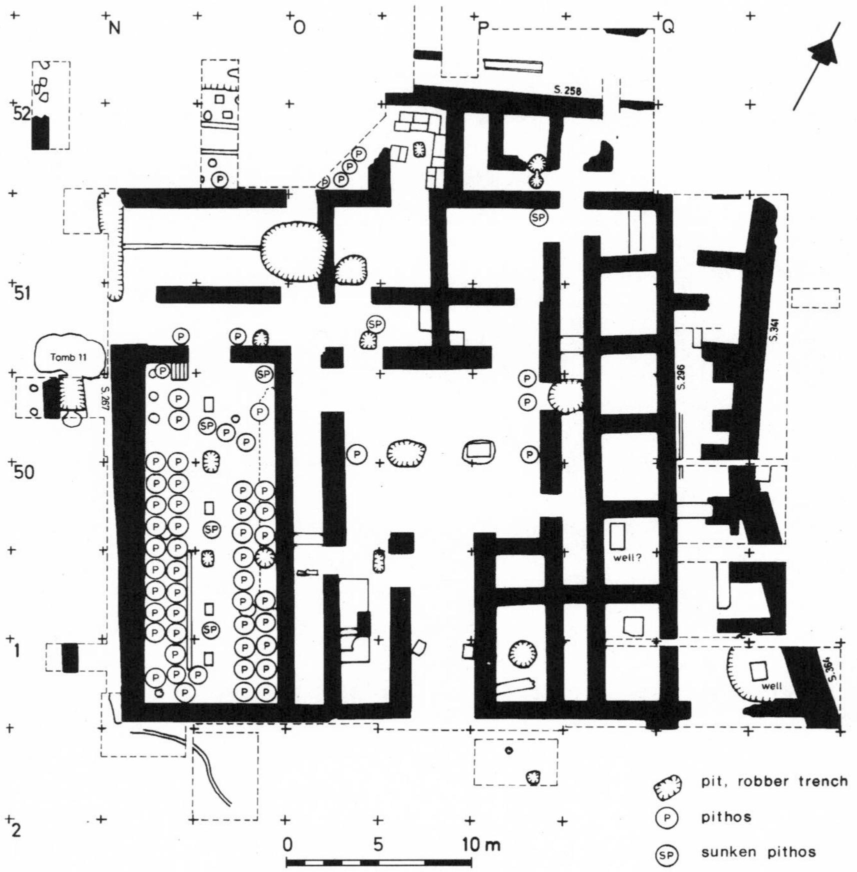

Figure 15. Plan of Building X at Ayios Dhimitrios at the end of the 1987 excavation season. Drawn by A. South.

Building X (fig. 15) is the largest building complex on the site; it is square in overall plan, measuring 30.5 × 30.5 m, with a tripartite plan around a central square courtyard. Ashlar masonry was extensively employed in its construction, which is also notable for its massive quality. A second story is likely, probably accessible by means of a staircase near the main entrance to the building. The largest room within the building (the "Pithos Hall"; fig. 16) measures ca. 19.5 × 7.25 m with a row of 6 rectangular stone pillars down its

Figure 16. The Pithos Hall in Building X at Ayios Dhimitrios, from south. Photograph by A. South.

center. Almost the entire hall was devoted to storage, with two rows of large pithoi (storage jars) standing on each side of the row of pillars. At least 47 jars stood on the floor, and 6 additional jars were sunk into the floor. A total capacity for the jars has been estimated at 33,500 liters, but no clear evidence was retrieved concerning the commodity or commodities stored within them.

The special character of Building X is readily apparent from its size and the quality of its construction. No evidence was found for a religious use, and a secular, perhaps administrative purpose may be surmised. This hypothesis may be supported by the discovery of five small clay cylinders bearing Cypro-Minoan inscriptions within and immediately adjacent to the building (Masson 1983). Otherwise, the excavation of Building X did not reveal the presence of notable quantities of artifacts, with the exception of a deposit of pottery found in a pit or well in the SE sector of the building (Area 173) (South 1988). The vessels comprise a high proportion of Mycenaean types, including several with pictorial decoration, and the deposit may represent discarded tableware, suggesting at least a partially residential character for the building.

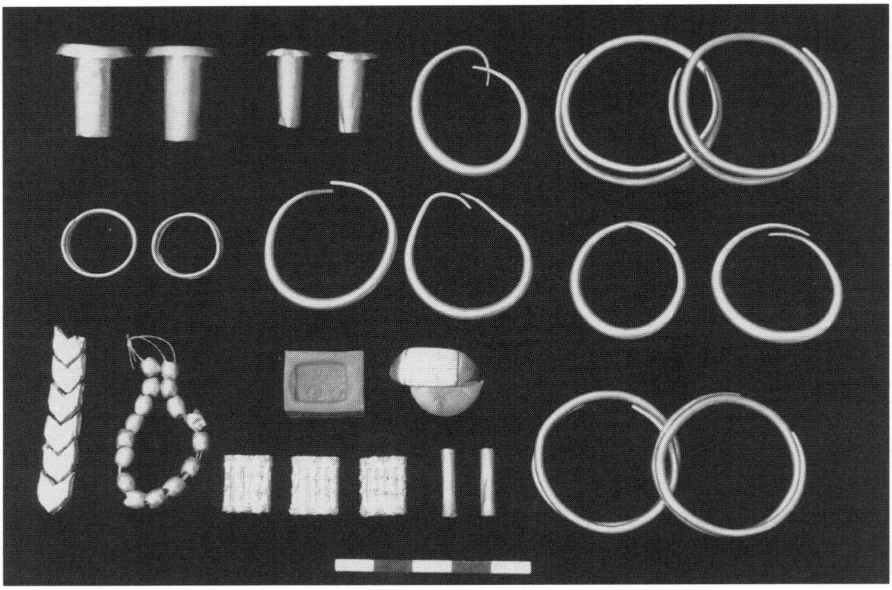

Figure 17. Gold jewelry found in Tomb 11 at Ayios Dhimitrios. Photograph by A. South.

Elsewhere on the site, artifacts of the usual Late Bronze Age categories occur in reasonable numbers, but the quantity of clear imports (mostly Mycenaean and Canaanite ceramics, with the occasional Minoan sherd) is less than might have been expected in view of the suggested connection between the location of the site and the procurement of and trade in copper. Evidence of metallurgical activities has been found on the site, especially in Building IX in the SE Area, but it is nowhere very extensive. Small quantities of slag occur in all excavated areas, but no evidence has yet been found for major smelting operations within the boundaries of the site, and it is likely that such operations would have been carried out in the vicinity of the mines. Bronze artifacts occur quite frequently on the site together with occasional fragments of oxhide ingots; a set of mainly bronze weights in the shape of animal figures and a negroid human head are among the finest artifacts found (Courtois 1983), but their place of manufacture is uncertain. Metal artifacts were clearly manufactured or repaired on a small scale at Ayios Dhimitrios, but no indications have yet been found for a more extensive metallurgical enterprise on the site.

The number of tombs so far located and excavated within the settlement area is small. The tombs cover the period LC IB–LC IIC (ca. 1575–1225 B.C.E.), and in the main they were in use at a slightly earlier period than that of the LC IIC settlement. All of the tombs are of the usual rock-cut chamber tomb type, with a square or rectangular *dromos* leading down to the burial chamber, the entrance to which was closed with a sizable stone. The condition of some tombs left much to be desired, but the now celebrated Tomb 11 (LC IIA:2, ca. 1375 B.C.E.) was found intact in 1984, with skeletal remains and grave goods still in their original positions (see South 1984b and articles by South and Goring in Peltenburg 1989). A rock-cut bench was located on either side of the burial chamber, and the skeletal remains comprised three young women, a young child, and three infants. All of the grave goods are of the highest quality and include numerous items of gold jewelry (fig. 17) together with imported and local ceramics (Mycenaean, Red Lustrous, White Slip, and Base Ring) and other gifts of silver, ivory, bone, glass, faience, bronze, amber, and stones, including alabaster. The tomb is one of the richest Bronze Age tombs found on the island and displays a degree of wealth and sophistication seldom seen even in Late Bronze Age funerary contexts.

In addition to the light shed on the nature of life in the Vasilikos valley in LC II, the Ayios Dhimitrios excavations have also shown that, despite a century of archaeological research, major Late Bronze Age settlements still await discovery in Cyprus, and the present distribution of such centers must be incomplete.

The Field Survey

The field survey of the Vasilikos valley[7] was designed from the outset of the project to provide information concerning the settlement system of the region from its earliest occupation until modern times, such a background being essential for the accurate interpretation of the excavated sites. Ceramic and lithic artifacts lying on the present ground surface betray the presence of unexcavated archaeological sites, and detailed recording of these occurrences should provide a reasonably accurate picture of the extent and nature of the utilization of the area in any given phase. The survey was begun in 1976 and continued sporadically thereafter. While it was hoped at first that complete coverage of the valley could be obtained, the initial reconnaissance survey

7. For the most recent published reports on the field survey, see Todd 1988 and 1989, where references to earlier publications are cited.

soon indicated that the density of sites was such that some form of sampling procedure had to be adopted. It was also apparent that certain types of small sites were missing. A system based on 100 m wide transects was, therefore, established, with a distance of 400 m separating the south side of one transect from the north side of the next transect to the south. The transects were aligned east–west across the valley and its side drainages, crosscutting the major environmental zones. The areas surveyed ranged from less than 1.5 km to more than 4.5 km in length. The results of this methodology were satisfactory, and the system was ultimately extended northward up to the area of the copper mines and the Kalavasos Dam. In all, 19 transects were surveyed between the dam and the coast.

A total of 135 sites has so far been recorded. The earliest occupation of the valley dates to the Aceramic Neolithic period (seventh millennium B.C.E., possibly starting earlier and continuing into the sixth millennium), attested mainly at the settlement sites of Kalavasos-Tenta and Mari-Mesovouni in the southern sector of the valley and at Ora-Klitari in the northern region toward the dam. It seems increasingly likely that there was a hiatus in settlement of more than a millennium following the Aceramic Neolithic period, prior to reoccupation of sites such as Tenta in the Ceramic Neolithic, ca. 4500 B.C.E.; no evidence for continuity of occupation was found at Tenta. The ensuing Early Chalcolithic phase is represented by 6 sites (including the excavated site of Ayious), but the later Chalcolithic is less well known, material of this phase only being found at 5 sites. Despite the size of the area surveyed, the Early Bronze Age seems to be almost unrepresented in the survey material, and excavation must clearly be undertaken at a suitable site to determine whether the Middle Bronze Age designation applied to so many sites is in fact accurate. The latter period is represented by considerable numbers of settlements and cemeteries, especially in the area of the village of Kalavasos and further north. Middle Bronze Age settlements do not occur on or near the coast. The settlement system in the Late Bronze Age comprises a major nucleation of population at the large settlement of Ayios Dhimitrios in the southern half of the valley, together with a considerable number of small sites stretching from the coast northward right up to near the copper mines.

Geometric period material was infrequently encountered during the course of the survey. Archaic period remains, on the other hand, occur widely throughout the valley, from near the mines down to the coast. Archaic sites are particularly numerous in the southern part of the valley, where settlements are located on the first terrace above the river and on some of the side streams; cemeteries are positioned on ridge tops and exposed bedrock areas of hill slopes in the vicinity of the settlements. The Classical period is poorly represented in the valley. The Hellenistic-Roman population of the valley was concentrated in three major settlements, two in the southern portion (Kalavasos-Kopetra and Sokopra) and one in the northern portion of the valley (Kalavasos-Spilios) close to the copper mines. Large slag heaps occur at Spilios and at the nearby site of Yirtomylos. Evidence for Roman period mining has also been located at the mines themselves. Medieval occupation is also attested widely in different parts of the valley.

The field survey has, therefore, demonstrated that settlement of the valley has been continuous for the past 9000 years or so with the notable exception of the period between the two Neolithic phases and perhaps also the Early Bronze Age, when occupation is not presently attested. The intensity of settlement clearly fluctuated, with peaks in the Middle Bronze and Archaic periods and phases of decline in the Geometric and Classical periods. The extent to which the pattern in the Vasilikos valley mirrors that in other parts of Cyprus remains to be determined, but it is very clear that the number of archaeological sites in an area such as the Vasilikos valley is vastly greater than was thought prior to the beginning of the survey a few years ago. This is an eloquent testimony to the need for further intensive field survey work in many areas of Cyprus, work that should be undertaken without delay in view of the rapidly changing agricultural landscape.

Results and Significance of the Research

During the past fourteen years archaeological excavations and field survey in the Vasilikos valley have been designed to provide information pertinent to the solution of the major problems of Cypriot prehistory. Although the project strategy has had to be modified on a number of occasions because of changing circumstances, the overall project aims have remained constant. Research in the valley is far from complete and a considerable period of future fieldwork is anticipated, probably with excavations at several different sites. Much effort is currently being directed toward the completion of the various excavation reports for publication, and an interim assessment of the achievements of the project is therefore timely. The following brief review of successes, failures, and outstanding problems will proceed in chronological order and will be restricted to the prehistoric period. Post-prehistoric problems are now being addressed by the staff of the Kalavasos-Kopetra project (cf. McClellan and Rautman 1989), a sister project of the V.V.P., and the results of the two projects are designed to be complementary.

The excavations at Tenta have illuminated various aspects of the Aceramic Neolithic period. New data were recovered concerning architecture, economy, and artifacts, and the first early prehistoric wall painting in Cyprus was discovered, probably depicting a rather fragmentary scene of two human figures side by side (Todd 1981). The artifacts included a scatter of obsidian blades or fragments thereof, indicating contact with the Anatolian mainland from which the raw material originated. One of the most important implications of the excavations relates to chronology. A mean settlement date of the mid–sixth millennium B.C.E. used to be assigned to the period (Stanley Price 1977: 69), but a series of radiocarbon dates from Tenta included dates as early as 7560 B.C.E. (5730 half-life, without recalibration), clearly indicating that an earlier date, at least for the beginning of the period, deserved serious consideration. The chronology of the Aceramic sites is not only of significance in itself, but it also has an important bearing on comparisons with the mainland (Todd 1985: 11). No evidence was found in the valley for pre-Aceramic Neolithic occupation, but such now appears to be attested in the Akrotiri Peninsula (Simmons 1989). No new data were retrieved concerning the origins of the settlers at the Aceramic Neolithic sites, and it is unclear whether or not there was continuity of settlement of the island between the period of Akrotiri Aetokremnos (ca. 8000 B.C.E.) and the occupation of sites such as Tenta (ca. 7000 B.C.E.?). At the end of the Aceramic Neolithic, the Tenta village was abandoned with no signs of widespread destruction. This confirms the situation at other sites. The complete lack of any evidence of settlement in the valley immediately following the end of the Aceramic Neolithic also mirrors the situation elsewhere, and the postulation of a gap in settlement over much if not all of Cyprus thus gains further credence.

Whereas in other regions of Cyprus, village settlements with substantial stone architecture have been found dating to the Ceramic Neolithic period ca. 4500 B.C.E. (Dikaios 1961 and Peltenburg 1982b), no architectural remains of this phase were found at Tenta, where a deep pit of uncertain purpose was the major Ceramic Neolithic feature encountered. Painted Combed Ware ceramics attest to the utilization of a small number of sites in the valley at this time, but the nature of the unexcavated sites is unknown. In the Early Chalcolithic period at Ayious there is also a total lack of standing structures, and it is possible that whatever factor was responsible for the avoidance of construction in stone in the Early Chalcolithic was also operative at an earlier date in the Kalavasos area. However, this is pure speculation and the situation can only be clarified by excavation at a suitable site.

Ayious is the only Chalcolithic site to have been extensively excavated in the Vasilikos valley, and it belongs to the early phase (ca. 3800 B.C.E.). In some respects the remains there offer parallels to the excavated features at Kissonerga-Mylouthkia in the Paphos region, where there are also pits (but generally larger than those at Ayious) (Peltenburg 1982a). Both sites are notable for a lack of preserved substantial standing structures, and it seems that this may have been a feature of Cypriot sites at this period. The strong contrast between the stone buildings of the Aceramic Neolithic (and the Ceramic Neolithic at Sotira-Teppes and Ayios Epiktitos-Vrysi) and the lack of these in the Early Chalcolithic supports the suggestion of a serious disruption at the end of the Ceramic Neolithic (Peltenburg 1982b). The Ayious excavations did not provide clear evidence indicating the reason for this disruption, although environmental deterioration remains a possibility. The Middle and Late Chalcolithic sequence recently documented in the Lemba-Kissonerga area north of Paphos (Peltenburg et al. 1987) is not so far evidenced in the Vasilikos valley, but Late Chalcolithic ceramics have been recognized there on the surface of several sites.

The problem of the nature of the Early Bronze Age (2500?–1900 B.C.E.) in the Vasilikos valley remains unresolved, as it does elsewhere in southern Cyprus (Herscher 1981: 81). If the present analysis is correct, there is a small but reasonable amount of Late Chalcolithic material in the valley, whereas there is virtually nothing that can be attributed to the Early Bronze Age. In contrast, large numbers of sites have been found during the field survey that may be dated to the Middle Bronze Age (Todd 1988, 1989). It could be argued that, for reasons unknown, the southern coastal zone of Cyprus was not occupied in the Early Bronze Age, but this seems an argument born of desperation. It is far more likely that among the surface collected pottery from the Vasilikos valley sites there is at least a modicum of Early Bronze Age material, but that it has so far remained unrecognized. Once again, the answer to this enigma can only be provided by further excavation.

The picture of the Middle Bronze Age (1900–1650 B.C.E.) in the Vasilikos valley and in southern Cyprus as a whole has changed dramatically in recent years. Catling's distribution map (1962: map after p. 144) shows no sites in the valley. The Bronze Age tombs in Kalavasos Village dated by Karageorghis to the Early Bronze Age (Karageorghis 1940–48) were then at least partially redated by Herscher to the Middle Cypriot period (Herscher 1976: 13) and numerous Middle Bronze Age sites were subsequently found by the field survey (cf. Todd 1989: fig. 1). The V.V.P. excavations of additional Middle Bronze Age tombs in Kalavasos Village amply demonstrated the wealth of this period in the valley. The ceramics provide evidence for extensive interregional connections, and although it cannot be proved, it is likely that the significance of the Kalavasos area in the Middle Bronze Age derives from the important copper deposits located north of Kalavasos Village. Excavation of one of the important settlement sites of this phase should cast light on the various Bronze Age problems that are still outstanding and provide antecedent information relevant to the Late Bronze Age site of Ayios Dhimitrios.

Views of the Late Bronze Age (1650–1050 B.C.E.) in the Kalavasos area have also been transformed in recent years as a result of the V.V.P. research. The existence of the town at Ayios Dhimitrios was unknown in 1976, and only a few Late Cypriot sites were known to Catling. The field survey in recent years has shown that there are also considerable numbers of Late Bronze Age sites in all parts of the valley, although these are probably not as numerous or, with the exception of Ayios Dhimitrios, as large as in the preceding Middle Bronze Age. The excavation of Building X and Tomb 11 at Ayios Dhimitrios has demonstrated the sophistication of Late Bronze Age life in an area where it had not previously been suspected. The existence of such an important center (which may be characterized as urban) at a strategic point in the Vasilikos valley in LC II must surely be connected with the acquisition of copper from the mines to the north of Kalavasos (South 1989: 322) and the supply of the material to the more important Late Bronze Age towns both at home and abroad. The relationship between the sites of Ayios Dhimitrios and nearby Maroni-Vournes (Cadogan 1988) remains to be established in detail, but both seem to have been abandoned at about the same time. Part of the Kalavasos Mine area is presently a restricted zone, but survey of the available mining area has not revealed any clear evidence of Late Bronze Age mining or metallurgical activities, although scattered sherds of this period do occur within a few hundred meters of fairly recent mining areas. If possible, further survey will be undertaken in the mining area, with Late Bronze Age considerations in mind.

The significance of the excavations and research in the Kalavasos area to date may now be examined within the broader Near Eastern context. Because of the central geographical position of the island, and despite the marked insularity of its inhabitants displayed in the earlier prehistoric phases, the data derived from major Cypriot excavation projects are of direct relevance to the mainland archaeological sequence and are of more than purely insular importance. The wide divergence between the prehistoric development of Cyprus and that of the various regions of the mainland has frequently been noted (e.g., Watkins 1981: 20; Todd in Todd and Croft forthcoming), and the research of the V.V.P. has not significantly altered this picture; it has, however, clarified the relationship with the mainland in some phases and suggested avenues for further enquiry.

In the Aceramic Neolithic phase, the Cypriot sites such as Tenta, with their curvilinear buildings, are greatly different from the mainland settlements of the seventh and sixth millennia B.C.E.[8] But if at least the beginning date for the Cypriot Aceramic is put back to the eighth millennium, a more plausible correlation can be postulated with the Pre-Pottery Neolithic A sites of the mainland, with their circular architecture (Todd 1985: 11). The excavations at Tenta and Ayious have also raised the question of the extent to which there may be a more general synchronism or parallel between the Cypriot archaeological record and that of Palestine, if not further north on the mainland. The gap following the end of the Cypriot Aceramic Neolithic might be mirrored in Palestine, where there is also a gap, together with uncertainty regarding the date of the subsequent Pottery Neolithic occupation.[9] It may also be significant that in the Early Chalcolithic phase in Cyprus (as it is known at present from the excavations at Kalavasos-Ayious and Kissonerga-Mylouthkia) and in the Chalcolithic period in the Beer-sheva region of Israel, subterranean features were widely employed for domestic or other purposes.[10] I have suggested elsewhere (Todd 1986b: 22) that the adoption of subterranean features in both areas may represent a similar reaction to the same conditions that affected both regions (whether the conditions be environmental or of some other nature), and this possibility needs to be investigated further.

Viewed from the mainland the greatest significance of the Vasilikos valley in the Bronze Age probably lay in its copper resources, and the recent V.V.P.

8. See Moore 1982 for a summary of the stages and characteristic features of the Neolithic sites in the Levant.

9. Moore (1982: 16) states that Palestine was "virtually deserted" for the earlier centuries of the sixth millennium B.C.E. Elsewhere (1983: 99), he postulates that environmental deterioration late in the seventh millennium B.C.E. was partly responsible for changes in the economy and settlement pattern in the Levant in Neolithic 3, which he dates 6000–5000 B.C.E. Further support for the existence of a gap prior to the Pottery Neolithic is provided by the striking change in architecture between the Pre-Pottery Neolithic B and the Pottery Neolithic A seen, for instance, at Jericho. The former period is characterized by well built mud-brick structures with a stone outer wall, the latter by pit dwellings (Kenyon 1979: chapters 2 and 3). The gap in the settlement of Palestine should be earlier in date than the gap in Cyprus, but this remains to be confirmed.

10. For the Beer-sheva region sites, see Perrot 1984. The use of the subterranean features in that area for habitation has recently been questioned by Gilead (1987), who suggests their use as storage facilities. The site of Ayious is probably approximately contemporary with sites such as Tell Abu Matar in the Beer-sheva area.

research has clarified the nature of settlement (size and density) in the valley in both Middle and Late Bronze Ages and revealed the presence of previously unknown major nucleations of population in both periods. As stated above the nature of Early Bronze Age occupation of the valley is unknown, and it is also unclear at what date the Kalavasos copper mines came into use. Middle and Late Bronze Age sites occur in the near vicinity of the mining area, but no evidence was found by the survey for actual Bronze Age mining or metallurgy at the mines themselves. Middle Bronze Age mining and metallurgical activities adjacent to the mine are attested at Ambelikou in NW Cyprus in MC I (nineteenth century B.C.E.) (Merrillees 1984), and more extensive survey of the entire Kalavasos mining area should be undertaken to try to resolve the problem of the earliest use of the mines. It seems very likely that the density of Middle Bronze Age sites in the Kalavasos area is to be connected with the mineral resources of the valley and the copper trade (Todd 1988: 140). While it may be true that the international trade in copper in the earlier centuries of the second millennium B.C.E. was on a comparatively small scale (Muhly, Maddin, and Stech 1988: 281), the almost continuous band of settlement (with at least several cemeteries) revealed by the field survey that stretches from south of Kalavasos Village northward to near the Kalavasos Mines on the west side of the valley (a distance of ca. 3.5 km) manifests the existence of very favorable conditions for Middle Bronze Age habitation, probably throughout all three phases of the period. From the agricultural point of view, the potential of the Vasilikos valley seems insufficient to warrant such a dense settlement pattern, and it seems clear to me that factors other than agriculture must have been operative, the most likely being copper mining and trade. A fragment of a crucible was found at Kalavasos-Laroumena (Todd 1989: 43), but no other evidence of metallurgy of proven Middle Bronze Age date has yet been found on sites in the valley.

The situation in the Vasilikos valley in the early part of the Late Bronze Age is not as clear as it was in the preceding Middle Bronze Age or as it is in LC II (especially LC IIC). LC I (ca. 1650–1475 B.C.E.) is represented only by a very small number of tombs and a handful of surface sherds on several sites;[11] no settlement evidence of this date has yet been excavated, and there is no clear evidence to indicate the significance of mining or metallurgy at this point. The tombs at the site of Ayios Dhimitrios cover all phases from LC IB through LC IIC, but the excavated settlement remains date only to LC

11. See South 1987 for a brief summary of the Late Bronze Age in the valley, with relevant references. See Todd 1989 for the most recent field survey results. The settlement and cemetery site of Kalavasos-Mitsingites may have continued in use into LC IA.

IIC. Presumably a somewhat earlier settlement area exists in the vicinity of Ayios Dhimitrios, but if so, it still awaits discovery. In view of the fact that Muhly, Maddin, and Stech have recently suggested (1988: 291) that Cypriot copper ingots only became a factor in the East Mediterranean metals trade in the thirteenth century B.C.E. (contemporary with the settlement at Ayios Dhimitrios), and that only at Enkomi is there evidence of extensive copper production in the sixteenth through the fourteenth centuries (Muhly, Maddin, and Stech 1988: 294), the discovery of the richly furnished Tomb 11 at Ayios Dhimitrios (dated to LC IIA:2, ca. 1375 B.C.E., contemporary with the Amarna period in Egypt) is of particular importance. It indicates the presence in the Vasilikos valley of people of high status with considerable wealth prior to the thirteenth century, and such wealth might also have been derived from the metals trade. If the equation of the ancient name of Alašiya with the island of Cyprus is accepted,[12] there is plentiful textual evidence for the overseas trading of copper from the island during the second millennium B.C.E. This includes the Amarna letters, which refer to Cypriot copper (and other goods) being sent to Egypt. Only future excavation of the settlement contemporary with Tomb 11 will show whether the Vasilikos valley was important in the supply of copper in the fourteenth century B.C.E. (and perhaps earlier).

The excavations at Ayios Dhimitrios and the field survey data have provided a picture of the Vasilikos valley in the thirteenth century B.C.E. as extensively occupied, with numerous small settlements or farmsteads with a single large (11.5 hectare) urban centre at Ayios Dhimitrios. Ingot fragments, metal artifacts, and furnace conglomerate all attest to the significance of metallurgy there, and the inhabitants of the site must have played an important role in supplying copper at a time of great international demand. The period was clearly prosperous, but the Ayios Dhimitrios settlement was short-lived and the site was abandoned at the end of LC II. No remains of the succeeding LC III period have been recognized anywhere in the valley. The reasons for this apparent abandonment are unknown, and it is notable that evidence of overall destruction of the site is lacking, evidence of fire only being found in the administrative Building X. The comparative lack of destruction and the short duration of the settlement (as so far excavated) set the site of Ayios Dhimitrios apart from other major Cypriot Late Bronze Age centers such as Kition, Hala Sultan Tekke, and Enkomi, where occupation continued in LC III. A momentous change appears to have occurred in the

12. For recent discussion of this equation see Muhly, Maddin, and Stech 1988: 292–94; see also Merrillees 1987, a reference quoted by Muhly, Maddin, and Stech, but not available to the writer.

settlement of the Vasilikos valley at about the end of LC II, ca. 1200 B.C.E., and occupation was not revived on a large scale until the Cypro-Archaic period 500 years or so later.

The recent years of archaeological research in the Vasilikos valley summarized in this paper have greatly enhanced our knowledge of prehistoric settlement in Cyprus, but more importantly they have also contributed to the understanding of the relationship between Cyprus and its mainland neighbors. The resources of the valley pertinent to the solution of the major problems of the Cypriot archaeological sequence have by no means been exhausted, and it is hoped that the continuation of the Vasilikos Valley Project for a number of future seasons will result in the further enrichment of the archaeology of the island and of the eastern Mediterranean region as a whole. Future excavations at Ayios Dhimitrios may be expected to cast further light on the international metals trade in the Late Bronze Age, a trade that encompassed the whole of the Aegean and Near Eastern world, and hopefully also on the mechanics of the mining and trade within Cyprus itself. Despite the very small size of the island, the significance of archaeological research there is often disproportionately large and stretches far beyond its shores. It is a privilege for a foreign archaeologist to work on the island, but the results of the research, however successful, are but scant repayment for the boundless hospitality and kindness of the Cypriot people.

Bibliography

Cadogan, G.

1988 Maroni IV. *Report of the Department of Antiquities Cyprus* (1988) part 1: 229–31.

Catling, H. W.

1962 Patterns of Settlement in Bronze Age Cyprus. *Opuscula Atheniensia* 4: 129–69.

Courtois, J-C.

1983 Le Trésor de poids de Kalavasos-Ayios Dhimitrios 1982. *Report of the Department of Antiquities Cyprus* (1983) 117–30.

Dikaios, P.

1953 *Khirokitia.* London: Oxford University Press.

1961 *Sotira.* Philadelphia: University Museum, University of Pennsylvania.

1962 The Stone Age. Pp. 1–204 in *The Swedish Cyprus Expedition*, volume 4, part 1A. Lund: Swedish Cyprus Expedition.

Gilead, I.
1987 A New Look at Chalcolithic Beer-Sheba. *BA* 50: 110–17.

Herscher, E.
1976 South Coast Ceramic Styles at the End of Middle Cypriote. *Report of the Department of Antiquities Cyprus* (1976) 11–19.
1981 Southern Cyprus, the Disappearing Early Bronze Age, and the Evidence from Phaneromeni. Pp. 79–85 in J. C. Biers and D. Soren (eds.), *Studies in Cypriote Archaeology.* Los Angeles: Institute of Archaeology, University of California.

Karageorghis, V.
1940–48 Finds from Early Cypriote Cemeteries. *Report of the Department of Antiquities Cyprus* (1940–48) 115–52.

Kenyon, K. M.
1979 *Archaeology in the Holy Land.* 4th ed. London: Ernest Benn.

Masson, E.
1983 Premiers Documents Chypro-Minoens du Site Kalavasos-Ayios Dhimitrios. *Report of the Department of Antiquities Cyprus* (1983) 131–41.

McClellan, M. C., and M. L. Rautman
1989 The 1987 and 1988 Field Seasons of the Kalavasos-Kopetra Project. *Report of the Department of Antiquities Cyprus* (1989) 157–66.

Merrillees, R. S.
1984 Ambelikou-Aletri: A Preliminary Report. *Report of the Department of Antiquities Cyprus* (1984) 1–13.
1987 *Alashia Revisited.* Cahiers de la Revue Biblique 22. Paris: Gabalda.

Moore, A. M. T.
1982 A Four-Stage Sequence for the Levantine Neolithic, ca. 8500–3750 B.C. *BASOR* 246: 1–34.
1983 The First Farmers in the Levant. Pp. 91–111 in T. C. Young, P. E. L. Smith, and P. Mortensen (eds.), *The Hilly Flanks and Beyond.* Studies in Ancient Oriental Civilizations 36. Chicago: The Oriental Institute.

Morris, D.
1985 *The Art of Ancient Cyprus.* Oxford: Phaidon.

Muhly, J. D., Maddin, R., and Stech, T.
1988 Cyprus, Crete and Sardinia: Copper Ox-Hide Ingots and the Bronze Age Metals Trade. *Report of the Department of Antiquities Cyprus* (1988) part 1: 281–98.

Pearlman, D.
1985 Kalavasos Village Tomb 51: Tomb of an Unknown Soldier. *Report of the Department of Antiquities Cyprus* (1985) 164–79

Peltenburg, E. J.
1982a *Recent Developments in the Later Prehistory of Cyprus.* Gothenburg: Åströms.
1982b *Vrysi: A Subterranean Settlement in Cyprus.* Warminster: Aris & Phillips.

Peltenburg, E. J., et al.

1987 Excavations at Kissonerga-Mosphilia 1986. *Report of the Department of Antiquities Cyprus* (1987) 1–18.

Peltenburg, E. J., ed.

1989 *Early Society in Cyprus.* Edinburgh: Edinburgh University Press.

Perrot, J.

1984 Structures d'habitat, mode de la vie et environnement: Les villages souterrains des pasteurs de Beershéva, dans le Sud d'Israel, au IVe millénaire avant l'ère chrétienne. *Paléorient* 10: 75–96.

Simmons, A.

1989 Preliminary Report on the 1988 Test Excavations at Akrotiri-Aetokremnos. *Report of the Department of Antiquities Cyprus* (1989) 1–5.

South, A. K.

1980 Kalavasos-Ayios Dhimitrios 1979: A Summary Report. *Report of the Department of Antiquities Cyprus* (1980) 22–53.

1982 Kalavasos-Ayios Dhimitrios 1980–1981. *Report of the Department of Antiquities Cyprus* (1982) 60–68.

1983 Kalavasos-Ayios Dhimitrios 1982. *Report of the Department of Antiquities Cyprus* (1983) 92–116.

1984a Kalavasos-Ayios Dhimitrios 1983. *Report of the Department of Antiquities Cyprus* (1984) 14–41.

1984b Riches of Late Bronze Age Cyprus. *ASOR Newsletter* 36/2: 3–5.

1985 Figurines and Other Objects from Kalavasos-Ayious. *Levant* 17: 65–79.

1987 Contacts and Contrasts in Late Bronze Age Cyprus: The Vasilikos Valley and the West. Pp. 83–91 in D. W. Rupp (ed.), *Western Cyprus: Connections.* Gothenburg: Åströms.

1988 Kalavasos-Ayios Dhimitrios 1987: An Important Ceramic Group from Building X. *Report of the Department of Antiquities Cyprus* (1988) part 1: 223–28.

1989 From Copper to Kingship: Aspects of Bronze Age Society Viewed from the Vasilikos Valley. Pp. 315–24 in E. J. Peltenburg (ed.), *Early Society in Cyprus.* Edinburgh: Edinburgh University Press.

South, A. K., P. Russell, and P. S. Keswani

1989 *Vasilikos Valley Project 3: Kalavasos-Ayios Dhimitrios II: Ceramics, Objects, Tombs, Specialist Studies.* Gothenburg: Åströms.

Stanley Price, N. P.

1977 Khirokitia and the Initial Settlement of Cyprus. *World Archaeology* 9: 66–89.

Todd, I. A.

1977 Vasilikos Valley Project: First Preliminary Report, 1976. *Report of the Department of Antiquities Cyprus* (1977) 5–32.

1978 Vasilikos Valley Project: Second Preliminary Report, 1977. *Journal of Field Archaeology* 5: 161–95.

1979 Vasilikos Valley Project: Third Preliminary Report, 1978. *Journal of Field Archaeology* 6: 265–300.

1981 A Cypriote Neolithic Wall Painting. *Antiquity* 55: 47–51.

1982 Vasilikos Valley Project: Fourth Preliminary Report, 1979–1980. *Journal of Field Archaeology* 9: 35–77.

1985 The Vasilikos Valley and the Chronology of the Neolithic/Chalcolithic Periods in Cyprus. *Report of the Department of Antiquities Cyprus* (1985) 1–15.

1986a Vasilikos Valley Project: Fifth Preliminary Report, 1980–1984. *Report of the Department of Antiquities Cyprus* (1986) 12–27.

1986b The Foreign Relations of Cyprus in the Neolithic/Chalcolithic Periods: New Evidence from the Vasilikos Valley. Pp. 12–24 in *Acts of the International Archaeological Symposium "Cyprus between the Orient and the Occident."* Nicosia: Department of Antiquities.

1987 *Vasilikos Valley Project 6: Excavations at Kalavasos-Tenta I.* Gothenburg: Åströms.

1988 The Middle Bronze Age in the Kalavasos Area. *Report of the Department of Antiquities Cyprus* (1988) part 1: 133–40.

1989 The 1988 Field Survey in the Vasilikos Valley. *Report of the Department of Antiquities Cyprus* (1989) 41–50.

Todd, I. A., and P. Croft

forthcoming *Vasilikos Valley Project 8: Excavations at Kalavasos-Ayious.* Gothenburg: Åströms.

Todd, I. A., ed.

1986 *Vasilikos Valley Project 1: The Bronze Age Cemetery in Kalavasos Village*, Gothenburg: Åströms.

Watkins, T.

1981 The Chalcolithic Period in Cyprus: The Background to Current Research. Pp. 9–20 in J. Reade (ed.), *Chalcolithic Cyprus and Western Asia.* London: British Museum.

*The "Word Pair" *qšt and *mṭ in Habakkuk 3:9 in the Light of Ugaritic and Akkadian*

D. T. Tsumura

In this short study I reexamine the items in the Ugaritic "word pair" *mṭ-qšt* on the basis of their Akkadian cognates so that Hab 3:9 might be better understood.

Ugaritic

It has been suggested that *mṭ* and *qšt* appear as a word pair in the Ugaritic mythological text KTU 1.3 [ᶜnt]: II:15–16, which reads (with Gordon's translation):

mṭm.tgrš / šbm.	With a stick she drives out *foes*
bksl.qšth.mdnt	Her bow *attacking* in the back (i.e., of her fleeing foes)

C. H. Gordon seems to take *mṭ* 'stick' and *qšt* 'bow' as a corresponding pair in this text.[1] M. Dahood, one of the first scholars to consider *mṭ* and *qšt* as a "word pair" common to Ugaritic and Hebrew, made this comment on Hab 3:9, the passage where *qešet* and *maṭṭôt* appear in parallel: "Though the line remains obscure, any advance in its understanding must take this [Ugaritic] parallelism into account."[2] F. M. Cross also takes this pair as "a formulaic

Author's note: It is a great pleasure for me to dedicate this modest article to my teacher and friend, Prof. D. W. Young, who stimulated me through his excellent scholarship and careful teaching. Both in literary studies and in linguistics I learned the valuable skills of applying the comparative method for analysis of texts, biblical and ancient Near Eastern.

1. C. H. Gordon, "Poetic Legends and Myths from Ugarit," *Berytus* 25 (1977) 77.

2. M. Dahood, "Ugaritic-Hebrew Parallel Pairs," *Ras Shamra Parallels* 1 (AnOr 49; Rome: Pontifical Biblical Institute, 1972) 258.

pair."[3] Most recently T. Hiebert, following Cross, also took the pair as "formulaic" in Hebrew and Ugaritic and suggested that "the key to understanding this line [Hab 3:9] is the relationship between *mṭ* [in v. 9b] and *qšt* [in v. 9a]."[4]

While it is certainly possible that in Hab 3:9 *qešet*, the term for 'bow,' is parallel to *maṭṭôt*, the Ugaritic term *mṭm* does not seem to be the exact counterpart of *qšt* in KTU 1.3 [ᶜnt]: II:15–16. Rather, the term *mṭ* is probably better understood as parallel to the phrase *ksl qšth* and *šb* as parallel to *mdnt* in this text, hence with the parallel structure a-b-c//A′-c′.[5]

Following this analysis, O. Loretz[6] translates the text:

> Mit einem Stock vertrieb sie die Angreifer,[7]
> mit der Sehne[8] ihres Bogens die Widersacher.

In his most recent translation,[9] J. C. de Moor uses the same structure, though individual terms are interpreted differently:

> With a staff she chased the old men
> with the stave[10] of her bow the veterans.[11]

The structure a-b-c//A′-c′, with the ellipsis of b′ (= VP), can be recognized in texts such as KTU 1.14: III:12–14[Krt 116–118] (Gibson's translation):

ḥẓk.al.tšᶜl / qrth.	do not discharge your arrows into the town,
abn.ydk / mšdpt	(nor) your slingstones (into) the citadel.[12]

3. F. M. Cross, *Canaanite Myth and Hebrew Epic* (Cambridge: Harvard University Press, 1973) 23 n. 59.

4. T. Hiebert, *God of My Victory: The Ancient Hymn in Habakkuk 3* (HSM 38; Atlanta: Scholars Press, 1986) 26.

5. A′: a ballast variant; b′: ellipsis. Grammatically, it may be analyzed as AdvPh-VP-NP(O)//AdvPh-NP(O). This pattern is well attested for Ugaritic poetic texts; cf. C. H. Gordon, *UT* 142 (13.157).

6. O. Loretz, "Ugaritische und hebräische Lexikographie," *UF* 12 (1980) 282.

7. See ibid., 282 on various interpretations of *šbm.*

8. Loretz follows M. Held's view: 'string'; cf. "Ugaritische und hebräische Lexikographie," 283 n. 58.

9. J. C. de Moor, *An Anthology of Religious Texts from Ugarit* (Nisaba 16; Leiden: Brill, 1987) 6.

10. For this interpretation, see J. C. de Moor, "The Anatomy of the Back," *UF* 12 (1980) 425.

11. See J. C. de Moor, "Ugaritic Smalltalk," *UF* 17 (1985) 222.

12. J. C. L. Gibson, *Canaanite Myths and Legends* (2d ed.; Edinburgh: T. & T. Clark, 1977) 85; note that Arabic *šadafa* means 'to be tall'.

Thus, it seems that, strictly speaking, the term *qšt* does not correspond to the term *mṭ* in KTU 1.3 [ᶜnt]: II:15–16 and that the text does not support the view that these two terms constitute a "formulaic pair" in Ugaritic.

mṭm: 'arrows'?

Cross and Hiebert[13] take *mṭm* as a plural form meaning 'arrows' in parallel with *qšt* 'bow' in KTU 1.3[ᶜnt]: II:15–16 and in Hab 3:9. Hiebert supports his position by referring to de Moor's earlier explanation: "In line 15 *mṭm* should be 'with her darts', because next to *bksl qšth* 'with the string of her bow' the word *mṭ* 'rod' can only be meant as a poetic designation of the arrow, as in Hab. 3:9, 14."[14] J. Day also translates *maṭṭôt* in Hab 3:9 as 'arrows'.[15] In a similar manner J. Gibson quotes Hab 3:9, 14 to explain the Ugaritic term *mṭm* and translates it 'shaft(s)'.[16]

However, as noted above, Gordon, Loretz, de Moor, and others[17] translate the word *mṭ* as 'stick, staff, rod', taking the suffixed *-m* as an adverbial enclitic *mem*[18] rather than as a plural ending. This interpretation is better supported, for the following reasons:

1. the term *mṭ* usually means 'a staff, stick, or rod' in Hebrew,[19] while its Akkadian cognate *miṭṭu* never refers to 'arrow(s)';[20]
2. a preposition is sometimes replaced in a poetic parallelism by the enclitic *mem* in Ugaritic;[21]
3. the verb *grš* 'to drive out' is also used when Baal drove out Yam with his 'stick, war club'[22] or 'mace'[23] (*ṣmd*) in KTU 1.2: IV[68]:12; arrows are never used for 'driving out' enemies in Hebrew[24] or in Ugaritic;

13. Cross, *Canaanite Myth and Hebrew Epic*, 23 n. 59; Hiebert, *God of My Victory*, 28.

14. J. C. de Moor, "(Review of) Arvid S. Kapelrud, *The Violent Goddess* . . . Oslo 1969," *UF* 1 (1969) 226.

15. J. Day, *God's Conflict with the Dragon and the Sea: Echoes of a Canaanite Myth in the Old Testament* (Cambridge: Cambridge University Press, 1985) 106.

16. Gibson, *Canaanite Myths and Legends*, 47.

17. A. Caquot, M. Sznycer, and A. Herdner, *Textes Ougaritiques* 1 (LAPO 7; Paris: du Cerf, 1974) 159 and note q; G. del Olmo Lete, *Mitos y leyendas de Canaan* (Madrid: Ediciones Cristiandad, 1981) 181, 576–77.

18. That is, 'with a staff' (Gordon, *UT* 443 [19.1642]).

19. BDB 641.

20. See below.

21. For example, KTU 1.14: II:13–15 [Krt 66–68], III:55–57 [Krt 159–161].

22. Gordon, *UT* 474 (19.2168).

23. Gordon, *UT* 537.

24. Note, however, that Josh 24:12 suggests the usual practice of 'driving out' the enemy with 'sword' (*ḥereb*) and 'bow' (*qešet*). While it is possible to take *mṭm*, if it means

4. the term *ksl*, which normally means 'the back',[25] the 'curved spine', would refer to the 'stave' (of a bow)[26] rather than the 'string';
5. in the poetic structure, a-b-c//A′-c′, 'arrows' for *mṭm*(a) would be less preferable as a parallel term for the expression 'the stave of a bow' *bksl.qšth* (A′) than 'a staff' or the like.

Even if one agrees that *mṭ* in Ugaritic refers to a weapon used in actual battle along with a bow (*qšt*), this does not automatically support the view that the term *mṭm* when used with *qšt* ('bow') in poetic parallelism means 'arrows' in Ugaritic. As Pope holds, "the parallelism of *mṭ* and *qšt* is no proof of synonymy, nor is it in Hab 3:9."[27] Since the two terms are not in exact parallelism with each other, the "synonymous" interpretation should not be accepted uncritically.

As for the term *mṭ* in KTU 1.23[52]: 37, 40, 44, 47, which Cross and Hiebert argue is another case of the use of *mṭ* for 'arrow',[28] there is no contextual reason why we should take it as meaning 'arrow'. Since the paired term, *ḫṭ*, refers to a kind of staff[29] or weapon[30] other than 'a bow', the term *mṭ* here also most likely has the usual meaning 'a staff, stick, or rod', rather than 'an arrow'.[31] This meaning, 'a staff, stick, or rod', for *mṭ* is also supported by its Akkadian cognate, *miṭṭu*.

'arrows', as part of the 'bow' and hence as intruments by which Anat 'drives out' her enemy in our Ugaritic text, Josh 24:12 rather suggests that *mṭ*, taken as 'a staff', and *qšt* 'a bow' are a similar pair of weapons by which a king or a warrior god/goddess would 'drive out' his/her enemy. In other words, 'staff' and 'bow' (lit., 'bowstave') are a better set of weapons for driving out enemies than 'arrows' and 'a bowstave' (see below).

25. Gordon, *UT* 421 (19.1280). Note another term, *bmt*, for 'back (of an animal or person)' (*UT* 373 [19.480]); cf. 'rib cage (= thorax), ribs' for *bmt* in A. F. Rainey, "Observations on Ugaritic Grammar," *UF* 3 (1971) 170.

26. Cf. de Moor, "The Anatomy of the Back," 425.

27. M. H. Pope, "Ups and Downs in El's Amours," *UF* 11 (1979) 706.

28. Cross, *Canaanite Myth and Hebrew Epic*, 23; Hiebert, *God of My Victory*, 28.

29. That is, 'staff, scepter' (Gordon, *UT* 401 [19.950]) or 'club' (554 [19.1710]). Note also that the Akkadian *ḫaṭṭu* means 'scepter, staff, stick'; cf. CAD Ḫ 154–55.

30. Cf. D. T. Tsumura, "A Ugaritic God, *MT-w-ŠR*, and His Two Weapons (*UT* 52:8–11," *UF* 6 (1974) 408 n.19.

31. Cross takes *ḫt* and *mṭ* in this text as 'bowstave' and 'shaft'; cf. *Canaanite Myth and Hebrew Epic*, 23 nn. 57, 59. He cites 2 Sam 22:35 for the "idiom" *nḥt qšt* 'to bend or stretch a bow' and renders the Ugaritic *il.ḫth.nḥt* as 'El bends his bowstave', but the biblical usage is "unique and problematic," as Pope comments; see M. H. Pope, "The Status of El at Ugarit," *UF* 19 (1987) 226; "Ups and Downs in El's Amours," 706. It should be noted that the term *ḫṭ* in KTU 1.19:I [1Aqht]: 14, which Cross cites in support of the meaning 'bowstave', probably means 'stick', not in the particular sense of 'bowstave', when

Akkadian

The Akkadian *miṭṭu* appears as a weapon in a god's hand with the sense 'staff' or 'mace', the Sumerian counterpart of which is giš.tukul.dingir ('a weapon of gods').[32] It is grouped with *ḫaṭṭu* 'scepter' several times[33] but is clearly distinguished from 'arrow' (*uṣṣu, mulmullu*)[34] and 'quiver' (*išpatu*)[35] and, like Ugaritic *mṭ*, seems never to mean 'an arrow'.

The mace, the god's majestic weapon, is sometimes mentioned as "the fifty-headed mace" in Sumerian, using the Akkadian loanword mitum (= *miṭṭum*), that is, giš.mi.tum.sag.50, mi.tum sag.ninnu, and others.[36] This expression appears in a description of Ninurta in a fully Sumerian expression, namely, giš.tukul.sag.ninnu (Angim III 36). Unfortunately, its Akkadian version is broken, but it is almost certain that the lacuna should be restored as having the Akkadian term *miṭṭu* written either syllabically or in Sumerograms.[37]

Lines 34–37 read as follows:

(34) mir lú.ra te.a.ta giš.pan a.ma.uru$_5$.mu:
(35) *šibba ša ana amēli iṭeḫḫû qaštu [abūbija]*
(I hold) the serpent which attacks man, the bow of my *abūbu* weapon
(36) a.má.uru$_5$.mè.a giš.tukul.sag.ninnu.mu:
(37) *abūb tāḫazi* [. . . . .]
(I hold) *abūbu*-of-Battle,[38] the mace with the fifty heads
(Angim III 34–37)[39]

---

used with *klb* 'a dog' and *mḫṣ* 'to strike'. Note Akkadian expressions: 'may the sorceress be chased away *kīma kalbi ina ḫaṭṭi* (GIŠ.PA) with a stick like a dog' (Maqlu V 43) and 'to strike with a stick' (**maḫāṣu* + *ina ḫaṭṭi* [GIŠ.GAR.PA]), cited by CAD Ḫ 155.

32. That is, 'the divine weapon' (CAD M/2 148; also CAD K 398). Cf. J. van Dijk, LUGAL UD ME-LÁM-*bi* NIR-GÁL: *Le récit épique et didactique des Travaux de Ninurta, du Déluge et de la Nouvelle Création* (Leiden: Brill, 1983) 52, line 5, which reads *bēlu ša ina qātišu elletum meṭṭa našû* 'le Seigneur dont le bras puissant fut prédestiné à (porter) l'arme meurtrière'.

33. See CAD M/2 148; K 398.

34. Cf. AHw 1439; CAD M/2 190–91.

35. Cf. CAD I/J 257–58.

36. Cf. CAD M/2 148.

37. Note, however, that ^{d}GIŠ.TUKUL SAG.NINNU is once identified with *kakku rešt[û] ša* ^{d}50 (= ^{d}EN.LIL) in BBR no. 27 rev. i 1ff., cf. CAD K 51.

38. For a similar phrase, *abūb tamḫāri* 'Deluge of Battle', see CAD A/1 79; AHw 8, 1314.

39. Cf. CAD A/1 79 and Q 147.

The last line (line 37) may be compared with the Sumerian phrase mi.tum giš.a.ma.ru (SAKI 128 Cyl. B vii 14)[40] 'the mace, the *abūbu* weapon' and a similar Akkadian phrase in a hymn to Marduk, [*mi*]*ṭṭukka abū*[*bu*] (KAR 337:14)[41] 'your mace, *abūbu* weapon'. In the present text, this *abūbu* weapon is also associated with 'bow' (*qaštu*) in line 35, thus combining both 'bow' and 'mace' as the two *abūbu* weapons in the hands of Ninurta. In other words, both 'mace' and 'bow' are described here as the two major weapons of a warrior god in Mesopotamia.[42]

This description matches well the image of another warrior god, Assur, "who is raising his bow, riding in his chariot and girt with the Deluge (*abūbu* [*ṣ*]*andu*)," as described in the text of the Annals of Sennacherib.[43] It is almost certain that the *abūbu*-weapon here refers to the mace (*miṭṭu*, mi.tum, giš.tukul, or giš.tukul.dingir) of Assur,[44] like those of Marduk and Ninurta[45] mentioned above.

These two weapons are probably those mentioned as granted to the human king Tiglath-pileser I by the warrior gods in the following text:

> *Ninurta u Nergal* GIŠ.TUKUL.MEŠ-*su-nu ezzūte u* GIŠ.BAN-*su-nu ṣīrta ana idi bēlūtija išruku*
> Ninurta and Nergal granted me their fierce weapons and their sublime bow to be worn at my lordly side (AKA 84 vi 59)[46]

Here, 'their weapons' (GIŠ.TUKUL.MEŠ-*šunu*) most likely refer to their 'maces', since Akkadian *miṭṭu* 'mace' is usually written in Sumerograms as GIŠ.TUKUL.DINGIR ('a weapon of gods') and the mace along with the bow is the weapon par excellence of a warrior god.[47]

40. Cited by CAD A/1 79.

41. Cited in CAD M/2 148.

42. It should be noted that *abūbu* symbolizes the destructive power of the warrior deity, not of an enemy such as Tiamat, Yam–Nahar, etc. See my "'The Deluge' (*mabbûl*) in Psalm 29:10," *UF* 20 (1988) 351–55.

43. OIP 2 140:7; cf. CAD A/1 80; CAD Q 150.

44. Note that the verbal adjective *ṣandu* also appears with weapons, which most likely mean 'maces' in the following text: *ummānišu . . . kakkēšunu ṣandūma* 'his army marched at his side, with their weapons tied up' (5R 35:16 [Cyr.]), cited by CAD Ṣ 92. See below on *kakku* as 'mace'.

45. The *abūbu*-weapon in the following text also probably refers to the mace of Nergal: "Nergal *šar tamḫāri bēl abāri u dunni bēl abūbi* king of the battle, lord of strength and might, lord of the Deluge (weapon)" (Streck Asb. 178:2); cf. CAD A/1 80.

46. Cf. CAD K 54.

47. Cf. CAD M/2 147–48. Note that GIŠ.TUKUL.DINGIR can also stand for Akkadian *kakku* 'weapon' (cf. CAD K 50–51) but, as CAD K 57 comments, "it seems that originally

A similar pair, *qaštu* ('bow') and *kakku* ('weapon'), is mentioned in a context that commands actual preparation for battle. Thus,

> *anantam kiṣṣar q[ašt]am iši šar[da]ppa turu[ṣ] kak[ka] tumu[ḫ]*
> get ready for battle, take up the bow, pull taut the reins, grasp the mace
> (2N-T343 rev. 6) [48]

The third action, 'to pull taut the reins', is definitely related to riding a war chariot. Thus, the three items—'bow', 'reins' (which stand for a chariot) and 'weapon' (*kakku*)—correspond exactly to the order of the three items—'bow', 'chariot', and 'the *abūbu*-weapon' (i.e., the mace)—that describe Assur's war activity.

In light of the above, it seems likely that the two terms 'bow' (*qaštu*) and 'mace' (*miṭṭu, kakku*) constitute a word pair in Akkadian, since they are the two major weapons in the hands of a king and also of a warrior god like Ninurta or Nergal. The Ugaritic warrior goddess Anat may also be taken as holding these two weapons in her hands in KTU 1.3[ᶜnt]: II:15–16.

Hebrew

The same pair appears in Hebrew in Hab 3:9, which reads:

ᶜryh tᶜwr qštk
šbᶜwt mṭwt ᵓmr

This is one of the most difficult passages in the entire Hebrew Bible, "a riddle which all the ingenuity of scholars has not been able to solve." [49] Unlike the other terms in v. 9, *qešet* and *maṭṭôt* are normally treated without emendation. While the meaning of *qešet* has never been doubted, *maṭṭôt* has been translated various ways, for example, as 'tribes', 'rods', 'shafts', 'arrows', or 'spears'. Modern scholars who emend the text [50] tend to take it as 'arrows' or the like, since they consider that the term is parallel to *qešet* 'bow' in v. 9a.

GIŠ.TUKUL denoted a mace or mace-like weapon (a stick with a stone or bitumen mace head), later on a dagger or the like worn in the belt."

48. CAD Q 147–48 and CAD K 51.

49. Davidson, cited by G. A. Smith, *The Book of the Twelve Prophets* (New York: A. C. Armstrong, 1899) 155. The syntactical structure of Hab 3:9a is discussed in detail in D. T. Tsumura, "Niphal with an Internal Object in Hab 3, 9a," *JSS* 31 (1986) 11–16.

50. The following are various suggestions and conjectural translations apparently based on emended texts:

(1) *šibᶜat* 'seven': 'seven arrows with a word' (Day assumes here "a reference to Yahweh's seven shafts or arrows of lightning" and compares them to Yahweh's seven thunders,

It should be noted, however, that elsewhere in Hebrew *maṭṭeh* has been taken as meaning 'staff' or 'rod' as in *mṭh* ᵓ*lhym* 'the staff of God' (Exod 4:20), and BDB (p. 641) suggests that Habakkuk 3 (vv. 9, 14) is a lone exception by its comment: "appar. *shafts*, i.e., arrows or spears, Hb 3:9, 14." However, as noted above, there is no support from cognate languages for taking this term as 'arrows'. Moreover, there is no proof that *maṭṭeh*, when paired with 'bow', means 'arrows', even when they are a word pair. Furthermore, in Hab 3:11 the words for 'arrow' and 'spear' appear as *ḥṣyk* 'your arrows' and *ḥnytk* 'your spear'.

Two objections against taking *maṭṭôt* (v. 9) as 'staff or mace' have been raised by scholars: "the plural form of *mṭ*" and "its use with *nqb* in v. 14a." On the first, Hiebert comments: "The divine warrior is never pictured carrying more than one mace into battle."[51] However, as noted above, Tiglath-pileser I is said to have been granted the fierce weapons (a plural form: GIŠ.TUKUL.MEŠ) by Ninurta and Nergal "to be worn at [his] lordly side." Another possibility is that the form *maṭṭôt* could be a "plural of intensity" and may possibly refer to a divine majestic 'mace' or 'staff' in the present context, because it is often described as "the fifty-headed mace" in Sumero-Akkadian expressions. It should be noted that an actual "gold mace-head with twelve mushroom-shaped knobs (heads)" from the Early Bronze period has been excavated in Alaçahöyük in central Anatolia.[52] The Hebrew *maṭṭôt* in Hab 3:9 could refer to a majestic mace of Yahweh. Therefore I would suggest the following translation of Hab 3:9b: 'the seven-headed mace *is* (your) word', taking *šb*ᶜ*wt* as 'heptad, sevenfold'.[53]

As for the second objection, Hiebert holds that "a mace would not 'pierce,' *nqb*, the head of the enemy, while arrows would."[54] However, it may

---

which he thinks are depicted in Psalm 29; cf. J. Day, "Echoes of Baal's Seven Thunders and Lightnings in Psalm xxix and Habakkuk iii 9 and the Identity of the Seraphim in Isaiah vi," *VT* 29 [1979] 146–47; *God's Conflict with the Dragon and the Sea*, 106–7);

(2) *śibba*ᶜ*tâ* 'thou hast sated with shafts thy quiver (ᵓ*šptk*): (Nowack); 'and charge thy quiver with shafts' (NEB); 'thy bow was satiated with shafts' (Marti). Cf. BHS: 𝔊 Barb ἐχόρτασας 𝔖 *wnsb*ᶜ*wn*;

(3) 'and put the arrows to the string' (RSV).

51. Hiebert, *God of My Victory*, 28.

52. Cf. The Middle Eastern Culture Center in Japan (ed.), *Land of Civilizations, Turkey* (Tokyo: Middle Eastern Culture Center, 1985) pl. 56.

53. Note a similar description of a divine word as a 'mace': "sein Wort ist *a-bu-bu* (// *a-ma-ru*) *tēbû*" (SBH: 4, 21), cited in AHw 8. Note also *ṣmd* 'double-headed axe'?, cf. J. C. de Moor, "The Semitic Pantheon of Ugarit," *UF* 2 (1970) 225.

54. Hiebert, *God of My Victory*, 28.

be suggested that the term *maṭṭāyw*[55] (v. 14a) refers to 'sticks' rather than 'maces' in its context. While it is 'Yahweh's majestic mace' *maṭṭôt* (v. 9b) that would 'crush' (**mḥṣ*) the head (*rōˀš*) in v. 13b, sticks would 'pierce' (**nqb*) the head (*rōˀš*) in v. 14a. It should be noted, however, that the use of the verb *nqb* here does not justify positing an exceptional meaning 'arrow' for *maṭṭeh*, since the verb does not necessarily indicate an arrow-like movement, 'to pierce through'. The noun form, *maqqebet* (< **nqb*) 'hammer',[56] as well as the Akkadian cognate *nakāpu*[57] (= *naqābu*[58]) 'to butt, gore, abut; knock down'[59] would rather suggest 'his sticks' as the meaning of *maṭṭāyw*.

In light of the above, *maṭṭôt* (Hab 3:9b) probably means 'a divine majestic mace', which is in parallel with Yahweh's 'bow' (*qešet*). This is supported by the extrabiblical usages of these terms, as noted above. It is possible then to think that *qšt* in this verse includes in itself the notion of 'arrows', following the principle of *pars pro toto*. The image of Yahweh as a warrior god, riding a chariot (v. 8) with a bow and a mace (v. 9), is thus in keeping with the general description of a human king in warfare and parallels that of Assur and other warrior gods in the ancient Near East. It is therefore hasty and unwarranted to conclude, as do Day[60] and others, that in Habakkuk 3 Yahweh is represented as a Baal-like figure, and thus that the text alludes to the Canaanite or Ugaritic *Chaoskampf* myth. The fact is that all these descriptions of the warrior gods simply reflect the actual image of a king in the Orient going to battle.[61]

55. Note that this word appears in Habakkuk 3 in both masculine and feminine plural forms, like *nhrym* (v. 8) and *nhrwt* (v. 9).

56. BDB 666; *HALAT* (3d ed.) 591; cf. AHw 607.

57. AHw 718; CAD N/2 156ff. *HALAT* 678 cites only *naqābu* (AHw 743a) as a cognate term for Hebrew *nqb* 'durchbohren', but AHw 743 (*naqābu* 'deflorieren') and AHw 718 (*nakāpu* 'stossen') as well as CAD N/2 156ff. suggest that Hebrew *nqb* and Akkadian *nakāpu* are cognate.

58. AHw 743.

59. Note that *nakāpu* appears in descriptions of attacking an enemy, for example:

> *tāḫassu ṣīru ezziš ittakkip*
> his superb attack keeps charging in fury (Angim IV 53)
> *ittakip kīma ūme ana māt nuku*[*rti*]
> like a storm, he hits the enemy country (Lugale II 33).

Cf. CAD N/2 157.

60. Day, *God's Conflict with the Dragon and the Sea*, 104ff. and passim.

61. For a detailed discussion of Habakkuk 3, see my article, "Ugaritic Poetry and Habakkuk 3," *TynBul* 40 (1988) 24–48.

Religious Conservatism and Political Invention in Ancient Sumer

Mary K. Wakeman

As a student of religion, I am interested in the way changes in theological reflection correlate with changes in polity. I particularly want to understand the origins and development of patriarchy. My starting point here is a statement by Thorkild Jacobsen. Discussing the Sacred Marriage rite in his essay on "Religious Drama in Ancient Mesopotamia," he notes "a shift of emphasis: from the god as source of all blessings, the goddess as receiving; to the goddess as the source, the god as recipient." He concludes that more recent, probably, "is the view of the god as recipient, since that would appear to represent a gradual fading of the divine identity in favor of the human one of the king in whom he was incarnate in the rite."[1] In what follows, I offer an interpretive framework to suggest how "divine identity faded in favor of the human one" in ancient Sumer, in an effort to make intelligible the confusing variety of conflicting evidence concerning the relation of human to divine power.

With growing social complexity, political power, by which I mean a person or group's authority to dispose of resources, human or material, comes increasingly to rest in male, elite, human hands. This was not always so. There was a time in ancient Sumer when the gods had power, when a community of people vested in the gods' divinity the power of their collectivity, and when the powers to which human beings were subject were experienced as female. Please do not misunderstand me: I do not think there ever was a time when women ruled over men, in a matriarchy. By the gods having power I mean that human and material resources were given or withheld

Author's note: This paper was first presented at the American Oriental Society Meeting in Ann Arbor, Michigan, April 16, 1985.

1. Thorkild Jacobsen, "Religious Drama in Ancient Mesopotamia," *Unity and Diversity* (ed. Hans Goedicke and J. J. M. Roberts; Baltimore: Johns Hopkins University Press, 1975) 68, 71.

depending on natural conditions. The communities to which I refer were the corporate kin groups of the early stages of Sumerian culture.

Each step of the process in ancient Sumer of enlarging the political unit entailed a corresponding change in religious understanding. How did the ways in which political power was religiously sanctioned work to effect a shift of power from female to male, temple to palace, god to human? The answer is: it worked as religion has always worked—conservatively, hanging onto traditional ways of speaking about what is happening so as to obscure the radical nature of change at the same time that it authorizes changes.

In the narrative that follows I will refer to familiar data to illustrate the process of political and religious change with respect to each of the three shifts. First, the convention that the powers that be are female is maintained while power is exercised by the male. Sargon, for instance, claimed authority for his empire with reference to Ishtar. Another example is the changed significance of the Sacred Marriage ritual as it functioned in the beginning and at the end of Sumer's history.

Second, the convention that leadership emerges by consensus to express the spirit of the community is maintained through the understanding that the king is the choice of the assembly of the gods, while what is authorized is a hierarchical form of government in which some people exert power over others with or without their consent. As military activity becomes increasingly important to the acquisition of political power, the temple comes to serve the palace rather than vice versa.

Third, the convention that the center of order in the human community is divine and that the community is ordered in accord with the immutable order of the universe is maintained by conferring divine status on the king, either as the husband of a goddess (e.g., Dumuzi) or the son of a god (e.g., Nanna or Ninurta) even though the office of kingship is a secular one and the man who holds it increasingly takes initiative to change the status quo.

When the convention of *communitas* could no longer be maintained, the king was given divinity to justify his dominion. It then became possible to forego the convention that power is female, and then, that power is divine. By Old Babylonian times, though the king's power was still justified by reference to the assembly of the gods, the transformation in the concept of the gods as a male hierarchy was complete.

The Narrative

Among the earliest evidences of religious activity in the ancient Near East are female figurines that testify to a time when the power of fertility was associated with the female. Eventually, this power was expressed through male figures as well. Many of the earliest temple communities of ancient Sumer belonged to male gods associated with the power for fertility in underground waters, the moon, the sun, the sky that brought the round of the seasons, and spring storms. Temples housed goddesses as well as gods; women as well as men were managers of temple estates.[2]

At the very beginning of Sumer's history the two most ancient Sumerian cities, Eridu and Uruk, provided the two types of religious ways to sanction political power that served as paradigms for every subsequent stage. The earliest concept of power that supported the more complex order of the city-state through its central temple was expressed in the cult of Enki, which celebrated the phallic force of fertility. In later stories about Enki, his priest is referred to as his servant (Adapa) or his son.[3] In the course of Sumerian history Enki came to incorporate the powers of his mother, of giving form and giving birth, and to supplant her in the god lists.[4] It is at this point and in this manner that power shifts from female to male. The shift in the balance of power from female to male divinities has to do with a lessening in the importance of natural relative to social forces.

Very early, Uruk took over from Eridu its role as the dominant city in southern Sumer, paving the way for an alternative method of asserting male authority under the power of a female deity: the man who managed the temple estate assumed the role of the husband chosen by its goddess, Inanna. So the two ways a man might claim authority in the earliest temple communities were (1) as the trusted servant or son or (2) as the husband of the divinity whose estate he managed.

As differences in wealth and resources among temple communities and between them and the unsettled countryside increased, kingship developed as

2. Thorkild Jacobsen, *The Treasures of Darkness* (New Haven: Yale University Press, 1976) 81.

3. If I may follow up Ann Kilmer's suggestion and find a connection between the hero of the flood story who receives warning from Enki, and Umul, the first baby, engendered by Enki; Anne Draffkorn Kilmer, "Speculations on Umul, the First Baby," *Cuneiform Studies in Honor of Samuel Noah Kramer* (ed. Barry L. Eichler; AOAT 25; Kevelaer: Butzon und Bercker / Neukirchen-Vluyn: Neukirchener Verlag, 1976).

4. "In the long run, the position of the [mother] goddess in the cosmic hierarchy proved untenable, and slowly she had to yield before a male god who, as she herself, represented numinous power in giving form and giving birth, the god of fresh waters, Enki/Ea. In the latter half of the Isin-Larsa period his name begins to precede that of Ninhursaga or other names of the birth goddess in the ranking of the highest gods, An, Enlil, Enki, Ninhursaga, etc. and eventually her name was completely replaced by that of Enki" (Thorkild Jacobsen, "Notes on Nintur," *Or* 42 [1973] 294).

an institution, the king being at first a commander in battle, then an adjudicator of boundary and other disputes, and eventually picking up magical and ritual duties associated with the priestly role. At a certain point the king came to be worshiped as a sacred symbol of unity, for the power of the center that he provided. Thus worship of authority at its center was substituted for the power of the spirit in the community (the divinity in the harvest rite). Religion validated the structures of power-over rather than empowering the community as a whole.

This did not happen all at once. In the course of the Early Dynastic period, which I will review next, as local communities were absorbed into regional kingdoms, the traditional religious means of celebrating the interdependency of human and divine energies served to authorize this shift to relative autonomy of palace from temple. The kind of authority that brought together and coordinated the affairs of several cities required a new level in the hierarchical order of gods and humans. Whereas the human had served the divine, now the temple, headed by the divine, served the palace (the religious elite served the political elite, who were religiously authorized). So the head of the palace had to be a special kind of divine figure, and the configuration of the gods in relation to each other shifted to accommodate this new level of power. The notion of the assembly of the gods on the one hand functioned as the temple community had, with An at its center representing the consensus, and on the other hand, as a kingdom with Enlil at its head representing the power to execute decisions. Thus by a sort of sleight of hand, through the same image (the assembly), religious convention managed to conserve the notion of *communitas* while authorizing the development of hierarchical social structure.[5]

During the Early Dynastic period (2900–2350 B.C.E.), important centers at Nippur in the north, Lagash to the east, and Ur in the south of Sumer experimented with a variety of ways of sanctioning male authority based on the two original paradigms. The title "King of Kish" was assumed during Early Dynastic times by various city chiefs who claimed that their authority to rule the whole area of Sumer was given to them by the god Enlil, as the executor of the will of the assembly of the gods of Sumer. His temple in the city of

5. The institution of dynastic succession presents a contradiction to all three conventions. (1) It presupposes male dominance: the patriarchal family in which men control their women so as to be sure of their sons; (2) it presupposes class dominance: the monopoly of certain families over positions of political power; and (3) it implies human dominance: reliance on laws of inheritance rather than the gods to assure stability in the transfer of rule.

Nippur was the chief shrine of the land, to which pilgrimages were made from the various cities of what Jacobsen refers to as the "Kengir League." [6] Of particular importance were the ritual journeys from the temple of Nanna at Ur to Nippur to exchange economic goods. The shift in balance of power from temple to palace resulting from the increased importance of military activity also gave Enlil prestige in Sumer as the god who authorized kings.

The title "King of Kish" was claimed by Mesanepada, founder of the first dynasty of Ur ca. 2490. Ur had a harbor on the Persian Gulf and presided over the southern sea trade. "Consequently every major kingdom formed in Babylon tried to gain possession of Ur." [7] Ilshu, who came from Mari far up the Euphrates River [during or before Eannatum's time] to lay claim to Sumer, was sufficiently concerned with the cult of Ur to dedicate his daughter Ninmetabarri as the human consort of its god Nanna. [8] We have a record of the names of the women who served as high priestess of Nanna at Ur for over 500 years. "This appointment was a royal prerogative which was exercised through numerous dynastic changes and provided in Sumer a unifying link even in periods of apparent disunity." [9] With reference to the two original paradigms, we might say that the priestess, the king's daughter who represented Ningal at Ur, paralleled the goddess Inanna at Uruk as the female figure through whom male power was authorized and complemented the powers of Enlil, who succeeded Enki as the male divinity through whom religious sanction was provided for the developing nation.

Jacobsen writes that "Uruk was ruled ca. 2400 by Lugal-kigennesh-dudud who, after concluding a brotherly pact with the expanding Lagash kingdom, succeeded in establishing a personal union between Ur and Uruk—the famous 'joining of lordship and kingship' . . . and eventually gained the title 'King of Kish.'" [10] The "joining of lordship and kingship," the authority of the male ruler in relation to the goddess Inanna at Uruk and in relation to the priestess of Nanna at Ur, brought together the oldest religious traditions of Sumer as exemplified in the worship of the goddess Inanna and of the god Enki. Nanna, like Enki, was a city god associated with male powers of

6. Thorkild Jacobsen, "Early Political Development in Mesopotamia," *Toward the Image of Tammuz* (ed. William L. Moran; Cambridge: Harvard University Press, 1970) 140ff.

7. Dietz Otto Edzard, "The Early Dynastic Period," *The Near East* (ed. Jean Bottéro, Elena Cassin, and Jean Vercoutter; New York: Delacorte Press, 1967) 85.

8. Jacobsen, "Early Political Development," 152.

9. Joan Oates, *Babylon* (London: Thames and Hudson, 1979) 38.

10. Jacobsen, "Early Political Development," 152.

fertility. Through marriage to the priestess at Ur, the god Nanna (son of Enlil, "prince of the gods" [11]) came to serve Enlil as his heir and appointed king.

Sacred Marriage as the rite involving a sexual union on which claims of dynastic succession to the rulership of all Sumer could be based may well have had its origins in Ur, as an expression of interdependency between the temple (Ur) and the palace (designated by the priesthood at Nippur). Authority continued to be exemplified in the priesthood of Ur as an intercity institution primarily concerned with economic cooperation, while the priesthood at Nippur vested political authority in the "King of Kish" (whatever his native city), who maintained peace among and protected or extended the boundaries of a league of cities. In ancient Uruk, the ruler had served the goddess; the priest served the temple community. At Ur, the goddess served the king, that is, the priestess served the palace on the assumption that the palace served the whole of Sumer. In the transition from local to national significance, the power balance between the divinity and the manager of the divinity's estate shifted. (At Uruk, the temple was the home of Inanna, incarnate in a woman who was served by the *en*-priest or manager of her estate. The king whose estate was the whole of Sumer was the god Nanna incarnate, who was served by the priestess of Nanna at Ur.)

To sum up, the three traditional ways of authorizing a king that had emerged by the end of the Early Dynastic period are expressed in the titles "King of Kish," "Lord of Uruk," and "King of Ur." With reference to the two original paradigms, the Eridu pattern of authorization through a male line was maintained by Enlil, while Uruk's Sacred Marriage was transformed at Ur to justify dynastic succession or provide for succession when a dynasty came to an end.

When Sargon conquered Lugalzagesi, he continued the dynastic union of Ur and Uruk in his own person, making his daughter Enheduanna priestess to Nanna at Ur and to An at Uruk. But it was Inanna (not Nanna or An) whose power was invoked to support Sargon's Semitic empire. By identifying her with the war-like Semitic goddess Ishtar and exalting her as the female counterpart of An, Enheduanna provided Sargon with a religious justification for his rule that appealed to the northern Semitic villagers who still associated divine power with femaleness. But when Enheduanna sang of Inanna as An's wife,[12] she was reflecting Sargon's policy of regularizing the

11. Jacobsen, *Treasures of Darkness*, 7.

12. Ibid., 137; W. W. Hallo and J. J. A. van Dijk, *The Exaltation of Inanna* (YNER 3; New Haven: Yale University Press) 97.

position of Inanna to conform to the Ur pattern, where the priestess served the god, thus demoting her, in relation to her consort, from divine to human, from the served to the servant.

Akkadian kings assumed the prerogative of the gods by interfering with city affairs. The convention of *communitas* could no longer be maintained. The king was deified, maintaining the convention that the exercise of power-over was a divine prerogative. With that, the way was open for finally dropping the convention that divine power was female, but the pendulum had to swing backward first, in the revival of the Uruk tradition during Ur III.

It was during the Ur III and Isin-Larsa periods at the end of Sumer's history (2100–1800) that the Urukian rite of Sacred Marriage was revived to express Sumer's religious and political self-understanding. Hymns to the Ur III king Shulgi indicate variously that he was adopted by Ninsun and Lugalbanda and given kingship by An, that he was blessed by Inanna as her husband, as well as being, at Nanna's request, Enlil's chosen steward. Iddin-Dagan of Isin was exalted as the incarnation, not of Nanna, but of Dumuzi. We come full circle back to the tradition of ancient Uruk, but in a way that marks the triumph of patriarchy in elevating a man to divine status through marriage to a goddess while lowering the status of female priestly authority at Ur, through whom that divine status had initially been conferred. As Jacobsen said, emphasis had shifted from god to goddess as the source of blessings, from goddess to god as their recipient, because divine identity had faded in favor of the human one of the king. As the goddess was to the god, so the king now was to the divinity. Power had shifted from divine to human, from female to male recipient of blessings, from temple (presided over by a priestess representing the goddess) to palace, where the king was the god incarnate. Meanwhile the conventions were upheld that power is female (the source of blessings), is dispensed by the temple (to the palace), and rests with the gods (among whom the king is now one).

Marriage as a metaphor for the union of equals, as it had been used to express the relationship between the community and the gods, the harmonious integration of cultural efforts and natural bounty to produce abundant crops and herds, had come to mask what was essentially a master/servant relationship, to authorize the institution of class domination first of all and of male dominance in particular.

All that remained was to drop the pretense to divinity, and allow that the king was a human being with the advantage mortality gives of being able to make mistakes and learn from them. Sumerian history came to an end, and with it, the divinity of the king and the role of the goddess in authorizing kingship. With the first dynasty of Babylon, the convention that the king is chosen by the gods to recreate their male hierarchy on earth was reaffirmed and persisted throughout the remainder of Mesopotamian history.[13]

13. Parallel developments in Lagash involving Ningirsu as husband of Bau, identified with Ninurta as son of Enlil, gave Ninurta the advantage over both Dumuzi and Nanna as divine prince, symbol of kingship. (I leave it to you to speculate why it was no longer necessary for the king to be so closely associated with the moon!)

Cambyses in Egypt

Edwin Yamauchi

Because it has been some fifty years since a comprehensive treatment of Cambyses in Egypt was published,[1] I would like to review this subject, especially in the light of new archaeological evidence.

Cambyses (529–522 B.C.E.) was the son of Cyrus the Great. Whereas his father was greatly honored, Cambyses' reputation has suffered by contrast. His greatest achievement was his conquest of Egypt in 525. Our most comprehensive historical account of the Persians in general and of Cambyses in particular is the Greek historian Herodotus.[2] But whereas Herodotus' accounts have been vindicated in many aspects (for example, his account of the Scythians[3]), his narrative of Cambyses in Egypt is directly contradicted by some Egyptological evidence.

Reasons for the Invasion of Egypt

Cambyses invaded Egypt to annex the country, which was the wealthiest area in the Near East. Herodotus sought the reason for the invasion in highly personal causes. He gives us three accounts. (1) The Persians said that Cambyses was angry that Amasis had sent the daughter of his deposed predecessor, Apries, instead of his own daughter for his harem (3.1). (2) The Egyptian

---

Author's note: It is a great privilege to contribute an essay in honor of Dwight Young, the scholar who first introduced me and many others to the basics of Akkadian and Egyptian at Brandeis University.

1. A. Klasens, "Cambyses en Egypte," *JEOL* 10 (1945–48) 339–49. Because this article is in Dutch, it has not been as widely cited as it might have been.

2. See my *Persia and the Bible* (Grand Rapids, Mich.: Baker, 1990).

3. See my *Foes from the Northern Frontier* (Grand Rapids, Mich.: Baker, 1982).

story, which Herodotus rejected, was that Cambyses was the son of the daughter of Apries (3.2). (3) Finally Herodotus tells us that when his mother became jealous of a newcomer from Egypt, Cambyses as a young boy vowed, "Mother, when I am grown a man, I will turn all Egypt upside down" (3.3).

At the height of the Egyptian Empire, the pharaohs of Egypt were happy to marry princesses from many countries but would not deign to send their own princesses abroad.[4] But in the post-Empire years after 1200, the Egyptians could not afford to be so particular. The fact that Solomon married a pharaoh's daughter is proof both of the prestige of the Israelite king and of the decline of Egypt in the tenth century.[5] We also have evidence that the pharaohs of the 21st and 22nd Dynasties gave away their daughters in marriage to foreigners.[6]

The first story, that Cambyses wished to marry a daughter of Apries, may have stemmed from Cambyses' attempt to lend an aura of legitimacy to his claim to be the heir to Apries.[7] This political fiction was also carried out in Cambyses' system of dating, which ignored the intervening reign of the usurper Amasis.

The Persian Invasion

The Egyptians, who early in the sixth century had many allies, were gradually isolated by the rapid expansion of the Persians under Cyrus. They were cut off from Lydia in 547 and from Babylon in 539. Cyprus, which had been won over by Amasis, defected to the Persians. Even Amasis' friend Polycrates

4. When the king of Babylonia, Burraburiaš II was refused a daughter of the pharaoh, Amenophis III, he wrote: ". . . grown daughters, beautiful women, must be available. Send me a beautiful woman as if she were [you]r daughter. Who is going to say: 'She is no daughter of the king!'" (William L. Moran, trans. and ed., *The Amarna Letters* (Baltimore: Johns Hopkins University Press, 1992) 9.

5. The doubts of Y. Aharoni (*The Land of the Bible* [2d ed.; Philadelphia: Westminster, 1979] 319 n. 42) that Solomon could have married a pharaoh's daughter are unfounded. See S. Horn, "Who Was Solomon's Egyptian Father-in-Law?" *BR* 12 (1967) 3–17; A. R. Green, "Solomon and Siamun," *JBL* 97 (1978) 353–67.

6. K. A. Kitchen, *The Third Intermediate Period in Egypt* (Warminster: Aris and Phillips, 1973) 282.

7. K. M. T. Atkinson, "The Legitimacy of Cambyses and Darius as Kings of Egypt," *JAOS* 76 (1956) 167–77. For a different analysis, see M. Lang, "War and Rape-Motif or Why Did Cambyses Invade Egypt?" *PAPS* 116 (1972) 410–14. See also T. Brown, "Herodotus' Portrait of Cambyses," *Historia* 31 (1982) 391–92.

of Samos was compelled to send a contingent to the Persian fleet (Her. 3.44). Polycrates obliged by sending his foes, including his brother Syloson.

Phanes, a mercenary from Halicarnassus (Herodotus' hometown), deserted the Egyptians (Her. 3.4) and advised Cambyses to seek the aid of the Arabs, who could supply camels and water (Her. 3.9). The Arabs controlled vast areas ranging from northeast Egypt to southern Palestine.[8]

The initial conflict between the Persians and the Egyptians took place at Pelusium in the northeast Delta, where Herodotus (3.12) was shown the skulls of the victims from the battle.[9] Herodotus believed that the Egyptians had thicker skulls than the Persians because they were accustomed to shaving their heads! After the victory at Pelusium, the Persians rapidly advanced to Memphis, the key city in Lower Egypt. With the capture of Memphis, open resistance subsided.

Cambyses now faced the task of establishing Persian control over a country that boasted one of the world's oldest civilizations. Our sources seem to be contradictory. On the one hand, Herodotus paints the picture of an erratic, willful conqueror who was determined to defy ancient conventions and to tread roughshod over religious sensibilities. On the other hand, some of the Egyptian sources depict Cambyses as accommodating himself to Egyptian customs.

Though there may be no completely satisfactory solution to some of these contradictions, a key may lie in the fact that Cambyses' policy was consistent but not uniform. That is, he behaved differently to different elements in Egypt, favoring those who accepted the Persians and punishing those who did not. Later, Xerxes likewise rewarded Greek oracles that favored him,

8. H. Grimme, "Beziehungen zwischen dem Staate Liḥjān und dem Achämenidenreiche," *OLZ* 44 (1941) 337–43. For the importance of the Arabs, see M. Elat, "The Economic Relations of the Neo-Assyrian Empire with Egypt," *JAOS* 98 (1978) 28–30; I. Eph^{c}al, *The Ancient Arabs* (Jerusalem: Magnes / Leiden: Brill, 1982).

9. In spite of his omissions, exaggerations, and errors, no one today doubts that Herodotus actually visited Egypt. See C. Sourdille, *La durée et l'étendue du voyage d'Hérodote en Égypte* (Paris: Leroux, 1910); W. Spiegelberg, *The Credibility of Herodotus' Account of Egypt in the Light of the Monuments* (Oxford: Blackwell, 1927); E. Lüddeckens, "Herodot und Ägypten," *ZDMG* 104 (1954) 330–46; T. W. Africa, "Herodotus and Diodorus on Egypt," *JNES* 22 (1963) 254–58; S. Benardette, *Herodotean Inquiries* (The Hague: Nijhoff, 1969) 32–68; R. Drews, *The Greek Accounts of Eastern History* (Cambridge: Harvard University Press, 1973) 80. O. K. Armayor ("Did Herodotus Ever Go to Egypt," *JARCE* 15 [1978] 59–74), while conceding that Herodotus visited Egypt, questions most of his information. For a defense of Herodotus, see A. B. Lloyd, *Herodotus Book II: Introduction* (Leiden: Brill, 1975).

while at the same time destroying the Temple of Athena. The stories about Cambyses' acts of desecration were probably derived from hostile sources, whether Egyptian or possibly Persian. On the other hand, some of the favorable accounts come from Egyptians who collaborated with the Persians.[10]

Udjahorresnet

One of the defectors to the Persian side left us a most valuable statue, inscribed with 48 lines. Udjahorresnet's statue, which is now in the Vatican Museum, is known as a *naophoros* figure because he holds in his hands a *naos* or 'shrine' containing the image of Osiris.[11] It is dated to the third year of Darius.

Udjahorresnet served Neith, the goddess of Sais in the western Delta. She was the goddess of hunting and war, the mistress of the bow and arrow. Udjahorresnet's inscription lists a long catalog of the titles so beloved of Egyptian nobility—"the Royal Chancellor, the Unique Companion, the True Acquaintance of the King. . . ."

Most important is the revelation that Udjahorresnet was the admiral of the royal navy under Amasis and Psammetichus III.[12] He reports:

> There came into Egypt the great king of all the foreign countries Cambyses (Kambujet), while the foreigners of all the foreign countries were with him. When he had taken possession of this entire land, they established their residence, and he was the great sovereign of Egypt, great lord of all the foreign countries.[13]

10. F. K. Kienitz, *Die politische Geschichte Ägyptens vom 7. bis zum 4. Jahrhundert vor der Zeitwende* (Berlin: Akademie, 1953) 56. One thinks of Josephus, who surrendered to the Romans and then attempted to absolve Titus of blame for the burning of the Jewish temple. See H. Montefiore, "Sulpicius Severus and Titus' Council of War," *Historia* 11 (1962) 156–70.

11. The Egyptian reads *wḏꜣ-ḥr-rś-n.t.* Because we are not sure of the vocalization of Egyptian, the name has been variously transcribed: Udjeharresnet, Udzahorresne, Wadjahoreresnet, etc. See A. B. Lloyd, "The Inscription of Udjaḥorresnet: A Collaborator's Testament," *JEA* 68 (1982) 166–80.

12. The defection of Udjahorresnet may be reflected in the garbled tradition found in Ctesias #9: "He (Cambyses) overcame Amyrtaeus, for the eunuch Combapheus, who had great influence with the Egyptian king, surrendered the dikes and betrayed the Egyptian cause. . . ." C. J. Ogden, "The Story of Cambyses and the Magus, as Told in the Fragments of Ctesias," *Madressa Jubilee Volume* (Bombay: Fort, 1914) 235; F. W. König, *Die Persika des Ktesias von Knidos* (Graz, Austria: Archiv für Orientforschung, 1972) 5.

13. G. Posener, *La première domination perse en Égypte* (Cairo: L'Institut Français d'Archéologie Orientale, 1936) 7; A. T. Olmstead, *History of the Persian Empire* (Chicago: University of Chicago Press, 1948) 90.

Udjahorresnet boasted that he instructed Cambyses about the greatness of Neith and her residence at Sais.[14] The site of Said (Sa el-Hagar) was at that time surrounded by a gigantic enclosure, filled with trees, sphinxes, and colossi.[15]

> I complained before the Majesty of the King of Upper and Lower Egypt, Cambyses, on the subject of all the foreigners, who had installed themselves in the temple of Neith, in order that they should be expelled from there, that the temple of Neith should appear in all its former splendor.[16]

Cambyses ordered the expulsion of these squatters,[17] destroying their dwellings and removing the rubble. Neith's temple was thus purified and its revenues and festivals restored.[18] Udjahorresnet claims that Cambyses not only visited the temple but that he also prostrated himself before the goddess, just as every pharaoh had done before him. He reports that Cambyses saved the residents of Sais from great calamity. Udjahorresnet may have considered it in the best interest of his district to cooperate with the Persians.[19]

As the Chief Physician, Udjahorresnet was empowered by the Persians to restore the medical colleges in Sais and throughout the whole of Egypt.[20] As part of his service to the new pharaoh, Udjahorresnet prepared the formal titulary whereby Cambyses was invested with the prenomen *Mesutre* 'Offspring of Re', emphasizing his legitimacy as the ruler of Egypt.[21]

14. Some have taken this passage as an initiation of Cambyses into the "Mysteries" of Neith, but Posener (*La première domination*, 14) disagrees.

15. W. M. Davis, "Egypt, Samos and the Archaic Style in Greek Sculpture," *JEA* (1981) 79; P. Montet, *Lives of the Pharaohs* (Cleveland: World, 1968) 261.

16. Posener, *La première domination*, 15.

17. Who were these squatters? Some have suggested that they were Greek mercenaries. Posener (*La première domination*, 16) believes they were Persian troops. P. G. Elgood (*The Later Dynasties of Egypt* [Oxford: Blackwell, 1951] 118) suggests that they were "the inhabitants of Sais too poor or too lazy to find accommodation elsewhere."

18. This parallels the expulsion of Tobiah from the temple in Jerusalem by Nehemiah (Neh 12:9). For other parallels with Ezra and Nehemiah, see J. Blenkinsopp, "The Mission of Udjahorresnet and Those of Ezra and Nehemiah," *JBL* 106 (1987) 409–21.

19. Posener, *La première domination*, 17. Lloyd ("The Inscription of Udjaḥorresnet," 173) suggests: "Cambyses made a genuine attempt to reconcile the Egyptians to Persian rule by adopting the traditional role of Pharaoh with all its implications; Udjaḥorresnet was, therefore, able to accept the change of government much more easily than might otherwise have been the case simply by applying the eminently straightforward principles: 'The King is dead. Long live the king.' "

20. A. H. Gardiner, "The House of Life," *JEA* 24 (1938) 158.

21. See Posener, *La première domination*, 12. After Cambyses, Alexander the Great was depicted as the son of the last pharaoh, Nectanebo II. In the Temple of Dendur, which was

Other Egyptians continued to hold office under the Persians.[22] A striking monument of such an Egyptian who served under the Persians is the Brooklyn Museum statue of Ptah-hotep. This is also a *naophoros* statue. Ptah-hotep's titles include: "The Prince and Count, Royal Treasurer and Sole Friend, . . . the Superintendent of all Royal Works, the Minister of Finance. . . ."[23] The only other material evidence from the century of Persian occupation in Egypt is a set of lion-figured unguentaria from Leontopolis, representing the lion god Mahes in a style that indicates they were probably made in Egypt for Persians.[24]

Cambyses inaugurated the 27th Dynasty, which lasted from 525 to 402.[25] Though he entered Egypt in the middle of 525 and left it about three years later, papyrus documents in Demotic claim as many as eight years for his reign in Egypt. This must mean that Cambyses, by a legal fiction, claimed jurisdiction over Egypt from the beginning of his reign in Persia in 529.[26]

The Desecration of Amasis' Body

An act that Herodotus (3.16) regarded as a senseless desecration may have been an attempt by Cambyses to strengthen his claim to be the legitimate

---

sent by Egypt to the Metropolitan Museum in New York, we behold the pharaoh Augustus pouring a libation to the god Khnum of Elephantine. The Roman emperor received the Egyptian titles: "The King of Upper and Lower Egypt, Lord of the Two Lands, Autocrator, the Son of Re, Lord of Crowns, Caesar, living forever"; C. Aldred, *The Temple of Dendur* (New York: Metropolitan Museum of Art, 1978) 27.

22. M. A. Dandamaev, *Persien unter den ersten Achämeniden* (trans. Heinz-Dieter Pohl; Wiesbaden: Reichert, 1976) 106. R. S. Bianchi, "Perser in Ägypten," *Lexicon der Ägyptologie* (ed. W. Helck and W. Westendorf; Wiesbaden: Harrassowitz, 1982) cols. 946, 950.

23. J. D. Cooney, "The Portrait of an Egyptian Collaborator," *Bulletin of the Brooklyn Museum* 15 (1953) 5.

24. B. V. Bothmer, *Egyptian Sculpture of the Late Period, 700 B.C. to A.D. 100* (Brooklyn: Brooklyn Museum, 1960) 77. Cf. J. D. Cooney, *Five years of Collecting Egyptian Art (1951–1956)* (Brooklyn: Brooklyn Museum, 1956) 56. For possible linguistic remains, see K. Sethe, "Spuren der Perserherrschaft in der späteren ägyptischen Sprache," *Festgabe für Theodor Nöldeke* (Göttingen: Königl. Gesellschaft der Wissenschaften, 1916) 112–33.

25. Some scholars date the end of Dynasty XXVII to 401 or even 398. Just before the conquest by Alexander, the Persians briefly reoccupied Egypt from 343 to 332 under Artaxerxes III. See J. H. Johnson, "The Demotic Chronicle as an Historical Source," *Enchoria* 4 (1974) 1–17.

26. Atkinson, "The Legitimacy of Cambyses," 168; M. F. Gyles, *Pharaonic Policies and Administration, 663–323 B.C.* (Chapel Hill: University of North Carolina Press, 1959) 98–100; W. Culican, *The Medes and Persians* (New York: Praeger, 1965) 61.

successor to Apries. Cambyses sought out the corpse of Amasis and attempted to mutilate it. But because the corpse had been embalmed, this proved to be in vain. He then had the corpse hurled into the fire. This was an especially terrible deed, because the Egyptians believed that the preservation of the body was necessary for the afterlife.[27]

Though many scholars have questioned this account,[28] there may have been method in his "madness." According to Manetho Shabako, the first king of the new Cushite (25th) Dynasty, burned alive Bocchoris, the last king of the 24th Dynasty. Atkinson believes that Cambyses desired to blacken the reputation of Amasis as a usurper.[29] Bresciani observes:

> In reality Cambyses' action was in line with the Egyptian point of view; since he did not want to recognize Amasis as a legitimate Pharaoh, he saw to it that his memory was accursed in exactly the manner that he knew would be final and convincing to the Egyptian mentality.[30]

The Expedition to Siwa

Cambyses planned an expedition far to the west against the Phoenician colony of Carthage (in present-day Tunisia), but this plan was frustrated when the Phoenician seamen of his fleet balked at the prospect of fighting against their countrymen (Her. 3.17, 19). The Libyans to the west of Egypt submitted to the Persians and sent gifts, as did the Greek colony of Cyrene (Her. 3.15).[31] As Cambyses sailed upstream to Thebes, he detached a contingent of 50,000 men to burn the oracle of Zeus-Ammon at Siwa (Her. 3.17, 25–26). After seven days' trekking into the desert, they came to the city of Oasis, probably the El-Khargeh oasis, where some Greeks from Samos

27. J. Davis, *Mummies, Men and Madness* (Grand Rapids, Mich.: Baker, 1972); R. S. Bianchi, "Egyptian Mummies: Myth and Reality," *Archaeology* 35/2 (1982) 18–25; E. F. Wente, "Funerary Beliefs of the Ancient Egyptians," *Expedition* 24/2 (1982) 17–26. For a fuller bibliography on the subject, see E. Yamauchi, "Magic or Miracle? Diseases, Demons and Exorcisms," *Gospel Perspectives 6* (ed. D. Wenham and C. Blomberg; Sheffield: JSOT Press, 1986) 160 n. 125.

28. For example, Kienitz, *Die politische Geschichte*, 57.

29. Atkinson ("The Legitimacy of Cambyses," 171) cites the desecration of the corpse of Oliver Cromwell at the time of the Restoration. See *The Diary and Correspondence of Samuel Pepys* (London: George Bell, 1900) 1.128–29 (entry for Dec. 4, 1660).

30. E. Bresciani, "Egypt and the Persian Empire," *The Greeks and the Persians* (ed. H. Bengston; London: Weidenfeld & Nicolson, 1968) 336.

31. See B. M. Mitchell, "Cyrene and Persia," *JHS* 86 (1966) 99–113.

were settled.[32] Halfway between the Oasis and Siwa, the Persian troops were overwhelmed by a tremendous sandstorm (Her. 3.26).

Siwa was located about 100 miles from the Mediterranean coast and the usual route to the shrine was from the north. Even then, because it was 400 miles west of the Nile, to reach Siwa required an arduous journey of at least 15 days through vast stretches of treacherous deserts.[33]

It was probably back in the 20th or possibly in the 18th Dynasty that Amon (later written Ammon), the god of Thebes, was introduced into Siwa. The same god was introduced into Napata in Nubia. Herodotus' account (2.42), which states that the Ammonium at Siwa was founded as a joint colony of Egyptians and Nubians, is supported by certain common elements.[34]

The shrine at Siwa became famed as an oracle. Answers to questions were indicated by the motion of the god's statue as it was borne on the shoulders of priests.[35] Its fame spread so that, by the middle of the seventh century, Greeks from Cyrene learned of the oracle.[36] When Croesus, the king of Lydia (560–546 B.C.E.), wished to test the seven most famous oracles in the world, he enquired of "Ammon in Lybia" (Her. 1.46).[37]

The oracle was supposedly consulted by Cimon, the son of Miltiades, ca. 450 and by the Athenians before the invasion of Sicily during the Peloponnesian War. The famous poet Pindar dedicated a hymn to the Siwan oracle, a copy of which, Pausanias (9.16.1) says, still stood in his day (ca. 160 C.E.).

The most famous visitor to Siwa was Alexander, who came in the winter of 332/331 after nearly losing his way in a sandstorm (Arrian 3.14). He was addressed by the priests as the "Son of Zeus-Ammon." The significance of the oracle's response, whose exact contents we do not know, has been the subject of intense debate.[38]

32. J. A. S. Evans, *Herodotus* (Boston: Twayne, 1982) 50: "the story is without proof, but it may be true, for Samos was one of the first Greek states to interest itself in Egypt." Cf. Davis, "Egypt, Samos," 69; U. Jantzen, "Ägyptische und orientalische Bronzen aus dem Heraion von Samos," *Gnomon* 47 (1975) 392–402.

33. Her. 4.181; Arrian *Alexander* 3.4.1; Plutarch *Alexander* 26–27. See G. Steindorff et al., "Der Orakeltempel in der Ammonsoase," *ZÄS* 69 (1933) 22; H. Kees, *Ancient Egypt* (Chicago: University of Chicago Press, 1961) 129.

34. Steindorff, "Der Orakeltempel," 23.

35. Diodorus Siculus 17.50.6; H. W. Parke, *Greek Oracles* (London: Hutchinson University Library, 1972) 110.

36. J. D. Ray, "Ancient Egypt," *Divination and Oracles* (ed. M. Loewe and C. Blacker; London: Allen & Unwin, 1981) 185.

37. Parke (*Greek Oracles*, 68), who mistrusts the tradition, does not believe that the Greeks came into contact with the Siwan oracle until the early fifth century B.C.E.

38. Ibid., 119–21; V. Ehrenberg, *Alexander und Ägypten* (Leipzig: Hinrichs, 1926) 30–42; G. C. Richards, "Proskynesis," *Classical Review* 48 (1934) 168–70; C. A. Robinson,

The oracle continued to function for still another thousand years until it was finally closed by Justinian (6th century C.E.), who built a sanctuary to *Theotokos* 'The God-Bearer' (Mary) at the site.[39]

A fine tomb at Siwa depicts a Greek by the name of *Si-Amun* 'Man of Amun' or 'Son of Amun'. He wears a Greek hairstyle but an Egyptian garment, while his son wears a Greek chiamys. This has been cited by some as a testimony to the intermarriages that must have taken place between the Greeks and the native women.[40]

Numerous travelers have described the ruins of the oracular temple, which rests on a limestone knoll in the village of Aghûrmi. The remains cover an area 120 by 80 meters wide; some of the walls stand to a height of 7.5 meters.[41] The plan of the sanctuary is not typically Egyptian. Some damaged inscriptions may possibly be attributed to Achoris of the 29th Dynasty (392–380 B.C.E.).[42] In 1970 an expedition recovered inscriptions from the 2nd–3rd century C.E.

The walls of the sanctuary are coated with white crystals formed from the soot of the camel dung burned by the priests. These crystals came to be called *sal ammoniac*, that is, 'salt of Ammon', hence the gas 'ammonia', which is derived from it.[43]

Scholars have been skeptical about the expedition of Cambyses' army into the western desert.[44] But there are indications that such disasters are far from impossible. The Siwans themselves tell a story of a tribe of attacking Tibbu from the western Sudan, who were providentially buried in a sandstorm before they could attack.[45] According to Fakhry, "In the year 1805, a caravan

---

"Alexander's Deification," *AJP* 64 (1943) 286–301; C. B. Welles, "The Discovery of Sarapis and the Foundation of Alexandria," *Historia* 11 (1962) 271–98; E. N. Borza, "Alexander and the Return from Siwah," *Historia* 16 (1967) 369; J. R. Hamilton, *Plutarch ALEXANDER: A Commentary* (Oxford: Clarendon, 1969) 69–73.

39. J. Leclant, "Per Africae Sitientia," *BIFAO* 49 (1950) 193–95.

40. Davis, "Egypt, Samos," 68; J. Boardman, *The Greeks Overseas* (2d ed.; London: Thames and Hudson, 1973) 159; T. F. R. G. Braun, "The Greeks in Egypt," *CAH* 3/3: *The Expansion of the Greek World, Eighth to Sixth Centuries B.C.*, 48.

41. Steindorff, "Der Orakeltempel," 4–10.

42. Ibid., 21.

43. F. El-Baz, "Siwa: Resort of Kings," *Aramco World Magazine* 30/4 (1979) 30–35. For alternative etymologies of 'ammonia', see G. Majno, *Healing Hand* (Cambridge: Harvard University Press, 1975) 487 n. 282.

44. For example, K. H. Waters, *Herodotus on Tyrants and Despots* (Wiesbaden: Steiner, 1971) 54.

45. A. Fakhry, *The Oases of Egypt I: Siwa Oasis* (Cairo: American University in Cairo, 1973) 66.

of 2,000 persons with their camels, en route from Dârfûr in the Western Sudan to Asyût, was buried under the sands of the same Libyan desert."[46]

Normally the Persian rulers were well disposed to foreign oracles, which tended to proffer favorable pronouncements.[47] We have reason to believe that Cambyses consulted the oracle at Buto (Her. 3.64), though he seems not to have believed its prophecy of his death until its fulfillment. His wrath against the oracle at Siwa may have been aroused by an unfavorable prediction.

The Expedition to Ethiopia

Herodotus (3.17–20) informs us that Cambyses wished to invade the land of the tall, long-living "Ethiopians," south of Egypt. This was a continuation of the policy maintained by the preceding Saite Dynasty.[48]

The king of Ethiopia presented a bow to the Persian scouts (Her. 3.21–22), warning Cambyses not to invade unless the Persians could draw such a bow. Haycock comments:

> Whether or not this incident is historical, as it may well be, it illustrates external attitudes and beliefs about Cush. The bow was indeed the weapon of the Nubians par excellence.[49]

For quite some time it was believed that a confirmation for Cambyses' invasion could be found in an inscription brought to Berlin in 1871, which mentions an enemy called KMBSWDN, who was identified as Cambyses by no less than J. H. Breasted.[50] But this clashes with the chronology of the Mero-

46. Ibid.

47. The Persians harshly treated the oracle at Didyma after the Ionian Revolt was suppressed in 494, exiling the Branchidae and carrying off the bronze statue of Apollo to Ecbatana; see E. Yamauchi, *New Testament Cities in Western Asia Minor* (Grand Rapids, Mich.: Baker, 1980) 130. For the key role of Delphi during the Persian conflict with the Greeks, see J. Elayi, "Le rôle de l'oracle de Delphes dans le conflit gréco-perse d'après 'Les Histoires' d'Hérodote," *Iranica Antiqua* 13 (1978) 93–118; 14 (1979) 67–150.

48. Bresciani, "Egypt and the Persian Empire," 337.

49. B. G. Haycock, "The Place of the Napatan-Meroitic Culture in the History of the Sudan and Africa," *The Sudan in Africa* (Khartoum: Khartoum University Press, 1974) 38. I. Hofmann and A. Vorbichler (*Der Äthiopenlogos des Herodot* [Vienna: Institut für Afrikanistik und Ägyptologie, 1979] 67, 172–77; idem, "Das Kambysesbild bei Herodot," *AfO* 27 [1980] 86–105) dismiss Cambyses' Ethiopian campaign as quite unhistorical. But their alternative explanation, that Cambyses represents, among other legendary and mythological motifs, Ahriman himself, the scion of the sun-god and the mad Nabonidus, is wildly speculative.

50. J. H. Breasted, *A History of Egypt* (New York: Bantam, 1964; reprint of 1909 ed.) 470.

itic kings established by Reisner,[51] who dates the Nubian king of his inscription, Nastasen, to the fourth century B.C.E.[52] Hintze, who has reexamined the inscription, now reads the name as ḤMBSWTN, to be identified with Khabbash, a ruler of the first and second cataracts.[53] The king who would have been the contemporary of Cambyses would have been Amani-natakelebte (538–519).[54]

Though the support from the Nastasen inscription proves to be illusory, there need be no doubt about the reality of Cambyses' invasion of Nubia. We have the inscription of a Persian official from Cambyses' reign in the Wadi Hammamat in Upper Egypt, indicating that quarrying operations were conducted there.[55] Later Darius and Xerxes counted Cush (Kusa) as part of the Persian Empire. Cushite troops, wearing leopard and lion skins, served in Xerxes' army (Her. 7.69). Darius used ivory from Cush for his palace at Susa. Biennial gifts of gold, ebony, and ivory were sent by the Cushites to the Persians. On the Apadana stairway at Persepolis, the Cushite delegation leads a long-necked animal, which looks like an okapi but that may have been intended to represent a giraffe—the tallest animal in the world and therefore a spectacular trophy.[56]

The Alleged Tauricide of the Apis

According to Herodotus (3.27), after the disastrous expedition to Siwa and the failure of the Ethiopian campaign, Cambyses returned to Memphis

51. G. A. Reisner, "The Meroitic Kingdom of Ethiopia: A Chronological Outline," *JEA* 9 (1923) 34–75.

52. J. M. Cook, "The Rise of the Achaemenids and Establishment of Their Empire," *Cambridge History of Iran II: The Median and Achaemenian Periods* (ed. I. Gershevitch; Cambridge: Cambridge University Press, 1985) 214.

53. F. Hintze, *Studien zur Meroitischen Chronologie und zu den Opfertafeln aus den Pyramiden von Meroe* (Berlin: Akademie, 1959) 17–20. See A. Spalinger, "The Reign of King Chabbash: An Interpretation," *ZÄS* 105 (1978) 142–54.

54. *Africa in Antiquity I: The Essays* (ed. S. Hochfield and E. Riefstahl; Brooklyn: Brooklyn Museum, 1978) 2.16.

55. Bianchi, "Perser in Ägypten," col. 944; G. A. Wainwright, "The Date of the Rise of Meroë," *JEA* 38 (1952) 75.

56. By early Dynastic times the giraffe could be found only south of the First Cataract. On the tomb of Rekhmire (1504–1450 B.C.E.) we see Nubians leading a giraffe. See *The Image of the Black in Western Art I: From the Pharaohs to the Fall of the Roman Empire* (New York: Menil Foundation, 1976) 48, fig. 14. A. Afshar, W. Dutz, and M. Taylor ("Giraffes at Persepolis," *Archaeology* 27 [1974] 114–17) suggest that the animal depicted was an okapi rather than a giraffe.

just as the Egyptians were celebrating the appearance of a new Apis bull. Cambyses misunderstood their festivities as exultation over his discomfiture.

When he was shown the calf, Cambyses, who was well nigh insane according to Herodotus (3.29), stabbed the Apis in the thigh, proclaiming: "Wretched wights, are these your gods, creatures of flesh and blood that can feel weapons of iron? That is a god worthy of the Egyptians!"[57]

The Apis (Egyptian *Hapi*) bull was regarded as the incarnation of Ptah, the creator god of Memphis.[58] It was held that Ptah inseminated Apis' mother with celestial fire. To qualify as the new Apis, a calf had to have special characteristics, according to Herodotus (3.28):

> The marks of this calf called Apis are these: he is black, and has on his forehead a three-cornered white spot, and the likeness of an eagle on his back; the hairs of the tail are double, and there is a knot under the tongue.

J. Ruffle comments, "They were selected by carefully observed signs, rather as a new Dalai Lama is chosen in Tibet, and taken to the temple where they were pampered throughout their life. . . ."[59]

After his ceremonious installation, the Apis would be extravagantly fed and cared for in the Apium (Greek *Apieion*), a special precinct opposite the temple of Ptah in Memphis. The Apis could be seen prancing in its courtyard each day at a fixed hour. Its movements, including its entrance into one room or another, were interpreted as oracular signs.[60]

Manetho claimed that the worship of the Apis went back to the 2d Dynasty. Actually it was known already in the 1st Dynasty, as shown by archaeological evidence, and no doubt had its roots in prehistoric times.[61] It is from

57. Diodorus Siculus (l.44.3) speaks of revolts by the Egyptians against the Persians because of "their lack of respect for the native gods." A later Persian king, Artaxerxes III (Ochus), was said by Plutarch (*De Iside et Osiride* 355B, #11) to have slain the Apis and to have eaten its flesh.

58. See H. Bonnet, "Apis," *Reallexikon der ägyptischen Religionsgeschichte* (Berlin: de Gruyter, 1952) 46–51. Other bulls include the Mnevis of Re at Heliopolis and the Buchis of Montu at Armant. H. Frankfort (*Ancient Egyptian Religion* [New York: Harper and Row, 1961] 10) argued that the Apis was the herald rather than the incarnation of Ptah. But see J. Vercoutter, "The Napatan Kings and Apis Worship," *Kush* 8 (1960) 64.

59. J. Ruffle, *The Egyptians* (Ithaca: Cornell University Press, 1977) 179; J. Vandier, *La religion égyptienne* (Paris: Presses Universitaires de France, 1949) 234–36.

60. E. Kiessling, "Die Götter von Memphis in griechisch-römischer Zeit," *Archiv für Papyrusforschung* 15 (1953) 26 n. 8.

61. W. B. Emery, *Archaic Egypt* (Baltimore: Penguin, 1961) 124.

the reign of Amenophis III in the New Kingdom (fourteenth century B.C.E.) that we begin to find inscriptions regarding these bulls.[62] The first stage of the Serapeum, where the bulls were to be buried, was constructed ca. 1300 B.C.E. The worship of the Apis reached its apogee from the 26th Dynasty (650 B.C.E.) on.

A complete Apis inscription would give the bull's birthday, its accession date, the date of its death and its burial, characteristically 70 days after (see Gen 50:3), and then its length of life.[63] The average life-span ranged from 16 to 19 years.[64]

The death of the Apis was announced in words similar to those used upon a pharaoh's demise, "The majesty of this god went forth to heaven," or "The god was conducted in peace to the Beautiful West." A stela dated to Psammetichus I (612 B.C.E.) describes the embalming of the Apis: "every craftsman was occupied with his task, anointing the body with unguent, wrapping it in royal cloth of very god; his casket was of *ḥd*, *mr*-wood, and cedar, the choicest of every terrace."[65] In 1941, near the temple of Ptah at Memphis, a number of objects associated with the Apis, dated to the reign of Shishak, were discovered.[66] These included four alabaster altars, a limestone manger, stands possibly used for an awning to shade the animal, and a large offering table (4 m × 2 m) used for washing or mummifying the bull.[67]

According to Ray,

62. Vandier, *La religion égyptienne*, 233.

63. See J. H. Breasted, *Ancient Records of Egypt* (Chicago: University of Chicago Press, 1906–7) 4.984, ## 974–75.

64. Kitchen, *Third Intermediate Period*, 156; M. Malinine, G. Posener, and J. Vercoutter, *Catalogue des stèles du Sérapéum de Memphis I* (Paris: Imprimerie Nationale, 1968) XIII.

65. Cited by K. S. Freedy and D. B. Redford, "The Dates in Ezekiel in Relation to Biblical, Babylonian, and Egyptian Sources," *JAOS* 90 (1970) 477.

66. Kitchen, *Third Intermediate Period*, 189; I. E. S. Edwards, T. G. H. James, and A. F. Short, *Introductory Guide to the Egyptian Collection* (London: British Museum, 1969) 148. Ptolemy I donated more than 50 silver talents and Ptolemy II 100 talents of myrrh for the burials of Apis bulls.

67. M. el Amir, "The *sēkos* of Apis at Memphis," *JEA* 34 (1948) 51–56; J. Dimick, "The Embalming House of the Apis Bulls," *Archaeology* 11 (1958) 183–89; idem, "The Embalming House of the Apis Bulls," *Mit Rahineh* (ed. R. Anthes; Philadelphia: University Museum, University of Pennsylvania, 1959) 75–79; M. Jones and A. M. Jones, "The Apis House Project at Mit Rahinah, First Season, 1982," *JARCE* 19 (1982) 51–58; idem, "The Apis House Project at Mit Rahinah: Preliminary Report of the Second and Third Seasons, 1982–1983," *JARCE* 20 (1983) 33–34; J. Kamil, "Ancient Memphis," *Archaeology* 38/4 (1985) 25–32. See R. L. Vos, *The Apis Embalming Ritual* (Leuven: Peeters, 1993).

> But nothing in the Apis's life quite became him like the leaving of it; amid national mourning, often displayed hysterically, the bull was embalmed, encoffined and escorted out to the western desert, finally to life in a massive granite sarcophagus in the catacomb known to modern visitors to Saqqâra as the Serapeum.[68]

The Serapeum

The bulls were carefully buried in mammoth sarcophagi carved from monolithic blocks of granite, about 10 feet high and 13 feet long, weighing between 60 and 70 tons. One of the most spectacular discoveries in the history of Egyptology was the recovery of these sarcophagi by Auguste Mariette in 1851 at the so-called Serapeum (Greek *Sarapieion*) at Saqqarah, approximately 20 miles southwest of Cairo. They were found in underground galleries more than 1,000 feet long.[69] Mariette and his successors found only two of the sarcophagi intact; the others had been plundered at an unknown date.[70] Mariette found numerous bronze statuettes of the Apis, depicted with the sun disc and the uraeus (cobra) between its horns.[71]

Near the Serapeum spectacular discoveries were made by W. B. Emery from 1964 until his lamented death in 1971 and then by his successors, G. T. Martin and H. S. Smith, until 1976.[72] They found a Sacred Animal Necropolis with terraces, temples, ramps, and galleries dedicated to the gods, containing 4 million mummified ibises and 500 baboons (both sacred to Thoth), 500,000 hawks (representing Horus), and a score of cows, representing Isis, the mother of the Apis bull.[73]

The Apis bull's mother had her Iseum built in the limestone cliffs on the desert edge north of the Serapeum perhaps as early as the sixth century B.C.E. Nearly 100 inscriptions of persons who took part in her burial have been recovered, the majority in Demotic.[74]

68. J. D. Ray, "The World of North Saqqâra," *World Archaeology* 10/2 (1978) 151.

69. Malinine, Posener, and Vercoutter, *Catalogue*, VII. The so-called Petits Souterrains contained burials from the reign of Ramesses II to that of Psammetichus I; the Grands Souterrains contained the most spectacular sarcophagi, including those of the Persian era.

70. C. W. Ceram, *Gods, Graves, and Scholars* (New York: Knopf, 1953) 132.

71. G. Kater-Sibbes and M. J. Vermaseren, *Apis* (3 vols.; Leiden: Brill, 1975–77).

72. See W. B. Emery, "Preliminary Report on the Excavations at North Saqqâra, 1969–70," *JEA* 57 (1971) 3–13; H. S. Smith, "Dates of the Obsequies of the Mothers of the Apis," *Revue d'Égyptologie* 24 (1972) 176–87.

73. Ray, "The World," 151. Also recovered were 1000 documents in Demotic, Greek, Aramaic, Carian, etc., primarily from the Ptolemaic period.

74. Emery, "Excavations at North Saqqâra, 1969–70," 11–12.

Apis Inscriptions of the Persian Era

Two of the sarcophagi from the Serapeum have a direct bearing on the question of whether Herodotus was correct regarding the tauricide by Cambyses.[75] In the case of Apis A, we have the following data:

BIRTH:	27th year (i.e., of Amasis) = 543
DEATH:	Unknown, but by subtracting 70 days from the date of the burial, one could reach a date late in August, 524.
BURIAL:	6th year (of Cambyses) = Nov. 6, 524
LENGTH OF LIFE:	19 years

For Apis B, we have the following data:

BIRTH:	5th year (of Cambyses) = May 29, 525
DEATH:	4th year (of Darius) = Aug. 31, 518
BURIAL:	70 days later
LENGTH OF LIFE:	8 years

What is highly unusual is the overlap of a year and three months, from the birth of Apis B (May, 525) to the death of Apis A (August, 524), during which there were apparently two Apis bulls.[76] We do know that during the reign of Shoshenq III ca. 798 one Apis died and another was installed in the same year.[77] Though ideally a new Apis was found soon after the death of the old Apis, during the Ptolemaic period there were often gaps of from one to three years between Apis bulls.[78]

Some have taken Apis A as the bull stabbed by Cambyses and have explained the overlap by assigning the years of the profaned bull to Apis B.[79] Klasens holds that neither Apis A nor Apis B can be the bull killed by

75. B. Porter and R. Moss, *Topographical Bibliography of Ancient Egyptian Hieroglyphic Texts, Reliefs, and Paintings III: Memphis* (Oxford: Clarendon, 1931) 213. See Bresciani, "Egypt and the Persian Empire," 334; E. Drioton and J. Vandier, *L'Égypte* (Paris: Presses Universitaires de France, 1952) 624.

76. Such a situation is regarded as unthinkable by Atkinson ("Legitimacy of Cambyses," 170) and Evans (*Herodotus*, 52).

77. See Kitchen, *Third Intermediate Period*, 340.

78. Ibid., 162. In 122 C.E., during the reign of Hadrian, a riot resulted upon this rediscovery of an Apis "after many years"; C. Birley, *Lives of the Later Caesars* (Harmondsworth: Penguin, 1976) 69–70.

79. This view was proposed by A. Wiedemann, *Der Tierkult der alten Ägypter* (Leipzig: Hinrichs, 1912), and accepted by H. R. Hall, *The Ancient History of the Near East* (London: Methuen, 1950) 312. Cf. also Elgood, *Later Dynasties*, 122.

Cambyses.[80] He argues that the coexistence of two Apis bulls was not inconceivable, citing one Apis bull who had to "wait in the wings" for three years before his predecessor died.

Klasens attempts to harmonize Herodotus' account with the inscriptional evidence of the two Apis sarcophagi by making the following assumptions: (1) Apis A died not in August, 524, but rather at the end of May, 525, just prior to Cambyses' invasion. (2) His burial was delayed because of the Persian invasion. (3) He interprets Her. 3.27 not as celebrating the birth but the accession of the Apis. (4) The bull killed by Cambyses was an Apis X, who was secretly interred. (5) Because we lack the accession date of Apis B, we do not know when he succeeded Apis A.[81]

While Klasens has demonstrated that it was possible for two Apis bulls to exist at the same time and that it is remotely possible to insert an unknown Apis X into the sequence between Apis A and B, there is a fatal flaw in his attempt to rehabilitate Herodotus on this crucial issue. It is quite clear that the sarcophagus of Apis A was dedicated by Cambyses himself.[82] As Culican points out:

> Cambyses takes the pharaonic titles "King of Upper and Lower Egypt, Son of Ra, Endowed with All Life" and is pictured wearing a pharaonic costume and kneeling before the Apis bull in an Egyptian posture of adoration.[83]

Thus, the difficulty is not ultimately the chronological problem—though given the relative rarity of these animals and the short time involved, this is also formidable—but rather the psychological improbability involved. It is simply difficult to believe that Cambyses would have honored the Apis A by providing it with a sarcophagus in November, 524, and then stabbed its successor a year later. He would certainly have been instructed in the significance of the rites by a counterpart of Udjahorresnet in Memphis and would not have misunderstood the rejoicing of the crowd at the acclamation of a new Apis.

The fact that we do not possess any Apis dedications for the reigns of Xerxes and Artaxerxes I may be the result of a gap in our archaeological records or indicate disruptions caused by periods of revolt.[84]

80. Klasens, "Cambyses en Egypte," 347.

81. Ibid., 346–48.

82. Kienitz, *Die politische Geschichte*, 58; Bresciani, "Egypt and the Persian Empire," 334; A. Gardiner, *Egypt of the Pharaohs* (London: Oxford University Press, 1961) 364.

83. Culican, *Medes and Persians*, 60.

84. Kitchen, *Third Intermediate Period*, 162 n. 330.

Regarding the origin of Herodotus' account, we can only speculate. Herodotus probably did not invent it out of whole cloth. I would suggest the following scenario: If we may assume that Cambyses did stab himself accidentally in the thigh (see below), the rumor may have spread in Egypt that the Persian invader had been punished by the Egyptian gods. Later elaborations may have tailored the crime to fit the punishment by maintaining that Cambyses had stabbed the Apis in the thigh. Because this Egyptian tale fit in so well with Herodotus' theme of *hubris* and avenging *nemesis*, Herodotus may have been happy to include it.[85]

We therefore have reason to believe that Cambyses, like Cyrus before him and Darius after him, tried to follow the general Persian policy of toleration and accommodation in order to pacify the Egyptians and to obtain the Egyptian gods' blessings.[86]

The Destruction of Temples

Though Cambyses did not murder the Apis bull, we need not doubt that the Persians destroyed some temples either to loot their contents or to punish resistance.[87] This is made quite clear by an explicit statement in a letter from the Jewish garrison in Elephantine to Bagohi, the Persian governor of Judah, on November 25, 407 B.C.E.:

> And during the days of the king(s) of Egypt our fathers had built that temple in Elephantine the fortress and when Cambyses (Aramaic KNBWZY) entered

85. Cf. K. H. Waters, "The Purpose of Dramatisation in Herodotus," *Historia* 15 (1966) 157–71. On the other hand J. M. Balcer (*Herodotus and Bisitun* [Stuttgart: Steiner, 1987] 99) rejects not only the story of the Apis episode but that of Cambyses' death. Balcer, who is skeptical not only of Herodotus but also of Darius, speculates that Cambyses may have been "stabbed by someone in his retinue," a crime possibly covered up in the Bisitun Inscription.

86. Vercoutter, "Napatan Kings," 67: "One thing at least is certain, Shabaka did not interfere with the Apis cult, but on the contrary paid his tribute to the god as soon as he reached Memphis by seeing that his name was inscribed in the burial chamber of the animal god and so ensuring that he should benefit by the god's blessing."

87. Diodorus Siculus (1.46.4) speaks of the looting of silver, gold, and costly stones from the temples; cf. Klasens, "Cambyses en Egypte," 345. There is an interesting parallel in the dual policies of Piankhy (25th Dynasty), when he invaded Lower Egypt. According to Vercoutter: "On the one hand wrath against the people who had dared to resist him, with the result that most of them were taken captive and the treasuries of the town were carried off; on the other hand the desire to be recognized as legal ruler by the priesthood of the god Ptah. . . ." ("Napatan Kings," 68).

> *Egypt* he found that temple built. And they overthrew the temples of the gods of Egypt, all (of them), but no one damaged anything in that temple.[88]

The burned layer at Naucratis may have also resulted from the Persian invasion.

Later classical writers, including some who saw ruined temples in Egypt, found it quite plausible to ascribe their destruction to the great arch-foe of Egypt, Cambyses. Diodorus Siculus (1.49.5), who visited Egypt ca. 60 B.C.E., wrote of the destruction of the mortuary temple of Ramesses II, a king whom he called Ozymandias, on the west bank of Thebes.[89] Strabo (17.1.27), who visited Egypt in 24 B.C.E., attributed many ruins to Cambyses:

> The city (Heliopolis) is now entirely deserted; it contains the ancient temple constructed in the Egyptian manner, which affords many evidences of the madness and sacrilege of Cambyses, who partly by fire and partly by iron sought to outrage the temples, mutilating them and burning them on every side, just as he did with the obelisks.[90]

Curtailment of Temple Donations

As Herodotus (2.37) observed, the Egyptian priests were well cared for:

> They neither consume nor spend aught of their own; sacred food is cooked for them, to each man is brought everyday flesh of beeves and geese in great abundance, and wine of grapes too is given to them.

One measure of Cambyses' that certainly alienated many of the influential priests[91] was his act of drastically curtailing the donations to all but a few favored temples. Our evidence for this measure comes from the reverse side of Demotic Papyrus 215 of the Bibliothèque Nationale in Paris. Of the three

88. B. Porten and J. C. Greenfield, *Jews of Elephantine and Arameans of Syene* (Jerusalem: Academon, 1976) 90. Cf. B. Porten, *Archives from Elephantine* (Berkeley: University of California Press, 1968) 19–20.

89. Immortalized by Percy Bysshe Shelley (1792–1822) in his poem: "My name is Ozymandias, king of kings: Look on my works, ye mighty, and despair!"

90. Pliny (*Nat. Hist.* 36.14.66–67) speaks of Cambyses' storming a city and burning it. Justin (9) relates that Cambyses, "disgusted at the superstitions of the Egyptians, ordered the temple of Apis and the other gods to be demolished."

91. Akhenaten likewise alienated the priests of Amon at Thebes, though in his case the blackening of the "heretic's" reputation came primarily not from the priests but from subsequent pharaohs; C. Aldred, *Akhenaten* (New York: McGraw-Hill, 1968) 257–60.

temples that were exempted, we are certain only of the name of Memphis. As for the other sites, scholars have suggested "Babylon" near the later site of Cairo and Hermopolis Parva in the Delta.[92] The decree stipulates:

> The cattle, which were given to the temples of the gods previously at the time of Pharaoh Amasis . . . with respect to them Cambyses commands, "Its half shall be given to them." As to the fowls, give them not to them. The priests themselves shall raise geese, and give (them) to their gods.

The text also mentions that the temples received gifts of grain, bread, wood, flax, incense, papyrus, and the equivalent of 16 tons of silver.[93]

Many historians believe that the jaundiced portrait of Cambyses that emerges in the pages of Herodotus was probably the result of misinformation fed to him by hostile Egyptian priests, who resented Cambyses' curtailment of their provisions.[94] An example of such a prejudiced source is a late text from the Horus temple of Edfu, which associates the "Medes," that is, the Persians, with the villainous god Seth.

The Death of Cambyses

In the spring of 522, Cambyses received bad news from Persia; he learned of a coup d'état and hastened home. According to Herodotus (3.64–66), as Cambyses was traveling homeward in Syria, possibly in the area of Hamath,[95] he jumped onto his horse. When the cap fell off the sheath of his sword,[96] he

92. Kienitz, *Die politische Geschichte*, 59; Klasens, "Cambyses en Egypte," 344 n. 37.

93. W. Spiegelberg, *Die sog. demotische Chronik des Pap. 215 der Bibliothèque National zu Paris* (Leipzig: Hinrichs, 1914) 32–33; Olmstead, *History of the Persian Empire*, 91; J. Prášek, *Kambyses* (Leipzig: Hinrichs, 1912) 12; W. Hinz, *Darius und die Perser* (Baden-Baden: Holle, 1976) 1.131.

94. Gardiner, *Egypt of the Pharaohs*, 364; Gyles, *Pharaonic Policies*, 39; Hinz, *Darius*, 131; Prášek, *Kambyses*, 30; Posener, *La première domination*, 164–66; R. N. Frye, *The Heritage of Persia* (Cleveland: World, 1963) 84.

95. Herodotus (3.64) gives the name of the site as *Agbatana*, which was also the name of the Median capital Ecbatana (modern Hamadan). Josephus (*Ant.* 11.30) places Cambyses' death at Damascus; Ctesias (#12) has him die in Babylon. Olmstead (*History of the Persian Empire*, 92) places the site near Mount Carmel; but most guess that Agbatana reflects Akmatha (i.e., Hamath).

96. Median and Persian scabbards had a tip that could fall off; see my *Foes from the Northern Frontier* (Grand Rapids, Mich.: Baker, 1982) 78, fig. 13; R. D. Barnett, "Median Arts," *Iranica Antiqua* 2 (1962) 77–95.

accidentally stabbed himself in the thigh. Because gangrene set in, Cambyses died some three weeks later.[97] His death was viewed by the classical writers as a just punishment for his misdeeds.[98]

A controversy has arisen over whether or not Cambyses' death can be interpreted as a suicide. Darius' Behistun Inscription, which is written in three languages, describes his death as follows:

OLD PERSIAN:	*uvāmaršiyuš amariyatā*	'he died his own death'
ELAMITE:	*hal-pi du-hi-e-ma hal-pi-ik*	'by his own death was dead'
AKKADIAN:	*mitūtu ramānišu mīti*	'he died his own death'[99]

Ernst Herzfeld interpreted this statement as meaning that Cambyses had committed suicide, an interpretation that has been followed by many scholars.[100] On the other hand, Wilhelm Schulze has cited parallels from twenty languages to argue that the phrase 'He died his own death' can mean a natural death.[101] M. Dandamaev points out that the phrase in Akkadian does not mean a normal death, nor is it the usual expression for suicide. It is rather an unusual phrase that intimates a premature, unexpected, and violent death.[102]

97. According to Ctesias (#12), Cambyses was carving a piece of wood with his knife when he accidentally stabbed himself; he died eleven days later.

98. Herodotus (3.64) has Cambyses struck in "the same part where he himself had once smitten the Egyptian god Apis." Justin (9) has the phrase *sponte evaginato* 'started out of its sheath', as though the sword was supernaturally moved against Cambyses.

99. R. G. Kent, *Old Persian* (rev. ed.; New Haven: American Oriental Society, 1953) 117, 120; E. von Voigtlander, *The Bisitun Inscription of Darius the Great* (London: Lund Humphreys, 1978) 55; J. P. Asmussen, "Iranica, A: The Death of Cambyses . . . ," *AcOr* 31 (1968) 9–20.

100. E. Herzfeld, "Der Tod des Kambyses," *BSOAS* 8 (1935–37) 589–97. Among those who have followed this interpretation are: W. W. How and J. Wells, *A Commentary on Herodotus* (Oxford: Clarendon, 1928) 1.396; Olmstead, *History of the Persian Empire*, 92; Kent, *Old Persian*, 177: H. S. Nyberg, *Der Reich der Achämeniden* (Bern: Francke, 1954) 75.

101. W. Schulze, "Der Tod des Kambyses," *Sitzungsberichte der Preussischen Akademie der Wissenschaften* 37 (1912) 685–703. See also J. Puhvel, "The 'Death of Cambyses' and Hittite Parallels," *A. Pagliaro Festschrift* (Rome: Istituto di Glottologia di Roma, 1969) 3.169–75.

102. Dandamaev, *Persien*, 146–48. Cambyses probably prepared a tomb for himself prior to his departure for Egypt. Some ruins 6 km (3.6 miles) north of Persepolis, called today Takht-i-Rustam, were identified by E. Herzfeld in 1932 as the unfinished grave of Cambyses. The striking similarities of the dimensions and orientation of the structure to those of Cyrus' own grave are convincing proofs that this was also a tomb. In 1973, less than 200 m east of Takht-i-Rustam, remains of a building that may have been Cambyses'

The Cambyses Legend

In 1899 a badly damaged Coptic manuscript that contained a highly garbled account of the invasion of Egypt by Cambyses was published. Cambyses is said to have sent a false letter in the name of the pharaoh calling for an assembly of the Egyptians at a festival for Apis. The Egyptian advisors, who are suspicious, have the people assemble, but armed. The pharaoh at first believes that the people are armed against himself but is then informed of their true intent. Unfortunately the text breaks off at this point.

The text is hopelessly confused. Cambyses is identified with Nebuchadnezzar and the Persians with the Assyrians! Quite surprisingly, the pharaoh places his trust in the Ammonites, Moabites, and Idumaeans. The references to the Gauls or Celts must indicate a date after the third century B.C.E.

Jansen believes that the text was originally composed in Demotic by a native Egyptian in the second century B.C.E. and then reworked by an Aramaic-speaking Jew.[103] But other scholars suggest a much later date, even as late as the eighth century C.E.[104] Cruz-Uribe points out some striking parallels with the Chronicle of Bishop John of Nikiu, which describes the Arab conquest of Egypt in the 640s. The Coptic author of the Cambyses Legend may have intended, in recalling the Persian tyrant, to pose "the veiled threat that any actions which harm the Egyptians will result in the death of the perpetrator."[105] MacCoull thinks that the legendary Cambyses was meant to represent the Caliph ᶜUmar.[106]

---

audience palace were discovered. See E. Herzfeld, *The Persian Empire* (Wiesbaden: Steiner, 1968) 36; W. Kleiss, "Der Takht-i Rustam bei Persepolis und das Kyros-grab in Pasargadae," *Archäologischer Anzeiger des Jahrbuches des deutschen archäologischen Instituts* 86 (1971) 157–62; A. B. Tilia, "Discovery of an Achaemenian Palace near Takhi-i Rustam to the North of the Terrace of Persepolis," *Iran* 12 (1974) 200–204; W. Kleiss and P. Calmeyer, "Das unvollendete achaemenidische Felsgrab bei Persepolis," *Archaeologische Mitteilungen aus Iran* n.s. 8 (1975) 81–98; W. Kleiss, "Zur Entwicklung der achaemenidischen Palastarchitektur," *Iranica Antiqua* 15 (1980) 199–211.

103. H. L. Jansen, *The Coptic Story of Cambyses' Invasion of Egypt* (Oslo: J. Dybwad, 1950).

104. G. Müller, "Zu den Bruchstücken des kopt. Kambysesromans," *ZÄS* 39 (1901) 113–17; H. Grapow, "Untersuchungen über Stil und Sprache des kopt. Kambysesromans," *ZÄS* 74 (1938) 55–68; J. Schwartz, "Les conquérants perses et la littérature égyptienne," *BIFAO* 48 (1948) 65–80.

105. E. Cruz-Uribe, "Notes on the Coptic Cambyses Romance," *Enchoria* 14 (1986) 56.

106. L. S. B. MacCoull, "The Coptic Cambyses Narrative Reconsidered," *GRBS* 23 (1982) 187.

Many centuries later, in sixteenth-century England in a play by Thomas Preston, Cambyses was once again resurrected to serve as the prototypical tyrant![107]

107. W. Armstrong, "The Background and Sources of Preston's *Cambises*," *English Studies* 31 (1950) 129–35; W. D. Wolf, "Recent Studies in Early Tudor Drama," *English Literary Renaissance* 8 (1978) 116–19.

Other articles that should be consulted are: Alan B. Lloyd, "Herodotus on Cambyses," in *Achaemenid History III: Method and History* (ed. A. Kuhrt and H. Sancisi-Weerdenburg; Leiden: Nederlands Instituut voor het Nabije Oosten, 1988) 55–66; Leo Depuydt, "Murder in Memphis: The Story of Cambyses' Mortal Wounding of the Apis Bull (ca. 523 B.C.E.)," *JNES* 54 (1995) 119–26; cf. idem, "Evidence for Accession Dating under the Achaemenids," *JAOS* 115 (1995) 193–204, esp. 201–2. Though admitting that the evidence is inconclusive, Depuydt believes that Herodotus may have been right after all about the killing of the Apis bull!

The Maturation Theme in the Adam and Eve Story

Anthony York

The great Swedish biblical scholar and orientalist, Ivan Engnell, once claimed that he had spent more than twenty-five years studying the creation story and the paradise myth of Genesis.[1] Surely, I remember thinking when I read that, to spend a quarter of a century studying a passage of three short chapters in the Bible is academic eccentricity enthroned. However, now that I have myself surveyed a minute portion of the secondary literature on the Adam and Eve story, my judgment of Engnell's dedication has become considerably more charitable.

It is undoubtedly true that this story's influence on Western literature and thought, out of all proportion to its size,[2] would take a lifetime to explore. Indeed, the dramatic statement of F. Parvin Sharpless concerning the relative worth of this passage is probably accurate: "The story in chapter three of the Book of Genesis carries more weight per line than any other literary document one can think of."[3] Moreover, the Adam and Eve story has been the object of intensive study for over 2300 years[4] and even today shows no signs of loosening its grip on our imaginations.[5]

Nevertheless, it is a curious fact that in spite of its enormous influence on postbiblical writers, we still lack a consensus on the meaning of the passage.[6]

1. I. Engnell, "'Knowledge' and 'Life' in the Creation Story," *Wisdom in Israel and in the Ancient Near East* (VTSup 3; ed. M. Noth and D. Winton Thomas; Leiden: Brill, 1969) 101.

2. From 2:4b to 3:24 there are just over 630 words!

3. F. Parvin Sharpless, *The Myth of the Fall: Literature of Innocence and Experience* (Hayden Humanities Series; Rochelle Park, N.J.: Hayden, 1974) 2.

4. That is, at least from the time of the Greek translation.

5. See the treatment by Nicolas Wyatt, "Interpreting the Creation and Fall Story in Genesis 2–3," *ZAW* 93 (1981) 10–21, for bibliography. *Semeia* 18 (1980) was given over to articles on Genesis 2–3.

6. I think it is in light of this communal frustration that we must evaluate D. R. G. Beattie's blunt article "What is Genesis 2–3 About?" *ExpTim* 92 (1980) 8–10. See the response by R. E. Williams on p. 339 of the same journal.

Given the great importance of the story in various systems of thought, this state of affairs is not only curious, it is astonishing. Moreover, when we reflect on the many different interpretations of this story offered through the ages, we are tempted to agree with Engnell that "every attempt to throw light upon the problem [of Genesis 2–3] must seem both presumptuous and doomed to failure."[7]

Problems of Methodology

Certainly, one reason for our difficulty is that scholars traditionally study the text with one eye on the story itself and another on its application to one of several systems of theology or cultural anthropology. Many scholars acknowledge this problem of divided loyalties and adjust their studies accordingly. Bo Reicke, for example, introduces his thoughtful article on the Adam and Eve story with a careful delimitation: "Although the subject has bearing upon all branches of Jewish and Christian theology, we think it wise, in treating this problem, to avoid certain questions which are usually directed to the Genesis text by advanced theology. Instead we shall try to explain the old narrative with regard to the sort of civilization in which it arose, in order to establish its original meaning. The application of the study of systematic theology is outside the scope of this little essay."[8]

Engnell, too, faces this problem: "A great deal of modern exegesis of Genesis has been precisely too 'modern', has too strong a flavour of an *interpretatio europeica*, indeed an *interpretatio christiana*," and he adds obligatorily, "the latter, of course, being justified from the point of view of faith and as being in the service of homiletics, but not at home in a strictly scientific treatment."[9]

Furthermore, to compound the problem, this strabismic approach to a biblical text is not, *pace* Engnell, modern. As Brevard Childs once wrote, "From the outset Jewish and Christian scholars wrestled with the problem of the various senses of Scripture."[10] The ancient rabbis, convinced as they were that great treasures were to be found in the biblical text if one mined with the proper tools, devised several systems of interpretation. Yet fundamental

7. Engnell, " 'Knowledge' and 'Life,' " 103.

8. B. Reicke, "The Knowledge Hidden in the Tree of Paradise," *JSS* 1 (1956) 194.

9. Engnell, " 'Knowledge' and "Life,' " 103.

10. B. Childs, "The *Sensus Literalis* of Scripture: An Ancient and Modern Problem," *Beiträge zur alttestamentlichen Theologie: Festschrift für W. Zimmerli* (ed. H. Donner et al.; Göttingen: Vandenhoeck and Ruprecht, 1977) 87.

to them all was the distinction they made between the *peshat*, the simple, unadorned meaning, and the *derash*, the embellished, the applied meaning in a given situation.[11]

In the modern context, Reicke's "original meaning" and Engnell's "strictly scientific treatment" (*peshat*) are then to be distinguished from the "homiletical" or "theological" meaning (*derash*).[12] Obviously, all sorts of difficulties and disagreements are going to arise in the *derash* aspect of this kind of interpretation, but even that is not the greatest problem, particularly for the Adam and Eve story. Here, to coin a phrase, one man's *peshat* is another man's *derash*. What, for example, is the simple, plain, "scientific," "original" meaning of the phrase "the tree of knowledge of good and bad"?[13] We can define each word in the phrase exhaustively—we can be especially profound with the word *knowledge*—and we still feel that the phrase means more than or something other than the sum total of its parts.

In brief, the theory of a two-tiered method of interpretation seems a worthy one, but the realities of two millennia of biblical studies would suggest that it has created as many problems as it has solved. While certainly we can applaud scholars like Engnell and Reicke for recognizing the problem and for attempting to present us with the "original" meaning alone, something inconceivable to the ancients, we must remember that most of us have formed our perception of the story from *derash* rather than *peshat* and so have not only the difficult problem of interpreting the story in its natural setting, but also the painful task of divesting ourselves of preconceived notions, of removing from the text the gauze of centuries of theological speculation.

Most of the speculation, of course, centers upon the interpretation of the story as an account of the "Fall of Man," but increasingly scholars are

11. My point is that the rabbis distinguished various levels of meaning in a biblical passage, not that the *peshat* was in fact the simple, plain meaning or what we might call the *sensus grammaticus et historicus*. See R. Loewe, "The 'Plain' Meaning of Scripture in Early Jewish Exegesis," *Papers of the Institute of Jewish Studies* (Jerusalem: Institute of Jewish Studies, 1964) 1.140–85, for an excellent discussion.

12. Surely Childs is incorrect when he writes that "after the end of the 18th century the issue of plural senses of the text hung on only in a vestigial form in most Protestant circles . . . ," (*Sensus Literalis*, 88). The influential (and Protestant), multivolumed *Interpreter's Bible* clearly adopts a double-barreled approach, with its commentary divided into "exegesis" and "exposition," that is, *peshat* and *derash*.

13. Apart from tradition, I see no good reason to render the Hebrew *ra*^{c} as 'evil'. Accordingly, in keeping with my attempt to see the story afresh, I follow the NAB in reading 'good and bad', even though at times the phrase is a bit jarring for ears more accustomed to the traditional.

recognizing that the "Fall" metaphor is inappropriate and misleading for our story.[14] Yahweh specifically says subsequent to the eating of the fruit (3:22), "The man has become like one of us." While certainly there is room for disagreement in these ambiguous words, a notion of "descent" seems a most remote option. If I may anticipate my argument, it is not so much the idea that man "falls," but that he "chooses" one thing over another, a knowledge of good and bad over immortality. For now it may suffice to remark that even the most traditional of commentators would agree, I venture, that only with a great deal of eisegesis can one find a "Fall of Man" doctrine in this passage.[15]

But, even if one could somehow manage to derive such an intent from the story,[16] he or she would still have to contend with the fact that such a doctrine is not clearly stated elsewhere in the literature of ancient Israel. This fact in itself should arrest the attention of those who seek to impute such a belief to the ancient writer. Were it, for example, a tenet available to the writer of Job, it would surely have been cited when the three friends appear to exhaust the current notions of sin and punishment to explain the horrors that befell Job. Yet not once is recourse taken to some primordial "Fall." Moreover, the doctrine of individual responsibility associated with Ezekiel primarily, but also with Jeremiah ("Do not say, Our fathers have eaten sour grapes and our teeth are set on edge," Ezek 18:2; Jer 31:29–30) positively militates against such a notion.

On the other hand, it is clear that this doctrine arose in the apocalyptic framework of postbiblical Judaism (cf. Wis 10:1–2; Sir 15:11–20; 2 Esdr 3:4–7), was then seized upon by subsequent writers such as Paul as an explanation of evil in the world, and was further expanded by Augustine. But, if the road from Adam to Augustine is historically understandable, it is not thereby

14. As many responsible writers have concluded. See, for example, the trenchant comments of Paul Ricoeur, *The Symbolism of Evil* (trans. Emerson Buchanan; Boston: Beacon, 1967) 233; Frederick W. Dillistone, "The Fall: Christian Truth and Literary Symbol," *Mansions of the Spirit* (ed. George A. Panichas; New York: Hawthorn, 1967) 137–54; C. Westermann, *Creation* (trans. J. J. Scullion; Philadelphia: Fortress, 1974) 108–9.

15. In this connection see the excellent article by Roberts W. French, "Reading the Bible: The Story of Adam and Eve," *College Literature* 9 (1982) 22–29. French correctly reads the story as literature, not as a sophisticated theological document.

16. And even then, does not Yahweh rescind his curse of 3:17—on the *ground*, incidentally, not the *man*—in 8:21? No less a biblical commentator than Ibn Ezra concluded just that (see *Torah Shlemah* [New York: American Biblical Encyclopedia Society, 1955] 2.50 n. 231). Among modern scholars, C. A. Simpson acknowledged the force of 8:21 when he wrote in the *Interpreter's Bible* (1.547) that this passage "is a reversal of the sentence found in 3:17 and can only be an addition by the hand of one who misunderstood the significance of the garden story." Misunderstanding, certainly; but whose?

inevitable. Further, the "Fall" metaphor, associated as it is with all sorts of doctrinal subtleties, which developed much later in Jewish and Christian thought, stands colossus-like, preventing immediate access to the narrative itself, thus compounding the already considerable difficulties of the passage.

In addition to the problem of theological predisposition, we have also the problem of context. Surely, all would agree that the axiom "interpret in context" is both necessary and desirable. Our problem, however, is defining the context. This difficulty has always been present in biblical studies,[17] but it has become more acute since the rise of source criticism. In the opinion of the majority of scholars, the Adam and Eve story is the initial story of J, which is still generally held to be the earliest of the four sources of the Pentateuch. Does one then interpret the Adam and Eve story in the context of J, or does he interpret it in terms of its new context provided by P, the latest of the four, whose themes, concerns, and style are noticeably different from those of J,[18] or does he isolate it from both sources and interpret

17. Is not "Canon Criticism," associated with James Sanders (*Torah and Canon*) and Brevard Childs (*Introduction to the Old Testament as Scripture*), essentially an attempt to define the context in which one interprets these writings? As E. D. Hirsch observes, "'significance' [as opposed to meaning alone] is textual meaning as related to some context, indeed any context, beyond itself" (*Aims of Interpretation* [Chicago: University of Chicago Press, 1976] 3). My impression of "Canon Criticism" is that it is an attempt to argue from "significance" to "meaning," or to recast the old cliché, to put the theological cart before the exegetical horse. Perhaps one reason for this is that with the rise of modern biblical criticism, it has become clear that the "original meaning" of an Old Testament text would not yield the "significance" that New Testament and later Christian writers attached to it. The solution, therefore, in Canon Criticism is to begin one's interpretive task at the end and work backward. Compare, too, the revealing comment by Bernhard W. Anderson: "Von Rad remarks, following R. Rosenzweig, that 'R' means 'Rabbenu' as well as 'Redactor' and that for Christians 'Rabbenu' means Jesus—i.e., we [Christians] should interpret the text as it has come to us through Jesus, the final Redactor" ("From Analysis to Synthesis: The Interpretation of Genesis 1–11," *JBL* 97 [1978] 29). I can only assume that, for these interpreters, the principal task of the modern biblical scholar is to determine how one's theological ancestors interpreted a given passage, in which case biblical studies becomes little more than History of Hermeneutics, that is, not the text itself but its significance and application are the object of one's study, or perhaps more fairly, the text in light of its application. In his excellent book *The Tenth Generation*, George Mendenhall also notes the distance between "meaning" and "significance," particularly as related to religious matters: "It is not the original intent or content of the Sacred Book that is important to religious communities, but its authority to undergird what the community holds at a particular time to be true" (p. ix).

18. P. E. S. Thompson, "The Jahwist Creation Story," *VT* 21 (1971) 197–208, argues persuasively, if not convincingly, for this approach.

synchronically,[19] or does he go further and analyze the story itself and break it down into its putative component parts?[20] In theory, of course, one can interpret the passage in any one of these ways or in all of them, as long as he makes it plain what he is doing.[21] The failure to define the precise context in which one interprets the story will inevitably lead to confusion.

In this paper, I am chiefly concerned with the Adam and Eve story in the context of J, which I take to be its natural setting. We now have to ask this question: was the Yahwist writer a creator, an interpreter, an editor, or a compiler? That is, were the stories that we now find in J created by him, or did they already exist in some form and were adapted by him to a new situation? For example, several studies suggest that in its original form Genesis 2–3 was a Canaanite story.[22] Peter Ellis in his book *The Yahwist: The Bible's First Theologian*, the most detailed analysis of the J source in English, suggests much the same thing when he writes, "It might even be conjectured that the Yahwist utilized these myths [Genesis 2–3] mediated through Canaanite writings, in order not only to demythologize them, but to appeal to those enlightened Canaanites in the kingdom who were well disposed to Yahwism."[23] Whether this specific genetic history of the text is true is difficult to say.[24] My own impression of the Yahwist is that he was neither a pure creator

19. As J. P. Fokkelman does so ably for the Tower of Babel story in his *Narrative Art in Genesis: Specimens of Stylistic and Structural Analysis* (Amsterdam: Van Gorcum, 1975). See too J. T. Walsh, "Genesis 2:4b–3:24: A Synchronic Approach," *JBL* 96 (1977) 161–77.

20. In the manner of J. Alberto Soggin, "The Fall of Man in the Third Chapter of Genesis," *Old Testament and Oriental Studies* (Biblica et Orientalia 29; Rome: Pontifical Biblical Institute, 1975) 88–111; Julius A. Bewer, *The Literature of the Old Testament in Its Historical Development* (New York: Columbia University Press, 1928) 61; I. Lewy, "The Two Strata in the Eden Story," *HUCA* 27 (1956) 92–99; and more recently Nicolas Wyatt, "Interpreting the Creation and Fall Story."

21. Of course, I have only mentioned *literary* contexts. If one wants to extend the matter into *theological* contexts, the problem becomes commensurately more complex.

22. F. T. Hvidberg, 'The Canaanite Background of Gen. I–III," *VT* 10 (1960) 285–94; also Wyatt, "Interpreting the Creation and Fall Story"; Thompson, "Jahwist Creation Story"; and Soggin, "The Fall of Man."

23. P. E. Ellis, *The Yahwist: The Bible's First Theologian* (Notre Dame: Fides, 1968) 60.

24. The difficulty with this approach is best exemplified by a passage from Soggin, a supporter of the Canaanite origin theory: "The origin of the story seems to have been Canaanite, that is, it came from the very milieu that the story was intended to oppose. Its original aim, however, is deliberately misunderstood by the biblical author and turned completely around for polemical reasons" ("Fall of Man," 88). In brief, if such a development or adaptation took place, its history is much too convoluted to reconstruct.

nor a mere editor or compiler. Rather, he used existing myths (see discussion below) to compose a new folk tale and myth.[25]

Regarding the "situational context," again there is great uncertainty. I will defer to the opinion of the great majority of scholars who date J in the ninth century B.C.E., while recognizing that there is a considerable body of opinion that would place it much later, even in exilic times.[26] I do not think it would seriously alter my interpretation if the later date should prove to be the correct one.

In brief, much of the methodological confusion surrounding the discussion of the Adam and Eve story is to be attributed on the one hand to external theological predispositions colliding with the narrative and on the other to a lack of precision in defining the context.

Literary Features of the Story

I take it as axiomatic that a proper understanding of a piece of literature includes a consideration of those formal aspects of the literature that at once relate it to other writings of the same genre and establish its own distinctive qualities. I wish to consider three principal literary features of the Adam and Eve story: (1) its relationship to other Near Eastern wisdom-mortality stories; (2) its emphasis on etiology; and (3) its fondness for paronomasia. A consideration of these features should aid us in understanding the writer's intent.

While in fact there are many aspects of our story that have parallels in other Ancient Near Eastern literature,[27] such as the deity forming man out of clay as a potter does a vessel (so the Egyptian god Khnum[28]), or the garden of

25. See H. J. Stoebe, "Gut und Böse in der jahwistischen Quelle des Pentateuch," *ZAW* 65 (1953) 188–204, for a good discussion of the relationship of J to his sources; also J. Scharbert, "Quellen und Redaktion in Gen. 2:4b–4:16," *BZ* 18 (1974) 45–64.

26. See George Mendenhall, "The Shady Side of Wisdom: The Date and Purpose of Gen. 3," *A Light Unto My Path* (Festschrift for Jacob Myers; ed. Howard N. Bream, Ralph D. Heim, and Carey A. Moore; Philadelphia: Temple University Press, 1974) 319–44; also see Nicolas Wyatt, "Interpreting the Creation and Fall Story."

27. See in particular Hans-Peter Müller, "Mythische Elemente in der jahwistischen Schöpfungerzählung," *ZTK* 69 (1972) 259–89; and H. Gese, "Der bewachte Lebensbaum und die Heroen: Zwei mythologische Ergänzungen zur Urgeschichte der Quelle J," *Wort und Geschichte* (Festschrift for Karl Elliger; Neukirchen-Vluyn: Neukirchener, 1973) 77–86.

28. See, for example, *Mythology of All Races* (ed. John Arnott MacCulloch; Boston: Archaeological Institute of America/Marshall Jones, 1918) vol. 12, chap. 3, pp. 50–51; and Henri Frankfort, *Ancient Egyptian Religion* (New York: Harper, 1948) 20.

the gods being located at the mouth of rivers, as in Canaanite mythology,[29] two ancient myths in particular warrant our close attention: the Gilgamesh Epic and the Adapa Myth.

Many recognize the Gilgamesh Epic as the source of the Flood Story in the Near Eastern world, but the Flood Story is only a small part of the total epic, which has as its theme the quest for immortality.[30] While surely it is unnecessary to recount the entire story, perhaps for our purposes we can rehearse Gilgamesh's brush with immortality. With the death of his beloved friend, Enkidu, Gilgamesh—part god and part man—realizes apparently for the first time that he too, although renowned for his wisdom and strength, is mortal. He then begins his quest to find the secret of immortality, and to that end visits Utnapishtim, the Babylonian Noah, who survived the flood and was rewarded with immortality. After recounting the story of the flood, Utnapishtim sends Gilgamesh on his way with a change of clothes and the promise that he will find the plant that will give him immortality. Gilgamesh does find the plant, the name of which is "Man Becomes Young in Old Age,"[31] only to have it stolen by a snake. Thus Gilgamesh is deprived of immortality.

The many parallels to the Adam and Eve story are obvious, but for our purposes, more important than the details is the theme of the great epic, which J. Pedersen admirably summarizes, "The lesson of the great epic is that even the man who attains the highest degree of wisdom . . . thus obtaining the greatest share in the divine is subject to the law of death."[32]

This is also fundamental in the Adam and Eve story. Adam, too, is like the gods, "The man has become like one of us, knowing good and bad"; and he too is denied immortality, "What if he now reaches out his hand and takes fruit from the tree of life also, eats it and lives forever?" (3:22). Then, and only then, is man driven out of the garden, and cherubim are stationed to guard the way to the tree of life. Note too that immortality in Gilgamesh is specifically defined in terms of youth ("Man Becomes Young in Old Age"), it obviously being the worst kind of pyrrhic victory to acquire immortality,

29. See W. F. Albright, *Archaeology and the Religion of Israel* (5th ed.; Garden City: Doubleday, 1968) 71ff.

30. I am referring to the Akkadian *Gilgamesh Epic.* See the invaluable study by Jeffrey H. Tigay, *The Evolution of the Gilgamesh Epic* (Philadelphia: University of Pennsylvania Press, 1982) for the different strands of the Epic.

31. So E. Speiser in *ANET,* 96. He notes that "the process is one of rejuvenation, not immortality." Surely, the notion is immortality *through* rejuvenation.

32. Pedersen, "Wisdom and Mortality," 241.

only to grow older and older. The only immortality worth having is the kind that somehow arrests development. This too is important for the Adam and Eve story.

The story of Adapa,[33] known throughout the Near East from Egypt to Mesopotamia, contains, like the Gilgamesh Epic, an account of man squandering an opportunity for gaining immortality, and this story too has the unfortunate mortal possessing great wisdom. The protagonist, Adapa, whose name very likely means 'Man' (as of course "Adam" does),[34] is granted power by Ea, the god of wisdom, to name everything. He is, as it were, the "Father of Nouns." Then the text has this significant line, "To him he [the god Ea] has given wisdom; immortality he has not given him." In the course of the story, Adapa is summoned to appear before the great sky god, Anu, because he has displeased him. Ea, the god of wisdom it will be recalled, tutors Adapa in how he should behave before the great deity. Specifically, he should refuse "the bread and water of life" when they are offered to him because, says Ea, they are really "the bread and water of death." Adapa dutifully obeys Ea. After Anu accepts Adapa's explanation for the displeasure and discomfort that he has brought the gods, he offers Adapa "the bread and water of life," as Ea said he would. Adapa, of course, refuses. Anu then asks him why he refused, and when Adapa tells him he is acting on Ea's advice, Anu laughs, clothes him with a garment, and sends him back to earth, full of wisdom but, alas, without the immortality that was within his grasp. By this ruse, Ea has prevented Adapa from gaining immortality.

Comparing the Adam and Adapa myths, John Skinner once observed: "In both we have the idea that wisdom and immortality combined constitute equality with the deity; in both we have a man receiving the first and missing the second; and in both the man is counseled in opposite directions by supernatural voices, and acts on that advice which is contrary to his interest."[35] The fundamental idea of all these stories—Gilgamesh, Adapa, and Adam—

33. See G. Buccellati, "Adapa, Genesis, and the Notion of Faith," *UF* 5 (1973) 61–66; Stephen H. Langdon, "The Myth of Adapa and Adam," vol. 5 (1931), chap. 4 of *Mythology of All Races.* Also in *ANET,* 101. Recent significant German studies of the Adapa story include B. Kienast, "Die Weisheit des Adapa von Eridu," *Symbolae Biblicae et Mesopotamicae Francisco Mario Theodoro de Liagre Böhl Dedicatae* (ed. M. Beek; Leiden: Brill, 1973) 234–39; and Hans-Peter Müller, "Mythos als Gattung archäischen Erzählens und die Geschichte von Adapa," *AfO* 29–30 (1983–84) 75–89.

34. So *ANET,* 101, citing Erich Ebeling, *Tod und Leben nach den Vorstellungen der Babylonier,* 27.

35. J. Skinner, *A Critical and Exegetical Commentary on Genesis* (ICC; New York: Charles Scribner's, 1917) 92.

is that while man may have great wisdom and so be like the gods in that respect, he is nevertheless unlike the gods in that he is mortal. Each of them also tells a story purporting to explain how man lost his chance at immortality. To be sure, the details are different. Each story is adapted to its own local setting and tells the story in its own way, but the same essential idea is present in all.

Incidentally, biblical literature might also provide us with another version of man's acquisition of divine wisdom. Eliphaz questions Job, "Were you born first of mankind? Were you brought forth before the hills? Did you listen in God's secret council and usurp all wisdom for yourself alone?" (Job 15:7–8). By the combination "born first of mankind" and "usurp all wisdom for yourself" the writer presupposes, in the opinion of many scholars, another account that must have explained man's acquisition of divine wisdom in another way, by listening in on the deity's secret council.

Be that as it may, we must now consider our writer's etiological emphasis. One of the most characteristic features of the J writer in general is his concern to explain how and why certain observable phenomena came to be the way they are. For example, in chap. 6, we read that the giants (the Nephilim), who were reputedly a part of Canaanite culture, came into being, according to J, as a result of the union of the sons of the gods and the daughters of men. In another place we are told that the Canaanites were an accursed people, fit only to be slaves of the Israelites, because their forefather, Ham, looked upon Noah's nakedness (chap. 9). Here, incidentally, the story is not so much an explanation of a phenomenon as of a perception, the perception that the Yahwist had of the Canaanites. Also, we are informed, mankind speaks many different languages because people of old attempted to build a tower reaching to the dwelling place of the deity, who promptly scattered the people over the face of the earth and confused their language "so that they can no longer understand one another" (Genesis 11:7). All these stories and many others are a part of J, and all of them are exercises in legendary and mythological causation. Because the Adam and Eve story is J's *creation* account, his account of the beginning of things, we should expect to find many such explanations, and we are not disappointed.

How did things get to be the way they are? This is the concern of etiology. Why is it that we call a certain four-legged creature on which a man rides in battle a *sûs* (horse)? Or why is it that we call a certain carnivore an *ʾaryēh* (lion)? They cannot have named themselves! The answer: the progenitor of our race named them, and that is what they are. Remember that Adapa too gave things, presumably everything, names. Why do snakes crawl in the dust? Why do people wear clothes? Animals do not. Why is childbirth so painful?

Why do women, in spite of that, desire a man? Why are women subordinate to men? Why is it that the bodies of the dead are reduced to dust, resembling soil? Indeed, so pronounced is this feature in the story that the writer cannot refrain from interrupting his narrative at one point to make sure the reader gets the message: "That is why," he informs us after the woman's creation, "a man leaves his father and mother, and is united to his wife" (2:24).

In this connection, there is certainly no need to say what one scholar, a representative of many, says of this etiological pattern, "These are problems which touch upon the elemental and eternal mysteries and with the solution of which the world is still in a certain sense wrestling."[36] I find it hard to imagine even the most reflective of men pondering why a snake crawls as one of the "elemental and eternal mysteries" of life. Like the inhabitants of the world of Chance, the gardener (Chauncey Gardiner) of Jerzy Kosinski's *Being There*, biblical scholars quite often appear predisposed to find profundity, even if they have to create it themselves.[37]

Yet, to describe the story as an etiological one is not to describe the full intent of the story, for of all the varied phenomena of life that cry out for explanation, the Yahwist selects only certain items to explain, and the feature that all these items have in common is the principle of hierarchy. In what ways is man different from animals? What is his relationship to them, specifically to the snake?[38] What is the relationship of man to woman? Of a man to his parents? Above all, how is man different from the gods? For overshadowing all the detailed etiological concerns is the larger question: what is the relationship of man to the divine? His answer—I think his unmistakable answer—is that man is like the gods in that he possesses, as they do, the knowledge of good and bad (I will present my understanding of that cloudy phrase in the appropriate place) and he is unlike them in that he is mortal.

This coincides with another fundamental idea of the Yahwist. There is, in his opinion, a hierarchy in the world, and our story establishes what that hierarchy is. When that hierarchy is in any way confused, trouble results. Abel offers the food of the gods, meat, to the deity, while Cain improperly offers the food of man, the produce of the soil, and murder is the result. The sons

36. Julian Morgenstern, *A Jewish Interpretation of Genesis* (Cincinnati: The Union of Hebrew Congregations, 1910) 50.

37. Compare the sobering words of Engnell, "Many exegetes . . . seem inclined to read too much of a modern 'philosophical' profoundness of thought into the Paradise myth" ("'Knowledge' and 'Life,'" 103–4).

38. See K. R. Joines, "The Serpent in Gen. 3," *ZAW* 87 (1975) 1–11, for the Near Eastern background.

of the gods cohabit with the daughters of men, and the disaster of the flood is the result. Ham sees his father's nakedness, a confusion of roles, and the Canaanites are cursed. Men attempt to enter the domain of the gods, and confusion (literally) results, the punishment being a reflection of the crime. Lot, a Hebrew, invites confusion by living among the Canaanites in Sodom, and the result is well known.

The third of the literary characteristics is the most difficult for the modern reader, the one who reads the Bible only in translation, to appreciate. It is the author's penchant for folk etymologies and puns.[39] Of course, most commentators call attention to this feature, but few attempt an explanation of the function of the wordplay in the meaning of the story. This aspect of his style is such an integral part of the story, however, that we have a right to expect it to be related to the author's intent.

Most non-Semitic translations of the story, that is, translations other than the Targums, the Peshiṭta, the Ethiopic, and the Arabic versions, make little or no attempt to reproduce this feature of the story. The earliest translation, the Septuagint, apparently attempts to capture some of the style of the Hebrew by its curious reading of Eden as E-d-e-*m*, so resembling *Adam* and *ʾadāmâ*. Other than that, it cannot hope to reproduce the original. Jerome's Vulgate also makes a valiant effort, but it cannot be said to have succeeded.[40]

Because every scholar knows the puns of the Adam and Eve story first hand, it will suffice to give but a few examples of those related to the theme of this paper. The first is the author's interesting use of the different Hebrew words for 'man'. In 2:7 we read, "The God Yahweh formed a 'man' from the dust of the ground," while 2:23 has "Now this, at last—bone of my bones, flesh from my flesh—this shall be called woman, for from 'man' was she taken." In the first passage, we have *ʾādām* because, the author says, *ʾādām* was formed from the dust of the *ʾadāmâ*. In the second, we have the word *ʾîš*, because, he says, "She shall be called *ʾiššâ*," feminine of *ʾîš*, "because from *ʾîš* was she taken." 'Man', rendered by two different words, is at once a product of the ground, and so *ʾādām*, and the source of woman, and so *ʾîš*.

Another well-known example, made even more interesting because of the proximity of the two words, is found in 2:25 and 3:1, where in the first passage we read, "They were both naked" and in the second, "The snake was

39. See J. de Fraine, "Jeux de mots dans le récit de la chute," *Mélanges bibliques redigés en l'honneur de André Robert* (Travaux de l'Institut Catholique de Paris 4; Paris, 1957) 48ff.

40. For instance, *vir* and *virago* for *ʾîš* and *ʾiššâ*. Calvin, among many others, rejected *virago* as bad Latin in his commentary on Genesis, but is his *virissa* better?

wiser[41] than any wild creature." The words 'naked' and 'wiser' are separated by only six words in the Hebrew text, but are virtually identical.[42] Obviously, we are to make some connection between 'naked' and 'wiser', given the literary propensities of the writer, and the connection is made for us in 3:7, "Then"—having eaten the fruit—"the eyes of both of them were opened, and they discovered that they were naked." That is, the nature of their newly acquired knowledge was the kind that made them aware of their nakedness. It is, I submit, our author's way of expressing that their maturity has now been acquired by the eating of the fruit. Bearing in mind our discussion of his etiological approach to his story, we can say that he will have observed that children are not ashamed of their nakedness, but mature people, wise people, those who have a knowledge of good and bad, are.

In brief, we may say that three principal literary characteristics of the Adam and Eve story—the relationship to other Near Eastern literature in retelling the same story, the etiological pattern, particularly in the items that the author chooses to "explain," and even the well known puns and paronomasia—all suggest that the story describes a condition wherein the primordial pair lost the opportunity of immortality ("the tree of life") but gained in the process the wisdom of maturity ("the tree of knowledge of good and bad") that separates them from the animals on the one hand but unites them to the gods on the other, thus establishing his principle of hierarchy, which we have said is very important to the J writer. It remains now to demonstrate that the phrase "knowledge of good and bad" does in fact denote "maturity" in biblical literature.

41. Modern translations, perhaps for theological reasons, wish to give to *ᶜārûm* a pejorative sense. So we have NEB's 'crafty' or NAB's 'cunning'. However, in Proverbs, the word is consistently used in contrast to terms for 'foolishness' (*ᶜiwwelet, kĕsîl*) as in 12:23, 13:16, 14:8, etc. Ordinarily, the antonym to 'foolish' is 'wise', and indeed the Septuagint uses the normal Greek word for 'wise' in 3:1 (*phronimōtatos*). But our notions of "wisdom" and "being wise," for better or worse, are such that a rendering of 'wise' here without a lengthy qualification can be infelicitous. Perhaps something like 'resourceful' will convey the idea without prejudice. See Saul's description of David in 1 Sam 23:22, where again *ᶜārûm* is the word. In any case, whatever the precise English equivalent, the word conveys in every instance that quality of judgment that is characteristic of "maturity" as opposed to "immaturity" or "foolishness."

42. 'Naked' is *ᶜărûmmîm* (plural, referring to Adam and Eve) and 'wiser' is *ᶜārûm.*

Knowledge of Good and Bad

Apart from the deity and man, the most pervasive element in this story is the tree of knowledge of good and bad. The garden of Eden, the woman, the snake, even the tree of life are all secondary to the tree of knowledge of good and bad. It figures in every part of the story, the beginning, the middle, and the conclusion, unlike the tree of life, which only appears at the beginning and the end (and even at the beginning, there is just the perfunctory notice that it was placed in the garden by Yahweh). There can be little question then that the tree of knowledge of good and bad is very important to the writer, but what does he intend by it? What is the primary meaning of the phrase?[43] We have a fairly clear idea of the meaning of the tree of life—that which conveys immortality—but what are we to make of the cumbersome phrase, the tree of knowledge of good and bad?

As one can well imagine, most of the disputes and interpretations of the story as a whole revolve around this phrase. We can, I think, dismiss out of hand those who see no significance in the tree beyond its being the focus of a test of obedience.[44] Anything, according to this reading, could have done just as well: "Do not take a nap in the afternoon," "Do not walk in the western part of the garden," or any one of a thousand other arbitrary commands that would test obedience equally well. It is clear in the story that there is something about this tree in particular that makes it a "tree of death" (so 2:17) when compared to the tree of life.

A very popular explanation equates our tree with omniscience. Knowledge of good and bad would then mean knowledge of everything between the range of good and the range of bad, that is, knowledge of everything.[45] Just as the phrase "heaven and earth" apparently means "everything" when it is used to describe the object of the deity's creative act, so a "knowledge of good and bad" would mean "all knowledge."

43. Among the many fine studies of this problem, the following have been particularly helpful to me: G. W. Buchanan, "The Old Testament Meaning of the Knowledge of Good and Evil," *JBL* 75 (1956) 114–20; H. S. Stern, "The Knowledge of Good and Evil," *VT* 8 (1958) 405–18; and W. Malcolm Clark, "A Legal Background to the Yahwist's Use of 'Good and Evil' in the Genesis 2–3," *JBL* 88 (1969) 266–78.

44. So Calvin and many others.

45. So G. von Rad in his commentary on Genesis; and P. Humbert, "Études sur le récit du paradis et de la chute dans la Genèse," *Mémoires de l'Université de Neuchâtel*, vol. 14 (Neuchâtel: Secretariat de l'Universite, 1940); also A. M. Honeyman, "*Merismus* in Biblical Hebrew," *JBL* 71 (1952) 11ff., and many others.

In evaluating this interpretation, we have to remember our discussion of the writer's etiological point of view. He intends to explain *what is* in terms of its *cause*, the *what* in terms of the *why*. This, as I have argued, is fundamental to the story. We cannot believe that this or any other writer seriously imputed omniscience to man at any point. In other words, there is no indication in the text or the literature as a whole that the writer believed that man acquired omniscience upon eating the fruit of this tree. His model, in brief, was not omniscient man. What did happen is expressed very simply: "Then the eyes of both of them were opened, and they discovered that they were naked." This is hardly a declaration of omniscience.

Ivan Engnell also rejects the notion of omniscience. He thinks that the knowledge in question is a knowledge of sex.[46] He and many others feel that the writer is attempting to convey specifically the sexual maturity of the first pair. I think this position has greater merit than the "omniscient" notion, and I think it is going in the proper direction. The problem is with the word *sex*. Whatever this knowledge is, according to the Yahwist, it specifically is a knowledge like that of the gods. "The man," Yahweh says, "has become like one of us, knowing good and bad" (3:22). Now, I have no objections a priori to the Hebrew deity having an empirical knowledge of sex, for such must be the meaning, but I rather doubt that the Yahwist would share my casualness concerning the subject. Whatever his perception of the deity might be, it certainly did not include Yahweh's sexual proclivities. However, I think that Engnell is partially correct. What is intended is not sex in itself but *maturity*, the full measure of one's powers, which indeed in a man may be characterized by sexual awakening, among other things. A study of several pertinent passages will support this interpretation.

There is first of all the story in Deuteronomy 1. Moses recalled the events leading up to the deity's decision to sentence the Israelites to a forty-year period of wandering in the wilderness for their faithlessness in not immediately seizing the land of Canaan. It seems they were discouraged upon hearing reports of giants in the land. Yahweh's response to this state of affairs was to forbid that generation to enter the promised land, but, he said, "Your little ones, who, you thought would become spoils of war, and your children who do not yet know *good and bad*, they shall enter. I will give it to them" (Deut 1:39). Here the writer distinguishes between "little ones" and "children who

46. Engnell, "Knowledge' and 'Life,'" passim; also J. Coppens, *La Connaissance du bien et du mal et le péché du Paradis* (Louvain: Nauwelaerts, 1948) and the same writer's subsequent work, "L'interprétation sexuelle du péché du Paradis dans la littérature patristique," *ETL* 24 (1948) 395–408.

do not yet know good and bad." The word for 'little ones' is the common word denoting small children—NEB renders it 'dependents'—while the second phrase is the common expression for children or people as in "children of Israel," and it is only to the second that the phrase "who do not yet know good and bad" is attached. We might say something like, "Those who are grown but not quite mature adults." Therefore, to say that someone has acquired a knowledge of good and bad is tantamount to saying that someone has reached maturity. But this maturity need not be thought of strictly in chronological terms. We recognize this in the modern idiom when we refer to someone as a "mature scholar" or when we say that a certain athlete has "matured into a fine runner." We mean by this that the person in question is exercising his full potential in a given capacity. And this is precisely what the Hebrew writers meant by the phrase, as we can see in a story featuring Solomon.

After Solomon has killed off his rivals for the throne and becomes king, he goes to Gibeon to offer a sacrifice. There, in a dream, Yahweh appears and asks him, "What shall I give you?" Solomon answers:

> Now Yahweh my God you have made your servant king in place of my father, David, though I am a mere child, unskilled in leadership. And I am here in the midst of your people, the people of your choice. Give to your servant therefore a heart with skill to listen, so that he may govern your people justly and distinguish good and bad (1 Kgs 3:7–9; NEB).

It is significant that when Solomon requests the ability to distinguish good and bad, he does so from the standpoint of "a mere child, unskilled in leadership." That is to say, this writer assumes his audience will know that a verb of cognition followed by the crucial phrase "good and bad" is idiomatic for acquiring maturity. Here of course it is not chronological maturity, but the maturity that is the mark of a good king.

We can see the idea from a slightly different perspective in a story about Barzillai, the man from Gilead. After King David has put down the abortive revolt of his son Absalom, he makes his way slowly back to Jerusalem, repaying old political debts. Along the way, he encounters his old comrade, Barzillai, who had befriended him in less auspicious times. David invites Barzillai to come to Jerusalem, where he will provide for his old age. Barzillai answers, "I am already eighty, and I cannot tell good from bad; I cannot taste what I eat or drink; I cannot hear voices of men and women singing. Why should I be a burden any longer on your majesty?" (2 Sam 19:35). It is clear here that the clause "I cannot tell good from bad" has nothing to do with a moral sense, but is rather parallel to the statement, "I cannot taste what I eat or drink." That is, Barzillai no longer has the full powers of manhood, or maturity, about him. That is precisely the sense that the phrase has in the Adam and Eve story.

It will be recalled that in both the Gilgamesh and Adapa myths the wisdom of the protagonists is strongly emphasized and contrasted to their mortality. As the Adapa story puts it, "Ea had given him wisdom, but immortality he had not given him." Also in both of those stories, the wisdom is a given; it is something the heroes possess at the outset of the stories. The Yahwist has taken the matter a step further. As far as human beings are concerned, unlike the gods, they can have either the wisdom of maturity, or they can have immortality. They cannot have both because they are opposites, one denoted by the tree of life and the other by the tree of knowledge of good and bad, which of course is also the tree of death. The gods do have both. That is, they obviously are mature; they exercise the full potential of their being. They are not children, yet they are also immortal. Our writer comes to this conclusion the same way he comes to all his conclusions: by observing life about him. He knows that every man has his own Eden, as it were, his golden age, and if he could in some way arrest his development, he could stay there, forever young, immortal. But man grows; he leaves his Eden, and the price for maturity is death; for whatever grows, he also observes, dies. The images he invokes after the pair have eaten the fateful fruit reinforces this idea. They realize that they are naked, just as adults do, having passed from childhood to maturity. The woman is to have pain in childbirth and is to feel a longing for the man, surely the characteristics of a mature woman. The man has now to work for a living, "With labor you shall win your food from the ground all the days of your life" (3:17). Above all, the two now possess the knowledge of good and bad, like the gods, but they possess it on their way to death, unlike the gods: "Dust you are and to dust you shall return" (3:19). Thus, our writer would conclude, man can have immortality like the gods and remain a child, or he can have maturity like the gods and die. He cannot have both. Johannes Pedersen once summarized the idea very nicely:

> Man is related to the gods, a relation which appears in his wisdom. The kinship would be complete if man were also given immortality. He has been close to immortality, but still he did not obtain it, and if he did so, he would no longer be human.[47]

Interestingly, the ancients did speculate on what would happen if an individual somehow did manage to acquire immortality without at the same time

47. Pedersen, "Wisdom and Mortality," 244.

arresting development. We have the essence of the story in the epigraph to T. S. Eliot's *The Waste Land*, taken from Petronius's *Dinner with Trimalchio.* It seems that the Sibyl at Cumae had been granted immortality by Apollo, but she forgot to ask for perpetual youth, for an arrest in development. The result was that she continued to wither until she was small enough to be put in a tear-sized bottle, and when the boys would ask her what she wanted, she would reply, "I want to die."

I wonder if that idea is not also expressed by our writer when he has Yahweh say, "What if he should now reach out his hand and take fruit from the tree of life and live forever?" (3:22), and then has Yahweh station cherubim before the tree to guard the way of the tree of life, for to partake now that he has achieved growth would be, like the Sibyl, to continue to grow and wither forever. In this case, Yahweh's act would be merciful, not punitive.

Index of Authors

Index of Scripture References

Deuterocanonical Literature

New Testament